Kian Guan Lim

Theory and Econometrics of Financial Asset Pricing

Kian Guan Lim

Theory and Econometrics of Financial Asset Pricing

DE GRUYTER

ISBN 978-3-11-067385-2
e-ISBN (PDF) 978-3-11-067395-1
e-ISBN (EPUB) 978-3-11-067401-9

Library of Congress Control Number: 2022939228

Bibliographic information published by the Deutsche Nationalbibliothek
The Deutsche Nationalbibliothek lists this publication in the Deutsche Nationalbibliografie; detailed bibliographic data are available on the Internet at http://dnb.dnb.de.

Cover image: Marcus Lindstrom / E+ / Getty Images
Typesetting: VTeX UAB, Lithuania
Printing and binding: CPI books GmbH, Leck

www.degruyter.com

To my family

Preface

This book is pedagogical in nature and will provide a firm foundation in the understanding of financial economics applied to asset pricing. The covered materials include analyses of stocks, bonds, futures, and options. Existing highly cited finance models are explained and useful references are provided. The discussion of theory is accompanied by rigorous applications of econometrics. Econometrics contain elucidations of both the statistical theory as well as the practice of data analyses. Linear regression methods and some nonlinear methods are covered.

The contribution of this book, and at the same time, its novelty, is in synergistically employing materials in probability theory, economics optimization, econometrics, and data analyses together to provide for rigorous learning in investment and empirical finance. This book is written at a level that is academically rigorous for masters level as well as advanced undergraduate courses in finance, financial econometrics, and quantitative finance. It is also useful for finance and banking professionals who wish to better equip themselves.

June 2022 Kian Guan Lim

https://doi.org/10.1515/9783110673951-201

Contents

1 Probability Distributions

1.1 Basic Probability Concepts

Probability is the mathematics of chances defined on possible events happening. A sample space Ω is the set of all possible simple outcomes of an experiment where each simple outcome or sample point ω_j is uniquely different from another, and each simple outcome is not a set containing other simple outcomes, i. e., not $\{\omega_1, \omega_2\}$, for example. An experiment could be anything happening with uncertainty in the outcomes, such as throwing of a dice in which case the sample space is $\Omega = \{1, 2, 3, 4, 5, 6\}$, and $\omega_j = j$ for $j = 1$ or 2 or 3 or 4 or 5 or 6, or a more complicated case of investing in a portfolio of N stocks, in which case the sample space could be $\Omega = \{(R_1^1, \ldots, R_1^N), (R_2^1, \ldots, R_2^N), \ldots\ldots\}$ where R_j^k denotes the return rate of the kth stock under the jth outcome. Another possible sample space could be $\Omega = \{R_1^P, R_2^P, R_3^P, \ldots\ldots\}$, where $R_j^P = \frac{1}{N}\sum_{k=1}^N R_j^k$ denotes the return rate of the equal-weighted portfolio P under the jth outcome.

Each simple outcome or sample point ω_j is also called an "atom" or "elementary event". A more complicated outcome involving more than a sample point, such as $\{2, 4, 6\}$ or "even numbers in a dice throw" which is a subset of Ω is called an event. Technically, a sample point $\{2\}$ is also an event. Therefore, we shall use "events" as descriptions of outcomes, which may include the cases of sample points as events themselves.

As another example, in a simultaneous throw of two dices, the sample space consists of 36 sample points in the form $(i, j) \in \Omega$ where each $i, j \in \{1, 2, 3, 4, 5, 6\}$. An event could describe an outcome whereby the sum of the two numbers on the dices is larger than 8, in which case the event is said to happen if any of the following sample points or simple outcomes happen, $(3, 6), (4, 5), (4, 6), (5, 4), (5, 5), (5, 6), (6, 3), (6, 4), (6, 5)$, and $(6, 6)$. This event is described by the set $\{(3, 6), (4, 5), (4, 6), (5, 4), (5, 5), (5, 6), (6, 3), (6, 4), (6, 5), (6, 6)\} \subset \Omega$. Another event could be an outcome whereby the sum of the two numbers on the dices is smaller than 4, in which case the event is described by $\{(1, 1), (1, 2), (2, 1)\} \subset \Omega$. Another event could be "either the sum is larger than 10 or smaller than 4", and represented by $\{(5, 6), (6, 5), (6, 6), (1, 1), (1, 2), (2, 1)\} \subset \Omega$. Thus, an event is a subset of the sample space.

1.1.1 Collection of Events

Suppose there is a sample space $\Omega = \{a_1, a_2, a_3, \ldots, a_6\}$. We may form events E_i as follows

$$E_1 = \{a_1, a_2\}$$
$$E_2 = \{a_3, a_4, a_5, a_6\}$$

https://doi.org/10.1515/9783110profile673951-001

$$E_3 = \{a_1, a_2, a_3\}$$
$$E_4 = \{a_4, a_5, a_6\}$$

$\phi = \{\}$, or the empty set, and Ω itself are also events. All these events are subsets of Ω.

The set of events is also called a collection of events or a family of events. (It is really a set of subsets of Ω.) We denote the collection by

$$\mathcal{F} = \{\phi, \Omega, E_1, E_2, E_3, E_4\}$$

If a collection $\mathcal{F}$ satisfies the following 3 properties, it is called an algebra or a field:

(1a) $\Omega \in \mathcal{F}$
(1b) If $E_j \in \mathcal{F}$, then $E_j^c \in \mathcal{F}$ (E_j^c is the complement of E_j.)
(1c) If $E_i \in \mathcal{F}$ and $E_j \in \mathcal{F}$, then $E_i \bigcup E_j \in \mathcal{F}$

If there is an infinite sequence of $E_n \in \mathcal{F}$, and if $\bigcup_{n=1}^{\infty} E_n \in \mathcal{F}$, then $\mathcal{F}$ is called a σ-algebra or σ-field in Ω. A σ-field is a field that is closed under countable unions. A field describes all possible events that can happen, including events that represent the non-occurrence (complement) of some events. Therefore each event in a field can be represented by a chance or probability measure. It will include a zero chance if it is an empty set ϕ.

For association between sets, we need to formalize the idea of mapping. A map is a function. A function $f(x)$ assigns to an element $x \in D(f)$, where $D(f)$ is called the domain set of f, a unique value $y = f(x) \in R(f)$, where $R(f)$ is called the range set of f. It is written $f : D(f) \longrightarrow R(f)$ (set to set) or equivalently, $f : x \mapsto y$ (element to element).

A function $f(x) = y$ is injective if and only if each unique element in $D(f)$ is mapped (paired) to a unique element in $R(f)$. This is also called one-to-one function. There may exist elements in $R(f)$ that are not paired to any element in $D(f)$. If all elements in $R(f)$ are mapped onto from elements of $D(f)$, the function is surjective. In this case there may be different elements in $D(f)$ that mapped onto the same element in $R(f)$. A function that is both injective and surjective is called bijective (or one-to-one correspondence).

A probability measure P is a function mapping $\mathcal{F}$ into the unit interval $[0, 1]$, $P : \mathcal{F} \longrightarrow [0, 1]$, or equivalently $P : E \in \mathcal{F} \mapsto x \in [0, 1]$, such that

(2a) $0 \le P(E) \le 1$ for $E \in \mathcal{F}$
(2b) $P(\Omega) = 1$
(2c) For any sequence of disjoint events E_n of $\mathcal{F}$

$$P\left(\bigcup_{n=1}^{\infty} E_n\right) = \sum_{n=1}^{\infty} P(E_n)$$

A probability measure is in general neither surjective nor injective. However, there are examples in which the probability measure is injective, e. g., the number of years n in which a firm survives before going bankrupt or closing down has a probability of $(1-p)^n p$ where $p > 0$ is the constant probability of default or closing down given that it survived the previous year. The triple $(\Omega, \mathcal{F}, P)$ is called a probability space. The probability space is a minimal structure for a formal analysis of events and their chances of happening in a static framework.

For finite sample space, the probability measure P poses no problem as each of the finite number of outcomes or sample points can carry a strictly positive probability number or P-measure. For example, if there are N equally likely occurrences in an experiment, each sample point has probability $\frac{1}{N} > 0$, no matter how large N is.

However, in a continuous sample space, where events can be points on a real line $[A, B] \in \mathcal{R}$, $A < B$, we cannot assign a positive probability measure q to each of the points like in a finite sample space. We know that a rational number is countably infinite or denumerable, which means the set of rational numbers can be put in a one-to-one correspondence with natural numbers. Real numbers in $[A, B]$ are a lot more in quantity than natural numbers $(1, 2, 3, \ldots)$; they are uncountable or nondenumerable. If each point or "elementary event" on $[A, B]$ has a probability $q > 0$, then the total of all probabilities of the outcomes of the real numbers in $[A, B]$ is infinite. Hence $P(\Omega) = 1$ in (2b) is not satisfied.

For continuous sample space, the "elementary events" have to be made up of something else, e. g., half-open sets $(A, B]$ with $A < x \leq B$. In this case, $A < B$. Each simple event as in $(A, B]$ has a non-zero length $B - A > 0$ which can be used to construct the probability measure, no matter how infinitesimally small the measure is. This "length" is also called a Lebesgue measure. As an immediate application of the Lebesgue measure, if an integral is taken over an indicator function f on support $[0, 1]$, where

$$
\begin{aligned}
f(x) &= 1 \quad \text{if } x \in [0,1] \text{ is a rational number} \\
&= 0 \quad \text{otherwise}
\end{aligned}
$$

the Riemann integral cannot be found. However, using the idea that this integral is basically the sum of 1× the total lengths of the rational numbers on $[0, 1]$, since Lebesgue measure of all these total lengths is zero, the Lebesgue integral of the above is zero. Another famous case of measure-zero set is the Cantor set where the elements are infinitely many, but they all add up to zero length. Half-open sets $\omega \subset \mathcal{R}$ and events equal to their intersections or unions that form elements of $\mathcal{F}$ are also called Borel sets on the real line.

In the above, we can define the probability of an event of half-open interval $(A, B]$ as $g(A, B) \times (B - A)$ where $g(A, B) < \infty$ is a function of A and B. Indeed such a function $g(A, B)$ can be found using the mean value theorem for integration on a continuous probability distribution, i. e. a continuous sample space on $\mathcal{R}$ with a probability measure defined on it. Suppose $f(x)$ is the probability density function on $x \in \mathcal{R}$. The mean value theorem states that there exists a real number $c \in (A, B]$ such that $\int_A^B f(x)\,dx \equiv F(B) - F(A) = f(c) \times (B - A)$ where $F(\cdot)$ is the cumulative distribution function (cdf), $F(B) - F(A)$ is the probability of event of half-open interval $(A, B]$ or $P(A < x \leq B)$, and $g(A, B) = f(c) = \frac{F(B)-F(A)}{B-A}$.

Given the probability space $(\Omega, \mathcal{F}, P)$ comprising half-open intervals E_n as "elementary events", the σ-field $\mathcal{F}$ contains events (as its elements) such as $\bigcup_{n=1}^{\infty} E_n$. But property (1b) of a σ-field implies $(\bigcup_{n=1}^{\infty} E_n)^c$ is also an element of $\mathcal{F}$. By De Morgan's Law, $(\bigcup_{n=1}^{\infty} E_n)^c = \bigcap_{n=1}^{\infty} E_n^c$. If E_n is an increasing interval, i. e. $E_{n+1} \supset E_n$, then $P(\bigcup_{n=1}^{\infty} E_n) = 1$ and $P(\bigcap_{n=1}^{\infty} E_n^c) = 0$. The latter event is a point. Technically, it is possible to assign a probability of zero to measurable sets that can be constructed as events in the field $\mathcal{F}$.

1.1.2 Random Variables

In a horse race involving 6 horses, simply called A, B, C, D, E, and F, a simple outcome of the race is a 6-tuple or 6-element vector viz. ω_B = (B, D, F, A, C, E) denoting horse B coming in first, D second, and so on. Assuming there is no chance of a tie, and no horse drops off, there are 6! permutations or $6\times5\times4\times3\times2\times1 = 720$ possible outcomes. However, for most people going to the Sunday derbies to wager, they are more interested in some function of the simple outcomes rather than the simple outcome itself. For example, if they had wagered on horse B for a payout of 3 to 1 for the winner, then the variables relevant to them are the returns to their wager.

There are 5! = 120 permutations with B as winner or a return rate of 200 %. There are $5 \times 5! = 600$ permutations where B is not a winner or a return rate of −100 %. The function $f : \omega_B \mapsto 200\,\%$, if ω_B is a 6-tuple (B, . . .), otherwise −100 %, is called a random variable.

Formally, let $(\Omega, \mathcal{F}, P)$ be an arbitrary probability space where $\mathcal{F}$ is a σ-field or collection of measurable subsets of Ω, or collection of events. Let X be a real-valued function on $\mathcal{F}$; in other words, $X : \mathcal{F} \longrightarrow \mathcal{R}$ or $X : E \in \Omega \mapsto x \in \mathcal{R}$, where E is an event.

X is a random variable (RV) if it is a measurable function from Ω to $\mathcal{R}$. It is a measurable function if for any Borel set $A \subset \mathcal{R}$, its inverse

$$X^{-1}(A) = \{\omega : X(\omega) \in A\} \in \mathcal{F}$$

Hence, $X^{-1}(A)$ is seen to be an element of $\mathcal{F}$ or a subset of Ω that is measurable or that can be assigned a suitable probability. (Note that $X^{-1}(A)$ can be $\phi \in \mathcal{F}$.) In other words, if the probability distribution of a RV X is (adequately) defined, there is a surjective mapping from the $\mathcal{F}$ in $(\Omega, \mathcal{F}, P)$ to each $x \in X$. If not, the RV is not well-defined.

Sometimes, when a RV is defined, it may not be necessary or convenient to refer to the more fundamental algebra $\mathcal{F}$ from which the RV is derived. In the example above, each horse race permutation may be the simple event $\omega_k \in \Omega$. However, the relevant RV outcome is either the return rate $-100\,\%$ or $R_K\,\%$ if the bet is on horse K. Or we can simply take the sample space as $\Omega = \{-100\,\%, R_K\%\}$, and directly define probability on the RV. In the same way that investment problems are studied by considering the stock i's return rate r_i as a RV taking values in $[-1, +\infty)$, we can regard the sample space as $\Omega = [-1, +\infty) \subset \mathcal{R}$. Now, X is a simple RV if it has a finite number of values of $X(\omega) = x$, for each real $x \in \mathcal{R}$ that is finite, and if $E_x = \{\omega : X(\omega) = x\} \in \mathcal{F}$. Graphically, this can be depicted in Figure 1.1 as follows.

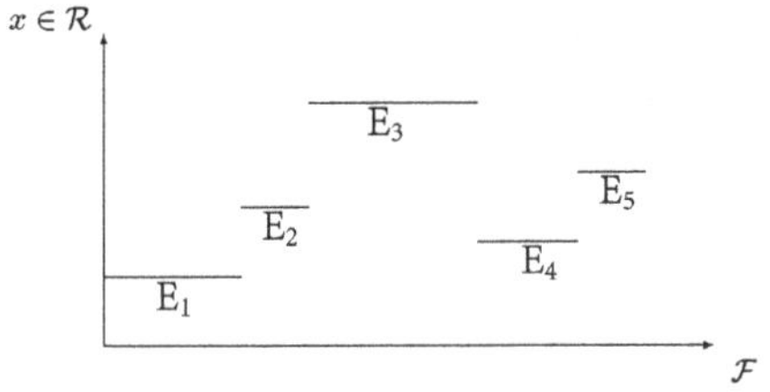

Figure 1.1: A Simple RV Function.

A note about the notation of a random variable is in order. A RV X takes different possible values x each with a particular probability $P(x)$. Thus a RV is sometimes differentiated by having a tilde sign above the alphabet. When we take expectation, we usually write $E(\tilde{X})$; but the equivalence in integration uses $\int x\,dF(x)$ since cdf function $F(\cdot)$ is defined on a value x. However, fixing notations in complicated equations can be tedious. We shall typically not use any differentiating signs and let the readers infer if it is a RV or its value in the context of the equations.

An example of a commonly used simple RV is the indicator variable $1_{\omega \in A}$ where this RV takes the value 1 when realized event ω is in set A, and 0 otherwise. The indicator variable is a useful tool in developing analytical solutions to some probability problems. For example, $E(1_{\omega \in A}) = P(A)$. This allows the concepts of expectation and probability distribution to be interconnected. A more general simple RV is $X = \sum_{i=1}^{N} x_i 1_{A_i}$ where X takes value x_i in the event $A_i = \{\omega : X(\omega) = x_i\} \in \mathcal{F}$, and $A_i \cap A_j = \phi$, for $i \neq j$. Simple RVs are easily measurable. Another example is as follows. Since $E_b = (-\infty, b]$ is a Borel set in $\mathcal{R}$, a measurable RV X can be defined as a mapping $X : \Omega \longrightarrow \mathcal{R}$ such that for any event $E_b \in \Omega$, $X(E_b) = b \in \mathcal{R}$.

1.1.3 Distribution Function

The probability distribution function, also called cumulative distribution function of a random variable X is a mapping from $\mathcal{R}$ to $[0, 1]$ defined by $F(b) = P(X \leq b)$. This distribution is a fundamental tool in statistical analyses. A distribution function has the following properties:

(3a) F is a nondecreasing (or monotone increasing) function, i. e. if $a \le b$, then $F(a) \le F(b)$

(3b) $\lim_{b\to-\infty} F(b) = 0$ and $\lim_{b\to+\infty} F(b) = 1$

(3c) F is right continuous, i. e. $\forall b \in \mathcal{R}$, $\lim_{h\downarrow 0} F(b + h) = F(b)$

If the cdf is continuous (without jumps), then it is both right continuous and left continuous, i. e., $\lim_{h\downarrow 0} F(b + h) = F(b) = \lim_{h\downarrow 0} F(b - h)$. This allows its derivative to be obtained at every point x, i. e., $\frac{dF(x)}{dx} = f(x)$ where $f(x)$ is the probability density function (pdf) of X. $f(x)$ is a non-negative function. To find probabilities of events on X, we require integration over the pdf, e. g., $P(a < x < b) = \int_a^b f(x)\,dx$. This is of course $\int_a^b dF(x) = F(b) - F(a)$. Note that the probability of any single point x in a continuous cdf is zero.

However, sometimes a pdf may not exist even if the cdf exists, e. g., a cdf defined on a Cantor set where the cdf function has no derivative on the points of the Cantor set. Thus cdf is a more general and robust way of defining a probability distribution that allows for jumps. Right continuity at b in (3c) facilitates a convenient statement of evaluating the probability of a jump occurring at point b, i. e. $P(X \le b) - P(X < b) = P(X = b)$, which is $F(b) - F(b_{-})$. If we were to use an alternative convention of left continuity, the probability $P(X = b) = F(b) - F(b_{-}) = 0$. To capture this probability under left continuity, one would require use of a different definition such as $P(X \le b) = F(b_{+})$, which is troublesome.

When a RV X is discrete, X takes only finitely many or countably many values, a_i, $i = 1, 2, \ldots$. The probability of event $\{X \le a_i\}$ occurring is cdf $F(a_i) = \sum_{x\le a_i} p(x)$. The probability of a_i occurring is $p(a_i) = F(a_i) - F(a_i-)$. In the above, $p(x)$ is called the probability mass function (PMF) for a discrete RV X. Note that pdf does not exist for discrete distributions.

1.1.4 Some Moments

For a RV X, its nth moment is $E(X^n)$ if it exists. The mean of X is its first moment when $n = 1$. For a continuous RV X with pdf $f(x)$

$$\mu = E(X) = \int_{-\infty}^{+\infty} x f(x) dx$$

In the discrete case, it is given by

$$\mu = E(X) = \sum_x x p(x)$$

where $p(x)$ is the PMF. The variance of X is

$$\sigma^2(X) = \text{var}(X) = E(X - \mu)^2$$

The moment-generating function (MGF) of RV X is

$$M(\theta) = E(e^{\theta X}) = \int_{-\infty}^{+\infty} e^{\theta x} dF(x)$$

Differentiating M w. r. t. its argument θ

$$M'(\theta) = \frac{d}{d\theta}E(e^{\theta X}) = E\left[\frac{d}{d\theta}(e^{\theta X})\right] = E[Xe^{\theta X}]$$

Likewise, the second derivative is

$$M''(\theta) = \frac{d}{d\theta}M'(\theta) = \frac{d}{d\theta}E(Xe^{\theta X}) = E\left[\frac{d}{d\theta}(Xe^{\theta X})\right] = E[X^2e^{\theta X}]$$

Similarly, we can show $\frac{d^n}{d\theta^n}M(\theta) = E[X^n e^{\theta X}]$. Thus, the nth non-central moment of X can be recovered by putting $\theta = 0$ in the nth derivative of the MGF $M(\theta)$. $E(X^n) = E[X^n e^{\theta X}]|_{\theta=0}$. If the moments are unique, then a moment generating function is uniquely identified with a probability distribution.

The covariance of two jointly distributed (both realizations occurring simultaneously) RVs X and Y is

$$\sigma_{XY} = \text{cov}(X, Y) = E(X - \mu_X)(Y - \mu_Y)$$

The correlation coefficient of two RVs X and Y is $(\sigma_{XY})/(\sigma_X\sigma_Y)$ where σ_X, σ_Y are the standard deviations (square roots of the variances) of RVs X and Y, respectively.

Continuous jointly distributed RVs X and Y have a joint pdf $f(x, y)$. The marginal distribution of any one of the joint RVs is obtainable by integration, viz.

$$f_X(x) = \int_y f(x, y)dy$$

Likewise for discrete RVs, the marginal PMF of RV X is

$$P_X(x) = \sum_y P(x, y)$$

1.1.5 Independence

For discrete RVs X and Y, they are independent if and only if (iff) $P(x,y) = P_X(x) \times P_Y(y)$. For continuous RVs X and Y, they are independent iff $f(x,y) = f_X(x) \times f_Y(y)$.

When X and Y are independent, their covariance is

$$\begin{aligned}
&\int_y \int_x (x-\mu_X)(y-\mu_Y) f(x,y)\, dx\, dy \\
&= \int_y \int_x (x-\mu_X)(y-\mu_Y) f_X(x) f_Y(y)\, dx\, dy \\
&= \int_y (y-\mu_Y)\left(\int_x (x-\mu_X) f_X(x) dx\right) f_Y(y)\, dy \\
&= 0
\end{aligned}$$

Therefore, independent RVs have zero covariance. However, the converse is generally not true. For the case of normal RVs, zero correlation does imply independence. More generally, a sequence of RVs $X_1, X_2, \ldots, X_n$ are independent if and only if (iff)

$$\begin{aligned}
&P(X_1 \in A_1, X_2 \in A_2, \ldots, X_n \in A_n) \\
&= P(X_1 \in A_1) \times P(X_2 \in A_2) \times \cdots \times P(X_n \in A_n)
\end{aligned}$$

1.2 Probability Distributions

1.2.1 Binomial Distribution

Suppose we have an experiment or trial in which there are only two outcomes. Without loss of generality, we call the two outcomes "head (H)" or "tail (T)" as in a coin toss. This type of trial is also called a Bernoulli trial. The probability of H is p, while the probability of T is therefore $1-p$.

Suppose the experiment is repeated and we perform N independent trials. Let X equal the number of observed H's in the N trials. X can take the values (outcomes) $0, 1, 2, \ldots, N$. The RV X is a binomial RV $B(N, p)$ with parameters N and p, and the discrete probability distribution of X is a binomial distribution. Note the surjective mapping of events $\langle H, T, T, \ldots, T\rangle$, $\langle T, H, T, \ldots, T\rangle$, $\langle T, T, H, \ldots, T\rangle, \ldots, \langle T, T, T, \ldots, H\rangle$ to $X = 1$.

For $0 \le k \le N$, $P(X = k) = \binom{N}{k} p^k (1-p)^{N-k}$.

$$\begin{aligned}
E(X) &= \sum_{j=0}^{N} j \binom{N}{j} p^j (1-p)^{N-j} \\
&= \sum_{j=1}^{N} j \frac{N!}{j!(N-j)!} p^j (1-p)^{N-j}
\end{aligned}$$

$$= \sum_{j=1}^{N} N\left(\frac{(N-1)!}{(j-1)!(N-j)!}\right)p^{j}(1-p)^{N-j}$$

$$= Np\sum_{j=1}^{N}\left(\frac{(N-1)!}{(j-1)!(N-j)!}\right)p^{j-1}(1-p)^{N-j}$$

$$= Np\sum_{i=0}^{N-1}\left(\frac{(N-1)!}{i!(N-1-i)!}\right)p^{i}(1-p)^{N-1-i}$$

$$= Np\sum_{i=0}^{N-1}\binom{N-1}{i}p^{i}(1-p)^{N-1-i} = Np$$

In the same way, we can show $\sigma_X^2 = Np(1-p)$. The moment-generating function of $B(N,p)$ is

$$\begin{aligned}
M(\theta) &= E[e^{\theta X}] \\
&= \sum_{x=0}^{N} e^{\theta x}\binom{N}{x}p^{x}(1-p)^{N-x} \\
&= \sum_{x=0}^{N}\binom{N}{x}(pe^{\theta})^{x}(1-p)^{N-x} \\
&= [pe^{\theta} + (1-p)]^{N}
\end{aligned}$$

From the MGF of X,

$$\begin{aligned}
\mu_X &= \left.\frac{dM}{d\theta}\right|_{\theta=0} = M'(0) = N[pe^{\theta} + (1-p)]^{N-1}(pe^{\theta})|_{\theta=0} = Np \\
E(X^2) &= M''(0) \\
&= \{N(N-1)[pe^{\theta} + (1-p)]^{N-2}(pe^{\theta})^2 + M'(\theta)\}|_{\theta=0} \\
&= N(N-1)p^2 + Np \\
&= (Np)^2 + Np(1-p) = \mu_X^2 + Np(1-p)
\end{aligned}$$

Hence, $\sigma^2(X) = E(X^2) - [E(X)]^2 = Np(1-p)$.

The Pascal arithmetic triangle shown in Figure 1.2 is closely associated with the development of the binomial distribution. Each interior number on any line in the Pascal triangle is the sum of the two adjoining numbers immediately above on the previous line.

Pascal (1623–1662) showed that numbers on the triangle can be interpreted as combinatorial numbers as in Figure 1.3. Pascal also showed that ${}^{n+1}C_k = {}^{n}C_{k-1} + {}^{n}C_k$. What is interesting is that each nth line on the Pascal triangle contains the (binomial) coefficients in the expansion of $(a+b)^n$. The binomial distribution probabilities are a special case of the binomial expansion where $a = p$ and $b = 1 - p$.

$$
\begin{array}{ccccccccccc}
 & & & & & 1 & & & & & \\
 & & & & 1 & & 1 & & & & \\
 & & & 1 & & 2 & & 1 & & & \\
 & & 1 & & 3 & & 3 & & 1 & & \\
 & 1 & & 4 & & 6 & & 4 & & 1 & \\
1 & & 5 & & 10 & & 10 & & 5 & & 1
\end{array}
$$

....

Figure 1.2: The Pascal Triangle.

$$
\begin{array}{ccccccccccc}
 & & & & & {}^{0}C_0 & & & & & \\
 & & & & {}^{1}C_0 & & {}^{1}C_1 & & & & \\
 & & & {}^{2}C_0 & & {}^{2}C_1 & & {}^{2}C_2 & & & \\
 & & {}^{3}C_0 & & {}^{3}C_1 & & {}^{3}C_2 & & {}^{3}C_3 & & \\
 & {}^{4}C_0 & & {}^{4}C_1 & & {}^{4}C_2 & & {}^{4}C_3 & & {}^{4}C_4 & \\
{}^{5}C_0 & & {}^{5}C_1 & & {}^{5}C_2 & & {}^{5}C_3 & & {}^{5}C_4 & & {}^{5}C_5
\end{array}
$$

....

Figure 1.3: The Pascal Triangle, in Combinatorial Numbers.

1.2.2 Application: Games of Chance

Games of chance or betting games have been around since the dawn of human history, and are succinct examples of combinatorial probabilities. In a casino roulette game, there are usually 38 (sometimes 37) numbers on the wheel, $00, 0, 1, 2, \ldots, 36$. Even numbers are red and odd numbers are black. "00" and zero are green. There are 18 reds and 18 blacks to bet on. If green shows up, the banker wins all. A \$1 bet on a red (black) returns \$2, including the bet amount, if red (black) turns up, or else \$0 with the loss of the bet amount. For each color-bet, there are 20 losing numbers to 18 winning ones. John decides to try his luck on red numbers. He will put \$1 bets 19 times on red. What is John's expected gain or loss after 19 games?

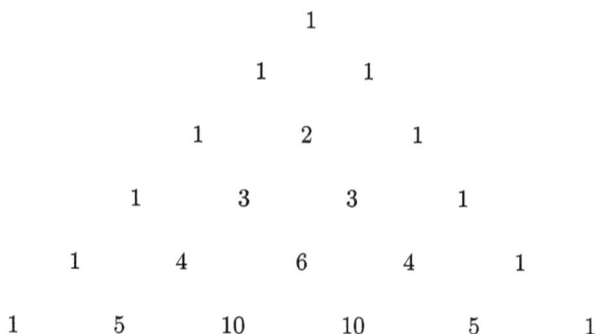

Assuming the wheel is fair, the probability of a win for John is 18/38. The probability of a loss is 20/38. His dollar win in each game is \$1. His dollar loss in each game is also \$1. Thus, John's outcome in each game is +\$1 with probability 18/38 and –\$1 with probability 20/38.

Let Z be the number of wins after 19 games. Z can take any of the values $0, 1, 2, \ldots,$ 19. Let X be John's dollar gain/loss after 19 games. $X = Z \times 1 + (19 - Z) \times (-1) = 2Z - 19$. Therefore, X takes values $-19, -17, -15, \ldots, -1, 1, \ldots, 15, 17, 19$, with a total of 20 possible outcomes from $B(19, \frac{18}{38})$.

After 19 games, his expected number of wins is $E(Z) = 19 \times \frac{18}{38} = 9$. His expected \$ gain/loss is $E(X) = 2E(Z) - 19 = -1$.

In the casino game of craps, two dice are rolled. The rules are that if you roll a total of 7 or 11 on the first roll, you win. If you roll a total of 2, 3, or 12 on the first roll, you lose. But if you roll a total of 4, 5, 6, 8, 9, or 10 on your first roll, the game is not ended and continues with more rolls. The total number in the first roll becomes your "point". This "point" is fixed for the game. If in subsequent rolls, you hit your "point" again before you hit a total of 7, then you win. If you roll a total of 7 before your hit your "point", then you lose. The rolling would continue until your "point" is hit or else 7 is hit. The game payoff is \$1 for a \$1 bet. You either win a dollar or you lose a dollar in each game. One wins or loses against the casino or banker.

First, we list all the possible outcomes in Table 1.1. The outcomes represent the total of the numbers on the two dice.

Table 1.1: Total of Numbers on Two Dice.

Total	1	2	3	4	5	6
1	2	3	4	5	6	7
2	3	4	5	6	7	8
3	4	5	6	7	8	9
4	5	6	7	8	9	10
5	6	7	8	9	10	11
6	7	8	9	10	11	12

There are 8 outcomes with "7" or "11" out of 36. Thus, the probability of a win out of a first roll is 8/36. There are 4 outcomes with a "2", "3", or "12". Thus, the probability of a loss out of a first roll is 4/36. If the first roll is "4", the game continues. The probability of the next roll being "4" and thus a win is 3/36. The probability of the next roll being "7" and thus a loss is 6/36. The game continues to a third and subsequent roll if the total is not "4" or "7". Thus, the probability of an eventual win if the first roll is "4" is $\frac{3}{36} + (1 - \frac{3}{36} - \frac{6}{36}) \times \frac{3}{36} + (1 - \frac{3}{36} - \frac{6}{36})^2 \times \frac{3}{36} + (1 - \frac{3}{36} - \frac{6}{36})^3 \times \frac{3}{36} + \cdots$, or $\frac{3}{36}(1 + \frac{27}{36} + [\frac{27}{36}]^2 + [\frac{27}{36}]^3 + \cdots) = \frac{3}{36} \times \frac{1}{1 - \frac{27}{36}} = \frac{1}{3}$. Notice that the idea of independence of the outcome in each roll is assumed in the probability computations.

The contingency table of the probabilities of the various outcomes is shown in Table 1.2. In Table 1.2, the last column shows that the probability of winning equals the probability of winning given first roll × probability of first roll.

Table 1.2: Outcome Probabilities in Craps.

First roll	Probability of first roll	Probability of winning given first roll	Probability of winning
4	3/36	1/3	1/36
5	4/36	4/10	4/90
6	5/36	5/11	25/396
8	5/36	5/11	25/396
9	4/36	4/10	4/90
10	3/36	1/3	1/36

Thus, the probability of winning in a game of craps by rolling is $\frac{8}{36} + 2 \times (\frac{1}{36} + \frac{4}{90} + \frac{25}{396})$. This is 49.2929 %. The probability of loss is 50.7071 %. Thus, the casino has a 1.4142 % advantage over your bet.

From a historical perspective, the Franciscan monk Friar Luca Pacioli (1445–1517) posed the following question in 1494. In those early days there were no computers, no video games, and no gadgets for people to play with, except perhaps coins. Two players would spend their leisure time tossing a coin in a match. If a head came up in a toss, player 1 won the game, otherwise player 2 won the game. The player who was the first to win a total of 6 games won the match and collected the entire prize pool that both had contributed to.

This sounds simple enough. However, Pacioli's question was: how would the prize pool be distributed if, for some reason, the games had to stop before the final winner was determined? This problem posed in the late 1400s came to be known as "the problem of points", and it remained unsolved for nearly 200 years until Fermat and Pascal came along. The issue was to decide how the stakes of a game of chance should be divided if that game was not completed for whatever reason. It appears that Pacioli had proposed that if player 1 was up by 5 game wins to player 2's 3 wins, then they could divide the stakes 5/8 to player 1 and 3/8 to player 2. However, there were fierce objections to this proposed solution.

Blaise Pascal (1623–1662) and Pierre de Fermat (1601–1665) began a series of letters around 1654 that led to the solution of the problem of points and expansion of the foundation for classical probability. Pascal's solution can be represented by a binomial tree shown in Figure 1.4. The full dot indicates the current state of 5 wins and 3 losses for player 1 (or equivalently 5 losses and 3 wins for player 2). The empty dots with number j indicate the completion of the match with j as winner.

Assuming that player 1 and 2 each has a probability 1/2 of winning in each game, player 1 will end up winning in 3 possibilities: {6 wins, 3 losses} with probability 1/2, {6

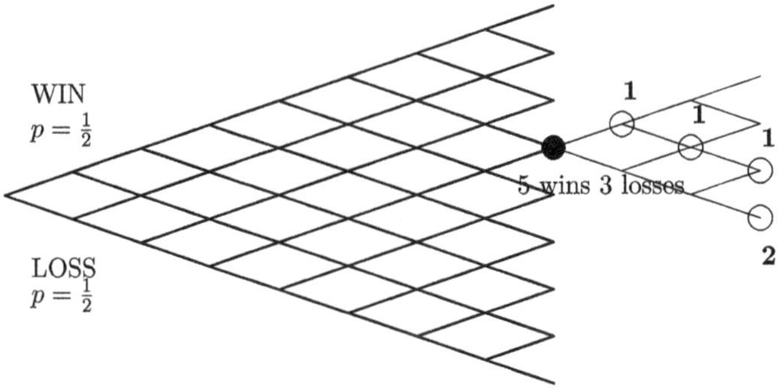

Figure 1.4: Binomial Tree for the Solution to the Problem of Points.

wins, 4 losses} with probability 1/4, {6 wins, 5 losses} with probability 1/8, and player 2 will win in only one possibility {6 wins, 5 losses} with probability 1/8. These 4 possibilities total up to a probability of 1. Hence, after 5 wins and 3 losses, player 1 has a total probability of winning the match of 1/2+1/4+1/8 = 7/8 while player 2 has a probability of winning at 1/8. A more reasonable way of dividing the stakes is therefore 7/8 to player 1 and 1/8 to player 2.

The concept is akin to looking forward in expected risk-return relationships instead of looking backward to sunk costs as in historical accounting.

1.2.3 Poisson Distribution

X is a Poisson RV with parameter λ if X takes values $0, 1, 2, \ldots$ with probabilities

$$P(X = k) = \frac{\lambda^k}{k!} e^{-\lambda}$$

If we sum all the probabilities

$$\sum_{k=0}^{\infty} P(X = k) = e^{-\lambda}\left(1 + \frac{\lambda}{1!} + \frac{\lambda^2}{2!} + \frac{\lambda^3}{3!} + \cdots\right) = e^{-\lambda} e^{\lambda} = 1$$

where we have used the Taylor series expansion of the exponential function e.

For a binomial RV $B(N, p)$ where N is large and p small such that the mean of X, $Np = \lambda$ is $O(1)$, then

$$\begin{aligned} P(X = k) &= \frac{N!}{(N-k)!k!} p^k (1-p)^{N-k} \\ &= \frac{N!}{(N-k)!k!} \left(\frac{\lambda}{N}\right)^k \left(1 - \frac{\lambda}{N}\right)^{N-k} \end{aligned}$$

$$= \frac{N(N-1)\cdots(N-k+1)}{N^k}\frac{\lambda^k}{k!}\frac{(1-\lambda/N)^N}{(1-\lambda/N)^k}$$
$$\approx 1 \times \frac{\lambda^k}{k!}\frac{e^{-\lambda}}{1}$$

when N is large. Parameter λ denotes the average number of occurrences over the time period whereby RV X is measured.

The MGF of a Poisson $X(\lambda)$ is

$$\begin{aligned} M(\theta) &= \sum_{x=0}^{\infty} e^{\theta x}\frac{\lambda^x e^{-\lambda}}{x!} \\ &= e^{-\lambda}\sum_{x=0}^{\infty}\frac{(\lambda e^{\theta})^x}{x!} \\ &= e^{-\lambda}e^{\lambda e^{\theta}} = e^{\lambda(e^{\theta}-1)} \end{aligned}$$

for all real values of θ.

Thus, the mean and variance of Poisson $X(\lambda)$ are found, respectively, as

$$\begin{aligned} \mu_X &= M'(0) = \lambda e^{\theta}e^{\lambda(e^{\theta}-1)}|_{\theta=0} = \lambda, \\ \sigma_X^2 &= M''(0) - \mu_X^2 \\ &= \lambda[\lambda e^{2\theta}e^{\lambda(e^{\theta}-1)} + e^{\theta}e^{\lambda(e^{\theta}-1)}]|_{\theta=0} - \mu_X^2 \\ &= \lambda(\lambda+1) - \lambda^2 = \lambda \end{aligned}$$

The Poisson process can be motivated and derived from a few reasonable axioms characterizing the type of phenomenon to be modeled.

A counting process $N(t)$, $t \geq 0$, taking values $0, 1, 2, \ldots$ at different higher time units t, is called a Poisson process if it has an occurrence rate λ per unit time, where at each occurrence the count increases by 1, and

(4a) $N(0) = 0$

(4b) $N(t+h) - N(t)$ and $N(t'+h) - N(t')$ are stationary regardless of t or t', and are independent for $t' \geq t + h$.

(4c) $P[N(h) = 1] = \lambda h + o(h)$ for small time interval h

(4d) $P[N(h) \geq 2] = o(h)$

Properties (4c) and (4d) indicate that the probability of a single occurrence of event is approximately proportional to the time that elapsed without an event. During a short period of time h, the probability of more than one event occurring is negligible. Clearly, (4b) indicates that the increments are stationary and independent, and thus memoryless. In other words, what happened in a previous period will not affect the probability of what will happen next.

Now

$$\begin{aligned}P[N(t+h)=0] &= P[N(t)=0, N(t+h)-N(t)=0]\\ &= P[N(t)=0]\,P[N(t+h)-N(t)=0]\\ &= P[N(t)=0]\,[1-\lambda h+o(h)]\end{aligned}$$

Then

$$\frac{P[N(t+h)=0]-P[N(t)=0]}{h} = -\lambda P[N(t)=0] + \frac{o(h)}{h}$$

By definition, $\lim_{h\to 0}\frac{o(h)}{h}=0$.

Let $P_0(t)=P[N(t)=0]$. As $h\downarrow 0$,

$$\frac{dP_0(t)}{dt} = -\lambda P_0(t)$$

Thus, $d\ln P_0(t) = -\lambda dt$, hence

$$P_0(t) = \exp(-\lambda t) \tag{1.1}$$

where $P_0(0)=1$.

More generally

$$\begin{aligned}P_n(t+h) &= P_n(t)P_0(h) + P_{n-1}(t)P_1(h) + P_{n-2}(t)P_2(h)\\ &\quad + \cdots + P_0(t)P_n(h)\\ &= (1-\lambda h)P_n(t) + \lambda h P_{n-1}(t) + o(h)\end{aligned}$$

Then

$$\frac{P_n(t+h)-P_n(t)}{h} = -\lambda P_n(t) + \lambda P_{n-1}(t) + \frac{o(h)}{h}$$

As $h\downarrow 0$

$$\frac{dP_n(t)}{dt} = -\lambda P_n(t) + \lambda P_{n-1}(t).$$

Thus

$$e^{\lambda t}[P_n'(t) + \lambda P_n(t)] = \lambda e^{\lambda t}P_{n-1}(t)$$

So

$$\frac{d}{dt}[e^{\lambda t}P_n(t)] = \lambda e^{\lambda t}P_{n-1}(t)$$

Suppose the solution is

$$e^{\lambda t}P_n(t) = \frac{(\lambda t)^n}{n!}, \quad \text{for any } t \tag{1.2}$$

To prove by mathematical induction, by first putting $n = 0$ in Eq. (1.2), $P_0(t) = \exp(-\lambda t)$ which is true as in Eq. (1.1). Second, for $n = 1$

$$\frac{d}{dt}[e^{\lambda t}P_1(t)] = \lambda e^{\lambda t}P_0(t) = \lambda$$

Integrating w. r. t. t, $e^{\lambda t}P_1(t) = \lambda t + c$. At $t = 0$, probability of $n = 1$ arrival is zero, so $c = 0$. Therefore, $P_1(t) = \lambda t \exp(-\lambda t)$, which follows Eq. (1.2).

Next, suppose Eq. (1.2) applies for $n = k - 1$. So

$$\frac{d}{dt}[e^{\lambda t}P_k(t)] = \lambda e^{\lambda t}P_{k-1}(t) = \lambda e^{\lambda t}e^{-\lambda t}\frac{(\lambda t)^{k-1}}{(k-1)!} = \frac{\lambda^k}{(k-1)!}t^{k-1}$$

Integrating w. r. t. t,

$$e^{\lambda t}P_k(t) = \frac{(\lambda t)^k}{k!} + c$$

Since $P_k(0) = 0$, $c = 0$. Thus, Eq. (1.2) is also satisfied for $n = k$. By mathematical induction, since $n = 1$ in Eq. (1.2) is true, then $n = 2$ in Eq. (1.2) is also true, and so on, for all $t \geq 0$.

Poisson events occur with a discrete time interval in-between that we call the interarrival or waiting time between events. Let T_n, for $n = 1, 2, \ldots$, be the interarrival time between the $(n-1)$th and the nth Poisson events.

$P[T_1 > t] = P[N(t) = 0|N(0) = 0] = \exp(-\lambda t)$ where $P[N(0) = 0] = 1$, from Eq. (1.1). Then, T_1 has an exponential distribution with rate λ. The cdf of RV T_1 taking a value less than or equal to t is $F(t) = 1 - \exp(-\lambda t)$ for time $t \geq 0$. Differentiating, its pdf is $\lambda \exp(-\lambda t)$ for time $t \geq 0$.

Its mean is

$$\int_0^\infty t\lambda \exp(-\lambda t)dt = -\int_0^\infty t\, d(e^{-\lambda t}) = -\left[e^{-\lambda t}\left(\frac{1}{\lambda} + t\right)\right]_0^\infty = \frac{1}{\lambda}$$

The variance is $(\frac{1}{\lambda})^2$.

From the above, it is seen that when the interarrival time of events or occurrences is exponentially distributed, the number of occurrences or events in a given time interval has a Poisson distribution, and vice-versa. A Poisson process can also be defined as an activity whose interarrival time has an exponential distribution. The exponential distribution is the only continuous distribution that has the memoryless property in (4b). Here

$$P[T_1 > t, T_1 > t + h] = P[T_1 > t + h|T_1 > t]P[T_1 > t]$$

or

$$P[T_1 > t + h] = P[T_1 - t > h|T_1 > t]P[T_1 > t]$$

Since the exponential distribution of the waiting time until an event happens, $P[T_1 \le t] = 1 - \exp(-\lambda t)$, is only a function of the waiting time t from the time of the last event regardless of the past, therefore we can also write $P[T_1 - t > h|T_1 > t] = P[T_1' > h] = \exp(-\lambda h)$ regardless of the time just past, t, and defining T_1' as the new waiting time starting at t.

1.2.4 Application: Credit Default Swap

A credit default swap (CDS) is a traded market instrument whereby one party agrees to pay a regular insurance premium X to a counterparty until such a time T_1 when the reference asset defaults, e. g., a bond that fails to make interest or principal payments. Upon default of the reference asset, the counterparty pays the insuree a one-time only fixed compensation amount P and the contract is terminated. If by the maturity of the CDS contract, $T < T_1$, the reference asset has not yet defaulted, the contract is terminated. For simplicity, suppose there are only two insurance premium payments until T, one at time $t = 0$ (now) and the other at $t = \frac{1}{2}T$. If default occurs, it is reported to happen possibly only at $t = \frac{1}{2}T$ for $(0 < T' \le \frac{1}{2}T)$ or at $t = T$ for $(\frac{1}{2}T < T' \le T)$. Insurer pays the compensation at the time when default is reported to have happened.

Using the exponential distribution to model the probability of no default of the bond by time $\frac{1}{2}T$, $P(T' > \frac{1}{2}T) = \exp(-\frac{1}{2}\lambda T)$ where in this application λ is sometimes called the risk-neutral default intensity parameter. Similarly, the probability of no default of the bond by time T, $P(T' > T) = \exp(-\lambda T)$. $P(T' = 0) = 0$. The probability of default occurring during $t \in (0, \frac{1}{2}T]$ is $1 - \exp(-\frac{1}{2}\lambda T)$, and the probability of default occurring during $t \in (\frac{1}{2}T, T]$ is $\exp(-\frac{1}{2}\lambda T) - \exp(-\lambda T)$. Hence the total probability of the mutually exclusive but all-inclusive events {default by $\frac{1}{2}T$}, {default during $(\frac{1}{2}T, T]$}, and {no default by T} is 1.

The present value of expected insurance payments by the insurance buyer is $X[1 + \delta \exp(-\frac{1}{2}\lambda T)]$ where δ is the constant risk-free discount factor on \$1 at time $\frac{1}{2}T$. The present value of expected compensation payment is $\delta P\ [1 - \exp(-\frac{1}{2}\lambda T)] + \delta^2 P\ [\exp(-\frac{1}{2}\lambda T) - \exp(-\lambda T)]$. At the start of the CDS contract, a fair value of λ is that which sets the present value of expected payments equal to the present value of compensation.

1.2.5 Uniform Distribution

A continuous RV X has a uniform distribution over interval (a, b) if its pdf is given by

$$f(x) = \begin{cases} \frac{1}{(b-a)} & a < x < b \\ 0 & \text{otherwise} \end{cases}$$

$$E(X) = \int_a^b \frac{x}{b-a} dx = \frac{b^2 - a^2}{2(b-a)} = \frac{a+b}{2}$$

$$E(X^2) = \int_a^b \frac{x^2}{b-a} dx = \frac{b^3 - a^3}{3(b-a)} = \frac{a^2 + ab + b^2}{3}$$

Thus

$$\operatorname{var}(X) = E(X^2) - [E(X)]^2 = \frac{a^2 + ab + b^2}{3} - \frac{(a+b)^2}{4} = \frac{(b-a)^2}{12}$$

There is a simple but useful theorem when the uniform distribution appears naturally.

Theorem 1.1. *Given any RV X with a distribution function $F(X) = U$, then $U \in (0,1)$ is a RV with standard uniform distribution.*

We provide proof for a more specific case where X is a continuous RV and $F(x)$ is continuous strictly increasing. The more general case can also be proved.

Proof. $P(F(x) \leq y) = P(x \leq F^{-1}(y))$. Note that to each y, a unique $F^{-1}(y)$ exists, since $F(y)$ is continuous strictly increasing. But $P(x \leq F^{-1}(y))$ by definition is $F(F^{-1}(y)) = y$.

If $F(X)$ is a RV denoted as U, then the above shows $P(U \leq y) = y$. Note that $0 \leq y \leq 1$. But this is the characterization of a uniform $U(0,1)$ distribution. Hence, $F(X) = U$ is $U(0,1)$. □

A very useful application of this theorem is to enable the generation of random values of X with any given cdf $F(X)$ where its inverse could be computed. Generate a random u from $U(0,1)$, then compute $x = F^{-1}(u)$ to obtain the random value of X.

1.2.6 Normal Distribution

Consider $\int_{-\infty}^{+\infty} e^{1-|y|} dy = \int_{-\infty}^{0} e^{1+y} dy + \int_{0}^{+\infty} e^{1-y} dy = [e^{1+y}]_{-\infty}^{0} - [e^{1-y}]_{0}^{+\infty} = 2e$.

For $y > 0$, $y^2 - 2|y| + 2 \equiv y^2 - 2y + 2 = (y-1)^2 + 1 > 0$. For $y < 0$, $y^2 - 2|y| + 2 \equiv y^2 + 2y + 2 = (y+1)^2 + 1 > 0$. Then, $y^2 - 2|y| + 2 > 0$ for all y. Or, $-\frac{y^2}{2} < 1 - |y|$. Hence, $\int_{-\infty}^{+\infty} e^{-y^2/2} dy < 2e$, and is bounded. This gives an idea that $\int_{-\infty}^{+\infty} e^{-y^2/2} dy$ has an interesting value.

We first find $I^2 = \int_{-\infty}^{\infty} \int_{-\infty}^{\infty} \exp(-\frac{x^2+y^2}{2}) dx\, dy$. Changing to polar coordinates by putting $x = r\cos\theta$ and $y = r\sin\theta$

$$I^2 = \int_0^{2\pi} \int_0^{\infty} e^{-r^2/2} |J|\, dr\, d\theta$$

where J is the Jacobian matrix and $|J|$ is its Jacobian determinant or simply "Jacobian":

$$|J| = \begin{vmatrix} \frac{dx}{dr} & \frac{dx}{d\theta} \\ \frac{dy}{dr} & \frac{dy}{d\theta} \end{vmatrix} = \begin{vmatrix} \cos\theta & -r\sin\theta \\ \sin\theta & r\cos\theta \end{vmatrix} = r\cos^2\theta + r\sin^2\theta = r$$

Each bivariate point (x, y) has a one-to-one correspondence to (r, θ) on the polar coordinate system.[1] Now

$$I^2 = \int_0^{2\pi}\int_0^{\infty} e^{-r^2/2} r\, dr\, d\theta = 2\pi$$

Hence,

$$\begin{aligned} 2\pi &= \int_{-\infty}^{\infty}\int_{-\infty}^{\infty} \exp\left(-\frac{x^2+y^2}{2}\right) dx\, dy \\ &= \int_{-\infty}^{\infty} \exp\left(-\frac{y^2}{2}\right)\left[\int_{-\infty}^{\infty} \exp\left(-\frac{x^2}{2}\right) dx\right] dy \\ &= \left[\int_{-\infty}^{\infty} \exp\left(-\frac{y^2}{2}\right) dy\right]^2 \end{aligned}$$

Thus, $\int_{-\infty}^{\infty} \frac{1}{\sqrt{2\pi}} e^{-\frac{y^2}{2}} dy = 1$. Applying a change of variable $y = \frac{x-\mu}{\sigma}$, we obtain

$$\int_{-\infty}^{\infty} \frac{1}{\sigma\sqrt{2\pi}} \exp\left[-\frac{(x-\mu)^2}{2\sigma^2}\right] dx = 1$$

so that the normal pdf is $f(x) = \frac{1}{\sigma\sqrt{2\pi}} \exp[-\frac{(x-\mu)^2}{2\sigma^2}]$.

We shall see that the normal distribution is indeed fascinating, if not one of the most celebrated results in mathematical statistics, via the central limit theorem. It comes naturally from common phenomena such as aggregation and averaging. Its distribution is also found to describe well the frequencies of occurrences in natural processes such as heights of people, IQs of students, spatial densities in plant growth, and so on. Not surprisingly, it is also used in describing the distributions of stock returns. While this is reasonable in normal times, it would appear from the many incidences of market turbulence in history, that unquestioned application could be greatly flawed. Even during normal times, stock returns generally display some skewness and

1 See Mood, Graybill, and Boes (1974) for transformations in probability distributions.

a larger kurtosis or fatter tails than those of a normal distribution. Some more complicated functions of the normal RV are often used to describe stock returns. In any case, normal distributions are excellent basic pillars to more complicated constructions.

The MGF of a standardized (or "unit") normal RV $X \sim N(0,1)$ is

$$\begin{aligned} M(\theta) &= \int_{-\infty}^{\infty} e^{\theta x} \frac{1}{\sqrt{2\pi}} e^{-\frac{1}{2}x^2}\, dx \\ &= \frac{1}{\sqrt{2\pi}} \int_{-\infty}^{\infty} \exp\left\{-\frac{(x^2 - 2\theta x)}{2}\right\} dx \\ &= \frac{1}{\sqrt{2\pi}} \int_{-\infty}^{\infty} \exp\left\{-\frac{(x-\theta)^2}{2} + \frac{\theta^2}{2}\right\} dx \\ &= e^{\frac{1}{2}\theta^2} \end{aligned}$$

Using the MGF, it can be shown that $E(X) = 0$, $E(X^2) = 1$, $E(X^3) = 0$, and $E(X^4) = 3$.

A related distribution is the lognormal distribution. A RV X has a lognormal distribution when $\ln(X) = Y$ is normally distributed:

$$Y \overset{d}{\sim} N(\mu, \sigma^2)$$

Then

$$\begin{aligned} E(X) = E(e^Y) &= \int_{-\infty}^{\infty} e^y \frac{1}{\sigma\sqrt{2\pi}} e^{-\frac{1}{2\sigma^2}(y-\mu)^2}\, dy \\ &= \int_{-\infty}^{\infty} \frac{1}{\sigma\sqrt{2\pi}} e^{-\frac{1}{2\sigma^2}[(y-\mu)^2 - 2\sigma^2 y]}\, dy \\ &= \int_{-\infty}^{\infty} \frac{1}{\sigma\sqrt{2\pi}} e^{-\frac{1}{2\sigma^2}[(y-(\mu+\sigma^2))^2 - \sigma^4 - 2\mu\sigma^2]}\, dy \\ &= e^{\mu + 1/2\sigma^2} \end{aligned}$$

Similarly, it can be shown that $\operatorname{var}(X) = e^{2\mu}[e^{2\sigma^2} - e^{\sigma^2}]$.

1.2.7 Related Distributions

Let $X \sim N(0,1)$ be a standardized or unit normal RV. Then RV X^2 has a chi-square distribution with one degree of freedom, i. e. χ_1^2. If $X_1, X_2, \ldots, X_k$ are k-independent unit normal RVs, then $\sum_{i=1}^k X_i^2$ has a chi-square distribution with k degrees of freedom, i. e. χ_k^2. The degree of freedom here refers to the number of independent observations in the sum of squares. If Y^2 and Z^2 are two independent chi-square RVs with k_1 and k_2 degrees of freedom, then their sum $Y^2 + Z^2$ is $\chi^2_{k_1+k_2}$. A chi-square RV is always positive and its pdf has a right skew. The mean of χ^2_k is k, and its variance is $2k$.

An important result for statistical inference is found in the following lemma.

Lemma 1.1. *If $X \sim N(\mu, \sigma^2)$, X_i for $i = 1, 2, \dots, n$ are independently identically distributed RV draws of X, and $S^2 = (n-1)^{-1} \sum_{i=1}^n (X_i - \bar{X})^2$, where $\bar{X} = n^{-1} \sum_{i=1}^n X_i$, then*

$$(n-1)\left(\frac{S^2}{\sigma^2}\right) \sim \chi^2_{n-1}$$

Proof. First we need to prove that $\bar{x}$ and S^2 are independent. $\bar{X} \sim N(\mu, \sigma^2/n)$, so

$$\begin{aligned}\bar{X} - X_j &= \frac{1}{n}(X_1 + \cdots + X_{j-1} + X_{j+1} + \cdots + X_n) - \frac{n-1}{n} X_j \\ &\sim N\left(0, (n-1)\frac{\sigma^2}{n^2} + (n-1)^2\frac{\sigma^2}{n^2}\right) = N\left(0, \frac{n-1}{n}\sigma^2\right)\end{aligned}$$

for any $j = 1, 2, \dots, n$. For any such j,

$$\operatorname{cov}(X_j - \bar{X}, \bar{X}) = \operatorname{cov}(X_j, \bar{X}) - \operatorname{var}(\bar{X}) = \frac{\sigma^2}{n} - \frac{\sigma^2}{n} = 0$$

Since $\bar{X}$ and $X_j - \bar{X}$ $\forall j$ are normally distributed, zero covariances imply they are statistically independent. Hence, $\bar{X}$ is also independent of $(n-1)^{-1} \sum_{i=1}^n (X_i - \bar{X})^2 = S^2$.

Next let $C = \sum_{i=1}^n (\frac{X_i - \mu}{\sigma})^2$. Then,

$$\begin{aligned}C &= \sum_{i=1}^n \left(\frac{(X_i - \bar{X}) + (\bar{X} - \mu)}{\sigma}\right)^2 \\ &= \sum_{i=1}^n \left(\frac{X_i - \bar{X}}{\sigma}\right)^2 + \sum_{i=1}^n \left(\frac{\bar{X} - \mu}{\sigma}\right)^2 + 2\left(\frac{\bar{X} - \mu}{\sigma^2}\right) \sum_{i=1}^n (X_i - \bar{X})\end{aligned}$$

The last term above equals to zero (whatever the realizations), so $C = \sum_{i=1}^n (\frac{X_i - \bar{X}}{\sigma})^2 + \frac{n(\bar{X}-\mu)^2}{\sigma^2}$. The latter is equal to $\frac{(n-1)S^2}{\sigma^2} + \frac{(\bar{X}-\mu)^2}{\sigma^2/n}$. The second term is the square of a unit normal RV since $\bar{X} \sim N(\mu, \sigma^2/n)$ and involves $\bar{X}$. It is a χ^2_1 RV. But C is χ^2_n. Both these χ^2_1 and χ^2_n are independent as $\bar{X}$ and S^2 are independent. Hence $\frac{(n-1)S^2}{\sigma^2}$ is χ^2_{n-1}. □

We note that $\frac{\bar{X}-\mu}{\sigma/\sqrt{n}} \sim N(0, 1)$. Another related distribution is obtained when this unit normal RV is divided by S/σ. We obtain the RV $\frac{\bar{X}-\mu}{S/\sqrt{n}}$. Since $S/\sigma \sim \sqrt{\frac{\chi^2_{n-1}}{n-1}}$, then $\frac{\bar{X}-\mu}{S/\sqrt{n}} \sim N(0,1)/\sqrt{\frac{\chi^2_{n-1}}{n-1}}$. The normal RV in the numerator and the chi-square RV in the denominator are statistically independent. $N(0,1)/\sqrt{\frac{\chi^2_{n-1}}{n-1}}$ is a Student's t-distribution RV with $(n-1)$ degrees of freedom, t_{n-1}.

From Lemma 1.1, taking expectations, $E[(n-1)S^2/\sigma^2] = E(\chi^2_{n-1}) = n-1$. Hence, $E(S^2) = \sigma^2$. Therefore, $S^2 = (n-1)^{-1}\sum_{i=1}^n (x_i - \bar{X})^2$ is the unbiased estimator of σ^2.

Suppose now $X \sim N(\mu_X, \sigma^2)$ and $Y \sim N(\mu_Y, \sigma^2)$ where X, Y are independent RVs. Observations x_i and y_j are independently drawn from these two RVs. Their unbiased sample variances are, respectively, RVs $S_X^2 = \sum_{i=1}^n \frac{(X_i-\bar{X})^2}{n-1}$ and $S_Y^2 = \sum_{i=1}^m \frac{(Y_i-\bar{Y})^2}{m-1}$. Their ratio is the F-distribution with two degrees of freedom, $n-1$ and $m-1$, i. e.,

$$\frac{S_X^2}{S_Y^2} = \frac{\sum_{i=1}^n (X_i - \bar{X})^2/(n-1)}{\sum_{j=1}^m (Y_i - \bar{Y})^2/(m-1)} \sim F_{n,m}$$

The F RV is in fact the ratio of two independent chi-square RVs each divided by their respective degree of freedom, $\frac{\chi^2_{n-1}/(n-1)}{\chi^2_{m-1}/(m-1)}$. Note that $1/F$ is also a F RV. There is an interesting relationship between the t-distribution RV with k degrees of freedom and the F RV. $t_k^2 = F_{1,k}$.

1.3 Estimation and Hypothesis Testing

Statistics is a major part of applied probability. A large part of applied statistics is about estimation of unknown parameters and about testing of statistical hypotheses concerning the parameter values. Suppose a random variable X with a fixed normal distribution $N(\mu, \sigma^2)$ is given. We do not know the value of the mean μ and the variance σ^2. Therefore the task is to estimate μ and σ^2. There are two common types of estimates – point estimate and interval estimate.

Suppose there is a random draw of a number or an outcome from this distribution. This is the same as stating that random variable X takes a (realized) value x. Let this value be x_1. Suppose we repeatedly make random draws and thus form a sample of n observations: $x_1, x_2, x_3, \ldots, x_{n-1}, x_n$. This is called a random sample with a sample size of n. Each x_i comes from the same distribution $N(\mu, \sigma^2)$.

We next consider a statistic, which is a RV and a function of the RVs $X_1, X_2, \ldots, X_n$, that is $\bar{X} = \frac{1}{n}\sum_{i=1}^n X_i$. Each time we select a random sample of size n, we obtain a realization of this statistic $\bar{x} = \frac{1}{n}\sum_{i=1}^n x_i$ which is a sample mean. In other words, $\bar{x}$ is a realized value of RV $\bar{X}$. With repeated or different samplings, we can obtain different values of $\bar{x}$. The probability distribution of $\bar{X}$ is called the sampling distribution of the mean or the distribution of the sample mean.

Another common sample statistic value is the unbiased sample variance estimator

$$S^2 = \frac{1}{n-1}\sum_{i=1}^n (X_i - \bar{X})^2$$

Its realized value s^2 is an unbiased estimate of the variance. Note we use "estimator" to denote the statistic or RV, and estimate to denote the (realized or computed) value of the statistic. The sample mean and the unbiased sample variance estimates are point estimates. When the sample size n is large, these estimates may be close to the actual μ and σ^2.

Suppose $X \sim N(\mu, \sigma^2)$, its cdf is

$$F(X) = \int_{-\infty}^{\frac{X-\mu}{\sigma}} f\left(\frac{X-\mu}{\sigma}\right) dz$$

where $f(\frac{X-\mu}{\sigma})$ is the standard normal pdf and $z = \frac{X-\mu}{\sigma}$. The standard normal cdf $f(z)$ is often written as $\Phi(z)$. For the standard normal Z,

$$P(a \leq z \leq b) = \Phi(b) - \Phi(a)$$

The normal distribution is a familiar workhorse in statistical estimation and testing. The normal distribution pdf curve is "bell-shaped". Areas under the curve are associated with probabilities. Figure 1.5 shows a standard normal pdf $N(0, 1)$ and the associated probability as area under the curve.

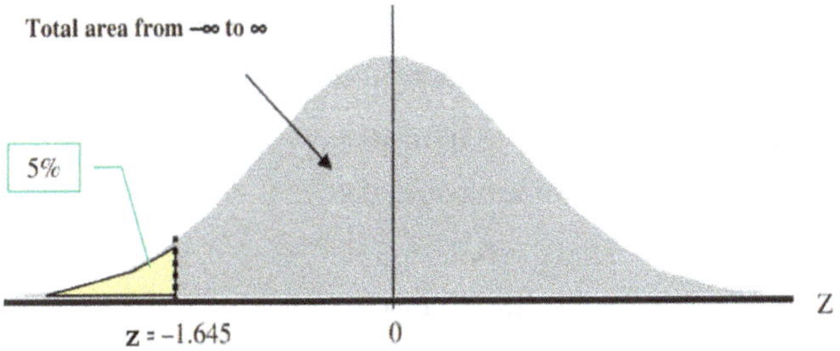

Figure 1.5: Standard Normal Probability Density Function of Z.

The corresponding z values of RV Z can be seen in the following standard normal distribution Table 1.3. For example, the probability $P(-\infty < z < 1.5) = 0.933$. This same probability can be written as $P(-\infty \leq z < 1.5) = 0.933$, $P(-\infty < z \leq 1.5) = 0.933$, or $P(-\infty \leq z \leq 1.5) = 0.933$. This is because for continuous pdf, $P(z = 1.5) = 0$.

From the symmetry of the normal pdf, $P(-a < z < \infty) = P(-\infty < z < a)$, we can also compute the following:

$$P(z > 1.5) = 1 - P(-\infty < z \leq 1.5) = 1 - 0.933 = 0.067.$$

$$P(-\infty < z \leq -1.0) = P(z > 1.0) = 1 - 0.841 = 0.159.$$

$$P(-1.0 < z < 1.5) = P(-\infty < z < 1.5) - (-\infty < z \leq -1.0) = 0.933 - 0.159 = 0.774.$$

$$P(z \leq -1.0 \text{ or } z \geq 1.5) = 1 - P(-1.0 < z < 1.5) = 1 - 0.774 = 0.226.$$

Table 1.3: Standard Normal Cumulative Distribution Curve.

z	Area under curve from $-\infty$ to z	z	Area under curve from $-\infty$ to z
0.000	0.500	1.600	0.945
0.100	0.539	1.645	0.950
0.200	0.579	1.700	0.955
0.300	0.618	1.800	0.964
0.400	0.655	1.960	0.975
0.500	0.691	2.000	0.977
0.600	0.726	2.100	0.982
0.700	0.758	2.200	0.986
0.800	0.788	2.300	0.989
0.900	0.816	2.330	0.990
1.000	0.841	2.400	0.992
1.100	0.864	2.500	0.994
1.282	0.900	2.576	0.995
1.300	0.903	2.600	0.996
1.400	0.919	2.700	0.997
1.500	0.933	2.800	0.998

Several values of Z under $N(0, 1)$ are commonly encountered, viz. 1.282, 1.645, 1.960, 2.330, and 2.576.

$$
\begin{aligned}
P(z > 1.282) &= 0.10 \text{ or } 10\,\%. \\
P(z < -1.645 \text{ or } z > 1.645) &= 0.10 \text{ or } 10\,\%. \\
P(z > 1.960) &= 0.025 \text{ or } 2.5\,\%. \\
P(z < -1.960 \text{ or } z > 1.960) &= 0.05 \text{ or } 5\,\%. \\
P(z > 2.330) &= 0.01 \text{ or } 1\,\%. \\
P(z < -2.576 \text{ or } z > 2.576) &= 0.01 \text{ or } 1\,\%.
\end{aligned}
$$

The case for $P(z < -1.645) = 5\,\%$ is shown in Figure 1.5.

Suppose we estimated the sample mean of a random sample of size $n = 100$ drawn from $X \sim N(\mu, \sigma^2)$ as $\bar{x} = 0.08$. This is a point estimate of μ. Suppose the variance is known, $\sigma^2 = 0.25$. Then $Z = \frac{\bar{X}-\mu}{0.5/\sqrt{100}} = \frac{\bar{X}-\mu}{0.05}$ is distributed as $N(0, 1)$. Suppose we find $a > 0$ such that $P(-a \leq z \leq +a) = 95\,\%$. Since z is symmetrically distributed, $P(-a \leq z) = 97.5\,\%$ and $P(z \leq +a) = 97.5\,\%$. Thus $a = +1.96$.

Then,

$$
P\left(-1.96 \leq \frac{\bar{x} - \mu}{0.05} \leq +1.96\right) = 0.95
$$

Re-arranging, $P(\bar{x} - 1.96(0.05) \le \mu \le \bar{x} + 1.96(0.05)) = 0.95$. Or, $P(-0.018 \le \mu \le 0.178)$. The interval estimate of μ at 95 % confidence level is thus $(-0.018, 0.178)$. This is also called the 95 % confidence interval estimate of μ based on the observed random sample. Different samples will give rise to different confidence intervals. Given a sample, there is 95 % probability or chance that the true μ is contained in the estimated interval.

In the above, suppose var(X) is not known. Suppose S^2 is the unbiased variance estimator. Then,

$$\frac{\bar{X} - \mu}{S/\sqrt{n}}$$

is distributed as t_{n-1}. We can find $a > 0$, such that $P(-a \le t_{n-1} \le +a) = 95\,\%$. Since t_{n-1} is symmetrically distributed about zero, $P(-a \le t_{99}) = 97.5\,\%$ and $\text{Prob}(t_{99} \le +a) = 97.5\,\%$. Thus $a = +1.9842$ (found from a t-distribution table).

Then,

$$P\left(-1.9842 \le \frac{\bar{x} - \mu}{s/\sqrt{100}} \le +1.9842\right) = 0.95$$

Re-arranging, $P(\bar{x} - 1.9842(s/10) \le \mu \le \bar{x} + 1.9842(s/10)) = 0.95$. In this case suppose sample mean and unbiased sample variance are computed as $\bar{x} = 0.08$, $s^2 = 0.36$. Thus $P(-0.03905 \le \mu \le 0.19905)$. The 95 % confidence interval estimate of μ based on the observed random sample is thus $(-0.03905, 0.19905)$.

1.3.1 Statistical Testing

In many situations, there is a priori (or ex-ante) information about the value of the mean μ, and it may be desirable to use observed data to test if the information is correct. μ is called a parameter of the population or fixed distribution $N(\mu, \sigma^2)$. A statistical hypothesis is an assertion about the true value of the population parameter, in this case μ. A simple hypothesis specifies a single value for the parameter, while a composite hypothesis will specify more than one value. We will work with the simple null hypothesis H_0 (sometimes this is called the maintained hypothesis), which is what is postulated to be true. The alternative hypothesis H_A is what will be the case if the null hypothesis is rejected. Together the values specified under H_0 and H_A should form the total universe of possibilities of the parameter. For example,

$$H_0 : \mu = 1$$
$$H_A : \mu \neq 1$$

Given the sample values and sampling distribution, a statistical test of the hypothesis is a decision rule based on the value of a test statistic to either reject or else not reject (informally similar in meaning to "accept") the null H_0. The set of sample outcomes or sample values that lead to the rejection of the H_0 is called the critical region. The set of sample outcomes or sample values that lead to the non-rejection of the H_0 is called the acceptance region. The critical region in many cases can be easily specified when the test statistic has a continuous distribution.

If H_0 is true but is rejected, a Type I error is committed. In colloquial parlance, this may be called a false negative. If H_0 is false but is accepted, a Type II error is committed or a false positive.

Suppose the test statistic has a t_{n-1} distribution. The statistical rule on $H_0 : \mu = 1$, $H_A : \mu \neq 1$, is that if the test statistic falls within the critical region (shaded), defined as $\{t_{n-1} < -a \text{ or } t_{n-1} > +a\}$, $a > 0$, as shown in Figure 1.6, then H_0 is rejected in favor of H_A. Otherwise, H_0 is not rejected and is "accepted".

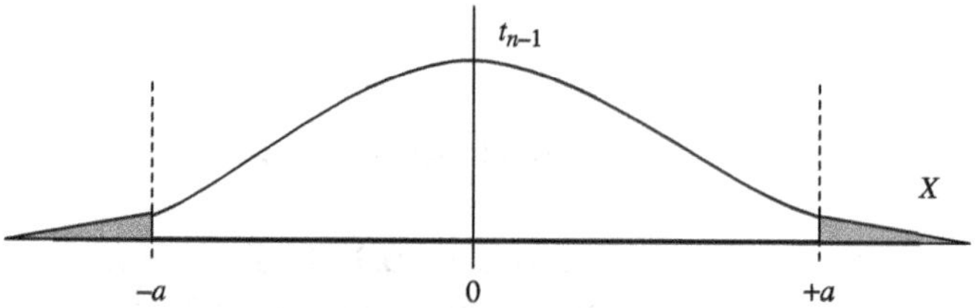

Figure 1.6: Critical Region Under the Null Hypothesis $H_0 : \mu = 1$.

If H_0 is true, the probability of rejecting H_0 would be the area of the critical region, say 5 % in this case. If $n = 100$, $P(-1.9842 < t_{99} < +1.9842) = 0.95$. Moreover, the t-distribution is symmetrical, so each of the right and left shaded tails has an area of 2.5 %. Using a left-tailed and a right-tailed critical region constitutes a two-tailed test with a significance level of 5 %. The significance level is the probability of committing a Type I error when H_0 is true. In the above example, if the sample t-statistic is 1.787, then it is < 1.9842, and we cannot reject H_0 at the two-tailed 5 % significance level. Given a sample t-value, we can also find its p-value which is the probability under H_0 of $|t_{99}|$ exceeding 1.9842 in a two-tailed test. In the above two-tailed test, the p-value of a sample statistic of 1.787 would be $2 \times P(t_{99} > 1.787) = 2 \times 0.0385 = 0.077$ or 7.7 %. Another way to verify the test is that if the p-value < test significance level, reject H_0; otherwise H_0 cannot be rejected.

In theory, if we reduce the probability of Type I error, the probability of Type II error increases, and vice versa. This is illustrated in Figure 1.7.

Suppose H_0 is false, and $\mu > 1$, so the true t_{n-1} pdf is represented by the dotted curve in Figure 1.7. The critical region $t_{99} < -1.9842$ or $t_{99} > +1.9842$ remains the same, so the probability of committing Type II error is 1− sum of shaded areas. Clearly, this probability increases as we reduce the critical region in order to reduce Type I error. Although it is ideal to reduce both types of errors, the tradeoff forces us to choose

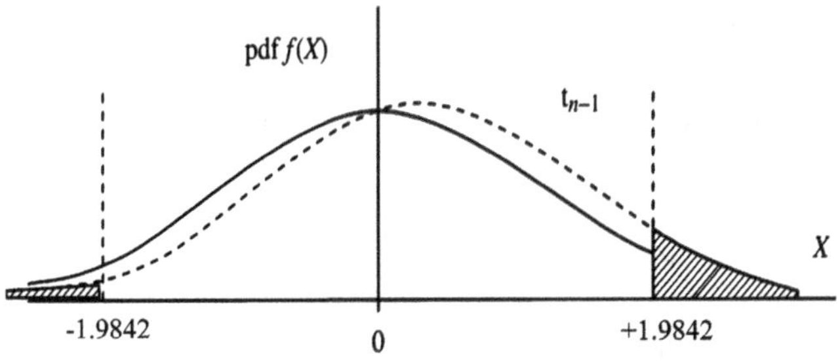

Figure 1.7: Depiction of Type II Error.

between the two. In practice, we fix the probability of Type I error when the prior belief is that H_0 is true, i. e. determine a fixed significance level, e. g., 10 %, 5 %, or 1 %. The power of a statistical test is the probability of rejecting H_0 when it is false. Thus, power $= 1 - P$(Type II error). Or, power equals the shaded area in Figure 1.7. Clearly, this power is a function of the alternative parameter value $\mu \neq 1$. We may determine such a power function of $\mu \neq 1$.

Reducing significance level also reduces power and vice versa. In statistics, it is customary to want to design a test so that its power function of $\mu \neq 1$ equals or exceeds that of any other test with equal significance level for all plausible parameter values $\mu \neq 1$ in H_A. If this test is found, it is called a uniformly most powerful test.[2]

We have seen the performance of a two-tailed test. Sometimes, we embark instead on a one-tailed test such as $H_0 : \mu = 1$, $H_A : \mu > 1$, in which we theoretically rule out the possibility of $\mu < 1$, i. e. $P(\mu < 1) = 0$. In this case, it makes sense to limit the critical region to only the right side. Thus, at the one-tailed 5 % significance level, the critical region under H_0 is {statistic value of $t_{99,95\,\%} > 1.661$} for $n = 100$.

Further Reading

Hogg, R. V., and A. T. Craig (1978), *Introduction to Mathematical Statistics*, Macmillan Publishing Co.
Mood, A. M., F. A. Graybill, and D. C. Boes (1974), *Introduction to the Theory of Statistics*, McGraw-Hill.

2 See Hogg and Craig (1978) in Further Reading.

2 Simple Linear Regression

2.1 Simple Linear Regression

A regression is an association between a dependent variable and other explanatory variables. The idea of checking out the association is basically for two major purposes: to provide some positive theory of how the dependent variable could be explained by, not necessarily caused by, other variables, and a normative or prescriptive theory of how to use the association to predict future occurrences of the dependent variable. In this chapter we consider simple linear regression involving only one explanatory variable. The dependent RV Y_i takes realized values $Y_1, Y_2, \ldots$ where i could denote time index or cross-sectional index, e. g., different stock i, or different sample points at different draws in repetitive sampling. The explanatory RV X_i makes sense if the bivariate cumulative probability distribution function cdf (X_i, Y_i) exists and is not null. The explanatory variable X_i should not be itself explained by Y_i nor dependent on parameters in the model explaining Y_i; hence it is often termed as independent or exogenous. In Figure 2.1, we show sample observations of Y and X variables.

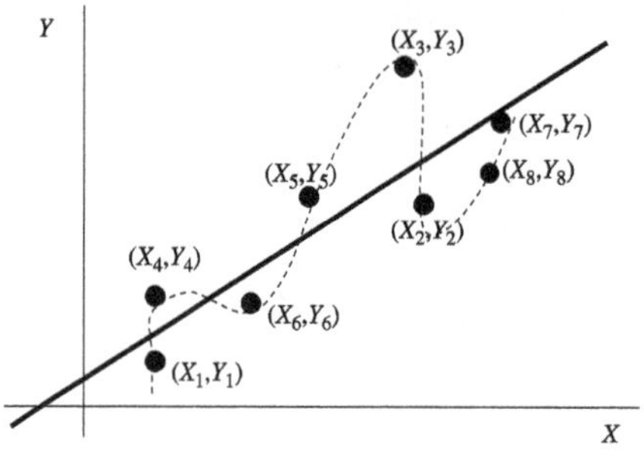

Figure 2.1: An Association Between Variables X and Y.

The bold line shows an attempt to draw a linear line as "close" to the observed occurrences as possible. The line is an attempt to provide a model that is able to indicate what is the associated Y_i value if another different X_i value is observed. Or, does it make sense for us to draw a nonlinear line that fits all the sample points exactly as seen in the dotted curve? Obviously not. This is because the bivariate points are just realized observations of bivariate random variables. Perfect fitting is only possible when the points are known ex-post. Drawing the dotted curve line through all the current eight points is like a model with eight parameters, e. g., an 8-degree polynomial equation. The dotted curve in-between points is arbitrary here. When another sample point (X_9, Y_9) is drawn, the 8-parameter curve clearly will not fit the new sample point. The 8-parameter model is an over-fitted model with no clear economic sense.

https://doi.org/10.1515/9783110673951-002

What we want is a straight line in a linear model, or else a curve in a nonlinear model, that is estimated in such a way that whatever the sample, as long as the size is sufficiently large, the line will pretty much remain at about the same position. This will then enable purposes of (1) explaining $Y_i \in$ RV Y given any $X_i \in$ RV X, and (2) forecasting given X_i. When the sample size is small, there will be large sampling errors of the model parameter estimates, i. e. the slope and intercept in Figure 2.1 of the fitted line may change by alot when a different sample is drawn.

Therefore, the idea of a regression model (need not be linear), $Y = f(X;\theta)+\varepsilon$, where ε is a random error or noise, is one where parameter(s) θ are suitably estimated as $\hat{\theta}$. $\hat{\theta}$ is "close to" true θ given a sample of $\{(X_i, Y_i)\}_{i=1,\ldots,n}$, size n, such that $\sum_{i=1}^{n} g[Y_i - f(X_i;\hat{\theta})]$ is small in some statistical sense where $g(.)$ is a criterion function. For example, $g(z) = z^2$ is one such criterion function. Thus, a linear regression model does not fit random variables X, Y perfectly, but allows for a residual noise ε in order that the model is not over-parameterized or over-fitted. This would then serve purposes (1) and (2).

A linear (bivariate) regression model is:

$$Y_i = a + bX_i + e_i$$

where a and b are constants. In the linear regression model, Y_i is the dependent variable or regressand. X_i is the explanatory variable or regressor. e_i is a residual noise, disturbance, or innovation. The i-subscript denotes a sample datum corresponding to an ith subject. There could be a sample of N subjects (sample size N) and the regression is a cross-sectional regression (across the subjects). For example, Y_i could represent the ith country's labor output, and X_i could represent the ith country's average schooling years. If a constant a has been specified in the linear regression model, then the mean of e_i is zero. If a constant has not been specified, then e_t may have a non-zero mean. It is common to add the specification that e_i is i. i. d. This means that the probability distributions of e_i, for $i = 1, 2, \ldots, N$, are all identical, and each is stochastically (probabilistically) independent of the others.

Often the linear regression is on time series. Thus, $Y_t = a + bX_t + e_t$ where t is the time index taking values $t = 1, 2, \ldots, T$. In this case, it is common to specify that e_t is stochastically independent of all other random variables, including its own lags and leading terms, implying $\text{cov}(e_t, e_{t-k}) = 0$ and $\text{cov}(e_t, e_{t+k}) = 0$ for $k = 1, 2, 3, \ldots, \infty$. An even stronger specification is that e_t is i. i. d. and also normally distributed, and we can write this as n. i. d. $N(\mu, \sigma_e^2)$. In trying to employ the model to explain, and also to forecast, the constant parameters a and b need to be estimated effectively, and perhaps some form of testing on their estimates could be done to verify if they accord with theory. This forms the bulk of the material in the rest of this chapter.

It is important to recognize that a linear model provides for correlation between Y_t and X_t (this need not be the only type of model providing correlation, e. g., nonlinear model $Y_t = \exp(X_t) + e_t$ also does the job) as we see occurred in joint bivariate distribution (X, Y). For example, in $Y_t = a + bX_t + e_t$, with i. i. d. e_t, we have

$\text{cov}(Y_t, X_t) = b\,\text{var}(X_t) \neq 0$ provided $b \neq 0$, and correlation coefficient $\rho(Y_t, X_t) = b\sqrt{\text{var}(X_t)}/\sqrt{\text{var}(Y_t)}$.

Sometimes, we encounter a timeplot (a timeplot shows a variable's realized values against time) or a scatterplot (a graph of simultaneous pairs of realized values of random variables) that does not look linear, unlike Figure 2.1. As an example, consider the following two regressions both producing straight lines that appear to cut evenly through the collection of points in each graph if we use the criterion that minimizes z^2.

The point is that using some intuitively appropriate criterion such as least squares minimization to fit linear lines is not enough. It is important to first establish that the relationship is plausibly linear before attempting to fit a linear regression model.

In Figure 2.2, the graph Y versus X is clearly a nonlinear curve. If it is quadratic, then it is appropriate in that case to use a nonlinear regression model such as $Y = \text{a} + \text{b}X + \text{c}X^2 + \varepsilon$. In Figure 2.3, for Y versus X, there is clearly an outlier point with a very high Y-value. As a result, the fitted line is actually above the normal points that form the rest of the sample. This can be treated either by excluding the outlier point if the assessment is that it is an aberration or recording error, or else by providing for another explanatory variable to explain that point that may be a rare event.

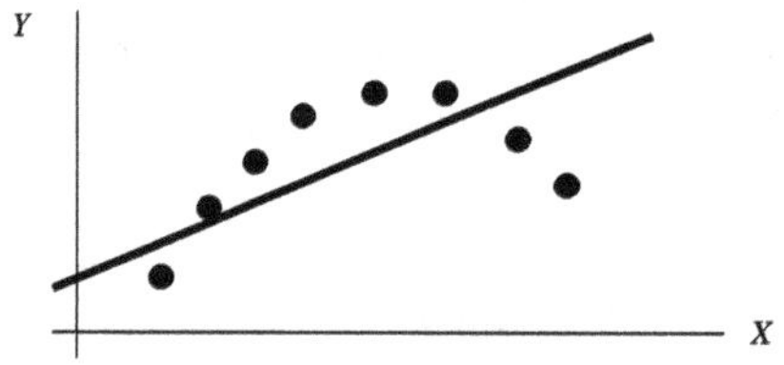

Figure 2.2: A Nonlinear Example.

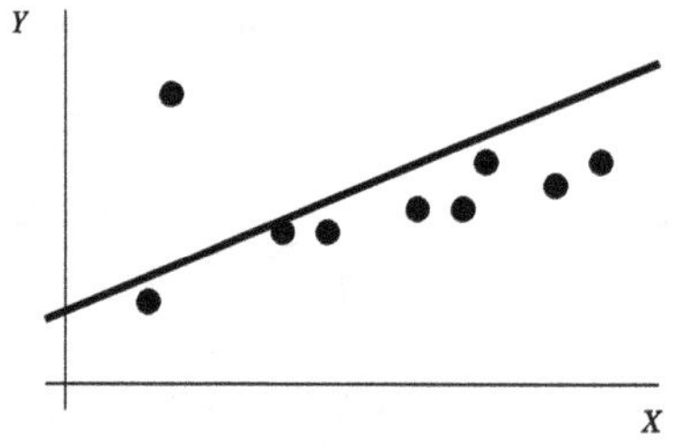

Figure 2.3: An Example of Outlier.

Thus, a visual check on the data plots is useful to ascertain if a linear regression model is appropriate and whether there are outliers. Sometimes, there are theoretical models that specify relationships between random variables that are nonlinear, but which can be transformed to linear models so that linear regression methods can be applied for estimation and testing. Examples are as follows.

When $Y = aX^b\varepsilon$, take log–log transformation (taking logs on both sides), so

$$\ln Y = \ln a + b \ln X + \ln \varepsilon$$

Note that here the disturbance noise ε must necessarily be larger than zero, otherwise $\ln \varepsilon$ will have non-feasible values. Here, $\ln \varepsilon$ can range from $-\infty$ to ∞. Sometimes, Y is called the constant elasticity function with respect to X since b is the constant elasticity (when $\ln \varepsilon$ is fixed at zero).

When $Y = \exp(a + bX + \varepsilon)$, taking logs on both sides ends up with a semi-log transformation, so $\ln Y = a + bX + \varepsilon$. This is also called a semi-log model.

When $e^Y = aX^b\varepsilon$, taking logs on both sides ends up again with a semi-log model $Y = \ln a + b \ln X + \ln \varepsilon$. Sometimes, when the regressor X is a fast increasing series relative to Y, then taking the natural log of X as regressor will produce a more stable result, as long as theory has nothing against this ad hoc data transformation practice.

There are examples of interesting nonlinear curves that are important in economics. An example is the Phillips curve shown as follows in Figure 2.4.

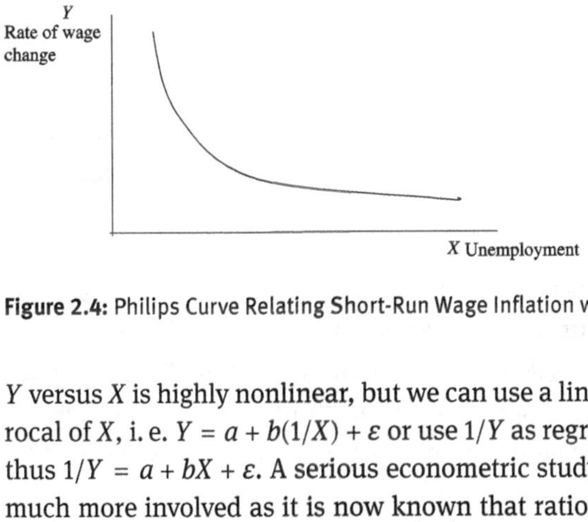

Figure 2.4: Philips Curve Relating Short-Run Wage Inflation with Unemployment Level.

Y versus X is highly nonlinear, but we can use a linear regression model on the reciprocal of X, i. e. $Y = a + b(1/X) + \varepsilon$ or use $1/Y$ as regressand or the dependent variable, thus $1/Y = a + bX + \varepsilon$. A serious econometric study of the Phillips curve is of course much more involved as it is now known that rational forces cause the curve to shift over time in the longer run. In other words, observed pairs of wage inflation and unemployment levels over time belong to different Phillips curves.

Next, we study one major class of estimators of the linear regression model and the properties of such estimators. This class is synonymous with the criterion method for deriving the estimates of the model parameters. This is the ordinary least squares (OLS) criterion.

2.2 OLS Method

In the linear regression model, the dependent variable is assumed to be a linear function of one or more explanatory variables plus a residual error (or noise or disturbance or innovation) variable introduced to account for all other factor(s) that are either not observed or are not known and which are random variable(s). It is important to note that the dependent variable, the explanatory variable, as well as the residual error variable are all RVs.

In a two-variable or simple linear regression model

$$Y_i = a + bX_i + e_i, \quad i = 1, 2, \ldots, N \tag{2.1}$$

Y_i is the dependent variable, X_i is the explanatory variable, and e_i is the residual error.

The random variables Y_i, X_i's are observed as sample bivariate points $\{X_i, Y_i\}$ (for different i). Disturbances or residual errors e_i's are not observed, and a, b are constants to be estimated. $E(e_i) = 0$, and var(e_i) is assumed to be a constant σ_e^2, which is also not observed. The task is to estimate parameters a and b and σ_e^2. Note that we have not specifically notate a RV with a tilde; the context should be clear which is a random variable and which is a realized value. Unlike Chapter 1, we do not denote realized values as lower case letters as otherwise the notations can become quite complicated.

The classical assumptions (desirable conditions) for OLS regression are:

(A1) $E(e_i) = 0$ for every i.

(A2) $E(e_i^2) = \sigma_e^2$, a same constant for every i.

(A3) $E(e_i e_j) = 0$ for every $i \neq j$.

(A4) X_i and e_j are stochastically independent (of all other random variables) for each i, j

In assumption (A2), the disturbances with constant variance are called homoskedastic. On the flip side, disturbances with non-constant variances are called heteroskedastic, a subject we shall study in more depth later. Condition (A3) implies zero cross-correlation if the sample is a cross-section, or zero autocorrelation if the sample is a time series. Such properties of the disturbance will be seen to simplify the estimation theory.

Assumption (A4) is perhaps the most critical and important assumption as it affects the feasibility of a good estimator and it also has to do with interpretation of the estimation and inference. As it is, the linear regression model essentially puts a probability distribution on X_i and e_i. Then RV Y_i is derived by adding $a + bX_i$ to e_i. Typically, but not necessarily, the probability distributions of X_i $\forall i$ are the same, and similarly, the probability distributions of e_i $\forall i$ are the same. We shall assume that sample points X_i $\forall i$ are from same probability distribution X, and unobserved e_i are also from same probability distribution e.

In addition to assumptions (A1) through (A4), we could also add a distributional assumption to the random variables, e. g.,

(A5) $e_i \sim N(0, \sigma_e^2)$

In Figure 2.5, the dots represent the data points (X_i, Y_i) for each i. The regression lines passing amidst the points represent attempts to provide a linear association between X_i and Y_i. The scalar value $\hat{e}_i$ indicate measure of the vertical distance between the point (X_i, Y_i) and the fitted regression line. The solid line provides a better fit than the dotted line, and we shall elaborate on this.

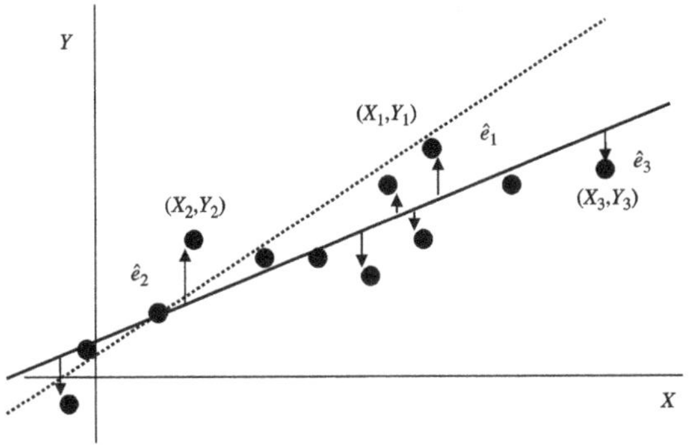

Figure 2.5: OLS Regression of Observations (X_i, Y_i).

The requirement of a linear regression model estimation is to estimate a and b. The OLS method of estimating a and b is to find $\hat{a}$ and $\hat{b}$ so as to minimize the residual sum of squares (RSS), $\sum_{i=1}^{N} \hat{e}_i^2$. Note that this is different from minimising the sum of squares of random variables e_i, which cannot be done as we do not observe the e_i's. This is an important concept that should not be missed. Given a particular sample, the computed numbers $\hat{a}$ and $\hat{b}$ are realized values of the estimators, and are called estimates. With different samples and hence different realizations of (X_i, Y_i)'s, there will be different sets of values of $\hat{a}$ and $\hat{b}$. These values are realizations from the estimators. Hence when $\hat{a}$, $\hat{b}$ are functions of RVs X, Y, they are themselves RVs. When they are functions of realizations X_i, Y_i, they are estimates. Although the same notation is used, the context should be distinguished.

The key criterion in OLS is to minimize the sum of the squares of vertical distances from the realized points (or data) to the fitted OLS straight line (or plane if the problem is of a higher dimension):

$$\min_{\hat{a},\hat{b}} \sum_{i=1}^{N} \hat{e}_i^2 \equiv \sum_{i=1}^{N} (Y_i - \hat{a} - \hat{b}X_i)^2$$

Since this is an optimization problem and the objective function is continuous in $\hat{a}$, and $\hat{b}$, we set the slopes with respect to $\hat{a}$ and $\hat{b}$ to zeros.

The First Order Conditions (FOC) yield the following two equations.

$$\frac{\partial \sum_{i=1}^{N} \hat{e}_i^2}{\partial \hat{a}} = -2\sum_{i=1}^{N}(Y_i - \hat{a} - \hat{b}X_i) = 0$$

$$\frac{\partial \sum_{i=1}^{N} \hat{e}_i^2}{\partial \hat{b}} = -2\sum_{i=1}^{N} X_i(Y_i - \hat{a} - \hat{b}X_i) = 0$$

Note that the above left-side quantities are partial derivatives. The equations above are called the normal equations for the linear regression of Y_i on X_i. From the first normal equation,

$$\sum_{i=1}^{N} Y_i = N\hat{a} + \hat{b}\sum_{i=1}^{N} X_i$$

we obtain

$$\hat{a} = \bar{Y} - \hat{b}\bar{X} \tag{2.2}$$

where $\bar{Y} = \frac{1}{N}\sum_{i=1}^{N} Y_i$ and $\bar{X} = \frac{1}{N}\sum_{i=1}^{N} X_i$ are sample means. It also shows that the fitted OLS line $Y = \hat{a} + \hat{b}X$ passes through $(\bar{X}, \bar{Y})$, the "centroid".

From the second normal equation,

$$\sum_{i=1}^{N} X_iY_i = \hat{a}\sum_{i=1}^{N} X_i + \hat{b}\sum_{i=1}^{N} X_i^2$$

Using Eq. (2.2) and the latter, we obtain:

$$\hat{b} = \frac{\sum_{i=1}^{N}(X_i - \bar{X})Y_i}{\sum_{i=1}^{N}(X_i - \bar{X})^2} \tag{2.3}$$

$\hat{b}$ can also be expressed as follows.

$$\hat{b} = \frac{\sum_{i=1}^{N}(X_i - \bar{X})(Y_i - \bar{Y})}{\sum_{i=1}^{N}(X_i - \bar{X})^2} = \frac{\sum_{i=1}^{N} x_i y_i}{\sum_{i=1}^{N} x_i^2}$$

where $x_i = X_i - \bar{X}$ and $y_i = Y_i - \bar{Y}$.

Given data set or sample data X_i, Y_i for $i = 1, 2, \ldots, N$, we can always find the estimates $\hat{a}$. $\hat{b}$ via Eqs. (2.2) and (2.3). When we treat X_i, Y_i as RVs, then $\hat{a}, \hat{b}$ are estimators. They are RVs as well.

What happens to the estimators $\hat{a}$ and $\hat{b}$ when the sample size N goes toward infinity? In such a situation when sample size approaches infinity (or practically when we are in a situation of a very large sample, though still finite sample size), we are discussing asymptotic (large sample) theory.

Consider the following sample moments as sample size increases toward ∞. Population means $E(X) = \mu_X$, $E(Y) = \mu_Y$, and population covariance $E(X - \mu_X)(Y - \mu_Y) = E(XY) - \mu_X\mu_Y$. The sample means are $\frac{1}{N}\sum_{i=1}^{N} X_i = \bar{X}$, $\frac{1}{N}\sum_{i=1}^{N} Y_i = \bar{Y}$. From the Law of Large Numbers, $\lim_{N\to\infty} \bar{X} = \mu_X$, $\lim_{N\to\infty} \bar{Y} = \mu_Y$, when X and Y are stationary. We deal with some of these statistical laws in more details in Chapter 5.

The sample covariance $\frac{1}{N-2}\sum(X_i - \bar{X})(Y_i - \bar{Y})$ is unbiased, but we can also employ $\frac{1}{N}\sum(X_i - \bar{X})(Y_i - \bar{Y}) = S_{XY}$ if N approaches ∞. Both the unbiased version and this S_{XY} will converge to population covariance σ_{XY} as $N \to \infty$. In dealing with large sample theory, we shall henceforth use the latter version of divisor N. Sample variance $\frac{1}{N}\sum(X_i - \bar{X})^2 = S_X^2$, and observe that S_X^2 also converges to σ_X^2 as N approaches ∞.

The population correlation coefficient is $\rho_{XY} = \frac{\sigma_{XY}}{\sigma_X\sigma_Y}$. The sample correlation coefficient is $r_{XY} = \frac{\sum(X_i-\bar{X})(Y_i-\bar{Y})}{\sqrt{\sum(X_i-\bar{X})^2\sum(Y_i-\bar{Y})^2}} = \frac{S_{XY}}{S_XS_Y}$. Likewise, when we take the limit, $\lim_{N\to\infty} r_{XY} = \rho_{XY}$. Theoretically, ρ_{XY} lies within $[-1, +1]$. Now, sample estimate r_{XY} is defined above so that it also lies within $[-1, +1]$. This can be shown using the Cauchy-Schwarz inequality:

$$\left(\sum xy\right)^2 \leq \left(\sum x^2\right)\left(\sum y^2\right)$$

Other definitions of sample correlation, though convergent to the population correlation, may not lie within $[-1, +1]$. One such example is when we use the unbiased sample covariance divided by the unbiased standard deviations.

Now, from Eq. (2.1), with stochastic Y_i and X_i,

$$\begin{aligned}\text{cov}(Y_i, X_i) &= \text{cov}(a + bX_i + e_i, X_i)\\ &= b\,\text{var}(X_i) + \text{cov}(e_i, X_i) = b\,\text{var}(X_i)\end{aligned}$$

since $\text{cov}(e_i, X_i) = 0$ via (A4). Thus in terms of population moments, $b = \text{cov}(Y_i, X_i)/\text{var}(X_i)$. We showed in Eq. (2.3) that

$$\hat{b} = \frac{\sum_{i=1}^{N} x_i y_i}{\sum_{i=1}^{N} x_i^2} = S_{XY}/S_X^2$$

Thus, when $N \to \infty$ for large sample, $\lim_{N\to\infty} \hat{b} = b$ under conditions of stationarity. If $\hat{b}$ is an estimator of b, and $\lim_{N\to\infty} \hat{b} = b$, $\hat{b}$ is said to be a consistent estimator. We can show likewise that $\lim_{N\to\infty} \hat{a} = a$, and hence $\hat{a}$ is also consistent. The concept of limit of RVs here will become clearer in Chapter 5.

The important question is: what are the desirable properties of the OLS estimators, assuming (A1) to (A5), in finite sample?

In Eq. (2.3), using $Y_i = a + bX_i + e_i$, we have

$$\hat{b} = \sum_{i=1}^{N}\left(x_i/\sum_{j=1}^{N}x_j^2\right)(a + bX_i + e_i)$$
$$= b + \sum_{i=1}^{N}\left(x_i/\sum_{j=1}^{N}x_j^2\right)e_i \tag{2.4}$$

Taking unconditional expectation and invoking (A4) and (A1), we have $E(\hat{b}) = b + \sum_{i=1}^{N} E(x_i/\sum_{j=1}^{N} x_j^2)E(e_i) = b$ since $E(e_i) = 0$.

From Eqs. (2.2) and (2.4):

$$\hat{a} = \bar{Y} - \hat{b}\bar{X}$$
$$= \bar{Y} - \left(b + \sum_{i=1}^{N}\left(x_i/\sum_{j=1}^{N}x_j^2\right)e_i\right)\bar{X}$$
$$= \bar{Y} - b\bar{X} - \sum_{i=1}^{N}\left(x_i\bar{X}/\sum_{j=1}^{N}x_j^2\right)e_i$$

Taking unconditional expectation and invoking (A4) and (A1), we have $E(\hat{a}) = E(\bar{Y}) - bE(\bar{X})$. Since $E(Y_i) = a + bE(X_i)$ $(\forall i)$, then $E(\bar{Y}) = a + bE(\bar{X})$. Hence $E(\hat{a}) = a$.

We just showed that estimators $\hat{a}$ and $\hat{b}$ have means at the true parameter values a and b, using (A4) and (A1). Thus OLS estimators $\hat{a}$ and $\hat{b}$ are accordingly unbiased. This is a desirable property of estimators, noting that X is stochastic.

Now to find the variances of estimators $\hat{a}$ and $\hat{b}$ and evaluate their efficiencies – the question of whether the variances are sufficiently small is more difficult. From Eq. (2.4), the variance of $\hat{b}$ is

$$E(\hat{b} - b)^2 = E\left[\sum_{i=1}^{N}\left(x_i/\sum_{j=1}^{N}x_j^2\right)e_i\right]^2$$
$$= \sum_{i=1}^{N}\left[E\left(x_i/\sum_{j=1}^{N}x_j^2\right)^2 E(e_i^2)\right]$$
$$= \sigma_e^2\sum_{i=1}^{N}E\left[x_i^2/\left(\sum_{j=1}^{N}x_j^2\right)^2\right]$$
$$= \sigma_e^2 E\left[1/\left(\sum_{j=1}^{N}x_j^2\right)\right]$$

using assumptions (A1) to (A4). Note that the unconditional variance involves expectations of functions of RVs X_1, X_2, and so on. These expectations are complicated moments of X, even as the distribution of X itself is not specified. It is a similar situation in the case of the variance of $\hat{a}$.

For inferences and computation of estimator variances in OLS, the conditional distributions of the estimators given X, i. e. given realized $X_1, X_2, \ldots, X_N$, are used. The mean and variance of the estimator under conditional distribution are the conditional mean and conditional variance, respectively. From Eq. (2.4), conditional mean of $\hat{b}$ is

$$E[\hat{b}|X] = b + \sum_{i=1}^{N}\left(x_i / \sum_{j=1}^{N} x_j^2\right)E[e_i|X] = b$$

since $E[e_i|X] = E[e_i] = 0$ with (A4) and (A1). Note that without (A4), $E[e_i|X]$ need not be equal to $E[e_i]$.

Conditional variance of $\hat{b}$ is

$$\begin{aligned} E[(\hat{b}-b)^2|X] &= \sum_{i=1}^{N}\sum_{j=1}^{N}\left(x_i / \sum_{k=1}^{N} x_k^2\right)\left(x_j / \sum_{k=1}^{N} x_k^2\right)E[e_ie_j|X] \\ &= \sum_{i=1}^{N}\left(x_i / \sum_{k=1}^{N} x_k^2\right)^2 E[e_i^2|X] \\ &= \sigma_e^2 / \sum_{i=1}^{N} x_i^2 \end{aligned} \tag{2.5}$$

since $E[e_ie_j|X] = 0$ via (A4) and (A3), and $E[e_i^2|X] = \sigma_e^2$ via (A4) and (A2). Note that without (A4), $E[e_ie_j|X]$ need not be equal to 0, and $E[e_i^2|X]$ need not be equal to σ_e^2,

From Eq. (2.2), conditional mean of $\hat{a}$ is

$$E[\hat{a}|X] = E[\bar{Y}|X] - \bar{X}E[\hat{b}|X] = (a + b\bar{X}) - \bar{X}b = a$$

since $E[Y_i|X_i] = a + bX_i + E(e_i|X_i)$ and $E(e_i|X_i) = 0$ via (A4) and (A1), for every i. The conditional variance of $\hat{a}$ is

$$\begin{aligned} \text{var}(\hat{a}|X) &= \text{var}(\bar{Y}|X) - 2\bar{X}\,\text{cov}(\bar{Y}, \hat{b}|X) + \bar{X}^2\,\text{var}(\hat{b}|X) \\ &= \frac{\sigma_e^2}{N} - 2\frac{\bar{X}}{N}\text{cov}\left(\sum_{i=1}^{N} a + bX_i + e_i, b + \sum_{i=1}^{N}\frac{x_ie_i}{\sum_{j=1}^{N} x_j^2}|X\right) \\ &\quad + \bar{X}^2\sigma_e^2 / \sum_{i=1}^{N} x_i^2 \\ &= \sigma_e^2\left(\frac{1}{N} + \bar{X}^2 / \sum_{i=1}^{N} x_i^2\right) \end{aligned} \tag{2.6}$$

since the middle term gives $\sum_{i=1}^{N} \text{cov}(e_i, (x_i / \sum_{j=1}^{N} x_j^2)e_i|X) = 0$ as $\sum_{i=1}^{N} x_i = 0$. It is also seen that $\text{var}(\hat{a}|X)$ and $\text{var}(\hat{b}|X)$ reduce toward zero as $N \to \infty$.

Conditional on X and employing (A1) to (A3), the estimators are unbiased and their variances can be readily computed as seen in Eqs. (2.5) and (2.6). By (A5), the conditional estimators are normally distributed. Statistical tests can then be conducted.

Any statistical tests of the estimators using the conditional distributions are valid, although the conditional variances will obviously change with different samples of X. For example, the distribution of X_i (for every i) may be largely concentrated in a particular range. If a sample of X is drawn such that its realized values are mostly out of this range, i. e. ex-ante low probability draws, then the estimator variance conditional on this sample X may be significantly different from conditional variances based on most other samples. However, this problem may not materialize in financial economics research dealing with market data (non-laboratory data) as the data, e. g. X, occurs only once and there is no further draw. The conditional variance is constant if there is repetitive sampling, i. e. using the same X each time but with different $(e_1, e_2, \ldots, e_N)$ added to form the Y_i's.

In summary, in linear regression model (2.1), OLS method produces estimators $\hat{a}$ and $\hat{b}$ that are unbiased in finite sample if classical assumptions (A1) to (A4) apply under the general context of stochastic X and e. The unbiasedness property applies to both unconditional and also conditional (on X) OLS estimators. When the sample size N is large, the estimates can be accurate and forecasting can be done using these estimates of $\hat{a}$ and $\hat{b}$. However, testing if the estimates are significantly different from some hypothesized values, e. g., zeros, requires use of the conditional on X distribution of the estimators in order to conveniently obtain computed conditional variances. This is typically not a problem with financial economics data. Together with the use of (A5), this allows for statistical inferences.

2.2.1 Forecasting

In forecast or prediction of Y_i based on an observed X_i, a useful result is that the best forecast of Y_i, in the sense of minimum mean square error, is the conditional expectation $E(Y_i|X_i)$.

Lemma 2.1. *For a bivariate distribution of RVs Y_i and X_i,*

$$E(Y_i - g(X_i))^2 \geq E(Y_i - E(Y_i|X_i))^2$$

for any function $g(X_i)$.

Proof.

$$\begin{aligned} E[(Y_i - g(X_i))^2|X_i] &= E[(Y_i - E[Y_i|X_i] + E[Y_i|X_i] - g(X_i))^2|X_i] \\ &= E[(Y_i - E[Y_i|X_i])^2|X_i] + E[(E[Y_i|X_i] - g(X_i))^2|X_i] \\ &\quad + 2E[(Y_i - E[Y_i|X_i])(E[Y_i|X_i] - g(X_i))|X_i] \end{aligned}$$

Given X_i, $E[Y_i|X_i] - g(X_i)$ is a function of X_i and can be considered a constant. Therefore the last term is zero since $E[(Y_i - E[Y_i|X_i])|X_i] = E(Y_i|X_i) - E(Y_i|X_i) = 0$. Hence the LHS $E[(Y_i - g(X_i))^2|X_i]$ is minimized by setting $g(X_i) = E[Y_i|X_i]$. □

Note that the lemma does not specify if $E[Y_i|X_i]$ is a linear forecast. In the case of a linear model, however, it becomes a linear forecast. With the result in the lemma, the best forecast of Y_{N+1} with linear regression model (2.1) is $E(Y_{N+1}) = a + bX_{N+1}$. In Eq. (2.1) $Y_i = a + bX_i + e_i$, $i = 1, 2, \ldots, N$, the OLS estimates $\hat{a}$ and $\hat{b}$ are unbiased using (A1) to (A4).

The OLS forecast of Y_{N+1} given X_{N+1} is thus:

$$\hat{Y}_{N+1} = \hat{a} + \hat{b}X_{N+1}.$$

The forecast or prediction error is $Y_{N+1} - \hat{Y}_{N+1}$. The forecast is unbiased since the conditional mean of the prediction error is zero, i. e. $E(\hat{Y}_{N+1} - Y_{N+1}|X_{N+1}) = E(\hat{a} - a) + E(\hat{b} - b)X_{N+1} = 0$. This OLS forecast also converges to the best forecast of Y_{N+1} when $\hat{a}$ and $\hat{b}$ converges toward a and b, respectively.

Now,

$$\hat{Y}_{N+1} = \hat{a} + \hat{b}X_{N+1} = (\bar{Y} - \hat{b}\bar{X}) + \hat{b}X_{N+1} = \bar{Y} + \hat{b}x_{N+1}$$

where $x_{N+1} = X_{N+1} - \bar{X}$.

But Eq. (2.1) gives $\bar{Y} = a + b\bar{X} + \frac{1}{N}\sum_{i=1}^{N} e_i$ and here we are dealing with a random variable rather than sample estimate. So,

$$\hat{Y}_{N+1} = \bar{Y} + \hat{b}x_{N+1} = a + b\bar{X} + \frac{1}{N}\sum_{i=1}^{N} e_i + \hat{b}x_{N+1}$$

which is again a representation as a random variable. However, $Y_{N+1} = a + bX_{N+1} + e_{N+1}$, so the forecast (or prediction) error is

$$\begin{aligned} Y_{N+1} - \hat{Y}_{N+1} &= bx_{N+1} - \hat{b}x_{N+1} + e_{N+1} - \frac{1}{N}\sum_{i=1}^{N} e_i \\ &= -(\hat{b} - b)x_{N+1} + e_{N+1} - \frac{1}{N}\sum_{i=1}^{N} e_i \\ \operatorname{var}(Y_{N+1} - \hat{Y}_{N+1} \mid x_{N+1}) &= x_{N+1}^2 \operatorname{var}(\hat{b}) + \sigma_e^2 + \frac{1}{N}\sigma_e^2 \\ &= \sigma_e^2\left(1 + \frac{1}{N} + \frac{x_{N+1}^2}{\sum_{i=1}^{N} x_i^2}\right) \end{aligned}$$

The forecast error (conditional on x_{N+1}) is normally distributed. So,

$$\frac{Y_{N+1} - \hat{Y}_{N+1}}{\hat{\sigma}_e\sqrt{(1 + \frac{1}{N} + \frac{x_{N+1}^2}{\sum_{i=1}^{N} x_i^2})}} \sim t_{N-2}$$

Therefore, a 90 % confidence interval for Y_{N+1} is

$$\hat{Y}_{N+1} \pm t_{N-2,95\,\%} \times \hat{\sigma}_e \sqrt{\left(1 + \frac{1}{N} + \frac{x_{N+1}^2}{\sum_{i=1}^{N} x_i^2}\right)}$$

One point to note is that in using the variance of $\hat{b}$ that is obtained from a sample $X_1, X_2, \ldots, X_N$, that variance is a conditional variance on $X_1, X_2, \ldots, X_N$. There is thus an assumption that this conditional variance is also the conditional variance when X_{N+1} is considered.

2.3 Gauss–Markov Theorem

There is an important result in linear regression called the Gauss-Markov theorem that justifies the use of OLS in (2.1). Linear estimators of a and b in Eq. (2.1) are those that take the form $\hat{A} = \sum_{i=1}^{N} \theta_i Y_i$ and $\hat{B} = \sum_{i=1}^{N} \gamma_i Y_i$, respectively, where θ_i and γ_i are fixed or deterministic functions of X only (and not in Y's or a or b). The estimators are expressed as linear functions (conditional on X) of Y.

The Gauss-Markov theorem states that amongst all linear and unbiased (conditional) estimators of the form:

$$\hat{A} = \sum_{i=1}^{N} \theta_i(X) Y_i$$
$$\hat{B} = \sum_{i=1}^{N} \gamma_i(X) Y_i$$

the OLS estimators $\hat{a}, \hat{b}$ have the minimum variances, i. e.

$$\text{var}(\hat{a}) \leq \text{var}(\hat{A})$$
$$\text{var}(\hat{b}) \leq \text{var}(\hat{B})$$

given the assumptions (A1) to (A4).

To prove the theorem, we develop more general characterizations of the OLS estimators.

From Eq. (2.4), conditional on X, $\hat{b}$ is a linear estimator with w_i's as fixed weights (function of X)[1] on the Y_i's.

$$\hat{b} = \sum_{i=1}^{N} w_i Y_i$$

where $w_i = x_i / \sum_{i=j}^{N} x_j^2$. It can be seen that the following properties of w_i hold. For convenience we drop the notations of index on the summation signs. We also do not show

1 Using the condition on X is sometimes called regression using “fixed” regressors.

explicitly the notation of conditioning on X, i. e. "$|X$".

$$\sum w_i = 0$$
$$\sum w_i^2 = \frac{1}{\sum x_i^2}$$
$$\sum w_i x_i = 1$$

Similarly, conditional on X, $\hat{a} = \bar{Y} - \hat{b}\bar{X}$ is a linear function of Y.

The weights for $\hat{a}$, v_i's, are as follows.

$$\hat{a} = \frac{1}{N}\sum_{i=1}^{N} Y_i - \sum_{i=1}^{N} w_i \bar{X} Y_i = \sum_{i=1}^{N} v_i Y_i$$

where

$$v_i = \left(\frac{1}{N} - \frac{x_i \bar{X}}{\sum_{i=1}^{N} x_i^2}\right)$$
$$\sum v_i = 1 - \frac{\bar{X}\sum x_i}{\sum x_i^2} = 1$$
$$\sum v_i X_i = \bar{X} - \bar{X}\frac{\sum x_i X_i}{\sum x_i X_i} = 0$$
$$\sum v_i^2 = \sum\left(\frac{1}{N^2} - \frac{2x_i\bar{X}}{N\sum x_i^2} + \frac{x_i^2\bar{X}^2}{(\sum x_i^2)^2}\right) = \frac{1}{N} + \frac{\bar{X}^2}{\sum x_i^2}$$

In the above, $\sum x_i = \sum(X_i - \bar{X}) = N\bar{X} - \sum \bar{X} = 0$.

Now, for the finite sample properties of the conditional OLS estimators:

$$\hat{b} = \sum w_i(a + bX_i + e_i) = b + \sum w_i e_i$$

Then, clearly $E(\hat{b}) = b$. Now, as seen earlier

$$\begin{aligned}\operatorname{var}(\hat{b}) &= E[(\hat{b} - b)^2] \\ &= E\left(\sum w_i e_i\right)^2 = \sum w_i^2 E(e_i^2) = \sigma_e^2\left(\frac{1}{\sum x_i^2}\right)\end{aligned}$$

Similarly, $\hat{a} = \sum v_i(a + bX_i + e_i) = a + \sum v_i e_i$. Thus, $E(\hat{a}) = a$. Then,

$$\operatorname{var}(\hat{a}) = E[(\hat{a} - a)^2] = E\left(\sum v_i e_i\right)^2 = \sigma_e^2\sum v_i^2 = \sigma_e^2\left(\frac{1}{N} + \frac{\bar{X}^2}{\sum x_i^2}\right)$$

The OLS estimators $\hat{a}$ and $\hat{b}$ are unbiased.

What is the probability distribution of $\hat{b}$? Using (A5), since $\hat{b}$ is a linear combination of e_i's that are normally distributed, $\hat{b}$ is also normally distributed.

$$\hat{b} \sim N\left(b, \sigma_e^2\left(\frac{1}{\sum x_i^2}\right)\right)$$

What is the distribution of $\hat{a}$? Similarly, we see that:

$$\hat{a} \sim N\left(a, \sigma_e^2\left(\frac{1}{N} + \frac{\bar{X}^2}{\sum x_i^2}\right)\right)$$

The covariance between the estimators $\hat{a}$ and $\hat{b}$ is obtained as follows.

$$\begin{aligned}\operatorname{cov}(\hat{a}, \hat{b}) &= E(\hat{a} - a)(\hat{b} - b)\\ &= E\left(\sum v_i e_i\right)\left(\sum w_i e_i\right) = \sigma_e^2 \sum v_i w_i = \sigma_e^2\left(-\frac{\bar{X}}{\sum x_i^2}\right)\end{aligned}$$

A proof of the Gauss-Markov theorem for the case of $\hat{b}$ is as follows. Let linear estimator of b be $\hat{B} = \sum_{i=1}^{N} \gamma_i Y_i$. Since we consider the class of linear unbiased estimators, let

$$E(\hat{B}) = \sum \gamma_i E(Y_i) = \sum \gamma_i (a + bX_i) = a \sum \gamma_i + b \sum \gamma_i X_i = b$$

This implies that
(1a) $\sum \gamma_i = 0$
(1b) $\sum \gamma_i X_i = 1$, and
(1c) $\operatorname{var}(\hat{B}) = \sum \gamma_i^2 \operatorname{var} Y_i = \sigma_e^2 \sum \gamma_i^2$, given the X_i's.

Define $\gamma_i = c_i + d_i$. Without loss of generality, let $c_i = x_i / \sum x_i^2$. From (1c), $\operatorname{var}(\hat{B}) = \sigma_e^2(\sum c_i^2 + \sum d_i^2 + 2\sum c_i d_i)$.

$$\begin{aligned}\text{But}\quad \sum c_i d_i &= \sum c_i(\gamma_i - c_i) = \sum \gamma_i \frac{x_i}{\sum x_i^2} - \sum\left(\frac{x_i}{\sum x_i^2}\right)^2\\ &= \left(\sum \gamma_i X_i - \bar{X}\sum \gamma_i\right)/\sum x_i^2 - 1/\sum x_i^2\end{aligned}$$

With (1b) and (1a), the RHS in the last equation equals to zero. Thus $\operatorname{var}(\hat{B}) = \sigma_e^2(\sum c_i^2 + \sum d_i^2)$. The minimum possible variance of $\hat{B}$ is to set $d_i = 0\ \forall i$.

Hence the minimum variance is $\sigma_e^2 \sum (x_i / \sum x_i^2)^2 = \sigma_e^2(1/\sum x_i^2)$ which is the variance of the OLS estimator $\hat{b}$. We can similarly prove the case for $\hat{a}$.

Now the estimated residual $\hat{e}_i = Y_i - \hat{a} - \hat{b}X_i$. It can be further expressed as:

$$\hat{e}_i = Y_i - (\bar{Y} - \hat{b}\bar{X}) - \hat{b}X_i = (Y_i - \bar{Y}) - \hat{b}(X_i - \bar{X}) = y_i - \hat{b}x_i$$

It is important to distinguish this estimated residual $Y_i - \hat{Y}_i$ from the actual unobserved e_i. From Eqs. (2.2) and (2.3), we see that:

$$\sum_{i=1}^{N} \hat{e}_i = 0 \quad \text{and} \quad \sum_{i=1}^{N} X_i\hat{e}_i = 0 \quad \text{or} \quad \sum_{i=1}^{N} (X_i - \bar{X})\hat{e}_i = 0$$

Their population equivalents are, respectively, $E(e_i) = 0$, $E(X_i e_i) = 0$ or $\text{cov}(X_i, e_i) = 0$.

With the Gauss-Markov theorem, OLS estimators (under the classical conditions) are called best linear unbiased estimators (BLUE) for the linear regression model in Eq. (2.1). They are efficient (best) estimators in the class of linear unbiased estimators. There may be some estimators that have smaller variances but these are biased, e. g., the Stein estimators.

2.4 Decomposition

We now analyse the decomposition of the Sum of Squares of $\sum_{i=1}^{N}(Y_i - \bar{Y})^2$. Recall that in the OLS method, we minimize the sum of squares of estimated residual errors $\sum_{i=1}^{N} \hat{e}_i^2$. Now,

$$\begin{aligned}
\sum_{i=1}^{N}(Y_i - \bar{Y})^2 &= \sum_{i=1}^{N}(\hat{Y}_i - \bar{Y} + Y_i - \hat{Y}_i)^2 = \sum_{i=1}^{N}(\hat{Y}_i - \bar{Y})^2 \\
&\quad + 2\sum_{i=1}^{N}(\hat{Y}_i - \bar{Y})(Y_i - \hat{Y}_i) + \sum_{i=1}^{N}(Y_i - \hat{Y}_i)^2 \\
&= \sum_{i=1}^{N}(\hat{Y}_i - \bar{Y})^2 + 2\sum_{i=1}^{N}(\hat{Y}_i - \bar{Y})\hat{e}_i + \sum_{i=1}^{N}\hat{e}_i^2 \\
&= \sum_{i=1}^{N}(\hat{Y}_i - \bar{Y})^2 + \sum_{i=1}^{N}\hat{e}_i^2
\end{aligned} \tag{2.7}$$

since

$$\sum_{i=1}^{N}(\hat{Y}_i - \bar{Y})\hat{e}_i = \sum_{i=1}^{N}\hat{Y}_i\hat{e}_i = \sum_{i=1}^{N}(\hat{a} + \hat{b}X_i)\hat{e}_i = 0$$

Let us define the Total Sum of Squares (TSS) $= \sum(Y_i - \bar{Y})^2$. Define Explained Sum of Squares (ESS) $= \sum(\hat{Y}_i - \bar{Y})^2$. Define Residual Sum of Squares (RSS) $= \sum \hat{e}_i^2 = \sum(Y_i - \hat{Y}_i)^2$.

From Eq. (2.7), TSS = ESS + RSS. RSS is also called the unexplained sum of squares (USS) or sum of squared residuals (SSR). Now,

$$\begin{aligned}
\text{ESS} &= \sum(\hat{Y}_i - \bar{Y})^2 = \sum(\hat{a} + \hat{b}X_i - \hat{a} - \hat{b}\bar{X})^2 = \hat{b}^2\sum(X_i - \bar{X})^2 \\
&= r_{XY}^2 \frac{S_Y^2}{S_X^2} NS_X^2 = r_{XY}^2 NS_Y^2 \\
\text{TSS} &= \sum(Y_i - \bar{Y})^2 = NS_Y^2
\end{aligned}$$

So, ESS/TSS $= r_{XY}^2$. In addition, $r_{XY}^2 = 1 -$ RSS/TSS.

ESS as a fraction of TSS or variation is the square of sample correlation coefficient in the two-variable linear regression model. But r_{XY}^2 lies between 0 and 1 inclusive since r_{XY} lies in $[-1, +1]$. This term

$$\frac{\text{ESS}}{\text{TSS}} = R^2$$

where $0 \leq R^2 \leq 1$, is called the coefficient of determination. This coefficient R^2 determines the degree of fit of the linear regression line to the data points in the sample. The closer R^2 is to 1, the better is the fit. Perfect fit occurs if all points lie on the straight line. Then $R^2 = 1$.

$$\frac{\text{ESS}}{\text{TSS}} = R^2 = 1 - \frac{\text{RSS}}{\text{TSS}}$$

Now, $\hat{e}_i = Y_i - \hat{a} - \hat{b}X_i$, so $\hat{e}_i$ is a normally distributed random variable since Y_i, $\hat{a}$, and $\hat{b}$, (given X_i) are normally distributed. This is obtained using the result that a linear combination of normal random variables is itself a normal random variable. Moreover, $E(\hat{e}_i) = E(Y_i) - a - bX_i = 0$. Conditional on X_i,

$$\begin{aligned}
\text{var}(\hat{e}_i) &= \text{var}(Y_i) + \text{var}(\hat{a}) + X_i^2\,\text{var}(\hat{b}) - 2\,\text{cov}(Y_i, \hat{a}) \\
&\quad - 2X_i\,\text{cov}(Y_i, \hat{b}) + 2X_i\,\text{cov}(\hat{a}, \hat{b}) \\
&= \sigma_e^2 + \sigma_e^2\left(\frac{1}{N} + \frac{\bar{X}^2}{\sum x_i^2}\right) + \sigma_e^2 X_i^2\left(\frac{1}{\sum x_i^2}\right) \\
&\quad - 2v_i\sigma_e^2 - 2X_i w_i \sigma_e^2 - 2\sigma_e^2 X_i\left(\frac{\bar{X}}{\sum x_i^2}\right) \\
&= \sigma_e^2\left[1 + \frac{1}{N} + \frac{\bar{X}^2}{\sum x_i^2} + \frac{X_i^2}{\sum x_i^2} - \frac{2}{N} + \frac{2x_i\bar{X}}{\sum x_i^2} - \frac{2x_iX_i}{\sum x_i^2} - \frac{2X_i\bar{X}}{\sum x_i^2}\right] \\
&= \sigma_e^2\left[1 - \frac{1}{N} + \frac{1}{\sum x_i^2}(\bar{X}^2 + X_i^2 + 2x_i\bar{X} - 2x_iX_i - 2X_i\bar{X})\right] \\
&= \sigma_e^2\left(1 - \frac{1}{N} - \frac{x_i^2}{\sum x_i^2}\right)
\end{aligned}$$

Similarly, we can show that

$$\begin{aligned}
\text{cov}(\hat{e}_i, \hat{e}_j) &= \text{cov}(Y_i - \hat{a} - \hat{b}X_i, Y_j - \hat{a} - \hat{b}X_j) \\
&= \text{cov}([a - \hat{a}] + [b - \hat{b}]X_i + e_i, [a - \hat{a}] + [b - \hat{b}]X_j + e_j) \\
&= \sigma_e^2\left(\left[\frac{1}{N} + \frac{\bar{X}^2}{\sum x_i^2}\right] - \frac{X_j\bar{X}}{\sum x_i^2} - \left[\frac{1}{N} - \frac{x_j\bar{X}}{\sum x_i^2}\right] - \frac{X_i\bar{X}}{\sum x_i^2} + \frac{X_iX_j}{\sum x_i^2}\right. \\
&\quad \left. - \frac{x_jX_i}{\sum x_i^2} - \left[\frac{1}{N} - \frac{x_i\bar{X}}{\sum x_i^2}\right] - \frac{x_iX_j}{\sum x_i^2}\right)
\end{aligned}$$

$$= \sigma_e^2\left(-\frac{1}{N} - \frac{1}{\sum x_i^2}[\bar{X}^2 - X_i\bar{X} - X_j\bar{X} + X_iX_j]\right)$$

$$= \sigma_e^2\left(-\frac{1}{N} - \frac{x_ix_j}{\sum x_i^2}\right)$$

Note that true e_i and e_j are independent according to the classical conditions, and their OLS estimates are asymptotically uncorrelated. Note also that $\frac{\sum_{i=1}^N \hat{e}_i^2}{\sigma_e^2} \sim \chi_{N-2}^2$ is a useful relationship involving unbiased sample estimate $\hat{\sigma}_e^2 = \sum_{i=1}^N \hat{e}_i^2/(N-2)$ and unknown population parameter σ_e^2.

After obtaining the OLS estimates $\hat{a}$ and $\hat{b}$, there is sometimes a need to perform statistical inference and testing, as well as forecasting and confidence interval estimation.

$$\begin{pmatrix} \hat{a} \\ \hat{b} \end{pmatrix} \sim N\left(\begin{pmatrix} a \\ b \end{pmatrix}, \begin{pmatrix} \sigma_e^2[\frac{1}{N} + \frac{\bar{X}^2}{\sum x^2}] & -\sigma_e^2[\frac{\bar{X}}{\sum x^2}] \\ -\sigma_e^2[\frac{\bar{X}}{\sum x^2}] & \sigma_e^2[\frac{1}{\sum x^2}] \end{pmatrix}\right)$$

So, $\frac{\hat{b}-b}{\text{s.e.}(\hat{b})} \equiv Z \sim N(0,1)$. For testing null hypothesis H_0: $b = 1$, employ sample estimate of σ_e^2 using $\hat{\sigma}_e^2$. Use

$$t_{N-2} = \frac{\hat{b} - 1}{\hat{\sigma}_e\sqrt{\frac{1}{\sum x^2}}}$$

For testing null hypothesis H_0: $a = 0$, use

$$t_{N-2} = \frac{\hat{a} - 0}{\hat{\sigma}_e\sqrt{\frac{1}{N} + \frac{\bar{X}^2}{\sum x^2}}}$$

It should be noted that most statistical or econometrics computing packages by default report tests of coefficients that are based on a null of zero, i. e. $H_0 : a = 0$, $H_0 : b = 0$.

As a final comment, suppose distributional assumption for e_i is made, e. g., normality, then another important class of estimators – maximum likelihood estimators (MLE) – can be developed. MLE essentially chooses estimators that maximize the sample likelihood function. There is equivalence of OLS and ML estimators in the specific case of normally distributed i. i. d. e_i's. However, MLE is in general a nonlinear estimator.

We use the simple regression tools to examine two important applications in finance: pricing stock index futures and futures hedging.

2.5 Stock Index Futures

Although the framework of linear regression can be applied to explain and also predict many financial variables, it is usually not enough to know just the econometric theory as seen so far in this chapter. To do a good job of exposition and predicting some financial variables, there would usually be a finance-theoretic framework and an appropriate way to think about how financial variables may interact and dynamically change over time as a result of investor actions and market conditions. Therefore, we will introduce these as the chapters proceed. In the rest of this section, we shall concentrate on a very important financial instrument used in the futures market as well as used by portfolio managers for hedging purposes.

A stock index is weighted average of index portfolio stock prices. The Standard and Poor's (S&P) 500 stock index, for example, is a market-capitalization weighted average price of 500 major stocks trading in U. S. The Nikkei 225 is a price-weighted average price of major 225 Japanese stocks. The FTSE 100 (The Financial Times and London Stock Exchange) index is a market-capitalization weighted average price of 100 large UK stocks. There are numerous stock indexes reflecting "average" prices of stocks in a country, in sectors of a country, and sometimes across bourses in a region.

These stock index numbers change every day, and usually more frequently on an intraday basis, as long as there is an agency or mechanism that computes the new average number as the constituent stocks change their traded prices in the market. While the index numbers themselves are not directly tradeable, derivatives or contracts written on them can be traded. One such type of contract is the stock index futures. Others include stock index options, exchange-traded funds, and so on.

We shall consider stock index futures that are traded in Stock or Futures Exchanges. In September, for example, one can trade on a Nikkei 225 Index futures contract that matures in December. This is called a December Nikkei 225 Index futures contract to reflect its maturity. After its maturity date, the contract is worthless. In September, however, the traded "price" (this is not a currency price, but an index price or a notional price) of this December contract will reflect how the market thinks the final at-maturity Nikkei 225 Index will be. If the September market trades the index futures at a notional price of 12,000, and you know that the December index number is going to be higher, then you will buy (long) say N of the Nikkei 225 Index December futures contracts. At maturity in December, if you still have not yet sold your position, and if the Nikkei 225 Index is really higher at 14,000, then you will make a big profit. This profit is calculated as the increase in futures notional price or 2000 points in this case $\times$ the Yen value per point per contract $\times$ number of contracts N.

Thus, a current stock index futures notional price is related to the index notional price at a future time. At maturity, the index futures notional price converges to the underlying stock index number. As stock index represents the average price of a large portfolio of stocks, the corresponding stock index futures notional price is related to the value of the underlying large portfolio of stocks making up the index. This relationship is sometimes called the no-arbitrage model pricing. It can be explained briefly as follows.

2.5.1 Cost of Carry Model

Suppose we define the stock index value to be S_t at current time t. This value is a weighted average of the underlying portfolio stock prices. The actual market capitalization currency value of the portfolio of stocks in the index is of course a very large multiplier of this index value. We assume that we can create a portfolio of diverse stocks those return tracks exactly the index return. (In reality, the tracking can be close for a large index portfolio but is not exact as the weight of each stock in the portfolio changes over time.) Given the assumption, the percentage return to the index changes reflects the overall portfolio's return. Suppose an institutional investor holds such a large diversified portfolio say of the major Japanese stocks whose portfolio return tracks the N225 index return.

Let the effective risk-free interest rate or the cost of carry be $r_{t,T}$ over $[t, T]$. An arbitrageur could in principle buy or short-sell the portfolio of N225 stocks in proportions equal to their weights in the index. Let the cost of this portfolio be αS_t whereby the simplifying assumption is that α is a constant multiplier reflecting the proportionate relationship of the portfolio value to the index notional value S_t. The percentage return on the index is also the same percentage return on the portfolio.

The arbitrageur either carries or holds the portfolio, or short-sells the portfolio until maturity T with a final cost at T of $\alpha S_t(1 + r_{t,T})$ after the opportunity cost of interest compounding is added. Suppose the Japanese stocks in the N225 Index issue an aggregate amount of dividends D over the period $[t, T]$. Since the N225 Index notional value is proportional to the overall 225 Japanese stocks' market value, the dividend yield d as a fraction of the total market value is the same dividend yield as a fraction of the N225 Index notional value. Then, the dividends issued to the arbitrageur's portfolio amount to $d \times \alpha S_t$. Suppose that the dividends to be received are perfectly anticipated, then the present value of this amount, $d^* \times \alpha S_t$ can be deducted from the cost of carry. Let $D^* = d^* S_t$. The net cost of carry of the stocks as at time T is then $\alpha[S_t - D^*](1 + r_{t,T})$.

Suppose the N225 Index futures notional price is now trading at $F_{t,T}$. The subscript notations imply the price at t for a contract that matures at T. The arbitrageur would enter a buy or long position in the stocks if at $t, F_{t,T} > [S_t - D^*](1 + r_{t,T})$. At the same time t, the arbitrageur sells an index futures contract at notional price $F_{t,T}$. For simplicity, we assume the currency value per point per contract is 1. Without loss of generality, assume $\alpha = 1$.

At T, whatever the index value, $S_T = F_{T,T}$, the arbitrageur would sell the portfolio at ¥S_T, gaining

$$¥S_T - [S_t - D^*](1 + r_{t,T})$$

Cash-settle the index futures trade, gaining

$$¥F_{t,T} - F_{T,T} \quad \text{or} \quad ¥F_{t,T} - S_T$$

The net gain is the sum of the two terms, i. e. $¥F_{t,T} - [S_t - D^*](1 + r_{t,T}) > 0$. Thus, the arbitrageur makes a riskless profit equivalent to the net gain above.

Conversely, the arbitrageur would enter a short position in the stocks if at t, $F_{t,T} < [S_t - D^*](1 + r_{t,T})$. At the same time t, the arbitrageur would buy an index futures contract at notional price $F_{t,T}$. At T, whatever the index value $S_T = F_{T,T}$, the arbitrageur would buy back the portfolio at S_T, gaining

$$¥[S_t - D^*](1 + r_{t,T}) - S_T$$

Cash-settle the index futures trade, gaining

$$¥F_{T,T} - F_{t,T} \quad \text{or} \quad ¥S_T - F_{t,T}$$

The net gain is the sum of the two terms, i. e. $¥[S_t - D^*](1 + r_{t,T}) - F_{t,T} > 0$. Thus, the arbitrageur risklessly makes a profit equivalent to the net gain above.

We have also ignored transaction costs in this analysis, which would mean that it is even more difficult to try to make riskless arbitrage profit. An early study by Lim (1992)[2] showed that such risk-free arbitrage in the Nikkei 225 Stock Index futures had largely disappeared, after transaction costs in the late 1980s. The cost-of-carry model price of the index futures $F_{t,T} = [S_t - D^*](1 + r_{t,T})$ is also called the fair value price. At this fair value price, no riskless arbitrage profit could be made. The fair value price is also the no-arbitrage equilibrium price.

As an illustration, we employ data from Singapore Exchange (SGX) that contain daily end-of-day Nikkei 225 Index values and Nikkei 225 Index December 1999 futures contract prices traded at SIMEX/SGX during the period September 1 to October 15, 1999. During this end 1999 period, the Japan money market interest rate was very low at 0.5 % p. a. We use this as the cost-of-carry interest rate. We also assume the Nikkei 225 stock portfolio's aggregate dividend was 1.0 % p. a. at present value. During these trade dates, the term-to-maturity on September 1 was 98 calendar days, so we use term-to-maturity of 98/365 or 0.2685. The term-to-maturity shortened to about 0.1534 on October 15. In addition to the no-arbitrage theory explained earlier, transactions costs considerations are added. It is assumed that in the arbitrage, if any, any buy/sell of stocks at t would entail a 0.5 % transactions cost (brokerage and exchange fees). Any subsequent sell/buy at T would also entail a 0.5 % transactions cost.

2 Kian Guan Lim (1992), Arbitrage and price behavior of the Nikkei Stock Index Futures, *Journal of Futures Markets*, 12 (2), 151–162.

If cash-and-carry arbitrage takes place, the arbitrageur would gain ¥$0.995S_T - [1.005S_t - D^*](1 + r_{t,T}) + F_{t,T} - S_T$ or approximately $F_{t,T} - 1.01[S_t - D^*](1 + r_{t,T})$. In this case, the fair price is approximately $F_{t,T} = 1.01[S_t - D^*](1 + r_{t,T})$. If reverse cash-and-carry arbitrage takes place, the arbitrageur would gain ¥$[0.995S_t - D^*](1 + r_{t,T}) - 1.005S_T + S_T - F_{t,T}$ or approximately $0.99[S_t - D^*](1 + r_{t,T}) - F_{t,T}$. In this case, the fair price is approximately $F_{t,T} = 0.99[S_t - D^*](1 + r_{t,T})$. Let $\tau = T - t$ be the term-to-maturity in terms of fraction of a year. Then $r_{t,T} \approx 0.005\tau$ and $D^* \approx 0.01\tau/(1 + 0.005\tau)$.

Based on the finance theory above, we plot in Figure 2.6 the two time series of the N225 futures price $F_{t,T}$, and the fair price F_t^*. We also compute a percentage difference $p_t = (F_{t,T} - F_t^*)/F_t^*$ indicating the percentage deviation from the fair price F_t^*. The time series plot of p_t is shown in Figure 2.7.

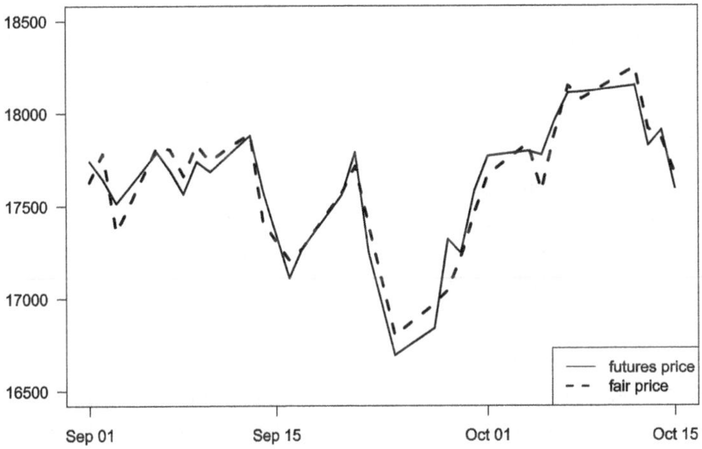

Figure 2.6: Prices of Nikkei 225 December Futures Contract from 9/1/1999 to 10/15/1999.

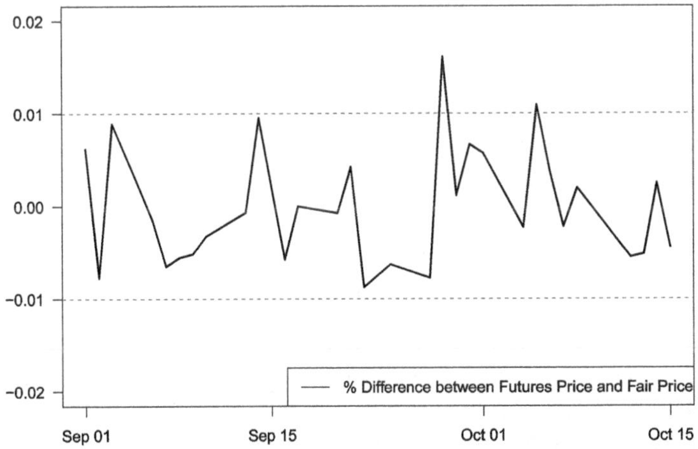

Figure 2.7: Percentage Difference Between Futures Price and Fair Price.

Figure 2.6 shows that both the futures price and the fair value are tracked closely together. The daily percentage differences p_t shown in Figure 2.7 were contained within 1 % of the fair value Yen price except for two outliers. The deviation of p_t from zero could be due to existence of arbitrage opportunities or other non-fee-based transactions costs such as bid-ask spread and slippage costs. Cost of bid-ask spread exists because at the point of selling (buying) futures, simultaneous action to buy (sell) the stocks need not be at the price indicated at that point in time since a buy (sell) action may hit a higher (lower) ask (bid) price. If the orders from more than one arbitrageur are triggered and buy (sell) orders on stocks and futures exceed the ask and bid volumes at the next price queue, then slippage occurs where some orders spill over into even higher ask or lower bid prices. These other costs and impacts could drive actual futures price away from the fair futures price but yet do not provide for any arbitrage profits.

The tendency for p_t in Figure 2.7 to mean-revert toward zero when it hits about 1 % or −1 % may imply that actual arbitrage took place only when the additional 1 % non-fee-based costs are considered. If $p_t > 0$ is too high (or futures price exceeds the fees-adjusted fair value by 1 % in the above context), arbitrageurs would sell the futures and buy the stocks in a cash-and-carry trade, pushing futures price downward and stock index upward, thus decreasing p_{t+1} toward zero. Conversely, if $p_t < 0$ is too low (or futures price drops below the fees-adjusted fair value by 1 % in the above context), arbitrageurs would buy the futures and short-sell the stocks in a reverse cash-and-carry trade, pushing futures price upward and stock index downward, thus increasing p_{t+1} toward zero. Once p_t moves away from the upper and lower bounds of +1 % and −1 % respectively, it can move randomly within these no-arbitrage bounds. However, Figure 2.7 indicates possible negative serial correlation in the change of p_t within the no-arbitrage bounds.[3]

The time series pattern of p_t in Figure 2.7 suggests that if there is practically little arbitrage, then (2a) deviation of p_t from zero is due to random disturbances, and (2b) change in p_t or Δp_t, would display negative daily correlation. (2a) is tantamount to a hull hypothesis $H_0 : E(p_t) = 0$, i. e. the expectation or mean of time series p_t is zero.

Instead of p_t we can use the variable $\ln(F_t/F_t^*)$ which is approximately the same as p_t. Their difference is that $\ln(F_t/F_t^*)$ has a range $(-\infty, +\infty)$ whereas $p_t \in (-1, +\infty)$ since F_t and F_t^* have the range $(0, +\infty)$. The ranges are theoretical possibilities. If we require assumption of normal distribution to perform statistical testing, then using the variable $\ln(F_t/F_t^*)$ to construct the test statistic is more suitable as this variable can be assumed to follow a normal distribution.

3 An early market microstructure study indicates that bid-ask bounce causes negative serial correlations even when there were no information and the market was efficient. See Richard Roll (1984), A simple implicit measure of the effective bid-ask spread in an efficient market, *The Journal of Finance*, 1127–1139.

The sample size for the two variables of F_t and F_t^* is 30. Assuming $q_t = \ln(F_t/F_t^*)$ is normally distributed, the t-statistic at d. f. 29, based on the null hypothesis that its mean is zero is $\sqrt{29} \times \bar{q}_t/s(q_t) = -0.0656$ where $\bar{q}_t$ is the sample mean of q_t and $s(q_t)$ is the sample standard deviation of q_t. Therefore the null hypothesis cannot be rejected at any reasonable level of test significance. Since p_t is a very close approximation of q_t the implication is that the mean of p_t is zero or $F_t = F_t^*$. Thus (2a) is supported. The futures price and its fees-adjusted fair price are statistically not different. There is support of the cost of carry model.

(2b) suggests that daily changes in p_t or Δp_t, are more likely to be negatively correlated. We can statistically examine the reversals in Δp_t by investigating a regression of the daily Δp_t on its lag. For the same reason, we use q_t instead of p_t. Specifically, we perform the linear regression $\Delta q_{t+1} = a + b\Delta q_t + e_{t+1}$, where $\Delta q_{t+1} = q_{t+1} - q_t$, a, b are coefficients, and e_{t+1} is assumed to be an i. i. d. residual error. In this case, the first data point $\Delta q_2 = q_2 - q_1$ is the change in q from 9/1 to 9/2; the last data point $\Delta q_{30} = q_{30} - q_{29}$ is the change in q from 10/14 to 10/15.

Since we employ a lag for regression, the number of sample observations used in the regression is further reduced by 1, so there are only $N = 28$ data points involving $\Delta q_3, \Delta q_4, \ldots, \Delta q_{30}$ as dependent values and $\Delta q_2, \Delta q_3, \ldots, \Delta q_{29}$ as explanatory values. The linear regression would produce t-statistic with $N - 2$ or 26 degrees of freedom. The linear regression results are reported in Table 2.1.

Table 2.1: Regression of $\Delta \ln(F_t/F_t^*)$ on Its Lag: $\Delta q_{t+1} = a + b\Delta q_t + e_{t+1}$.

Variable	**Coefficient**	**Std. Error**	***t*-Statistic**	**Prob.**
Constant	0.00005	0.0014	0.032	0.9751
Lagged Δq_t	−0.57340	0.1534	−3.739	0.0009***
R-squared	0.3497	F (d. f. 1,26)-statistic		13.98
Adjusted R-squared	0.3247	Prob(F-statistic)		0.0009***
S. E. of regression	0.0076	Sum squared resid.		0.00151

Note: *** indicates significance at the 0.1 % level whether one-tailed or two-tailed tests.

Table 2.1 shows the usual statistical values reported in most statistical software. The regression results using the ordinary least squares method show that the estimated coefficient that is the regression constant a is $\hat{a} = 0.00005$ with a two-tailed p-value of 0.9751, i. e. $P(|\hat{a}| > 0.00005) = 0.975$. Hence we cannot reject $H_0 : a = 0$ at any reasonable significance level. The estimated coefficient of lagged Δq_t, that is the regression slope b, is $\hat{b} = -0.57340$ with a two-tailed p-value of 0.0009, i. e. $P(|\hat{b}| > 0.57340) = 0.0009$. This means that the probability of observing any estimate larger in magnitude than 0.57340 is very small at 0.09 %. If we test the null $H_0 : b = 0$ at 1 % significance level which provides a very small 1 % chance of type I error (rejecting when null is true), the smaller than 1 % p-value means that we reject the null. Thus the statistical evidence is that $b \neq 0$ (basically $b < 0$ in this case). This shows the presence of reversals in Δq_t across days.

Several notes regarding the relations of the reported numbers in the Table are in order. The sum of squared residuals SSR or the residual sum of squares RSS is 0.00151. The residual standard error or the standard error (S. E.) of regression can be found as $\hat{\sigma}_e = \sqrt{SSR/26} = 0.0076$. In this simple two-variable regression, the square of the t-statistic for the slope coefficient, $t_{26}^2 = (-3.739)^2 = 13.98$ which is the F-statistic with 1,26 degrees of freedom. The F-statistic is used to test the null hypothesis $H_0 : a = 0$, $b = 0$. The one-tailed (right-tail) p-value of the F-statistic is 0.00092. Hence we can reject the null for any reasonable significance level. The coefficient of determination of the linear regression or R-squared is $R^2 = 0.3497$. It is the proportion of the variance in the dependent variable that is explained by the independent variables.

The problem with R^2 is that its value increases when more regressors are added to the linear regression, regardless of whether the added variables help in fact to explain the regressand or not. This problem arises when one is comparing different regression models on the same dependent variable but using different numbers of regressors or explanatory variables. To mitigate this issue, an adjustment is made to R^2 to impose a penalty when the number of regressors excluding the constant is increased. This resulted in the adjusted R^2 that is equal to $1 - \frac{(1-R^2)(N-1)}{N-k-1}$ where k is the number of regressors excluding the constant. When $k = 0$, adj $R^2 = R^2$. In our case, $k = 1$, so adj. $R^2 = 1-(1-0.3497)27/26 = 0.3247$. Adjusted R^2 decreases with k if R^2 is held constant; but it may increase when R^2 itself increases fast enough with more regressors.

In statistics, quantiles are RV X values that divide the cumulative distribution function cdf of the RV into equal intervals. If cdf $(X = x_1) = 0.10$, cdf $(X = x_2) = 0.20$, cdf $(X = x_3) = 0.30$, and so on, then $x_1, x_2, x_3, \ldots$ are called the deciles. If cdf $(X = x_1)$ $= 0.25$, cdf $(X = x_2) = 0.50$, cdf $(X = x_3) = 0.75$, and so on, then $x_1, x_2, x_3, \ldots$ are called the quartiles. In the latter case, x_2 is also called the median or the 50th percentile. x_1 is called the lower quartile or the 25th percentile. x_3 is called the upper quartile or the 75th percentile.

The quantile-quantile (Q-Q) plot is a graphical technique for visually comparing two probability distributions by plotting their quantiles side by side. A special case is to check if a sample set of points comes from a particular distribution such as the normal distribution. Suppose the equidistant points of $1/28, 2/28, \ldots, n/28, \ldots, 27/28, 1$ form the range set of variable X with cdf as the mapping function from $x_n \in X$ to the range set. Suppose X follows a normal distribution $N(\mu, \sigma^2)$. Then $z_n = (x_n - \mu)/\sigma$ are realizations of a standard $N(0, 1)$. cdf $(x_n) =$ cdf $(z_n) \equiv \Phi(z_n) = n/28$. The inverse function can be obtained as $x_n = \mu + \sigma\Phi^{-1}(n/28)$. Clearly, the series of numbers $\{x_n\}$ is ordered from low to high.

At the same time, there is an empirical distribution describing the sample set of points. In our case we try to check if the regression error RV e_{t+1} comes from a normal distribution. Let the estimated residuals in the regression in Table 2.1 be $\hat{e}_t$ for $t =$

$1, 2, \ldots, 28$. Suppose we order the 28 points of $\hat{e}_t$ from low to high as $\hat{e}_j$. In our case $\hat{e}_{j=1} = -0.01098$, $\hat{e}_{j=2} = -0.01023$, and so on. $\hat{e}_{j=27} = 0.01162$ and $\hat{e}_{j=28} = 0.02294$. Let the empirical cdf function be $M(\cdot)$ such that $M(\hat{e}_{j=n}) = n/28$. Then $\hat{e}_{j=n} = M^{-1}(n/28)$.

If $\hat{e}_j$ is normally distributed with a general mean μ and variance σ^2, then we can set $\hat{e}_{j=n} = x_n$ for $n = 1, 2, \ldots, 28$. In other words, $M(\hat{e}_{j=n}) = \Phi(z_n)$, so $M^{-1}(n/28) = \mu + \sigma\Phi^{-1}(n/28)$ for $n = 1, 2, \ldots, 28$. In a Normal Q-Q plot (or Q-Q plot based on a theoretical normal distribution), the x-axis measures the theoretical quantiles for the standardized normal variate $\Phi^{-1}(n/28)$ while the y-axis measures the sample quantiles $M^{-1}(n/28)$. Then, each point on the plot corresponds to a value n with coordinates $(\Phi^{-1}(n/28), M^{-1}(n/28))$, and the points should fall on a straight line with constant μ and slope σ. However, if the empirical points $\hat{e}_t$ are not normally distributed, then the Normal Q-Q plot would not produce a straight line. We compute the Normal Q-Q plot of the estimated residuals from Table 2.1, The plot is shown in Figure 2.8 as follows.

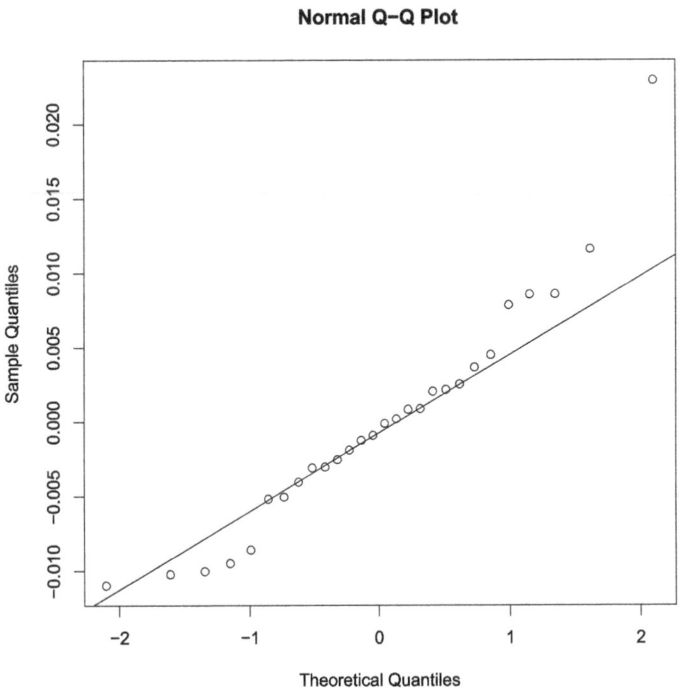

Figure 2.8: Normal Q-Q Plot of Residuals.

There are two outliers with values 0.01162 and 0.02294. Most of the other values of $\hat{e}_t$ appear to fall on the straight line indicating closeness to the normal distribution. However, several points with $\Phi^{-1}(n/28)$ below -1 have $M^{-1}(n/28)$ values below the straight line, indicating a fatter left tail than that of the normal distribution. Similarly, several points with $\Phi^{-1}(n/28)$ above +1 have $M^{-1}(n/28)$ values above the straight line, indicating a fatter right tail.

2.6 Hedging

We can also use linear regression to study optimal hedging. Suppose a large institutional investor holds a huge well-diversified portfolio of Japanese stocks that has returns following closely that of the N225 Stock Index return or rate of change. Suppose in September 1999, the investor was nervous about an imminent big fall in Japan equity prices, and wished to protect his/her portfolio value over the period September to mid-October 1999. He/She could liquidate his stocks. But this would be unproductive since his/her main business was to invest in the Japanese equity sector. Besides, liquidating a huge holding or even a big part of it would likely result in loss due to impact costs. Thus, the investor decided to hedge the potential drop in index value by selling h Nikkei 225 Index futures contracts. If the Japanese stock prices did fall, then the gain in the short position of the futures contracts would make up for the loss in the actual portfolio value.

The investor's original stock position has a total current value ¥V_t. For example, this could be 10 billion Yen. We make the simplifying assumption that his/her stock position value is a constant factor $f\times$ the N225 Index value S_t. Then, $\Delta V_{t+1} = f\Delta S_{t+1}$, and the portfolio return rate $\Delta V_{t+1}/V_t = \Delta S_{t+1}/S_t$. (In reality, the equivalence of return is approximate.)

By the simplifying assumption, the investor essentially forms a hedged portfolio comprising ¥$f \times S_t$, and h number of short positions in N225 Index futures contracts. The contract with maturity T has notional traded price $F_{t,T}$ and an actual price value of ¥500 $\times F_{t,T}$ where the contract is specified to have a value of ¥500 per notional price point. At the end of the risky period, his hedged portfolio ¥ value change would be:

$$P_{t+1} - P_t = f \times (S_{t+1} - S_t) - h \times 500 \times (F_{t+1,T} - F_{t,T}) \tag{2.8}$$

In effect, the investor wished to minimize the risk or variance of $P_{t+1} - P_t \equiv \Delta P_{t+1}$. Now, simplifying notations, from Eq. (2.8):

$$\Delta P_{t+1} = f \times \Delta S_{t+1} - h \times 500 \times \Delta F_{t+1}$$

So, $\text{var}(\Delta P_t) = f^2 \times \text{var}(\Delta S_t) + h^2 \times 500^2 \times \text{var}(\Delta F_t) - 2h \times 500f \times \text{cov}(\Delta S_t, \Delta F_t)$. Note that it does not matter here if the subscript is $t+1$ or t as we are treating their variances and covariances as similar whatever the time index. This is a property of a stationary RV that we shall discuss in a later chapter.

The FOC for minimising $\text{var}(\Delta P_t)$ with respect to decision variable h yields:

$$2 \times h(500^2)\,\text{var}(\Delta F_t) - 2 \times (500f)\,\text{cov}(\Delta S_t, \Delta F_t) = 0$$

or a risk-minimising "optimal" hedge of

$$h^* = \frac{f \times \text{cov}(\Delta S_t, \Delta F_t)}{500\, \text{var}(\Delta F_t)}$$

This is a positive number of contracts since S_t and $F_{t,T}$ would move together and recall that at maturity T of the futures contract, $S_T = F_{T,T}$. h^* can be estimated by substituting in the sample estimates of the covariance in the numerator and of the variance in the denominator.

The optimal hedge can also be estimated through the following linear regression[4] employing OLS method:

$$\Delta S_t = a + b\Delta F_t + e_t$$

where e_t is residual error that is uncorrelated with ΔF_t. We run this regression and the results are shown in Table 2.2.

Table 2.2: OLS Regression of Change in Nikkei Index on Change in Nikkei Futures Price: $\Delta S_t = a + b\Delta F_t + e_t$. Sample size = 29.

Variable	Coefficient	Std. Error	*t*-Statistic	Prob.
Constant	4.666338	24.01950	0.194	0.8474
ΔF_t	0.715750	0.092666	7.724	0.0000***
R-squared	0.6884	*F* (d. f. 1,27)-statistic		59.6597
Adjusted *R*-squared	0.6769	Prob(*F*-statistic)		0.0000***
S. E. of regression	129.325	Sum squared resid.		451573.2

Note: *** indicates significance at the 0.1 % level whether one-tailed or two-tailed tests.

Theoretically, $b = \text{cov}(\Delta S_t, \Delta F_t)/\text{var}(\Delta F_t) = 500/f \times h^*$. (Recall that earlier in the chapter, when dealing with two-variable linear regression, $b = \text{cov}(X_i, Y_i)/\text{var}(X_i)$.) Hence h^* estimate is found as $\hat{b} \times f/500$ number of the futures contracts to short in this case. From Table 2.2, $\hat{b}$ is 0.71575. With a ¥10 billion portfolio value and spot N225 Index on September 1, 1999 at 17479, f = 10 billion/17479 = 572,115. Thus the number of futures contract to short in this case is estimated as:

$$h^* = \hat{b} \times f/500 = 0.71575 \times 572{,}115/500 \approx 819$$

number of N225 futures contracts.

4 One of the earliest studies to highlight use of least squares regression in optimal hedging is Louis H. Ederington (1979), The hedging performance of the new futures markets, *The Journal of Finance*, 34, 157–170.

Further Reading

Gujarati, D. N. (1995), *Basic Econometrics*, Third edition, McGraw-Hill.
Johnston, J., and J. DiNardo (1997), *Econometric Methods*, Fourth edition, McGraw-Hill.

3 Capital Asset Pricing Model

A capital asset pricing model (CAPM) is a theoretical model to explain the level of expected return over a specific horizon of an asset using systematic risks. The asset is typically a traded financial instrument such as a stock (a major form of equity or ownership), a bond, a futures, a swap, an option, etc. A systematic risk is often described as the expected value of systematic risk factors that are RVs that affect all assets within the market at the same time, although having different degrees of impact on different assets. The different impacts are due to the different sensitivities of the assets to the risk factors. In this chapter we focus on the two-parameter (mean-variance) CAPM that was the mainstream of financial asset pricing in the sixties through the eighties. This is often mentioned as the Sharpe–Lintner (sometimes Sharpe–Lintner–Mossin) capital asset pricing model.[1] The theory and the econometrics will be discussed. To provide a good grasp of the basic theory of supply and demand in the financial economics of asset pricing, we lead the readers through some fundamental aspects of microeconomic decision theory involving utility or preference.

3.1 Expected Utility Theory

A rational framework for decision-making starts with preference – how a consumer would choose to consume among different consumption bundles, each of which is affordable by his/her budget. A consumption vector is $(x_1, x_2, \ldots, x_n)$ where x_i is number of units consumed of good i, and so on. If the consumer strictly prefers bundle $X = (x_1, \ldots, x_n)$ to bundle $Y = (y_1, \ldots, y_n)$, then we write $X \succ Y$. If consumer indeed chooses X over Y, this is called his/her revealed preference or choice. If the consumer has equal preference or is indifferent between bundles X and Y, then we write $X \sim Y$.

Suppose there is a utility function $U(\cdot)$ on the vector of consumption goods bundle such that $X \succ Y$ if and only if (iff) $U(X) > U(Y)$, $X \prec Y$ iff $U(X) < U(Y)$, and $X \sim Y$ iff $U(X) = U(Y)$. The actual number of the utility function, "utils", is just an ordering that indicates which bundle is preferred. Thus $U(\cdot)$ is an ordinal or ordering number, and not a cardinal or counting number (which would have some implications on relative magnitudes). Note that the assumption of existence of such a utility function $U : X \mapsto u \in \mathcal{R}$ is not trivial as it projects a consumption vector to a scalar number, i. e., it collapses a higher dimension object to a single dimension object.

Revealed preferences can in theory be used to build, for example in a two-goods world, a set of indifference curves quantified by the ordinal numbers of utils for each consumer. Then, one can tell if another bundle is preferred to existing ones or not by

1 See W. Sharpe (1964), Capital asset prices: A theory of market equilibrium under conditions of risk, *The Journal of Finance*, 19, 425–442.

https://doi.org/10.1515/9783110673951-003

looking at the indifference curves. But this is as far as it gets; there is nothing else in the cookie jar for understanding choices under uncertainty situations.

3.1.1 Choices Under Uncertainty

In order to build choice theory and decision-making on preferences of risky or uncertain outcomes, the von Neumann–Morgenstern (VM) expected utility representation or framework is very useful and popular in economics and financial research. A risky outcome is generically represented by a lottery which is characterized as a chance game in which there are two probabilistic outcomes: a probability p of winning X and a probability $(1 - p)$ of winning Y. X and Y can be monetary amounts, need not be consumption bundles, and can also be lotteries.

The lottery is expressed as $[p \odot X + (1 - p) \odot Y]$. Even though X or Y may be a vector of units of goods, the operation $\odot$ is not a multiplication, but simply denotes the association of probability p with lottery claim X in $p \odot X$ and of probability $(1 - p)$ with claim Y in $(1-p) \odot Y$. The idea is represented by the lottery diagrams in Figure 3.1.

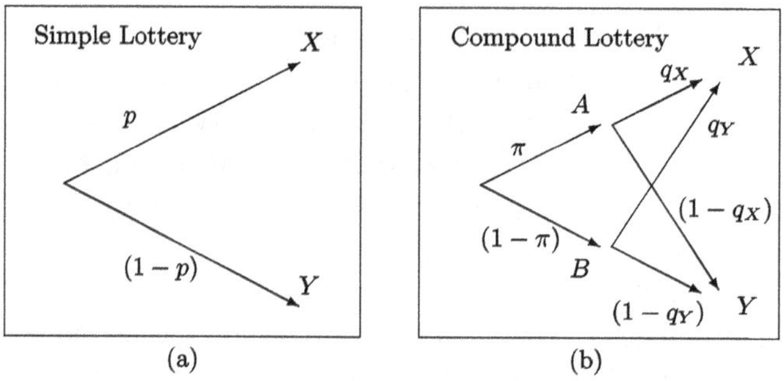

Figure 3.1: Simple and Compound Lotteries.

The simple lottery diagram, Figure 3.1(a), shows the lottery $[p \odot X + (1-p) \odot Y]$. Entities on the nodes represent consumption bundles or lotteries, while those on the branches represent probabilities. For the compound lottery diagram, Figure 3.1(b), A and B are themselves lotteries, with A being $[q_X \odot X+(1-q_X) \odot Y]$, and B being $[q_Y \odot X+(1-q_Y) \odot Y]$. This compound lottery is the same as $[(\pi q_X+(1-\pi)q_Y) \odot X+(\pi(1-q_X)+(1-\pi)(1-q_Y)) \odot Y]$ when we consider that the probability of winning X is now $p = \pi q_X + (1 - \pi)q_Y$.

We require a few axioms to construct the useful class of VM utility functions. There are three assumptions as follows.

(A1) Any two lotteries X, Y can be put into one or both of the preference relations: $X \succeq Y, X \preceq Y$.

(A2) If $X \succeq Y$, then for any other lottery Z, $[p \odot X + (1-p) \odot Z] \succeq [p \odot Y + (1-p) \odot Z]$, where $p \in [0,1]$.

(A3) Suppose $X \succ Y \succ Z$ are any 3 lotteries, then $p, q, r \in [0,1]$ can be found such that $[p \odot X + (1-p) \odot Z] \succ Y \sim [q \odot X + (1-q) \odot Z] \succ [r \odot X + (1-r) \odot Z]$

(A1) is called the completeness axiom. It includes the case $X \sim Y$ when both $X \succeq Y$ and $X \preceq Y$.

(A2) is sometimes called the substitution axiom or the independence axiom. This is intuitive, but is not some natural fixture, so it has to be axiomatized. For example, if I prefer a China holiday to a European holiday, it may also be that I prefer an even lottery of a European versus Mediterranean holiday to an even lottery of a China versus Mediterranean holiday, perhaps because of the lesser anxiety in the locational differences of the lottery outcomes. The axiom does compel some rationality onto the probability structure so as to make it a bit like a physical fraction p of outcome 1 and fraction $(1-p)$ of outcome 2 in the lottery.

In addition, this axiom yields (a) the reflexivity principle, i. e., put $p = 0$ in (A2), and for any Z, $Z \succeq Z$; and (b) the transitivity principle, i. e., $X \succeq Y \Longrightarrow [p \odot X + (1-p) \odot Z] \succeq [p \odot Y + (1-p) \odot Z]$; $Y \succeq Z \Longrightarrow [p \odot Y + (1-p) \odot Z] \succeq [p \odot Z + (1-p) \odot Z] = Z$, hence $[p \odot X + (1-p) \odot Z] \succeq Z$, and $X \succeq Z$ by putting $p = 1$.

(A2) also implies that if $X \sim Y$ (or $\{X \succ Y$ and $X \prec Y\}$), then for any other lottery Z, $[p \odot X + (1-p) \odot Z] \sim [p \odot Y + (1-p) \odot Z]$ (or $\{[p \odot X + (1-p) \odot Z] \succeq [p \odot Y + (1-p) \odot Z]$ and $[p \odot X + (1-p) \odot Z] \preceq [p \odot Y + (1-p) \odot Z]\}$).

(A3) is a continuity axiom and is sometimes called the Archimedean axiom. It buys a lot of things. First, it allows one to put a lottery of X and Z in equal preference with possibly a non-lottery Y. Thus $U(Y)$ is some weighted average of the $U[p \odot X + (1-p) \odot Z]$ and $U[r \odot X + (1-r) \odot Z]$. Thus the utility function cannot be just ordinal as otherwise it is difficult to define $U(Y)$. The utility function $U(\cdot)$, that is continuous and increasing in the sense that $U(X) \geq (\leq)\ U(Y)$ iff $X \succeq (\preceq)\ Y$, is now extended to a cardinal utility function that measures levels of absolute satisfaction or preference such that changes in the levels are comparable in different situations. The latter comparison is not possible under ordinal utility function. Measures of level changes also provide for measures of marginal utility which is an important analytical concept in decision theory. We consider the class of cardinal utility functions under positive affine transformation, i. e. if $U(X)$ is a feasible utility function, so is $V(X) = aU(X) + b$ (for constants a and b). This preserves the ranking of marginal utility, i. e. $dU(X) > dU(Y) > dU(Z) \Leftrightarrow dV(X) > dV(Y) > dV(Z)$.

Without loss of generality, we define $U : X \rightarrow [0,1] \in \mathcal{R}$. Unit utility is associated with the best or most preferred lottery B, i. e. $U(B) = 1$, while zero utility is associated with the worst or least preferred lottery W, i. e. $U(W) = 0$. Use of these two extreme reference points simplifies the construction, but are not really necessary. By the affine transformation, any analytical results obtained using $U(X) \in [0,1]$ can be similarly obtained using utility $V(X) = aU(X) + b \in [b, a+b]$ for arbitrary $a, b < \infty$. Probability

p lies in $[0,1]$. "$\succ$" means strict preference while "$\succeq$" means preference and includes indifference "$\sim$".

Using B and W, (A3) allows any lottery to be put into equal preference with a lottery on B and W, i. e. any lottery $X \sim [\pi \odot B + (1-\pi) \odot W]$ for a $\pi \in [0,1]$. (A3) also gives rise to the following lemma.

Lemma 3.1. $[p \odot B + (1-p) \odot W] \succ [q \odot B + (1-q) \odot W]$ *iff* $p > q$.

Proof. Suppose $X \succ Y$. By (A3), $\exists$ (there exists) $p_X, p_Y \ni$ (such that)

$$X \sim [p_X \odot B + (1-p_X) \odot W] \succ [p_Y \odot B + (1-p_Y) \odot W] \sim Y$$

Since $X \succ Y \succ W$, by (A3) again, $\exists\, \pi \ni$

$$[\pi \odot X + (1-\pi) \odot W] \sim Y$$

Left-hand side (LHS) is

$$\begin{aligned}[\pi \odot X + (1-\pi) \odot W] &\sim [\pi \odot [p_X \odot B + (1-p_X) \odot W] + (1-\pi) \odot W] \\ &\sim [\pi p_X \odot B + (1-\pi p_X) \odot W]\end{aligned}$$

where we have used (A2).

Therefore, $[\pi p_X \odot B + (1-\pi p_X) \odot W] \sim Y \sim [p_Y \odot B + (1-p_Y) \odot W]$. Thus, $\pi p_X = p_Y$. As $0 < \pi < 1$, we have $p_X > p_Y$, which is the proof of the "only if" part when we put $X = B \succ W = Y$.

Conversely, if $p_X > p_Y$, and $X \sim [p_X \odot B + (1-p_X) \odot W]$, while $Y \sim [p_Y \odot B + (1-p_Y) \odot W]$, we can find $0 < \pi < 1$, such that $\pi p_X = p_Y$. Thus, $Y \sim [\pi p_X \odot B + (1-\pi p_X) \odot W] \sim [\pi \odot X + (1-\pi) \odot W]$. By (A3), $X \succ Y$. □

Theorem 3.1 (VM Expected Utility Representation). *There is a utility function on the lottery space X, $U : X \to [0,1] \in \mathcal{R}$, such that*

$$U(p \odot X + (1-p) \odot Y) = pU(X) + (1-p)U(Y)$$

where p is the probability of outcome X, and $1-p$ is the probability of outcome Y.

Proof. By (A3), we can characterize lotteries X and Y as $X \sim [p_X \odot B + (1-p_X) \odot W]$ and $Y \sim [p_Y \odot B + (1-p_Y) \odot W]$ for $p_X, p_Y \in [0,1]$. By Lemma 3.1, $X \succ Y$ iff $p_X > p_Y$. Let function $U : X \to [0,1] \in \mathcal{R}$. We can thus fix $U(X) = p_X$ and $U(Y) = p_Y$ without loss of generality. This preserves the ranking of $X \succ Y$ given $p_X > p_Y$, and vice-versa, $X \succ Y \Rightarrow U(X) > U(Y) \Rightarrow p_X > p_Y$. Next

$$\begin{aligned}&p \odot X + (1-p) \odot Y \\ &\quad \sim p \odot [p_X \odot B + (1-p_X) \odot W] + (1-p) \odot [p_Y \odot B + (1-p_Y) \odot W]\end{aligned}$$

$$\sim [(pp_X + (1-p)p_Y) \odot B + (1 - pp_X - (1-p)p_Y) \odot W]$$
$$\sim [(pU(X) + (1-p)U(Y)) \odot B + (1 - pU(X) - (1-p)U(Y)) \odot W]$$

Since the LHS lottery is again expressed as a compound lottery of B and W, we can assign its utility as the probability of B in the compound lottery, i. e.,

$$U(p \odot X + (1-p) \odot Y) = pU(X) + (1-p)U(Y) \qquad \square$$

The utility function $U(\cdot)$ that satisfies axioms (A1), (A2), (A3) and thus the relationship $U(p \odot X + (1-p) \odot Y) = pU(X) + (1-p)U(Y)$ is called the VM utility function. It adds more properties to a primitive ordinal utility function. The VM $U(\cdot)$ has a strong advantage over a primitive ordinal utility as it is able to provide cardinality in terms of expectation, optimization, and is able to rank preferences by the expected outcome. It is also characterized as an expected utility function since any utility can be expressed as an expected utility with a trivial probability of one.

Is $U(X)$ function limited to characterization by p_X in $X \sim [p_X \odot B + (1-p_X) \odot W]$? We see what happens when we broaden it to be $U(X) = ap_X + b$ where $a > 0$ and b are constants. This includes the case when $U(X) = p_X$. Now

$$\begin{aligned}
&p \odot X + (1-p) \odot Y \\
&\quad \sim p \odot [p_X \odot B + (1-p_X) \odot W] + (1-p) \odot [p_Y \odot B + (1-p_Y) \odot W] \\
&\quad \sim [(pp_X + (1-p)p_Y) \odot B + (1 - pp_X - (1-p)p_Y) \odot W] \\
&\quad \sim \left[\left(p\left\{\frac{U(X)-b}{a}\right\} + (1-p)\left\{\frac{U(Y)-b}{a}\right\}\right) \odot B \right. \\
&\qquad \left. + \left(1 - p\left\{\frac{U(X)-b}{a}\right\} - (1-p)\left\{\frac{U(Y)-b}{a}\right\}\right) \odot W\right]
\end{aligned}$$

And so

$$\begin{aligned}
&U(p \odot X + (1-p) \odot Y) \\
&\quad = a\left(p\left\{\frac{U(X)-b}{a}\right\} + (1-p)\left\{\frac{U(Y)-b}{a}\right\}\right) + b \\
&\quad = pU(X) + (1-p)U(Y)
\end{aligned}$$

Thus, the expected utility representation is preserved and $U(\cdot)$ is unique up to a positive affine transformation. Any expected utility function or VM function $aU(\cdot) + b$, where $a > 0$ and b are constants, is equivalent to expected utility function $U(\cdot)$, producing the same preference outcomes.

There have been refutations of the VM representation via offered empirical paradoxes showing inconsistencies of VM utility implications, e. g., the Ellsberg and Allais paradoxes, being two of the most famous. However, the camp of rationalists remains very strong, and VM framework remains a major tool in economics and financial-theoretic modeling.

Hirshleifer and Riley commented,[2] “The dissident literature claims that the discrepancies revealed by these results refute the economist's standard assumption of rationality, or at least the expected utility hypothesis as a specific implication of that assumption. We reject this interpretation. A much more parsimonious explanation, in our opinion, is that this evidence merely illustrates certain limitations of the human mind as a computer. It is possible to fool the brain by the way a question is posed, just as optical illusions may be arranged to fool the eye”.

3.2 Utility Functions

Under market mechanism where goods $i = 1, 2, \ldots, n$ are traded, suppose the market prices $\{p_i\}_{i=1,2,\ldots,n}$ are competitive and strictly positive (taken as given; in other words, individual consumer choices cannot affect the prices), a representative individual's demand on the goods $\{x_i\}_{i=1,2,\ldots,n}$ is restricted by his/her income Y accordingly. Denote X as the vector $(x_1, x_2, \ldots, x_n)$. The budget constraint is

$$\sum_i p_i x_i \leq Y$$

As a consumer, he/she chooses x_i's to

$$\max_X U(X) \quad \text{subject to} \quad \sum_i p_i x_i \leq Y \quad \text{and} \quad X > 0$$

Note that vector $X \geq 0 \Rightarrow$ any element is either > 0 or $= 0$. Vector $X > 0 \Rightarrow$ at least one element $x_i > 0$ while the others are ≥ 0. $X \gg 0 \Rightarrow$ all x_i's > 0. U as a function of direct consumption goods amounts is called a direct utility function and the optimal demands x_i as a solution is called the Marshallian demand function.

How do we solve this constrained optimization problem? Let us consider necessary conditions for a maximum. In Figures 3.2(a) and (b), it is seen that keeping all other variables constant while varying x_i, if a maximum point occurs in the closed interior set where $x_i \geq 0$, as in Figure 3.2(a), then in this case, $U_i' = 0$ at the maximum point. However, in Figure 3.2(b), the maximum point occurs at $x_i = 0$. At this point, the slope U_i' is clearly negative. The slope could also be zero here.

Hence, under constraint $x_i \geq 0$, $U_i' \leq 0$ at the maximum point. This is one necessary condition. In fact, either $\{U_i' = 0, x_i > 0\}$ or $\{U_i' \leq 0, x_i = 0\}$, so we can use another necessary condition for maximum, i. e. $U_i' \times x_i = 0$.

2 J. Hirshleifer and J. G. Riley (1992), *The Analytics of Uncertainty and Information*, Cambridge University Press, p. 34.

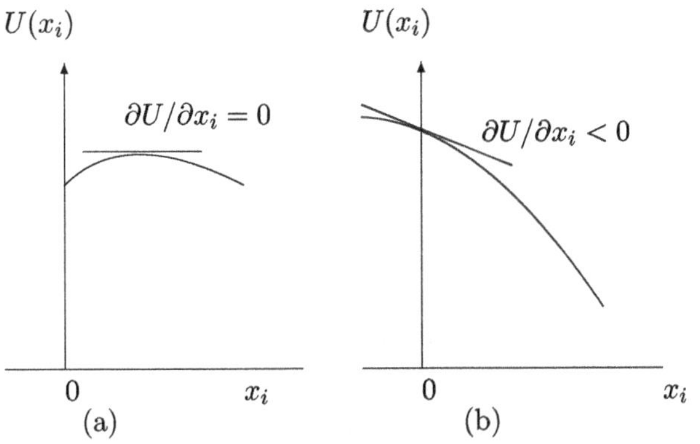

Figure 3.2: Unconstrained and Constrained Maximums.

Form the "Lagrangian" function with Lagrange multiplier λ; $L \equiv U(X) + \lambda(Y - \sum_i p_i x_i)$. Then, maximize the objective function

$$\max_{X,\lambda} U(X) + \lambda\left(Y - \sum_i p_i x_i\right) \quad \text{s.t.} \quad X > 0$$

Note that in L, if the maximum occurs within the constraint $(Y - \sum_i p_i x_i) > 0$, or in its interior, then the solution should be as if solving max $U(X)$ without the constraint, hence λ necessarily equals zero. If the maximum is right at the boundary where $(Y - \sum_i p_i x_i) = 0$, then $\lambda > 0$ since any increase of Y in the constraint set would increase L by the shadow price λ, which must necessarily be strictly positive in this case.

In fact, either $\{(Y - \sum_i p_i x_i) = 0, \lambda > 0\}$ or $\{(Y - \sum_i p_i x_i) > 0, \lambda = 0\}$, so we can use another necessary condition for maximum, i. e. $(Y - \sum_i p_i x_i)\lambda = 0$.

The first-order necessary conditions (FOC) are:

(C1) $\frac{\partial L}{\partial x_i} : U_i(X) - \lambda p_i \leq 0, \forall i$

(C2) $(U_i(X) - \lambda p_i)x_i = 0, \forall i$

(C3) $\frac{\partial L}{\partial \lambda} : Y - \sum_i p_i x_i \geq 0,$

(C4) $(Y - \sum_i p_i x_i)\lambda = 0$

(C5) $x_i \geq 0, \forall i$, and

(C6) $\lambda \geq 0$.

Second-order conditions for maximum are met as $U(\cdot)$ is assumed to be strictly concave.

Conditions (C1) and (C2) follow the same arguments laid out for diagrams in Figures 3.2(a) and (b) when $x_i \geq 0$. (C4) is sometimes called the complementary slackness condition.

Suppose we have an interior solution in (C1)–(C6), then $\lambda > 0$, and $x_i > 0 \quad \forall i$.

(C2) $\Rightarrow U_i = \lambda p_i$. (C4) $\Rightarrow Y = \sum_i p_i x_i$, so $\lambda = \frac{\sum_i U_i x_i}{Y}$. Then, we have

$$U_i = \frac{p_i}{Y}\left(\sum_i U_i x_i\right) \quad \forall i$$

and a solution $x_1^*, x_2^*, \ldots, x_n^*$ can be found. Each x_i^* is a function of p_i's and Y, or $x_i^*(Y;p)$ where p is the vector of p_i's. When expressed in terms of given prices and income Y, the demand function is called a Hicksian demand function.[3]

Utility function $U(Y;p)$ based on Hicksian demand or income or wealth Y is called an indirect utility function. It is this indirect form of utility function in terms of available income or wealth that is most often used in finance theory.

Under preference relations that can be represented as VM expected utility formulated above, an individual determines the probabilities of lottery payoffs, assigns an index U to each possible payoff, and then makes a decision to maximize the expected value of the index. The index or sometimes "utils" is a function of income or wealth. We shall refer to the use of utility under the representation as VM utility function.

Suppose there is an investment A that leads to final wealth W_A which is a RV with probability distribution $P(W_A)$. Another investment B leads to final wealth W_B with probability distribution $P(W_B)$. A is preferred to B iff $E(U(W_A)) > E(U(W_B))$ or $\sum U(W_A)P(W_A) > \sum U(W_B)P(W_B)$. Henceforth, we shall use money in the argument of $U(\cdot)$. Even if we use a certain good (say, gold) and its amount x in the argument, we can treat it as "money" or as a numéraire, so all other goods can be denominated in terms of the amount of gold.

3.2.1 Taylor Series Expansion

For more analytical development of the utility function, a convergent Taylor series expansion is required. We explain this as follows. The Taylor series expansion is an important analytical linear approximation to continuously differentiable functions using polynomials and plays a major role in mathematical analysis. A polynomial function in x to degree n can be written in the form

$$a_0 + a_1 x + a_2 x^2 + a_3 x^3 + \cdots + a_{n-1} x^{n-1} + a_n x^n$$

where a_k $\forall k$ is a constant. The Taylor series expansion is explained by the Taylor's Theorem as follows.

Theorem 3.2 (Taylor's Theorem). *Let f be a function that is $n+1$ times differentiable on an open interval containing points a and X. Then, for a fixed a,*

3 For more microeconomics, see Varian (1992).

$$f(x) = f(a) + (x-a)f'(a) + (x-a)^2\frac{f''(a)}{2!} + (x-a)^3\frac{f'''(a)}{3!} + \cdots + (x-a)^n\frac{f^{(n)}(a)}{n!} + R_n(x)$$

where $f^{(n)}(a)$ is the nth derivative evaluated at point a, and remainder term $R_n(x) = (x-a)^{n+1}\frac{f^{(n+1)}(y)}{(n+1)!}$ for some number y such that $a < y < x$.

Proof. We can always define a function

$$F(t) = f(x) - f(t) - (x-t)f'(t) - (x-t)^2\frac{f''(t)}{2!} - \cdots - (x-t)^n\frac{f^{(n)}(t)}{n!}$$

for a fixed t such that $a \le t \le x$. In general, this function will contain x and t. However, specifically, $F(x) = 0$ and $F(a) = f(x) - f(a) - (x-a)f'(a) - (x-a)^2\frac{f''(a)}{2!} - \cdots - (x-a)^n\frac{f^{(n)}(a)}{n!}$. The proof is completed when it can be shown that $F(a) = R_n(x) = (x-a)^{n+1}\frac{f^{(n+1)}(y)}{(n+1)!}$ for some number y such that $a < y < x$. Now

$$F'(t) = -f'(t) - (x-t)f''(t) + f'(t) - (x-t)^2\frac{f'''(t)}{2!} + (x-t)f''(t) - \cdots - (x-t)^n\frac{f^{(n+1)}(t)}{n!} + (x-t)^{n-1}\frac{f^{(n)}(t)}{(n-1)!}$$
$$= -(x-t)^n\frac{f^{(n+1)}(t)}{n!}$$

Define $H(t) = F(t) - (\frac{x-t}{x-a})^{n+1}F(a)$. We have $H(a) = 0$, and $H(x) = F(x) = 0$. There is a y between a and x such that $H'(y) = 0$ (Rolle's theorem). But $H'(y) = F'(y) + (n+1)\frac{(x-y)^n}{(x-a)^{n+1}}F(a)$. Hence, $F'(y) + (n+1)\frac{(x-y)^n}{(x-a)^{n+1}}F(a) = 0$. Or, $-(x-y)^n\frac{f^{(n+1)}(y)}{n!} + (n+1)\frac{(x-y)^n}{(x-a)^{n+1}}F(a) = 0$.

Hence, $F(a) = (x-a)^{n+1}\frac{f^{(n+1)}(y)}{(n+1)!}$. □

The Taylor series expansion is very useful for analysis. When the remainder term $R_n(x)$ is very small or ≈ 0, then $f(x)$ can be well approximated by $f(a) + (x-a)f'(a) + (x-a)^2\frac{f''(a)}{2!} + \cdots + (x-a)^n\frac{f^{(n)}(a)}{n!}$. The Taylor series expansion can also be used to determine if a stationary point a (when $f'(a) = 0$) is a local minimum or a local maximum or a local point of inflection. The local feature refers to only a section or part of the domain while a global feature refers to the whole domain of the function. Suppose $f'(a) = \cdots = f^{(n-1)}(a) = 0$, but $f^{(n)}(a) \neq 0$. By Theorem 3.1, $f(x) - f(a) = R_{n-1}(x) = (x-a)^n\frac{f^{(n)}(y)}{n!}$ for $a < y < x$. If n is even, $(x-a)^n > 0$. In this case, if $f^{(n)}(y) > 0$, and supposing a is sufficiently close to y, so $f^{(n)}(a) > 0$, then $f(x) > f(a)$, hence point a is a local minimum. The special case of $f'(a) = 0$ and $f''(a) > 0$ implies a local minimum at a on $f(x)$. In the same case, if $f^{(n)}(y) < 0$, and supposing a is sufficiently close to y, so $f^{(n)}(a) < 0$, then $f(x) < f(a)$, hence point a is a local maximum. For a special case such as a quadratic function, the local minimum (maximum) is also the global minimum (maximum). If n is odd, $f(x)-f(a)$ have opposite signs for $x < a$ and for $x > a$ (whichever sign is $f^{(n)}(a)$). In this case, point a is a point of inflection.

3.2.2 Maclaurin Series

Theorem 3.1 can be specialized to the case of Maclaurin series which is a particular power series (a polynomial with an infinitely differentiable function) by fixing $a = 0$. Then,

$$f(x) = \sum_{n=0}^{\infty} \frac{f^{(n)}(0)}{n!} x^n$$

where $f^{(0)}(0)$ is defined as $f(0)$. The infinite Taylor series needs to be convergent so that when computation is done at a particular cutoff of large n, the resulting polynomial is a good approximation. If the higher derivative $f^{(n+1)}(a)$ grows at a rate much faster than n itself, then the series may not converge and the Taylor series is not valid. Many important convergent Maclaurin series are as follows.

$$\begin{aligned}
e^x &= 1 + x + \frac{x^2}{2!} + \frac{x^3}{3!} + \cdots = \sum_{n=0}^{\infty} \frac{x^n}{n!} \\
\ln(1+x) &= x - \frac{x^2}{2} + \frac{x^3}{3} - \cdots = \sum_{n=1}^{\infty} \frac{(-1)^{n+1} x^n}{n} \\
\sin x &= x - \frac{x^3}{3!} + \frac{x^5}{5!} - \cdots = \sum_{n=0}^{\infty} \frac{(-1)^n x^{2n+1}}{(2n+1)!} \\
\cos x &= 1 - \frac{x^2}{2!} + \frac{x^4}{4!} - \cdots = \sum_{n=0}^{\infty} \frac{(-1)^n x^{2n}}{(2n)!}
\end{aligned}$$

From the last two expressions, one can see that $d \sin x/dx = \cos x$.

3.3 Risk Aversion

First, we note that by the basic axiom of nonsatiation in human economic behavior (generically, excepting some self-sacrificial souls or instances), $U(x) > U(y)$ iff $x > y$ where x, y are money units. This is because for fixed x greater than fixed y, $x \succ y$, so by VM expected utility (which after this point we shall always assume, unless it is otherwise indicated), $E[U(x)] > E[U(y)]$. Hence $U(x) > U(y)$ as x, y are constants in this case. If for any $x > y$, $U(x) > U(y)$, then $U(\cdot)$ is a strictly increasing function of its argument. Assuming continuous function $U(\cdot)$ with existence of at least the first and second derivatives, for purposes of easy analysis and exposition of basic theoretical results, then clearly, $U'(\cdot) > 0$. Similarly, if $U(x) > U(y)$ and hence $E[U(x)] > E[U(y)]$, then $x \succ y$.

We shall define that a person (or agent or investor) is risk neutral if he (or she) is indifferent between doing nothing or value 0 and an actuarially (probabilistically in the expectations sense) fair amount $E(X) = 0$ where X is a RV or a lottery, and $r > 0$:

$$X = \begin{cases} \pi r & \text{with probability } (1-\pi) \\ -(1-\pi)r & \text{with probability } \pi \end{cases}$$

The agent is defined to be risk averse if he or she prefers doing nothing to accepting the gamble, i. e., prefers certainty to an actuarially fair game. He/she is defined to be risk loving if he or she prefers the gamble to certainty.

Theorem 3.3. *An agent is risk averse iff $U(W)$, where W is his or her wealth, is a strictly concave function.*

Proof. By Jensen's inequality, if $U(\cdot)$ is strictly concave (which means $-U(\cdot)$ is strictly convex), $E[U(W+X)] < U(E[W+X]) = U(W)$ since $E(X) = 0$ for an actuarially fair lottery. Thus, the agent always prefers certainty to the actuarially fair gamble X, and is thus risk averse.

For the "only if" part, suppose the agent is risk averse, then

$$U(W) > \pi U(W - [1-\pi]r) + (1-\pi)U(W + \pi r)$$

for all $r > 0$ and $\pi \in (0,1)$. Since

$$U(W) = U(\pi(W - [1-\pi]r) + (1-\pi)(W + \pi r))$$

strict concavity of $U(\cdot)$ is shown. □

We shall henceforth assume all agents are risk averse unless otherwise specified. Suppose an agent faces a risky lottery of RV X, with $E(X) = 0$, so his/her final wealth is $W + X$, where W is a constant. An insurance company charges him/her an insurance amount I to remove any uncertainty in his/her final wealth. Then

$$E[U(W+X)] = U(W-I)$$

Using Taylor series expansion, considering I is small relative to variance in X, then

$$E\left[U(W) + XU'(W) + \frac{1}{2}X^2U''(W) + o(U)\right] = U(W) - IU'(W) + o(U)$$

where $o(U)$ denotes an approximation to a little (small) order, i. e. $o(U)$ tends toward zero as U grows larger. Conversely, big order $O(U)$ would mean that $O(U)/U$ remains as some finite constant that does not approach zero. Thus,

$$\frac{1}{2}E[X^2]U''(W) \approx -IU'(W)$$

or $I \approx -\frac{1}{2}\frac{U''(W)}{U'(W)}\,\mathrm{var}(X)$.

Intuitively, for any agent, $-\frac{U''(W)}{U'(W)} = A(W)$ is a positive number such that insurance premium I increases with this number $A(W)$ for a given risk X. If the agent is willing to pay a higher risk premium, he/she is more risk averse. Thus, $A(W)$ is a measure of risk aversion: the higher the $A(W)$, the higher the risk aversion. $A(W) > 0$ since concave $U(\cdot)$ implies $U''(\cdot) < 0$.

$A(W) = -\frac{U''(W)}{U'(W)}$ is called the absolute risk aversion function; $T(W) = 1/A(W)$ is called the risk-tolerance function; $R(W) = W \times A(W)$ is called the relative risk aversion function. In some VM utility, when these functions become constants, we have the associated "risk aversion coefficients". For example, $U(W) = -e^{-aW}$, where a is a constant, is a negative exponential utility function. $U' = -aU$, and $U'' = a^2U$, so $A(W) = -U''/U' = a$, and $a > 0$ is called the constant absolute risk aversion coefficient.

Another example is $U(W) = \frac{W^{1-\gamma}-1}{1-\gamma}$, where γ is a constant, and U is a power utility function. $U' = W^{-\gamma}$, and $U'' = -\gamma W^{-\gamma-1}$. So, $R(W) = -WU''/U' = \gamma$, and $\gamma > 0$ is called the constant relative risk aversion coefficient. Another form or an affine transform of the power utility function is $U(W) = \frac{W^{1-\gamma}}{1-\gamma}$ that is also called an isoelastic utility function since $dU/dW \times W/U = 1-\gamma$, a constant.

The logarithmic utility function $\ln(W)$ is a special case of the power utility, as seen below, when $\gamma \to 1$. Apply L'Hôpital's rule:

$$\lim_{\gamma\to 1}\frac{W^{1-\gamma}-1}{1-\gamma} = \lim_{\gamma\to 1}\frac{d(W^{1-\gamma}-1)/d\gamma}{d(1-\gamma)/d\gamma} = \ln(W)$$

Note $\frac{d}{dW}\ln W = 1/W > 0$, so log utility is increasing in W. Next, $\frac{d^2}{dW^2}\ln W = -1/W^2 < 0$, so log utility exhibits strict concavity and thus risk aversion.

$U(W) = \frac{t}{1-t}(\frac{cW}{t}+d)^{1-t}$, $d > 0$, is a class of hyperbolic absolute risk aversion (HARA) utilities. $U' = c(\frac{cW}{t}+d)^{-t}$, and $U'' = -c^2(\frac{cW}{t}+d)^{-t-1}$. So, $A(W) = -U''/U' = c(\frac{cW}{t}+d)^{-1}$. Thus, $T(W) = 1/A(W) = \frac{W}{t}+\frac{d}{c}$. HARA utility functions are linear risk tolerance functions (in wealth).

It is interesting to note that since the 1980s there have been increasing attempts to model non-standard utility, i. e. non-VM utility that does not necessarily obey Theorem 3.1. A non-standard utility may have the advantage of higher flexibility to explain some of the aberrations or anomalies occurring that could not be satisfactorily explained by VM-type preferences. An example of non-standard utility is the recursive Epstein–Zin utility function[4] that is used frequently in life-cycle modeling where

4 L. G. Epstein and S. E. Zin (1989), Substitution, risk aversion, and the temporal behavior of consumption growth and asset returns I: A theoretical framework, *Econometrica*, 57(4), 937–969.

intertemporal substitutional issues are significant. In the Epstein–Zin utility, an extra elasticity of intertemporal substitution parameter allows its disentanglement from the coefficient of risk aversion so that both intertemporal substitution or resolution of uncertainty in near versus far risks and also risk aversion in degree of overall uncertainty can be separately considered.

3.3.1 Application of VM Expected Utility

Nicholas Bernoulli in 1713 posed the "St. Petersburg Paradox" as follows. It was commonly accepted at that time that the price of a lottery would be its expected value. The lottery pays 2^{n-1} if the first head occurs in the nth toss of a coin.

The probability of a head at the nth toss follows a geometric distribution (special case of negative binomial) $p(1-p)^{n-1}$ where $p = 1/2$ is the probability of a head. The expected payoff of the lottery is then

$$\sum_{i=1}^{\infty} \frac{1}{2}\left(\frac{1}{2}\right)^{i-1} 2^{i-1} = \sum_{i=1}^{\infty} \frac{1}{2} = \infty$$

The paradox is that no one would pay a large amount to buy this lottery with an expected payoff of ∞.

Now suppose people are risk averse and not risk neutral (who would then play actuarially fair games). Suppose they have log utility $\ln(W)$. Then, a fair price π is $\ni$ (such that):

$$\ln(\pi) = \sum_{i=1}^{\infty} \frac{1}{2}\left(\frac{1}{2}\right)^{i-1} \ln(2^{i-1}) = \sum_{i=1}^{\infty} \left(\frac{1}{2}\right)^{i} (i-1)\ln 2 = \ln 2$$

Hence, $\pi = 2$ which is a much smaller sum to pay given the risk aversion, and can thus explain the paradox!

3.3.2 Value of Information

Suppose a market offers shares that give rise to a payoff (RV X_i) for every \$1 invested in a future state (event) i share as follows. There are N finite states of the world, thus N types of shares:

$$\$\text{payoff} = \begin{cases} X_i & \text{with probability } p_i \\ 0 & \text{with probability } (1-p_i) \end{cases}$$

An investor or individual has a budget of \$1 with which to allocate amount $a_i \geq 0$ to the ith share such that $\sum_{i=1}^{N} a_i = 1$. His/her payoff if state j occurs next period is $\$a_j X_j$. He/she maximizes his/her expected utility subject to budget constraints, i. e.

$$\max_{a_i} \sum_{i=1}^{N} p_i U(a_i X_i) \quad \text{s. t.} \sum_{i=1}^{N} a_i = 1 \quad \text{and} \quad a_i > 0 \quad \forall i$$

If Lagrangian function $L \equiv \sum_{i=1}^{N} p_i \; U(a_i X_i) + \lambda(1 - \sum_i a_i)$ is maximized, assuming the budget constraint is exactly met, and that all $a_i > 0$, then the necessary conditions (FOCs) are

$$p_i X_i U'(a_i X_i) = \lambda, \forall i, \quad \text{and} \quad \sum_{i=1}^{N} a_i = 1$$

For log utility $U(\cdot)$, the necessary FOCs are

$$p_i X_i \frac{1}{a_i X_i} = \frac{p_i}{a_i} = \lambda, \forall i, \quad \text{and} \quad \sum_{i=1}^{N} a_i = 1$$

Solving, $\lambda = \sum_{i=1}^{N} p_i = 1$, so $a_i = p_i$. Then, the maximum value of the objective function is

$$\sum_{i=1}^{N} p_i \ln(p_i X_i) = \sum_{i=1}^{N} p_i \ln p_i + \sum_{i=1}^{N} p_i \ln X_i \tag{3.1}$$

Now, the uncertainty in the problem has to do with which state i will eventually occur. Suppose the investor is given an information set on which state occurred before he or she makes an investment decision about a_i. Suppose there is perfect information (or perfect knowledge) about which state i would occur. Then, the investor's ex-ante objective function, given this full information each time before he or she decides, is

$$\max_{a_i} E(U(a_i X_i)|X) = \sum_{i=1}^{N} p_i \ln(1 \times X_i) = \sum_{i=1}^{N} p_i \ln(X_i) \tag{3.2}$$

where all \$1 budget is allocated to state i when $X = X_i$.

Maximum expected log utility is obtained in (3.1) without information while that in (3.2) is obtained with full information from X. The information value (in util sense, not \$ sense here) is therefore

$$\left[\sum_{i=1}^{N} p_i \ln X_i\right] - \left[\sum_{i=1}^{N} p_i \ln p_i + \sum_{i=1}^{N} p_i \ln X_i\right] = -\sum_{i=1}^{N} p_i \ln p_i > 0$$

In statistical information theory, $-\sum_{i=1}^{N} p_i \ln p_i$ is also called the entropy of RV X and is a measure of the uncertainty embodied in the randomness of X. For example, $X = 2$ with probability 0.5 and $X = 1$ with probability 0.5 has an entropy of $-\ln 0.5 = 0.6931$. Another RV has distribution $X = 2$ with probability 0.9 and $X = 1$ with probability 0.1. This has entropy $-0.9 \ln 0.9 - 0.1 \ln 0.1 = 0.3251$. Hence the former X is a lot more uncertain than the latter in that one is more able to predict the latter with the higher probability of which value will occur.

3.4 Single-Period CAPM

The Sharpe–Lintner CAPM is a single-period model. From about 1964 until the 1980s, it was a predominant model for understanding the pricing of stocks as well as projects through extensive use of its concept of systematic risk in beta. It is still relevant, although there have been much improvements in the understanding of how stocks are priced, including behavioral aberrations and extensions to multi-factor models. The CAPM is a single-factor model relying on the market index to explain systematic variations in stock returns.

Suppose there are N risky stocks and 1 risk-free bond with risk-free rate r_f over the period. Utility function is strictly increasing and concave. We shall assume either stock return rates r_i's are jointly normally distributed[5] (which means any portfolio or linear combination of return rates is normally distributed) and/or the investor has quadratic utility functions.

Investor k maximizes expected utility based on current wealth W_0 and investment decisions or portfolio weights (percentage investment) on the stocks, x_i:

$$\max_{\{x_i\}_{i=1,2,\ldots,N}} E[U(W_1)]$$

where $W_1 = W_0(1 + r_P)$, r_P being the portfolio return rate, and

$$\begin{aligned} r_P &= \sum_{i=1}^{N} x_i r_i + \left(1 - \sum_{i=1}^{N} x_i\right) r_f \\ &= r_f + \sum_{i=1}^{N} x_i (r_i - r_f) \\ &= r_f + x^T (r - r_f 1) \end{aligned}$$

5 A more general class that includes the normal distribution is the class of elliptical distributions. This assumption has the disadvantage that W_1 may become negative. We can assume that the joint normal distributions of r_i's produce a negligibly small probability as such, or else use $W_1 = W_0 \exp(r_P)$ where r_P is lognormally distributed. However, in the latter, linear combinations of lognormal returns in a portfolio do not yield exactly a lognormal portfolio return.

Note that the weights of the N stocks and the risk-free bond sum to 1. In the last step, we switch to matrix[6] notations, where $x^T = (x_1, x_2, \ldots, x_N)$, $r^T = (r_1, r_2, \ldots, r_N)$, and $1^T = (1, 1, \ldots, 1)_{1\times N}$. Note also that the investor's portfolio defined above consists of optimal portions of the N risky stocks and also a portion on the risk-free bond.

For the portfolio return r_P which is normally distributed, note that

$$E(r_P) = \mu_P = r_f + x^T(\mu - r_f 1),$$
$$\mathrm{var}(r_P) = \sigma_P^2 = x^T \Sigma x$$

and

$$\mathrm{cov}(r, r_P) = \begin{pmatrix} \mathrm{cov}(r_1, r_P) \\ \mathrm{cov}(r_2, r_P) \\ \vdots \\ \mathrm{cov}(r_N, r_P) \end{pmatrix} = \Sigma x$$

where Σ is the covariance matrix of the N risky stock returns. Note the above results are obtained even when the portfolio return r_P contains a non-zero fraction $(1 - x^T 1)$ of the risk-free bond.

Either the multivariate normal return distribution assumption or the quadratic utility assumption has the effect of ensuring that the investor's preference ultimately depends only on the mean and variance of the return distribution. In the multivariate normal assumption, the third and higher wealth level moments in a Taylor expansion of $E[U(\cdot)]$ (assuming the expansion is convergent) based on normally distributed wealth W_1 at end of period, can be expressed as functions of the first two moments of the normal distribution. Hence, for any arbitrary preferences, the VM expected utility $E[U(W_1)]$ of end-of-period wealth depends only on the mean and variance. However, there has been strong empirical evidence that stock return distributions tend to be skewed and have tails fatter than those of a normal distribution.

In the quadratic utility assumption, investor's preference depends only on the mean and variance of returns because third and higher orders of derivatives of $E[U(\cdot)]$ in a Taylor expansion of $U(\cdot)$ are zeros. Thus, only the first and second moments of return enter into the VM expected utility $E[U(W_1)]$ of end-of-period wealth. However, quadratic utility has the disadvantage that at some wealth level that is sufficiently high, expected utility may decrease, thus violating a standing axiom of nonsatiability. Moreover, there is increasing absolute risk aversion with respect to wealth, which is not very intuitive.

Despite the caveats discussed above where we see that mean–variance optimization (as in Markowitz's portfolio optimization)[7] may be inconsistent at times with ex-

6 For microeconomic analysis using matrix operations, see Takayama (1985).

7 H. Markowitz (1952), Portfolio Selection, *The Journal of Finance*, 7, 77–91. See also Huang and Litzenberger (1988) for a rigorous discussion of portfolio optimization mathematics.

pected utility maximization, it is still a very powerful framework to derive meaningful and positive financial economic theories and understanding. We express $E(U)$ as a function of only μ_P and σ_P^2 for the mean–variance analysis. Thus, we maximize VM expected utility, $E[U(W_1)] \equiv V(\mu_P, \sigma_P^2)$.

The FOC becomes (in vector notation)

$$\frac{\partial V}{\partial x}_{N\times 1} = 0 = \frac{\partial V}{\partial \mu_P}(\mu - r_f 1) + \frac{\partial V}{\partial \sigma_P^2}(2\Sigma x) \tag{3.3}$$

Rearranging,

$$\begin{aligned} x &= -\frac{1}{2}\left(\frac{\frac{\partial V}{\partial \mu_P}}{\frac{\partial V}{\partial \sigma_P^2}}\right)\Sigma^{-1}(\mu - r_f 1) \\ &= t\Sigma^{-1}(\mu - r_f 1) \end{aligned} \tag{3.4}$$

where $t = -\frac{1}{2}\left(\frac{\frac{\partial V}{\partial \mu_P}}{\frac{\partial V}{\partial \sigma_P^2}}\right) > 0$ since $\frac{\partial V}{\partial \mu_P} > 0$ due to nonsatiation, and $\frac{\partial V}{\partial \sigma_P^2} < 0$ due to risk aversion. Thus $t = \frac{1}{2}\left(\frac{\partial \sigma_P^2}{\partial \mu_P}\right) > 0$ (holding V constant), which is a measure of risk tolerance.

We see that investors optimally invest in only two funds. The first fund is a portfolio of stocks as given by x in Eq. (3.4), while the second fund is $\$W_0(1 - x^T 1)$ in risk-free bonds. This is sometimes called a two-fund separation theorem, and implies that under mean–variance optimization, investors can achieve optimality by simply investing in two properly construed funds rather than having to worry about deciding weights for every stock. This has in the past been used as an argument for passive market index fund investment, such as in Vanguard.

The model is actually not quite complete yet. The optimization above is for a kth investor in the market. Suppose there are Z number of non-homogeneous or heterogeneous investors in the market. When all their stock demands are aggregated, the total vector dollar demand on risky stocks is given by

$$\sum_{k=1}^{Z} x_k W_0^k$$

where superscript k denotes association of the quantity with the kth investor. We allow different investors to have different original wealth, hence W_0^k. They may also have different utility functions $V(\mu_P, \sigma_P^2)$, hence different t^k values although they all have the same information of market return parameters, μ and Σ. Suppose the total market wealth is $M = \sum_{k=1}^{Z} W_0^k$, we can then define $N \times 1$ vector of weights $x_M = \frac{\sum_{k=1}^{Z} x_k W_0^k}{M}$. Thus, x_M acts like the optimal portfolio of stocks of a representative investor (or the aggregated average of all non-homogeneous investors), when aggregate demand is equated to aggregate supply of dollars for each security, i. e. the ith element of $\sum_{k=1}^{Z} x_k W_0^k$ equated to the ith element of $x_M M$.

This equation of demand and supply is called an equilibrium condition and is necessary for any good solution to a problem involving the whole set of investors in the market. x_M is the equilibrium market portfolio (weight vector).

$$x_M M = \sum_{k=1}^{Z} x_k W_0^k = \sum_{k=1}^{Z} t^k W_0^k \Sigma^{-1}(\mu - r_f 1)$$

Thus

$$x_M = \left(\frac{\sum_{k=1}^{Z} t^k W_0^k}{M}\right)\Sigma^{-1}(\mu - r_f 1)$$

which implies

$$\Sigma x_M = \text{cov}(r, r_M) = t^M(\mu - r_f 1) \tag{3.5}$$

where $t^M = (\frac{\sum_{k=1}^{Z} t^k W_0^k}{M}) > 0$ is the market-averaged or representative investor's risk tolerance, and $r_M = r_f + x_M^T(r - r_f 1)$ is the market portfolio return. The market portfolio in this case consists of a positive supply of all risky stocks as well zero net supply of the risk-free bond. We may sometimes distinguish the risky part as the risky market portfolio. It is seen that $\text{cov}(r_i, r_M) = \text{cov}(r_i, \sum_{j=1}^{N} x_j r_j), \forall j$, where $x_M^T = (x_1, x_2, \dots, x_N)$.

Multiplying by x_M^T, Eq. (3.5) becomes

$$x_M^T \Sigma x_M = \sigma_M^2 = t^M(\mu_M - r_f)$$

$$\text{or} \quad t^M = \frac{\sigma_M^2}{(\mu_M - r_f)} \tag{3.6}$$

Note that $x_M^T(\mu - r_f 1) = x_M^T \mu - r_f X_M^T 1 = \mu_M - r_f$ as the expected risky market portfolio return is $E(r_M) = \mu_M$, and $x_M^T 1 = 1$ with net zero borrowing and lending.

Substituting Eq. (3.6) into Eq. (3.5), we obtain

$$\mu - r_f 1 = \frac{\Sigma x_M}{\sigma_M^2}(\mu_M - r_f) \tag{3.7}$$

Eq. (3.7) is the securities market line (SML) of the CAPM. Its ith element is

$$E(r_i) - r_f = \beta_i(E(r_M) - r_f) \tag{3.8}$$

where $\beta_i = \frac{\text{cov}(r_i, r_M)}{\sigma_M^2}$.

Equation (3.8) says that the expected excess return of any security is equal to a risk premium (required compensation by a risk-averse investor for holding risky stock) which is proportional to its beta, β_i, a measure of its systematic risk. Since systematic risk cannot be diversified away, the CAPM shows importantly that only diversifiable risk does not cost, but non-diversifiable risk fetches a positive risk premium. This positive risk premium is the market risk premium, $(E(r_M) - r_f)$.

From Eq. (3.4), for a mean-variance efficient portfolio (i. e. a portfolio return with minimum variance σ_p given mean μ_p),

$$\Sigma x = t(\mu - r_f 1) \quad \text{and} \quad \sigma_p^2 = x^T \Sigma x = t(\mu_p - r_f)$$

The last equation is a parabola of μ_p versus σ_p^2.

Similarly from Eq. (3.4), we have $x^T = t(\mu - r_f 1)^T \Sigma^{-1}$, and evaluate $x^T(\mu - r_f 1) = \mu_p - r_f$ as

$$t(\mu - r_f 1)^T \Sigma^{-1}(\mu - r_f 1) = td$$

where $d = (\mu - r_f 1)^T \Sigma^{-1}(\mu - r_f 1)$ is a constant. Thus $t = (\mu_p - r_f)/d$.

Then,

$$\sigma_p^2 = t(\mu_p - r_f) = (\mu_p - r_f)^2/d \qquad \text{or} \qquad (\mu_p - r_f)^2 = d\sigma_p^2$$

The last equation is a hyperbola of μ_p versus σ_p.[8] The hyperbola is shown in Figure 3.3.

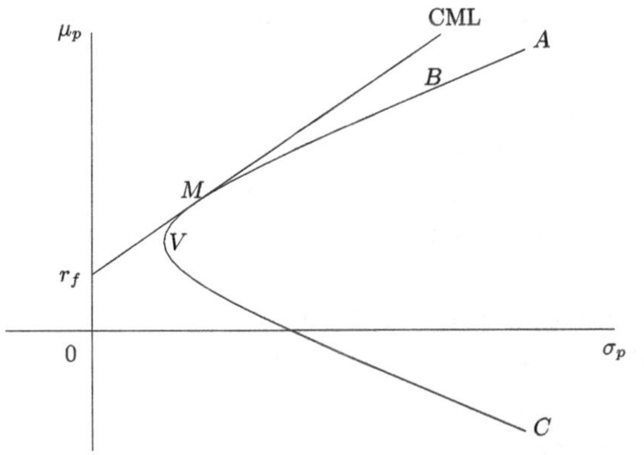

Figure 3.3: Mean-Variance Risky Portfolio Efficient Frontier.

Curve A-B-M-V-C is the hyperbola of μ_p versus σ_p. Portfolio V is called the minimum variance (or minimum standard deviation) portfolio as it is formed of all the N risky stocks and has the minimum variance. Segment of curve A-B-M-V is called the mean-variance portfolio efficient frontier as no other risky portfolio can be formed whereby

8 See Robert C. Merton (1972), An analytic derivation of the efficient portfolio frontier, *The Journal of Financial and Quantitative Analysis*, 7 (4), 1851–1872.

its variance would be smaller than that on the efficient frontier for the same given level of return. Segment VC is the inefficient frontier as for any portfolio on this frontier, there is another portfolio on the efficient segment with the same variance but higher mean return.

A geometrical interpretation of the CAPM can be done using this frontier. Suppose an investor invests some amounts in the risk-free asset with return rate r_f and the rest of the wealth in a frontier portfolio. Clearly, his/her optimal risk-return would now lie on the straight line that has intercept at r_f and has the point of tangency at M on the hyperbola. If all investors behave the same, M is the equilibrium market portfolio. Points on the tangent line below M comprises lending at the risk-free rate and buying the risky market portfolio M. Points on the tangent line above M comprises borrowing at the risk-free rate and buying the risky market portfolio M with leverage, i. e. investing own wealth plus borrowed money. This tangent line is also called the Capital Market Line (CML). The equation for the CML is

$$\mu_p = r_f + \frac{E(r_M) - r_f}{\sigma_M}\sigma_p$$

where the mean and standard deviation of market portfolio M's return are μ_M and σ_M.

3.4.1 Estimation

The CAPM model or the Eq. (3.8) is testable if we can observe the risky market portfolio return as well as the returns of individual stocks or returns of portfolios of stocks. (CAPM is typically a model used on stock returns instead of general securities such as bonds or options as these other assets have different return characteristics that are not consistent with having a normal distribution.)

Equation (3.8) can be expressed as a regression equation that implies (3.8), i. e. is consistent with (3.8). If returns are multivariate normal, then this regression specification is plausible, viz.

$$r_{it} = r_{ft} + \beta_i(r_{mt} - r_{ft}) + e_{it}, \quad \forall i, t \tag{3.9}$$

where $E(e_{it}) = 0$, and we have added time indexing for the risk-free rate r_{ft} and risky market portfolio return r_{mt} in order to allow the rates to vary over time. The familiar CAPM equation we usually see is the expectation condition (take expectation of Eq. (3.9):

$$E(r_{it}) = r_{ft} + \beta_i E(r_{mt} - r_{ft}) \tag{3.10}$$

that holds good for each time period t. In other words, this CAPM is actually a single-period model where the cross-sectional expected returns of stocks are related to the excess expected market portfolio return. It has become common for empirical reason, assuming stationary processes in the returns, to treat the estimation and testing of CAPM in the time series version of Eq. (3.9) rather than just the expected condition above.

In Eq. (3.9), when we take the covariance of r_{it} with r_{mt}, we obtain

$$\mathrm{cov}(r_{it}, r_{mt}) = \mathrm{cov}(r_{ft}, r_{mt}) + \beta_i \,\mathrm{var}(r_{mt}) + \mathrm{cov}(e_{it}, r_{mt})$$

Since r_{ft} is supposed to be a constant at t, $\mathrm{cov}(r_{it}, r_{ft}) = 0$. By the CAPM model in Eq. (3.8), in order for $\beta_i = \frac{\mathrm{cov}(r_i, r_M)}{\sigma_M^2}$, we must have $\mathrm{cov}(e_{it}, r_{mt}) = 0$ for each i and t. We can re-write Eq. (3.9) in a simple linear regression form as:

$$r_{it} - r_{ft} = \alpha_i + \beta_i(r_{mt} - r_{ft}) + e_{it}, \quad \forall i, t \tag{3.11}$$

where $\alpha_i = 0$ and $\mathrm{cov}(e_{it}, r_{mt}) = 0$ for each i, t. Hence, Eq. (3.11) provides for OLS estimators that are BLUE under the classical conditions. In particular, estimate $\hat{\alpha}_i$ should not be significantly different from zero under equilibrium situations, and then the stock i's beta or β_i is estimated as:

$$\hat{\beta}_i = \frac{\sum_{t=1}^{T}(X_t - \overline{X})(Y_t - \overline{Y})}{\sum_{t=1}^{T}(X_t - \overline{X})^2}$$

where $X_t = r_{mt} - r_{ft}$, $Y_t = r_{it} - r_{ft}$, $\overline{X} = \frac{1}{T}\sum_{t=1}^{T} X_t$, and $\overline{Y} = \frac{1}{T}\sum_{t=1}^{T} Y_t$. $\hat{\beta}_i$ is BLUE. It is also consistent, converging asymptotically to $\beta_i = \frac{\sigma_{im}}{\sigma_m^2}$.

The regression version in Eq. (3.11) involves regression of excess stock i return rate $r_{it} - r_{ft}$ on excess market return rate $r_{mt} - r_{ft}$, and a constant. α_i is also called the alpha of stock i. It is theoretically 0 in equilibrium, but could become positive or negative in actual regression. The interpretation of the latter then becomes one of financial performance:
$\alpha_i > 0$, positive abnormal return and
$\alpha_i < 0$, negative abnormal return.

In the investment context, suppose r_{it} is the return of a stock or a portfolio over time. Positive alpha indicates that the stock or portfolio is providing returns above normal or above the equilibrium which according to CAPM α_i should be zero. Negative alpha indicates that the stock or portfolio is providing returns below normal or below the equilibrium which according to CAPM α_i should be zero. Strictly speaking, if the CAPM is plausible, then this disequilibrium occurs only for a small number of stocks over the sample period in which alpha is measured. Stocks with positive (negative) alphas are said to outperform (underperform) their benchmark returns, i. e. their ex-post realized returns exceed (undershoot) significantly their ex-ante expected returns as indicated by the benchmark model, in this case the CAPM (although other benchmark models may be used.)

Alpha is also called the Jensen measure in a portfolio context. Good quantitative strategy portfolio managers hunt for stocks with significant positive alphas in order to form their super-performing portfolio. The advantage of using Eq. (3.11) is not only to provide for possibility of some stocks in disequilibrium situations and uncovering of abnormal returns in the form of alphas that are significantly different from zero, but the use of excess returns as dependent and explanatory variables purges any inflationary components in the return rates. The theoretical model deals strictly with real rates of returns, so it is good to use real excess rates of returns for this reason.

There are some practical issues. What is the ideal sampling size for estimating betas, alphas, and the other risk and performance measures? It is observed that in practice one can only obtain in any case a finite sample. Between 5 years of monthly data and 10 years of monthly data, it may make sense to use only 5 years or 60 monthly sampling points. This is because the market changes over time in the sense of changing its distribution so that beta or the slope may also change over time. An example is when there were five years of recession followed by five years of boom. In such a case, taking a sample from the entire 10 years for a simple regression may provide incorrect inferences. How long should a time series be used in the regression is however an empirical issue as there is no rigid theory about it. Some studies also recommend adjustments to the estimation of beta to minimize sampling errors. For details, see Blume (1975).[9]

3.4.2 Application: CAPM Regression

Devon Energy Corporation is a large American company that engages in the acquisition, exploration, development, and production of natural gas and oil in the United States and Canada. It is involved in the transportation and processing of the oil and natural gas. Monthly stock return data of Devon Energy and of the Standard and Poor's (S&P) 500 index return are collected in the sampling periods January 2005 to December 2009, and January 2010 to December 2014. Devon Energy Corporation stock is traded on the New York Stock Exchange. The S&P 500 is a capitalization-weighted stock market index comprising 500 of the largest companies listed on stock exchanges in the U. S. The risk-free return rate is the U. S. 1-month Treasury bill rate obtained from the Federal Reserve statistics. The monthly return rates of the stock are obtained by taking the natural logarithms of the end-of-month stock prices plus any dividends issued during that month relative to the previous end-of-month prices. The S&P 500 index is used as a proxy for the market portfolio. Thus the market portfolio returns are obtained by taking the natural logarithms of the end-of-month S&P 500 indexes relative to the previous end-of-month S&P 500 indexes.

9 M. Blume (1975), Betas and their regression tendencies, *The Journal of Finance*, 10 (3), 785–795.

To compute the excess monthly stock returns, we subtract from the monthly stock returns the monthly 1-month risk-free return rates. Similarly, to compute the excess monthly market returns, we subtract from the monthly market portfolio returns the monthly 1-month risk-free return rates. The linear regression model using Eq. (3.11) is employed to estimate alpha and beta.

The case of Devon Energy Corporation is illustrated as follows. The dependent variable is the monthly excess return rate of the stock.

The formulae for the various reported statistics in Table 3.1 are explained as follows. The number of regressors, $k = 2$, as shown by number of explanatory variables in the Variable column. $\hat{\alpha}$ is estimated coefficient of constant term in the table. $\hat{\beta}$ is slope estimate and is reflected as coefficient of the excess market return explanatory variable. The standard error of $\hat{\alpha}$ is

$$\hat{\sigma}_e \sqrt{\frac{1}{T} + \frac{\bar{X}^2}{\sum_{t=1}^{T}(X_t - \bar{X})^2}}$$

where we use $X_t = r_{mt} - r_{ft}$. The standard error of $\hat{\beta}$ is

$$\hat{\sigma}_e \sqrt{\frac{1}{\sum_{t=1}^{T}(X_t - \bar{X})^2}}$$

Table 3.1: Regression of Monthly Excess Stock Return of Devon Energy on Monthly Excess Market Return, Jan 2005–Dec 2009.

Variable	Coefficient	Std. Error	*t*-Statistic	Prob.
Constant	0.0141	0.0108	1.307	0.196
Excess Market Return	1.1871	0.2278	5.211	0.0000***
R-squared	0.3189	*F* (d. f. 1,58)-statistic		27.16
Adjusted *R*-squared	0.3072	Prob(*F*-statistic)		0.0000***
S. E. of regression	0.0832	Sum squared resid.		0.4013

Note: *** indicates significance at the 0.1 % level whether one-tailed or two-tailed tests.

The SSR, or sum of squared residuals, is SSR $= \sum_{t=1}^{T} = \hat{e}_t^2$. The standard error of e, "S. E. of regression", is $\hat{\sigma}_e = \sqrt{\frac{1}{T-2}\text{SSR}}$.

"F-statistic" in the table is $F_{k-1,T-k} = \frac{R^2/(k-1)}{(1-R^2)/(T-k)}$. This is the test statistic under the null hypothesis $H_0 : \alpha_i = 0, \beta_i = 0$ for $k = 2$. For the case $k = 2$, the t-statistic for $\hat{\beta}_i$, is also the square-root of the $F_{1,T-k}$ statistic where the first degree of freedom in the F-statistic is one, i. e. $t_{T-k}^2 = F_{1,T-k}$. This result does not generalize to $k > 2$. The"Prob (F-statistic)" refers to the p-value of the computed $F_{1,58}$ test-statistic. This p-value is the probability of the $F_{1,58}$ RV exceeding the computed statistic. The smaller this p-value, the less likely the null $H_0 : \alpha_i = \beta_i = 0$ is true. So if we set the significance level as 0.1 %, we would only accept H_0 if the p-value is larger than this critical value of 0.1 % or 0.001. By setting a lower significance level, we establish a lower type I error. In the above, clearly the null hypothesis is rejected.

3.4.3 Interpretation of Regression Results

What is the OLS estimate of alpha? $\hat{\alpha}_i = \overline{r_i - r_f} - \hat{\beta}_i \overline{r_m - r_f}$, where the bar denotes the sampling average. From Table 3.1, alpha was not significantly different from zero at 10 % significance level. In the latter period as seen in Table 3.2, estimated alpha is negative at −0.0143 with a two-tailed p-value of 0.0607. It is significantly negative at a test significance level of 10 %. Thus the stock appeared to underperform in the period after the global financial crisis of 2008–2009. Another possible interpretation is that the benchmark CAPM model was not adequate and the negative alpha could be explained by missing factors.

Table 3.2: Regression of Monthly Excess Stock Return of Devon Energy on Monthly Excess Market Return, Jan 2010–Dec 2014.

Variable	Coefficient	Std. Error	t-Statistic	Prob.
Constant	−0.0143	0.0075	−1.913	0.0607
Excess Market Return	1.3144	0.1943	6.764	0.0000***
R-squared	0.4409	F (d. f. 1,58)-statistic		45.75
Adjusted R-squared	0.4313	Prob(F-statistic)		0.0000***
S. E. of regression	0.0558	Sum squared resid.		0.1808

Note: *** indicates significance at the 0.1 % level whether one-tailed or two-tailed tests.

From Tables 3.1 and 3.2, it is noted that the t-statistics of the beta estimates in both periods are above 5 with p-values lesser than 0.00005, so the betas are certainly significantly positive. The estimated betas of the Devon Energy stock was 1.1871 in the sample period Jan. 2005–Dec. 2009, but increased to 1.3144 in the sample period Jan. 2010–Dec. 2014. Thus, the stock return is highly positively correlated with market movements. The F-statistics with degrees of freedom $k - 1 = 2 - 1 = 1$, and $T - k = 60 - 2 = 58$, are 27.16 and 45.75, respectively, in both periods. Notice that the higher the coefficient of determination R^2, the higher the F-value. This is a test on null $H_0 : \alpha_i = \beta_i = 0$. Thus, a good fit with reasonably high R^2's of 0.3189 and 0.4409, respectively, imply that $\hat{\alpha}_i$ and $\hat{\beta}_i$ fit well and are unlikely to be zero. Therefore, $H_0 : \alpha_i = \beta_i = 0$ is rejected since p-value for the $F_{1,58}$ test-statistic is < 0.00005 for both periods.

The estimate of the stock's systematic risk is

$$\hat{\beta}_i\sqrt{(1/T-1)\sum_{t=1}^{T}(X_t-\overline{X})^2}$$

where $X_t = r_{mt} - r_{ft}$.

The estimate of the stock's unsystematic risk is $\hat{\sigma}_e = \sqrt{\text{RSS}/(T-2)}$. From the standard error of regression, $\hat{\sigma}_e$, and the standard error of $\hat{\beta}_i$ in Table 3.1, we can compute $\sum_{t=1}^{T}(X_t - \bar{X})^2 = 0.1334$. The systematic risk of the stock is thus estimated as $1.1871 \times \sqrt{0.1334/59} = 0.0564$ or 5.64 %. Unsystematic risk is estimated as $\hat{\sigma}_e = 0.0832$ or 8.32 %. It is seen that idiosyncratic risk for Devon Energy during the 2005 to 2009 period is larger than the systematic risk induced by market movements. From Table 3.2, systematic risk of the stock is similarly estimated as $1.3144 \times \sqrt{0.0825/59} = 0.0492$ or 4.92 %. Unsystematic risk is estimated as $\hat{\sigma}_e = 0.0558$ or 5.58 %. It is seen that idiosyncratic risk for Devon Energy during the 2010 to 2014 period is only slightly larger than the systematic risk.

The regression line as a result of the OLS method can be written as:

$$\text{Excess Stock Return} = \hat{\alpha}_i + \hat{\beta}_i \text{ Excess Market Return}$$

This linear relationship, or the line if expressed graphically, is called Devon Energy Corporation's (DVN) Security Characteristic Line (SCL). It shows the slope as Devon Energy stock's beta, the intercept as its alpha, and indications of unsystematic risks as dispersions of the returns about the SCL. We produce such plots in Figures 3.4 and 3.5 for the two periods.

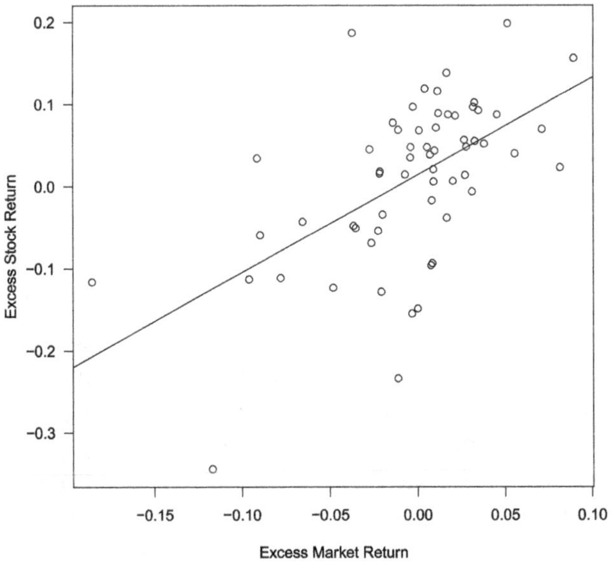

Figure 3.4: DVN Characteristic Line 2005–2009.

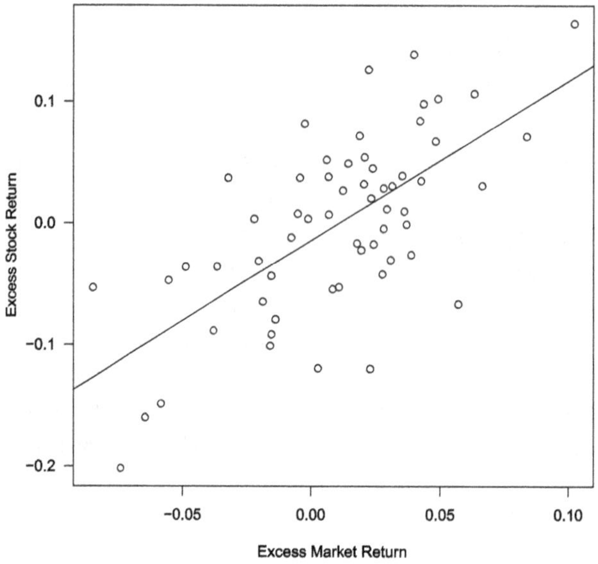

Figure 3.5: DVN Security Characteristic Line 2010–2014.

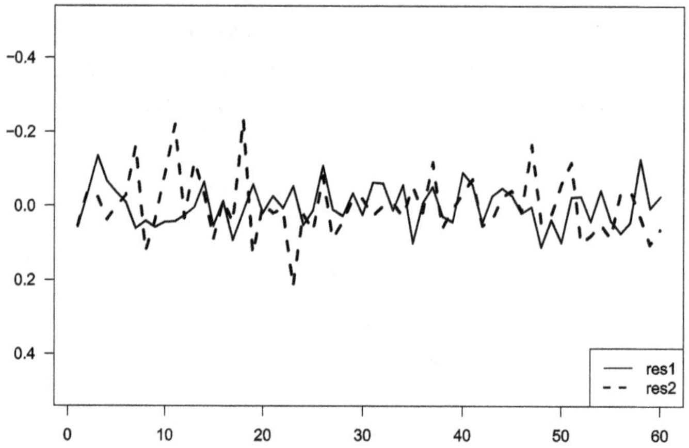

Figure 3.6: Fitted residuals in Tables 3.1 and 3.2.

The stock's SCL should not be confused with the market's security market line (SML) which is represented by a graph of expected returns versus their corresponding betas. We also plot the estimated (or fitted) residuals of the SCL in Figure 3.6. The fitted residuals $\hat{e}_i$ from Table 3.1 in period 2010–2014, res1, and the fitted residuals $\hat{e}_i$ from Table 3.2 in period 2005–2009, res2, are shown in Figure 3.6. The fitted residual plot allows a visual inspection of whether the residuals follow the classical assumptions of zero mean and constant variance. In Figure 3.6, the higher volatility of the fitted residuals in the earlier 2005–2009 period is seen. There also appears to be clustering of higher volatility around 2005 to 2006. It could be that the CAPM model is not well specified during such a period or that the classical assumptions about the residuals are not appropriate.

3.4.4 Testing

The two-parameter CAPM model or CAPM Eq. (3.8) has been tested in various ways. Black, Jensen, and Scholes (BJS) (1972)[10] used the equal-weighted portfolio of all stocks traded on the New York Stock Exchange as proxy for the market portfolio. By sorting the stocks into ranked betas, they also formed 10 portfolios of these stocks according to the beta ranks. Stocks with the largest betas were put into the first portfolio; then the next ranked beta stocks were put into the second portfolio, and so on. The idea in grouping the stocks into portfolios before measuring the betas of the portfolios (instead of betas of individual stocks) is to reduce measurement or estimation errors of the betas. The portfolio betas are estimated by averaging the betas of the individual stocks within each of the 10 portfolios. This has the effect of averaging out (presumably random) sampling errors of beta estimates of each stock within each portfolio. The study also considered the higher likelihood of very high betas or very low betas due to random chance being grouped together, producing selection bias in the portfolio grouping and portfolio beta estimation. This is mitigated by estimating each stock beta (before averaging into portfolio betas) using lagged 60 months for ranking and sorting into portfolios. Subsequent months' returns are then used to re-estimate betas of the portfolios. BJS tested the CAPM in Eq. (3.8) using both a time series approach and a cross-sectional approach.

In the time series approach, BJS ran regressions on each portfolio based on Eq. (3.11) and tested if the estimated α_i for each portfolio i was statistically not significantly different from zero. They found that the estimated intercept or $\hat{\alpha}_i$ were consistently negative for the high-beta ($\hat{\beta}_i > 1$) portfolios and consistently positive for the low-beta ($\hat{\beta}_i < 1$) portfolios. BJS also performed cross-sectional regression between the returns on the 10 portfolios and their estimated betas for different holding periods. There was some evidence of linearity between the average monthly portfolio returns and the portfolio betas, indicating significantly positive risk premium of $E(r_{mt} - r_{ft})$ as in Eq. (3.8).

The cross-sectional regression procedures are further improved by Fama-MacBeth (1973).[11] For each month t of the test period, the beta of each stock is estimated using

---

10 F. Black, M. Jensen, and M. Scholes (1972), The Capital Asset Pricing Model: Some Empirical Tests, *Studies in the Theory of Capital Markets*, Praeger, New York, 79–121.

11 E. F. Fama and James D. MacBeth (FM) (1973), Risk, return, and equilibrium: empirical tests, *The Journal of Political Economy*, Vol. 81, No. 3. (May–June, 1973), 607–636. See also E. F. Fama and James D. MacBeth (1974), Tests of the multiperiod two-parameter model, *Journal of Financial Economics*, 1, 43–66.

data from earlier months. At t, the sorted portfolios are used to obtain the average estimated beta for each portfolio j of stocks. This portfolio j beta, $\hat{\beta}_{jt}$, at t is then used in the cross-sectional regression Eq. (3.12), i. e. regression across portfolio returns $j = 1, 2, \ldots, N$ at t. FM also used other cross-sectional explanatory variables at t besides $\hat{\beta}_{jt}$, including $(\hat{\beta}_{jt})^2$ and also estimates of the standard deviation of the residual returns, $\hat{\sigma}_{jt}$.

$$r_{jt} - r_{ft} = \gamma_{0t} + \gamma_{1t}\hat{\beta}_{jt} + \gamma_{2t}(\hat{\beta}_{jt})^2 + \gamma_{3t}\hat{\sigma}_{jt} + \eta_{jt} \tag{3.12}$$

where η_{jt} is the residual error of the cross-sectional regression at t. The OLS estimates of $\hat{\gamma}_{0t}$, $\hat{\gamma}_{1t}$, $\hat{\gamma}_{2t}$, and $\hat{\gamma}_{3t}$ are collected for each t in the test period. These formed time series of N months each in the test period. The t-statistics were then computed to test if the mean of each of these time series was zero. For each t, $\hat{\gamma}_{0t}$ should be zero according to CAPM. But since the estimated $\hat{\gamma}_{0t}$ is a RV with small sample errors, treating each time estimate as a stationary independent RV in the time series, the t-statistic testing the sample mean of this time series would indicate if indeed its expected value is zero according to CAPM.

Likewise, for each t, $\hat{\gamma}_{1t}$ should be the expected market risk premium according to CAPM. But since the estimated $\hat{\gamma}_{1t}$ is itself a RV, treating each time estimate as a stationary independent RV in the time series, the t-statistic testing the sample mean of this time series would indicate if indeed its expected market risk premium is not zero but positive according to CAPM. By CAPM, the t-statistics for the time series tests of the means of sampling estimates $\hat{\gamma}_{2t}$, and $\hat{\gamma}_{3t}$ should indicate expected values of zeroes. In general there was support of the CAPM with data from the 1940s through the 1970s.

We started off in the estimation section by stating that the CAPM model or the Eq. (3.8) is testable if we can observe the risky market portfolio return. We note that the literature has mostly employed a proxy for the market return such as return on a broad liquid index, e. g., S&P 500 index. Roll's critique[12] states that since we cannot actually observe the market portfolio return (the market conceivably could be much larger than stocks on NYSE, including global stocks, bonds, real estates, and other investment assets), the tests cannot be conclusive. Specifically, as shown in Figure 3.3, if B is any point on the efficient frontier, then the same CAPM equation $E(r_i) - r_f = \beta_i(E(r_B) - r_f)$, where now $\beta_i = \text{cov}(r_i, r_B)/\text{var}(r_B)$, can be obtained. In other words, if the CAPM test does not reject the CAPM equation, then it is just a verification that the market proxy B lies on the efficient frontier, and not necessarily that B is equivalent to M. Roll's critique leads to the understanding that all CAPM tests may be construed more appropriately as tests that the market proxy is an efficient portfolio.[13]

---

12 Richard Roll (1977), A critique of the asset pricing theory's tests Part I: On past and potential testability of the theory, *Journal of Financial Economics*, 4(2): 129–176.

13 See Michael R. Gibbons, Stephen A. Ross, and Jay Shanken (1989), A test of the efficiency of a given portfolio, *Econometrica*, 57, 1121–1152.

3.5 Performance Measures

The Jensen measure of portfolio performance is given by the alpha estimate in regressions similar to Eq. (3.11) where excess return is used as dependent variable, and the explanatory variables may include other risk factors besides the excess market return. Jensen alpha is also called risk-adjusted return or abnormal return.

The Treynor measure of portfolio performance is given by realized excess portfolio return rate per unit of estimated beta, over the sampling period, i. e.

$$\frac{\overline{r_{pt} - r_{ft}}}{\hat{\beta}_p}$$

where subscript p denotes association with a portfolio. Conditional on the true beta, the expected Treynor measure is $E(r_{pt} - r_{ft})/\beta_p$. Theoretically, in equilibrium when there is no abnormal performance as in zero Jensen measure, the expected Treynor measure is equivalent to the expected excess market portfolio return rate. Therefore, the realized Treynor measure shows whether a portfolio is performing better than or equal to, or worse than the market portfolio when it is compared with the realized excess market portfolio return rate.

It can be shown that if the Jensen measure, conditional on beta, indicates superior (inferior) performance, then the expected Treynor measure indicates performance better than (worse than) the market's.

$$\begin{aligned} \alpha &= E(r_{pt} - r_{ft}) - \beta_p E(r_{mt} - r_{ft}) > (<)\, 0 \\ &\Leftrightarrow \frac{E(r_{pt} - r_{ft})}{\beta_p} > (<)\, E(r_{mt} - r_{ft}) \end{aligned}$$

Hence, conditional on beta, realized Treynor measure exceeding (below) realized excess market return rate is tantamount to a positive (negative) alpha.

The above performance measures are useful for well-diversified portfolios, but could also be interpreted for individual stocks. For portfolios that are not well diversified, their total risk σ_p becomes important. Realized Sharpe measure or Sharpe ratio is

$$\frac{\overline{r_{pt} - r_{ft}}}{\hat{\sigma}_p}$$

where $\overline{r_{pt} - r_{ft}}$ is realized excess portfolio return rate per unit of estimated standard deviation of the portfolio from the sampling period. It shows how well the portfolio is performing relative to the realized capital market line with estimated slope $\overline{r_{mt} - r_{ft}}/\hat{\sigma}_m$. Theoretically,

$$\frac{E(r_{pt} - r_{ft})}{\sigma_p} > (<) \frac{E(r_{mt} - r_{ft})}{\sigma_m}$$

$$\Leftrightarrow E(r_{pt} - r_{ft}) - \frac{\sigma_p}{\sigma_m} E(r_{mt} - r_{ft}) > (<)\ 0$$

$$\Rightarrow E(r_{pt} - r_{ft}) - \frac{\rho_{pm}\sigma_p\sigma_m}{\sigma_m^2} E(r_{mt} - r_{ft}) > \text{(uncertain)}\ 0$$

$$\Leftrightarrow \alpha > \text{(uncertain)}\ 0$$

Hence a Sharpe ratio larger than the CML slope implies positive alpha. A smaller Sharpe ratio does not have any certain implication about alpha. Thus, there is also some relationship between the expected Sharpe performance measure and the other two expected measures. All the expected measures identify superior performance consistently with one another. The realized measures are estimates of the expected measures and have approximately similar relationships as indicated.

There is also the appraisal ratio α_p/σ_e, which is estimated by $\hat{\alpha}_p/\hat{\sigma}_e$, where the numerator is Jensen's measure and the denominator is residual or idiosyncratic risk, not total risk. The appraisal ratio ranks portfolios or funds with positive alphas relative to the specific portfolio risk. The higher the ratio, the better is the portfolio or fund for investment, all other things being equal. An excellent discussion of some these issues on performance measures and attribution can be found in Bodie, Kane, and Marcus (1999).

More recently, sortino ratio has been added to the list of popular portfolio performance measures. The sortino ratio, like the Sharpe ratio, is a return-to-risk ratio. It has realized portfolio return rate less its expected return in the numerator, and square root of estimated semi-variance in the denominator. The estimated semi-variance in this case is $\frac{1}{T}\sum_{t=1}^{T}[\min(r_{pt} - \bar{r}_p, 0)]^2$. The semi-variance is also called a lower partial moment. It is supposed to measure the downside risk of a portfolio instead of variance that includes upside variation that strictly is not considered a risk to the investor (ignoring the utility assumptions). Hence the sortino ratio is meant to rank a portfolio performance as lower where its Sharpe ratio is similar to another portfolio but where its downside risk is higher. Many popular sources of investment literature uses the risk-free rate as the expected return rate. Strictly speaking this is incorrect. An equilibrium asset pricing model accounting for the downside risk should be used to derive the benchmark expected return.[14] However, there are other issues relating to the appropriate utility function supporting such downward risk pricing.

14 See W. W. Hogan and J. M. Warren (1974), Toward the development of an equilibrium capital market model based on semivariance, *Journal of Financial and Quantitative Analysis* 9, 1–12, and V. S. Bawa and E. B. Lindenberg (1977), Capital market equilibrium in a mean lower partial moment framework, *Journal of Financial Economics* 5, 189–200.

An early study by Banz (1981)[15] documented an important observation that stock capitalization value or size matters (at least during the sampling period and in many subsequent studies well into 2000s) during in-sample and also ex-post realized returns. This is an aberration from the CAPM that prescribes the market index as the only common factor affecting all stock returns. It is also termed the size anomaly.

We employ stock data from the Center for Research in Security Prices (CRSP) database divided into 10 value-weighted portfolios with each portfolio containing a decile ranked by capitalization value or firm size. Market returns (S&P 500 index returns) and one-month U. S. Treasury bill rates of returns for the sampling period January 2002 to December 2006 are also used. Monthly (end-of-month) return rates are used in the regression of Eq. (3.11) for each of the portfolio.

The alphas and betas for each sized-portfolio are obtained and plotted in Figure 3.7 against the size deciles. On the horizontal axis, decile 1 denotes the smallest capitalization portfolio while decile 10 denotes the largest capitalization portfolio.

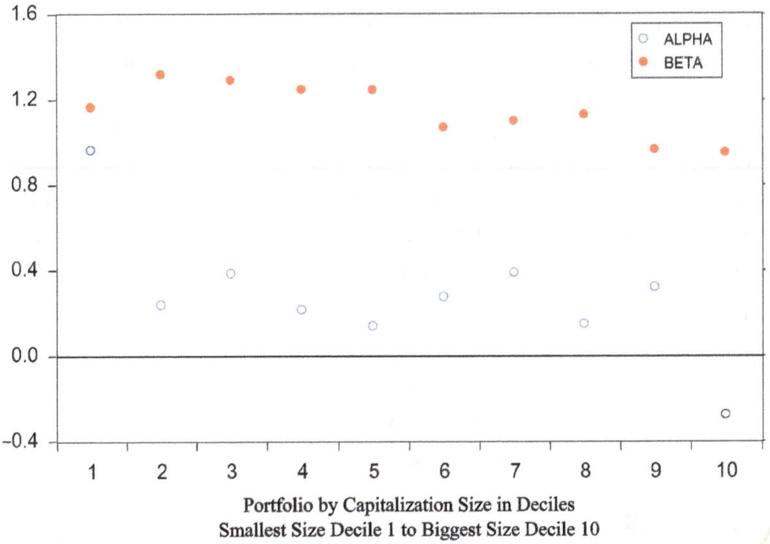

Figure 3.7: $\hat{\alpha}_i$'s and $\hat{\beta}_i$'s in CAPM Regressions Using Monthly Returns of 10-Sized-Portfolios in Sampling Period Jan. 2002 to Dec. 2006.

In Figure 3.7, all the betas are significantly different from zero at very small p-values of less than 0.0005. Only three of the alpha values are significantly different from zero at the 1 % significance level. It is seen that the smallest size firms in decile 1 realizes

15 R. W. Banz (1981), The relationship between return and market value of common stocks, *Journal of Financial Economics*, 3–18.

the largest positive Jensen's alpha, while the biggest size firms in decile 10 realizes the only negative alpha among all portfolios. This result appears to be consistent with the empirical observations by Banz. Betas are seen to fall slightly and converge toward 1 as size increases. However, perhaps due to arbitrageurs, the size anomaly may have weakened considerably since the 1980s.

The investment performance measures of alpha and also risk measures (systematic risk and total risk), however, need to be applied with care, when dealing with hedge funds and investment strategies such as market timing.

Since the 1990s, hedge funds have become quite fashionable. These funds, unlike traditional investment funds or unit trusts that go long and hold in selected assets over selected horizons, can go short, rollover derivatives, and perform all kinds of investments in virtually any asset classes that are in the financial markets. Therefore, it is not appropriate to measure the performance of hedge funds using the traditional performance measures described above. The hedge funds may display very high return to risk (Sharpe) ratio, but a lot of risks could be contained in huge negative skewness or huge kurtosis that do not show up readily in variance. Fung and Hsieh (2001)[16] have described a method using complicated lookback straddles to track these funds performances. Research in hedge fund strategies has been especially voluminous in recent years.

Market timing refers to the ability of funds managers to shift investment funds into the market portfolio when market is rising, and to shift out of the stock market into money assets or safe treasury bonds when market is falling, particularly if the market falls below risk-free return. If a particular fund can perform in this way, then its returns profile over time will look as follows (Figure 3.8).

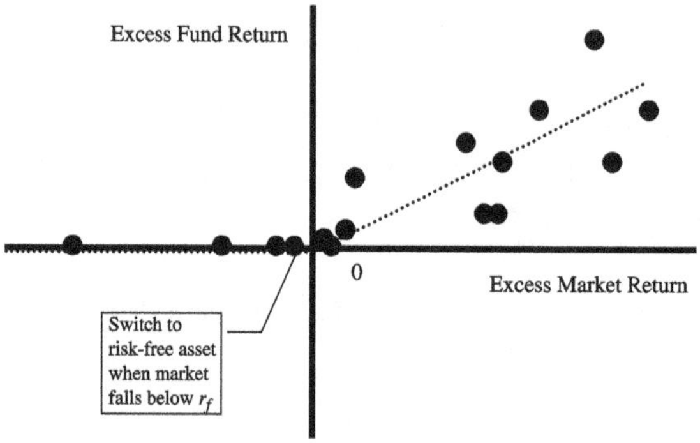

Figure 3.8: Display of Timing Abilities.

16 W. Fung and D. A. Hsieh (2001), The risk in hedge fund strategies: Theory and evidence from trend followers, *Review of Financial Studies*, 14 (2), 313–342.

Note the nonlinear profile of the returns realizations over time in Figure 3.8. Suppose we represent the above by a different set of axes as follows by squaring the X variable, i. e. squaring the excess market returns (see Figure 3.9).

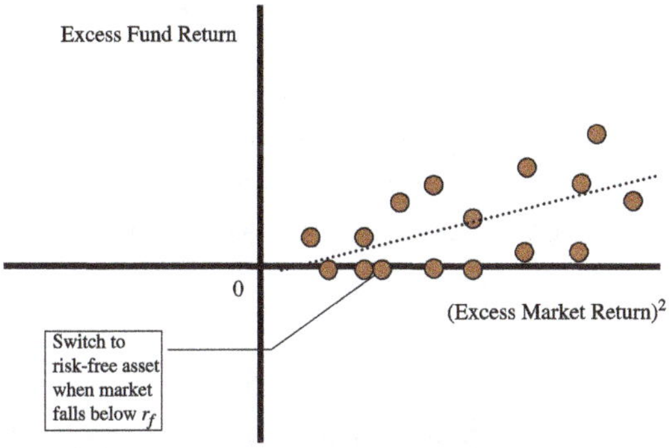

Figure 3.9: Alternative Display of Timing Abilities.

It can be seen that the existence of market timing abilities in a fund portfolio will show up as a slope when we regress excess fund return on the square of excess market return as Figure 3.9 indicates. If there is no market-timing ability, there will be as many points in the negative fourth quadrant, and the slope of a fitted line will be flat or close to zero. This idea was first proposed by Treynor and Mazur (1966).[17] Many important subsequent studies include Merton (1981).[18] If we employ a multiple linear regression using another explanatory variable that is the square of the market excess return,

$$r_{it} - r_{ft} = \alpha_i + \beta_i(r_{mt} - r_{ft}) + \gamma_i(r_{mt} - r_{ft})^2 + e_{it}$$

where e_{it} is independent of r_{mt}, then market timing abilities in a fund will show up as a significantly positive $\hat{\gamma}_i$. Unfortunately, many mutual funds that were studied did not display such market timing abilities.

Further Reading

Bodie, Z., A. Kane, and A. J. Marcus (1999), *Investments*, Fourth edition, Irwin McGraw Hill.
Huang, C. F., and R. H. Litzenberger (1988), *Foundations for Financial Economics*, North-Holland Publishing.
Takayama, A. (1985), *Mathematical Economics*, Second edition, Cambridge University Press.
Varian, H. R. (1992), *Microeconomic Analysis*, Third edition, W. W. Norton.

---

17 J. L. Treynor and K. Mazur (1966), Can mutual funds outguess the market? *Harvard Business Review*, 43.

18 R. C. Merton (1981), On market timing and investment performance, I: An equilibrium theory of value for market forecasts, *Journal of Business*, 54, 363–406.

4 Event Studies

Event studies in financial econometrics are about the role of information in affecting market stock prices. Given new information (or conditional on the new information), investors adjust their demand and supply of stocks and thus move stock prices into a new equilibrium if indeed the information has value. If the new information is irrelevant or of no economic value to the stock pricing, then the stock price would remain unchanged. The statistical tool of conditional probability is thus of great importance in understanding the role of information. We review the fundamental Bayes' formula, and then discuss the critical idea of market efficiency related to asset pricing.

4.1 Set Operations

Consider the sample space Ω and events A, B, C represented by sets in the Venn diagram, Figure 4.1, shown below. Suppose simple sample points or elements of Ω are shown as $e_1, e_2, e_3, e_4, e_5, e_6$. By definition, only one of the sample points can occur in any one experimental outcome. Events may contain one or more sample points, and as discussed in Chapter 1, are subsets of the universal set Ω. When e_1 occurs, event A is also said to occur. Likewise, when e_2 occurs, event B is said to have occurred. When e_4 occurs, both events A and B are said to have occurred, and we can say that the intersection event $A \cap B$ has occurred.

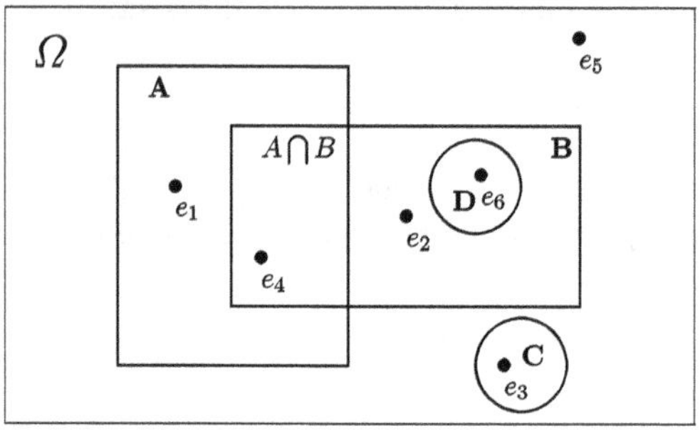

Figure 4.1: Venn Diagram.

De Morgan's law in set theory states that

$$(A \cup B)^c = A^c \cap B^c, \quad \text{and}$$
$$(A \cap B)^c = A^c \cup B^c$$

Event $\Omega \backslash A$ is the same as A^c, the complement of set A. $A \backslash B$ is the same as $A \cap B^c$.

https://doi.org/10.1515/9783110673951-004

When e_5 occurs, event $\Omega\backslash(A \cup B \cup C)$ has occurred. Using the above relationship

$$\Omega\backslash(A \cup B \cup C) = (A \cup B \cup C)^c = A^c \cap B^c \cap C^c$$

Hence, $e_5 \in A^c \cap B^c \cap C^c$.

From the diagram, clearly $A \cap C = B \cap C = \phi$, where ϕ is the empty or null set. In addition, $D \subset B$, which means that if event D occurs, then B is also said to have occurred.

Suppose there are $n_{A\backslash B}$, $n_{B\backslash A}$, $n_{A\cap B}$, and n_Ω sample points in events $A\backslash B$, $B\backslash A$, $A\cap B$, and Ω, respectively. Assume each sample point can occur with equal probability. Using the frequentist notion of probability (taking "long-run" relative frequency as probability), the probability of A happening is $\frac{(n_{A\backslash B}+n_{A\cap B})}{n_\Omega}$. That of B happening is $\frac{(n_{B\backslash A}+n_{A\cap B})}{n_\Omega}$. That of event $A \cap B$ happening is $\frac{(n_{A\cap B})}{n_\Omega}$. Since $A \cup B = A\backslash B + A \cap B + B\backslash A$, where "+" denotes union of disjoint sets, then probability of event $A \cup B$ is $\frac{(n_{A\backslash B}+n_{A\cap B}+n_{B\backslash A})}{n_\Omega}$.

Suppose we are given the information that event B has happened. Conditional on (or given) this information, what is the probability that another event, say A, has happened?

The conditional probability of A given B is

$$P(A|B) = \frac{P(A \cap B)}{P(B)} \tag{4.1}$$

which is $\frac{n_{A\cap B}}{n_B}$.

Intuitively this is correct since $P(A \cap B) = P(A|B) \times P(B) = \frac{n_{A\cap B}}{n_B} \times \frac{n_B}{n_\Omega} = \frac{n_{A\cap B}}{n_\Omega}$. For the case of D, $P(B|D) = \frac{P(B\cap D)}{P(D)} = P(D)/P(D) = 1$.

Suppose there are disjoint sets G_i, $i = 1, 2, 3, \ldots, M$, such that $B \subseteq \bigcup_{i=1}^M G_i$. Then, Bayes' formula is obtained as follows.

4.1.1 Bayes' Formula

$$\begin{aligned} P(A|B) &= \frac{P(A \cap B)}{P(B)} \\ &= \frac{P(B \cap A)}{P(B \cap G_1) + P(B \cap G_2) + \cdots + P(B \cap G_M)} \\ &= \frac{P(B|A)P(A)}{P(B|G_1)P(G_1) + P(B|G_2)P(G_2) + \cdots + P(B|G_M)P(G_M)} \\ &= \frac{P(B|A)P(A)}{\sum_{i=1}^M P(B|G_i)P(G_i)} \end{aligned} \tag{4.2}$$

The denominator on the right-hand side (RHS) of Eq. (4.2) exists if $B \subseteq \bigcup_{i=1}^M G_i$. A stronger sufficient condition is that there is a partition of Ω by sets G_i, $i = 1, 2, 3, \ldots, M$,

i. e., disjoint sets G_i such that $\bigcup_{i=1}^{M} G_i = \Omega$, and hence, necessarily $B \subseteq \bigcup_{i=1}^{M} G_i$. The probability of an event B as a union of sub-events $(B \cap G_i)$, resulting in $P(B) = \sum_{i=1}^{M} P(B|G_i)P(G_i)$, is sometimes called the Law of Total Probability.

4.2 Market Efficiency

The concept of (informational) market efficiency was investigated by Fama (1970)[1] and many others. Fama surveyed the idea of an informationally efficient capital market, and made the following famous definition: "A market in which prices always 'fully reflect' available information is called 'efficient' ". Three forms of the efficient market hypothesis (EMH) are often cited. The weak-form asserts that all past market prices or their history are fully reflected in securities prices. An immediate implication of this version of the EMH is that charting and technical analyses are of no use in making abnormal profit. Technical analysis and charting rely on the belief that past stock prices show enough patterns and trends for profitable forecasting. This possibility is opposed to the notion of stock prices "following" random walks (i. e. the next price change is an independent random movement). When prices adjust instantaneously, past returns are entirely useless for predicting future returns. The semi-strong form asserts that all publicly available information, including historical prices, is fully reflected in securities prices. The implication is that fundamental analyses such as analyses of a company's balance sheet, income statement, and corporate news and development, are of no use in making abnormal profit. Finally, the strong-form asserts that all available information including public and private information is fully reflected in securities prices. If true, the implication is that even insider information is of no use in making abnormal profit.

We shall consider semi-strong form market efficiency in more detail. The market is represented by the collective body of investors at time t who make the best use of whatever available information (thus rational investors) to predict future period stock price at time $t+1$, i. e., price S_{t+1}. Suppose Φ_t is all relevant publicly available information available at t. Think of information Φ_t as a conditioning RV (i. e. a RV that takes a certain value that is being conditioned upon) that is jointly distributed with S_{t+1}. In addition, Φ_M is the information actually used by the market, and is at most all of Φ_t. The true conditional probability of next period price is $P(S_{t+1}|\Phi_t)$ while the market's conditional probability is $P(S_{t+1}|\Phi_M)$. The market is semi-strong form informationally efficient if and only if

$$P(S_{t+1}|\Phi_M) \stackrel{d}{=} P(S_{t+1}|\Phi_t)$$

1 E. Fama (1970), Efficient capital markets: A review of theory and empirical work, *The Journal of Finance*, 25(2), 383–417.

i. e. distributionally the same. One implication is that the market forecast $E(S_{t+1}|\Phi_M) = E(S_{t+1}|\Phi_t)$.

Suppose not all of the available information Φ_t is used by the market, and $E(S_{t+1}|\Phi_M) \neq E(S_{t+1}|\Phi_t)$, then the market is informationally inefficient. In this case, all available information is not instantaneously incorporated into price at t, S_t. In the next instance, when more of the information gets absorbed by the market, the price S_t will adjust toward equilibrium. Hence, an informationally inefficient market will see price adjustments over a discrete time interval, and not instantaneously, to any substantive news.

Many tests of asset pricing in the literature employ the framework of rational investors and (informational) market efficiency. A framework such as the Sharpe-Lintner CAPM typically employs additional assumptions such as exogenous price processes and an explicit or implicit homogeneous preference function (typically a standard strictly monotone concave utility function) for all investors making up the market. In addition, explicitly or implicitly, the von Neumann–Morgenstern expected utility hypothesis is usually employed. Aberrations or non-validation in the test results were pointed out as evidence of market inefficiencies or sometimes coined as market anomalies (meaning something yet to be explained). Behavioral finance arose in this context to help explain the anomalies. It may agree with informational efficiency, but not with the rationality framework mostly to do with the standard preference assumption and the expected utility hypothesis. Some examples of early anomalies were the size effect, day-of-the-week, month-of-the-year effects, value versus growth premium, and so on. Later anomalies against the implication of random walk or approximate random walk by rational asset pricing models include contrarian strategies and momentum trading profits.[2] We provide an illustration of market efficiency as follows.

Suppose at time $t = 0$, there was information about whether the December 2008 GM, Ford, Chrysler bailout plan of \$25 billion would pass through Senate. Suppose GM stock price at $t = 0$ was \$3. If the bailout were successful, the stock price would increase to either \$5 or \$4 at $t = 1$. The latter variation is due to other risk factors and uncertainties. If the bailout were unsuccessful, the stock price would drop to either \$2 or \$1 at $t = 1$. All probabilities of the Bernoulli outcomes were 50 %. Assume that the risk-adjusted discount rate from $t = 0$ to $t = 1$ was 0. This is depicted in Figure 4.2.

If the market did not know about the outcome (i. e., did not process the information even when it was known), then at $t = 0$, its expected stock price at $t = 1$ was $\frac{1}{4}(\$5 + \$4 + \$2 + \$1) = \$3$. However, if the market was informationally efficient, then at $t = 0_+$, its conditional (upon the bailout outcome information) expectation of price at

2 A useful undergraduate investment textbook for reference in these background readings is Bodie, Kane, and Marcus (1999).

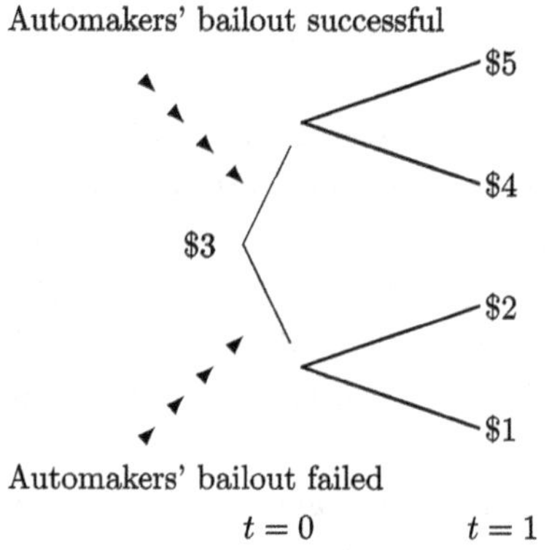

Figure 4.2: Stock Price Changes Contingent on Bailout News.

$t = 1$ was either $4.50 if the outcome were successful or $1.50 if the outcome were unsuccessful. Looking at this simple setup, it is easy to see that if at $t = 0_+$, the stock price did not quickly move away from $3, then the market was informationally inefficient as it did not capture the information immediately.

4.3 Conditional Expectation

A conditional probability is constituted by a joint probability and the marginal probabilities. We analyze this from a building-blocks perspective. The automakers' story is depicted as follows in a Venn diagram (Figure 4.3).

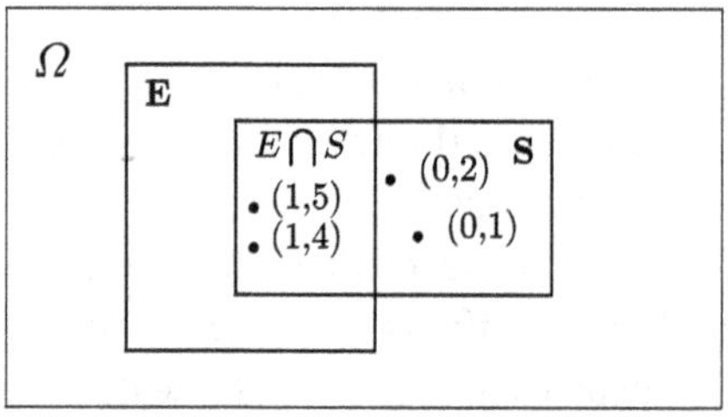

Figure 4.3: Venn Diagram on Automakers' Events.

In Figure 4.3, one and only one sample point can occur, represented by the bullets. E is the event that the automakers' bailout is successful. We can also represent this by a RV that is an indicator function, X (or denoted using indicator notation 1_E) where $x = 1$ if the bailout is successful, i. e. event E, and $x = 0$ if the bailout is not successful, i. e. event E^C. Let S be the event that a stock takes strictly positive prices, and the RV Y corresponds to elements of S taking dollar values $y \in \{5, 4, 2, 1\}$. Let each sample point be a joint outcome of the automakers' bailout and the stock price, (x, y). Note that we may allow an event S^c to denote the firm's bankruptcy and hence a stock price of zero. However, in our probability model here, $P(S^c) = 0$.

$\Omega = \{(1,5), (1,4), (0,2), (0,1)\}$. Each point occurs with equal probability 1/4. Therefore, conditional probability

$$P(y \in S|x = 1) = \frac{P(S \cap E)}{P(E)} = \frac{P(1,5) + P(1,4)}{1/2} = 1$$

This may be a trivial exercise in verifying the framework of the Bayesian formula since the Venn diagram clearly implies that $P(S) = 1$ independent of whatever the outcome of X. We had seen that $P(S^c) = 0$ earlier.

Conditional expectation

$$\begin{aligned} E(Y|x = 1) &= \sum_{y \in S} yP(y|x = 1) \\ &= \sum_i y_i P(x = 1, y_i)/P(x = 1) \\ &= 5 \times P(1,5)/0.5 + 4 \times P(1,4)/0.5 \\ &= 5 \times \frac{1}{2} + 4 \times \frac{1}{2} = 4.50 \end{aligned}$$

Similarly, we can show $E(Y|x = 0) = 1.50$.

In a more general setting involving two random variables $X \in \mathcal{R}$ and $Y \in \mathcal{R}$, the outcome probabilities may be represented by Table 4.1 and also the Venn diagram in Figure 4.4. The table shows $P(X = x, Y = y)$.

Table 4.1: Joint Probabilities of Events (x, y).

	$x = 1$	$x = 2$	$x = 3$	$x = 4$	...
$y = 1$	0.02	0.03	0.01	0.05	...
$y = 2$	0.03	0.03	0.02	0.01	...
$y = 3$	0.04	0.03	0.01	0.02	...
$y = 4$	0.05	0.02	0.01	0.05	...
$\vdots$	$\vdots$	$\vdots$	$\vdots$	$\vdots$	$\ddots$

Sample points in the Venn diagram are (x, y). The set $\{x = k\}$ denotes $\{(k,1), (k,2), \ldots\}$, and the set $\{y = j\}$ denotes $\{(1,j), (2,j), \ldots\}$. Thus in a multivariable sample space, using the Venn diagram, it is often that we use marginal variable values $x = 1$, $x = 2$, etc. as defining sets, i. e., all elements with $x = 1$, or with $x = 2$, etc. It is easily seen that $P(Y = j) = P(1,j) + P(2,j) + \cdots$ etc., and $P(X = k) = P(k,1) + P(k,2) + \cdots$ etc. $P(Y = j|X = k) = P(k,j)/P(X = k)$.

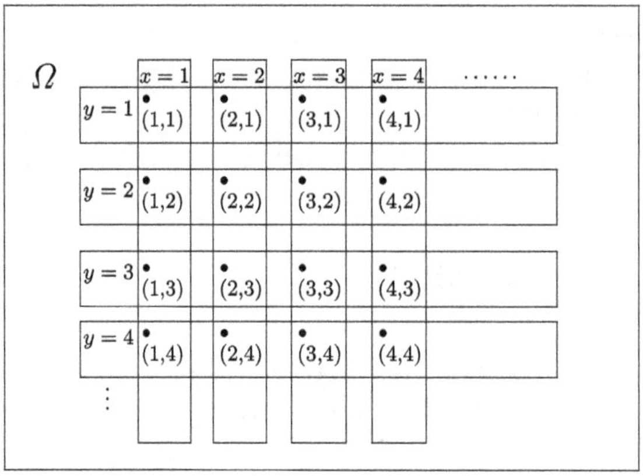

Figure 4.4: Venn Diagram of Joint Probabilities.

When the probability distribution is continuous and that pdf $f(x,y)$ is used, it is often more convenient to employ analytical methods than use Venn diagrams which are suitable only for relatively small discrete sets.

For continuous $x \in R(x)$ and $y \in R(y)$, where $R(x)$, $R(y)$ denote the support sets over which the integrations take place,

$$E^{X,Y}(Y) = \int_{R(x)} \int_{R(y)} yf(x,y)\, dy\, dx$$

$$= \int_{R(y)} y\left(\int_{R(x)} f(x,y)\, dx \right) dy$$

$$= \int_{R(y)} yf_Y(y)\, dy = E^Y(y)$$

where $f_Y(y)$ indicates the marginal pdf of RV Y integrated out from the joint pdf $f(x,y)$. For clarity, we have put superscripts on the expectation operator $E(\cdot)$ denoting the joint distribution (X,Y) or else the marginal distribution Y underlying the integration.

In addition,

$$E^{X,Y}(Y) = \int_{R(x)} \int_{R(y)} yf(x,y)\, dy\, dx$$

$$= \int_{R(x)} \int_{R(y)} y \frac{f(x,y)}{f_X(x)} f_X(x)\, dy\, dx$$

$$= \int_{R(x)} \left(\int_{R(y)} yf(y|x)\, dy \right) f_X(x)\, dx$$

$$= \int_{R(x)} E^{Y|X}(Y|X) f_X(x)\, dx$$
$$= E^X E^{Y|X}(Y|X)$$

Conditional probability is just a special case of conditional expectation if we put $Y = 1_{y \le k}$ taking values 1 or 0. In this case

$$E^{Y|X}(Y|X) = \int_{R(y)} 1_{y\le k} f(y|x)\, dy = P(Y \le k|x)$$

It should also be noted that $E^{Y|X}(Y|X)$ is a RV varying with X, and can be expressed as a certain function $g(X)$ of X.

4.3.1 Application: Value-at-Risk

Suppose RV X is distributed as $N(\mu, \sigma^2)$ and X is the change in capital of a financial institution as a result of market forces on its investments. If $X > (<)\ 0$, there is a gain (loss). At $(1 - q)$ level of confidence, the worst loss situation is $v < 0$ whereby $\int_{-\infty}^{v} f(x)dx = q$ where the left-hand side (LHS) is the area under the curve of the normally distributed X from $-\infty$ to v. $f(x)$ is the pdf of the normal X. By risk convention, typically a loss is expressed as a positive number. Hence the absolute value $|v|$ is called the investment's (absolute) Value-at-Risk (VaR) at the $(1 - q)$ level of confidence.

Suppose $|v|$ is established as the VaR(q) at qth percentile, or equivalently VaR at the $(1 - q)$ level of confidence. The expected loss conditional on hitting the VaR or the tail conditional expectation is by convention the absolute value of

$$E(X|X < v) = \frac{\int_{-\infty}^{v} x f(x)dx}{\int_{-\infty}^{v} f(x)dx}$$

In risk language, this quantity is also called the Conditional Value-at-Risk (CVaR) or Expected Shortfall. We shall find this quantity as follows, remembering that $X \sim N(\mu, \sigma^2)$.

First, let $z = \frac{x-\mu}{\sigma}$, so $z \in$ RV $Z \sim N(0, 1)$. Now,

$$E(X|X < v) = E(\mu + \sigma Z|\mu + \sigma Z < v)$$
$$= \mu + \sigma E\left(Z|Z < \frac{v - \mu}{\sigma}\right)$$

The second step is to find $E(Z|Z < v')$ where $v' = \frac{v-\mu}{\sigma}$.

Let $c = \frac{1}{\sqrt{2\pi}}$. Since

$$d(ce^{-\frac{1}{2}z^2}) = -z(ce^{-\frac{1}{2}z^2})dz$$

integrating over $(-\infty, v']$, we have

$$[ce^{-\frac{1}{2}z^2}]_{-\infty}^{v'} = -\int_{-\infty}^{v'} zce^{-\frac{1}{2}z^2}dz + k$$

Therefore

$$\phi(v') - 0 = -\int_{-\infty}^{v'} zce^{-\frac{1}{2}z^2}dz + k$$

As $v' \uparrow +\infty$, the LHS approaches zero. First term on the RHS approaches the mean of the standard normal RV, which is zero. Therefore, constant of integration $k = 0$. Hence

$$\int_{-\infty}^{v'} zce^{-\frac{1}{2}z^2}dz = -\phi(v')$$

Then,

$$E(Z|Z < v') = \frac{\int_{-\infty}^{v'} zf(z)dz}{\int_{-\infty}^{v'} f(z)dz} = -\frac{\phi(v')}{\Phi(v')}$$

Thus,

$$E(X|X < v) = \mu - \sigma\frac{\phi(v')}{\Phi(v')} < v$$

4.4 Moving Across Time

So far, we have dealt with joint pdf $f^{X,Y}(x, y)$ and conditional pdf $f^{Y|X}(y|x)$ where each of these yields a certain number in $\mathcal{R}^1$. Random variables X and Y occur at one point in time. When we are in a single time period or instance, conditioning is quite simple using the conditional probability rule in Eq. (4.1) or the extended Bayes' formula in (4.2). It all happens within the same time–space and it is easy to visualize on the same Venn diagram.

However, when events unfold across time, more apparatus is needed.[3] To generate some more serious results involving conditional probability distributions (over and above the conditional probabilities of events shown earlier), and which leads to martingale theory at a deeper end of probability theories and applications, we need a more formal structure and architecture with regard to the probability space and σ-fields. We shall more explicitly relate σ-fields to information sets.

First, it is needful to explain some ideas about information structure and information sets. Suppose the sample space is $\Omega = \{\omega_1, \omega_2, \omega_3\}$. The largest field or algebra is the set

$$\mathcal{F}_b = \{\phi, \Omega, \{\omega_1\}, \{\omega_2\}, \{\omega_3\}, \{\omega_1, \omega_2\}, \{\omega_1, \omega_3\}, \{\omega_2, \omega_3\}\}$$

consisting of $2^3 = 8$ events $E_i \in \mathcal{F}$. It is also called a field generated by $\{\{\omega_1\}, \{\omega_2\}, \{\omega_3\}\}$ which means the smallest field containing $\{\omega_1\}$, $\{\omega_2\}$, and $\{\omega_3\}$. Thus we can always find a field by picking a subset of Ω and using it to generate a field satisfying conditions (1a), (1b), and (1c) of Chapter 1.

Obviously, the bigger the subset, the bigger the generated field. Fields will always include ϕ and Ω. The largest field associated with sample space Ω, i. e. generated by Ω, will contain all elements of Ω and all possible unions of these elements, as well as ϕ. In a continuous state space, $\mathcal{F}$ will be a σ-field. Note that in the above case, $\mathcal{F}_b = \mathcal{F}$, the field generated by Ω. The smallest field is $\mathcal{F}_0 = \{\phi, \Omega\}$.

A smaller field than $\mathcal{F}_b$ could be $\mathcal{F}_a = \{\phi, \Omega, \{\omega_3\}, \{\omega_1, \omega_2\}\}$, being generated by $\{\{\omega_3\}, \{\omega_1, \omega_2\}\}$. The fields or algebras are collections of subsets of Ω or more conveniently termed as collections of events.

Let there be two time periods, $t = 1$ followed by $t = T = 2$. For events $E_i \in \mathcal{F}_b$ at $t = 2$,

$$\begin{aligned}
E_0 &\equiv e_0^b = \phi \quad \text{with } P(e_0^b) = P(\phi) = 0 \\
E_\Omega &\equiv e_\Omega^b = \Omega \quad \text{with } P(e_\Omega^b) = P(\Omega) = 1 \\
E_1 &\equiv e_1^b = \{\omega_1\} \quad \text{with } P(e_1^b) = P(\{\omega_1\}) = p_1 \\
E_2 &\equiv e_2^b = \{\omega_2\} \quad \text{with } P(e_2^b) = P(\{\omega_2\}) = p_2 \\
E_3 &\equiv e_3^b = \{\omega_3\} \quad \text{with } P(e_3^b) = P(\{\omega_3\}) = p_3 \\
E_4 &\equiv e_4^b = \{\omega_1, \omega_2\} \quad \text{with } P(e_4^b) = P(\{\omega_1, \omega_2\}) = p_1 + p_2 \\
E_5 &\equiv e_5^b = \{\omega_1, \omega_3\} \quad \text{with } P(e_5^b) = P(\{\omega_1, \omega_3\}) = p_1 + p_3 \\
E_6 &\equiv e_6^b = \{\omega_2, \omega_3\} \quad \text{with } P(e_6^b) = P(\{\omega_2, \omega_3\}) = p_2 + p_3
\end{aligned}$$

For events $E_i \in \mathcal{F}_a$ at $t = 1$,

$$E_0 \equiv e_0^a = \phi \quad \text{with } P(e_0^a) = P(\phi) = 0$$

3 See Pliska (1997) for a more detailed description of some of the concepts here.

$$E_\Omega \equiv e^a_\Omega = \Omega \quad \text{with } P(e^a_\Omega) = P(\Omega) = 1$$
$$E_1 \equiv e^a_1 = \{\omega_1, \omega_2\} \quad \text{with } P(e^a_1) = P(\{\omega_1, \omega_2\}) = p_1 + p_2$$
$$E_2 \equiv e^a_2 = \{\omega_3\} \quad \text{with } P(e^a_2) = P(\{\omega_3\}) = p_3$$

Now, over time in the period $[0, T]$, the information structure in the market is a time-sequence of increasing fields or algebras such that each future field is a superset of past fields (or past fields are subsets of future fields). An information structure can be conveniently represented by an evolving tree in Figure 4.5 as follows. The events corresponding to nodes on the information tree show increasing partitioning of existing sets as time moves forward into the future.

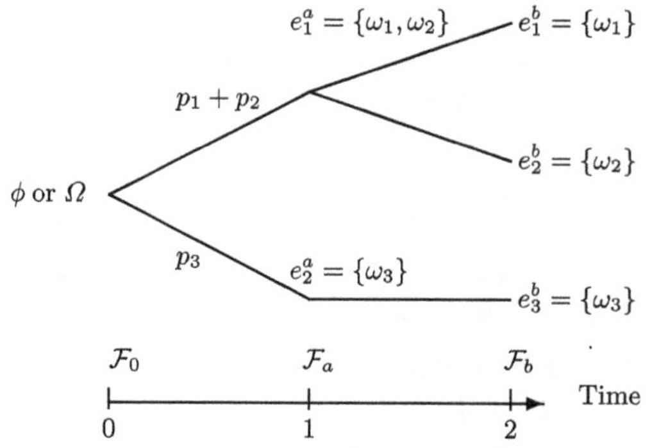

Figure 4.5: Information Structure.

Clearly, $\mathcal{F}_0 \subset \mathcal{F}_a \subset \mathcal{F}_b$. The information structure, which is assumed to be known by all investors at the start $t = 0$, says that at $t = 0$, there is trivial information: either null event ϕ or that all future events are possible, i. e. Ω, with probability 1. At $t = 1$, events are either e^a_1 with probability $p_1 + p_2$ or e^a_2 with probability p_3. Then, at $t = 2$, it is either e^b_1 or e^b_2 if e^a_1 at $t = 1$, or e^b_3 if e^a_2 at $t = 1$. Thus, at $t = 1$, the information set is $\mathcal{F}_a$ whereby investors can tell which event in $\mathcal{F}_a$ has occurred. At $t = 1$, investors cannot tell which of e^b_1 or e^b_2 has occurred since these events do not belong to $\mathcal{F}_a$. If an investor at a time before $t = 1$ knows that the information set at $t = 1$ is $\{\{\omega_1, \omega_2\}, \{\omega_3\}, \phi, \Omega\}$, then the ex-ante probability of occurrence of either event $\{\omega_1, \omega_2\}$ or event $\{\omega_3\}$ can be known. Ex-post, the investor could observe if $\{\omega_1, \omega_2\}$ or $\{\omega_3\}$ had occurred at $t = 1$.

At $t = 2$, there is greater resolution of uncertainty, and the information set enlarges to become field $\mathcal{F}_b$ (becoming finer) so that the investors can know which of e^b_1, e^b_2, or e^b_3 has occurred.

For the field or algebra on the LHS in Figure 4.6, we can find a RV Y as a mapping $Y : E_i \mapsto Y(E_i)$, for $i = 1, 2, 3, \ldots$.

Clearly, the RV is a function from events in $\mathcal{F}_a$ to $\mathcal{R}$. Sometimes, more than one sample point maps to the same value that the RV takes. But when we collect all those

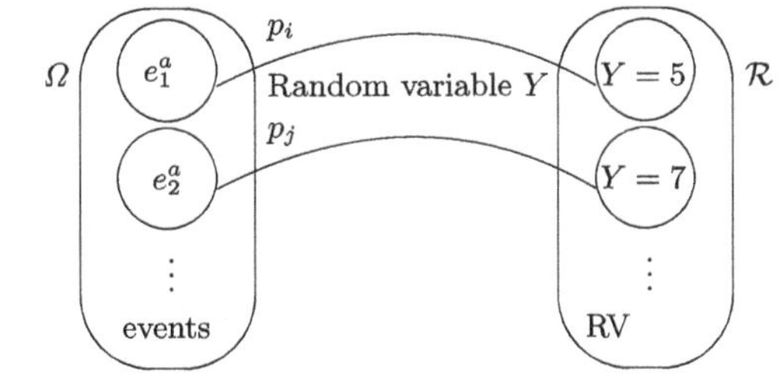

Figure 4.6: Random Variable as a Function Y at $t = 1$.

sample points that map to the same value on the RHS in $\mathcal{R}$, we can group those points as belonging to the same event and redefine the RV if necessary. Then, there is a one-to-one correspondence or bijection between disjoint events and unique values in $\mathcal{R}$ when the range set is appropriately defined. In the earlier example, a RV can be defined so that event $E_1 \equiv e_1^a$ or $E_1 = \{\omega_1, \omega_2\}$ is equivalent to RV Y with its value $y = 5$. Similarly, event $E_2 \equiv e_2^a$ or $E_2 = \{\omega_3\}$ is equivalent to RV Y with its value $y = 7$.

Thus, $P(Y = 5) = P(E_1)$, and $P(Y = 7) = P(E_2)$. Since we say field or algebra $\mathcal{F}_a$ is generated by E_1 and E_2, we can equivalently say $\mathcal{F}_a$ is generated by $Y = 5$ and $Y = 7$. Thus, in general, we can say a field at $t = j$ is generated by events at $t = j$ or generated by the RV Y at $t = j$, i. e., $\mathcal{F}_t = \sigma(Y_t)$. In this case, when we say a RV Y is measurable on field $\mathcal{F}$, we may also say that it is measurable on $\sigma(Y)$, the field generated by Y.

For discrete RV, it is mapped onto at most countably infinite numbers in $\mathcal{R}$. For continuous RVs, a properly defined RV may be constructed as a bijection from a σ-field to Borel sets in $\mathcal{R}$, so any probability measure p on the events in the σ-field is equivalent to the probability measure p on the corresponding Borel sets in $\mathcal{R}$.

We have shown how an information set at time t, Φ_t, corresponds to a particular σ-field at t, $\mathcal{F}_t$. Consider information set $\Phi_b \equiv \mathcal{F}_b$ where $\mathcal{F}_b = \{\phi, \Omega, \{\omega_1\}, \{\omega_2\}, \{\omega_3\}, \{\omega_1, \omega_2\}, \{\omega_1, \omega_3\}, \text{or } \{\omega_2, \omega_3\}\}$. With a properly defined probability space, we can always find the conditional probability $P(E_i|\Phi_t)$, or equivalently $P(E_i|\mathcal{F}_t)$, on the measurable events $\{E_i\}$.

The probability Table 4.2 for RV X at $t = 0$ can be shown as follows. The probabilities are in the distribution $P(X|\mathcal{F}_0)$ or $P(X|\phi, \Omega)$. There is no information about which event E_i has occurred, so the unconditional probabilities are p_i's.

Table 4.2: Unconditional Distribution.

State ω	RV $X(\omega)$	Probability
ω_1	$X_1 = X(\omega_1)$	p_1
ω_2	$X_2 = X(\omega_2)$	p_2
ω_3	$X_3 = X(\omega_3)$	p_3

When we condition on an information set or algebra $\mathcal{F}_t$, the defined meaning is that we are conditioning on events in $\mathcal{F}_t$ or RV Y that could occur at t. On an ex-ante basis, the conditioning is done on all events of $\mathcal{F}_t$ so that $P(E_i|\mathcal{F}_t)$ is really a conditional probability $P(E_i|E_j \in \mathcal{F}_t)$ which is a function of E_j.

Based on the last statement, we are looking at a two-sided table as follows for $\mathcal{F}_a$. The events in $\mathcal{F}_a$ are $\{\omega_1, \omega_2\}$, and ω_3. We omit the trivial events of null and Ω. Each column in the following Table 4.3 shows conditional probability of a sample point (or possible future event) given the various events in $\mathcal{F}_a$.

Table 4.3: Conditional Probabilities Given $\mathcal{F}_a$.

Event $E_i \in \mathcal{F}_a$:	$P(\{\omega_1\}\|E_i)$	$P(\{\omega_2\}\|E_i)$	$P(\{\omega_3\}\|E_i)$
$\{\omega_1, \omega_2\}$	$\frac{p_1}{p_1+p_2}$	$\frac{p_2}{p_1+p_2}$	0
$\{\omega_3\}$	0	0	1

Note that when event $\{\omega_1, \omega_2\}$ occurred, it is not possible to distinguish which state ω_1 or ω_2 had occurred.

Earlier we see how events and RV values may be put in one-to-one correspondence. Conditioning on the events of algebra $\mathcal{F}_a$ can also be written as conditioning on RV Y. In particular, $P(\{\omega_j\}|\{\omega_1, \omega_2\}) \equiv P(\{\omega_j\}|Y = 5)$. In addition, $P(\{\omega_j\}|\{\omega_3\}) \equiv P(\{\omega_j\}|Y = 7)$.

For $\mathcal{F}_b$, the conditional probabilities are shown in Table 4.4.

Table 4.4: Conditional Probabilities Given $\mathcal{F}_b$.

Event $E_i \in \mathcal{F}_b$:	$P(\{\omega_1\}\|E_i)$	$P(\{\omega_2\}\|E_i)$	$P(\{\omega_3\}\|E_i)$
$\{\omega_1\}$	1	0	0
$\{\omega_2\}$	0	1	0
$\{\omega_3\}$	0	0	1

For RV $X(\omega_i)$, we may define $P(X|\mathcal{F}_t)$ as a $M \times N$ matrix or table in which the ijth element is $P(\{\omega_j\}|E_i)$, (recall in Table 4.2, $\exists$ (there exists) RV $X \ni$ (such that) $\omega_j \mapsto x \in X$) and there are N simple sample points $\{\omega_j\}$ in Ω. M is the number of events, $E_1, E_2, \ldots, E_M$, $M \leq N$, excluding ϕ, Ω, in $\mathcal{F}_t$. We can also write $P(X|\mathcal{F}_t)$ as $P(X|\Phi_t)$. When $\exists$ RV Y with bijection $g : E_i \mapsto y \in Y$, then we can also write $P(X|\mathcal{F}_t) \equiv P(X|Y)$.

For conditional expectation, we define $E(X|\mathcal{F}_t) \equiv E(X|\Phi_t) \equiv E(X|Y)$ as a $M \times 1$ vector

$$\begin{pmatrix} E(X|E_1) \\ E(X|E_2) \\ \vdots \\ E(X|E_M) \end{pmatrix}$$

Back to the example of $\Omega = \{\omega_1, \omega_2, \omega_3\}$ in Table 4.2 and information $\mathcal{F}_0$, $\mathcal{F}_a$, and $\mathcal{F}_b$, conditional on event $E_1 = \{\omega_1, \omega_2\}$ at $t = 1$,

$$\begin{aligned} E(X|\{\omega_1, \omega_2\} \in \mathcal{F}_a) &= \sum_{i=1}^{3} X(\omega_i) \times P(\omega_i|E_1) \\ &= X_1 \frac{p_1}{p_1 + p_2} + X_2 \frac{p_2}{p_1 + p_2} + X_3 \times 0 \\ &= \frac{X_1 p_1 + X_2 p_2}{p_1 + p_2} \end{aligned}$$

Conditional on event $E_2 = \{\omega_3\}$,

$$\begin{aligned} E(X|\{\omega_3\} \in \mathcal{F}_a) &= \sum_{i=1}^{3} X(\omega_i) \times P(\omega_i|E_2) \\ &= X_1 \times 0 + X_2 \times 0 + X_3 \times 1 \\ &= X_3 \end{aligned}$$

Hence

$$E(X|\mathcal{F}_a) = \begin{pmatrix} \frac{X_1 p_1 + X_2 p_2}{p_1 + p_2} \\ X_3 \end{pmatrix}$$

If we take the unconditional expectation, the scalar

$$\begin{aligned} E[E(X|\mathcal{F}_a)] &= P(\{\omega_1, \omega_2\}) \times E(X|E_1) + P(\{\omega_3\}) \times E(X|E_2) \\ &= (p_1 + p_2) \frac{X_1 p_1 + X_2 p_2}{p_1 + p_2} + p_3 X_3 \\ &= p_1 X_1 + p_2 X_2 + p_3 X_3 \end{aligned}$$

which is equal to $E[X]$.

Under information set $\mathcal{F}_b$, $E(X|\mathcal{F}_b)$ is a vector $[E(X|E_i \in \mathcal{F}_b)]$. For event $\{\omega_1\}$,

$$\begin{aligned} E(X|\{\omega_1\} \in \mathcal{F}_b) &= \sum_{i=1}^{3} X(\omega_i) \times P(\omega_i|\omega_1) \\ &= X_1 \times 1 + 0 + 0 \\ &= X_1 \end{aligned}$$

For event $\{\omega_2\}$,

$$
\begin{aligned}
E(X|\{\omega_2\} \in \mathcal{F}_b) &= \sum_{i=1}^{3} X(\omega_i) \times P(\omega_i|\omega_2) \\
&= 0 + X_2 \times 1 + 0 \\
&= X_2
\end{aligned}
$$

For event $\{\omega_3\}$,

$$
\begin{aligned}
E(X|\{\omega_3\} \in \mathcal{F}_b) &= \sum_{i=1}^{3} X(\omega_i) \times P(\omega_i|\omega_3) \\
&= 0 + 0 + X_3 \times 1 \\
&= X_3
\end{aligned}
$$

Hence, if X is measurable w. r. t. $\mathcal{F} \equiv \sigma(X)$, $E(X|X = x) = x$ or we can write it more generally as $E(X|X) = X$. Note that $E(X|X) \neq E(X)$.

If we take the unconditional expectation

$$
E[E(X|\mathcal{F}_b)] = p_1 X_1 + p_2 X_2 + p_3 X_3
$$

which is equal to $E[X]$. How about $E[E(X|\mathcal{F}_b)|\mathcal{F}_a]$? We saw how conditioning on $\mathcal{F}_a \supset \mathcal{F}_0$ produces a RV.

Let $Z = E(X|\mathcal{F}_b)$ so Z is a function $Z(\omega_i)$. We saw earlier that $Z(\omega_i) = X_i$. Conditional on event $E_1 = \{\omega_1, \omega_2\} \in \mathcal{F}_a$,

$$
\begin{aligned}
E(Z|E_1) &= \sum_{i=1}^{3} Z(\omega_i) \times P(\omega_i|E_1) \\
&= X_1 \frac{p_1}{p_1 + p_2} + X_2 \frac{p_2}{p_1 + p_2} + X_3 \times 0 \\
&= \frac{X_1 p_1 + X_2 p_2}{p_1 + p_2}
\end{aligned}
$$

Conditional on event $E_2 = \{\omega_3\} \in \mathcal{F}_a$,

$$
\begin{aligned}
E(Z|E_2) &= \sum_{i=1}^{3} Z(\omega_i) \times P(\omega_i|E_2) \\
&= X_1 \times 0 + X_2 \times 0 + X_3 \times 1 \\
&= X_3
\end{aligned}
$$

The probability table for $E[E(X|\mathcal{F}_b)|\mathcal{F}_a]$ can be shown as follows (see Table 4.5).

This is identical with $E(X|\mathcal{F}_a)$. It is important to recapitulate the usage of information sets. When we say an investor has an information set Φ_t equivalent to the field or algebra $\mathcal{F}_t$, we mean that the investor will know which particular event will eventually occur in that set. The vector $P(X(\omega_i)|\Phi_t) \equiv P(X(\omega_i)|\mathcal{F}_t)$ provides the conditional probability on an ex-ante basis of each $\{\omega_i\}$ given each event in $\Phi_t \equiv \mathcal{F}_t$.

Table 4.5: The probability table for $E[E(X|\mathcal{F}_b)|\mathcal{F}_a]$.

Event $E_i \in \mathcal{F}_a$:	$E[E(X|\mathcal{F}_b)|\mathcal{F}_a]$
$\{\omega_1, \omega_2\}$	$\frac{X_1p_1+X_2p_2}{p_1+p_2}$
$\{\omega_3\}$	X_3

4.4.1 Law of Iterated Expectations

From the previous section, we have the law of iterated expectations. To be more precise, consider the law as expressed in the following lemma.

Lemma 4.1. *Suppose $\mathcal{G} \subset \mathcal{F}$, then*

$$E(E(X|\mathcal{F})|\mathcal{G}) = E(X|\mathcal{G}) = E(E(X|\mathcal{G})|\mathcal{F})$$

where $\mathcal{G}$ is a sub-field of $\mathcal{F}$.

Proof. Let $\mathcal{F} = \sigma(W)$ and $\mathcal{G} = \sigma(Z)$ where W, Z are RVs. Since $E(X|W)$ is a RV in W,

$$\begin{aligned} E(E(X|W)|Z) &= \int\limits_{R(w)} \Big(\int\limits_{R(x)} x f_{X|W}(x|w) dx \Big) f_{W|Z}(w|z)\, dw \\ &= \int\limits_{R(w)} \Big(\int\limits_{R(x)} x f_{X|W,Z}(x|w,z)\, dx \Big) \frac{f_{W,Z}(w,z)}{f_Z(z)} dw \end{aligned}$$

where we use the fact $\mathcal{G} \subset \mathcal{F} \Leftrightarrow f(x|w,z) = f(x|w)$ since z yields no additional information over w. Then

$$\begin{aligned} E(E(X|W)|Z) &= \int\limits_{R(w)} \Big(\int\limits_{R(x)} x \frac{f_{X,W,Z}(x,w,z)}{f_{W,Z}(w,z)}\, dx \Big) \frac{f_{W,Z}(w,z)}{f_Z(z)} dw \\ &= \int\limits_{R(x)} x \Big(\int\limits_{R(w)} \frac{f_{X,W,Z}(x,w,z)}{f_Z(z)}\, dw \Big) dx \\ &= \int\limits_{R(x)} x \frac{1}{f_Z(z)} \Big(\int\limits_{R(w)} f_{X,W,Z}(x,w,z)\, dw \Big) dx \\ &= \int\limits_{R(x)} x \frac{1}{f_Z(z)} f_{X,Z}(x,z)\, dx \\ &= \int\limits_{R(x)} x f_{X|Z}(x|z)\, dx = E(X|Z) \end{aligned}$$

Also, $E(E(X|Z)|W) = E(h(Z)|W,Z) = h(Z)$ where $h(Z) = E(X|Z)$. □

Consider another useful result:

$$\begin{aligned} E(E[X|Y]g(Y)) &= \int_{R(y)} \left(\int_{R(x)} xf(x|y)dx \right) g(y)f_Y(y)dy \\ &= \int_{R(y)} \left(\int_{R(x)} xg(y)f(x|y)f_Y(y)\, dx \right) dy \\ &= \int_{R(y)} \int_{R(x)} yg(y)f(x,y)\, dx\, dy \\ &= E^{XY}(Xg(Y)) \end{aligned} \tag{4.3}$$

As a corollary from Eq. (4.3), we put $g(Y) \equiv 1$.

Corollary 4.1.

$$E(E[X|Y]) = E^{XY}(X) = E(X) \triangleq E(X|\mathcal{F}_0)$$

This is sometimes called a smoothing lemma as $h(Y) \equiv E(X|Y)$ could be a smoother and more convenient function to integrate than $E(X)$.

Corollary 4.2. *From Lemma 4.1, we also obtain*

$$E(E(X|Z)|Z) = E(X|Z)$$

In the earlier discussion, there is a time dimension, and information set $\mathcal{F}_0 = \{\phi, \Omega\}$ occurs at time $t = 0$, $\mathcal{F}_a \equiv \mathcal{F}_1$ at time $t = 1$, and $\mathcal{F}_b \equiv \mathcal{F}_2$ at time $t = 2$. We can see that the information sets become finer and richer as time progresses: $\mathcal{F}_0 \subseteq \mathcal{F}_1 \subseteq \mathcal{F}_2 \ldots$. This fits with intuition about how rational agents would know more as time progresses (assuming no loss of memory)! In such a time setup, the information set stochastic process (probabilistic process over time) $\mathcal{F}_t$ is called a filtration. Sometimes the probability space is enhanced to show a filtration, i. e., a filtered probability space $(\Omega, \mathcal{F}, \{\mathcal{F}_t\}, \mathcal{P})$.

If there is a sequence of RVs Y_t that are measurable with respect to each $\mathcal{F}_t$, then we say the sequence $\{Y_t\}$ is adapted w. r. t. the filtration $\{\mathcal{F}_t\}$. $\{\omega_1, \omega_2\}$ and $\{\omega_3\}$ are adapted to $\mathcal{F}_a$, so are $\{\omega_1\}$, $\{\omega_2\}$, $\{\omega_3\}$, $\{\omega_1, \omega_2\}$, $\{\omega_1, \omega_3\}$, and $\{\omega_2, \omega_3\}$ adapted to $\mathcal{F}_b$. If $E_i \in \mathcal{F}_a \mapsto Y_i^a \in Y^a$ and $E_i \in \mathcal{F}_b \mapsto Y_i^b \in Y^b$, then RV Y^a is adapted to $\mathcal{F}_a$ and RV Y^b is adapted to $\mathcal{F}_b$.

4.4.2 Application: Asset Pricing

The Law of Iterated Expectations in application to a filtration says that if $\mathcal{F}_t \subseteq \mathcal{F}_{t+1} \subseteq \mathcal{F}_{t+2} \subseteq \ldots$, then

$$E(E(X|\mathcal{F}_{t+1})|\mathcal{F}_t) = E(X|\mathcal{F}_t)$$

This result is used commonly in testing asset pricing models in the empirical finance and economics literature. In finance theory under rational expectations, a traded asset price is determined by

$$p_t = E(m_{t+1}p_{t+1}|\Phi_t)$$

where $m_{t+1} = (\beta\frac{U'(C_{t+1})}{U'(C_t)})$ is the marginal rate of substitution or pricing kernel of an economy agent consuming C_t with von Neumann–Morgenstern utility function $U(\cdot), p_t$ is the asset price and Φ_t is the agent's information set. However, in trying to test this model, an econometrician cannot observe the agent's information Φ_t. At time t, p_t is known, so it can be treated as a constant. Then, we can take iterated expectations on the asset pricing formula to obtain the unconditional version $p_t = E(m_{t+1}p_{t+1})$ consistent with the conditional one, and be able to test it using econometric methods such as the generalized method of moments.

The Law of Iterated Expectations can also be used to show that the best predictor (in the sense of minimum mean square error) of a random variable Y that is correlated with random variable X is given by the conditional mean of Y given $X = x$, or $E(Y|X = x)$. Y and X are jointly distributed.

Suppose function $\pi(X)$ is the best predictor of Y. The mean square error of prediction is

$$\begin{aligned}
&E[Y - \pi(X)]^2\\
&\quad = E\{[Y - E(Y|X)] + [E(Y|X) - \pi(X)]\}^2\\
&\quad = E[Y - E(Y|X)]^2 + E[E(Y|X) - \pi(X)]^2\\
&\qquad + 2E\{[Y - E(Y|X)][E(Y|X) - \pi(X)]\}\\
&\quad = E[Y - E(Y|X)]^2 + E[E(Y|X) - \pi(X)]^2\\
&\quad \geq E[Y - E(Y|X)]^2
\end{aligned}$$

Therefore, the best predictor in the sense of minimum possible mean square error is $\pi(X) = E(Y|X)$ which is a RV varying with X. For now, let $E(Y|X) = g(X)$. In the above derivation, the middle term becomes zero as seen below:

$$\begin{aligned}
&E\{[Y - E(Y|X)][E(Y|X) - \pi(X)]\}\\
&\quad = E\{YE(Y|X)\} - E\{Y\pi(X)\}\\
&\qquad - E\{E(Y|X)E(Y|X)\} + E\{E(Y|X)\pi(X)\}\\
&\quad = E\{Yg(X)\} - E\{Y\pi(X)\}\\
&\qquad - E\{E(Yg(X)|X)\} + E\{E(Y\pi(X)|X)\}\\
&\quad = E\{Yg(X)\} - E\{Y\pi(X)\} - E\{Yg(X)\} + E\{Y\pi(X)\}\\
&\quad = 0
\end{aligned}$$

The minimum mean square error criterion allows the simple result of $E(Y|X)$ being best predictor, and since $E(Y|X)$ is analytically more tractable when joint distributions of (X, Y) are provided, the same criterion is used commonly in ordinary least squares econometric estimation methods.

4.5 Events

In this section, we study how financial events such as dividend payout, rights issue, bonus issue, earnings announcements, and so on, may affect the market prices of the corresponding stocks. The change in the probability distribution of the stock return conditional on the event is measured by t-statistics. The events are usually publicly available information at the time of announcement or happening. In event study, an underlying benchmark asset pricing model is assumed in order to make proper or meaningful inferences about significant return changes.

Event studies are therefore typically not about tests of an asset pricing model, but are tests of (1) whether the market is informationally efficient given the public information of the event, assuming the benchmark model, and also assuming we know or have a prior belief of whether the event has positive, negative, or neutral impact on returns, or (2) whether and how the event has positive, negative, or neutral impact on returns, assuming the benchmark model, and also assuming the market is informationally efficient.

The distinction between (1) and (2) should be kept in view in the interpretation of event study results in order not to confuse things. In most practical situations dealing with positive economics and in policy implications, it is usually more useful to apply (2), i. e. assuming benchmark model and market efficiency. For testing informational efficiency via (1), it is also common to assume strong-form market efficiency, so that significant return deviations before the time of the publicly announced event may be interpreted as information leakage or inside information revelation.

There are three stages in an event study analysis. First, we need to define the event of interest and identify the period over which the event will be examined. Next, we have to design a testing framework to define the way to measure impact and to test its significance. Finally, we need to collect appropriate data to perform the testing of the event's impact and draw conclusions in a model-theoretic and statistical sense.

Event studies are of various types. It is typically in the form of an announcement.

(1a) Firm-specific event, e. g., insider trading, announcement of board change, announcement of major strategic change, unusual rights issue announcement, announcement to file or seek "Chapter 11" (reorganization in U. S. in a last effort to avoid bankruptcy and liquidation which is "Chapter 7"), executive stock option issues, employee stock option issues, etc.

(1b) Across firms system-wide event, e. g., unanticipated better-than-forecast earnings announcement (good news), unanticipated worse-than-forecast earnings announcement (bad news), anticipated better-than or else worse-than forecast earnings announcement (no news). Others include announcement of bonus issues, stock splits, mergers and acquisitions, better than expected dividends or worse than expected dividends, new debt issues, seasoned equity issues, block sales, purchase of other companies' assets and stocks, etc.

(1c) Macro events, e. g., increase in CPF employer contribution, GDP growth and decline projection, regulatory changes, etc.

Event studies focus on the performance of stock prices (or equivalently stock returns) before, during, and after the event announcement. On the flip side, it is also about the reaction of stock investors to news or information, if any, from the event.

4.5.1 Testing Framework

The subject of event studies in finance is usually approached using a formal treatment of statistical and data analyses. The sampling frame or study period must also be clearly designed and stated. The event sampling time frame and the announcement windows/periods are shown graphically in Figures 4.7 and 4.8. The study period is depicted as follows. The measurement (or estimation) period is used for estimating the parameters of the stock return process employing historical data during the period. Daily (continuously compounded) stock return, i. e., $\ln(P_{t+1}/P_t)$, using typically end of day prices, is the variable commonly employed in conjunction with the daily continuously compounded market return, and also the daily risk-free rate.

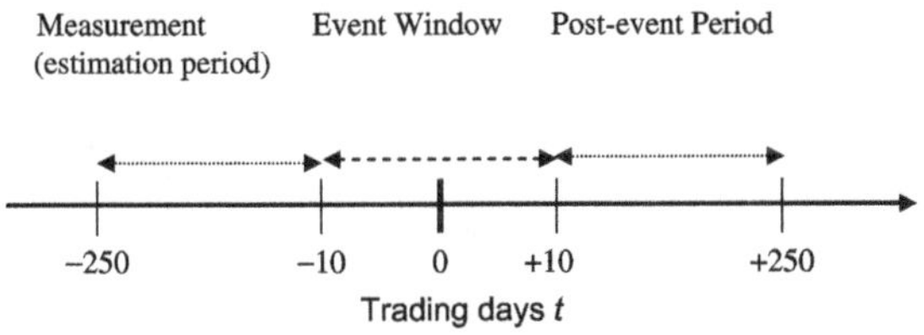

Figure 4.7: Event Sampling Frame.

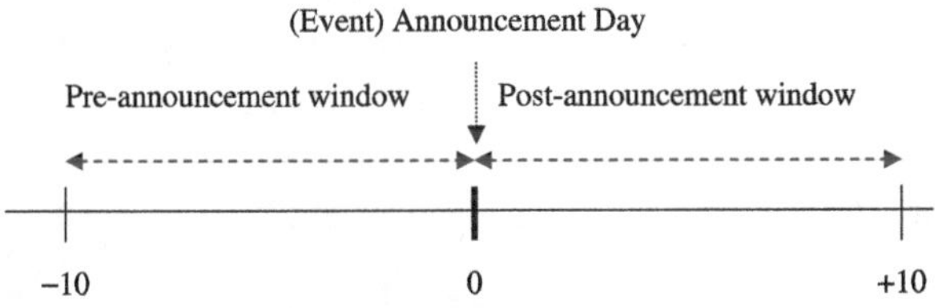

Figure 4.8: Announcement Windows.

Days are measured according to number of trading days before Event Day 0 (the event announcement day), or number of trading days after Event Day 0. In the above, the measurement or estimation is about 240 sample points from $t = -250$ to $t = -11$. Sometimes, when we suspect that the market is disruptive and beta may have changed over the nearly one calendar year (about 250+ trading days), then we use a shorter time series, e. g., 60 trading days ($t = -70$ to -11). During a stable measurement period, a longer or large sample is better in order to reduce sampling errors in the parameter estimators.

The post-event period that goes up to one calendar year is less often used except for studies such as mergers and acquisitions, buyouts, IPOs, when a longer time is required before the effect of the event is to be seen. The Event Window (or period) is the most important part of the time frame and is further delineated as follows.

The number of days to use in the event window typically includes two calendar weeks (or 10 trading days) before the announcement day, the announcement day itself, and 10 trading days after the announcement day. This window should be large enough to show up any possible changes to returns due to the event. The event date is the day when the event becomes public information, e. g., when the announcement or news is broadcast as public information. It is denoted as Day 0 in the event study calendar.

The parameters estimated from the measurement period are used in the event period to compute the defined deviation from normal return as a measure of impact of event, if any.

4.5.2 Benchmark

A benchmark or conditional expected return rate will have to be defined. Various benchmark models are used. In what follows, we shall take "returns" to mean return rates.

(A) Market Model

Suppose r_{it} is the return rate of stock i at time t, and r_{mt} is the market portfolio return rate (or alternatively return rate of a market index) at time t. If r_{it} and r_{mt} are bivariate normally distributed (all stock returns being MVN (multivariate normally distributed) is sufficient to give this bivariate relationship), then conditional probability distribution of $r_{it}|r_{mt}$ is normal with (conditional) mean and (conditional) variance

$$\begin{aligned} E(r_{it}|r_{mt}) &= E(r_{it}) + \frac{\sigma_{im}}{\sigma_m^2}[r_{mt} - E(r_{mt})] \\ &= \left[E(r_{it}) - \frac{\sigma_{im}}{\sigma_m^2}E(r_{mt})\right] + \frac{\sigma_{im}}{\sigma_m^2}r_{mt} \end{aligned} \tag{4.4}$$

and

$$\text{var}(r_{it}|r_{mt}) = \sigma_i^2 - \frac{\sigma_{im}^2}{\sigma_m^2} \tag{4.5}$$

where $\text{cov}(r_{it}, r_{mt}) = \sigma_{im}$, $\text{var}(r_{mt}) = \sigma_m^2$, and $\text{var}(r_{it}) = \sigma_i^2$. Then, we can write the linear regression model of r_{it} on r_{mt} as

$$r_{it} = a_i + b_i r_{mt} + e_{it} \tag{4.6}$$

where

$$a_i = \left[E(r_{it}) - \frac{\sigma_{im}}{\sigma_m^2} E(r_{mt})\right], \quad b_i = \frac{\sigma_{im}}{\sigma_m^2}, \quad \text{and} \quad E(e_{it}|r_{mt}) = 0 \tag{4.7}$$

The last condition in (4.7) can be taken as a specification that e_{it} is uncorrelated with r_{mt}, which in the context of MVN, amounts to stochastic independence. It also implies via the law of iterated expectations that $E(e_{it}) = 0$. The above regression model Eq. (4.6) is called the market model. This is purely a statistical model, but it is consistent with the two-parameter CAPM. The market model does not necessarily imply the Sharpe-Lintner CAPM as parameter a_i is not necessarily constrained to be the CAPM intercept. Nevertheless, a_i is a constant that can possibly follow that constraint. CAPM does not necessarily imply the market model as quadratic utility and not MVN can be a sufficient condition for CAPM. But, MVN is both a sufficient condition for CAPM and for the market model together with some mild preference conditions. Note that in general, $\text{cov}(e_{it}, e_{it-1})$ is not necessarily zero. If we restrict this covariance to zero, then we are looking at what had been called a single-index model. In the latter case, the index actually need not be the market portfolio return, although it is natural to identify the appropriate single index or factor as the market return.

The verification of Eq. (4.4) is straightforward as in a bivariate normal distribution. If we take the unconditional variance of r_{it} or $\text{var}(r_{it})$ in Eq. (4.6),

$$\sigma_i^2 = b_i^2 \sigma_m^2 + \sigma_e^2 = \frac{\sigma_{im}^2}{\sigma_m^2} + \sigma_e^2$$

where $\sigma_e^2 = \text{var}(e_{it})$. Now, $b_i \sigma_m$ is called the systematic risk and σ_e is called the unsystematic or idiosyncratic or diversifiable risk of stock *i* return. But conditional variance $\text{var}(r_{it}|r_{mt}) = \sigma_e^2$. Hence, by Eq. (4.5), $\sigma_e^2 = \sigma_i^2 - \frac{\sigma_{im}^2}{\sigma_m^2}$. This is essentially Eq. (4.6).

Henceforth we construe the market model for stock *i* return as

$$r_{it} = \alpha_i + \beta_i r_{mt} + e_{it} \tag{4.8}$$

satisfying the following assumed conditions.

(2a) $\text{cov}(r_{mt}, e_{it}) = 0$;
(2b) $\text{var}(e_{it}) = \sigma_i^2$, a constant;
(2c) $(e_{it}, e_{it-k}) = 0$ for $k \neq 0$

Then OLS regression for data set, $t = -250$ to $t = -11$, will yield BLUE $\hat{\alpha}_i$ and $\hat{\beta}_i$ that are also consistent. In addition, estimate of σ_i^2,

$$\hat{\sigma}_i^2 = \frac{1}{L-2}\sum_{t=-L-10}^{-11}(r_{it} - \hat{\alpha}_i - \hat{\beta}_i r_{mt})^2 = \frac{1}{L-2}\sum_{t=-L-10}^{-11}\hat{e}_{it}^2$$

is unbiased and consistent. Note that L is number of sample points in the measurement window, and could be 240 or 60 or in-between.

The market model (A) is a more popular benchmark used in event studies. In (A), the benchmark or normal return during the Event Window is defined as $\hat{r}_{i\tau} = \hat{\alpha}_i + \hat{\beta}_i r_{m\tau}$ where the time subscript is now τ (to distinguish from t) outside the Event Window. So, $\tau = -10$ to $+10$ in the Event Window.

The normal return on day τ is an expected return conditional on information available up to and including day τ. In the case of market model, this relevant information is just $r_{m\tau}$.

The abnormal return to stock i at time $\tau \in [-10, +10]$ is

$$\text{AR}_{i\tau} = r_{i\tau} - \hat{r}_{i\tau} = r_{i\tau} - \hat{\alpha}_i - \hat{\beta}_i r_{m\tau} \tag{4.9}$$

(B) CAPM Equation Model

$$r_{it} = r_{ft} + \beta_i(r_{mt} - r_{ft}) + u_{it}$$

In (B), the normal return during the Event Window is defined as

$$\hat{r}_{i\tau} = r_{f\tau} + \hat{\beta}_i(r_{m\tau} - r_{f\tau})$$

The abnormal return would then be

$$\text{AR}_{i\tau} = r_{i\tau} - \hat{r}_{i\tau} = r_{i\tau} - (r_{f\tau} + \hat{\beta}_i(r_{m\tau} - r_{f\tau}))$$

Other supplementary measures of abnormal return include the following. They can be used to check the robustness of the results in case the benchmark model is not correct.
(C) Market Adjusted Excess Return

In (C), the abnormal return during the Event Window is defined as $r_{i\tau} - r_{m\tau}$. This measure may be a robustness check of whether the CAPM or Market model may be incorrect as it depends on just the market factor, e. g., there could be other factors but with market as main positive factor. Different abnormal return signs from (A) or (B) may warrant relook at those benchmark models. After relook, it could be benchmark models (A), (B) are correct but market adjusted excess return is too rough without an exact beta estimate.

(D) Mean Adjusted Excess Return

In (D), the abnormal return is defined as $r_{i\tau} - \bar{r}_i$ where $\bar{r}_i$ is a an estimate of expected return based on lagged returns, $\frac{1}{L}\sum_{t=-L-10}^{-11} r_{it}$.

Suppose our event is a systematic one such as bonus issue information effect (whether bonus dividend announcement is good news, bad news, or no news?) We can test this over not just one firm with a bonus dividend announcement, but over N (e. g., 30) firms each with a bonus dividend announcement not all at the same time but scattered through time, e. g., all within several years. Figure 4.9 shows how N similar events (Event date "0") can take place at different calendar time.

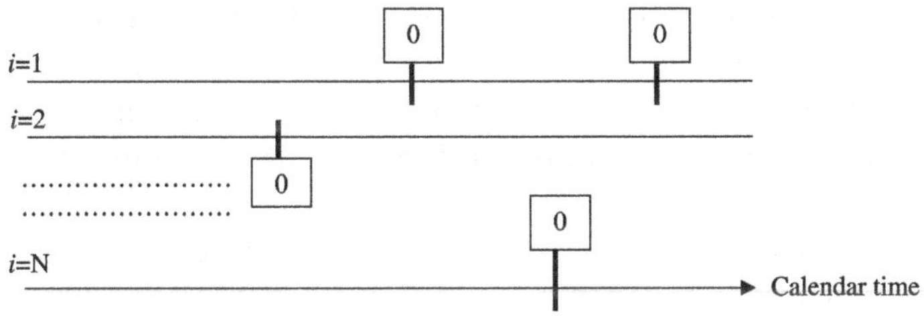

Figure 4.9: Grouping Events.

The announcement date (day of announcement of the bonus dividend event) for each firm is denoted Event Day 0 even though they are from different calendar dates. Also, event day −3 would refer to three days before announcement relative to all Day 0 of each firm event. Note also that we could have two events from the same firm if the firm happened to make two bonus issue announcements separated by time. Avoiding clustering of the events in time prevents confounding events, e. g., 9/11 when all stocks dived. If we had done an event study of positive announcements and all firm-events lined up around the month of late November–December 2001, then the 9/11 would produce a negative effect on all the stocks that is certainly not due to the event of positive earnings. Spreading out also has the advantage of ensuring the various $AR_{i\tau}$'s of the various firms do not correlate so that it is easier to estimate the variance of a portfolio of the $AR_{i\tau}$'s across firms. In other words, if the firm-events all cluster together at the same time, then since firm returns (even after adjusting for market) may still possess contemporaneous correlations, the portfolio variance will be harder to measure because of the covariance terms.

Suppose we use the Market Model (A) as our correct benchmark model. Then, the $AR_{i\tau}$'s computed during the Event Window for any day τ would, in a situation without news impact or no fresh news, be randomly varying about zero provided (a) the model is true (which we assumed already) and (b) the market is efficient (quick to process information and update price if there is new information) and rational (will process relevant information correctly if given the information). The implication is that residual noise does not display a mean > 0 or < 0 when there is no fresh news to alter the firm or stock's mean and volatility. In an efficient and rational market, without significant information impact, the expected value of $\text{AR}_{i\tau}$ is zero, conditional on market information up to and including those at τ. However, a zero expected $\text{AR}_{i\tau}$ despite information would mean market informational inefficiency.

Significant information in the event announcement is taken to be unanticipated news that causes the market to either (a) re-evaluate the stock's expected future earnings (thus also dividends), and/or (b) re-evaluate the stock's risk-adjusted discount rate, resulting in the immediate efficient adjustment of the stock price. With significant information impact, the expected value of $\text{AR}_{i\tau}$ is non-zero (positive if good news on stock and negative if bad news on stock), conditional on market information up to and including those at τ. Average abnormal return on day τ in the event window would then be significantly different from zero. The abnormal return essentially reflects a change in the conditional expectation of the stock return by the market. Immediate reflection of publicly announced information in price shows semi-strong form informational efficiency.

We define the null hypothesis H_0: event has no impact on stock returns (or more specifically – no impact on stock's abnormal returns). This same hypothesis can be made more detailed in several ways as follows. From Eq. (4.9) the market model abnormal return under the zero impact null is

$$\text{AR}_{i\tau} = r_{i\tau} - \hat{\alpha}_i - \hat{\beta}_i r_{m\tau}$$

so that

$$\begin{aligned} E(\text{AR}_{i\tau}|r_{m\tau}) &= E(r_{i\tau}|r_{m\tau}) - E(\hat{\alpha}_i|r_{m\tau}) - r_{m\tau}E(\hat{\beta}_i|r_{m\tau}) \\ &= E(r_{i\tau}|r_{m\tau}) - \alpha - \beta r_{m\tau} \\ &= 0 \end{aligned}$$

and

$$\begin{aligned} \text{var}(\text{AR}_{i\tau}|r_{m\tau}) &= \text{var}(r_{i\tau}|r_{m\tau}) + \text{var}(\hat{\alpha}_i|r_{m\tau}) + r_{m\tau}^2\,\text{var}(\hat{\beta}_i|r_{m\tau}) \\ &\quad + 2r_{m\tau}\,\text{cov}(\hat{\alpha}_i, \hat{\beta}_i|r_{m\tau}) - 2\,\text{cov}(r_{i\tau}, \hat{\alpha}_i|r_{m\tau}) \\ &\quad - 2r_{m\tau}\,\text{cov}(r_{i\tau}, \hat{\beta}_i|r_{m\tau}) \\ \text{var}(\text{AR}_{i\tau}|r_{m\tau}) &= \sigma_i^2 + \sigma_i^2\left(\frac{1}{L} + \frac{\bar{r}_m^2}{\sum_{t=-L-10}^{-11}(r_{mt} - \bar{r}_m)^2}\right) \\ &\quad + r_{m\tau}^2\sigma_i^2\frac{1}{\sum_{t=-L-10}^{-11}(r_{mt} - \bar{r}_m)^2} \end{aligned}$$

$$- 2r_{m\tau}\sigma_i^2 \frac{\bar{r}_m}{\sum_{t=-L-10}^{-11}(r_{mt} - \bar{r}_m)^2}$$

$$= \sigma_i^2\left(1 + \frac{1}{L} + \frac{(r_{m\tau} - \bar{r}_m)^2}{\sum_{t=-L-10}^{-11}(r_{mt} - \bar{r}_m)^2}\right)$$

where

$$\bar{r}_m = \frac{1}{L}\sum_{t=-L-10}^{-11} r_{mt}$$

Recall that while t ranges from $-L-10$ to -11 within the estimation period, τ ranges from -10 to $+10$ within the event window. The last two terms in $\text{var}(\text{AR}_{i\tau}|r_{m\tau})$, i. e., $\text{cov}(r_{i\tau}, \hat{\alpha}_i|r_{m\tau})$ and $\text{cov}(r_{i\tau}, \hat{\beta}_i|r_{m\tau})$, are zero because $r_{i\tau}|r_{m\tau}$ involves $e_{i\tau}$ whereas $\hat{\alpha}_i$ and $\hat{\beta}_i$ involve e_{it} ($t = -L - 10$ to -11), and $e_{i\tau}$ and e_{it} are uncorrelated or perhaps even stronger, independent. Note that estimator errors are added to the variance of $\text{AR}_{i\tau}$.

4.5.3 Test Statistics

If the estimation period sample size L is large, we can use the argument of asymptotic result to show $\text{var}(\text{AR}_{i\tau}|r_{m\tau})$ converges to σ_i^2, or use the latter as an approximation in the case when L is fairly large, e. g., $L = 240$.

So,

$$\text{AR}_{i\tau}|r_{m\tau} \overset{d}{\sim} N(0, \sigma_i^2)$$

Test for each stock i using

$$\frac{\text{AR}_{i\tau}}{\hat{\sigma}_i} \overset{d}{\sim} N(0,1) \quad \text{or more accurately,} \quad t_{L-2} \tag{4.10}$$

This is sometimes called the $\text{SAR}_{i\tau}$, the standardized abnormal return. The distribution is sometimes also interpreted as Student's t with $L - 2$ degrees of freedom. This is because $\hat{\sigma}_i^2$ is estimated via

$$\hat{\sigma}_i^2 = \frac{1}{L-2}\sum_{t=-L-10}^{-11}(r_{it} - \hat{\alpha}_i - \hat{\beta}_i r_{mt})^2 \cong \frac{\sigma_i^2}{L-2}\chi_{L-2}^2$$

and

$$\frac{\text{AR}_{i\tau}}{\hat{\sigma}_i} = \frac{\text{AR}_{i\tau}}{\sigma_i} \times \frac{\sigma_i}{\hat{\sigma}_i} = Z\Big/\sqrt{\frac{\hat{\sigma}_i^2}{\sigma_i^2}} \cong t_{L-2}$$

where $Z \sim N(0,1)$.

If we have N firm-events, at any time τ within the Event Window, the average abnormal return (in some instances, it has been called aggregated abnormal return),

$$\mathrm{AAR}_\tau = \frac{1}{N}\sum_{i=1}^{N} \mathrm{AR}_{i\tau}$$

Assuming independence of disturbance across events because they are not clustered, for large L,

$$\mathrm{var}(\mathrm{AAR}_\tau | r_{m\tau}) \approx \frac{1}{N^2}\sum_{i=1}^{N} \sigma_i^2$$

So,

$$\mathrm{AAR}_\tau | r_{m\tau} \approx N\left(0, \frac{1}{N^2}\sum_{i=1}^{N} \sigma_i^2\right)$$

Test for each Event Window day τ using

$$\frac{\mathrm{AAR}_\tau}{\sqrt{\frac{1}{N^2}\sum_{i=1}^{N} \hat{\sigma}_i^2}} \approx N(0,1) \tag{4.11}$$

There is another way to represent this test statistic in terms of the $\mathrm{SAR}_{i\tau}$. $\sqrt{N}[\frac{1}{N}\sum_{i=1}^{N} \frac{\mathrm{AR}_{i\tau}}{\hat{\sigma}_i}] \approx N(0,1)$. This is approximately equal to Eq. (4.11).

In order to test for the persistence of the impact of the event during period $\tau_k - \tau_1$ (where τ_1 is start of Event Window, and τ_{21} is end of Event Window, and $\tau_1 \leq \tau_k \leq \tau_{21}$), the abnormal return can be added to obtain the cumulative abnormal return for each i,

$$\mathrm{CAR}_i(\tau_1, \tau_k) = \sum_{\tau=\tau_1}^{\tau_k} \mathrm{AR}_{i\tau}$$

Assuming independence of disturbance across time viz. $\mathrm{cov}(e_{it}, e_{it-k}) = 0$ for $k \neq 0$:

$$\mathrm{var}(\mathrm{CAR}_i(\tau_1, \tau_k) | r_{m\tau_k}, \ldots) = \sum_{\tau=\tau_1}^{\tau_k} \mathrm{var}(\mathrm{AR}_{i\tau} | r_{m\tau}) \approx (\tau_k - \tau_1 + 1)\sigma_i^2$$

So, $\mathrm{CAR}_i(\tau_1, \tau_k) | r_{m\tau_k,\ldots} \approx N(0, (\tau_k - \tau_1 + 1)\sigma_i^2)$. Test for each event window period (τ_1, τ_k) using

$$\frac{\mathrm{CAR}_i(\tau_1, \tau_k)}{\sqrt{(\tau_k - \tau_1 + 1)\hat{\sigma}_i^2}} \approx N(0,1) \tag{4.12}$$

The cumulative average abnormal return

$$\mathrm{CAAR}(\tau_1, \tau_k) = \frac{1}{N}\sum_{i=1}^{N}\sum_{\tau=\tau_1}^{\tau_k} \mathrm{AR}_{i\tau} = \sum_{\tau=\tau_1}^{\tau_k}\frac{1}{N}\sum_{i=1}^{N}\mathrm{AR}_{i\tau}$$

$$\mathrm{var}(\mathrm{CAAR}(\tau_1, \tau_k)|r_{m\tau_k}, \ldots) \approx \frac{1}{N^2}\sum_{i=1}^{N}(\tau_k - \tau_1 + 1)\sigma_i^2$$

So,

$$\mathrm{CAAR}(\tau_1, \tau_k)|r_{m\tau_k} \ldots \approx N\left(0, \frac{1}{N^2}\sum_{i=1}^{N}(\tau_k - \tau_1 + 1)\sigma_i^2\right)$$

CAAR may be construed as average of CAR or cumulation of AAR. Now test for each event window period (τ_1, τ_k) using

$$\frac{\mathrm{CAAR}(\tau_1, \tau_k)}{\sqrt{(\tau_k - \tau_1 + 1)\frac{1}{N^2}\sum_{i=1}^{N}\hat{\sigma}_i^2}} \approx N(0, 1) \tag{4.13}$$

The z-statistics in Eqs. (4.10)–(4.13) can be used to test the H_0. The interpretation in each case will be slightly different. For example, in Eq. (4.10) a rejection says that there is an unexpected large increase or decrease in return for that event day, while in Eq. (4.12), a rejection says that there is an unexpected large increase or decrease in cumulative return.

The tests are based on the null that the returns mean level and variance or volatility remain constant. A rejection could mean that the conditional mean had changed due to the event announcement. On the other hand, it is also possible that a rejection or non-rejection could be due to a change in volatility due to the event. If we want to test if there is a conditional mean change considering changed volatility as a result of the event, then we can use the sample variance of AAR_τ during the event window, $\tau \in (1, 21)$, i. e.,

$$\hat{\sigma}^2(\mathrm{AAR}(1, 21)) = \frac{1}{20}\sum_{\tau=1}^{21}(\mathrm{AAR}_\tau - \overline{\mathrm{AAR}})^2$$

where

$$\overline{\mathrm{AAR}} = \frac{1}{21}\sum_{\tau=1}^{21}\mathrm{AAR}_\tau$$

to construct the approximate t_{20} test statistic

$$\frac{\mathrm{AAR}_\tau}{\sqrt{\hat{\sigma}^2(\mathrm{AAR}(1, 21))}} \approx t_{20}$$

for testing, where $\tau \in (1, 21)$. It is important to interpret the CAR or CAAR graph appropriately.

We illustrate how CAR could be interpreted using three events as depicted in Figure 4.10.

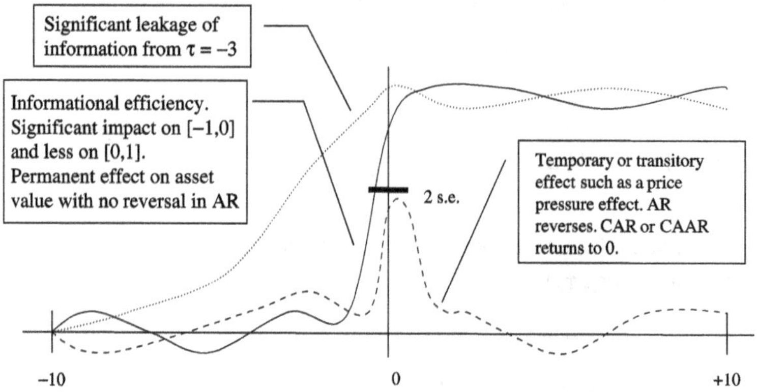

Figure 4.10: Graph of Cumulative Abnormal Returns Based on Events.

The three events in Figure 4.10 show different paths of CAR. In the dotted event path, CAR is significant only at event date due to a significantly positive AR. After that, AR is negative, and thus CAR falls back to zero. CAR remains at zero thereafter. This shows a price pressure effect that could be due to excessive buying (or selling) not because of information but liquidity. Because of temporary inelasticity, large volume selling will drive down price temporarily and large volume buying will drive up price temporarily. As there is no information, the prices will revert, thus showing a reversal in AR over one or two days: CAR reverts back to zero after that. The positive AR is possibly due to buying pressure and illiquidity. Such price pressure effects do not last and are said to be temporary or transitory.

However, if there is excessive buying pressure, but sellers are plentiful and can easily substitute into other shares, then the supply curve is flat or highly elastic, so the buying pressure will not force up price. This substitution effect will not produce any significant AR or CAR in the first place.

Similarly, if there is excessive selling pressure, but buyers are plentiful and can easily substitute from other shares, then the demand curve is flat or highly elastic demand, so the selling pressure will not force down the market share price. It is more plausible that the market operates under information effect as well as substitution effect, so dotted event paths illustrated in Figure 4.10 will be rare.

At times, even when a piece of information is known to produce asset price changes, but if this information is already known or anticipated, then its announcement at day 0 will not produce any significant AR or CAR.

However, the solid line event shown in Figure 4.10 illustrates significant event with a positive impact on price and returns, e. g., a positive earnings announcement. The impact is permanent. The news is also quickly absorbed and the price adjusted quickly so that after Day 1 of event, there is no more price adjustment, and AR is zero, so CAR stays constant thereafter.

In the other small dotted event with positive CAR, the news appeared to hit before event date, at about $\tau = -3$. The AR and thus CAR are significantly positive. This may indicate information leakage. It appears that inside information has caused the significant price changes before the public news. The slow leakage and not one-time jump may indicate a bit of strong-form market informational inefficiency, but it could also be efficient but with slow adjustments due to slow release of private information.

In what follows, we study an actual event on a firm, and show how to conduct the various event study tests. The data is collected from Center for Research in Security Prices (CRSP) database managed at the University of Chicago.

4.6 Case Study: Bank of America Acquires Merrill Lynch

At about the beginning of the recent global financial crisis, the Bank of America (BOA) announced on September 15, 2008 (Monday), that she was acquiring Merrill Lynch (ML) in a $50-billion stock-for-stock exchange. BOA would exchange 0.8595 share for each ML share. The offer price for ML's share in terms of the BOA share market value at that time represented about US$29 a share.

It was to be one of the most tumultuous weeks in the financial history of global capital markets. Early on that Monday, Lehman Brothers, the Number 4 investment bank in U. S. had filed for Chapter 11 bankruptcy. Earlier in March, JP Morgan Chase had bought out ailing Bear Stearns at a deep discount. These investment firms had gotten into deep trouble by sinking huge chunks of investment capital in real estate derivatives and collaterized debt obligations (CDOs), and these instruments were either becoming a tiny fraction of their original values or could not be traded as liquidity had dried up upon the fear of troubled mortgages.

Merrill Lynch's share was last traded the close of the previous week at US$17.05 a share, so BOA appeared to pay a premium of 70 % above the last market price. At its peak, in 2007, ML's share was selling above US$98. The deal also carried substantial risks for BOA as ML had billions of dollars in assets tied to mortgages that had dived in value. Merrill had reported four straight quarterly losses.

Our task in this single-event single-firm study is to try as scientifically as possible to test (a) if the acquisition announcement on September 15, 2008 (event day 0) contained significant information whether good news or bad news for the stockholders and (b) if there was a leakage[4] of information during the two weeks (10 trading days)

---

4 All information and data are collected from known published sources such as Yahoo Finance, CRSP, and SGX database. The term "leakage" is purely a technical word denoting information being known by a subset of investors. There is no connotation of wrong-doing or of issues that would be implicated by law. The above qualifications apply to the present case.

before announcement. We use daily traded data during one calendar year (about 252 market price observations) before the event window [−10, +10] to estimate the market model (A) as benchmark. The $\hat{\alpha}_i$ and $\hat{\beta}_i$ estimates of the market model parameters for BOA are then used to estimate the abnormal returns

$$\mathrm{AR}_{i\tau} = r_{i\tau} - \hat{\alpha}_i - \hat{\beta}_i r_{m\tau}$$

in the Event Window. The abnormal returns during the Event Window 10 days prior to announcement date until 10 days post-announcement are shown in Figure 4.11. The cumulative abnormal return is shown in Figure 4.12.

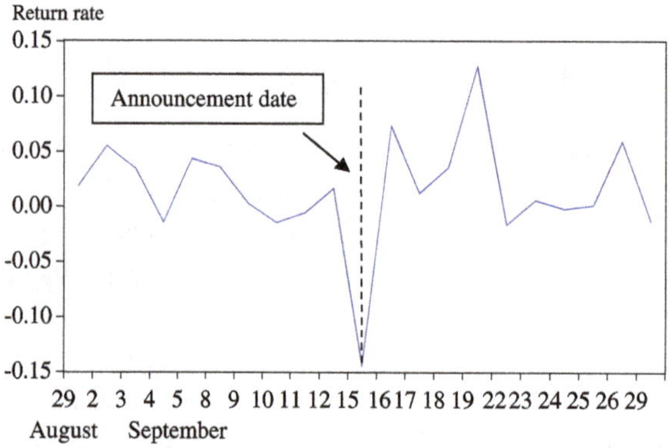

Figure 4.11: Abnormal Returns Around the Event that Bank of America (BOA) Announced Acquisition of Merrill Lynch on September 15, 2008.

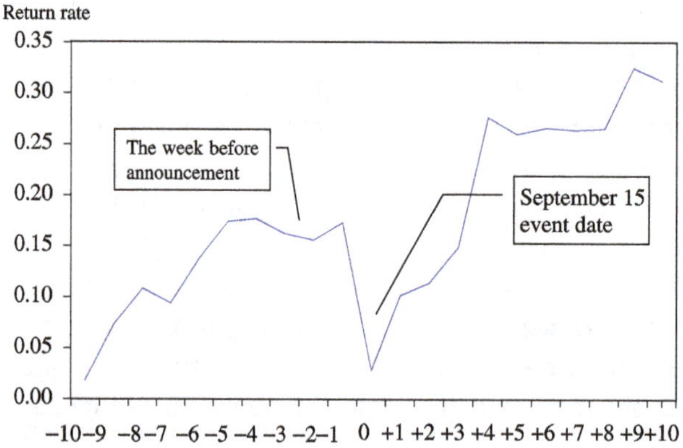

Figure 4.12: Cumulative Abnormal Returns of Bank of America (BOA) from August 29 to September 29, 2008.

The t-statistics (approximated by standard normal variate) in Eq. (4.12) for testing if the CAR is significant are also computed for different event days during the event window. They are shown in Table 4.6.

Table 4.6: T-Statistics of the CAR from $\tau = -10$ to $\tau = +9$.

Dates	$N(0, 1)$	Dates	$N(0, 1)$
Aug 29	0.7719	Sep 15	0.3517
Sep 2	2.1730*	Sep 16	1.2196
Sep 3	2.6002**	Sep 17	1.3112
Sep 4	1.9566	Sep 18	1.6551
Sep 5	2.5640**	Sep 19	2.9633**
Sep 8	2.9481**	Sep 22	2.6989**
Sep 9	2.7704**	Sep 23	2.6798**
Sep 10	2.3756*	Sep 24	2.5824**
Sep 11	2.1583*	Sep 25	2.5253*
Sep 12	2.2696*	Sep 26	3.0170**

Note: CAR values that are significantly different from 0 at the 5 % two-tailed significance level are indicated by * whereas those significant at the 1 % two-tailed level are indicated by **.

Figures 4.11, 4.12, and Table 4.6 indicate that BOA's prices had increased two weeks prior to announcement date. At event date on September 15, there was a significant drop in price. There did not appear to be any leakage as the price did not show any marked changes in the few days before the event date. The significant drop was probably due to the market taking the news as bad, believing BOA was undertaking a high risk in acquiring ML.

However, in the 2–4 days subsequent to announcement, BOA's prices showed reversion back to normality and in fact climbed somewhat. This may be due to stockholders realising after all that the acquisition was actually good for the future business development of BOA.

The news reported that BOA was combining its own large consumer and corporate banking business with ML's global wealth management, advisory expertise, and financial services capabilities and capacities, creating a huge finance corporation that would rival Citigroup Inc.[5]

5 There have been numerous studies on various events of corporate finance involving announcement effects. Two examples are J. Aharony and I. Swary (1980), Quarterly dividend and earnings announcements and stockholders' return: An empirical analysis, *The Journal of Finance*, 35, 1–12, and A. Keown and J. Pinkerton (1981), Merger announcements and insider trading activity, *The Journal of Finance*, 36.

Further Reading

Bodie, Z., A. Kane, and A. J. Marcus (1999), *Investments*, Fourth edition, Irwin McGraw Hill.
Pliska, S. R. (1997), *Introduction to Mathematical Finance: Discrete Time Models*, Blackwell Publishers.

5 Time Series Modeling

A time series is a sequence of random variables at successive times, often, though not necessarily, at regular time intervals. If the realized values are observed, it is a realization of the time series and is sometimes called “time series data”. Sometimes “time series” refers to this realized data series. When we are modeling, we treat it as a sequence of RVs. But when we are doing estimation, it is a series of data. If the data is observed continuously, it is a continuous time series. In this chapter we shall study the probability concepts behind a time series and also discuss time series models used to fit time series data for explanation and for forecasting. We begin by considering a stochastic process that gives rise to a time series. Since the probability results apply more generally, we shall use study stochastic processes when the sequence is indexed more generally according to other possible variables and not just time index.

5.1 Stochastic Process

A stochastic process is a sequence of RVs X_1, X_2, $X_3,\ldots$, and so on. Each X_i has a cumulative distribution function (cdf). A common type of sequence is indexed by time $t_1 < t_2 < t_3 < \ldots$ for $X_{t_1}, X_{t_2}, X_{t_3}, \ldots$, and so on.

A stochastic process $\{X_i\}_{i=1,2,\ldots}$ is said to be weakly (covariance) stationary if each X_i has the same mean and variance, and $\text{cov}(X_i, X_{i+k}) = \gamma(k)$, i. e. a function only dependent on k. As an example, suppose monthly stock return rates r_t where r_1 = return rate in Jan 2009, r_2 = return rate in Feb 2009, etc. form a stochastic process that is weakly stationary. If $\text{var}(r_1) = 0.25$, what is $\text{var}(r_5)$? Clearly, this is the same constant 0.25. If $\text{cov}(r_1, r_3) = 0.10$, what is $\text{cov}(r_7, r_9)$? Clearly, this is 0.10 since the time gap between the two random variables is similarly two months in either case.

The past history or realized values of the return process, $\{r_t\}_{t=1,2,\ldots,60}$, e. g., $\{0.010, -0.005, 0.003, 0.008, -0.012, \ldots, 0.008\}$ is called a time series, which is a time-indexed sequence of sample points of each random variable r_t in the stochastic process $\{r_t\}_t$.

A stochastic process $\{X_i\}_i$ is said to be strongly stationary if each set of $\{X_i, X_{i+1}, X_{i+2}, \ldots, X_{i+k}\}$ for any i and the same k has the same joint multivariate pdf independent of i. As an example, consider joint multivariate normal distribution, MVN. Suppose the following is strongly stationary,

$$\{r_1, r_2, r_3\} \stackrel{d}{\sim} \text{MVN}(M_{3\times1}, \Sigma_{3\times3})$$

then clearly the joint multivariate pdf of $\{r_3, r_4, r_5\}$ has the same MVN (M, Σ).

There are two very important and essential theorems dealing with stochastic processes and, therefore, applicable to the study of time series of empirical data. They are the Law of Large Numbers and the Central Limit Theorem. For the basic proofs of

https://doi.org/10.1515/9783110673951-005

some of the probability laws, we also present several lemmas regarding inequalities and convergences.

5.1.1 Some Important Inequalities

Lemma 5.1 (Markov's Inequality). *If X is a nonnegative* RV, *then for* $a > 0$,

$$P(X \geq a) \leq \frac{E(X)}{a}$$

Proof.

$$E(X) = \int_0^{\infty} xf(x)dx \geq \int_a^{\infty} xf(x)dx \geq a \int_a^{\infty} f(x)dx = aP(X \geq a)$$

Then,

$$\frac{E(X)}{a} \geq P(X \geq a)$$ □

Another way to prove makes use of the indicator function and its expectation as a probability. Suppose RV Y is defined on the same probability space $(\Omega, \mathcal{F}, \mathcal{P})$ as X.

$$Y(\omega) = \begin{cases} 1 & \text{if } X(\omega) \geq a \\ 0 & \text{if } X(\omega) < a \end{cases}$$

Since $X(\omega) \geq 0$, $Y(\omega) \leq \frac{X}{a}$. Thus, $E(Y) \leq \frac{E(X)}{a}$. As $E(Y) = P(X \geq a)$, the inequality is obtained.

Lemma 5.2 (Chebyshev's Inequality). *If X is a RV with mean* μ *and variance* σ^2, *then for* $a > 0$,

$$P(|X - \mu| \geq a) \leq \frac{\sigma^2}{a^2}$$

Proof. Using the Markov inequality, if we use $(X - \mu)^2 > 0$ as a nonnegative RV, and note that $(X - \mu)^2 \geq a^2$ if and only if $(\Leftrightarrow)|X - \mu| \geq a$, then we obtain the result. □

Another version is to use $\frac{(X-\mu)^2}{\sigma^2}$ as the nonnegative RV, then $P(|X - \mu| \geq a\sigma) \leq \frac{1}{a^2}$.

5.2 Law of Large Numbers

Theorem 5.1 (Weak Law of Large Numbers, WLLN). *Let* $\{X_i\}_{i=1,2,\ldots}$ *be a sequence of uncorrelated identical RVs each with mean* μ *and variance* σ^2. *Then, for any* $\epsilon > 0$,

$$P\left(\left|\frac{X_1+X_2+\cdots+X_n}{n}-\mu\right|\geq\epsilon\right)\downarrow 0,\quad as\ n\uparrow\infty$$

Proof. Note that

$$E\left(\frac{X_1+X_2+\cdots+X_n}{n}\right)=\mu$$

and

$$\operatorname{var}\left(\frac{X_1+X_2+\cdots+X_n}{n}\right)=\frac{\sigma^2}{n}$$

From Chebyshev's inequality, therefore,

$$P\left(\left|\frac{X_1+X_2+\cdots+X_n}{n}-\mu\right|\geq\epsilon\right)\leq\frac{\sigma^2}{n\epsilon^2}$$

Thus, as $n\uparrow\infty$, for any given $\epsilon>0$, no matter how small, the probability that the sample mean deviates from μ can be made ever closer to zero. □

The WLLN says that the sample mean in the uncorrelated identical variables case (and obviously also for the special case of i. i. d.) converges in probability to the population mean μ. RVs X above do not need to be identical. The same WLLN result can be obtained if the RVs X have constant finite mean and constant finite variance, and are uncorrelated (but not exactly identical). Stochastic process with constant mean and variance as well as zero covariance is weakly stationary. The WLLN may hold for weakly stationary process in general, i. e. allowing some non-zero covariance, as long as there is some ergodicity, i. e. correlations disappear in longer term. The WLLN gives us some degree of confidence in estimating population parameters such as mean or variance using sample mean or sample variance, respectively, when the sample size is large and the underlying RV is weakly stationary.

5.2.1 Convergence Concepts

Let x be a real number on $(0,1]\in\mathcal{R}$. Let x be represented by a nonterminating (in the sense there are no infinite zeros at the end of the expansion) dyadic expansion, where

$$x=\sum_{n=1}^{\infty}\frac{d_n(x)}{2^n}=\frac{d_1(x)}{2}+\frac{d_2(x)}{2^2}+\frac{d_3(x)}{2^3}+\cdots$$

and $d_n(x)=0$ or 1. Thus, $x=0.d_1(x)d_2(x)\ldots$ in base 2, where $\{d_1(x),d_2(x),d_3(x),\ldots\}$ is an infinite sequence of binary digits 0 or 1. We always use the infinite expansion when there is a choice, e. g., $1/2=0.011111\ldots$ instead of 0.1. Or $3/8=0.01011111\ldots$ instead of 0.011.

The probability of drawing a particular number x from $(0,1] \in \mathcal{R}$ is thus equivalent to the probability of having a particular infinite sequence of binary digits where "1" may denote head and "0" may denote tail as in an infinite number of coin tosses of a fair coin. There will be some elements of $x \in (0,1]$ where the infinite sequence ends with an infinite number of "1" 's or the infinite sequence ends with an infinite repetition of some patterns of "1" 's and "0" 's, e. g., 0.001001001001001... These patterned numbers can be shown as a number indicating fraction of "1" 's in the total number of digits. In this case it is 1/3. Since rational numbers are countable, these patterned numbers form a set M that has zero Lebesgue probability measure.

The event of drawing a particular number $x \in (0,1]$ can be mapped to a particular fraction of the heads or "1" 's, i. e. $\lim_{n\to\infty} \frac{1}{n}\sum_{i=1}^{n} d_i(x)$ associated with a particular infinite sequence of binary digits. The way to formally relate the event of $x \in \Omega$ to the infinite sequence of Bernoulli RVs $d_i(x)$ and its fraction of "1" 's is to think of the probability space $(\Omega, \mathcal{F}, P)$ as comprising an outcome x that is bijective with a time series $\{d_1(x), d_2(x), d_3(x), \ldots\}$. Subsets of x form the σ-field $\mathcal{F}$. P is the probability measure on these subsets. The time series $\{d_1(x), d_2(x), d_3(x), \ldots\}$ itself when each $d_i(x)$ is a Bernoulli RV is a stochastic process. But given the realization of time series $\{d_1(x), d_2(x), d_3(x), \ldots\}$, it is a sample path. Each sample path maps to a fraction of "1" 's. Thus we can evaluate the probability of an event x as probability of a bijective event $\lim_{n\to\infty} \frac{1}{n}\sum_{i=1}^{n} d_i(x)$.

For events or numbers in M, it is possible that

$$\lim_{n\to\infty} \frac{1}{n}\sum_{i=1}^{n} d_i(x) \neq \frac{1}{2}$$

The fraction of "1" 's for the binary number 0.001001001... is 1/3, while that of 0.100010001000... is 1/4, and so on.

However, outside of set M, i. e. in $\Omega\backslash M$, each d_i is a Bernoulli RV with probability 1/2 of taking value 1 and probability 1/2 of taking value 0. Thus, if we perform an infinite number of random fair coin tosses and count the fraction of head occurrences as $\lim_{n\to\infty} \frac{1}{n}\sum_{i=1}^{n} d_i(x_1)$, this limit is 1/2.

Then, for all $x \in A = \Omega\backslash M$, $d_i(x)$ occurs infinitely often as 0 and also infinitely often as 1 as realizations across i, so:

$$P\left(\left[x \in A : \lim_{n\to\infty} \frac{1}{n}\sum_{i=1}^{n} d_i(x) = \frac{1}{2}\right]\right) = 1$$

We see that for any $x \in A$ and therefore any sample path of Bernoulli $d_i(x)$, $\frac{1}{n}\sum_{i=1}^{n} d_i(x)$ converges to 1/2. Since $P(A) = 1$, we say that the almost all events (excepting those with measure zero) are convergences to 1/2, i. e. convergence to 1/2 with probability 1 (w. p. 1).

We also say that $\frac{1}{n}\sum_{i=1}^{n} d_i(x)$ converges to 1/2 almost everywhere (a. e.), or almost surely (a. s.), i. e., it converges to 1/2 except on a set M of probability measure zero.

The a. e. or a. s. convergence is also called a strong convergence. Note the difference of the above strong convergence with convergence in probability discussed earlier via the Chebyshev's inequality and the WLLN, i. e.

$$\lim_{n\to\infty} P\left(\left|\frac{1}{n}\sum_{i=1}^{n} d_i(x) - \frac{1}{2}\right| > \epsilon\right) = 0$$

for any $\epsilon > 0$.

It is seen that convergence in probability is weaker than the almost sure convergence since a sequence $d_i(x)$ could have average $\frac{1}{n}\sum_{i=1}^{n}(d_i(x)-\frac{1}{2})$ with decreasing variance $1/(4n)$ (for uncorrelated sequence) toward zero but for any n, no matter how large, there is a non-zero probability that $\frac{1}{n}\sum_{i=1}^{n}(d_i(x)-\frac{1}{2}) \neq 0$. The latter means that convergence to 1/2 is not everywhere, i. e. there is some set with positive probability measure. no matter how large n is, where convergence is not to 1/2. But with stronger condition of i. i. d. sequence, the almost sure convergence implies convergence in probability since probability of divergence from 1/2 is zero.

In probability, there is another type of convergence in L^p of RVs $X_n \equiv f_n(x) = \frac{1}{n}\sum_{i=1}^{n} d_i(x)$ to $X \equiv f(x) = 1/2$, viz.

$$\lim_{n\to\infty} E(|X_n - X|^p) = 0$$

X_n is said to converge in pth mean to X. For $p = 2$, X_n is said to converge in mean square to X, or notationally as is commonly seen, $X_n \xrightarrow{\mathcal{L}^2} X$.

As an example of convergence in mean square, consider that

$$E\left(\left|\frac{1}{n}\sum_{i=1}^{n} d_i(x) - \frac{1}{2}\right|^2\right) = \text{var}\left(\frac{1}{n}\sum_{i=1}^{n} d_i(x)\right)$$

since $E(\frac{1}{n}\sum_{i=1}^{n} d_i(x)) = \frac{1}{2}$. Now, $\text{var}(\frac{1}{n}\sum_{i=1}^{n} d_i(x)) = \frac{1}{4n}$ for the case of i. i. d. Bernoulli RV d_i, then

$$\lim_{n\to\infty} E\left(\left|\frac{1}{n}\sum_{i=1}^{n} d_i(x) - \frac{1}{2}\right|^2\right) \equiv \lim_{n\to\infty} \text{var}\left(\frac{1}{n}\sum_{i=1}^{n} d_i(x)\right) = 0$$

The result of convergence in mean square can be obtained as long as $\text{var}(\frac{1}{n}\sum_{i=1}^{n} d_i(x))$ converges to zero as $n \uparrow \infty$. By the Chebyshev two-tailed inequality,

$$\lim_{n\to\infty} P\left(\left|\frac{1}{n}\sum_{i=1}^{n} d_i(x) - \frac{1}{2}\right| \geq \epsilon\right) \leq \frac{\text{var}(\frac{1}{n}\sum_{i=1}^{n} d_i(x))}{\epsilon^2}$$

Since the numerator on the RHS approaches zero in the limit as $n \uparrow \infty$, therefore

$$\lim_{n\to\infty} P\left(\left|\frac{1}{n}\sum_{i=1}^{n} d_i(x) - \frac{1}{2}\right| > \epsilon\right) = 0$$

for any $\epsilon > 0$. In the above, we show that convergence in $\mathcal{L}^2 \Rightarrow$ convergence in probability (in P). More generally, convergence in $\mathcal{L}^p (1 \le p < \infty) \Rightarrow$ convergence in P. The converse is not necessarily true.

Convergence a. s. $\Rightarrow$ convergence in P. Hence, convergence a. s. and $\mathcal{L}^p$ convergence are stronger convergence than convergence in P. We show below an example in which for measurable $\omega \in (0,1]$, a sequence of RVs $X_n(\omega)$ converges to 0 in P but not a. e. Note that each event ω gives rise to a sample path of values $X_1, X_2, \ldots$. In terms of notations, the event ω here is equivalent to x in the earlier example on convergence concepts, and $X_n(\omega)$ is equivalent to $d_n(x)$.

$$\begin{array}{lll} X_1 = 1_{(0,1]} & & \\ X_2 = 1_{(0,\frac{1}{2}]} & X_3 = 1_{(\frac{1}{2},1]} & \\ X_4 = 1_{(0,\frac{1}{3}]} & X_5 = 1_{(\frac{1}{3},\frac{2}{3}]} & X_6 = 1_{(\frac{2}{3},1]} \\ \ldots & & \end{array}$$

Each line represents a partition of the interval $(0,1]$. For any $\omega \in (0,1]$, there is one $X_n(\omega)$ value equal to 1 in each line. Hence, as $n \to \infty$, $X_n(\omega)$ will take the value 1 infinitely often. Thus for each $\omega \in (0,1]$, $X_n(\omega)$ does not converge to 0. Neither does it converge to 1. It is like an infinitely alternating series between values 0 and 1. Since

$$P\left(\omega : \lim_{n\to\infty} X_n(\omega) = 0\right) = 0$$

$X_n \nrightarrow 0$ a. s.

For arbitrarily small $\epsilon > 0$, when $n = 1$,

$$P(|X_1 - 0| > \epsilon) = 1 \quad \text{since all } X_1(\omega) = 1 \text{ for all } \omega \in (0,1]$$

When $n = 2$,

$$P(|X_2 - 0| > \epsilon) = 1/2 \quad \text{since } P(\omega : X_2 = 1) = 1/2$$

When $n = 4$,

$$P(|X_4 - 0| > \epsilon) = 1/3 \quad \text{since } P(\omega : X_4 = 1) = 1/3$$

We can see that as $n \to \infty$, $P(\omega : X_n = 1)$ becomes smaller and smaller and tends toward zero. Hence,

$$\lim_{n\to\infty} P(\omega : |X_n(\omega) - 0| > \epsilon) = 0$$

Thus, in this case, X_n converges to zero in P.

A diagrammatic explanation of the two types of a. s. and probability or P convergence of $X_n(\omega)$ is shown in Table 5.1. For a. s. or a. e. convergence, $X_n(\omega_i) \to X(\omega_i)$ for a set $\{\omega_i\} \in A$ such that $P(A) = 1$. For convergence in probability, $P(|X_n - X| > \epsilon)$ converges to zero.

Table 5.1: Illustration of Different Convergence Modes.

Ω	1	...	i	...	n	∞
ω_1	$X_1(\omega_1)$	...	$X_i(\omega_1)$	...	$X_n(\omega_1)$	$\to X(\omega_1)$
ω_2	$X_1(\omega_2)$	...	$X_i(\omega_2)$	...	$X_n(\omega_2)$	$\to X(\omega_2)$
ω_3	$X_1(\omega_3)$	...	$X_i(\omega_3)$	...	$X_n(\omega_3)$	$\to X(\omega_3)$
$\vdots$	$\vdots$	$\vdots$	$\vdots$	$\vdots$	$\vdots$	$\vdots$
All ω:	$P(\|X_1 - X\| > \epsilon)$	...	$P(\|X_i - X\| > \epsilon)$	...	$P(\|X_n - X\| > \epsilon)$	$\to 0$

With the concept of a. e. convergence explained, we now present the Borel–Cantelli lemma before proceeding to the Strong Law of Large Numbers.

Lemma 5.3 (Borel-Cantelli lemma). *If the sum of the probabilities of events $E_n \equiv \{\omega : X_n(\omega) \in A\}$, for A being a set of values, is finite, $\sum_{n=1}^{\infty} P(E_n) < \infty$, then*

$$P\Big(\limsup_{n\to\infty} E_n\Big) = 0$$

The limit supremum (lim sup) or $\lim_{n\to\infty} \sup_{k\geq n} x_k$ of an infinite sequence of numbers $\{x_n\}$ is the least upper bound that occurs infinitely often (i. o.) or else is the limit itself. The limit infimum (lim inf) or $\lim_{n\to\infty} \inf_{k\geq n} x_k$ of an infinite sequence of numbers $\{x_n\}$ is the greatest lower bound that occurs infinitely often (i. o.) or else is the limit itself. However, the limit supremum of an infinite sequence of events $X_n \in A$ (or set $\{\omega\}$ of the σ-field yielding $X_n \in A$) is

$$\limsup_{n\to\infty} \bigcap_{n=1}^{\infty} \bigcup_{k=n}^{\infty} (X_k \in A)$$

If there are elements $\{a \in A\} \in \bigcup_{k=n}^{\infty} X_k, \forall k$, then the limit supremum is the set of $\{a\}$, the set that occurs infinitely often (i. o.) in the sequence of events $(X_n \in A)$.

An example of limit supremum of an infinite sequence of events involving RVs X_n is as follows. Event E_n is defined as $X_n > 0$ with probability $P(E_n) = (\frac{1}{2})^n$, so that $\sum_{n=1}^{\infty} P(E_n) = 1 < \infty$. (Note that this sum is across infinite number of RVs each with a total probability of 1, so $\sum_{n=1}^{\infty} P(\Omega_n) = \infty$.) The Borel-Cantelli lemma states that as $\limsup E_n$ consists of the event that the RV takes value larger than zero, the probability of this event $E_n \equiv (X_n > 0)$ is zero in the limit case of $(X_n > 0)$ where $n \uparrow \infty$. This is obvious since the probability is $(\frac{1}{2})^n \downarrow 0$.

Proof. The sequence of events $\bigcup_{n=k}^{\infty} E_n$ for increasing k is non-increasing, i. e.

$$\bigcup_{n=1}^{\infty} E_n \supseteq \bigcup_{n=2}^{\infty} E_n \supseteq \cdots \supseteq \bigcup_{n=k}^{\infty} E_n \supseteq \cdots \limsup_{n\to\infty} E_n$$

Since

$$P\Big(\limsup_{n\to\infty} E_n\Big) = \lim_{k\to\infty} P\bigg(\bigcup_{n=k}^{\infty} E_n\bigg)$$

and (by sub-additivity), $P(\bigcup_{n=k}^{\infty} E_n) \leq \sum_{n=k}^{\infty} P(E_n)$, then if $\sum_{n=1}^{\infty} E_n < \infty$, $\lim_{k\to\infty} \sum_{n=k}^{\infty} P(E_n) = 0$. Hence

$$P\Big(\limsup_{n\to\infty} E_n\Big) = 0$$

□

Theorem 5.2 (Strong Law of Large Numbers, SLLN).[1] *Let $\{X_i\}_{i=1,2,\ldots}$ be a sequence of i. i. d. RVs each with finite mean μ and finite second and fourth moments. Then, with probability* 1 *or a. s.,*

$$P\bigg(\omega : \lim_{n\to\infty} \frac{X_1(\omega) + X_2(\omega) + \cdots + X_n(\omega)}{n} = \mu\bigg) = 1$$

Proof. Let $S_n(\omega) = X_1(\omega)+X_2(\omega)+\cdots+X_n(\omega)$. Let event E_n be equivalent to $|S_n(\omega)-n\mu| > n\epsilon$ for some small $\epsilon > 0$. By Markov's Inequality,

$$P(|S_n(\omega) - n\mu|^4 \geq n^4\epsilon^4) \leq \frac{E(S_n(\omega) - n\mu)^4}{n^4\epsilon^4}$$

Finite second and fourth moments of $X_n(\omega)$ (for each n across all $\omega \in \Omega$ in the probability space) implies $E(S_n(\omega) - n\mu)^4 \leq Dn^2$ for every n and for some constant D. Hence, for a given small $\epsilon > 0$,

$$\sum_{n=1}^{\infty} P(|S_n(\omega) - n\mu| \geq n\epsilon) \leq \frac{D}{\epsilon^4} \sum_{n=1}^{\infty} \frac{1}{n^2} < \infty$$

since $\sum_{n=1}^{\infty} \frac{1}{n^2} = \frac{\pi^2}{6} < \infty$.[2] Then apply the Borel-Cantelli lemma to obtain

---

1 There are many versions of the law as many mathematical results are intertwined. See Billingsley (2012) for more details.

2 This is the solution by Euler to the Basel problem in 1735. The finiteness on the RHS is not possible with just assumption on finite variance and using Chebyshev's Inequality as it will result in summation $\sum_{n=1}^{\infty} \frac{1}{n}$ which is a harmonic series that is divergent.

$$P\Big(\omega : \limsup_{n\to\infty}(|S_n(\omega)/n - \mu| \geq \epsilon)\Big) = 0$$ □

There is a weak type of convergence – convergence in distribution. First, we define the empirical distribution function (edf) and visit the Glivenko–Cantelli theorem.

Suppose $X_1, X_2, \ldots, X_n$ are i. i. d. random variables with a common distribution function $F(X)$. For a given value y, we can determine if for each i,

$$1_{[X_i \leq y]}(\omega) = \begin{cases} 1 & \text{if } X_i(\omega) \leq y \\ 0 & \text{otherwise} \end{cases}$$

Note that each ω, e. g., a sample path, constitutes a set of values of the random sample of size n. Define an edf of $F(X)$ as

$$\hat{F}_n(y, \omega) = \frac{1}{n}\sum_{i=1}^{n} 1_{[X_i \leq y]}(\omega)$$

across all $\omega \in \Omega$.

Theorem 5.3 (Glivenko–Cantelli). *For a sequence of i. i. d. X_i's, with probability 1 (or for all $\omega \in A \ni$ (such that) $P(A) = 1$),*

$$\lim_{n\to\infty} \sup_{-\infty<y<\infty} |\hat{F}_n(y, \omega) - F(y)| = 0$$

Clearly, given y, for all y, each $1_{[X_i \leq y]}(\omega)$ is an i. i. d. Bernoulli RV with probability $F(y)$ of 1 and probability $1 - F(y)$ of 0. Then by the SLLN, its average $\hat{F}_n(y)$ converges to the population fraction $F(y)$. The "supremum" tells of a stronger, uniform convergence, or convergence at a rate regardless of point y.

We now show the most important result in the convergence of distribution – the Central Limit Theorem.

5.3 Central Limit Theorem

Theorem 5.4. *Suppose $\{X_i\}_{i=1,2,\ldots}$ is a sequence of i. i. d. random variables, each having mean μ and variance σ^2. Then, the RV $\frac{\sum_{i=1}^n X_i - n\mu}{\sigma\sqrt{n}}$ converges in distribution to the standard normal RV as $n \uparrow \infty$.*

(Note that the numerator of the RV has mean 0 and the denominator is the standard deviation of the numerator.)

Proof. We can rewrite the RV $\frac{\sum_{i=1}^n X_i - n\mu}{\sigma\sqrt{n}}$ as $Y_n =^d \sum_{i=1}^n \frac{1}{\sqrt{n}} Z_i$ where $Z_i = \frac{X_i - \mu}{\sigma}$ is i. i. d. with mean 0 and variance 1. For a given n, the MGF of $\sum_{i=1}^n \frac{Z_i}{\sqrt{n}}$ is

$$
\begin{aligned}
M_Y(\theta) &= E\left(\exp\left(\theta\sum_{i=1}^{n}\frac{Z_i}{\sqrt{n}}\right)\right)\\
&= E\left(\prod_{i=1}^{n}\left[\exp\left(\frac{\theta}{\sqrt{n}}Z_i\right)\right]\right)\\
&= \left[M_Z\left(\frac{\theta}{\sqrt{n}}\right)\right]^n
\end{aligned}
$$

where $M_Z(\frac{\theta}{\sqrt{n}}) = E(\exp(\frac{\theta}{\sqrt{n}}Z))$.

Let $t = \theta/\sqrt{n}$ and $Q(t) = \ln M_Z(t)$. Taking derivatives w. r. t. the argument, $\frac{dM(t)}{dt} = M'(t)$, and so on, we have

$$
Q'(t) = \frac{M_Z'(t)}{M_Z(t)}, \quad \text{and} \quad Q''(t) = \frac{M_Z(t)M_Z''(t) - [M_Z'(t)]^2}{[M_Z(t)]^2}
$$

Now, putting $t = 0$, $M_Z(0) = 1$. $Q(0) = \ln M_Z(0) = \ln 1 = 0$. $M_Z'(0) = E(Z) = 0$. Hence $Q'(0) = 0$. $M_Z''(0) = E(Z^2) = 1$. Hence $Q''(0) = 1$. Now, let $t = m\theta$, where $m = 1/\sqrt{n}$. Using the L'Hôpital's rule,

$$
\begin{aligned}
\lim_{m\to 0}\frac{Q(t)}{m^2} &= \lim_{m\to 0}\frac{\frac{dt}{dm}\frac{dQ}{dt}}{2m}\\
&= \lim_{m\to 0}\frac{\theta dQ/dt}{2m}\\
&= \lim_{m\to 0}\frac{\theta^2 d^2Q/dt^2}{2} = \frac{\theta^2}{2}
\end{aligned}
$$

since the argument t in Q goes to zero as $m \to 0$. Re-expressing in terms of n instead of m,

$$
\lim_{n\to\infty} nQ\left(\frac{\theta}{\sqrt{n}}\right) = \frac{\theta^2}{2}
$$

or,

$$
\lim_{n\to\infty}\left[M_Z\left(\frac{\theta}{\sqrt{n}}\right)\right]^n = e^{\frac{\theta^2}{2}}
$$

$M_Y(\theta)$ converges to $e^{\frac{\theta^2}{2}}$ which is the MGF of a standard normal RV. Hence Y_n converges to $N(0,1)$. □

The above result is usually called the Lindeberg-Levý Central Limit Theorem. There are other more complicated versions of the CLT, some dealing with weaker requirements such as independence but allowing heterogeneous variances such as in the Lindeberg–Levy–Feller theorem. In such cases, the variances also have to be bounded in some way to enable convergence. The speed toward convergence or rate of convergence, i. e. how large n must be in order to get to within certain probabilistic deviation or "closeness" of the limit, is obviously slower when the conditions for CLT become more relaxed. When $E|X_i|^3 < \infty$, i. e., it is bounded, the Berry–Esseen theorem gives an idea of the rate of convergence in CLT.

We have seen how convergence to 0 of $\sum_i^n X_i - n\mu$ is achieved by suitable division (or "normalization") by n, and convergence to RV $N(0,1)$ is achieved by a different normalization by $\sigma\sqrt{n}$. Thus, normalization by anything between n and $\sigma\sqrt{n}$ can produce interesting results. CLT enables meaningful statistical testing and inference. Another related law, the law of iterated logarithm deals with characterizing how the partial sum $\sum_i^n X_i - n\mu$ would behave as n increases.

Convergence in distribution or in law is, however, a weak convergence, and generally does not imply the stronger a. s. convergence or convergence in P. For example, given a binomial distribution $X_n \sim B(n,p)$, $X_n' = \frac{X_n - np}{\sqrt{np(1-p)}}$ converges to a standard normal distribution. But the discrete values of the binomial RV are just a countable set of points $\in \mathcal{R}$ with measure zero in continuous $\mathcal{R}$. Thus, convergence of RV X_n' in distribution to $Z \sim N(0)$ does not imply that RV X_n' converges to Z in probabiliy or converges a. s. (w. p. 1). On the contrary, convergence in P and also convergence w. p. 1 imply convergence in distribution. Here, unlike convergence a. s. or convergence in probability where the sample space of general X_n and X are the same, convergence in distribution does not necessarily imply X_n' shares the same sample space as the convergent RV Z as seen in the binomial case.

We show below how convergence in probability implies convergence in distribution. The converse is true only when the convergence in distribution is to a constant or a degenerate distribution. Suppose sequence of RVs X_n converges to RV X in probability. The corresponding continuous cdfs are $F_n(X_n)$ and $F(X)$.

For any $\varepsilon > 0$, consider joint event $\{X_n \le u, X \le u+\varepsilon\} \subseteq \{X \le u+\varepsilon\}$, hence $P(X_n \le u, X \le u+\varepsilon) \le P(X \le u+\varepsilon) = F(u+\varepsilon)$. Also consider joint event $\{X_n \le u, X > u+\varepsilon\}$ that implies event $\{X_n - X < -\varepsilon\}$. The latter implies event $\{|X_n - X| > \varepsilon\}$. Hence $P(X_n \le u, X > u+\varepsilon) \le P(|X_n - X| > \varepsilon)$. Therefore, for any $\varepsilon > 0$,

$$\begin{aligned} P(X_n \le u) &= P(X_n \le u, X \le u+\varepsilon) + P(X_n \le u, X > u+\varepsilon) \\ &\le F(u+\varepsilon) + P(|X_n - X| > \varepsilon) \end{aligned}$$

Similarly, consider joint event $\{X_n \le u, X \le u-\varepsilon\} \subseteq \{X_n \le u\}$, hence $P(X_n \le u, X \le u-\varepsilon) \le P(X_n \le u) = F_n(u)$. Also consider joint event $\{X_n > u, X \le u-\varepsilon\}$ that implies event $\{X_n - X > \varepsilon\}$. The latter implies event $\{|X_n - X| > \varepsilon\}$. Hence $P(X_n > u, X \le u-\varepsilon) \le P(|X_n - X| > \varepsilon)$. Therefore, for any $\varepsilon > 0$,

$$\begin{aligned} P(X \le u-\varepsilon) &= P(X \le u-\varepsilon, X_n \le u) + P(X \le u-\varepsilon, X_n > u) \\ &\le F_n(u) + P(|X_n - X| > \varepsilon) \end{aligned}$$

Thus for any $\varepsilon > 0$,

$$F(u-\varepsilon) - P(|X_n - X| > \varepsilon) \le F_n(u) \le F(u+\varepsilon) + P(|X_n - X| > \varepsilon)$$

If X_n converges to X in probability, then $\lim_{n\to\infty} P(|X_n - X| > \varepsilon) = 0$. If $F(\cdot)$ is continuous, then as $n \uparrow \infty$, $F_n(u)$ converges to $F(u)$, that is convergence in distribution of X_n.

5.3.1 Applications

The normal distribution can be used as an approximation to both the binomial and the Poisson distributions . Consider a random sample $\{X_i\}_{i=1,2,\ldots}$ with each RV $X_i = 1$ or 0 from a Bernoulli distribution of an event happening, and $X_i = 1$ has probability p. The mean and variance of X_i are p and $p(1-p)$. Suppose the random sample consists of n such Bernoulli RVs. Then aggregate outcome $Y_n = X_1 + X_2 + \cdots + X_n$ follows the binomial distribution with mean np and variance $np(1-p)$.

By the CLT, therefore $\frac{\sum_{i=1}^n X_i - np}{\sqrt{np(1-p)}}$ or $\frac{Y_n - np}{\sqrt{np(1-p)}}$ converges toward a $N(0,1)$ as $n \to \infty$. For large n, therefore, $Y_n \approx N(\mu, \sigma^2)$ where $\mu = np$, and $\sigma^2 = np(1-p)$.

Consider a stock price process that increases in price by factor 1.01 with probability 0.6 and decreases in price by factor 0.99 with probability 0.4 over each short time interval. After 60 such intervals, the binomial probability of exactly $Y = 40$ price increases (and 20 price decreases) is

$$\begin{aligned} &P(Y = 40; p = 0.6, n = 60) \\ &= \binom{60}{40}(0.6)^{40}(0.4)^{20} \\ &= 0.0616 \end{aligned}$$

This is also the case that the stock price after 60 intervals had risen by a factor of $1.01^{40}(0.99)^{20} = 1.2178$.

Using normal approximation $P(Y = 40) \approx P(39.5 \le Z \le 40.5)$ where Z is normally distributed with mean $60(0.6) = 36$ and variance $60(0.6)(0.4) = 14.4$. Hence,

$$\begin{aligned} P(Y = 40) &\approx P(39.5 \le Z \le 40.5) \\ &= P\left(\frac{39.5-36}{\sqrt{14.4}} \le \frac{Z-36}{\sqrt{14.4}} \le \frac{40.5-36}{\sqrt{14.4}}\right) \\ &= \Phi(1.185854) - \Phi(0.922331) = 0.0603 \end{aligned}$$

A Poisson approximation to the binomial problem would yield $P(Y = 40; \lambda = np = 36) = e^{-36}(36)^{40}/40! = 0.0508$. The CLT also affords a way in which the standardized Poisson RV $\frac{X-\lambda}{\sqrt{\lambda}}$ (where X is Poisson(λ)) with mean 0 and variance 1 may approximately be normal for large λ.

To show this, we consider the MGF of $\frac{X-\lambda}{\sqrt{\lambda}}$. We use the fact that the MGF of X, $M_X(\theta)$, is $\exp(\lambda(e^\theta - 1))$. We also employ the Taylor series expansion of an exponential function.

$$E\left(\exp\left[\theta\left(\frac{X-\lambda}{\sqrt{\lambda}}\right)\right]\right)$$
$$= \exp(-\theta\sqrt{\lambda})E\left(\exp\left[\frac{\theta}{\sqrt{\lambda}}X\right]\right)$$
$$= \exp(-\theta\sqrt{\lambda})\exp(\lambda(e^{\theta/\sqrt{\lambda}}-1))$$
$$= \exp(-\theta\sqrt{\lambda})\exp\left(\lambda\left[\theta/\sqrt{\lambda}+\frac{1}{2!}(\theta/\sqrt{\lambda})^2+\frac{1}{3!}(\theta/\sqrt{\lambda})^3+\cdots\right]\right)$$
$$= \exp(-\theta\sqrt{\lambda})\exp\left(\theta\sqrt{\lambda}+\frac{1}{2!}\theta^2+\frac{1}{3!}(\theta^3/\sqrt{\lambda})+o(\lambda)\right)$$
$$= \exp\left(\frac{1}{2!}\theta^2+\frac{1}{3!}(\theta^3/\sqrt{\lambda})+o(\lambda)\right)$$
$$\to \exp\left(\frac{1}{2}\theta^2\right) \quad \text{as } \lambda\uparrow\infty$$

5.4 Stock Return Rates

In finance, the lognormal distribution is important. A pertinent example is a stock price at time t, P_t. There are several empirically observed characteristics of stock price that are neat and could be appropriately captured by the lognormal probability distribution model.

(1a) $P_t > 0$, i. e. prices must be strictly positive.
(1b) Return rates derived from stock prices over time are normally distributed when measured over a sufficiently long interval, e. g., a month.
(1c) Returns could display a small trend or drift, i. e., they increase or decrease over time.
(1d) The ex-ante anticipated variance of return rate increases with the holding period.

We examine the case when P_t is lognormally distributed to see if this distribution offers the above characteristics. Lognormally distributed P_t means that $\ln P_t \overset{d}{\sim} N$, Normal. Thus, $P_t = \exp(N) > 0$ where N is a normal random variable. Hence, (1a) is satisfied. Likewise, $\ln P_{t+1} \overset{d}{\sim}$ Normal. Therefore, $\ln P_{t+1} - \ln P_t \overset{d}{\sim}$ Normal or, $\ln(P_{t+1}/P_t) \overset{d}{\sim}$ Normal.

Now $\ln(P_{t+1}/P_t) \equiv r_{t,t+1}$ is the continuously compounded stock return over holding period or interval $(t, t+1]$. If the time interval or each period is small, this is approximately the discrete return rate $(P_{t+1}/P_t) - 1$. However, the discrete return rate is bounded from below by -1. Contrary to that, the return $r_{t,t+1}$ has $(-\infty, \infty)$ as support, as in a normal distribution.

We can justify how $r_{t,t+1}$ can reasonably be assumed as being normally distributed, or equivalently, that the price is lognormally distributed, over a longer time interval.

Consider a small time interval or period $\Delta = 1/T$, such that $\ln(P_{t+\Delta}/P_t)$, the small interval continuously compounded return, is a random variable (not necessarily normal) with mean $\mu\Delta = \mu/T$, and variance $\sigma^2\Delta = \sigma^2/T$. The allowance of small $\mu \neq 0$ in the above satisfies (1c). We may assume that each continuously compounded return over the small interval is i. i. d.

Aggregating the returns,

$$\ln\left(\frac{P_{t+\Delta}}{P_t}\right) + \ln\left(\frac{P_{t+2\Delta}}{P_{t+\Delta}}\right) + \ln\left(\frac{P_{t+3\Delta}}{P_{t+2\Delta}}\right) + \cdots + \ln\left(\frac{P_{t+T\Delta}}{P_{t+(T-1)\Delta}}\right) = \ln\left(\frac{P_{t+T\Delta}}{P_t}\right) \tag{5.1}$$

The right-hand side of Eq. (5.1) is simply the continuously compounded return $\ln(P_{t+1}/P_t) \equiv r_{t,t+1}$ over the longer period $[t, t+1)$, where the length is made up of $T = 1/\Delta$ number of Δ periods. The left-hand side of Eq. (5.1), invoking the Central Limit Theorem, for large T, is $N(T\mu\Delta, T\sigma^2\Delta)$ or $N(\mu, \sigma^2)$ since $T\Delta = 1$. Hence, $r_{t,t+1} \sim N(\mu, \sigma^2)$, which satisfies (1b) and justifies the use of lognormal distribution for prices.

Moreover, $P_{t+k} = P_t e^{r_{t,t+k}} > 0$ even if return $r_{t,t+k}$ may sometimes be negative. Suppose the returns $r_{t,t+1}, r_{t+1,t+2}, r_{t+2,t+3}, \ldots, r_{t+k-1,t+k}$ are independent. Then,

$$\operatorname{var}\left(\ln \frac{P_{t+k}}{P_t}\right) = \operatorname{var}\left(\sum_{j=0}^{k-1} r_{t+j,t+j+1}\right) = k\sigma^2$$

Thus, ex-ante variance of return increases with holding period $(t, t+k]$. This satisfies characteristic (1d).

It is important to recognize that the simple holding period return rate $(P_{t+1}/P_t) - 1$ does not display some of the appropriate characteristics. The simple returns have to be aggregated geometrically in the following way.

$$\frac{P_{t+1}}{P_t} = 1 + R_{t,t+1}$$

$$\frac{P_{t+k}}{P_t} = \prod_{j=0}^{k-1} \frac{P_{t+j+1}}{P_{t+j}} = \prod_{j=0}^{k-1} (1 + R_{t+j,t+j+1}) \in [0, \infty)$$

The lower boundary of zero is implied by the limited liability of owners of listed stocks. This return computation is cumbersome and poses analytical intractability when it comes to computing drifts and variances. It is straightforward to compute the means and variances of the sums of random variables as in the case of the continuously compounded returns, but not so for the products of random variables when they are not necessarily independent, as in the case of the discrete period simple returns here.

5.4.1 Test of Normality

Given the importance of the role of the normal distribution in financial returns data, it is not surprising that many statistics have been devised to test if a given sample of data $\{r_i\}$ comes from a normal distribution. One such statistic is the Jarque-Bera (JB) test of normality.[3] The test is useful only when the sample size n is large (sometimes, we call such a test an asymptotic test).

The JB test statistic $= n[(\hat{\gamma}^2/6)+((\hat{\kappa}-3)^2/24)] \sim^d \chi_2^2$, where $\hat{\gamma}$ is the skewness estimate of $\{r_i\}$ and $\hat{\kappa}$ is the kurtosis estimate of $\{r_i\}$. Note that the inputs of these measures to the JB test statistic are sample estimates where

$$\hat{\gamma} = \frac{\frac{1}{n}\sum_{i=1}^{n}(r_i - \bar{r})^3}{\hat{\sigma}^3}$$

$$\hat{\kappa} = \frac{\frac{1}{n}\sum_{i=1}^{n}(r_i - \bar{r})^4}{\hat{\sigma}^4}$$

$$\bar{r} = \frac{1}{n}\sum_{i=1}^{n} r_i$$

$$\text{and} \quad \hat{\sigma}^2 = \frac{1}{n}\sum_{i=1}^{n}(r_i - \bar{r})^2$$

For $\{r_i\}$ to follow a normal distribution, its skewness sample estimate $\hat{\gamma}$ should converge toward 0, since the normal distribution is symmetrical with third moment being zero, and its kurtosis sample estimate $\hat{\kappa}$ should converge toward 3. If the JB statistic is too large, exceeding say the 95th percentile of a χ^2 distribution with two degrees of freedom, or 5.99, then the null hypothesis, H_0, of normal distribution is rejected. The JB statistic is large if $\hat{\gamma}$ and $(\hat{\kappa} - 3)$ deviate materially from zero.

5.4.2 Case Study: American Express Company Stock Returns

We provide an example of the stock return sample distributions of the American Express Company. The American Express Company (AXP) is one of the Dow Jones Industrial Average's 30 companies, and is a large diversified international company specialising in financial services including the iconic AMEX card services. It is globally traded. The AXP daily stock returns in a five-year period from 1/3/2003 to 12/31/2007 are collected from public source Yahoo Finance and processed as follows.

The return rates are daily continuously compounded return rates $\ln(P_{t+1}/P_t)$. Thus, weekly as well as monthly stock returns can be easily computed from the daily

3 See C. M. Jarque and A. K. Bera (1987), A test for normality of observations and regression residuals, *International Statistical Review*, 55, 163–172.

return rates. The continuously compounded weekly return rate would be the sum of the daily return rates for the week, Monday to Friday. The continuously compounded monthly return rate would be the sum of the daily return rates for the month. As there are typically about five trading days in a week, and stocks are traded mainly through Stock Exchanges that operate on a five-day week, the weekly return is computed from the sum of five daily return rates. Similarly, there are only about 21 to 22 trading days on average in a month for adding up to the monthly return. Yearly or annual return will be summed over about 252–260 trading days in a year. (An outlier of more than 12 % drop in a single day in the database on 2005 October 3rd was dropped.)

Tuesday's (one-day) return rate is usually computed as the log (natural logarithm) of close of Tuesday's stock price relative to close of Monday's price. Unlike other days, however, one has to be sensitive to the fact that Monday's return cannot be usually computed as the log (natural logarithm) of close of Monday's stock price relative to close of Friday's price. The latter return spans three days, and some may argue that the Monday daily return should be a third of this, although it is also clearly the case that Saturday and Sunday have no trading. Some may use closing price relative to the opening price on the same day to compute daily returns. Open-to-close return signifies return captured during daytime trading when the Exchange is open. However, close-to-open return signifies the price change that has taken place overnight. We shall not be concerned with these issues for the present purpose.

The three series of daily, weekly, and monthly return rates are tabulated in histograms. Descriptive statistics of these distributions such as mean, standard deviation, skewness, and kurtosis are reported. The Jarque-Bera tests for the normality of the distributions are also conducted.

In Figure 5.1, the JB test statistic shows a p-value of < 0.000, thus normality is rejected at significance level 0.0005 or 0.05 % for the daily returns. The mean return in the sampling period is 0.0377 % per day, or about $252 \times 0.0377 = 9.5$ % per annum. The daily return standard deviation or volatility is 1.333 %.

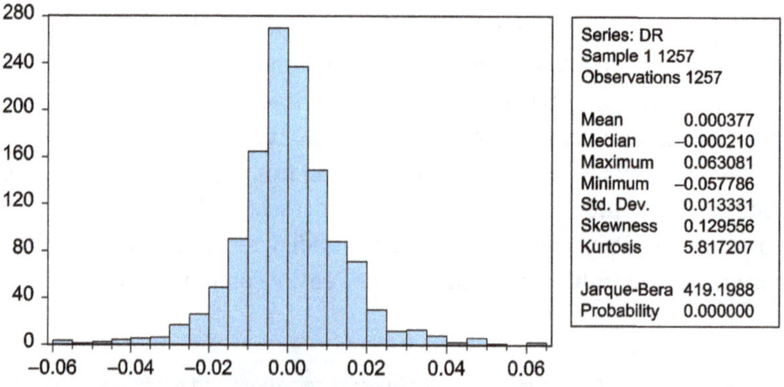

Figure 5.1: Histogram and Statistics of Daily AXP Stock Return Rates.

If the continuously compounded return were independently identically distributed, the annual volatility may be computed as $\sqrt{252} \times 0.01333 = 21.16\,\%$. Figure 5.1 indicates AXP stock has positive skewness during this sampling period. Its kurtosis of 5.817 exceeds 3.0, which is the kurtosis of a normally distributed random variable.

In Figure 5.2, the JB test statistic shows a p-value of < 0.000, thus normality is also rejected at significance level 0.0005 or 0.05 % for the weekly returns.

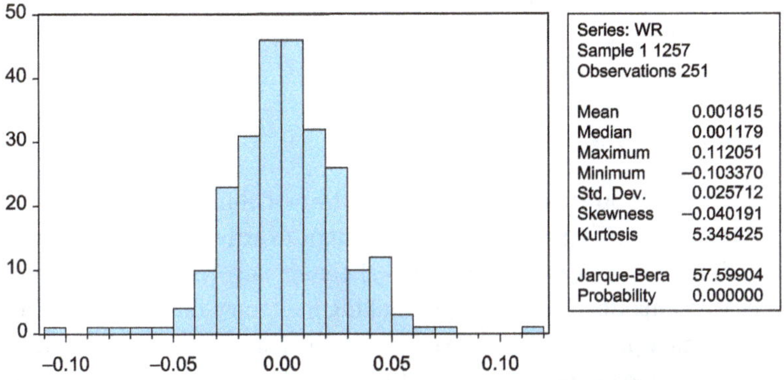

Figure 5.2: Histogram and Statistics of Weekly AXP Stock Return Rates.

In Figure 5.3, the JB test statistic shows a p-value of 0.799. Thus, normality is not rejected at significance level 0.10 or 10 %. (Indeed, it is not rejected even at significance level of 75 %. Sometimes, we may call the p-value the exact significance level.)

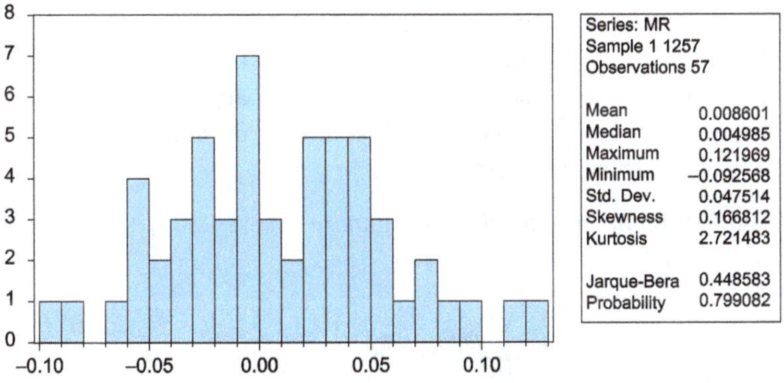

Figure 5.3: Histogram and Statistics of Monthly AXP Stock Return Rates.

In the legend boxes of the figures, note that sample size $n = 1257$ for the daily returns, $n = 251$ for the weekly returns, and $n = 57$ for the monthly returns. It is interesting to note that daily and weekly stock return rates are usually not normal, but aggregation to monthly return rates produces normality as would be expected by our earlier discussion on Central Limit Theorem. This result has important implications in financial modelling of stock returns. Short interval return rates such as daily returns should not be modeled as normal given our findings. In fact, the descriptive statistics of the return rates for different intervals above show that shorter interval return rates tend to display higher kurtosis or "fat" tail in the pdf. Many recent studies of shorter interval return rates introduce other kinds of distributions or else stochastic volatility and jump processes to produce returns with "fatter" tails or higher kurtosis than that of the normal distribution.

5.5 Time Series Models

In this section, we study the Box-Jenkins approach[4] to the modelling of time series. The approach is systematic, involving a recipe of careful steps to arrive at the appropriate process for modelling and forecasting purposes. The steps involve identification of the time series process, making it stationary or making it as some differencings of an underlying nonstationary process, estimating the identified model, then validating it. We shall also study an important application to the modelling of inflation rates in the economy.

A basic building block of stationary processes is a white noise. A white noise process $\{u_t\}$ is one where each u_t has zero mean, constant variance $\sigma_u^2 < \infty$, and in addition has zero serial correlation. Call this the weak-form white noise. It is a special case of weakly or covariance-stationary process with zero mean and zero autocorrelation. A stronger version of white noise has u_t that is independent of u_{t-k} and u_{t+k} for any $k \neq 0$. Here (probability density function, if it exists), $\text{pdf}(u_t|u_{t-k}, u_{t+k}) \equiv \text{pdf}(u_t)$ for $k \neq 0$. An even stronger version is where $u_t \sim \text{i. i. d.}$

Most covariance-stationary processes can be formed from linear combinations of weak-form white noises. We shall use the covariance-stationary (weak-form) white noise in the following. The Wold Theorem states that any covariance-stationary process can be constructed from white noises.

Theorem 5.5 (Wold Theorem). *Any covariance-stationary time series $\{Y_t : t \in \mathbb{Z}\}$ can be represented in the form*

$$Y_t = \sum_{j=0}^{\infty} \psi_j u_{t-j} + \eta_t$$

where $\psi_0 = 1$, $\sum_{j=1}^{\infty} \psi_j^2 < \infty$, u_t is white noise and has zero correlation with Y_{t-j} (for $j > 0$), and η_t is deterministic.

4 Refer to Box and Jenkins (1970).

Proof. Given $\{Y_t : t \in \mathbb{Z}\}$ is a covariance-stationary process, define an orthogonal projection of RV Y_t on lagged variables of itself:

$$P[Y_t|Y_{t-1},\ldots,Y_{t-n}] = b_0(n) + b_1(n)Y_{t-1} + \cdots + b_n(n)Y_{t-n}$$

for any integer $n > 0$, where the projection constants $b_j(n) < \infty$ (for $0 \le j \le n$) are determined by minimizing $E(u_t^2)$ where $u_t = Y_t - b_0(n) - b_1(n)Y_{t-1} - \cdots - b_n(n)Y_{t-n}$. Minimization gives first order conditions such that $E(u_t) = 0$ and $E(u_t Y_{t-j}) = 0$ (for every $j = 1, 2, \ldots, n$), hence the orthogonality, i. e. u_t has zero correlation with all Y_{t-j} for $1 \le j \le n$. Note also that coefficients $b_j(n)$ for $0 \le j \le n$ may be different for different n as different numbers of lagged variables are used.

Since $u_{t-k} = Y_{t-k} - b_0(n) - b_1(n)Y_{t-k-1} - \cdots - b_n(n)Y_{t-k-n}$ (for $k \ge 1$), $\text{cov}(u_t, u_{t-k}) = 0$ as the covariances of u_t with all terms involving Y_{t-k}, $Y_{t-k-1} \ldots$ etc. are zeros. Also, $\text{var}(u_{t-k})$ is a sum involving variances of Y_{t-k-j} and covariances of Y_{t-k-j}'s. This variance is constant σ_u^2 for every k as Y_t is covariance-stationary. Hence u_t is a white noise.

We assume the projection limit exists, i. e.

$$\lim_{n\to\infty} P[Y_{t+k}|Y_{t-1},\ldots,Y_{t-n}] = P[Y_{t+k}|Y_{t-1},Y_{t-2},\ldots]$$

or,

$$\begin{aligned} Y_t &= u_t + P[Y_t|Y_{t-1},Y_{t-2},\ldots] = u_t + b_0 + b_1 Y_{t-1} + b_2 Y_{t-2} + b_3 Y_{t-3} + \cdots \\ &= u_t + b_0 + b_1(u_{t-1} + b_0 + b_1 Y_{t-2} + \cdots) + b_2(u_{t-2} + b_0 + b_1 Y_{t-3} + \cdots) + \cdots \end{aligned}$$

Hence $Y_t = u_t + (\psi_1 u_{t-1} + \psi_2 u_{t-2} + \psi_3 u_{t-3} + \cdots) + \eta_t$ where η_t equals sum of terms involving products of b_j's (assume this sum converges) and is deterministic. $\psi_1 = b_1$, $\psi_2 = b_1^2 + b_2$, and so on. Moreover, $\text{var}(Y_t) = \sigma_u^2 \sum_{j=1}^{\infty} \psi_j^2 < \infty$, so $\sum_{j=1}^{\infty} \psi_j^2 < \infty$. □

The Wold Theorem is sometimes referred to as the "Wold Decomposition Theorem" due to the decomposition into the stochastic sum of white noises and the deterministic part. If we are working with covariance-stationary process $\{Y_t\}$ that has zero mean, then by Wold theorem, it can be represented by $Y_t = \sum_{j=0}^{\infty} \psi_j u_{t-j}$ without the deterministic component.

The use of lag (or backward-shift) and forward-shift operators are convenient in time series models. A lag operator L is an operation on a time series that shifts the entire series or else one RV one step back in time. For example, $LY_t = Y_{t-1}$. Lag operator has properties similar to multiplication:

(2a) commutative: $L(aY_t) = aL(Y_t)$
(2b) distributive over addition: $L(Y_t + X_t) = LY_t + LX_t$
(2c) operating on constant c: $Lc = c$
(2d) operator exists in the limit: $\lim_{j\to\infty}(1 + \phi L + \phi^2 L^2 + \cdots + \phi^j L^j) = (1 - \phi L)^{-1}$

For any covariance-stationary zero mean time series, the Wold representation $Y_t = \sum_{j=0}^{\infty} \psi_j u_{t-j} = \psi(L)u_t$, where $\psi(L) = \sum_{j=0}^{\infty} \psi_j L^j$, has an infinite number of parameters ψ_j's to be estimated, hence it is not feasible for statistical work with finite sample. As a practical matter, the principle of parsimony advocates using time series models that have fewer parameters. The Wold representation can be approximated by the ratio of two finite-lag polynomials:

$$\psi(L) \approx \frac{\theta(L)}{\phi(L)}$$

Suppose a covariance-stationary process is modeled by $Y_t = \frac{\theta(L)}{\phi(L)} u_t$ or, $\phi(L)Y_t = \theta(L)u_t$ where u_t is white noise $\sim (0, \sigma_u^2)$. $\phi(L) = 1 - \phi_1 L - \phi_2 L^2 - \cdots - \phi_p L^p$ and $\theta(L) = 1 + \theta_1 L + \theta_2 L^2 + \cdots + \theta_q L^q$.

Here process $\{Y_t\}$ is autoregressive (AR) with order p and also has a moving average (MA) noise with order q, i. e., it is an ARMA(p, q) process. We shall be concerned to ensure that the $\{Y_t\}$ process we use involving arbitrary $\theta(L)$ and $\phi(L)$ must be stationary. For the part on the RHS which is a MA(q) process, $\theta(L)u_t$ is covariance-stationary if q is finite since $E[\theta(L)u_t] = 0$ and $\text{var}[\theta(L)u_t]$ is a sum of q terms of finite weights θ_j^2 with σ_u^2.

But we have to check that the LHS $\phi(L)Y_t$ is indeed covariance-stationary, This is also a check in general if any AR(p) process, for finite p, is covariance-stationary. Let $\phi(L)Y_t = v_t$ where v_t is white noise $\sim (0, \sigma_v^2)$. Thus $(1 - \phi_1 L - \phi_2 L^2 - \cdots - \phi_p L^p)Y_t = v_t$.

Replacing the L operator with variable z, $1 - \phi_1 z - \phi_2 z^2 - \cdots - \phi_p z^p = 0$ is called the characteristic equation. The p number of solutions z^* are called the characteristic roots. Note that if any root $|z^*| = 1$ (we use modulus $|z|$ as a measure since some roots may be complex), the process is non-stationary. For example, for AR(1), if $1 - \phi_1 z = 0$ has a solution $z^* = 1$, then $\phi_1 = 1/z^* = 1$. Therefore the process is $Y_t = Y_{t-1} + v_t$. So $\text{var}(Y_t)$ increases with t, and Y_t is non-stationary. But if $|z^*| > 1$ (i. e., characteristic root is outside the unit circle), then $\phi_1 < 1$ so $Y_t = \phi_1 Y_{t-1} + v_t$ and $\text{var}(Y_t) = \sigma_v^2/(1 - \phi_1^2) < \infty$. Hence Y_t is covariance-stationary.

In economic and financial modeling, typically a low order ARMA(p, q) process is used. Consider the following time series process to model how random variable Y_t evolves through time. They are all constructed from the basic white noise process $\{u_t\}_{t=-\infty,\ldots,+\infty}$ where u_t has zero mean, variance σ_u^2, and zero serial correlations. For estimation purposes, we add the assumption of u_t being i. i. d.

(3a) Autoregressive order one, AR(1), process:

$$Y_t = \theta + \lambda Y_{t-1} + u_t, \quad \lambda \neq 0, \tag{5.2}$$

where Y_t depends on or autoregresses on its lag value, Y_{t-1}.

(3b) Moving average order one, MA(1), process:

$$Y_t = \theta + u_t + \alpha u_{t-1}, \quad \alpha \neq 0 \tag{5.3}$$

where the residual is made of a moving average of two white noises u_t and u_{t-1}.

(3c) Autoregressive Moving Average order one-one process, ARMA:

$$Y_t = \theta + \lambda Y_{t-1} + u_t + \alpha u_{t-1}, \quad \lambda \neq 0, \quad \alpha \neq 0 \tag{5.4}$$

where Y_t autoregresses on its first lag, and the residual is also a moving average.

5.6 Autoregressive Process

Consider the AR(1) process:

$$Y_t = \theta + \lambda Y_{t-1} + u_t, \quad (\lambda \neq 0), \ t = -T, \ldots, T \tag{5.5}$$

where $\{u_t\}$ is i. i. d. with zero mean, i. e. $E(u_t) = 0$ for every t, and $\text{var}(u_t) = \sigma_u^2$. Note that this is a regression of a stationary random variable Y_t on its lag Y_{t-1}.

It is important to recognize that since the process holds for $t = -T, \ldots, T$, the process is equivalent to a system of equations as follows.

$$\begin{aligned}
Y_T &= \theta + \lambda Y_{T-1} + u_T \\
Y_{T-1} &= \theta + \lambda Y_{T-2} + u_{T-1} \\
&\vdots \\
Y_1 &= \theta + \lambda Y_0 + u_1 \\
&\vdots \\
Y_{-T+1} &= \theta + \lambda Y_{-T} + u_{-T+1}
\end{aligned}$$

These equations are stochastic, not deterministic, as each equation contains a random variable u_t that is not observable.

By repeated substitution for Y_t in this AR(1) process,

$$\text{Eq. (5.5)} \Rightarrow Y_t = \theta + \lambda(\theta + \lambda Y_{t-2} + u_{t-1}) + u_t$$

or

$$\begin{aligned}
Y_t &= (1 + \lambda)\theta + \lambda^2 Y_{t-2} + (u_t + \lambda u_{t-1}) \\
&= \cdots \\
&= (1 + \lambda + \lambda^2 + \lambda^3 + \cdots)\theta + (u_t + \lambda u_{t-1} + \lambda^2 u_{t-2} + \cdots)
\end{aligned}$$

For each t,

$$\begin{aligned}
E(Y_t) &= (1 + \lambda + \lambda^2 + \lambda^3 + \cdots)\theta \\
&= \frac{\theta}{1 - \lambda} \quad \text{provided } |\lambda| < 1
\end{aligned}$$

Otherwise if $|\lambda| \geq 1$, either a finite mean does not exist or the mean is not constant under an initial condition $E(Y_{-T}) = c_0$ an arbitrary constant not related to θ.

$$\begin{aligned}\text{var}(Y_t) &= \text{var}(u_t + \lambda u_{t-1} + \cdots + \lambda^k u_{t-k} + \cdots) \\ &= \sigma_u^2(1 + \lambda^2 + \lambda^4 + \cdots) \\ &= \frac{\sigma_u^2}{1-\lambda^2} \quad \text{provided } |\lambda| < 1\end{aligned}$$

Otherwise if $|\lambda| \geq 1$, either a finite variance does not exist or the variance is not constant under an initial condition $\text{var}(Y_{-T}) = c_1$, a constant.

Autocovariance of Y_t and Y_{t-1}, or

$$\begin{aligned}\text{cov}(Y_t, Y_{t-1}) &= \text{cov}(\theta + \lambda Y_{t-1} + u_t, Y_{t-1}) \\ &= \lambda \frac{\sigma_u^2}{1-\lambda^2}. \\ \text{corr}(Y_t, Y_{t-1}) &= \lambda\end{aligned}$$

The autocorrelation coefficient lag k, $\rho(k)$, is obtained by dividing the autocovariance lag k of Y_t and Y_{t-k}, $\gamma(k)$, by the variance of Y_t. As $\gamma(k) = \lambda^k \frac{\sigma_u^2}{1-\lambda^2}$, corr $(Y_t, Y_{t-k}) \equiv \rho(k) = \lambda^k$.

Hence, we see that the AR(1) Y_t process is covariance-stationary with constant mean $= \theta/(1-\lambda)$, constant variance $= \sigma_u^2/(1-\lambda^2)$, and autocorrelation lag k, $\rho(k) = \lambda^{|k|}$, a function of k only, provided $|\lambda| < 1$.

As a numerical example, suppose

$$Y_t = 2.5 + 0.5Y_{t-1} + u_t \tag{5.6}$$

Assume Y_{t-1} and u_t are stationary normally distributed, and not correlated. It is given that $E(u_t) = 0$, and $\text{var}(u_t) = 3$.

Stationarity implies $E(Y_t) = E(Y_{t-1}) = \mu_Y$, and $\text{var}(Y_t) = \text{var}(Y_{t-1}) = \sigma_Y^2$. If we take unconditional expectation on Eq. (5.6),

$$E(Y_t) = 2.5 + 0.5E(Y_{t-1}) + E(u_t)$$

So, $\mu_Y = 2.5 + 0.5\mu_Y$, then $\mu_Y = \frac{2.5}{(1-0.5)} = 5$.

If we take unconditional variance on Eq. (5.6),

$$\text{var}(Y_t) = 0.5^2\,\text{var}(Y_{t-1}) + \text{var}(u_t)$$

So, $\sigma_Y^2 = 0.25\sigma_Y^2 + 3$. Then, $\sigma_Y^2 = 3/(1-0.25) = 4$.

The first-order autocovariance (or autocovariance at lag 1)

$$\begin{aligned}\operatorname{cov}(Y_t, Y_{t-1}) &= \operatorname{cov}(2.5 + 0.5Y_{t-1} + u_t, Y_{t-1}) \\ &= 0.5\operatorname{cov}(Y_{t-1}, Y_{t-1}) \\ &= 0.5 \times 4 = 2\end{aligned}$$

Since Y_t is stationary, $\operatorname{cov}(Y_{t+k}, Y_{t+k+1}) = \operatorname{cov}(Y_{t+k}, Y_{t+k-1}) = \gamma(1) = 2$ for any k.

First-order autocorrelation (autocorrelation at lag 1):

$$\operatorname{corr}(Y_{t+k}, Y_{t+k+1}) = \operatorname{corr}(Y_{t+k}, Y_{t+k-1}) = \rho(1) = \frac{\gamma(1)}{\sigma_Y^2} = 0.5$$

Second-order and higher order autocovariance:

$$\operatorname{cov}(Y_t, Y_{t-j}) = \operatorname{cov}(2.5 + 0.5Y_{t-1} + u_t, Y_{t-j}) = \gamma(j) \neq 0 \quad \text{for } j > 1$$

Note that we can also write $\operatorname{var}(Y_t) = \sigma_Y^2 = \gamma(0)$. So in general, $\rho(k) = \frac{\gamma(k)}{\gamma(0)}$.

5.7 Moving Average Process

Consider the MA(1) process:

$$Y_t = \theta + u_t + \alpha u_{t-1}\ (\alpha \neq 0), \quad t = -T, \ldots, T \tag{5.7}$$

where $\{u_t\}$ is i. i. d. with zero mean and variance σ_u^2. We have

$$\begin{aligned}E(Y_t) &= \theta \\ \operatorname{var}(Y_t) &= \sigma_u^2(1 + \alpha^2) \\ \operatorname{cov}(Y_t, Y_{t-1}) &= \operatorname{cov}(\theta + u_t + \alpha u_{t-1}, \theta + u_{t-1} + \alpha u_{t-2}) \\ &= \alpha\sigma_u^2 \\ \operatorname{corr}(Y_t, Y_{t-1}) &= \frac{\alpha}{1 + \alpha^2} \\ \operatorname{corr}(Y_t, Y_{t-k}) &= 0 \quad \text{for } k > 1\end{aligned}$$

Hence, we see that MA(1) Y_t is covariance-stationary with constant mean $= \theta$, constant variance $= \sigma_u^2(1 + \alpha^2)$, and autocorrelation lag k, a function of k only:

$$\rho(k) = \begin{cases} \frac{\alpha}{1+\alpha^2}, & k = 1 \\ 0, & k > 1 \end{cases}$$

5.8 Autoregressive Moving Average Process

Consider the ARMA(1,1) process $Y_t = \theta + \lambda Y_{t-1} + u_t + \alpha u_{t-1}$ $(\lambda \neq 0, \alpha \neq 0)$, $t = -T, \ldots, T$, where $\{u_t\}$ is i. i. d. with zero mean and variance σ_u^2. It implies

$$\begin{aligned}Y_t &= \theta + \lambda(\theta + \lambda Y_{t-2} + u_{t-1} + \alpha u_{t-2}) + u_t + \alpha u_{t-1}\\ &= (1+\lambda)\theta + \lambda^2 Y_{t-2} + (u_t + \lambda u_{t-1}) + \alpha(u_{t-1} + \lambda u_{t-2})\\ &= (1+\lambda+\lambda^2+\cdots)\theta + (u_t + \lambda u_{t-1} + \lambda^2 u_{t-2} + \cdots)\\ &\quad + \alpha(u_{t-1} + \lambda u_{t-2} + \lambda^2 u_{t-3} + \cdots)\\ &= (1+\lambda+\lambda^2+\cdots)\theta + u_t + (\lambda+\alpha)u_{t-1}\\ &\quad + (\lambda+\alpha)\lambda u_{t-2} + (\lambda+\alpha)\lambda^2 u_{t-3} + \cdots\end{aligned}$$

For each t,

$$\begin{aligned}E(Y_t) &= \frac{\theta}{1-\lambda} \quad \text{provided } |\lambda| < 1,\\ \operatorname{var}(Y_t) &= \sigma_u^2[1 + (\lambda+\alpha)^2 + (\lambda+\alpha)^2\lambda^2 + (\lambda+\alpha)^2\lambda^4\\ &\quad + (\lambda+\alpha)^2\lambda^6 + \cdots]\\ &= \sigma_u^2\left[1 + \frac{(\lambda+\alpha)^2}{1-\lambda^2}\right] \quad \text{provided } |\lambda| < 1,\\ \operatorname{cov}(Y_t, Y_{t-1}) &= \operatorname{cov}(\theta + \lambda Y_{t-1} + u_t + \alpha u_{t-1}, Y_{t-1})\\ &= \lambda \operatorname{var}(Y_{t-1}) + \alpha \operatorname{cov}(u_{t-1}, Y_{t-1})\\ &= \lambda \operatorname{var}(Y_{t-1}) + \alpha \operatorname{cov}(u_{t-1}, \lambda Y_{t-2} + u_{t-1} + \alpha u_{t-2})\\ &= \lambda \operatorname{var}(Y_{t-1}) + \alpha\sigma_u^2,\\ \text{and} \quad \operatorname{cov}(Y_t, Y_{t-k}) &= \lambda^k \operatorname{var}(Y_{t-k}) + \alpha\lambda^{k-1}\sigma_u^2 \quad \text{for } k \ge 1\end{aligned}$$

Hence, we see that ARMA(1,1) Y_t is covariance stationary with constant mean = $\theta/(1-\lambda)$, constant variance = $\sigma_u^2[1 + (\lambda+\alpha)^2/(1-\lambda)^2] = \sigma_Y^2$, and autocovariance lag k, a function of k only, provided $|\lambda| < 1$.

It is important to know that while we are dealing with covariance-stationary processes, e. g., AR(1) ($|\lambda| < 1$), or MA(1), their conditional mean will change over time. This is distinct from the constant mean we talk about, which is the unconditional mean, and the distinction is often a source of confusion among beginning students, but it is important enough to elaborate.

5.8.1 Changing Conditional Means

Consider AR(1) process $Y_t = \theta + \lambda Y_{t-1} + u_t$ ($\lambda \neq 0$) and also $Y_{t+1} = \theta + \lambda Y_t + u_{t+1}$. At $t+1$, information Y_t is already known, so

$$E(Y_{t+1}|Y_t) = \theta + \lambda Y_t + E(u_{t+1}|Y_t)$$

The last term is 0 since u_{t+1} is not correlated with Y_t. Therefore, conditional mean at t is $\theta + \lambda Y_t$. The conditional mean also serves as forecast when estimated parameters are used, e. g., $\hat{\theta} + \hat{\lambda} Y_t$. This is different from the constant unconditional mean $\frac{\theta}{1-\lambda}$. As Y_{t+k} changes with k, the conditional mean changes with Y_{t+k}. However, the conditional variance at t is

$$\text{var}(Y_{t+1}|Y_t) = \text{var}(u_{t+1}|Y_t) = \sigma_u^2$$

which is still a constant no matter what Y_t is.

This conditional variance, however, is smaller than the unconditional variance $\frac{\sigma_u^2}{1-\lambda^2}$ ($|\lambda| < 1$). This is because the unconditional variance includes variance $\lambda^2 \sigma_Y^2$ on the regressor since Y_{t-1} is not assumed to be known yet.

Next, consider another example, an MA(1) process: $Y_{t+1} = \theta + u_{t+1} + \alpha u_t$ ($\alpha \neq 0$).

$$E(Y_{t+1}|u_t) = \theta + \alpha u_t \neq \theta$$
$$\text{var}(Y_{t+1}|u_t) = \sigma_u^2 < \sigma_u^2(1 + \alpha^2)$$

Likewise for MA(1) covariance stationary process, conditional mean changes at each t, but conditional variance is constant and is smaller than the unconditional variance.

Given a time series and knowing it is from a stationary process, the next step is to identify the statistical time series model or the generating process for the time series. Since AR and MA models produce different autocorrelation function (ACF) $\rho(k)$, $k > 0$, we can find the sample autocorrelation function $r(k)$ and use this to try to differentiate between an AR or MA or perhaps ARMA model. To get to the sample autocorrelation function, we need to estimate the sample autocovariance function.

5.9 Sample Autocorrelation Function

Given a sample $\{Y_t\}$, $t = 1, 2, 3, \ldots, T$, the sample autocovariance lag k is:

$$c(k) = \frac{1}{T} \sum_{t=1}^{T-k} (Y_t - \bar{Y})(Y_{t+k} - \bar{Y})$$

for $k = 0, 1, 2, 3, \ldots, p$. As a rule of thumb, $p < T/4$, i. e., given a sample size T, we usually would not want to estimate a sample autocovariance with a lag that is larger than $T/4$. To use a larger lag means we will have a lesser number of terms in the summation, and this may affect convergence.

Note the divisor is T and $c(k)$ is consistent, i. e., $\lim_{T\uparrow\infty} c(k) = \gamma(k)$. The sample autocorrelation lag k is then

$$r(k) = \frac{c(k)}{c(0)}$$

for $k = 0, 1, 2, 3, \ldots, p$.

In the above estimator of autocorrelation function, there are sometimes different versions in different statistical packages due to the use of different divisors, e. g.,

$$r(k) = \frac{\frac{1}{T-k-2}\sum_{t=1}^{T-k}(Y_t - \bar{Y})(Y_{t+k} - \bar{Y})}{\frac{1}{T-1}\sum_{t=1}^{T}(Y_t - \bar{Y})^2}$$

which is the ratio of two unbiased estimators of covariances. Asymptotically, there is no difference as T gets to be very large. However, in finite sample, the estimates will look slightly different. A more convenient formula is

$$r(k) = \frac{\sum_{t=1}^{T-k}(Y_t - \bar{Y})(Y_{t+k} - \bar{Y})}{\sum_{t=1}^{T}(Y_t - \bar{Y})^2} \tag{5.8}$$

This formulation implicitly assumes division by T on both the numerator and the denominator, and thus represents the consistent estimates of both autocovariances, rather than unbiased finite sample estimates. There may be sampling possibilities when $r(k)$ lies outside $[-1, +1]$. $c(k)$ and $r(k)$ are symmetrical functions about $k = 0$, i. e., $c(k) = c(-k)$, and $r(k) = r(-k)$.

The sample autocorrelation function $r(k)$ can also be represented as an autocorrelation matrix. The following may be that of an AR(1) process $Y_t = 2.5 + 0.5Y_{t-1} + u_t$.

corr	Y_t	Y_{t-1}	Y_{t-2}	Y_{t-3}
Y_t	1	0.53	0.24	0.12
Y_{t-1}	0.53	1	0.53	0.24
Y_{t-2}	0.24	0.53	1	0.53
Y_{t-3}	0.12	0.24	0.53	1

$r(k)$ is a random variable with a sampling distribution of the autocorrelation.

The general shapes of sample autocorrelation function for AR and MA processes are depicted in Figure 5.4.

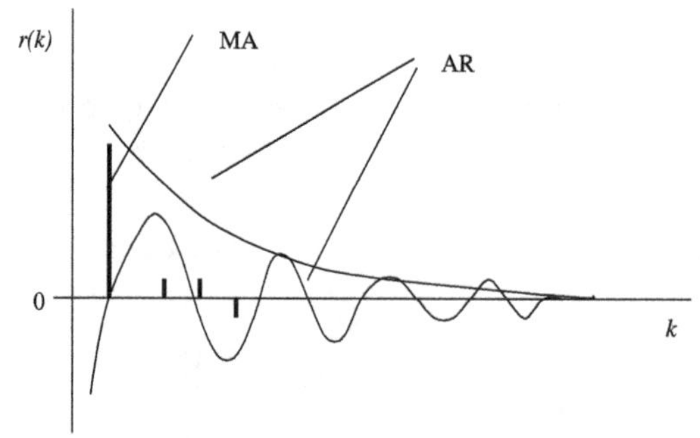

Figure 5.4: Sample Autocorrelation Functions of AR and MA Processes.

Based on the AR(1) process in Eq. (5.5) and the sample autocorrelation measure $r(k)$ in Eq. (5.8),

$$\operatorname{var}(r(k)) \approx \frac{1}{T}\left[\frac{(1+\lambda^2)(1-\lambda^{2k})}{1-\lambda^2} - 2k\lambda^{2k}\right]^5 \tag{5.9}$$

For $k = 1$, $\operatorname{var}(r(1)) \approx \frac{1}{T}[1-\lambda^2]$. For $k = 2$,

$$\begin{aligned}\operatorname{var}(r(2)) &\approx \frac{1}{T}\left[\frac{(1+\lambda^2)(1-\lambda^4)}{(1-\lambda^2)} - 4\lambda^4\right] \\ &= \frac{1}{T}(1-\lambda^2) + \frac{3}{T}\lambda^2(1-\lambda^2) > \operatorname{var}(r(1))\end{aligned}$$

5.10 Test of Zero Autocorrelations for AR(1)

For the AR(1) process, autocorrelation lag k, $\rho(k) = \lambda^k$, provided $|\lambda| < 1$. Suppose we test the null hypothesis $H_0\colon \rho(k) = 0$ for all $k > 0$. This is essentially a test of the null hypothesis $H_0\colon \lambda = 0$. Then,

$$\operatorname{var}(r(k)) \approx \frac{1}{T}$$

for all $k > 0$. Under H_0, Eq, (5.2) becomes $Y_t = \theta + u_t$, where $\{u_t\}$ is i. i. d. Hence, $\{Y_t\}$ is i. i. d.

Therefore, asymptotically as sample size T increases to $+\infty$,

$$\begin{pmatrix} r(1) \\ r(2) \\ \vdots \\ r(m) \end{pmatrix} \sim N\left(\begin{pmatrix} 0 \\ 0 \\ \vdots \\ 0 \end{pmatrix}, \begin{bmatrix} \frac{1}{T} & 0 & 0 & 0 \\ 0 & \frac{1}{T} & 0 & 0 \\ 0 & 0 & \ddots & 0 \\ 0 & 0 & 0 & \frac{1}{T} \end{bmatrix}\right)$$

As T becomes large, the MVN distribution is approached. To test that the jth autocorrelation is zero, evaluate $z_j \sim N(0,1)$ statistic as follows.

$$z_j = \frac{r(j) - 0}{\sqrt{\frac{1}{T}}}$$

Reject $H_0\colon \rho(j) = 0$ at 95 % significance level if the $|z|$ value exceeds 1.96 for a two-tailed test.

---

5 For derivation of the var($r(k)$) above, see M. S. Bartlett (1946), On the theoretical specification of sampling properties of autocorrelated time series, *Journal of Royal Statistical Society B*, 27.

Since it is known that AR processes have ACF $\rho(k)$, approximated by $r(k)$, that decay to zero slowly, but MA(q) processes have ACF $\rho(k)$, approximated by $r(k)$, that are zero for $k > q$, a check of the autocorrelogram (graph of $r(k)$) in Figure 5.5 shows that we reject $H_0 : \rho(k) = 0$ for $k > 1$ at the 95 % significance level for the AR(3) process. For MA(q) processes where $\rho(k) = 0$ for $k > q$,

$$\text{var}(r(k)) \approx \frac{1}{T}\left[1 + 2\sum_{j=1}^{q} \rho(j)^2\right]$$

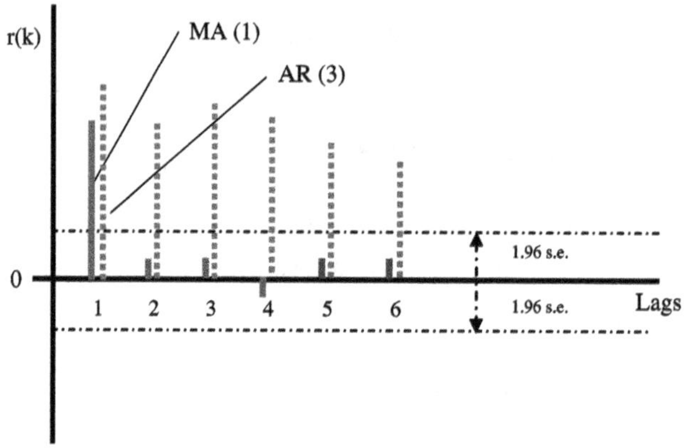

Figure 5.5: Identification Using Sample Autocorrelogram.

Thus, for MA(1), var($r(1)$) may be estimated by $T^{-1}[1+2r(1)^2] > 1/T$. In Figure 5.5, MA(1) is identified. Compare this with the AR(3) that is also shown. The standard error used in most statistical programs is $1/\sqrt{T}$. This standard error is reasonably accurate for AR(1) and for MA(q) processes when q is small.

To test if all autocorrelations are simultaneously zero, $H_0 : \rho(1) = \rho(2) = \cdots = \rho(m) = 0$ (it is common practice to set m at 6, 12, 18, provided $T > 4m$ as a rule of thumb), we can apply the Box and Pierce (1970) Q-statistic:

$$\hat{Q}_m = T\sum_{k=1}^{m}[r(k)]^2 = \sum_{k=1}^{m}[\sqrt{T}r(k)]^2 = \sum_{k=1}^{m} z_k^2 \sim \chi_m^2 \qquad (5.10)$$

This is an asymptotic test statistic. The Ljung and Box (1978) test statistic provides for approximate finite sample correction to the above asymptotic test statistic:

$$\hat{Q}'_m = T(T+2)\sum_{k=1}^{m}\frac{[r(k)]^2}{T-k} \sim \chi_m^2 \qquad (5.11)$$

This Ljung-Box test is appropriate in situations when the null hypothesis is a white noise or approximately white noise such as stock return rate.

5.10.1 Invertible MA Processes

The MA processes can sometimes be represented by infinite order AR processes. As an example, consider MA(1):

$$Y_t = \theta + u_t + \alpha u_{t-1} \; (\alpha \neq 0), \quad \text{or} \quad Y_t = \theta + (1 + \alpha B)u_t$$

So, $(1 + \alpha B)^{-1} Y_t = (1 + \alpha B)^{-1}\theta + u_t$.

Note that $(1 + x)^{-1} = 1 - x + x^2 - x^3 + x^4 - \cdots$ for $|x| < 1$. Also, let constant $c = (1 + \alpha B)^{-1}\theta = \theta/(1 + \alpha)$. Then,

$$(1 - \alpha B + \alpha^2 B^2 - \alpha^3 B^3 + \alpha^4 B^4 - \cdots)Y_t = c + u_t$$

or

$$Y_t - \alpha Y_{t-1} + \alpha^2 Y_{t-2} - \alpha^3 Y_{t-3} + \alpha^4 Y_{t-4} - \cdots = c + u_t$$

Thus,

$$Y_t = c + \alpha Y_{t-1} - \alpha^2 Y_{t-2} + \alpha^3 Y_{t-3} - \alpha^4 Y_{t-4} + \cdots + u_t$$

which is an infinite order AR process.

This AR(∞) process is not a proper representation that allows infinitely past numbers of Y_{t-k}'s to forecast a finite Y_t unless it is stationary with finite mean and variance. If it is not stationary, Y_t may increase by too much, based on an infinite number of explanations of past Y_{t-k}'s.

It is covariance-stationary provided $|\alpha| < 1$. If a stationary MA(q) process can be equivalently represented as a stationary AR(∞) process, then the MA(q) process is said to be invertible. Although all finite order MA(q) processes are stationary, not all are invertible. For example, $Y_t = u_t - 0.3u_{t-1}$ is invertible, but $Y_t = u_t - 1.3u_{t-1}$ is not. Also, MA(1) process $Y_t = \theta + u_t + \alpha u_{t-1}$ ($\alpha \neq 0$) and another MA(1) process $Y_t = \theta + u_t + \frac{1}{\alpha} u_{t-1}$ ($\alpha \neq 0$) are both stationary and have same lag-one autocorrelation $\rho(1) = \frac{\alpha}{1+\alpha^2}$, and $\rho(k) = 0$ for $k > 1$, but only the MA(1) with $\alpha < 1$ is invertible. Invertibility of an MA(q) process to stationary AR(∞) allows expression of current Y_t and future Y_{t+k} in terms of past Y_{t-k}, $k > 0$. This could facilitate forecasts and interpretations of past impact.

A mixed autoregressive moving average process of order (p, q) is

$$\begin{aligned} Y_t = \theta + \lambda_1 Y_{t-1} + \lambda_2 Y_{t-2} + \cdots + \lambda_p Y_{t-p} + u_t \\ + \alpha_1 u_{t-1} + \alpha_2 u_{t-2} + \cdots + \alpha_q u_{t-q} \end{aligned}$$

This may also be invertible to an infinite order AR or less interestingly, an infinite order MA.

5.10.2 Yule-Walker Equations

Consider a stationary AR(p) process $Y_t = \theta + \lambda_1 Y_{t-1} + \lambda_2 Y_{t-2} + \cdots + \lambda_p Y_{t-p} + u_t$. Note that u_t is i. i. d. and has zero correlation with Y_{t-k}, $k > 0$. Multiply both sides by Y_{t-k}. Then,

$$Y_{t-k}Y_t = Y_{t-k}\theta + \lambda_1 Y_{t-k}Y_{t-1} + \lambda_2 Y_{t-k}Y_{t-2} + \cdots + \lambda_p Y_{t-k}Y_{t-p} + Y_{t-k}u_t$$

Taking unconditional expectation on both sides, and noting that $E(Y_{t-k}Y_t) = \gamma(k) + \mu^2$ where $\mu = E(Y_{t-k})$ for any k, then

$$\begin{aligned}\gamma(k) + \mu^2 = \mu\theta + \lambda_1[\gamma(k-1) + \mu^2] + \lambda_2[\gamma(k-2) + \mu^2] + \cdots \\ + \lambda_p[\gamma(k-p) + \mu^2]\end{aligned} \tag{5.12}$$

However, the unconditional mean is

$$\mu = \theta + \lambda_1\mu + \lambda_2\mu + \cdots + \lambda_p\mu$$

Using this in Eq. (5.12), we have

$$\gamma(k) = \lambda_1\gamma(k-1) + \lambda_2\gamma(k-2) + \cdots + \lambda_p\gamma(k-p) \quad \text{for } k > 0$$

Dividing both sides by $\gamma(0)$,

$$\rho(k) = \lambda_1\rho(k-1) + \lambda_2\rho(k-2) + \cdots + \lambda_p\rho(k-p) \quad \text{for } k > 0$$

If we set $k = 1, 2, 3, \ldots, p$, we obtain p equations. Put $\rho(0) = 1$. Note also that $\rho(k) = \rho(-k)$. These equations derived from AR(p) are called the Yule-Walker equations.

$$\begin{aligned}\rho(1) &= \lambda_1 + \lambda_2\rho(1) + \cdots + \lambda_p\rho(p-1)\\ \rho(2) &= \lambda_1\rho(1) + \lambda_2 + \cdots + \lambda_p\rho(p-2)\\ \rho(3) &= \lambda_1\rho(2) + \lambda_2\rho(1) + \cdots + \lambda_p\rho(p-3)\\ &\ \vdots\\ \rho(p) &= \lambda_1\rho(p-1) + \lambda_2\rho(p-2) + \cdots + \lambda_p\end{aligned}$$

They solve for the p parameters in $\lambda_1, \lambda_2, \ldots, \lambda_p$ using $\rho(k)$, $k = 1, 2, \ldots, p$. If we replace the $\rho(k)$ by sample $r(k)$ as approximates, then the p Yule-Walker equations can be solved as follows for the parameter estimates $\hat{\lambda}_k$'s.

$$\mathrm{R} = \begin{pmatrix} r(1)\\ r(2)\\ \vdots\\ r(p)\end{pmatrix} \qquad \Phi = \begin{bmatrix} 1 & r(1) & r(2) & \cdots & r(p-1)\\ r(1) & 1 & r(1) & \cdots & r(p-2)\\ r(2) & r(1) & 1 & \cdots & r(p-3)\\ \vdots & \vdots & \vdots & \ddots & \vdots\\ r(p-1) & r(p-2) & r(p-3) & \cdots & 1\end{bmatrix}$$

$$\hat{\Lambda} = \begin{pmatrix} \hat{\lambda}_1 \\ \hat{\lambda}_2 \\ \vdots \\ \hat{\lambda}_p \end{pmatrix}$$

and $R = \Phi\hat{\Lambda}$. Therefore,

$$\hat{\Lambda} = \Phi^{-1}R \tag{5.13}$$

The other parameters can be estimated as follows.

$$\hat{\mu} = \frac{1}{T}\sum_{t=1}^{T} Y_t, \quad \hat{\theta} = \hat{\mu}(1 - \hat{\lambda}_1 - \hat{\lambda}_2 - \cdots - \hat{\lambda}_p)$$

The estimate of the variance of u_t can be obtained from

$$\frac{1}{T-p-1}\sum_{t=p+1}^{T} (Y_t - \hat{\theta} - \hat{\lambda}_1 Y_{t-1} - \cdots - \hat{\lambda}_p Y_{t-p})^2$$

It is important to note that the identification of the appropriate process must be done before estimation of the parameters is possible since the correct approach to the estimation requires knowledge of the underlying process.

5.11 Partial Autocorrelation Function

The sample ACF allows the identification, respectively, of either an AR or an MA process depending on whether the sample $r(k)$ decays (reduces to zero) slowly or is clearly zero after some lag k. However, even if an AR is identified, it is still difficult to identify the order of the lag, p, since all AR(p) processes show similar decay patterns of ACF. A complementary tool using the partial autocorrelation function (PACF) is used to identify p in the AR(p) process. The PACF also helps to confirm MA(q) processes.

If $p = 1$, let $Y_t = \theta + \lambda_{11}Y_{t-1} + u_t$, so applying the Yule-Walker Equations for $p = 1$, we have (using double subscripts to λ: the first denotes the order of p, and the second denotes the position of the parameter)

$$\rho(1) = \lambda_{11}$$

If $p = 2$, let $Y_t = \theta + \lambda_{21}Y_{t-1} + \lambda_{22}Y_{t-2} + u_t$, so applying the Yule-Walker Equations for $p = 2$, we have

$$\rho(1) = \lambda_{21} + \lambda_{22}\rho(1)$$
$$\rho(2) = \lambda_{21}\rho(1) + \lambda_{22}$$

If $p = 3$, let $Y_t = \theta + \lambda_{31}Y_{t-1} + \lambda_{32}Y_{t-2} + \lambda_{33}Y_{t-3} + u_t$, so applying the Yule-Walker Equations for $p = 3$, we have

$$\rho(1) = \lambda_{31} + \lambda_{32}\rho(1) + \lambda_{33}\rho(2)$$
$$\rho(2) = \lambda_{31}\rho(1) + \lambda_{32} + \lambda_{33}\rho(1)$$
$$\rho(3) = \lambda_{31}\rho(2) + \lambda_{32}\rho(1) + \lambda_{33}$$

Thus we can form k equations using the Yule-Walker equations if $p = k$.

If $p = 1$, λ_{11} is estimated as $\hat{\lambda}_{11} = r(1)$ using the Yule-Walker Equations. If $p = 2$, λ_{22} is estimated as $\hat{\lambda}_{22} = \frac{r(2)-[r(1)]^2}{1-[r(1)]^2}$. If $p = k$, solve for $\hat{\lambda}_{kk}$ as the last element of $\hat{\Lambda}$ in $\Lambda_{k\times1} = \Phi^{-1}_{k\times k}R_{k\times1}$.

The estimate $\hat{\lambda}_{11}$ is a sample partial autocorrelation of Y_t with its lagged Y_{t-1}. In this case of $p = 1$, it is also the sample autocorrelation since there are no other explanatory variables in AR(1). The estimate $\hat{\lambda}_{22}$ is a sample partial autocorrelation of Y_t with its lagged Y_{t-2}. In this case of $p = 2$, it is partial since the effect by Y_{t-1} is held constant. The estimate $\hat{\lambda}_{kk}$ is a sample partial autocorrelation of Y_t with its lagged Y_{t-k}. In this case of $p = k$, it is partial since the effect by $Y_{t-1}, Y_{t-2}, \ldots, Y_{t-k+1}$ is held constant.

What is interesting to note is that given true order p or AR(p), theoretically $\lambda_{11} \neq 0$, $\lambda_{22} \neq 0$, $\lambda_{33} \neq 0, \ldots, \lambda_{pp} \neq 0$, $\lambda_{p+1\,p+1} = 0$, $\lambda_{p+2\,p+2} = 0$, $\lambda_{p+3\,p+3} = 0$, and so on. Or, $\lambda_{kk} \neq 0$ for $k \leq p$, and $\lambda_{kk} = 0$ for $k > p$. Therefore, while an AR(p) process has a decaying ACF that does not disappear to zero, it has a PACF that disappears to zero after lag p.

For $k > p$, $\text{var}(\hat{\lambda}_{kk}) = T^{-1}$. Therefore, we can apply hypothesis testing to determine if for a particular k, H_0: $\lambda_{kk} = 0$, should be rejected or not by considering if statistic $|\frac{\hat{\lambda}_{kk}}{\sqrt{T^{-1}}}| > 1.96$ at the 5 % level of significance.

For any MA(q) process, if it is invertible, it is an AR(∞), so its PACF will not disappear, but will decay. In addition to the sample ACF shown in Figure 5.5, sample PACF shown in Figure 5.6 indicates that the AR(3) process is identified as its PACF becomes insignificant at $k = 4$.

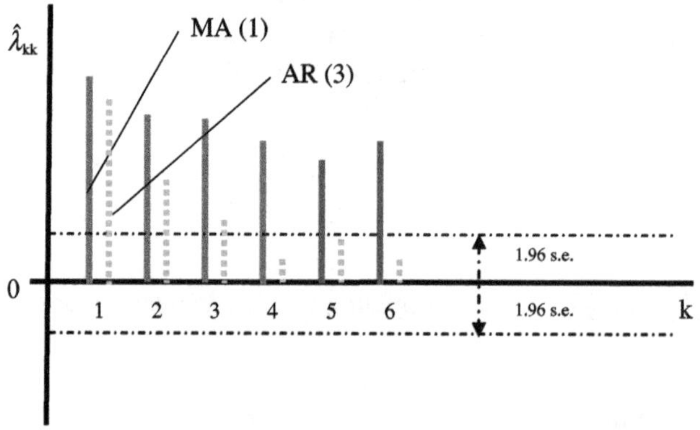

Figure 5.6: Sample Partial Autocorrelogram.

5.11.1 Application: GDP Growth

In growing economies, GDP dollars, or the national output, is usually on an upward trend with obviously increasing means. Thus, the process is not stationary per se, and some form of transformation is required to arrive at the stationary process. We shall see how the Box Jenkins approach deals with such a nonstationary process. In Figure 5.7, we show the quarterly time series US$ per capita GDP graph of a fast-growing Singapore economy from 1985 to 1995. The data are available from the Singapore Government's Department of Statistics.

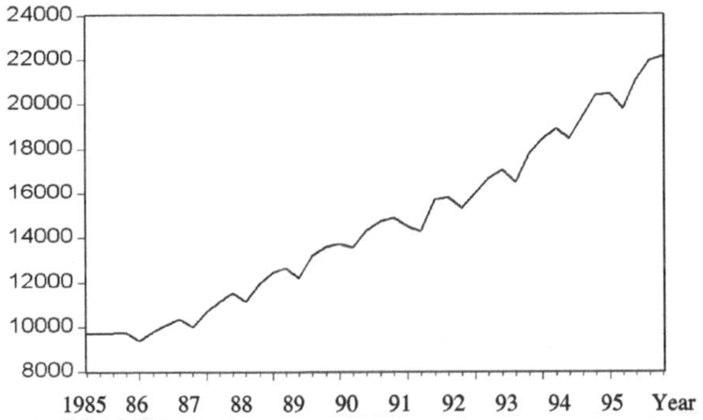

Figure 5.7: Singapore's Per Capita GDP in US$ from 1985 to 1995.

This is the gross domestic output in an economy, and is seen to be rising with a time trend. If we input a time trend variable T, and then run an OLS regression on an intercept and time trend, we obtain

$$Y = 7977.59 + 292.74^* T$$

where Y is GDP and $T = 1, 2, \ldots, 44$ quarters from 1985 to 1995.

We then perform a time series analysis on the estimated residuals of this regression, i. e., $\hat{e} = Y - 7977.59 - 292.74^* T$. Sample ACF and PACF correlograms are plotted for the estimated residuals $\hat{e}$ to determine its time series model. This is shown in Figure 5.8.

Figure 5.8 indicates significant ACF that decays slowly so AR(p) process is suggested. PACF is significant only for lag 1, so an AR(1) is identified. The residual process is not i. i. d. since the Ljung-Box Q-statistic indicates rejection of zero correlation for $m = 1, 2, 3, \ldots$, etc. Then, we may approximate the process as

$$\begin{aligned}(Y_t - 7977.59 - 292.74^* T)\\ = 0.573^* (Y_{t-1} - 7977.59 - 292.74^* [T - 1]) + u_t\end{aligned}$$

Sample: 1 44
Included observations: 44

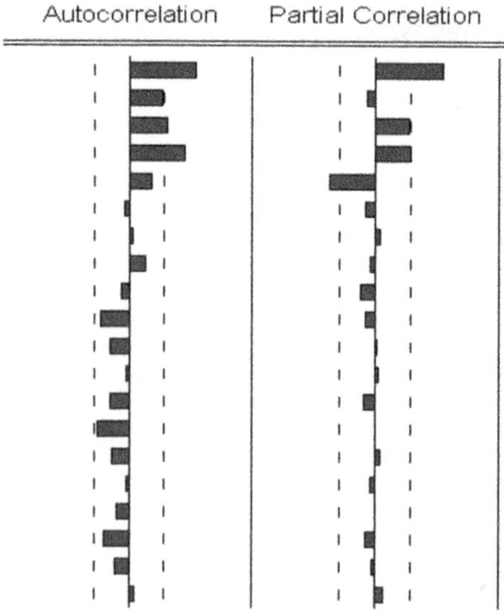

	AC	PAC	Q-Stat	Prob
1	0.573	0.573	15.430	0.000
2	0.279	-0.072	19.192	0.000
3	0.323	0.289	24.351	0.000
4	0.482	0.295	36.101	0.000
5	0.191	-0.383	37.993	0.000
6	-0.043	-0.076	38.091	0.000
7	0.018	0.048	38.109	0.000
8	0.131	-0.033	39.081	0.000
9	-0.071	-0.123	39.375	0.000
10	-0.253	-0.075	43.174	0.000
11	-0.165	0.011	44.849	0.000
12	-0.023	0.032	44.881	0.000
13	-0.160	-0.095	46.555	0.000
14	-0.275	0.004	51.654	0.000
15	-0.150	0.043	53.232	0.000
16	-0.020	-0.047	53.261	0.000
17	-0.105	0.005	54.093	0.000
18	-0.217	-0.076	57.747	0.000
19	-0.116	-0.022	58.840	0.000
20	0.033	0.073	58.932	0.000

Figure 5.8: Sample Autocorrelation and Partial Autocorrelation Statistics.

where u_t is i. i. d. Then, $Y_t = 3598 + 126T + 0.573Y_{t-1} + u_t$. We create a fitted (in-sample fit) series

$$\hat{Y}_t = 3598 + 126T + 0.573Y_{t-1}$$

and plot this fitted $\hat{Y}_t$ and Y_t together, we obtain Figure 5.9.

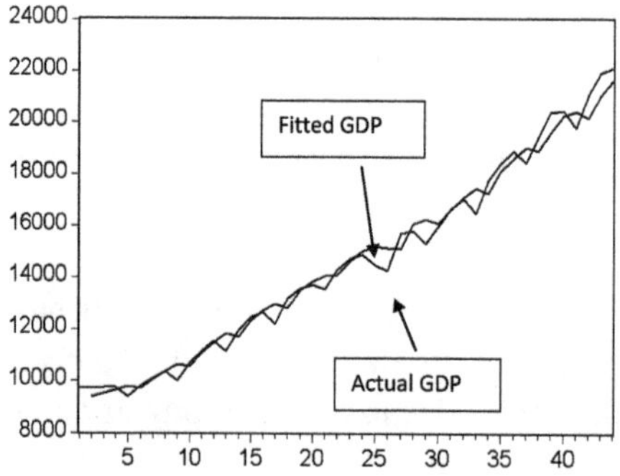

Figure 5.9: Fitted GDP Equation $\hat{Y}_t = 3598 + 126T + 0.573Y_{t-1}$, 1985–1995.

5.12 Autoregressive Integrated Moving Average Process

Suppose for a stationary time series $\{Y_t\}$, both its ACF and PACF decay slowly or exponentially without reducing to zero, then an ARMA(p, q), $p \neq 0$, $q \neq 0$, model is identified. Sometimes, a time series ACF does not reduce to zero, and yet its PACF also does not reduce to zero, not because it is ARMA(p, q), but rather it is an autoregressive integrated moving average process ARIMA(p, d, q). This means that we need to take d number of differences in $\{Y_t\}$ in order to arrive at a stationary ARMA(p, q). For example, if $\{Y_t\}$ is ARIMA(1, 1, 1), then $\{Y_t - Y_{t-1}\}$ is ARMA(1, 1). In such a case, we have to take differences and then check the resulting ACF, PACF in order to proceed to determine ARMA.

There is a special case ARIMA(0, 1, 1) that is interesting, amongst others.

$$\Delta Y_t \equiv Y_t - Y_{t-1} = u_t - \alpha u_{t-1}, \quad |\alpha| < 1$$

Then, $(1 - B)Y_t = (1 - \alpha B)u_t$. So,

$$\begin{aligned}
&\frac{(1-B)}{(1-\alpha B)} Y_t = u_t \\
&\Leftrightarrow \frac{(1-\alpha B) - (1-\alpha)B}{(1-\alpha B)} Y_t = u_t \\
&\Leftrightarrow [1 - (1-\alpha)(B + \alpha B^2 + \alpha^2 B^3 + \cdots)] Y_t = u_t \\
&\Leftrightarrow Y_t = Y^*_{t-1} + u_t, \quad Y^*_{t-1} \equiv \delta \sum_{j=1}^{\infty} (1-\delta)^{j-1} Y_{t-j}, \quad \delta = 1 - \alpha \\
&\Leftrightarrow E(Y_t | Y_{t-1}, Y_{t-2}, \ldots,) = Y^*_{t-1} = \delta Y_{t-1} + (1-\delta) Y^*_{t-2}
\end{aligned}$$

Thus, the forecast of next Y_t at time $t - 1$ is the weighted average of last observation Y_{t-1} and the exponential-weighted moving average of past observations of Y_{t-1}.

Another special application of ARIMA is deseasonalization. Suppose a time series $\{S_t\}$ is monthly sales. It is noted that every December (when Christmas and New Year comes around) sales will be higher because of an additive seasonal component X (assume this is a constant for simplicity). Otherwise, $S_t = Y_t$. Assume Y_t is stationary.

Then, the stochastic process of sales $\{S_t\}$ will look as follows.

$$Y_1, Y_2, \ldots, Y_{11}, Y_{12} + X, Y_{13}, Y_{14}, \ldots, Y_{23}, Y_{24} + X, Y_{25}, Y_{26}, \ldots, Y_{35}, Y_{36} + X, Y_{37}, Y_{38}, \ldots$$

This is clearly a nonstationary series even if $\{Y_t\}$ by itself is stationary. This is because the means will jump by X each December. A stationary series can be obtained from the above for purpose of forecast and analysis by performing the appropriate differencing.

$$(1 - B^{12})S_t = Y_t - Y_{t-12}$$

The differenced series becomes

$$Y_{13} - Y_1, Y_{14} - Y_2, \ldots, Y_{23} - Y_{11}, Y_{24} - Y_{12}, Y_{25} - Y_{13}, Y_{26} - Y_{14}, \ldots, Y_{35} - Y_{23}, Y_{36} - Y_{24}, Y_{37} - Y_{25}, Y_{38} - Y_{26}, \ldots$$

that is stationary provided Y_t is stationary.

Suppose $(1 - B^{12})S_t = u_t$, a white noise. Then, this can be notated as a $(0,1,0)_{12}$ process. If $(1-\theta B^{12})S_t = u_t$, then it is $(1,0,0)_{12}$. Notice that the subscript 12 denotes the power of B. If $(1-\theta B)(1-B^{12})S_t = u_t$, then it is $(1,0,0)\times(0,1,0)_{12}$. $(1-B^{12})S_t = (1-\alpha B)u_t$ is $(0,1,0)_{12} \times (0,0,1)$.

5.12.1 Application: Modeling Inflation Rates

Modelling inflation rates using the Box-Jenkins approach is an important application in finance, especially during periods in which the economy is experiencing significant inflation.

We define monthly inflation rate I_t as the change from month $t-1$ to month t in the natural log of the Consumer Price Index (CPI) denoted by P_t.

$$I_t = \ln\left(\frac{P_t}{P_{t-1}}\right)$$

Using U. S. data for the period 1953–1977, Fama and Gibbons (1984)[6] reported the following sample autocorrelations in their Table 1 (shown as follows in Table 5.2).

Table 5.2: Autocorrelations of Monthly Inflation Rates and Rate Changes.

	$r(1)$	$r(2)$	$r(3)$	$r(4)$	$r(5)$	$r(6)$
I_t	0.55	0.58	0.52	0.52	0.52	0.52
$I_t - I_{t-1}$	0.53	0.11	0.06	0.01	0.00	0.03
	$r(7)$	$r(8)$	$r(9)$	$r(10)$	$r(11)$	$r(12)$
I_t	0.48	0.49	0.51	0.48	0.44	0.47
$I_t - I_{t-1}$	0.04	0.04	0.06	0.02	0.08	0.09

Given sample size $N = 299$, the standard error of $r(k)$ is approximately 0.058. Using 95 % significance level or a critical region outside of 1.96 standard errors, or about 0.113, $r(k)$'s for the I_t process are all significantly greater than 0, but $r(k)$'s for $I_t - I_{t-1}$

6 See E. Fama and M. R. Gibbons (1984), A comparison of inflation forecasts, *Journal of Monetary Economics*, 13, 327–348.

process are all not significantly different from 0 except for $r(1)$. The autocorrelation of I_t is seen to decline particularly slowly, suggesting plausibility of an ARIMA process. The ACF of $I_t - I_{t-1}$ suggests an MA(1) process. Thus, I_t is plausibly ARIMA(0,1,1). Using this identification,

$$I_t - I_{t-1} = u_t + \alpha u_{t-1}, \quad |\alpha| < 1 \tag{5.14}$$

From Eq. (5.14), $E_{t-1}(I_t) = I_{t-1} + \alpha u_{t-1}$ since u_t is i. i. d. Substitute this conditional forecast or expectation back into Eq. (5.14), then

$$I_t = E_{t-1}(I_t) + u_t \tag{5.15}$$

But $E_t(I_{t+1}) = I_t + \alpha u_t$ and $E_{t-1}(I_t) = I_{t-1} + \alpha u_{t-1}$ imply that

$$\begin{aligned} E_t(I_{t+1}) - E_{t-1}(I_t) &= I_t - I_{t-1} + \alpha(u_t - u_{t-1}) \\ &= u_t + \alpha u_{t-1} + \alpha(u_t - u_{t-1}) \\ &= (1 + \alpha)u_t \end{aligned} \tag{5.16}$$

Hence the first difference of the forecasts is a white noise $(1+\alpha)u_t$. From Eq. (5.15), $u_t = I_t - E_{t-1}(I_t)$ can also be interpreted as the unexpected inflation rate realized at t.

Suppose α is estimated as −0.8. Then, Eq. (5.14) can be written as:

$$I_t - I_{t-1} = u_t - 0.8u_{t-1}$$

From Eq. (5.16), the variance in the change of expected inflation is $(1 - 0.8)^2\sigma_u^2$ or $0.04\sigma_u^2$, while the variance of the unexpected inflation is σ_u^2. Thus, the latter variance is much bigger. This suggests that using past inflation rates in forecasting future inflation as in the time series model (5.15) above is not as efficient. Other relevant economic information could be harnessed to produce forecast with less variance in the unexpected inflation, which is to produce forecast with less surprise. Fama and Gibbons (1984) show such approaches using the Fisher effect which says that

$$R_t = E_{t-1}(r_t) + E_{t-1}(I_t)$$

where R_t is the nominal risk-free interest rate from end of period $t-1$ to end of period t, and this is known at $t - 1$, r_t is the real interest rate for the same period as the nominal rate, and I_t is the inflation rate.

Notice that the right-side of the Fisher equation contains terms in expectations. This is because inflation at $t - 1$ when R_t is known, has not happened, and so is only an ex-ante conditional expectation. If the real rate r_t is known at $t-1$, then the equation would be $R_t = r_t + E_{t-1}(I_t)$, and this creates an immediate contradiction in that $E_{t-1}(I_t) = R_t - r_t$ becomes known at $t - 1$ which is not. Thus, at $t - 1$, real rate, like inflation, is ex-ante and not known.

Further Reading

Billingsley, P. (2012), *Probability and Measure*, John Wiley & Sons.
Box, G., and G. Jenkins (1970), *Time Series Analysis: Forecasting and Control*, Holden-Day Publishers.
Hamilton, James D. (1994), *Time Series Analysis*, Princeton University Press.

6 Multiple Linear Regression

In this chapter, we consider linear regression models with more than one stochastic explanatory variable. This is called multiple linear regression. Under classical assumptions, including the regressors (explanatory variables) being independent, i. e. exogenous and not dependent on the regressand (dependent variable) nor the parameters, the estimators of the parameters possess desirable properties such as unbiasedness and efficiency in finite sample, and consistency and asymptotic efficiency in large sample. We then consider the estimation and testing issues when some of the classical assumptions are violated. The latter are called specification errors (deviations from the classical assumptions) and in their presence the estimators may not have the desirable properties. Adjustment methods are also suggested to show how some of the problems due to specification errors may be overcome. The background comments in Chapter 2 regarding the stochastic explanatory variables and use of conditional estimators in inferences and efficiency matters as in the Gauss–Markov theorem also apply in the multiple regression framework.

6.1 Multiple Linear Regression

When we extend the linear regression analyses to more than one random explanatory variable, we are dealing with multiple linear regression model viz.

$$Y_i = b_0 + b_1 X_{i1} + b_2 X_{i2} + b_3 X_{i3} + \cdots + b_{k-1} X_{i,k-1} + u_i \tag{6.1}$$

where subscripts ij of X denotes the ith sample point for $i = 1, 2, \ldots, N$, and the jth non-constant explanatory variable for $j = 1, 2 \ldots, k-1$. We can also use t instead of i when we deal with a time series, for $t = 1, 2, \ldots, T$. Note that, including the constant, there are k explanatory "variables". An example of multiple linear regression is when Y_i denotes a performance measure of factory i for $i = 1, 2, \ldots, N$, and $X_{i,j}$ denotes a jth characteristic of factory i, for $j = 1, 2, \ldots, k-1$. In this case, the multiple linear regression is a cross-sectional regression explaining the cross-sectional performance of factories with associated characteristics as explanatory variables. Another example of multiple linear regression is when Y_t is return rate of a stock at time t for $t = 1, 2, \ldots, T$, and $X_{t,j}$ denotes a jth characteristic of the stock at time t, for $j = 1, 2, \ldots, k-1$. In this case, the multiple linear regression is a time-series regression explaining the stock return performance across time using associated characteristics at each time t as explanatory variables.

https://doi.org/10.1515/9783110673951-006

6.1.1 Partial Correlation Coefficient

In a simple two-variable linear regression,

$$Y_i = b_0 + b_1 X_i + u_i, \quad \text{for } i = 1, 2, \ldots, N$$

If $\text{cov}(X_i, u_i) = 0$, then $b_1 = \text{cov}(Y_i, X_i)/\text{var}(X_i) = \rho(Y_i, X_i)\sqrt{\text{var}(Y_i)}/\sqrt{\text{var}(X_i)}$ where $\rho(Y_i, X_i)$ is the (zero order) correlation coefficient between Y_i and X_i.

Suppose an additional explanatory variable Z_i is introduced. Now there is multiple linear regression:

$$Y_i = c_0 + c_1 X_i + c_2 Z_i + v_i, \quad \text{for } i = 1, 2, \ldots, N$$

In this case, even if $\text{cov}(X_i, v_i) = 0$, c_1 is not equal to $\text{cov}(Y_i, X_i)/\text{var}(X_i)$ as other explanatory variable is present, except when $\text{cov}(X_i, Z_i) = 0$.

The sample correlation coefficients can be more readily evaluated when we consider the linear regressions in deviation forms i. e.

$$y_i = c_1 x_i + c_2 z_i + \varepsilon_i, \quad \text{for } i = 1, 2, \ldots, N$$

where $y_i = Y_i - \bar{Y}$, $x_i = X_i - \bar{X}$, $z_i = Z_i - \bar{Z}$, and $\varepsilon_i = v_i - \frac{1}{N}\sum_{i=1}^N v_i$. $\bar{Y} = \frac{1}{N}\sum_{i=1}^N Y_i$, $\bar{X} = \frac{1}{N}\sum_{i=1}^N X_i$, $\bar{Z} = \frac{1}{N}\sum_{i=1}^N Z_i$, and $E(\varepsilon_i) = 0$. Also assume for simplicity that ε_i is independent of x_i and z_i. Assume all the variables are stationary.

The zero order sample correlation coefficient between y_i and x_i is:

$$r_{yx} = \frac{\sum_i y_i x_i}{\sqrt{\sum_i y_i^2 \sum_i x_i^2}}$$

where we left out the notation of sample size N. However, the sample partial correlation coefficient between y_i and x_i after controlling for z_i or removing effect of z_i (on y_i and on x_i) is:

$$r_{yx.z} = \frac{r_{yx} - r_{yz} r_{xz}}{\sqrt{1 - r_{yz}^2}\sqrt{1 - r_{xz}^2}}$$

It is seen that if the sample correlations of y_i and z_i and of x_i and z_i are both positive, then the partial correlation effect of x_i on y_i, after removing the effect of z_i, is lower than r_{yx}.

The sample partial correlation coefficient between y_i and x_i after controlling for z_i can also be computed as follows. First, OLS linear regressions are run of y_i on z_i, and also of x_i on z_i. The fitted errors of these regressions are

$$\hat{e}_{yz,i} = y_i - \left(\frac{\sum_i y_i z_i}{\sum_i z_i^2}\right) z_i \quad \text{and} \quad \hat{e}_{xz,i} = x_i - \left(\frac{\sum_i x_i z_i}{\sum_i z_i^2}\right) z_i$$

These fitted residuals contain variations in y_i and x_i after the effects of z_i are removed.

The sample correlation coefficient of $\hat{e}_{yz,i}$ and $\hat{e}_{xz,i}$ is:

$$\frac{\sum_{i=1} \hat{e}_{yz,i}\hat{e}_{xz,i}}{\sqrt{\sum_i e^2_{yz,i} \sum_i e^2_{xz,i}}}$$

that can be shown to be exactly $r_{yx.z}$, the sample partial correlation coefficient of y_i and x_i controlling for effects of z_i.

If $\hat{e}_{yz,i}$ is regressed on $\hat{e}_{xz,i}$, the OLS estimate of the slope based on these partial variables is also the OLS estimate of the partial slope of c_1 in the multiple linear regression. Similarly, it can be shown that the OLS estimate of the slope based on the regression of partial variables $\hat{e}_{yx,i}$ on $\hat{e}_{zx,i}$ is also the OLS estimate of the partial slope of c_2 in the multiple linear regression.

The matrix formulation of Eq. (6.1) can be written concisely as:

$$Y_{N\times1} = X_{N\times k}B_{k\times1} + U_{N\times1} \tag{6.2}$$

where

$$Y_{N\times1} = \begin{pmatrix} Y_1 \\ Y_2 \\ \vdots \\ Y_N \end{pmatrix}, \quad X_{N\times k} = \begin{pmatrix} 1 & X_{11} & \cdots & X_{1,k-1} \\ 1 & X_{21} & \cdots & X_{2,k-1} \\ \vdots & \vdots & \ddots & \vdots \\ 1 & X_{N1} & \cdots & X_{N,k-1} \end{pmatrix}$$

$$B_{k\times1} = \begin{pmatrix} b_0 \\ b_1 \\ \vdots \\ b_{k-1} \end{pmatrix}, \quad \text{and} \quad U_{N\times1} = \begin{pmatrix} u_1 \\ u_2 \\ \vdots \\ u_N \end{pmatrix}$$

The classical conditions in matrix format are:

(A1) $E(U) = 0_{N\times1}$

(A2) $\text{var}(U) = \sigma_u^2 I_{N\times N}$, where $E(u_i^2) = \sigma_u^2$, a same constant for every i, and $E(u_i u_j) = 0$ for every $i \neq j$. Thus, this matrix condition provides for both conditions of variance homoskedasticity (constant variance), and cross-variable zero correlation that are separately specified in the univariate case in Chapter 2.

(A3) X and U are stochastically independent of each other. Being matrix and vector, respectively, this means any pairs of elements from X and U are stochastically independent.

(A4) $U \sim N(0, \sigma_u^2 I)$

The classical conditions (A1), (A2), (A3) can be relaxed (weakened slightly) to

(A1′) $E(U|X) = 0_{N\times1}$
(A2′) $\text{var}(U|X) = E(UU^T|X) = \sigma_u^2 I_{N\times N}$

Note that (A1), (A2), (A3) together are stronger conditions as they imply (A1′) and (A2′). But (A1′) and (A2′) do not imply (A3) which is a strong independence assumption, though (A1′) implies (A1) and (A2′) implies (A2).

(A1′) implies $E(E(U|X)) = E(U) = 0$ by the Law of Iterated Expectations. This means that $E(u_i) = 0, \forall i$. (A1′) also implies $E(u_i|X_{jk}) = 0$, for any i, j, k. This includes $\text{cov}(u_i, X_{ij}) = 0$ for every i. If i is a time index t, this means $E(u_t|X_{tj}) = 0$ for every t, given $j = 1, 2, \ldots, k-1$. The latter is described as contemporaneous zero correlation between u_t and characteristic X_{tj} at same time t.

(A2′) gives $E(u_i^2|X) = \sigma_u^2$ for every i, and also $E(u_i u_j|X) = 0$ for every pair of i, j such that $i \neq j$. By the Law of Iterated Expectations, $E(u_i^2) = \sigma_u^2$ for every i and $E(u_i u_j) = 0$ where $i \neq j$. It also implies u_i^2 and $u_i u_j$, second moments of U, have zero correlations with any elements of X.

6.1.2 Least Squares Theory

The idea of least squares can be thought of as a linear orthogonal (least distance) projection. Think of the $N \times 1$ vector of Y as a vector in N-dimensional Euclidean space (or R^N vector space with Cartesian co-ordinates and a distance metric) and vectors XB in the same N-dimensional space but lying on a subspace which is a k-dimensional hyperplane. This is a non-trivial departure in concept. For example, in the two-variable case, we look at Y versus X in two dimension on a Cartesian plane, but here we think of Y and XB in N dimension. The idea is to find a projection vector.

If $Y - X\hat{B}$ is the orthogonal projection from Y to the hyperplane formed by XB, then $(XB)^T(Y - X\hat{B}) = 0$ or $B^T X^T(Y - X\hat{B}) = 0$. Thus, $X^T(Y - X\hat{B}) = 0$. Therefore, we obtain $\hat{B} = (X^T X)^{-1} X^T Y$. The projection represents minimum perpendicular distance from Y to the fitted vector $X\hat{B}$. The geometric idea is illustrated as follows in Figure 6.1.

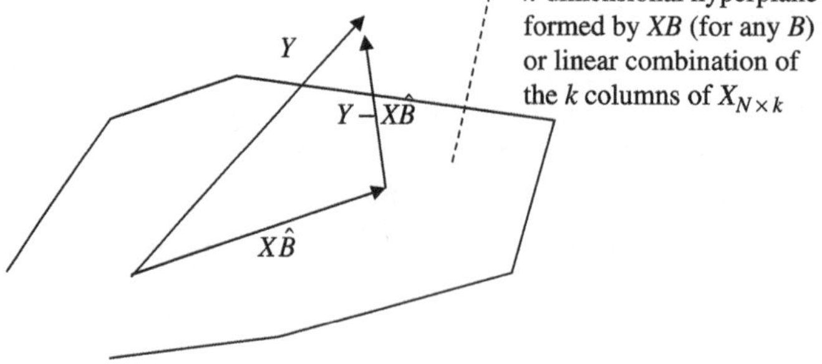

Figure 6.1: Least Squares Theory.

Now we derive the ordinary least squares estimator $\hat{B}$ using optimization. Let the estimated residuals be $\hat{U} = Y - X\hat{B}$. The sum of squared residuals (or residual sum of squares RSS) is $\sum_{t=1}^{N} \hat{u}_t^2 = \hat{U}^T\hat{U}$.

Applying the OLS method to obtain the OLS estimate for B:

$$\min_{\hat{B}} \hat{U}^T\hat{U} \equiv (Y - X\hat{B})^T(Y - X\hat{B}) = Y^TY - 2\hat{B}^TX^TY + \hat{B}^TX^TXB$$

The first-order condition gives:

$$\frac{\partial \hat{U}^T\hat{U}}{\partial \hat{B}} = -2X^TY + 2X^TX\hat{B} = 0$$

Therefore,

$$\hat{B} = (X^TX)^{-1}X^T \tag{6.3}$$

provided that inverse of (X^TX) exists. (X^TX) is of dimension $k \times k$. For inverse of (X^TX) to exist, (X^TX) must have full rank of k. The rank of $X_{N\times k}$ is at most $\min(N, k)$. Thus, k must be smaller than N. This means that when we perform a regression involving k explanatory variables (including the constant), we must employ at least a sample size of k and larger.

6.1.3 Properties of OLS Estimators

$$\hat{B} = (X^TX)^{-1}X^T(XB + U) = B + (X^TX)^{-1}X^TU$$

If X and U are stochastically independent as in (A3), then $E(\hat{B}) = B + E[(X^TX)^{-1}X^T] \times E[U] = B$ as $E[U] = 0$ with (A1). If we employ (A1′) instead, $E(\hat{B}) = B + E[(X^TX)^{-1}X^TU] = B + E(E[(X^TX)^{-1}X^TU|X]) = B + E[(X^TX)^{-1}X^TE(U|X)] = B$.

It is shown that the OLS estimators in $\hat{B}$ are unbiased. Now,

$$\hat{B} - B = (X^TX)^{-1}X^TU$$

The $k \times k$ covariance matrix of $\hat{B}$ is

$$\begin{aligned}\text{var}(\hat{B}) &= E(\hat{B} - B)(\hat{B} - B)^T = E((X^TX)^{-1}X^TU)((X^TX)^{-1}X^TU)^T \\ &= E[(X^TX)^{-1}X^TUU^TX(X^TX)^{-1}]\end{aligned}$$

Applying (A3) and (A2),

$$\begin{aligned}\text{var}(\hat{B}) &= E[(X^TX)^{-1}X^TE(UU^T)X(X^TX)^{-1}] \\ &= \sigma_u^2 E[(X^TX)^{-1}X^TIX(X^TX)^{-1}] \\ &= \sigma_u^2 E[(X^TX)^{-1}]\end{aligned}$$

If we apply (A2′) instead, we obtain the same result.

$$\begin{aligned}\text{var}(\hat{B}) &= E[E((X^TX)^{-1}X^TUU^TX(X^TX)^{-1}|X)]\\ &= E[(X^TX)^{-1}X^TE(UU^T|X)X(X^TX)^{-1}]\\ &= \sigma_u^2E[(X^TX)^{-1}X^TIX(X^TX)^{-1}]\\ &= \sigma_u^2E[(X^TX)^{-1}]\end{aligned}$$

For statistical inference, we now use conditional variance, so

$$\text{var}(\hat{B}|X) = \sigma_u^2(X^TX)^{-1} \tag{6.4}$$

By (A4), $\hat{B}_{k\times 1} \sim N(B_{k\times 1}, \sigma_u^2(X^TX)^{-1})$.

As in the two-variable case, OLS estimator $\hat{B}$ is BLUE. Note also that in this case, there is no restriction on X (i. e., it is not necessary that there must be a constant regressor among X, for $\hat{B}$ to be BLUE).

Now, the unbiased sample estimate of σ_u^2 is $\hat{\sigma}_u^2 = \frac{\hat{U}^T\hat{U}}{N-k}$. If $H_0 : B_j = 1$, the statistical distribution of test statistic

$$\frac{\hat{B}_j - 1}{\hat{\sigma}_u\sqrt{j\text{th diag element } (X^TX)^{-1}}} \quad \text{is } t_{N-k}$$

6.2 Tests of Restrictions

Consider a linear combination, $R_{q\times k}\hat{B}_{k\times 1}$. Suppose the null hypothesis is based on q linear restrictions on the coefficients, $H_0 : R_{q\times k}B_{k\times 1} = r_{q\times 1}$. Then, $R_{q\times k}\hat{B}_{k\times 1} - r_{q\times 1}$, where R and r are constants, is normally distributed since $\hat{B}$ is normally distributed given the classical assumptions, and conditional on X. The idea is to test if deviation of $R\hat{B} - r$ is attributed to insignificant sampling error (i. e., we cannot reject H_0) or whether it is significant (i. e., we reject H_0).

$$E(R\hat{B}) = RB$$

The covariance matrix of $R\hat{B} - r$ is the covariance matrix of $(R\hat{B})_{q\times 1}$ since r is constant. This is also the covariance matrix of $R(\hat{B} - B)$ since B is constant.

$$\text{var}(R\hat{B} - r) = E[R(\hat{B} - B)(\hat{B} - B)^TR^T] = \sigma_u^2R(X^TX)^{-1}R^T,$$

or

$$\text{var}(R\hat{B} - r) = R[\text{var}(\hat{B})]R^T$$

We provide an illustration as follows. Note in what follows that $\text{var}(R_{2\times3}\hat{B}_{3\times1})$ yields a 2×2 covariance matrix.

$$\text{var}\left[\begin{pmatrix} x_1 & x_2 & x_3 \\ y_1 & y_2 & y_3 \end{pmatrix}\begin{pmatrix} \hat{a} \\ \hat{b} \\ \hat{c} \end{pmatrix}\right] = \text{var}\left[\begin{pmatrix} x_1\hat{a} + x_2\hat{b} + x_3\hat{c} \\ y_1\hat{a} + y_2\hat{b} + y_3\hat{c} \end{pmatrix}\right]$$

$$= \begin{bmatrix} x^T V x & x^T V y \\ y^T V x & y^T V y \end{bmatrix}$$

$$= \begin{pmatrix} x_1 & x_2 & x_3 \\ y_1 & y_2 & y_3 \end{pmatrix} V \begin{pmatrix} x_1 & y_1 \\ x_2 & y_2 \\ x_3 & y_3 \end{pmatrix} = RVR^T$$

where

$$x^T = (x_1 x_2 x_3), \quad y^T = (y_1 y_2 y_3) \quad \text{and} \quad V_{3\times3} = \text{cov}\begin{pmatrix} \hat{a} \\ \hat{b} \\ \hat{c} \end{pmatrix}$$

Next we discuss some fundamental matrix results before arriving at the distribution of the test statistic of $RB = r$. The quadratic form of a square matrix $A_{q\times q}$ is $x^T Ax$ where vector x is of dimension q, and $x^T Ax$ is a quadratic function in the elements of x. We consider only real matrix A. If A is real symmetric, $A^T = A$. The eigenvalues λ_i's of A are real but not necessarily all distinct for different i. The eigenvalues are found by solving $Av_i = \lambda_i v_i$ where v_i is the corresponding $q \times 1$ eigenvector. If the eigenvalues are distinct, then their eigenvectors (for real symmetric A) are orthogonal. Even when there are eigenvalues with multiplicity, one can always find eigenvectors such that they are orthogonal (for real symmetric A).

We can write $AV = V\Lambda$ where $\Lambda_{q\times q}$ is a diagonal matrix with real elements λ_i in the diagonal and zeros off-diagonal. $V_{q\times q}$ is the matrix containing the q columns of eigenvectors $v_1, v_2, \ldots, v_q$. For real symmetric A, we can always find an orthonormal V such that $V^T V = I_{q\times q}$. The last equality also implies that $V^T = V^{-1}$ or that an inverse to this orthonormal V exists. Then $A = V\Lambda V^{-1} = V\Lambda V^T$ and $\Lambda = V^T AV$. The last two implications given real symmetric A are part of the Spectral Theorem in matrices, basically allowing a real symmetric A to be diagonalizable.

If for any real $x \neq 0$, $x^T Ax > (\geq)\ 0$, then A is positive definite (semi-definite). A positive definite matrix A can be expressed as $Y^T Y$ where Y (not all elements zeros) has dimensions $q \times q$. Hence a positive definite matrix is also symmetric. We shall now consider A as a real positive definite matrix. A has real positive eigenvalues. On the other hand, if all eigenvalues of A are real positive, then A is real positive definite. It is also diagonalizable, i. e., $A = V\Lambda V^T$.

The covariance matrix $\Sigma_{q\times q}$ of a random vector $Z_{q\times1}$ (with elements or RVs that are not linearly dependent) is always positive definite. This can be easily shown as

$\text{var}(x^T Z)$ for any real $x_{q\times 1}$ is $x^T\Sigma x$ that must be positive. Hence the covariance matrix can be decomposed as $\Sigma = V\Lambda V^T$. And $\Sigma^{-1} = V\Lambda^{-1}V^T = V\Lambda^{-\frac{1}{2}}\Lambda^{-\frac{1}{2}T}V^T$.

If random vector $Z_{q\times 1} \sim N(0, \Sigma_{q\times q})$, then $Z^T\Sigma^{-1}Z = P^T P$ where $P_{q\times 1} = \Lambda^{-\frac{1}{2}T}V^T Z$. Now, P is a linear combination of q RVs, being elements of Z. $E[PP^T] = E[\Lambda^{-\frac{1}{2}T}V^T ZZ^T \times V\Lambda^{-\frac{1}{2}}] = \Lambda^{-\frac{1}{2}T}V^T E[ZZ^T]V\Lambda^{-\frac{1}{2}} = \Lambda^{-\frac{1}{2}T}V^T\Sigma V\Lambda^{-\frac{1}{2}} = I_{q\times q}$ since $V^T\Sigma V = \Lambda$. Each element in P has zero correlation (hence independence under normality) with other elements. Thus

$$Z^T\Sigma^{-1}Z \sim \chi^2_q$$

So,

$$(R\hat{B} - r)^T [\sigma_u^2 R(X^T X)^{-1} R^T]^{-1} (R\hat{B} - r) \sim \chi^2_q$$

where $\hat{B}$ is the OLS estimate of B in $Y = XB + U$. This is also called the Wald criterion. It may be used as a Wald χ^2-test if the sample size is very large so that unknown σ_u^2 can be substituted by estimate $\hat{\sigma}_u^2$.

Now, $\hat{U} = Y - X\hat{B} = U + X(B - \hat{B}) = U + X(-(X^T X)^{-1}X^T U) = (I - X(X^T X)^{-1}X^T)U$. Let $M = I - X(X^T X)^{-1}X^T$. Here M is an idempotent matrix. By definition, any idempotent matrix has the property that when multiplying by itself, the product remains the same as the original matrix. Here, in addition, M is symmetric: $M^T = M$. Further, for a symmetric idempotent matrix, it can be shown that in its diagonalization where $M = V\Lambda V^T$, Λ diagonal elements are either ones or zeros.

With $\hat{U} = MU$ and $U_{N\times 1} \sim N(0, \sigma_u^2 I_{N\times N})$, $\frac{\hat{U}^T\hat{U}}{\sigma_u^2} \sim \chi^2_{N-k}$ where the trace of M is $N - k$. Moreover it can be shown that $\hat{U}^T\hat{U}$ is independent of $\hat{B}$ and also independent of $(R\hat{B} - r)^T[\sigma_u^2 R(X^T X)^{-1}R^T]^{-1}(R\hat{B} - r)$. Thus,

$$\frac{(R\hat{B} - r)^T [R(X^T X)^{-1} R^T]^{-1} (R\hat{B} - r)/q}{\hat{U}^T\hat{U}/(N-k)} \sim F_{q,N-k} \tag{6.5}$$

This provides a test of $H_0 : RB = r$.

The test of this restriction, $H_0 : RB = r$, can also be constructed in another way. Suppose we run OLS on a restricted regression by imposing $RB = r$. Hence, $\min(Y - XB)^T(Y - XB)$ subject to $RB = r$. Solve the Lagrangian

$$\min_{\hat{B}^c, \hat{\lambda}} (Y - X\hat{B}^c)^T (Y - X\hat{B}^c) + 2\hat{\lambda}^T (R\hat{B}^c - r)$$

where $\hat{B}^c$ denotes the constrained estimator.

The first-order conditions are:

$$-2X^T(Y - X\hat{B}^C) + 2R^T\hat{\lambda} = 0$$

and also $2(R\hat{B}^C - r) = 0$.

Therefore,

$$\begin{bmatrix} X^T X & R^T \\ R & 0 \end{bmatrix} \begin{pmatrix} \hat{B}^C \\ \hat{\lambda} \end{pmatrix} = \begin{bmatrix} X^T Y \\ r \end{bmatrix}$$

Then,

$$\begin{pmatrix} \hat{B}^C \\ \hat{\lambda} \end{pmatrix} = \begin{bmatrix} X^T X & R^T \\ R & 0 \end{bmatrix}^{-1} \begin{bmatrix} X^T Y \\ r \end{bmatrix}$$
$$= \begin{bmatrix} (X^T X)^{-1}(I + R^T CR(X^T X)^{-1}) & -(X^T X)^{-1} R^T C \\ -CR(X^T X)^{-1} & C \end{bmatrix} \begin{bmatrix} X^T Y \\ r \end{bmatrix}$$

where $C = (-R(X^T X)^{-1} R^T)^{-1}$ using partitioned matrix inverse.[1] Thus,

$$\begin{aligned} \hat{B}^C &= (X^T X)^{-1}(I + R^T CR(X^T X)^{-1}) X^T Y - (X^T X)^{-1} R^T Cr \\ &= (X^T X)^{-1} X^T Y + (X^T X)^{-1} R^T C[R(X^T X)^{-1} X^T Y - r] \\ &= \hat{B} + (X^T X)^{-1} R^T C(R\hat{B} - r) \\ &= \hat{B} - (X^T X)^{-1} R^T (R(X^T X)^{-1} R^T)^{-1} (R\hat{B} - r) \end{aligned}$$

Therefore,

$$\hat{B}^C - \hat{B} = -(X^T X)^{-1} R^T (R(X^T X)^{-1} R^T)^{-1} (R\hat{B} - r)$$

Now, constrained estimated residual

$$\hat{U}^C = Y - X\hat{B} - X(\hat{B}^C - \hat{B}) = \hat{U} - X(\hat{B}^C - \hat{B})$$

Hence,

$$\hat{U}^{CT} \hat{U}^C = \hat{U}^T \hat{U} + (\hat{B}^C - \hat{B})^T X^T X (\hat{B}^C - \hat{B}) \text{ since } X^T \hat{U} = 0$$

Then, $\hat{U}^{CT} \hat{U}^C - \hat{U}^T \hat{U} = (R\hat{B} - r)^T (R(X^T X)^{-1} R^T)^{-1} (R\hat{B} - r)$ which is the numerator in Eq. (6.5) before dividing by q. Hence, we see that

$$\frac{\frac{\text{(CSSR-USSR)}}{q}}{\frac{\text{USSR}}{(N-k)}} \sim F_{q,N-k}$$

where CSSR is constrained sum of squared residuals $\hat{U}^{CT} \hat{U}^C$ and USSR is unconstrained sum of squared residuals $\hat{U}^T \hat{U}$.

1 See Johnson and Wichern (2002).

If we apply $R = I_{k\times k}$ in the restriction $RB = 0$, then we are really testing $H_0 : b_0 = b_1 = b_2 = \cdots = b_{k-1} = 0$. The test statistic for this H_0 is:

$$\frac{\hat{B}^T[(X^TX)^{-1}]^{-1}\hat{B}/k}{\hat{U}^T\hat{U}/(N-k)} = \frac{\hat{B}^T(X^TX)\hat{B}/k}{\hat{U}^T\hat{U}/(N-k)} \sim F_{k,N-k}$$

The above is a test of whether the X's explain Y or allow a linear fitting of Y. Suppose the X's do not explain Y. But if the mean of Y is not zero, then the constraint $b_0 = 0$ should not be used as part of the null hypothesis. If used, there will be rejection of H_0, but this will lead to the wrong conclusion that X's explain Y.

In other words, if we allow or maintain the mean of Y to be non-zero, a more suitable test of whether X's affect Y is $H_0 : b_1 = b_2 = \cdots = b_{k-1} = 0$. We leave out the constraint $b_0 = 0$. How do we obtain such a test statistic?

The restrictions $H_0 : b_1 = b_2 = \cdots = b_{k-1} = 0$ are equivalent to the matrix restriction of $R_{k-1\times k}B = 0_{k-1\times 1}$ where $R = [0|I_{k-1}]$ with its first column containing all zeros. Partition $X = [1|X^*]$ where the first column 1 contains all ones, and X^* is $N \times (k-1)$. Then

$$X^TX = [1|X^*]^T[1|X^*] = \begin{bmatrix} N & 1^TX^* \\ X^{*T}1 & X^{*T}X^* \end{bmatrix}$$

Now $R(X^TX)^{-1}R^T = [0|I_{k-1}](X^TX)^{-1}[0|I_{k-1}]^T$. This produces the bottom right $(k-1) \times (k-1)$ submatrix of $(X^TX)^{-1}$. But by the partitioned matrix result in linear algebra, this submatrix is

$$\left[(X^{*T}X^*) - X^{*T}1\left(\frac{1}{N}\right)1^TX^*\right]^{-1} = \left[X^{*T}\left(I - \frac{1}{N}11^T\right)X^*\right]^{-1}$$

where $(I - 1/N11^T) \equiv M^0$ is symmetrical and idempotent, and transforms a matrix into deviation form, i. e.,

$$M^0X^* = \begin{bmatrix} X_{11} - \bar{X}_1 & X_{12} - \bar{X}_2 & \cdots & X_{1(k-1)} - \bar{X}_{k-1} \\ X_{21} - \bar{X}_1 & X_{22} - \bar{X}_2 & & X_{2(k-1)} - \bar{X}_{k-1} \\ \vdots & \vdots & \ddots & \\ X_{N1} - \bar{X}_1 & X_{N2} - \bar{X}_2 & \cdots & X_{N(k-1)} - \bar{X}_{k-1} \end{bmatrix} = X^{**}$$

Hence $R(X^TX)^{-1}R^T = (X^{*T}M^0X^*)^{-1} = [X^{**T}X^{**}]^{-1}$. So, $[R(X^TX)^{-1}R^T]^{-1} = [X^{**T}X^{**}]$. It can be shown easily that $(I - 1/N11^T) \times (I - 1/N11^T) = (I - 1/N11^T)$.

From the OLS definition of estimated residual $\hat{U}$, $\hat{U} = Y - X\hat{B}$. It can shown that $X^T\hat{U} = 0$. This is because $X^T\hat{U} = X^T(Y - X\hat{B}) = X^TY - X^TX[(X^TX)^{-1}X^TY] = 0$. Hence $[1|X^*]^T\hat{U} = 0$ which gives $1^T\hat{U} = 0_{1\times 1}$ and also $X^{*T}\hat{U} = 0_{k-1\times 1}$.

Now, $M^0Y = M^0X\hat{B} + M^0\hat{U}$. But $M^0\hat{U} = (I - 1/N11^T)\hat{U} = \hat{U} - 1[1/N1^T\hat{U}] = \hat{U}$. Then, $M^0Y = [0|X^{**}]\hat{B} + \hat{U}$. Let

$$M^0 Y = \begin{bmatrix} Y_1 - \bar{Y} \\ Y_2 - \bar{Y} \\ \vdots \\ Y_N - \bar{Y} \end{bmatrix} \text{ be } Y^{**}$$

Then, from the above,

$$Y^{**} = X^{**} \begin{bmatrix} \hat{b}_1 \\ \hat{b}_2 \\ \vdots \\ \hat{b}_{k-1} \end{bmatrix} + \hat{U}$$

where constant estimate $\hat{b}_0$ is left out. If we define

$$\hat{B}^{**} = \begin{bmatrix} \hat{b}_1 \\ \hat{b}_2 \\ \vdots \\ \hat{b}_{k-1} \end{bmatrix}$$

then, $Y^{**} = X^{**}\hat{B}^{**} + \hat{U}$. Thus,

$$Y^{**T}Y^{**} = \hat{B}^{**T}X^{**T}X^{**}\hat{B}^{**} + \hat{U}^T\hat{U}$$

since

$$X^{**T}\hat{U} = (M^0X^*)^T\hat{U} = X^{*T}M^0\hat{U} = X^{*T}\hat{U} = 0$$

Now, using $[R(X^TX)^{-1}R^T]^{-1} = [X^{**T}X^{**}]$,

$$(R\hat{B})^T[\sigma_u^2 R(X^TX)^{-1}R^T]^{-1}(R\hat{B}) = \frac{\hat{B}^{**T}(X^{**T}X^{**})\hat{B}^{**}}{\sigma_u^2}$$

$$= \frac{(X^{**}\hat{B}^{**})^T(X^{**}\hat{B}^{**})}{\sigma_u^2} \sim \chi_{k-1}^2$$

Hence, the test statistic is

$$\frac{\frac{(X^{**}\hat{B}^{**})^T(X^{**}\hat{B}^{**})}{(k-1)}}{\frac{\hat{U}^T\hat{U}}{(N-k)}} \sim F_{k-1,\, N-k}$$

Moreover, the numerator is ESS/$(k-1)$, then

$$\frac{\frac{\text{ESS}}{[\text{TSS}(k-1)]}}{\frac{\text{RSS}}{[\text{TSS}(N-k)]}} \sim F_{k-1,N-k}$$

Therefore,

$$\frac{\frac{R^2}{(k-1)}}{\frac{(1-R^2)}{(N-k)}} \sim F_{k-1,N-k}$$

Note that if R^2 is large, the F statistic is also large. What happens to the test on H_0 : $B_2 = B_3 = \cdots = B_k = 0$? Do we tend to reject or accept? We reject H_0.

While R^2 determines how well is the fit of the regression line $X\hat{B}$, usually adjusted R^2 or $\bar{R}^2$ is used to check how well Y is explained by the model XB:

$$\bar{R}^2 = 1 - \frac{\frac{RSS}{(N-k)}}{\frac{TSS}{(N-1)}} = \frac{1-k}{N-k} + \frac{N-1}{N-k}R^2$$

As we can arbitrarily increase R^2 by using more explanatory variables or overfitting, then for any fixed N, increase in k will be compensated for by a reduction to a smaller $\bar{R}^2$, ceteris paribus.

Three other common criteria for comparing the fit of various specifications or model XB are:

Schwarz Criterion: $\text{SC} = -2\frac{L^*}{N} + \frac{k}{N}\ln N$

Akaike Information Criterion: $\text{AIC} = -2\frac{L^*}{N} + \frac{2k}{N}$

Hannan-Quinn criterion: $\text{HQC} = -2\frac{L^*}{N} + \frac{2k}{N}\ln(\ln N)$,

where

$$L^* = \ln\left[\left(2\pi\hat{\sigma}_u^2\right)^{-N/2}\exp\left(-\frac{1}{2\hat{\sigma}_u^2}\sum_{i=1}^{N}\hat{u}_i^2\right)\right], \quad \text{and} \quad \sum_{i=1}^{N}\hat{u}_i^2 \text{ is SSR}$$

Unlike $\bar{R}^2$, when a better fit yields a larger $\bar{R}^2$ number, here, smaller SC, AIC, and HQC indicate better fits. This is due to the penalty imposed by larger k.

6.3 Forecasting

For prediction or forecasting involving multiple explanatory variables, let the new variables be $c^T = (1X_2^*X_3^* \cdots X_k^*)$. So, the forecast is

$$\hat{Y} = c^T\hat{B}$$

The variance of the forecast is $\text{var}(c^T\hat{B}) = c^T\,\text{var}(\hat{B})c$. Note that the variance of forecast is not the variance of forecast error.

However, in terms of prediction or forecast error in the next period

$$Y = c^T B + U^*_{1\times 1}$$
$$Y - \hat{Y} = U^* - c^T(\hat{B} - B)$$

So, conditional on X,

$$\text{var}(Y - \hat{Y}) = \sigma_u^2[1 + c^T (X^T X)^{-1} c]$$

There is the implicit assumption that this conditional variance also applies to the new c values. And,

$$\frac{Y - \hat{Y}}{\hat{\sigma}_u \sqrt{1 + c^T(X^T X)^{-1} c}} \sim t_{N-k}$$

Thus, the 95 % confidence interval of next Y is:

$$\hat{Y} \pm t_{0.025} \hat{\sigma}_u \sqrt{1 + c^T (X^T X)^{-1} c}$$

After considering the desirable properties of OLS estimators of the multiple linear regression (MLR) under the classical conditions of disturbances, it is time to consider specification errors. A specification error or a misspecification of the MLR model is a problem with an assumption of the model such that the problem will lead to OLS not being BLUE. Some specification errors are practically not serious enough to lose sleep over, but some can be pretty serious to merit detailed investigation.

We shall consider different types of specification errors as follows, and then suggest remedies. Specifically, we shall consider the misspecifications of disturbances or residual errors, the misspecifications of explanatory variables, misspecifications of the relationship between the explanatory variables and disturbances, and misspecifications of coefficients. Special cases of misspecifications of disturbances such as heteroskedasticity and serial correlations will be considered in more details.

6.4 Misspecification with Disturbances

The classical conditions state that $E(UU^T|X) = \sigma_u^2 I_N$ in which the disturbances are spherical (both homoskedastic and serially uncorrelated). Suppose instead $E(UU^T|X) = \sigma_u^2 \Omega_{N\times N} \neq \sigma_u^2 I_N$, where each element of the covariance matrix $\Omega_{N\times N}$ may be a non-zero constant. Taking iterated expectations, $E(UU^T) = \sigma_u^2 \Omega_{N\times N} \neq \sigma_u^2 I_N$. If $\Omega_{N\times N}$ is known, i. e.

$$Y_{N\times 1} = X_{N\times k} B_{k\times 1} + U_{N\times 1}$$
$$U \sim N(0, \sigma_u^2 \Omega_{N\times N}) \quad \text{and} \quad \Omega \neq I$$

we can apply generalized least squares (GLS) estimation.

Since Ω is a covariance matrix, any $x_{N\times 1}$ vector must yield $\sigma_u^2 x^T \Omega x \geq 0$ as the variance of $x^T U$. Hence, Ω is positive definite. In Linear Algebra, there is a theorem that if Ω is positive definite, then it can be expressed as:

$$\Omega = PP^T \tag{6.6}$$

where P is a $N \times N$ non-singular matrix. Note that P is fixed and non-stochastic. Now Eq. (6.6) implies

$$P^{-1}\Omega P^{-1T} = I \tag{6.7}$$

and also

$$\Omega^{-1} = P^{-1T}P^{-1} \tag{6.8}$$

Define $Y^* = P^{-1}Y, X^* = P^{-1}X$, and $U^* = P^{-1}U$. Pre-multiply the original model $Y = XB + U$ by P^{-1}. Then,

$$P^{-1}Y = P^{-1}XB + P^{-1}U$$

or $Y^* = X^*B + U^*$. Thus,

$$\begin{aligned} \text{cov}(U^*) &= E(U^*U^{*T}) = E(P^{-1}UU^TP^{-1T}) = P^{-1}E(UU^T)P^{-1T} \\ &= \sigma_u^2 P^{-1}\Omega P^{-1T} \end{aligned}$$

By Eq. (6.7), $\text{cov}(U^*) = \sigma_u^2 I$.

Thus, $Y^* = X^*B + U^*$ satisfies the classical conditions. The OLS regression of Y^* on X^* gives

$$\hat{B} = (X^{*T}X^*)^{-1}X^{*T}Y^* \tag{6.9}$$

This $\hat{B}$ is BLUE. This is not the original OLS estimator of $\hat{B}_{\text{OLS}} = (X^TX)^{-1}X^TY$ since the regression is made using transformed Y^* and X^*. Call this new generalized least squares estimator $\hat{B}_{\text{GLS}}$.

We can express $\hat{B}_{\text{GLS}}$ in terms of the original Y and X. We do this by substituting the definitions of X^* and Y^* into Eq. (6.9) and utilising Eq. (6.8).

$$\begin{aligned} \hat{B}_{\text{GLS}} &= (X^{*T}X^*)^{-1}X^{*T}Y^* = [(P^{-1}X)^T(P^{-1}X)]^{-1}(P^{-1}X)^T(P^{-1}Y) \\ &= (X^TP^{-1T}P^{-1}X)^{-1}X^TP^{-1T}P^{-1}Y \end{aligned}$$

Or,

$$\hat{B}_{\text{GLS}} = (X^T\Omega^{-1}X)^{-1}X^T\Omega^{-1}Y$$

Note that σ_u^2 does not appear in the formula for $\hat{B}_{\mathrm{GLS}}$. Given Ω, the latter is the Generalized Least Squares (GLS) estimator of B in the regression of Y on X. This GLS (exactly the same as $\hat{B}$ in Eq. (6.9)) is BLUE. It is interesting to note that OLS regression of Y on X based on $Y_{N\times 1} = X_{N\times k}B_{k\times 1} + U_{N\times 1}$, with non-spherical disturbances U, produces OLS estimator $\hat{B}_{\mathrm{OLS}}$ that is unbiased, i. e. $E(X^TX)^{-1}X^TY = B$, but unlike $\hat{B}_{\mathrm{GLS}}$, is not best in the sense of efficiency.

Given that Ω is known, an unbiased estimate for σ_u^2 is (since $\mathrm{cov}(U^*)$ is $\sigma_u^2 I$)

$$\begin{aligned}\hat{\sigma}_u^2 &= \frac{1}{N-k}(Y^* - X^*\hat{B}_{\mathrm{GLS}})^T(Y^* - X^*\hat{B}_{\mathrm{GLS}})\\ &= \frac{1}{N-k}(P^{-1}Y - P^{-1}X\hat{B}_{\mathrm{GLS}})^T(P^{-1}Y - P^{-1}X\hat{B}_{\mathrm{GLS}})\\ &= \frac{1}{N-k}(Y - X\hat{B}_{\mathrm{GLS}})^T P^{-1T}P^{-1}(Y - X\hat{B}_{\mathrm{GLS}})\\ &= \frac{1}{N-k}\hat{U}^T\Omega^{-1}\hat{U}\end{aligned}$$

where above $\hat{U} = Y - X\hat{B}_{\mathrm{GLS}}$. Note also that

$$\mathrm{cov}(\hat{B}_{\mathrm{GLS}}) = \sigma_u^2(X^{*T}X^*)^{-1} = \sigma_u^2(X^TP^{-1T}P^{-1}X)^{-1} = \sigma_u^2(X^T\Omega^{-1}X)^{-1}$$

Thus, the usual procedures of confidence interval estimation and testing of the parameters can be carried out.

6.4.1 Heteroskedasticity

Heteroskedasticity (or non-homoskedasticity) refers to the case when the variances of the disturbances representated as diagonal elements in $\Omega_{N\times N}$ are not constants. Suppose

$$\mathrm{cov}(U) = \sigma_u^2\Omega,$$

where

$$\Omega_{N\times N} = \begin{pmatrix} X_{1j}^2 & 0 & \cdots & 0\\ 0 & X_{2j}^2 & \cdots & 0\\ \vdots & \vdots & \ddots & \vdots\\ 0 & 0 & \cdots & X_{Nj}^2\end{pmatrix}$$

This is a special case when Ω is of a known form. Here, $Y = XB + U$, $X = (X_1|X_2|X_3|\cdots|X_k)$ where the first column of X is $X_1 = (1\cdots 1\cdots 1)^T$ and the jth column is $X_j = (X_{1j}X_{2j}\cdots X_{Nj})^T$. The N disturbances have variances proportional to the square of a certain jth explanatory variable X_{ij} as follows.

Now,

$$\Omega_{N\times N}^{-1} = \begin{pmatrix} \frac{1}{X_{1j}^2} & 0 & \cdots & 0 \\ 0 & \frac{1}{X_{2j}^2} & \cdots & 0 \\ \vdots & \vdots & \ddots & \vdots \\ 0 & 0 & \cdots & \frac{1}{X_{Nj}^2} \end{pmatrix}$$

Therefore,

$$\hat{B} = (X^T\Omega^{-1}X)^{-1}X^T\Omega^{-1}Y = (X^{*T}X^*)^{-1}X^{*T}Y^*,$$

where

$$Y^* = \begin{pmatrix} \frac{Y_1}{X_{1j}} \\ \frac{Y_2}{X_{2j}} \\ \vdots \\ \frac{Y_N}{X_{Nj}} \end{pmatrix} \quad \text{and} \quad X^* = \begin{pmatrix} \frac{1}{X_{1j}} & \frac{X_{12}}{X_{1j}} & \cdots & \frac{X_{1k}}{X_{1j}} \\ \frac{1}{X_{2j}} & \frac{X_{22}}{X_{2j}} & \cdots & \frac{X_{2k}}{X_{2j}} \\ \vdots & \vdots & \ddots & \vdots \\ \frac{1}{X_{Nj}} & \frac{X_{N2}}{X_{Nj}} & \cdots & \frac{X_{Nk}}{X_{Nj}} \end{pmatrix}$$

For the notation in X_{ij}, the first subscript i represents time/cross-sectional position $1, 2, \ldots, N$, and second subscript j represents the column number of X or the jth explanatory variable. The above GLS estimator $\hat{B}$ is also called the weighted least squares estimator since we are basically weighing each observable $(Y_i, X_{i1}, X_{i2}, \ldots, X_{ij}, \ldots, X_{ik})$ by $1/X_{ij}$ for every i.

Then, to test $H_0 : B_j = 0$, we use

$$\frac{\hat{B}_j - 0}{\hat{\sigma}_u \times \sqrt{j\text{th diagonal element of } (X^{*T}X^*)^{-1}}}$$

that is distributed as t_{N-k}.

Suppose the N disturbances have variances proportional to the αth power of a certain jth explanatory variable X_{ij} as follows. X and U are not correlated.

$$\text{cov}(U) = \sigma_u^2\Omega$$

$$\Omega_{N\times N} = \begin{pmatrix} X_{1j}^{\alpha} & 0 & \cdots & 0 \\ 0 & X_{2j}^{\alpha} & \cdots & 0 \\ \vdots & \vdots & \ddots & \vdots \\ 0 & 0 & \cdots & X_{Nj}^{\alpha} \end{pmatrix}$$

However, α is not known and has to be estimated.

The suggested estimation procedure is as follows.

(1a) Use OLS to obtain $\hat{B}_{\text{OLS}} = (X^T X)^{-1} X^T Y$ that is unbiased, but not BLUE.
(1b) Find estimated residual $\hat{u}_i = Y_i - \sum_{j=1}^{k} \hat{B}_{j,\text{OLS}} X_{ij}$ (Note: $E(\hat{U}) = U$).
(1c) Since $\text{var}(u_i) = \sigma_u^2 X_{ij}^{\alpha}$ for $i = 1, 2, \ldots, N$, then

$$\ln[\text{var}(u_i)] = \ln \sigma_u^2 + \alpha \ln X_{ij}.$$

α is estimated by OLS regression using

$$\ln[\hat{u}_i^2] = \text{constant} + \alpha \ln X_{ij} + \text{residual error}.$$

Obtaining $\hat{\alpha}$, this is used as follows to estimate $\hat{\Omega}$.

(1d)

$$\hat{\Omega}_{N\times N} = \begin{pmatrix} X_{1j}^{\hat{\alpha}} & 0 & \cdots & 0 \\ 0 & X_{2j}^{\hat{\alpha}} & \cdots & 0 \\ \vdots & \vdots & \ddots & \vdots \\ 0 & 0 & \cdots & X_{Nj}^{\hat{\alpha}} \end{pmatrix}.$$

Then, $\hat{B} = (X^T \hat{\Omega}^{-1} X)^{-1} X^T \hat{\Omega}^{-1} Y$ will be approximately BLUE (subject to sampling error in $\hat{\alpha}$).

In situations where Ω is unknown and the form is approximately $I_{N\times N}$, then we may stick to OLS. It is still unbiased, and approximately BLUE.

Suppose the heteroskedasticity implies

$$\Omega_{N\times N} = \begin{pmatrix} \sigma_1^2 & 0 & \cdots & 0 \\ 0 & \sigma_2^2 & \cdots & 0 \\ 0 & \vdots & \ddots & 0 \\ 0 & 0 & 0 & \sigma_N^2 \end{pmatrix}$$

where $\sigma_u^2 = 1$ here, and the $\{\sigma_t^2\}_{t=1,2,3,\ldots,N}$ are not known, but are finite constants. Assume (A1′) $E(U|X) = 0$ and (A2′) $E(UU^T|X) = \Omega_{N\times N}$. The OLS estimator $\hat{B} = (X^T X)^{-1} X^T Y$ is still unbiased but inefficient.

The covariance matrix of OLS $\hat{B}$ conditional on X is

$$(X^T X)^{-1} X^T \Omega X (X^T X)^{-1}$$

Since Ω is diagonal with constants, $X^T \Omega X = \sum_{t=1}^{N} \sigma_t^2 X_t^T X_t$, where

$$X_{N\times k} = \begin{pmatrix} X_1 \\ X_2 \\ \vdots \\ X_t \\ \vdots \\ X_N \end{pmatrix}$$

and X_t is $1 \times k$ vector containing all the explanatory variables at the same time-point.

White (1980)[2] suggests a heteroskedasticity-consistent covariance matrix estimator (HCCME), $\text{cov}(\hat{B})$, as $(X^TX)^{-1}X^T\hat{\Omega}X(X^TX)^{-1}$ that is consistent.

First, run OLS and obtain $\hat{u}_t = Y_t - X_t\hat{B}_{\text{OLS}}$.

Let

$$\hat{\Omega} = \begin{pmatrix} \hat{u}_1^2 & 0 & \cdots & 0 \\ 0 & \hat{u}_2^2 & \cdots & 0 \\ \vdots & \vdots & \ddots & \vdots \\ 0 & 0 & \cdots & \hat{u}_N^2 \end{pmatrix}$$

where N is the sample size.

Based on (A1′) and (A2′),

$$\begin{aligned} E[X^T\hat{\Omega}X] &= E\left[\sum_{t=1}^{N} \hat{u}_t^2 X_t^T X_t\right] \\ &= \sum_{t=1}^{N} E[\hat{u}_t^2]E[X_t^T X_t] \\ &= \sum_{t=1}^{N} \sigma_t^2 E[X_t^T X_t] \\ &= E[X^T\Omega X] \end{aligned}$$

where the expectation is taken over each of the N periods, i. e. a multiple integral.

Assume $\frac{1}{N}\sum_{t=1}^{N} \sigma_t^2 E[X_t^T X_t] < \infty$ when $N \uparrow \infty$. Thus there is some restriction on the sum of unconditional moments of $\sigma_t^2 X_t^T X_t$. Then,

$$\lim_{N\to\infty} E\left(\left[\frac{1}{N}\sum_{t=1}^{N} \hat{u}_t^2 X_t^T X_t\right] - \left[\frac{1}{N}\sum_{t=1}^{N} \sigma_t^2 X_t^T X_t\right]\right) = 0$$

that shows convergence in mean of $1/N \sum_{t=1}^{N} \hat{u}_t^2 X_t^T X_t$. This implies convergence in probability. Hence

$$\frac{1}{N}(X^T\hat{\Omega}X) \xrightarrow{P} \frac{1}{N}(X^T\Omega X)$$

Conditional on X, we should obtain the same result as above.

2 See Halbert White, A heteroskedasticity-consistent covariance matrix estimator and a direct test for heteroskedasticity, *Econometrica*, 48, 817–838, 1980. A reference text book is Halbert White (1984), *Asymptotic Theory for Econometricians*, Academic Press.

Therefore, the OLS estimator covariance matrix in this case is estimated by

$$(X^T X)^{-1} X^T \hat{\Omega} X (X^T X)^{-1}$$

that is consistent for large N. We can then apply

$$N(X^T X)^{-1} X^T \hat{\Omega} X (X^T X)^{-1}$$

as the HCCME estimator of the covariance of $\sqrt{N}\hat{B}_{OLS}$. Thus, statistical inference on $\hat{B}$ using this HCCME can be done when the sample size is large. In practice, sometimes a finite-sample correction is used, and HCCME of $\text{cov}(\hat{B}_{OLS})$ is computed as

$$\frac{N}{N-k}(X^T X)^{-1} X^T \hat{\Omega} X (X^T X)^{-1}$$

There are several tests of the presence of heteroskedasticity.[3] If the form is such that the disturbance variance is positively associated with the corresponding explanatory variable level, Goldfeld-Quandt test may be used. In this test, the sample data is sorted in order of the value of the explanatory variable that is associated with the disturbance variance, starting with data with the lowest disturbance variance. OLS regression is then performed using the first third and the last third of this sorted sample. If the association is true, then the disturbance of the first third will have smaller variance (approximately homoskedastic) than the variance of the disturbance of the last third. Since the SSR/$(N-k)$ (or RSS/$(N-k)$) is the unbiased estimate of the variance of the residuals, the ratio of SSR(last third)/SSR(first third) $\times (n_1-k)/(n_3-k)$, where n_1 and n_3 are the sample sizes of the first third and last third, respectively, is distributed as $F_{n3-k,n1-k}$ under the null of no heteroskedasticity. If the ratio statistic under the F-distribution is too large and the null is rejected, then this form of heteroskedasticity is detected.

If heteroskedasticity is suspected to be of the form $\sigma_t^2 = f(Z_t)$ linked linearly to some $k-1$ exogenous variables Z_t, then the Breusch-Pagan & Godfrey test (LM test) can be performed. Here estimated $\hat{u}_t^2$ is regressed against a constant and Z_t and an asymptotic χ_{k-1}^2 test statistic and an equivalent $F_{k-1,N-k}$-statistic are reported based on the null hypothesis of zero restrictions on the slope coefficients of Z_t. If the null hypothesis is rejected, then there is evidence of the heteroskedasticity.

If the form of the heteroskedasticity is unknown, except that $\{\sigma_t^2\}$ for various $t = 1, 2, 3, \ldots, N$ are not constants but are functions of variables possibly dependent on X, then White's test can be applied. There are two cases. Either estimated $\hat{u}_t^2$ is regressed against a constant and X and its squared nonconstant terms, e. g., X_{1t}^2, X_{2t}^2, etc., or estimated $\hat{u}_t^2$ is regressed against a constant and X, its squared nonconstant terms, e. g.,

3 For more information, refer to R. Davidson and J. G. MacKinnon (1993), *Estimation and Inference in Econometrics*, Oxford University Press, 560–564.

X_{1t}^2, X_{2t}^2, etc., as well as cross-sectional terms, e. g., $X_{1t}X_{2t}, X_{1t}X_{3t}$, etc. In either case, an asymptotic χ_{k-1}^2 test statistic and an equivalent $F_{k-1,N-k}$ statistic are reported based on the null hypothesis of zero restrictions on the slope coefficients of the $k-1$ number of regressors. If the null hypothesis is rejected, then there is evidence of the heteroskedasticity.

6.4.2 Serial Correlation

Disturbances are serially correlated if u_t is a time series or cross-correlated if u_i is cross-sectional. For example, if Y's, X's, and U's are stochastic processes (over time), then if u_t is AR(1) or MA(1), the autocorrelation is not zero for at least one lag. Then $E(UU^T) = \sigma_u^2 \Omega_{N\times N} \neq \sigma_u^2 I_N$. Specifically, the off-diagonal elements are not zero.

Suppose disturbance

$$u_{t+1} = \rho u_t + e_{t+1}$$

where e_{t+1} is zero mean i. i. d., then

$$\Omega_{N\times N} = \begin{pmatrix} 1 & \rho & \rho^2 & \cdots & \rho^{N-1} \\ \rho & 1 & \rho & \cdots & \rho^{N-2} \\ \rho^2 & \rho & 1 & \cdots & \rho^{N-3} \\ \vdots & \vdots & \vdots & \ddots & \vdots \\ \rho^{N-1} & \rho^{N-2} & \rho^{N-3} & \cdots & 1 \end{pmatrix}$$

What happens? If ρ is known, then we can apply GLS and obtain a BLUE estimator of B. If ρ can be accurately estimated, then Estimated or Feasible GLS can be applied. Specifically the Cochrane-Orcutt (iterative) procedure is explained here. It tries to transform the disturbances into i. i. d. disturbances so that the problem is less severe, and then FGLS estimators are approximately consistent and asymptotically efficient.

Suppose ρ is known, we transform the data into

$$Y_N^* = Y_N - \rho Y_{N-1}$$
$$\vdots$$
$$Y_2^* = Y_2 - \rho Y_1$$

and

$$X_N^* = X_N - \rho X_{N-1}$$
$$\vdots$$
$$X_2^* = X_2 - \rho X_1$$

Recall X_t is $1 \times k$ matrix containing all explanatory variables at time t. The system of regression equations is:

$$\begin{aligned} Y_N &= X_N B + u_N \\ Y_{N-1} &= X_{N-1} B + u_{N-1} \\ &\vdots \\ Y_2 &= X_2 B + u_2 \\ Y_1 &= X_1 B + u_1 \end{aligned}$$

Therefore,

$$\begin{aligned} Y_N^* &= Y_N - \rho Y_{N-1} = X_N B + u_N - \rho(X_{N-1}B + u_{N-1}) = X_N^* B + e_N \\ &\vdots \\ Y_2^* &= X_2^* B + e_2 \end{aligned}$$

Thus, we are back to the classical conditions, and OLS is BLUE on the transformed data. Of course, this is equivalent to GLS on the original data.

In practice, however, since ρ is not known, it has to be estimated. First run OLS on the original data. Obtain the estimated residuals

$$\hat{u}_t = Y_t - X_t \hat{B}_{\text{OLS}}$$

Next, estimate ρ using

$$\hat{\rho} = \frac{\frac{1}{N}\sum_{t=2}^{N} \hat{u}_t \hat{u}_{t-1}}{\frac{1}{N}\sum_{t=2}^{N} \hat{u}_{t-1}^2}$$

Note that the index starts from 2. $\hat{\rho}$ is the sample first-order autocorrelation coefficient of residual error u_t in $U = Y - XB$ regression.

Then, the transformations are done, viz.

$$\begin{aligned} Y_N^* &= Y_N - \hat{\rho} Y_{N-1} \\ &\vdots \\ Y_2^* &= Y_2 - \hat{\rho} Y_1 \\ Y_1^* &= \sqrt{1-\hat{\rho}^2}\, Y_1 \\ X_N^* &= X_N - \hat{\rho} X_{N-1} \\ &\vdots \\ X_2^* &= X_2 - \hat{\rho} X_1 \end{aligned}$$

$$X_1^* = \sqrt{1-\hat{\rho}^2}X_1$$

The last transformation involving X_1 may be added to allow an extra sample point; it approximately keeps the structure of the variance of X_t's similar. Then, OLS is run again using the transformed $\{Y_t^*\}$ and $\{X_t^*\}$. The estimators are approximately consistent and asymptotically efficient. Iterations can be performed using the updated OLS $\hat{u}_t$ and $\hat{\rho}$ for another round of OLS regression until the estimates converge.

The presence of serial correlations, hence non-homoskedastic disturbances and breakdown of the classical conditions, can be tested using the Durbin-Watson (DW) tests, the Box-Pierce-Ljung Q-tests, and Breusch-Pagan & Godfrey test (LM test).

The DW d-test statistic is reported in most standard regression output tables. It is related to the estimated $\hat{\rho}$.

$$d = \frac{\sum_{t=2}^{N}(\hat{u}_t - \hat{u}_{t-1})^2}{\sum_{t=2}^{N}\hat{u_t^2}}$$

where $\hat{u}_t$ is the estimated residual. $d \approx 2(1-\hat{\rho})$. In a linear regression, when the fitted residuals indicate a high DW-d statistic above 2, there is negative correlation in the disturbance. When the fitted residuals indicate a low DW-d statistic below 2, there is positive correlation in the disturbance. When the DW d-statistic is about 2, there is zero correlation.

The d-statistic follows a Durbin-Watson distribution when the null is zero correlation. When the null of the disturbance is an AR(1) process, then the Durbin-Watson h-statistic is used. The DW d-statistic distribution is complex, being dependent on sample size N, significance level, number of regressors k, and whether there is a constant or not in the regressors. The DW d-distribution is reported in table form giving two numbers d_L and d_H where $d_L < d_H$ under the null hypothesis of $H_0 : \rho = 0$.

If DW $d < 2$, then if $d < d_L$, reject H_0 in favor of alternative hypothesis $H_A : \rho > 0$. But if DW $d > d_H$, then we cannot reject (thus "accept") H_0. If DW $d > 2$, then if $4\text{-}d < d_L$, reject H_0 in favor of alternative hypothesis $H_A : \rho < 0$. But if DW $4\text{-}d > d_H$, then we cannot reject (thus "accept") H_0. If $d < 2$, and $d_L < d < d_H$, or if $d > 2$, and $d_L < 4 - d < d_H$, then we cannot conclude whether to reject or accept H_0.

The other tests of serial correlation viz. the Box-Pierce-Ljung Q-test and Breusch-Pagan & Godfrey test (LM test) overcome the DW test limitations. The essential idea of the LM test is to test the null hypothesis that there is no serial correlation in the residuals up to the specified order. Here estimated $\hat{u}_t$ is regressed against a constant and lagged $\hat{u}_{t-1}, \ldots, \hat{u}_{t-k+1}$, and an asymptotic χ^2_{k-1} test statistic and an equivalent $F_{k-1,N-k}$ statistic are reported based on the null hypothesis of zero restrictions on the slope coefficients of $\hat{u}_{t-j}$'s. Strictly speaking, the F-distribution is an approximation since ρ is estimated.

6.5 Misspecification with Explanatory Variable

There are several categories of specification errors with explanatory variable X.

6.5.1 Exclusion of Relevant Explanatory Variables

Exclusion or omission of relevant explanatory variables can lead to serious finite sample bias and also large sample inconsistency. This is sometimes called an error of omission.

For example, in Singapore, demand (proxied by number of bids for COEs) for car D_t is specified as follows.

$$D_t = B_0 + B_1 P_{t-1} + u_t$$

where P_t is average price of car at t. What have we left out? What happens to OLS $\hat{B}_0, \hat{B}_1$ if the true model is

$$D_t = b_0 + b_1 P_{t-1} + b_2 Y_t + b_3 Q_t + b_4 M_t + \xi_t$$

where Y_t is average income level at t, Q_t is the amount of quota allocated for bidding at t, and M_t is unemployment rate in the economy at t. Thus, there is an error of omission.

$E(\hat{B}_0) \neq b_0$ and $E(\hat{B}_1) \neq b_1$. Thus, the OLS estimators are biased and not consistent.

An exception when omission is not as problematic is when the omitted explanatory variable is orthogonal to all the existing explanatory variables, i. e., the omitted variable has zero correlations with all the existing explanatory variables.

Suppose the true model is $Y_{N\times 1} = X_{N\times k} B_{k\times 1} + Z_{N\times 1} D_{1\times 1} + V_{N\times 1}$, but the linear regression is performed on $Y_{N\times 1} = X_{N\times k} B_{k\times 1} + U_{N\times 1}$ where the variable Z is omitted. Then, $U_{N\times 1} = Z_{N\times 1} D_{1\times 1} + V_{N\times 1}$.

Assume $E(V|X,Z) = 0$ and $E(VV^T|X,Z) = \sigma_u^2 I_{N\times N}$ so that OLS estimators on the true model are BLUE. But OLS estimator on the performed regression is $(X^T X)^{-1} X^T Y$. Now, the expected value of this estimator is:

$$\begin{aligned} E[(X^T X)^{-1} X^T Y] &= E[(X^T X)^{-1} X^T (XB + ZD + V)] \\ &= B + E[(X^T X)^{-1} X^T (ZD + V)] \\ &= B + E[E[(X^T X)^{-1} X^T ZD|X,Z]] \\ &\quad + E[E[(X^T X)^{-1} X^T V|X,Z]] \\ &= B + E[(X^T X)^{-1} X^T ZD] \neq B \end{aligned}$$

Hence it is seen that the OLS estimator is generally biased. The bias is caused by the omitted variable that appears in the second term on the RHS above. Assuming X, Z, and V are stationary, the OLS estimator is also generally not consistent as

$$\begin{aligned}\lim_{N\to\infty}(X^TX)^{-1}X^TY &= B + \lim_{N\to\infty}[(X^TX)^{-1}X^T(ZD+V)]\\ &= B + \Sigma_{XX}^{-1}\Sigma_{XZ}D + \Sigma_{XX}^{-1}\left(\lim_{N\to\infty}X^TV\right)\\ &= B + \Sigma_{XX}^{-1}\Sigma_{XZ}D \neq B\end{aligned}$$

where $\lim_{N\to\infty}X^TX = \Sigma_{XX}$, $\lim_{N\to\infty}X^TZ = \Sigma_{XZ}$, and $\lim_{N\to\infty}X^TV = 0$ since $E(X^TV) = 0_{k\times1}$.

However, if $E(Z|X) = 0$ which implies $E(X^TZ) = 0$, i. e. Z and X are orthogonal, then

$$\begin{aligned}E[(X^TX)^{-1}X^TY] &= B + E[E[(X^TX)^{-1}X^TZD|X]]\\ &\quad + E[E[(X^TX)^{-1}X^TV|X]]\\ &= B + E[(X^TX)^{-1}X^TE[Z|X]D] + 0 = B\end{aligned}$$

in which case the estimator is still unbiased even though there is an omitted orthogonal variable. It can be seen that we can re-write the performed regression as $Y = XB + (ZD + V)$ where $E(ZD + V|X) = 0$ and $E[(ZD + V)(ZD + V)^T]$ is in general not a homoskedastic covariance matrix. Hence the OLS estimator is in general not efficient.

6.5.2 Inclusion of Irrelevant Explanatory Variables

The unnecessary inclusion of irrelevant variables for explanation is sometimes called an error of commission. Suppose the true specification of demand for cars/COEs in Singapore, D_t, is

$$D_t = b_0 + b_1P_{t-1} + b_2Y_t + b_3Q_t + b_4M_t + \xi_t$$

but additional explanatory variables

$$\begin{aligned}Z_{1t} &= \text{number of cars in Hong Kong}\\ Z_{2t} &= \text{number of cars in New York}\\ Z_{3t} &= \text{number of cars in Tokyo}\\ &\vdots\\ Z_{kt} &= \text{number of cars in Mexico City}\end{aligned}$$

are employed in the MLR.

Clearly, the $\{Z_{it}\}_{i,t}$ variables should have no explanation on D_t. They are irrelevant variables. However, given the finite sample size $t = 1, 2, \ldots, N$, it is highly likely that some of the irrelevant variables may help to explain the variation in D_t and thus increase the coefficient of determination, R^2, of the MLR.

This is a statistical artifact and has nothing to do with economic theory. If the sample is sufficiently large relative to the number of included irrelevant variables, we should find the estimates of their coefficients not to be significantly different from zero. Estimates of b_0, b_1, b_2, b_3, b_4, and σ_u^2 are still unbiased. However, the sampling error may increase if the superfluous variables are correlated with the relevant ones. If the estimated regression model is employed to do forecast, then it could lead to serious errors especially when the variances of the irrelevant variables are large.

One approach to reduce the problem of irrelevant inclusion is to start with a large set of plausible explanatory variables. Take note of the adjusted R^2 or the Akaike Information Criteria. Then reduce the number of explanatory variables until the adjusted R^2 is maximized or the AIC is minimized. Since the problem of unnecessary inclusion is not as serious, it is useful to observe the estimates with the larger set of explanatory variables, and then compare with estimates of a subset of explanatory variables. If an appropriate set of explanatory variables is selected, the estimates should not change much from the results in the regression with the larger set. This procedure is part of an area in econometrics called model selection.

6.5.3 Multi-collinearity

Suppose we partition $X_{N \times k} = (X_1 | X_2 | X_3 | \cdots | X_k)$ where X_j is a $N \times 1$ column. If at least one X_j is nearly a linear combination of other X_i's, i. e. there is a strong degree of collinearity among the columns of X, or multi-collinearity problem, then the determinant $|X^T X|$ is very close to zero which generally means diagonal elements of $(X^T X)^{-1}$ are very large.

But $\text{var}(\hat{B}_j) = j$th diagonal element of $\sigma_u^2 (X^T X)^{-1}$ so this would be very large. This means that the sampling errors of the estimators in $\hat{B}$ are large in the face of multi-collinear X. It leads to small t-statistic based on $H_0 : B_j = 0$, and thus the zero null is not rejected. Hence it is difficult to obtain accurate estimators. Even if B_j is actually $>$ (or $<$) 0, we cannot reject $H_0 : B_j = 0$.

What can we do to fix the problem? We can fall back on a priori restrictions based on theory. For example, if explanatory variable X_j is highly correlated with $X_1, X_2, \ldots, X_{j-1}, X_{j+1}, \ldots, X_k$ but b_j theoretically is close to zero, we can restrict $b_j = 0$ and thus avoid inclusion of X_j. This will eliminate the multi-collinearity problem.

Or else we live with the shortcoming that is a data problem, and not a model problem. The problem can of course be mitigated when the sample size increases. It should be noted that the OLS estimators are still BLUE, and asymptotically, the OLS estimators are still consistent.

6.5.4 Nonstationarity

When X has a time trend, e. g., $X_{it} = a_0 + a_1 t + u_{it}$, u_{it} being i. i. d., then it is problematic to regress Y_{it} on X_{it} because X_{it} is not stationary. When Y_{it} is also nonstationary, there is the problem of "false" correlation between Y_{it} and X_{it}. This problem will be explored more fully in the chapter on unit roots.

6.6 Misspecification of Independence between *X* and *U*

When there is dependence between regressor X and disturbance U, this dependence can take two major forms. The two major misspecification forms are contemporaneous zero correlation but stochastic dependence, and contemporaneous non-zero correlation.

6.6.1 Contemporaneous Zero Correlation but Stochastic Dependence

Suppose lagged dependent variable Y_{t-1} is included as an explanatory variable in MLR with

$$Y_t = B_0 + B_1 X_{t1} + B_2 X_{t2} + \cdots + B_{k-2} X_{tk-2} + CY_{t-1} + u_t$$

Then even if Y_{t-1} and u_t are contemporaneously not correlated, because Y_t is correlated with u_t, then process $\{Y_t\}$ and $\{u_t\}$ are not stochastically independent. (Stochastic independence would require all past and future Y_{t+k}'s to be uncorrelated with u_t.) What happens? OLS estimator is not BLUE, but is still consistent. This is also referred to as the lagged endogenous variable problem.

We can show that as follows. In matrix notation, $Y_{N\times1} = (Y_1 Y_2 \cdots Y_N)^T$. $X_{N\times k} = (1|X_1|X_2|\cdots|Y^*)$ where 1 is $N \times 1$, X_i is $N \times 1$, and $Y^* = (Y_0 Y_1 \cdots Y_{N-1})^T$.

$$U_{N\times1} = (u_1 u_2 \cdots u_N)^T \cdot B_{k\times1} = (B_0 B_1 B_2 \ldots B_{k-2} C)^T$$

Then, OLS $\hat{B} = (X^T X)^{-1} X^T Y$. The expected value of this OLS estimator is:

$$\begin{aligned} E(\hat{B}) &= E[(X^T X)^{-1} X^T (XB + U)] = E[B + (X^T X)^{-1} X^T U] \\ &= B + E[(X^T X)^{-1} X^T U] \end{aligned}$$

If $\{X_1, X_2, \ldots\}$ or $X_{N\times k}$ is stochastically independent of U, then the expectation of the last term above becomes:

$$E[(X^T X)^{-1} X^T U] = E[(X^T X)^{-1} X^T] E(U)$$

which is $0_{k\times1}$ since $E(U) = 0$.

However, if one element of $X_{N\times k}$, e. g. Y^*, is not independent of U, then the term $E[(X^TX)^{-1}X^TU]$ is not zero since the expectation cannot be taken as the product of expectations of $(X^TX)^{-1}X^T$ and U as some random elements in $(X^TX)^{-1}X^T$ will be dependent on U. In other words, under this scenario, the assumptions (A3) or else (A1′) do not hold. Hence dependence even with contemporaneous zero correlation leads to biased estimator in finite sample as the bias $E[(X^TX)^{-1}X^TU] \neq 0$.

Nevertheless, in large sample, the estimator can be shown to be consistent when X and U are stationary. The OLS estimator is: $\hat{B} = B + (X^TX)^{-1}X^TU$. Therefore, if Y_{t-1} and u_t are contemporaneously uncorrelated, and X_{ti}'s ($\forall i$) are also uncorrelated with u_t, then

$$\frac{X^TU}{N} = \begin{pmatrix} \frac{1}{N}\sum_{t=1}^{N} u_t \\ \frac{1}{N}\sum_{t=1}^{N} X_{t1}u_t \\ \frac{1}{N}\sum_{t=1}^{N} X_{t2}u_t \\ \vdots \\ \frac{1}{N}\sum_{t=1}^{N} X_{tk-2}u_t \\ \frac{1}{N}\sum_{t=1}^{N} Y_{t-1}u_t \end{pmatrix}_{k\times 1} \xrightarrow[N\uparrow\infty]{} \begin{pmatrix} E(u_t) \\ \operatorname{cov}(X_{t1}, u_t) \\ \operatorname{cov}(X_{t2}, u_t) \\ \vdots \\ \operatorname{cov}(X_{tk-2}, u_t) \\ \operatorname{cov}(Y_{t-1}, u_t) \end{pmatrix} = 0_{k\times 1}$$

Assume X^TX/N converges to a nonsingular $k \times k$ matrix, say Q, then:

$$\underset{N\uparrow\infty}{p\lim}\,\hat{B} = B + \underset{N\uparrow\infty}{p\lim}\left(\frac{X^TX}{N}\right)^{-1} \underset{N\uparrow\infty}{p\lim}\,\frac{X^TU}{N} = B + Q\cdot 0 = B$$

Thus, zero contemporaneous correlation, but not independence, does not yield BLUE for OLS $\hat{B}$, but yields consistency. In other words, $\hat{B}$ is biased in finite sample but is consistent.

6.6.2 Contemporaneous Non-Zero Correlation

In addition to $Y_t = B_0 + B_1X_{t1} + B_2X_{t2} + \cdots + B_{k-2}X_{tk-2} + CY_{t-1} + u_t$, suppose u_t is AR(1) process, i. e. $u_t = \rho u_{t-1} + e_t$, then

$$\begin{aligned} &\operatorname{cov}(Y_{t-1}, u_t) \\ &\quad = \operatorname{cov}(B_0 + B_1X_{t-11} + \cdots + B_{k-2}X_{t-1k-2} + \cdots + CY_{t-2} + u_{t-1}, u_t) \\ &\quad = \operatorname{cov}(u_t, u_{t-1}) \neq 0 \end{aligned}$$

Thus, Y_{t-1} and u_t are contemporaneously correlated. What happens? OLS estimator is not BLUE, and is also not consistent.

There are some special situations as follows when stochastic dependence between X and U arises and causes problems.

6.7 Measurement Error Problem

Measurement error problem in X (errors-in-variables problem) occurs when observed X_t^* is not the intended explanatory variable X_t, but is X_t measured with error. Suppose the true model is $Y_t = a + bX_t + u_t$, but we employ X_t^* as regressor instead.

$$X_t^* = X_t + e_t$$

is what is observed and used for the regressor in place of X_t. e_t is measurement error from the actual but unobserved X_t, and $\text{cov}(e_t, u_t) = 0$.

Under the true model, $Y_t = a + bX_t + u_t \Leftrightarrow Y_t = a + b(X_t^* - e_t) + u_t$. Therefore,

$$Y_t = a + bX_t^* + (u_t - be_t)$$

Now $\text{cov}(X_t^*, [u_t - be_t]) = \text{cov}(X_t + e_t, u_t - be_t) = -b\,\text{var}(e_t) \neq 0$ when $\text{cov}(X_t, u_t) = 0$. Thus, the MLR with measurement error induces a contemporaneous non-zero correlation. If we regress Y_t on X_t^*, the OLS estimator is not BLUE, and is not consistent. Does measurement error in dependent variable cause inconsistency? No.

6.7.1 Simultaneous Equations Model

Some regression specifications require simultaneous equations model. For example, if demand D_t is modeled as a regression equation with price P_t as explanatory variable:

$$D_t = B_0 + B_1P_t + e_t$$

then there could be another simultaneous equation of supply S_t, viz.

$$S_t = A_0 + A_1P_t + u_t$$

Assume that in general, $\text{cov}(u_t, e_t) = 0$.

The two regressions constitute the simultaneous equations model. In economic equilibrium, $D_t = S_t$. Then,

$$\begin{aligned} B_0 + B_1P_t + e_t &= A_0 + A_1P_t + u_t \\ \text{or} \quad (A_1 - B_1)P_t &= (B_0 - A_0) + (e_t - u_t) \end{aligned}$$

From the last equation, we have $\text{cov}(P_t, e_t) = \text{var}(e_t)/(A_1 - B_1) \neq 0$ and $\text{cov}(P_t, u_t) = -\text{var}(u_t)/(A_1 - B_1) \neq 0$. Thus, simultaneous equations induce contemporaneous non-zero correlation when MLR is performed on only one of the regression equations. This is called the simultaneous equations bias. If we regress D_t on P_t or else S_t on P_t, without considering simultaneous equations, the OLS estimator is not BLUE, and not consistent.

The simultaneous equations bias can be shown graphically in Figure 6.2. The issue of endogeneity bias also arises in structural equations model that may look similar to simultaneous equations though structural equations are more often used in the context where explanatory variables contain latent variables that are not directly observable but which may be also explained by the dependent variable. The issue is that the X variables are endogenous.

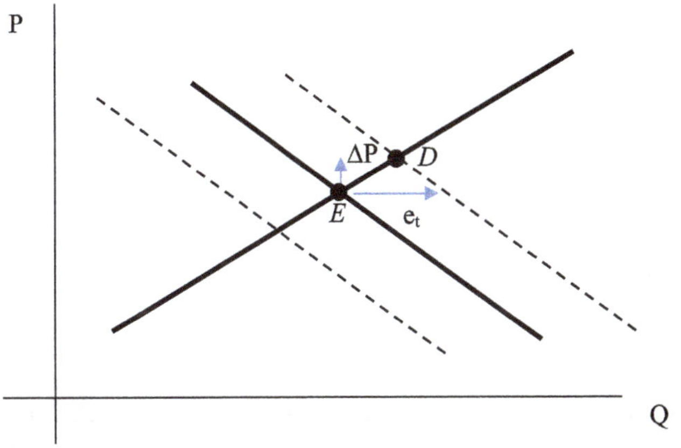

Figure 6.2: Simultaneous Equations Bias under Demand and Supply Equations.

In Figure 6.2, Y-axis "P" represents price, and X-axis represents equilibrium quantity "Q" demanded and supplied. The negatively sloping line represents the demand curve or demand schedule indicating demand as a decreasing function of price. The positively sloping line represents the supply curve or supply schedule indicating supply as an increasing function of price. The intersection of the two lines denotes the equilibrium price and quantity point "E". Given P_t, when demand D_t moves right ("up") or left ("down") by disturbance e_t, and assuming the supply curve is not changed, then the equilibrium point displaces to "D". At "D", the new equilibrium price has increased, i. e. $\triangle P > 0$. Because of the elastic supply curve, movement in the demand curve due to e_t induces equilibrium price change along the supply curve, and thus P_t also changes. It is seen that $\text{cov}(P_t, e_t) \neq 0$. Similarly, supply curve movement induces price change along the demand curve, hence $\text{cov}(P_t, u_t) \neq 0$.

6.8 Instrumental Variables

To overcome the problem of inconsistency when there is contemporaneous correlation, instrumental variables regression can be performed. Suppose we can find k explanatory variables (maybe including some of the original X columns that do not have contemporaneous correlation with U) $Z_{N\times k}$ such that

(2a) they are (contemporaneously) correlated with X and
(2b) they are not (contemporaneously) correlated with U.

Property (2a) yields $p\lim(\frac{1}{N}Z^TX) = \Sigma_{ZX} \neq 0_{k\times k}$ and assume Σ_{ZX} is nonsingular.
Property (2b) yields $p\lim(\frac{1}{N}Z^TU) = \Sigma_{ZU} = 0_{k\times 1}$.
As $p\lim(\frac{1}{N}Z^TZ) = \Sigma_{ZZ} \neq 0_{k\times k}$, an instrumental variables (IV) estimator is

$$\hat{B}_{\text{IV}} = (Z^TX)^{-1}Z^TY$$

Therefore,

$$\hat{B}_{\text{IV}} = (Z^TX)^{-1}Z^TY = B + (Z^TX)^{-1}Z^TU$$

and

$$\begin{aligned} p\lim \hat{B}_{\text{IV}} &= B + p\lim\left(\frac{1}{N}Z^TX\right)^{-1}\left(\frac{1}{N}Z^TU\right) \\ &= B + \Sigma_{ZX}^{-1}\Sigma_{ZU} = B + 0_{k\times 1} = B \end{aligned}$$

Thus, $\hat{B}_{\text{IV}}$ is consistent. The asymptotic covariance of $\hat{B}_{\text{IV}}$ conditional on Z, X, is

$$\begin{aligned} E[(\hat{B}_{\text{IV}} - B)(\hat{B}_{\text{IV}} - B)^T|X,Z] &= E[(Z^TX)^{-1}Z^TUU^TZ(X^TZ)^{-1}|X,Z] \\ &= \sigma_u^2(Z^TX)^{-1}Z^TZ(X^TZ)^{-1} \end{aligned}$$

which in finite sample is approximated by $\hat{\sigma}_u^2(Z^TX)^{-1}Z^TZ(X^TZ)^{-1}$.

6.9 Misspecification with Coefficients

In the study of MLR so far, we have assumed B is constant. When B is not constant, e. g., there is a structural break, then not accounting for changing B would yield incorrect estimates. Other types of nonconstant parameters are when B is a random coefficient, or when B is a switching regression model within a business cycle. For example, B could take different values B_G or B_B conditional on the state of the economy, good or bad, respectively. The states of the economy could be driven by a Markov Chain model. Each period the state could be good G or bad B. If the state at $t-1$ is G, next period probability of G is 0.6 and probability of B is 0.4. This is shown in Table 6.1.

Table 6.1: Random Coefficient in Two States.

	State G at t	State B at t
State G at $t-1$	0.6	0.4
State B at $t-1$	0.2	0.8

Assume $\text{cov}(U) = \Omega$ whatever the state at $t-1$. Then

$$\begin{aligned} Y_t &= X_t B_G + u_t \quad \text{with probability 0.6 if state at } t-1 \text{ is } G \\ Y_t &= X_t B_B + u_t \quad \text{with probability 0.4 if state at } t-1 \text{ is } G \\ Y_t &= X_t B_G + u_t \quad \text{with probability 0.2 if state at } t-1 \text{ is } B \\ Y_t &= X_t B_B + u_t \quad \text{with probability 0.8 if state at } t-1 \text{ is } B \end{aligned}$$

where X_t is the tth row of $X_{N\times k}$. The estimation can be done to produce estimators with desirable asymptotic properties using maximum likelihood method if the probability distribution of U is known.

In simple structural breaks such as a change in B coefficient in $Y = XB + U$ at time $t = N_1 + 1$, the MLR may be constructed as follows. Let the slope coefficients before the break be $B^B_{k\times 1}$ and those after the break be $B^A_{k\times 1}$. Let $X_{N\times k}$ be partitioned into two $X^B_{N_1\times k}$ and $X^A_{N_2\times k}$, where $N_1 + N_2 = N$, $X^T = ((X^B)^T|(X^A)^T)$. Then the MLR is $Y = X^*B^* + U^*$ where

$$X^*_{N\times 2k} = \begin{pmatrix} X^B_{N_1\times k} & \mathbf{0}_{N_1\times k} \\ \mathbf{0}_{N_2\times k} & X^A_{N_2\times k} \end{pmatrix}, \quad \text{and} \quad B^*_{2k\times 1} = \begin{pmatrix} B^B_{k\times 1} \\ B^A_{k\times 1} \end{pmatrix}$$

and $\text{cov}(U) = \Omega^*$. The OLS estimators of B^* under the classical assumptions are BLUE.

We can test if there is a simple structural break at $t = N_1 + 1$ by using Chow's Test. There is no structural break under the null hypothesis $H_0 : B^B = B^A = B$. There are k constraints in the null hypothesis. We make use of the constrained versus unconstrained residual sum of squares error. Under no constraint, USSR $= \hat{U}^{*T}U^*$. Under the constraint of the null hypothesis, CSSR $= \hat{U}^T\hat{U}$. Hence a test of the null hypothesis uses test statistic

$$\frac{(\text{CSSR} - \text{USSR})/k}{\text{USSR}/(N-2k)}$$

that has a F-distribution with $k, N-2k$ degrees of freedom under the null. If the test statistic is too large, the null or no structural break is rejected.

Further Reading

Fujikoshi Yasunori, V. V. Ulyanov, and R. Shimizu (2010), *Multivariate Statistics: High Dimensional and Large-Sample Approximations*, John Wiley & Sons.

Johnson, Richard A., and D. W. Wichern (2002), *Applied Multivariate Statistical Analysis*, Prentice-Hall.

Johnston, J., and J. DiNardo (1997), *Econometric Methods*, Fourth edition, McGraw-Hill.

7 Multi-Factor Asset Pricing

In this chapter, we discuss the important topics about arbitrage pricing theory and the intertemporal asset pricing model and their connection to multi-factor asset pricing models. The pricing models are at the heart of many quantitative investment strategies aimed at portfolio selection and rebalancing to capture positive alphas and hence above market returns.

The capital asset pricing model (CAPM) is a single factor asset pricing model with the market as the factor. The implication is that systematic risk connected to the covariation with market returns is the only risk that is priced. However, there is no reason why the universe of assets in the economy could not have their prices and returns dependent on more than one economy-wide systematic factor.

Several remarks are in order to place the roles of the asset pricing models in the context of pragmatic investment contexts. We shall mostly apply the results to stocks as the asset since the nature of the stock returns described in earlier chapters fits the use of linear regressions.

(1a) If systematic factors are found to explain the stock returns, i. e. factors that affect all stock returns, then knowing what are the factors can help in constructing profitable portfolios with high positive expected returns in the next period if the factors can be anticipated.

(1b) If the factors are not contemporaneous with the dependent stock return in the linear regression, but are lagged factors, then the latter serves as natural predictors since they are pre-determined. In general, using lagged explanatory variables has this advantage, but it also has the disadvantage that the regression has more uncertain residual noise, having larger variances. Some factors may be associated with the stock returns contemporaneously but their lags may not.

(1c) Even if next period factors cannot be anticipated, knowing the factors enables more accurate estimation of stock return covariance matrix that can help in portfolio risk-return optimization involving the inverse of the covariance matrix as shown in Chapter 3.4. It can also help in hedging investments.

(1d) An asset pricing model provides a benchmark expected return in that if the model is correct and correctly estimated, then on average the stock return should equal to the fitted stock return according to the model. However, if the time-series stock return on average is larger (smaller) than the fitted return, e. g., $\hat{\alpha} > (<) 0$, as seen in Chapter 3.5, then there is implication of superior or abnormal return.

(1e) If the model is correct with the requisite systematic factors that are typically publicly available information, then positive (negative) $\hat{\alpha}$ is likely due to private information assuming the market has strong-form efficiency (otherwise the private information would not be revealed in $\hat{\alpha}$ different from zero). Thus finding significant $\hat{\alpha}$ is like trying to learn about factors or information affecting the stock return that are not publicly observed. If it is assumed that this information persists over

https://doi.org/10.1515/9783110673951-007

the next period, then it makes sense to go long (short) on stocks with positive (negative) alphas.

In what follows, we describe the framework to think about systematic factors that require risk-adjusted return compensation, discuss the Arbitrage Pricing Theory and the Merton's Intertemporal Capital Asset Pricing Model (ICAPM), and then move on to empirical spadeworks.

7.1 Arbitrage Pricing Theory

Ross's Arbitrage Pricing Theory[1] (APT) has come to be understood as essentially a statistical model of equilibrium asset prices. In a very large economy with no friction and many assets, no-arbitrage argument (without the need to specify investors' risk-return preferences) gives rise to equilibrium expected returns. These returns are related to an unknown number of factors in the economy that exogenously affect the returns in a statistical way. Merton's ICAPM[2] is an intertemporal equilibrium model where investors make optimal consumption versus investment decisions constrained by their preferences and resources. The risks in the economy are driven by some finite number of economic state factors. Expected returns are related to the nature of these economic factors as well as investor preferences. Although the characters of both APT and ICAPM are quite different, they both have a common intention of explaining equilibrium expected returns based on some systematic factors, whether observed or not.

Assume asset returns R_i's are generated by a K-factor model ($K < N$ where N is the total number of assets in the economy):

$$R_i = E(R_i) + \sum_{j=1}^{K} b_{ij}\delta_j + \varepsilon_i, \quad i = 1, 2, \ldots, N \tag{7.1}$$

where $E(R_i) = E_i$; δ_j's are zero mean common risk factors (i. e., they affect asset i's return R_i via b_{ij}'s); b_{ij}'s are the factor loadings (or sensitivity coefficients to factors) for asset i, and ε_i is mean zero asset i's specific or unique risk.

Also,

$$\begin{aligned} \mathrm{cov}(\varepsilon_i, \varepsilon_j) &= 0 \quad \text{for } i \neq j \\ \mathrm{cov}(\varepsilon_i, \delta_j) &= 0 \quad \text{for every } i, j \end{aligned}$$

Using matrix notations for Eq. (7.1):

1 See A. S. Ross (1976), The arbitrage theory of capital asset pricing, *Journal of Economic Theory*, 13, 341–360.

2 See Robert C. Merton (1973), An intertemporal capital asset pricing model, *Econometrica* 41, 867–887.

$$R_{N\times1} = E_{N\times1} + B_{N\times K}\delta_{K\times1} + \varepsilon_{N\times1}$$
$$E(\varepsilon\varepsilon^T) = \sigma_\varepsilon^2 I_{N\times N}$$
$$E(\delta\varepsilon^T) = 0_{K\times N}$$

An example of Eq. (7.1) for stock returns may be:

$$R_i = E(R_i) + b_{ig}g + b_{ip}p + \varepsilon_i$$

where $E(R_i)$ is the stock's unconditional expected return in the absence of any other news, and RVs g and p are unexpected deviations, with zero means, in GDP and in prime interest rate, that will affect R_i. The factor betas (or factor loadings or sensitivities) are $b_{ig} > 0$, and $b_{ip} < 0$. When GDP is unexpectedly high with a booming economy, the firm's revenues will unexpectedly rise and give rise to a higher return R_i, hence positive b_{ig}. When prime rate or business cost unexpectedly rises, firm's revenues will suffer unexpectedly, leading to fall in return R_i, hence negative b_{ip}.

Suppose we can find a portfolio $x_{N\times1}$ where the element are weights or fractions of investment outlay, such that

$$x^T l = 0; \quad l = \begin{bmatrix} 1 \\ 1 \\ \vdots \\ 1 \end{bmatrix}_{N\times1} \tag{7.2}$$

$$x^T B = 0_{1\times K} \tag{7.3}$$

Now Eq. (7.2) implies that x is an arbitrage portfolio, i. e. zero outlay, with zero systematic risk via Eq. (7.3).

Suppose that x is a well-diversified portfolio, so $x^T\varepsilon \approx 0_{1\times1}$. Hence, portfolio return is:

$$x^T R = x^T E + x^T B\delta + x^T\varepsilon \doteqdot x^T E \; (= x^T E \text{ as } N \uparrow \infty)$$

But since x is costless and riskless, then to prevent arbitrage profit, the return to x must be zero, i. e.

$$x^T E = 0 \tag{7.4}$$

Since Eqs. (7.2) and (7.3) economically imply Eq. (7.4) always, then

$$E_{N\times1} = \gamma_0 \underset{N\times1}{l} + \underset{N\times K}{B}\gamma \tag{7.5}$$

where γ_0 is a scalar constant and γ is a $K \times 1$ constant vector. To verify Eq. (7.5), pre-multiply the LHS and RHS by x^T:

$$x^T E = \gamma_0 x^T l + x^T B\gamma = 0 + 0 = 0$$

using Eqs. (7.2) and (7.3).

Equation (7.5) can be explained by the standard linear algebra result that if any vector orthogonal to l and columns of B is also orthogonal to E, then this implies that E is a linear combination of l and the columns of B, i. e. Equation (7.5).

Equation (7.5) is sometimes called the Arbitrage Pricing Model. Ex-ante unconditional expected return, E, is related to economy-wide constant γ_0 and to risk premia $\gamma_{K\times1}$ for each of the K factor risks. If we put $B = 0$, then clearly γ_0 is the risk-free rate. Note that if B increases, then the systematic risks $B\gamma$ increase, and thus E also increases.

For a single asset i, Eq. (7.5) implies:

$$E(R_i) = r_f + b_{i1}\gamma_1 + b_{i2}\gamma_2 + \cdots + b_{iK}\gamma_K \tag{7.6}$$

Putting Eq. (7.6) side by side the underlying process

$$R_i = E(R_i) + \sum_{j=1}^{K} b_{ij}\delta_j + \varepsilon_i$$

it is seen that

$$R_i = r_f + b_{i1}(\gamma_1 + \delta_1) + b_{i2}(\gamma_2 + \delta_2) + \cdots + b_{iK}(\gamma_K + \delta_K) + \varepsilon_i \tag{7.7}$$

where γ_j's are constants, and δ_j's are zero mean r. v.'s.

Equation (7.7) can be expressed in matrix form as:

$$R_{N\times1} - r_f l_{N\times1} + B_{N\times K}\theta_{K\times1} + \varepsilon_{N\times1} \tag{7.8}$$

where $E(R_{N\times1}) = E_{N\times1}$,

$$\begin{aligned} E(\theta) &= E(\gamma + \delta) = \gamma_{K\times1}, \quad \text{a } K\times1 \text{ vector of risk premia,} \\ E(\varepsilon) &= 0 \\ E(\theta\varepsilon^T)_{K\times N} &= 0 \end{aligned} \tag{7.9}$$

Each equation in the system in Eq. (7.8) at time t is

$$R_i - r_f = b_{i1}\theta_1 + b_{i2}\theta_2 + \cdots + b_{iK}\theta_K + \varepsilon_i \tag{7.10}$$

for stocks i, where $i = 1, 2, \ldots, N$.

b_{ij} is the sensitivity of stock i to the jth risk premium factor variable θ_j that is common to all stocks. We may call θ_j the jth risk factor, and its mean γ_j the jth factor risk premium. b_{ij} is the same sensitivity to the risk premium form of the APT equation in

Eq. (7.5). Except for the special case of single-period CAPM where $K = 1$ and $E(\theta_1)$ is the market premium or expected excess market return, the risk premia factor variables θ_j's, or the common risk factors, are generally not observable nor known.

The APT model is strictly speaking a single period asset pricing model. Equation (7.6) holds for each period t. Over time t, however, we can put a time series structure onto each of the variables in Eq. (7.6) in order to be able to use time series data to estimate and test the model. Thus over time t,

$$R_{it} - r_{ft} = b_{i1}\theta_{1t} + b_{i2}\theta_{2t} + \cdots + b_{iK}\theta_{Kt} + \varepsilon_{it} \tag{7.11}$$

where θ_{jt} is the jth risk (premium) random factor. Its mean at t is $E(\theta_{jt}) = \gamma_j$, the jth risk premium, where $\theta_{jt} = \gamma_{jt} + \delta_{jt}$ and also $E(\varepsilon_{it}) = 0$. This risk premium γ_j may vary over time. In the regression specification in Eq. (7.11), θ_{1t} can be defined as ones, i. e., allowing for a constant intercept. We shall add a bit more restrictions to enable nice econometric results, i. e., we assume $E(\varepsilon_{it}\theta_{jt}) = 0$, for every t, i, and j, $\text{var}(\delta_{jt})$ is constant over time for each j, and $\text{var}(\varepsilon_{it})$ is constant over time.

An equivalent specification is:

$$R_{it} - r_{ft} = b_{i1}\gamma_{1t} + b_{i2}\gamma_{2t} + \cdots + b_{iK}\gamma_{Kt} + \xi_{it}, \tag{7.12}$$

where $\xi_{it} = \sum_{j=1}^{K} b_{ij}\delta_{jt} + \varepsilon_{it}$, and $E(\xi_{it}) = 0$

There are some empirical problems in estimating and testing the APT. Firstly, the number of factors, K, is not known theoretically. Setting different K will affect the estimation of the factor loadings B. Secondly, even if K is known, it is not known what the factors are. One can only make guesses about economic variables that may have an impact on R_{it}. One may also make guesses about the factor loadings instead of the factors. This APT framework can be linked with the linear multi-factor asset pricing model that are multiple linear regression models using factors to explain stock returns.

7.2 Merton's Intertemporal CAPM

Another approach to deriving multi-factor model is to start with a risk-preference framework in financial economics instead of a statistical specification. Assume the representative agent in the economy maximizes his/her lifetime $[0, T]$ consumption as follows.

$$\max_{C,w} E_0\left[\int_0^T U(C_t, t)dt + B(W_T, T)\right]$$

subject to

$$dW = \sum_{i=1}^{N} w_i(\mu_i - r)Wdt + (rW - C)dt + \sum_{i=1}^{N} w_i W\sigma_i\, dz_i$$

where

$$\begin{aligned} dP_{it}/P_{it} &= \mu_i(x)dt + \sigma_i(x)dz_i \quad \text{for } i = 1, 2, \ldots, N \\ dP_{0t}/P_{0t} &= r(x)dt \\ dx &= \mu_x(x)dt + \sigma_x(x)dz_x \end{aligned}$$

x (longer notation: x_t) is a state variable at t that affects N risky asset prices P_{it} via their means and volatilities and also the risk-free asset P_0 via its mean, over $(t, t + dt]$. z_{it} and z_{xt} are Wiener processes with product $\rho_{ix}dt$.

Indirect utility at any t is

$$J(W, x, t) = \max_{C,w} E_t\left[\int_t^T U(C_s, s)ds + B(W_T, T)\right]$$

Bellman equation at t is

$$J(W, x, t) = \max_{C,w}[U(C_t, t) + E_t(J(W + dW, x + dx, t + dt)]$$

Or,

$$0 = \max_{C,w}[U(C_t, t) + E_t(dJ(W, x, t)]$$

Applying Itô's lemma on dJ:

$$\begin{aligned} 0 = \max_{C,w}\Bigg[& U(C_t, t) + J_t + J_W\left\{\sum_{i=1}^{N} w_i(\mu_i - r)W + (rW - C)\right\} + J_x\mu_x \\ & + \frac{1}{2}J_{WW}W^2\sum_{i=1}^{N}\sum_{j=1}^{N}\sigma_{ij}w_i w_j + \frac{1}{2}J_{xx}\sigma_x^2 + J_{Wx}W\sum_{i=1}^{N} w_i\sigma ix\Bigg] \end{aligned}$$

The first order conditions w.r.t. C and w_i are

$$\begin{aligned} 0 &= U_C - J_W \\ 0 &= J_W W(\mu_i - r) + J_{WW}W^2\sum_{j=1}^{N} w_j\sigma_{ij} + J_{Wx}W\sigma_{ix} \quad \text{for } i = 1, 2, \ldots, N \end{aligned}$$

The second equation can be re-arranged as

$$w_j W = A\Sigma^{-1}(\mu - rl) + H\Sigma^{-1}V$$

where w_j on the LHS is optimal allocation to jth risky asset, $A = -J_W/J_{WW}$, $H = -J_{Wx}/J_{WW}$, μ is $N \times 1$ vector of $\{\mu_i\}$, l is vector of ones, V is $N \times 1$ vector of $\{\sigma_{ix}\}$, and Σ is covariance matrix of $\{\sigma_{ij}\}$.

$A > 0$ acts like inverse of risk aversion (i. e. risk rolerance): higher tolerance or A implies more allocations to assets with higher expected returns and less to the risk-free asset. $H = -\frac{\partial C/\partial x}{\partial C/\partial W}$. The second term adjustment to allocation is a hedge demand against increase in x that reduces C at a given W. Then $H > 0$, and more allocation is given to assets with positive σ_{ix} that tends to give higher returns when x increases.

Then

$$A^k(\mu - rl) = \Sigma w_j^k W^k - H^k V$$

where k is added as superscript to denote that the allocation w_j, wealth W^k, risk tolerance A^k and hedge propensity H^k are unique to each individual k out of T. Sum across all individuals, then divide through by $\sum_{k=1}^{T} A^k$.

$$(\mu - rl)_{N\times1} = c\Sigma_{N\times N}\omega_{N\times1} - hV_{N\times1} \tag{7.13}$$

where $c = \sum_{k=1}^{T} W^k / \sum_{k=1}^{T} A^k$, $\omega = \sum_{k=1}^{T} w_j^k W^k / \sum_{k=1}^{T} W^k$, and $h = \sum_{k=1}^{T} H^k / \sum_{k=1}^{T} A^k$. ω is the vector of fraction of total market wealth invested in each asset.

Each asset in the market in Eq. (7.13) has excess return as follows.

$$(\mu_i - r) = c\sigma_{iM} - h\sigma_{ix} \tag{7.14}$$

Pre-multiplying Eq. (7.13) by ω' we obtain:

$$(\mu_M - r) = c\sigma_M^2 - h\sigma_{Mx} \tag{7.15}$$

The optimal hedge demand (for maximal correlation with the stochastic factor x in dollar terms) is $H\Sigma^{-1}V$. This can be constructed as an optimal hedge portfolio $\theta = \Sigma^{-1}V/(l'\Sigma^{-1}V)$ where the portfolio weights sum to one, i. e., $l'\theta = 1$.

Pre-multiply Eq. (7.13) by θ':

$$(\mu_\theta - r) = c\sigma_{\theta M} - h\sigma_{\theta x} \tag{7.16}$$

where μ_θ is the expected return of the hedge portfolio, $\sigma_{\theta M}$ is covariance between the optimal hedge portfolio return and market return, and $\sigma_{\theta x}$ is covariance between the optimal hedge portfolio return and the state variable x.

Now solve Eqs. (7.15) and (7.16) for values of c and h. Substitute these into Eq. (7.14) to obtain:

$$\mu_i - r = \beta_i^M(\mu_M - r) + \beta_i^\theta(\mu_\theta - r) \tag{7.17}$$

where $\beta_i^M = \frac{\sigma_{iM}\sigma_{\theta x} - \sigma_{ix}\sigma_{M\theta}}{\sigma_M^2\sigma_{\theta x} - \sigma_{Mx}\sigma_{M\theta}}$ and $\beta_i^\theta = \frac{\sigma_{ix}\sigma_M^2 - \sigma_{iM}\sigma_{Mx}}{\sigma_M^2\sigma_{\theta x} - \sigma_{Mx}\sigma_{M\theta}}$.

Note that when there is no stochastic opportunity set and $dx = 0$, then $\sigma_{ix} = \sigma_{Mx} = 0$, and so Eq. (7.17) gives:

$$(\mu_i - r) = \frac{\sigma_{iM}}{\sigma_M^2}(\mu_M - r)$$

which is similar in form to the single-period CAPM although this continuous time CAPM holds over small time intervals dt, but can be aggregated to approximately the discrete CAPM. More importantly, the continuous time CAPM addresses the multi-period issue within its theory.

Equation (7.17) can be re-expressed as

$$\mu_i - r = \eta_1 \sigma_{iM} + \eta_2 \sigma_{ix} \tag{7.18}$$

where

$$\begin{aligned}
\sigma_{ix} &= \text{cov}(dP_i/P_i, dx) \\
\eta_1 &= \frac{\sigma_{\theta x}(\mu_M - r) - \sigma_{Mx}(\mu_\theta - r)}{\sigma_M^2 \sigma_{\theta x} - \sigma_{Mx}\sigma_{M\theta}} \\
\eta_2 &= \frac{-\sigma_{M\theta}(\mu_M - r) + \sigma_M^2(\mu_\theta - r)}{\sigma_M^2 \sigma_{\theta x} - \sigma_{Mx}\sigma_{M\theta}}
\end{aligned}$$

If x_t is a vector of S unique state variables, the intertemporal CAPM (ICAPM) can be derived with $S + 2$ fund separation (or S optimal hedge portfolios + market portfolio + risk-free asset):

$$\mu_i - r = \eta_1 \sigma_{iM} + \eta_2 \sigma_{ix_1} + \eta_3 \sigma_{ix_2} + \cdots + \eta_{S+1} \sigma_{ix_S} \tag{7.19}$$

where $\sigma_{ix_j} = \text{cov}(dP_i/P_i, dx_j)$ for $j = 1, 2, \ldots, S$. For x_t being a vector S unique state variables, Eq. (7.17) is also extended to:

$$\mu_i - r = \beta_i^M(\mu_M - r) + \beta_i^{\theta_1}(\mu_{\theta_1} - r) + \beta_i^{\theta_2}(\mu_{\theta_2} - r) + \cdots + \beta_i^{\theta_S}(\mu_{\theta_S} - r)$$

Discretization gives, at each end of $t-1$ or start of t over period $(t, t+\triangle]$:

$$E(R_{it+\triangle} - r_{t+\triangle}) = \sum_{k=1}^{S+1} b_{ik} y_k$$

where factor $y_1 = E(R_{Mt+\triangle} - r_{t+\triangle})$, factors $y_k = E(R_{\theta_k t+\triangle} - r_{t+\triangle})$ for $k = 2, 3, \ldots, S+1$. $b_{i1} = \beta_i^M$, $b_{ik} = \beta_i^{\theta_{k-1}}$ (for $k = 2, 3, \ldots, S+1$) are stock i's factor loadings on the unique state variables. This equation looks similar to the APT Eq. (7.6) for each t. Hence the ICAPM can also be employed to check out dynamic factors in the form of the market portfolio $(R_{Mt+\triangle} - r_{t+\triangle})$ and the hedge portfolios $(R_{\theta_k t+\triangle} - r_{t+\triangle})$ $\forall k = 1, 2, 3, \ldots, S$. Recall that each of the additional factors corresponds to a state variable innovation. For econometric estimation and testing, we can assume that over the sample data time-space, joint distributions of stock returns and state vector is stationary, so scalars γ_k's are intertemporal constants.

In Eq. (7.19), for any state variable x_j, given the other state variables are held constant at $\underline{x}$, $dx_{jt} = \mu_x(x_{jt}, \underline{x})dt + \sigma_x(x_{jt}, \underline{x})\, dz_{x_{jt}}$. Also, $dP_{it}/P_{it} = \mu_i(x_{jt}, \underline{x})dt + \sigma_i(x_{jt}, \underline{x})\, dz_{it}$. We apply discretization, replacing dt with $\triangle$ to obtain approximate relationships.

$$x_{jt+\triangle} - x_{jt} = \mu_x(x_{jt}, \underline{x}) \triangle + \sigma_x(x_{jt}, \underline{x}) \triangle z_{x_{jt}} \tag{7.20}$$

$$R_{it+\triangle} = \mu_i(x_{jt}, \underline{x}) \triangle + \sigma_i(x_{jt}, \underline{x}) \triangle z_{it} \tag{7.21}$$

where $R_{it+\triangle} = \triangle P_{it}/P_{it}$. Note return is over period $(t, t+\triangle]$.

The one-period ahead version of Eq. (7.21) is:

$$R_{it+2\triangle} = \mu_i(x_{jt+\triangle}, \underline{x}) \triangle + \sigma_i(x_{jt+\triangle}, \underline{x}) \triangle z_{it+\triangle} \tag{7.22}$$

From Eq. (7.22), the intertemporal nature of the model (not a single period model) implies $x_{jt+\triangle} - x_{jt}$ in Eq. (7.20) has non-zero covariance with $R_{it+2\triangle}$ in Eq. (7.22). Thus in general, $\text{cov}_t(R_{Mt+2\triangle}, x_{jt+\triangle} - x_{jt}) \neq 0$, i. e., state variable innovation at t in $(t, t+\triangle]$ can predict future market returns. See Maio and Santa-Clara (2012)[3] for such tests. This covariance $\text{cov}_t(R_{Mt+2\triangle}, x_{jt+\triangle} - x_{jt})$ should have the same sign as σ_{ix_j} in Eq. (7.19).

Suppose in Eq. (7.19), stock i return's covariance with state variable innovation $x_{jt+\triangle} - x_{jt}$ (same sign as stock i return's factor loading on the hedge portfolio return associated with the state variable) is positive, i. e., $\sigma_{ix_j} > 0$. Then $\text{cov}_t(R_{Mt+2\triangle}, x_{jt+\triangle} - x_{jt}) > 0$, i. e., positive jth state variable innovation at t in $(t, t+\triangle]$ leads on average to increase in future market returns. Then, stock i's return is not a good hedge for the intertemporal risk since its return as well as the future market's return increase with the jth state variable innovation. Investors in stock i will demand an intertemporal risk premium, so in Eq. (7.19), $\eta_j > 0$. This is similar to single period Sharpe CAPM model where if stock's return covariance with the market is more positive, the stock's risk premium increases.

But if $\sigma_{ix_j} < 0$, then $\text{cov}_t(R_{Mt+2\triangle}, x_{jt+\triangle} - x_{jt}) < 0$, i. e., positive jth state variable innovation at t in $(t, t+\triangle]$ leads on average to decrease in future market returns. Then, stock i's return is also not a good hedge for the intertemporal risk since its return as well as the future market's return decrease with increase in the jth state variable innovation. Investors in stock i will demand an intertemporal risk premium, so in Eq. (7.19), $\eta_j > 0$.

Thus an intertemporal theoretical test should include testing if $\eta_j > 0$ in Eq. (7.19) over and above testing for significance in the factor loadings. This is a difference between testing for multi-factor model Eq. (7.11) under APT or under Merton's ICAPM.

---

3 Paulo Maio and Pedro Santa-Clara (2012), Multifactor models and their consistency with the ICAPM, *Journal of Financial Economics* 106, 586–613.

7.3 Estimating and Testing Multi-Factor Models

Tests of APT tend to utilize statistical methods such as principal components method, factor analysis, etc. with a view to understand how many factors there are in the economy. There have been various debates about whether APT is testable, but we shall not worry about that here. In some sense, ICAPM is more natural in suggesting a regression relationship between asset returns and market variables that are possibly the ones producing risks that investors must hedge.

We now discuss the estimation and testable specifications of APT in Eqs. (7.11) and (7.12) when it is extended to a multi-period setting. There are several intuitive approaches. Supposing K is known. In Eqs. (7.11) and (7.12), suppose we identify the set of stocks to investigate and this set forms observations for the dependent variable.

Approach (i) is to postulate what the risk factors θ_{jt} are, $\forall t$. Given these, it is not possible to perform a cross-sectional regression at any t. This is because at t, there are only K number of observations for explanatory variable θ_j (left out t subscript) but a larger NK number of parameters b_{ij}'s to be estimated. However, getting the loadings or b_{ij}'s for each t is a necessary step to progress. To get them we can perform time series regressions based on Eq. (7.11) separately for each stock i using $T \times 1$ $R_{it} - r_{ft}$ as dependent variable and θ_{jt}, $j = 1, 2, \ldots, K$, and $t = 1, 2 \ldots, T$ as explanatory variables. The estimated $\hat{b}_{ij}$ $(i = 1, 2, \ldots, N; j = 1, 2, \ldots, K)$ using sample period $[1, T]$ data are obtained. In the next step, we can then perform a cross-sectional regression based on Eq. (7.12) employing $N \times 1$ dependent variable $R_{it} - r_{ft}$ at a time $T + 1$ and $\hat{b}_{ij}$, $(i = 1, 2, \ldots, N; j = 1, 2, \ldots, K)$ as explanatory variables. The coefficient estimates via OLS are $\hat{\gamma}_{jT+1}$ for $j = 1, 2, \ldots, K$. The use of time series data over $[1, T]$ but cross-sectional data at $T + 1$ outside of $[1, T]$ is intentional. Note that $\hat{b}_{ij}$ estimates from $[1, T]$ involve covariances between stocks' excess returns and the factor risks θ_{jt}. In the cross-sectional regression of Eq. (7.12), ξ_{it} would have dependency with $\hat{b}_{ij}$ if the stock i's excess return were from a period in $[1, T]$. Thus, by using different periods possibly on a rolling basis, e. g., $[2, T + 1]$, $[3, T + 2]$, etc., we can repeat the steps to perform cross-sectional regressions at $T + 2$, $T + 3$, and so on. Then we would obtain time series of estimates $\hat{\gamma}_{jT+n}$ for each j and for $n = 0, 1, 2, \ldots$. We can interpret each $\hat{\gamma}_{jT+n}$ as a conditional estimate. By taking sample average of these we can arrive at the unconditional estimates.

Approach (ii) is to postulate instead what the risk factor loadings b_{ij} $(\forall i, j)$ are. In this case, we can directly perform a cross-sectional regression based on Eq. (7.12) employing $N \times 1$ dependent variable $R_{it} - r_{ft}$ $(\forall i = 1, 2, \ldots, N)$ at time t. The coefficient estimates via OLS are $\hat{\gamma}_{jt}$ for $j = 1, 2, \ldots, K$. For $t \in [1, T']$, we would obtain time series of estimates $\hat{\gamma}_{jt}$ for each j and for $t = 0, 1, 2, \ldots, T'$. We can interpret each $\hat{\gamma}_{jt}$ as a conditional estimate. By taking sample average of these we can arrive at the unconditional estimates.

Approach (iii), like in approach (i), is to postulate what the risk factors θ_{jt} are, $\forall t$. Then directly perform time series regressions based on Eq. (7.11) but using portfolio stock returns as dependent variable instead of individual stock returns. θ_{jt}, $(\forall j, t)$

are explanatory variables. OLS estimates $\hat{b}_{ij}$ are then tested for significance where i is a portfolio. Grouping the stock returns into portfolio returns as dependent variable has the advantage of reducing the variance of the residual error ε_{it} in Eq. (7.11) and hence also the standard errors of the b_{ij} estimators. Portfolios can also be constructed to maximize the covariation between $R_{it} - r_{ft}$ and θ_{jt} (hence increasing slope magnitudes), assuming the risk factors are true. (If the risk factors are false, then the artificial construction of portfolios to heighten the covariations could lead to spurious results.)

These three approaches to finding the multiple systematic risk factors in asset pricing are shown in the several studies that we discuss next. As in approach (i), Chen, Roll, and Ross (1986)[4] and others specify macroeconomic and financial market variables that intuitively make economic sense in explaining co-movements with stock returns in a systematic fashion. For example, industrial production in an economy could increase and correlate with higher stock prices especially for firms that have business exposures to industrial activities, and this is in addition to the general stock market movement. They used the following five macroeconomic variables in their MLR:

(2a) monthly industrial production growth, MP_t
(2b) monthly change in expected inflation, DEI_t
(2c) monthly unexpected inflation, UI_t
(2d) unexpected monthly risk premium, URP_t, that is the difference between monthly yields on long-term Baa corporate bonds and yields on long-term government bonds. This proxied for default risk premium.
(2e) unexpected monthly term structure factor, UTS_t that is the differences in promised yields to maturity on long-term government bond and short-term Treasury bill, or approximately the slope of the government yield curve.

Keim and Stambaugh (1986) found[5] the following three ex-ante observable variables that affected risk premia of stocks and bonds:

(3a) difference between yields on long-term Baa grade and below corporate bonds and yields on short-term Treasury bills (This proxied for default premium.)
(3b) $\log_e$ of ratio of real S&P composite index to previous long-run S&P level, (This might proxy for inflationary tendencies.)
(3c) $\log_e$ of average share price of the lowest market value quintile of firms on NYSE. There appeared to be some business cycle and size effect.

4 N. F. Chen, R. Roll, and S. A. Ross (1986), Economic forces and the stock market, *Journal of Business*, 59, 383–403.

5 D. B. Keim and R. F. Stambaugh (1986), Predicting returns in the bond and stock markets, *Journal of Financial Economics*, 17, 357–390.

There have been many other similar studies. All suggest that there are at most 3 to 5 significant factors or economic variables that affect variation in the cross-sectional returns.

Chen, Roll, and Ross (1986) ran the following MLR:

$$R_{it} = a + b_{i,\mathrm{MP}}\mathrm{MP}_t + b_{i,\mathrm{DEI}}\mathrm{DEI}_t + b_{i,\mathrm{UI}}\mathrm{UI}_t + b_{i,\mathrm{URP}}\mathrm{URP}_t + b_{i,\mathrm{UTS}}\mathrm{UTS}_t + e_{i,t} \tag{7.23}$$

where the betas are the factor loadings on the state variables (risk factors) MP_t, DEI_t, UI_t, URP_t and UTS_t. e_t is an idiosyncratic (unsystematic) error. Support of the MLR as consistent with the APT or ICAPM is to check if the identified economic variables are risk factors that can systematically explain each of the N stock returns (1) cross-sectionally, i. e., across N at each time t; (2) dynamically over time, i. e., across t for each stock at a time (here we require to assume the betas b_{ij}'s are constant over time), and that R^2 is reasonable indicating the chosen factors can explain well and that possibly no other explanatory variables are left out.

The cross-sectional test of the multi-factor asset pricing model (with identified factors via economic reasonining or empirical statistical correlations) can be performed using the Fama-MacBeth (1973) technique.[6]

7.3.1 Fama-MacBeth Method

Equilibrium expected return of any asset i in any period t is about cross-sectional relationship between all assets' expected returns at t and the factor risk premiums $\gamma_{K\times1}$ at t. Thus in the Sharpe CAPM, the testable implication is about whether given loadings or betas β_i, $\forall i$, asset returns R_i $\forall i$, at t are related cross-sectionally to risk premium at t via $R_i - r_f = \beta_i E(R_M - r_f) + e_i$, i. e. Eq. (7.8).

A simple verification would be to find cross-sectional regression of excess returns $R_i - r_f$ on estimated β_i and test if the estimated coefficient of $\hat{b}$ in $R_i - r_f = a + b\hat{\beta}_i + e_i$ is indeed significantly positive. This estimated coefficient is the risk premium at t and could be interpreted as $E_t(R_M - r_f)$ at t that may change over time. Simultaneously one could check if $\hat{a}$ is not significantly different from 0.

If we perform one cross-sectional regression at each time t, we may have different risk premium estimates for different t since risk premium can conditionally change over time. After the cross-sectional estimates of $E_t(R_M - r_f)$ are obtained for each t in the sample space $[1, T]$, we can average them over T and find the mean. This mean is

6 E. Fama and MacBeth J. (1973), Risk, return, and equilibrium: Empirical tests, 1973, *Journal of Political Economy*, 81 (3), 607–636.

an estimate of $E[E_t(R_M - r_f)]$ or the unconditional market risk premium $E(R_M - r_f)$. If this is statistically positive, it is verification of the positive risk premium.

In applying the FM method to Eq. (7.23), there are formally three steps. Step one is data preparation. This involves selecting the sampling period, the stocks to be tested (as comprehensive as is possible), and the best sources of the data. The stocks are grouped into 20 equally weighted portfolios formed by size. This is done for different sub-periods e. g., 1958–84, 1958–67, 1968–77, 1978–84. Using the portfolio returns as dependent variable allows for beta estimates (of the portfolio – think of each portfolio as a complex stock) with less sampling error, i. e. a very small standard error, since a portfolio return's unsystematic risk is much smaller than that of a single stock return. Thus using portfolios in the second step of time series regressions to obtain the beta loadings wouild minimize errors-in-variables bias when the estimated betas are used as explanatory variables in the third step.[7]

Step two is time series regressions in the estimation of the factor loadings $b_{i,\mathrm{MP}}$, $b_{i,\mathrm{DEI}}$, $b_{i,\mathrm{UI}}$, $b_{i,\mathrm{URP}}$, $b_{i,\mathrm{UTS}}$ for each i. Five years of monthly data, e. g., year $XX + 1$ January to year $XX + 5$ December, are used to find OLS estimates $\hat{b}_{i,\mathrm{MP}}$, $\hat{b}_{i,\mathrm{DEI}}$, $\hat{b}_{i,\mathrm{UI}}$, $\hat{b}_{i,\mathrm{URP}}$, $\hat{b}_{i,\mathrm{UTS}}$ for each i. These estimates are defined as the betas for cross-sectional regressions on each months of year $XX + 6$. The next window of five years data from $XX + 2$ January to $XX + 6$ December could be used for the next set of beta estimates for cross-sectional regressions on each months of year $XX + 7$, and so on. The rolling window could be moving forward month by month instead of year by year. For month by month rolling window, it is then natural to apply the beta estimates for cross-sectional regression of data in the month immediately after the rolling window, i. e. post-window. Note also that the estimated betas in post-windows are not constant and would change.

Step three is cross-sectional regression (across portfolios i) month by month in the post-window.

$$\begin{aligned} R_i = a &+ E(\mathrm{MP})\hat{b}_{i,\mathrm{MP}} + E(\mathrm{DEI})\hat{b}_{i,\mathrm{DEI}} + E(\mathrm{UI})\hat{b}_{i,\mathrm{UI}} \\ &+ E(\mathrm{URP})\hat{b}_{i,\mathrm{URP}} + E(\mathrm{UTS})\hat{b}_{i,\mathrm{UTS}} + e_i \end{aligned} \tag{7.24}$$

For each cross-sectional regression using dependent variable and estimated betas defined at time (month) t, a set of OLS estimates of the risk premiums $\widehat{E(\mathrm{MP}_t)}$, $\widehat{E(\mathrm{DEI}_t)}$, $\widehat{E(\mathrm{UI}_t)}$, $\widehat{E(\mathrm{URP}_t)}$, $\widehat{E(\mathrm{UTS}_t)}$ at t is found. For the sub-period, find the time series averages of these premium estimates. Test for their significance using simple t-statistics of sample means, i. e., the sample mean divided by sample standard deviation is approximately distributed as a t-distribution.

7 Fischer Black, Michael C. Jensen, and Myron Scholes (1972), The capital asset pricing model: Some empirical tests, in M. Jensen, ed., *Studies in the Theory of Capital Markets*, Praeger, NY, was an early study to consider reducing error-in-variable bias by forming portfolios stock returns as dependent variables.

An abridged illustration of Chen, Roll, and Ross (1986) Table 4B results is shown in Table 7.1.

Table 7.1: Regression Results of Eq. (7.23) Using Monthly Data.

Period	$\hat{a}$	$\widehat{E(\text{MP})}$	$\widehat{E(\text{DEI})}$	$\widehat{E(\text{UI})}$	$\widehat{E(\text{URP})}$	$\widehat{E(\text{UTS})}$
1958–84	4.124	13.589***	−0.125	−0.629**	7.205***	−5.211*
	(1.361)	(3.561)	(−1.640)	(−1.979)	(2.590)	(−1.690)
1958–67	4.989	13.155*	0.006	−0.191	5.560*	−0.008
	(1.271)	(1.897)	(0.092)	(−0.382)	(1.935)	(−0.004)
1968–77	−1.889	16.966***	−0.245***	−1.353***	12.717***	−13.142**
	(−0.334)	(2.638)	(−3.215)	(−3.320)	(2.852)	(−2.554)

Note: The t-statistics are shown in the parentheses. For example, in the sample period 1958–84 (total of 324 months), t_{323} can be approximated by the standard normal distribution. ***, **, *, indicate significance at the two-tailed 1 %, 5 %, and 10 % level, respectively, using the normal distribution as approximation.

To summarize their results, the risk premiums for factors related to industrial growth and default risk are positive and those for factors related to unexpected inflation and yield curve slope are negative. The risk premium associated with DEI was found to be generally not significant. Their results for the sub-period 1978–1984 were not significant, i. e., coefficient estimates were not significantly different from zeros. The economic intuition behind these results. similar to the reasoning behind the Sharpe-Lintner CAPM is as follows.

Equation (7.11) provides the betas or factor loadings b_{ij} for all stock i returns at time t. Pick a factor θ_j. If stocks have ex-post returns that on average increase with the jth factor loadings b_{ij}, ceteris baribus, then it implies that expected jth risk factor or the jth risk premium is positive. Higher b_{ij} or higher partial correlation of stock i's excess return with the jth risk factor means that stock i is less valuable for portfolio risk diversification, as in high market beta stocks. Assuming most stocks have positive correlations with the factor, thus it is compensated with a higher expected return for the higher systematic θ_j risk.

Examples are the estimated positive risk premiums, $\widehat{E(\text{MP}_t)}$ and $\widehat{E(\text{URP}_t)}$ corresponding to risk factors MP_t and URP_t. The economic intuition is that higher MP_t or increase in industrial growth leads to higher consumer demands of goods and hence better profitability and higher stock returns on average. Increases in URP_t could be due to increasing default risks of some firms in the market leading to switch of demand from some bonds to shares that are safe. This flight to quality could drive up most other shares' prices while some other shares that are linked to the bonds with increased default risks would sink in prices.

If stocks have ex-post returns that on average decrease with the jth factor loadings b_{ij}, ceteris baribus, then it implies that expected jth risk factor or the jth risk premium is negative. Lower $b_{ij} > 0$ in this case means contribution to expected return is more since the premium is negative. If we would explain the risk compensation in the case of a negative risk premium, it is more convenient to express the MLR as excess stock return regressed on factor $1/b_{ij}$ multiplied by θ_j' where ex-post return on average now increases with $1/b_{ij}$ (decreases with b_{ij}). Risk premium in this representation would be $E(\theta_j') > 0$. Then the usual explanation under positive premium goes through, i. e., smaller b_{ij} increases partial correlation with θ_j', provides less diversification, and hence is more risky and is thus compensated with higher expected returns.

Examples are the estimated negative risk premiums, $\widehat{E(\text{UI}_t)}$ and $\widehat{E(\text{UTS}_t)}$ corresponding to risk factors UI_t and UTS_t. The economic intuition for mostly negative correlations of stock returns with UI_t is due to increases in inflation possibly increasing firms' costs and thus reducing profitability. This would decrease market demand of stocks and hence decrease share prices and returns. Mostly negative correlations of stock returns with UTS_t could be that increasing (decreasing) yield curve slope signals confidence (diffidence) in borrowing to invest in the long-term, and hence share prices would be more (less) valuable. Given next period payoff, rising (falling) share price today would imply a lower (higher) return in the next period.

To find the multiple risk factors, another approach is to look for factors which represent systematic categorizations of all firms such that identifiable characteristics of firms, e. g., their financial accounts, impact on returns.

Banz (1981)[8] found low (high) market equity ME (number of shares outstanding × share price) correlates with high (low) residual error if market return is the only factor. In other words, if we run cross-sectional OLS

$$R_i - r_f = c_0 + c_1\hat{\beta} + c_2\text{ME}_i + \eta_i$$

we would get a significantly negative estimate of c_2. Stattman (1980)[9] and Rosenberg, Reid, and Lanstein (1985)[10] found that average returns on U.S. stocks are positively related to the ratio of a firm's book value of common equity, BE, to its market value. ME. Chan, Hamao, and Lakonishok (1991)[11] found that book-to-market equity, BE/ME, has a strong role in explaining the cross-section of average returns on Japanese stocks. In other words, if we run OLS

8 R. Banz (1981), The relation between return and market value of common stocks, *Journal of Financial Economics* 9,3–18.

9 D. Stattman (1980), Book values and stock returns, *The Chicago MBA: A Journal of Selected Papers*, 4, 25–45.

10 B. Rosenberg, K. Reid, and R. Lanstein (1985), Persuasive evidence of market inefficiency, *Journal of Portfolio Management* 11:9–17.

11 Louis K. C. Chan, Y. Hamao, and J. Lakonishok (1991), Fundamentals and stock returns in Japan, *The Journal of Finance*, 46 (5), 1739–1764.

$$R_i - r_f = c_0 + c_1\hat{\beta} + c_2\text{ME}_i + c_3\text{BE/ME}_i + \eta_i$$

across firms denoted i, we would get a significantly positive estimate of c_3.

These studies highlighted a firm's capitalization (size) and its book equity to market equity ratio (BE/ME) as important empirical determinants of its ex-post returns. High BE/ME also implies a value stock, i. e., its traded price is low relative to its accounting fundamentals.

In more results related to multi-factor asset pricing, Basu (1983)[12] showed that earnings-price ratios (E/P) help explain the cross-section of average returns on U.S. stocks in tests that also include size and market beta. E/P is likely to be higher (prices are lower relative to earnings) for stocks with higher risks and expected returns. In other words, if we run cross-sectional OLS

$$R_i - r_f = c_0 + c_1\hat{\beta} + c_2\text{ME}_i + c_3 E/P_i + \eta_i$$

we would get a significantly positive estimate of c_3. Bhandari (1988)[13] reported positive relation between leverage and average return. It is plausible that leverage is associated with risk and expected return.

Like Reinganum (1981),[14] and Lakonishok and Shapiro (1986),[15] Fama and French (1992)[16] found that the relation between beta and average return disappears during the more recent 1963–1990 period, even when beta is used alone to explain average returns. The simple relation between beta and average return is also weak in the 50-year 1941–1990 period.

At any time t, different firms have different measures of characteristics e. g. size, book-to-market ratios, earnings-price ratios, etc. Therefore these characteristic measures are not the systematic factors that affect all the firms. These characteristic measures behave more like the beta or factor loadings that can differ at different levels for different firms. But each particular identifiable characteristic, e. g. size, should be related to a common risk factor such that the realization of the risk factor multiplied by the loading contributes to the ex-post stock return. For example, the systematic risk factor linked to the size loading could be variations in economy-wide loanable funds.

12 S. Basu (1983), The relationship between earnings yield, market value and return for NYSE common stocks: Further evidence, *Journal of Financial Economics* 12, 129–156.

13 L. Bhandari (1988), Debt/Equity ratio and expected common stock returns: Empirical evidence, *The Journal of Finance*, 43, 507–528.

14 M. Reinganum (1981), A misspecification of capital asset pricing: Empirical anomalies based on earnings yields and market values, *Journal of Financial Economics*, 9, 19–46.

15 J. Lakonishok and A. C. Shapiro (1986), Systematic risk, total risk and size as determinants of stock market returns, *Journal of Banking and Finance* 10, 115–132.

16 E. Fama and K. R. French (1992), The cross-section of expected stock returns, *The Journal of Finance*, 47(2), 427–465.

More loanable funds for businesses would mean lower interest rates and is generally good for small businesses, hence positive impact on returns of smaller firms. But insufficient loanable funds mean high interests and small firms would be negatively impacted. Another intuitive explanation of size effect could be economy-wide distress risks that would impact on small cap firms more, hence higher expected return as risk-compensation for the small cap firms. The characteristic of BE/ME or value could be associated with higher operating leverages, i. e. higher proportion of fixed costs. Higher fixed cost effect could be linked with risk factors such as business cycles or economic-wide sales activities.

7.3.2 Cross-Sectional Regressions

In any period t, the ability to explain the cross-sectional expected returns on assets is the essence of a workable asset pricing model. Suppose we add a regression constant in Eq. (7.12):

$$R_{it} - r_{ft} = a + b_{i1}\gamma_{1t} + b_{i2}\gamma_{2t} + \cdots + b_{iK}\gamma_{Kt} + \xi_{it}$$

where $E(\xi_{it}) = 0$. As in approach (ii), Fama and French (1992) used U.S. NYSE, AMEX, and NASDAQ exchange stocks that are recorded in CRSP database for cross-sectional regressions. Individual stock return is employed as dependent variable, and CAPM beta $\hat{b}_i$, ln(ME), ln(BE/ME), ln(A/ME), ln(A/BE), E/P Dummy, and E(+)/P of stock i in month t are used as factor loadings $b_{i1}, b_{i2}, b_{i3}, \ldots, b_{iK}$.

ME = market equity \$ value is stock i's last price × number of stock i's shares outstanding in the market
BE = book equity value
A = total book asset value is BE + BL where BL is book liability value
E is per share earnings
P is \$ price per share

ln(ME) represents size of market equity. Small size firms have lower ln(ME) values than larger firms. We expect smaller firms to be systematically more risky with higher distress costs and default risks and thus the market will require higher ex-post returns.

ln(BE/ME) represents book-to-market equity value. Higher BE/ME with higher operating leverages are systematically more risky and thus the market will require higher ex-post returns. ln(A/ME) represents relative leverage. Higher ln(A/ME) implies a relatively higher component of debt. This increases beta, but beyond that it also increases default risk, which leads to higher expected return. E/P Dummy is 0 if E/P is positive and 1 if E/P is negative. E(+)/P is the ratio of total earnings to market equity, but is assigned a value of 0 if E/P is negative. High E/P indicates underpriced stock (in the case where earnings are not too low due to high stress cost) and will explain higher expected returns.[17]

For the dependent variable of stock return measured from July of year n to June of year $n+1$, BE, A, and E for each firm are measured using accounts from the fiscal year ending in calendar year $n-1$. The accounting ratios are measured using market equity ME in December of year $n-1$. Firm size ln(ME) is measured in June of year n. These accounting variables of each firm measured by year end $n-1$ are used as monthly explanatory variables for the monthly returns in July n to June $n+1$. Hence the explanatory variables are available to investors prior to the returns. Market β_i, corresponding to the excess market portfolio return as factor for each firm, is obtained using estimates based on a portfolio of stocks with approximately similar betas. This beta for the portfolio is then used as beta for each of the stocks in the portfolio.

In the Fama and French studies on cross-sectional regressions, for each period such as a month, the cross-sectional multiple linear regression in Eq. (7.12) yields coefficient estimates of risk premiums $\hat{\gamma}_1, \hat{\gamma}_2, \ldots, \hat{\gamma}_K$ and their t-statistics. The estimated coefficients at each month t such as $\hat{\gamma}_{jt}$ form a time series, and its time-averaged "t-statistics" can be obtained as:

$$\frac{\frac{1}{\sqrt{T}}\sum_{t=1}^{T}\hat{\gamma}_{jt}}{\sqrt{\frac{1}{T}\sum_{t=1}^{T}(\hat{\gamma}_{jt}-\frac{1}{T}\sum_{t=1}^{T}\hat{\gamma}_{jt})^2}}$$

to test if the estimates are significantly different from zero assuming they are randomly distributed about zero over time under the null of zero coefficient values. The test of the model would include testing if $\hat{a}$ is not significantly different from zero. Note that instead of using just one cross-sectional regression at a specific time period, approach (ii) is used in which many cross-sectional regressions are performed and the tests are done on the sample averages of the time series of the estimates for each cross-sectional regression. The approach yields more accurate testing with more data across time.

An abridged illustration of Fama and French (1992) Table 3 result is shown in Table 7.2.

The results showed that by itself market beta β does not appear to explain cross-sectional returns as the t-statistic of 0.46 shows the estimated coefficients were not significantly different from zeros. However, the estimated risk premiums corresponding to loads ln(M/E) and ln(BE/ME) were, respectively, negatively and positively significant. By itself, E/P risk premium also appeared to be positively significant. Estimated risk premium for ln(A/ME) is similar to that of ln(BE/ME) as both the loadings are strongly correlated. Estimated risk premium for ln(A/BE), which resembled somewhat the size effect, was negative. When ln(ME) and ln(BE/ME) were entered together in the MLR, their estimated coefficients or risk premiums remained significantly nega-

17 K. Jaffe, D. B. Keim, and R. Westerfield (1989), Earnings yields, market values, and stock returns, *The Journal of Finance*, 44, 135–148, suggested a U-shape for average return versus E/P ratio.

Table 7.2: Average Slopes Using Monthly Regression Results of Eq. (7.12) from July 1963 to December 1990.

β	ln(ME)	ln(BE/ME)	ln(A/ME)	ln(A/BE)	E/P Dummy	E(+)/P
0.15 (0.46)	NA	NA	NA	NA	NA	NA
NA	−0.15 (−2.58)	NA	NA	NA	NA	NA
NA	NA	0.50 (5.71)	NA	NA	NA	NA
NA	NA	NA	NA	NA	0.57 (2.28)	4.72 (4.57)
NA	−0.11 (−1.99)	0.35 (4.44)	NA	NA	NA	NA
NA	−0.11 (−2.06)	NA	0.35 (4.32)	−0.50 (−4.56)	NA	NA
NA	−0.13 (−2.47)	0.33 (4.46)	NA	NA	−0.14 (−0.90)	0.87 (1.23)

Note: The t-statistics are shown in the parentheses. For example, in the sample period July 1963 to December 1990 (330 months), the t-statistics for the slope time series average, t_{329} can be approximated by the standard normal distribution.

tive and positive, respectively. Hence Fama and French (1992) showed that there were at least two significant risk factors closely associated with firms' characteristics such as size and value.

In Table 7.3, we show an abridged illustration of Fama and French (1992) Table 5 results. Average Monthly Returns (%) on Portfolios Formed on Size and Book-to-Market Equity, July 1963 to December 1990, were reported. V1, V3, V5, V7, V10 represent equal-weighted portfolios of the first, third, fifth, seventh, and tenth decile of stocks sorted by Book equity to Market equity ratios. ME1, ME3, ME5, ME7, and ME10 represent equal-weighted portfolios of the first, third, fifth, seventh, and tenth decile of stocks sorted by capitalization or market equity.

Table 7.3: Average Returns of Different Portfolios Formed by the Intersection of the Value and Size Decile Portfolios.

	Book-to-Market Portfolios					
	All	**V1**	**V3**	**V5**	**V7**	**V10**
Size Portfolios						
All	1.23	0.64	1.06	1.24	1.39	1.63
ME1	1.47	0.70	1.20	1.56	1.70	1.92
ME3	1.22	0.56	1.23	1.36	1.30	1.60
ME5	1.24	0.88	1.08	1.13	1.44	1.49
ME7	1.07	0.95	0.99	0.99	0.99	1.47
ME10	0.89	0.93	0.84	0.79	0.81	1.18

The averages of portfolio returns in any of the 10×10 intersection portfolios of the value and size decile portfolios are similar to a linear regression of returns on dummies denoting each of 10 by 10 deciles based on lagged ME, BE/ME measures of each stock. Clearly, the average ex-post returns of stocks decrease with size but increase with book-to-market ratio.

In terms of a direct factor modeling approach (iii), Fama and French (1993) provided such a technique to empirically identify several suitable factors for the multi-factor asset pricing models.[18] This path-breaking technique is also called the Fama-French 3-factor Model.

7.3.3 Fama-French Three Factor Model

Suppose $\text{cov}(R_{it}, R_{jt}) \neq 0$ at t for any two stocks i, j. Suppose there exists a group of stocks $j \in S$ with similar characteristics of small capitalizations, and another group of stocks $k \in B$ with big capitalizations. For all small cap stocks, $\text{cov}(R_{it}, \frac{1}{N}\sum_{j\in S} R_{jt})$ at t is high and $\text{cov}(R_{it}, \frac{1}{N}\sum_{k\in B} R_{kt})$ at t is low. The latter is consistent with the empirical observations of capitalization being a determinant of returns. For all large cap stocks, $\text{cov}(R_{it}, \frac{1}{N}\sum_{j\in S} R_{jt})$ at t is low and $\text{cov}(R_{it}, \frac{1}{N}\sum_{k\in B} R_{kt})$ at t is high.

If we form an index $F_t = \frac{1}{N}\sum_{j\in S} R_{jt} - \frac{1}{N}\sum_{k\in B} R_{kt}$, then for small cap stocks, $\text{cov}(R_{it}, F_t)$ at t is high, while for large cap stocks $\text{cov}(R_{it}, F_t)$ at t is low (possibly negative). Hence we see that F_t is a good candidate for a systematic risk factor that affects all stocks cross-sectionally since stocks vary cross-sectionally by capitalizations.

Similarly suppose high value stocks' ($\in H$) returns have high positive correlations, low value stocks' ($\in L$) returns have high positive correlations, but high and low value stock returns have low correlations. If we form an index $G_t = \frac{1}{N}\sum_{j\in H} R_{jt} - \frac{1}{N}\sum_{k\in L} R_{kt}$, then for high value stocks, $\text{cov}(R_{it}, G_t)$ at t is high, while for low value stocks $\text{cov}(R_{it}, G_t)$ at t is low (possibly negative). Hence G_t is a another good candidate for a systematic risk factor that affects all stocks cross-sectionally since stocks vary cross-sectionally by BE/ME ratios. The factors need not be, but can be constructed as self-financing portfolios if the outlay on the long positions equal to the shortsale value of the short positions.

Fama and French (1993) constructed micmicking portfolios of indexes F_t and G_t as follows. In June of each year n from 1963 to 1991, stocks on NYSE, Amex, and NASDAQ are divided into a small cap S and a big cap B group. For the size sort, market equity or capitalization is measured at the end of June. The same stocks are also sorted into three book-to-market ratio groups comprising bottom 30 % ratios (L group), medium 40 % (M group), and top 30 % ratios (H group). To be more precise, the ratio in year n is

18 E. Fama and K. R. French (1993), Common risk factors in the returns on stocks and bonds, *Journal of Financial Economics*, 33, 3–56.

formed using the book common equity for fiscal year ending in calendar year $n-1$. This is typically December $n-1$. Market equity is measured at end December of year $n-1$. Six portfolios are constructed each year from the intersection of these two sorts: S/L, S/M, S/H, B/L, B/M, and B/H portfolios. Monthly value-weighted returns on the six portfolios are computed from July of year n top June of $n+1$. The portfolios are rebalanced in June of $n+1$ based on the yearly updated ME and BE/ME firm numbers. The SMB ("small-minus-big") micmicking portfolio monthly return is constructed as the difference between the simple average of S/L, S/M, S/H monthly returns and the simple average of B/L, B/M, B/H monthly returns. The HML ("high-minus-low") micmicking portfolio monthly return is constructed as the difference between the simple average of S/H and B/H monthly returns and the simple average of S/L and B/L monthly returns.

The key regression model is:

$$R_{it} - r_{ft} = a + b(R_{Mt} - r_{ft}) + s\text{SMB}_t + h\text{HML}_t + e_t \tag{7.25}$$

where R_{Mt} is a value-weighted market portfolio return, and r_{ft} is one-month Treasury bill rate at month t. e_t is the residual innovation.

The dependent variable R_{it} is a portfolio return for the month t. Fama and French (1993) included studies on bond returns but we shall not discuss them here. In June of each year n, size sort into 5 quintiles was performed based on market equity measured at the end of June. The same stocks are also sorted into 5 quintiles based on book-to-market ratio groups where BE/ME ratios are measured in the same way as when constructing the micmicking portfolios. 25 portfolios are constructed each year from the intersection of these two sorts. Monthly value-weighted returns of stocks in the 25 portfolios are computed from July of year n top June of $n+1$. The latter form the monthly dependent variables.

As in the first and second steps of the macroeconomic factors model above, time series regression is performed on Eq. (7.11) for each portfolio i of the 25 portfolios. Fama and French (1993) used this time series regression approach essentially to test for the significance of factor loadings. Significant factor loadings for stock returns are necessary for showing the selected factors in the regression are systematic according to APT.

An abridged illustration of Fama and French (1993) Table 6 results is shown in Table 7.4. We name their portfolios as follows. Stocks in the ith size quintile are denoted as in the group Si, while stocks in the jth BE/ME or value quintile are denoted as in the group Vj. Stocks in the intersection of the smallest cap and third value quintile are denoted as in the group S1V3. Thus S1V3 portfolio denotes the value-weighted return of stocks in the S1V3 group. Each line in the table denotes a regression using a different portfolio return as dependent variable.

The outstanding feature of the results is that all the coefficients are significantly different from zero at p-values much less than 1 % level. The R^2 for the regressions are very high at close to one. Moreover, the estimated coefficients $\hat{s}$ on the size micmicking portfolio are significantly positive except that of S5V3 that is significantly negative. The estimated coefficients reduce in magnitudes as size increases (see S1V3 to S5V3), indicating that increasing size reduces expected returns. This could be due to smaller cap firms facing higher (default and other funding) risks, and thus having their stocks compensated with higher expected returns.

Table 7.4: Regression Results of Eq. (7.25) Using Monthly Data from July 1963 to December 1991.

Dependent Variable	b	s	h	R^2
S1V3 Portfolio	0.95	1.19	0.26	0.97
	(60.44)	(52.03)	(9.66)	
S2V3 Portfolio	1.00	0.88	0.26	0.95
	(55.88)	(34.03)	(8.56)	
S3V3 Portfolio	−0.98	0.60	0.32	0.93
	(50.78)	(21.23)	(9.75)	
S4V3 Portfolio	1.04	0.29	0.30	0.91
	(51.21)	(9.81)	(8.83)	
S5V3 Portfolio	0.98	−0.23	0.21	0.88
	(46.57)	(−7.58)	(5.80)	
S3V1 Portfolio	1.12	0.76	−0.38	0.95
	(56.88)	(26.40)	(−11.26)	
S3V2 Portfolio	1.02	0.65	−0.00	0.94
	(53.17)	(23.39)	(−0.05)	
S3V4 Portfolio	0.97	0.48	0.51	0.93
	(54.38)	(18.62)	(16.88)	
S3V5 Portfolio	1.09	0.66	0.68	0.93
	(52.52)	(21.91)	(19.39)	

Note: The t-statistics are shown in the parentheses. For example, in the sample period July 1963 to December 1991 (342 months), the t-statistics for the coefficient estimates, t_{338} can be approximated by the standard normal distribution.

The estimated coefficients $\hat{h}$ on the value micmicking portfolio increase in magnitudes as BE/ME increases (see S3V1 to S3V5), indicating that increasing BE/ME increases expected returns. This could be due to value or high book-value firms facing higher operating leverage risks. Market risks as in the Sharpe-Lintner CAPM is also seen as significant with significantly positive $\hat{b}$ for all portfolios.

This study suggests that the market beta and two other firm attributes viz. capitalization size and book-to-market equity ratio are three variables that correspond each to a common risk factor affecting the cross-section of stocks. Together with the earlier 1992 study, Fama and French broke completely new and fascinating ground in the world of investment finance by pointing out presumably better explanations for the cross-sectional expected returns of stocks than what single-factor CAPM does. It is in explaining every stock's return variations that these risk factors are considered as systematic across the market. The new proxies of systematic risk factors they suggested led to voluminous research that followed. Unlike factors linked to macroeconomic variables, these Fama-French risk factors can be constructed like funds that can be traded and used for hedging. Thus, there is greater plausibility in their use by the market, and hence their role as systematic risk factors.

Carhart 4-Factor Model[19] is an extension of the Fama-French 3-Factor Model to include a momentum factor. The monthly momentum factor is formed by equal-weighted average of returns of highest performing firms in the previous year less the equal-weighted average of returns of the worst performing firms. It is called the winners minus losers or up minus down (UMD) factor. The factor however appeared to reverse correlation in events of momentum crashes during strong economic downturns.

Fama and French 5-Factor model[20] also extended the 3-Factor Model to include the return spread between firms with high operating profitability and firms with low or negative operating profitability, RMW (robust minus weak), as a factor, and also the return spread between firms that invested conservatively and those that invested aggressively, CMA (conservative minus aggressive), as another factor. These factors are thought to have positive correlations with ex-post stock returns. However including the latter two factors appeared to dilute the effect of the value factor.

As stock market and portfolio performance research continue, it is interesting to know that empirical data research oftentimes come up with evidence of new systematic factors that are valuable to be considered. Over time some proved to be spurious results, some due to data-snooping,[21] some over-shadowed by new factors that seem to subsume the old ones, and some disappeared with new and more recent market development and data.

In recent years, Karolyi and Stijn (2020) discussed that there are hundreds or even more of so called new anomalies or factors. Many of these may not survive rigorous empirical tests and many are just linear combinations of other factors. Relatively new perspectives of cross-sectional and time series analyses of the factor models were discussed.[22]

---

19 M. M. Carhart (1997), On persistence in mutual fund performance, *The Journal of Finance*, 52, 57–82.

20 E. Fama and K. French (2015), A five-factor asset pricing model, *Journal of Financial Economics* 116, 1–22.

21 This is similar in idea to over-fitting a regression with too many explanatory variables to get a high R^2, but which does not promise, and sometimes work adversely in forecasting. Data snooping is more about using models and specifications, including searching for constructions of data variables to try to explain cross-sectional return variations. Heuristically, if a relationship can be rejected at 5 % significance level if the null that there is no relationship is true, then there is 5 % chance that if we search hard enough within a dataset, we just may be able to find a relationship that cannot be rejected 5 % of the times..

22 See the special 2020 volume 33 of the *Review of Financial Studies*. See also G. Andrew Karolyi and Stijn Van Nieuwerburgh (2020), New methods for the cross-section of returns, *The Review of Financial Studies*, 33(5), 1879–1890.

7.4 Forecasting Returns

We discussed the purposes of estimating the mult-factor models and in (1a), (1b), we indicated how forecasting or prediction of next period returns can be carried out. Consistently better than average prediction will no doubt be useful for investing decisions. Lewellen (2015)[23] provided some results in forecasting using Fama and French (1992) approach or approach (ii).

In Lewellen (2015), cross-sectional regressions of stock returns were first run on their pre-determined or lagged characteristics. His Model 1 used size, BE/ME, and past 12-month stock returns as characteristics. Model 2 added 3-year share issuance (log growth in split-adjusted outstanding shares) and one-year accruals, profitability, and asset growth as characteristics. Model 3 included 8 additional characteristics such as beta, dividend yield, one-year share issuance, 3-year stock returns, 12-month volatility, 12-month turnover, market leverage, and sales-to-price ratio. Each month t, estimates of the Fama-MacBeth slopes or premiums related to these characteristics, $\hat{\gamma}_{jt}$ (via Eq. (7.12)) are collected, and then used to form ten-year rolling averages or else cumulative averages.

For example, if monthly (conditional) premiums (corresponding to each characteristic) are estimated via cross-sectional regressions from January 1964 to December 2013, the averages of the estimates from Jan. 1964 to Dec. 1973 over 120 months form the 10-year averages. It is also the first cumulative averages. The averages of the estimates from Feb. 1964 to Jan. 1974 form the next 10-year average. Jan. 1964 to Jan. 1974 averages are the cumulative averages. Averages of Mar. 1964 to Feb. 1974 are the next 10-year rolling averages. Jan. 1964 to Feb. 1974 are the next cumulative averages. There are other ways to form rolling averages.

Let the averages (or else cumulative averages) over window $[d_1, d_2]$ be denoted as follows.

$$\overline{\hat{\gamma}_j}[d_1, d_2] = \frac{1}{d_2 - d_1 + 1} \sum_{t=1}^{d_2 - d_1 + 1} \hat{\gamma}_{jt}$$

for each $j = 1, 2, \ldots, K$. This is used as the expected premium for the future month d_2+1. Equation (7.12) is then used to make a forecast or prediction of stock i excess return at $d_2 + 1$. The forecast is

$$E_{d_2}(R_{id_2+1}) = r_{fd_2+1} + b_{i1}\overline{\hat{\gamma}_1}[d_1, d_2] + b_{i2}\overline{\hat{\gamma}_2}[d_1, d_2] + \cdots + b_{iK}\overline{\hat{\gamma}_K}[d_1, d_2]$$

where $b_{i1}, b_{i2}, \ldots, b_{iK}$ characteristics or loadings of stock i are pre-determined at a time just prior to month $d_2 + 1$.

23 J. Lewellen (2015), The cross-section of expected stock returns, *Critical Finance Review*, 4, 1–44.

Hence as the window $[d_1, d_2]$ rolls forward in time to $[d_1 + 1, d_2 + 1], [d_1 + 2, d_2 + 2], \ldots, [d_1 + t, d_2 + t]$, we obtain a time series of return forecasts, $F_{id_2+1} = E_{d_2}(R_{id_2+1})$ for each stock i. We can then compare the realized stock i returns at $t + 1$ versus the forecast return for $t + 1$. This is done for all stocks i. Time series regressions for each i of $R_{i,t}$ on $F_{i,t}$ can be performed and the slope S_i is noted. Averages of the slopes and their t – *statistics* across i provide an idea of the predictive performances under each model and each method of rolling or cumulative windows. Good predictive or forecast performances would produce average slopes close to one and high average t-statistics. Average slopes of between 0.63 to 0.82 were reported in the Lewellen (2015) study using the 3 models and the 2 types of windows.

Another approach to the forecasting could be based on Fama and French (1993) or approach (iii) for the first step. Assume the time series over window $[d_1, d_2]$ of the risk factors θ_{jt} are given or observable. For each stock i, employ Eq. (7.11) using time series regression to estimate the stock's loadings $\hat{b}_{ij}[d_1, d_2]$ for $j = 1, 2, \ldots, K$. These are constants over $[d_1, d_2]$. Use $\hat{b}_{ij}[d_1, d_2]$ $(\forall j)$ as loadings for next month $d_2 + 1$. Also estimate $E_{d_2}(\theta_{jd_2+1}) = \gamma_{jd_2+1}$ using a time series model on each θ_{jt} over $[d_1, d_2]$. Next, use Eq. (7.12) to forecast next period return for each stock i:

$$E_{d_2}(R_{id_2+1}) = r_{fd_2+1} + \hat{b}_{i1}[d_1, d_2]E_{d_2}(\theta_{1d_2+1}) + \hat{b}_{i2}[d_1, d_2]E_{d_2}(\theta_{2d_2+1}) + \cdots$$
$$+ \hat{b}_{iK}[d_1, d_2]E_{d_2}(\theta_{Kd_2+1})$$

This is then repeated as the window $[d_1, d_2]$ rolls forward in time to $[d_1 + 1, d_2 + 1], [d_1 + 2, d_2 + 2], \ldots, [d_1 + t, d_2 + t]$. We can then compare the realized stock i returns at $t + 1$ versus the forecast return for $t + 1$. This is done for all stocks i. Time series regressions for each i of $R_{i,t}$ on its forecast can be performed and the slope S_i is noted. As the variation in $\hat{b}_{ij}[d_1, d_2]$ $(\forall j)$ from month to month may be small, much of any predictive accuracy if any would come from estimating $E_{d_2}(\theta_{jd_2+1})$.

7.5 Anomalies and Behavioral Finance

Traditional finance asset pricing models or paradigms based on rationality, i. e., optimization (of utility), rational expectations using all available information, and arbitraging away mispricings (no-arbitrage equilibrium) do not appear to explain all asset pricing aberrations. Many of these aberrations or anomalies, not currently explainable by rational equilibrium asset pricing models, may be explainable using human behaviors. Behavioral finance is such an alternative explanation of some systematic cases of apparent irrationality. What could lead to prices keeping away (at least temporarily) from no-arbitrage equilibrium or being apparent irrational at any point in time under behavioral finance are due to three key reasons:

(4a) Irrationality or else bounded rationality[24]
(4b) Limits to Arbitrage
(4c) Psychological (behavioral) biases that affect how people make investment decisions despite the information. It is how they add their values/beliefs to the information.

Limited investor attention, an aspect of bounded rationality, refers to an anomaly in which investors purchase attention grabbing stocks that have bigger price changes and higher trading volumes or are linked with significant press events though the stocks do not have objective evidence of such movement possibilities. Barber abd Odean (2008)[25] explained that attention-driven buying is caused by the search costs when investors are faced with an enormous number of stocks they can purchase. Stocks that caught their attention reduce the search costs but also reduce their ability to compute rationally.

Limits to arbitrage itself could be due to three sources of market frictions. (1) There is no perfect substitutes for mispriced security, e. g., Long-Term Capital Management (LTCM). Buying cheap Russian debt cannot be hedged by selling more expensive US debt. (2) There are transactions costs including short-selling constraints. The costs could prevent swift arbitrage. (3) Interruption by noisy traders (or uninformed liquidity traders) can prolong mispricings for a bit. The increased mispricing gap due to noisy trades in the opposite direction means arbitrageur suffers temporary loss even while he/she is trying to set up convergence trades. Arbitrageur may not want to take this risk if his/her trading capital is limited.

Before the 1990s, the Chicago School of full rational expectations modeling dominated the thinking behind asset pricing and investments. As an alternative, the competing behavioral finance school argues that many financial phenomena can plausibly be understood using models in which at least some if not many agents are not fully rational. There are other behavioral schools of thought originating from the field of psychology that suggest bounded rationality, ecological rationality, and so on.

One major implication of behavioral finance is that risky arbitrage opportunities and abnormal profit opportunities may appear to arise in the market because investor behavior is governed by psychology and behavioral biases. These prompt deviations from full rationality that we might otherwise expect. There is a huge variety of psychological effects modeled to explain aberrations from empirical validations of rational asset pricing models. Some examples are regret theory, anchoring behavior, prospect

24 See Herbert A. Simon (1957), *Models of Man*, NY: John Wiley.

25 B. M. Barber and T. Odean (2008), All that glitters: The effect of attention and news on the buying behavior of individual and institutional investors, *The Review of Financial Studies*, 21(2), 785–818.

theory by Kahneman and Tversky (1979),[26] mental accounting by Thaler (1980),[27] and so on.

For example, regret theory is a theory that says people expect to regret if they make a wrong choice, and the regret will cause aversion especially to the type of decisions that in the past had produced regrets. It could run both ways, implying more risk aversion if in the past the decision-maker had taken risk and suffered heavy losses, or less risk aversion if in the past the decision-maker had been conservative and regretted missing multiplying his or her wealth during the boom.

Anchoring behavior is the use of irrelevant information as a reference for estimating or expecting some unknown quantities. For example, in assessing the fair price of a small firm's stock, the investor could be using the price of another small firm's stock for comparison, even though the latter information is irrelevant because the two stocks are in different industries and at different levels of risks.

Prospect theory postulates that preferences will depend on how a problem is framed. Preference is a function of decision weights on outcomes, and the weights do not correspond exactly to the outcome probabilities. Specifically, prospect theory predicts that most decision-makers tend to overweigh small probabilities on huge losses and underweigh moderate and high probabilities on moderate gains or returns. Hence, prospect theory is better able to explain phenomenon such as loss aversion, as in selling stocks after a major drop for fear of further drop.

Mental accounting theorists argue that people behave as if their assets are compartmentalized into a number of non-fungible (non - interchangeable) mental accounts such as current income or current wealth. The marginal propensities to consume out of the different accounts are all different, and thus an investor with a larger mental account in current income may indeed invest more, while a similarly wealthy investor with a larger mental account in current wealth may consume more and invest less.

As an illustration of loss aversion tendency, Kahneman and Tversky (1979) discussed – "Would you take a gamble with a 50 % chance of losing $100 vs. a 50 % chance of winning $101? Most people would say no. Despite the positive expected payoff, the possibility of losing $100 is enough to deter participation". This explains why investors hesitate to sell when there is a loss and sell too soon when there is a gain (as it "costs" more to take loss). Sometimes the tendency to hold on to loss stocks and realize gains too soon in rising stocks is called "Disposition Effect" – see Odean (1998).[28]

---

26 D. Kahneman and A Tversky (1979), Prospect theory: An analysis of decision under risk, *Econometrica*, 47(2), 263–292.

27 See R. H. Thaler (1980), Toward a positive theory of consumer choice, *Journal of Economic Behavior and Organization*, 1, 39–60, and also R. H. Thaler (1985), Mental accounting and consumer choice, *Marketing Science*, 4, 199–214.

28 Terrance Odean (1998), Are investors reluctant to realize their losses? *The Journal of Finance*, 53(5), 1775–1798.

In ambiguity aversion, people do not like situations where they are uncertain about the probability distribution of a gamble (ambiguity situations). This ambiguity aversion can be illustrated by the Ellsberg (1961) paradox.

Suppose that there are two urns, 1 and 2. Urn 1 contains a total of 100 balls, 50 red and 50 blue. Urn 2 also contains 100 balls, again a mix of red and blue, but the subject does not know the proportion of each. Subjects are asked to choose one of the following two gambles (a1 or a2), each of which involves a possible payoff to subject of $100, depending on the color of a ball drawn at random from the relevant urn.
a1: a ball is drawn from Urn 1, subject receives $100 if red, $0 if blue,
a2: a ball is drawn from Urn 2, subject receives $100 if red, $0 if blue.

Subjects are then next also asked to choose between the following two gambles (b1 or b2):
b1: a ball is drawn from Urn 1, subject receives $100 if blue, $0 if red,
b2: a ball is drawn from Urn 2, subject receives $100 if blue, $0 if red.

If subject chooses a1 and then b1, the irrationality is as follows. If subject chooses a1 over a2, then by rationality, the subject should believe there are more than 50 blue balls in urn 2. But given the latter, a rational subject would choose b2 in the second set of gambles. Subject's choices of a1 and then b1 clearly are not consistent with rational choices. The choices are, however, due to behavioral biases of ambiguity aversion since a2 and b2 face uncertain probability distributions.

Investor sentiment is another behavioral factor affecting stock returns. Sentiment is the propensity to speculate and hence stocks that are more difficult to value (more speculation required) or stocks that have higher idiosyncratic volatility are more susceptible to sentiment biases. See Daniel, Hirshleifer, and Subrahmanyam (1998, 2001),[29] and Hirshleifer (2001).[30] Informed investor can exploit such investor sentiments to sell more when the sentiment is to hold and buy more when the sentiment is to sell. On average, strong sentiments would lead to underperformance, i. e. negative alpha. Thus informed investors can profit more from trading in hard-to-value and high idiosyncratic volatility stocks.

Overconfidence is another behavioral trait affecting full rationality. Overconfident investors assign high chances of obtaining higher returns than indicated by historical or objective data. Investors exhibit greater overconfidence when the market uncertainty is higher and sometimes also when the most recent returns are higher. Some

---

29 K. Daniel, D. Hirshleifer, and A. Subrahmanyam (1998), Investor psychology and security market under- and overreactions, *The Journal of Finance*, 53, 1839–1885, and K. Daniel, D. Hirshleifer, and A. Subrahmanyam (2001), Overconfidence, arbitrage and equilibrium asset pricing, *The Journal of Finance*, 56, 921–965.

30 David Hirshleifer (2001), Investor psychology and asset pricing, *The Journal of Finance*, 56, 1533–1597.

individual investors commit larger investment mistakes and exhibit stronger behavioral biases in more uncertain environments. Thus ex-post returns to investing in hard-to-value and also high idiosyncratic volatility stocks are lower for general market investors.

7.6 Calendar Effect Anomalies

Some anomalies are specifically related to the calendar such as day of the week, month of the year, seasons, festive events, or major events tied to specific time of the year.

Many researchers reported that the mean daily stock returns on Monday tended to be lower than those of other weekdays.[31] On average. Monday returns appeared to be significantly lower than those of Friday returns. This is called the Monday effect or the weekend effect.

The Monday effect could be due to the practice of firms releasing negative news on Friday nights so Monday closing stock prices were lower than Friday closing. It could also be a technical reason that short-selling typically occurs more on Monday than on Friday as traders need to close the short positions sometimes within a day or two. There could also be behavioral reasons such as traders experiencing a decline in optimism over the weekend. However, some studies in the 1990s showed that the day-of-the-week effect in the U.S. stock market may have largely disappeared in the 1990s.

The January effect[32] is when stock prices tended to rise in January, especially the prices of small firms and firms whose stock price has declined substantially over the recent years. The significantly positive January return was typically driven by heavy selling during December and aggressive buying during January. Investors tended to sell off low-performing stocks at the end of each year and then buy back those stocks a few weeks later. Investors often sold off underperforming stocks in December so that they could use the losses to offset capital gains taxes – this is called "tax-loss harvesting."[33] The "tax-selling" can depress stock prices to low levels where they become attractive to buyers in January. In January, investors who had received year-end work cash bonuses could also add these to buying shares. Besides the institutional tax reason, there are plausible pyschological and behavioral reasons. Some investors

31 See M. Gibbons and P. Hess (1981), Day of the week effects and asset returns, *Journal of Business*, 54, D. Keim, and R. Stambaugh (1984), A further investigation of the weekend effect in stock returns, *The Journal of Finance*, 39, J. Jaffe, and R. Westerfield (1985), The weekend effect in common stock returns: The international evidence, *The Journal of Finance*, 40, and G.N. Pettengill (2003), A survey of the Monday effect literature, *Quarterly Journal of Economics.*

32 R. H. Thaler (1987), Anomalies: The January effect, *Journal of Economic Perspectives*, 1(1), 197–201.

33 R. H. D'Mello, S. P. Ferris, and C. Y. Hwang (2003), The tax-loss selling hypothesis, market liquidity, and price pressure around the turn-of-the-year, *Journal of Financial Markets*, 6(1), 73–98.

believed that January might be the suitable month to start investing toward some objectives upon a New Year's resolution.

In major Asian stock markets such as in China, Hong Kong, Japan, Malaysia, South Korea and Taiwan, the Chinese Lunar New Year holiday effect[34] during 1999 to 2012 was seen in the form of significantly positive pre-CLNY returns. It would appear that positive emotion played a role in contributing to the higher returns.

Of course, many anomalies do not survive closer analysis once transaction costs are taken into account. If a so-called anomaly exists, but which cannot be profitably exploited because transaction costs are too high, then it cannot be anomalous by definition. Time anomalies are interesting in finance and useful for instruction from the point of teaching basic econometrics when it comes to using dummy variables. We provide an example as follows.

7.6.1 Day-of-the-Week Effect

Let the daily continuously compounded return rate R_t of a market portfolio or else a well traded stock on day t be expressed as

$$R_t = c_1 D_{1t} + c_2 D_{2t} + c_3 D_{3t} + c_4 D_4 t + c_5 D_{5t} + u_t \tag{7.26}$$

where c_j's are constants and D_{jt}'s are dummy variables. These dummy variables take values as follows.

$$D_{1t} = \begin{cases} 1 & \text{if return is on a Monday at time } t \\ 0 & \text{otherwise} \end{cases}$$

$$D_{2t} = \begin{cases} 1 & \text{if return is on a Tuesday at time } t \\ 0 & \text{otherwise} \end{cases}$$

$$D_{3t} = \begin{cases} 1 & \text{if return is on a Wednesday at time } t \\ 0 & \text{otherwise} \end{cases}$$

$$D_{4t} = \begin{cases} 1 & \text{if return is on a Thursday at time } t \\ 0 & \text{otherwise} \end{cases}$$

$$D_{5t} = \begin{cases} 1 & \text{if return is on a Friday at time } t \\ 0 & \text{otherwise} \end{cases}$$

u_t is a disturbance term that is assumed to be n. i. d. Notice that we choose to regress without a constant. If we perform OLS on Eq. (7.26), with a time series sample size of N, the matrix form of the regression is:

34 See Tian Yuan and Rakesh Gupta (2014), Chinese Lunar New Year (CLNY) effect in Asian stock markets, 1999–2012, *The Quarterly Review of Economics and Finance*, 54(4), 529–537.

$$\underbrace{\begin{pmatrix} R_1 \\ R_2 \\ \vdots \\ \vdots \\ \\ R_N \end{pmatrix}}_{Y} = \underbrace{\begin{pmatrix} 1 & 0 & 0 & 0 & 0 \\ 0 & 1 & 0 & 0 & 0 \\ \vdots & \vdots & \vdots & \vdots & \vdots \\ 0 & 0 & 0 & 1 & 0 \\ \vdots & \vdots & \vdots & \vdots & \vdots \\ 0 & 0 & 0 & 0 & 1 \end{pmatrix}}_{X} \underbrace{\begin{pmatrix} c_1 \\ c_2 \\ c_3 \\ c_4 \\ c_5 \end{pmatrix}}_{B} + \underbrace{\begin{pmatrix} u_1 \\ u_2 \\ \vdots \\ \vdots \\ \\ u_N \end{pmatrix}}_{U}$$

Each row of the $X_{N\times5}$ matrix contains all zero elements except for one unit element. Assume $U \sim N(0, \sigma_u^2)$.

The day-of-the-week effect refers to a price anomaly whereby a particular day of the week has a higher mean return than the other days of the week. To test for the day-of-the-week effect, a regression based on Eq. (7.26) is performed.

To test if the day-of-the-week effect occurred in the Singapore stock market, we employ Singapore Stock Exchange data. Continuously compounded daily returns are computed based on the Straits Times Industrial Index (STII) from July 18, 1994 to August 28, 1998 and on the reconstructed Straits Times Index (STI) from September 7, 1998 until the end of the sample period as at October 18, 2002. The data were collected from Datastream. At that time, STI was a value-weighted index based on 45 major stocks that made up approximately 61 % of the total market capitalization in Singapore. Since the STII and STI were indexes that captured the major stocks that were the most liquidly traded, the day-of-the-week effect, if any, would show up in the returns based on the index movements.

We use 1075 daily traded data in each period: July 18, 1994 to August 28, 1998 (period 1), and September 7, 1998 to October 18, 2002 (period 2). Table 7.5 shows descriptive statistics of return rates for each trading day of the week. Table 7.6 shows the multiple linear regression result of daily return rates on the weekday dummies using returns from period 1.

The OLS regression result shows that the coefficient $\hat{c}_1 = -0.002278$ is the only one that is significantly different (smaller) than zero. This corresponds to D_1, the Monday dummy variable. Thus, there is a significantly negative mean return on Monday. This Monday day-of-the-week effect in Singapore is similar to evidence elsewhere in the U.S. and in other exchanges in Asia.

Why do we interpret this as negative mean return on Monday? Equation (7.26) implies that:

$$R_t = c_1 D_{1t} + u_t$$

since the other c_j coefficients are not significantly different from zero. Then, $E(R_t) = c_1 D_{1t}$. For Mondays, $D_{1t} = 1$. So, mean Monday return, $E(R_t \mid \text{Monday}) = c_1$. This is

Table 7.5: Return Characteristics on Different Days of the Week.

	Mon	Tue	Wed	Thu	Fri
Mean	−0.002278	−0.001052	0.001194	−0.000394	−0.000359
Median	−0.002272	−0.001255	0.000269	−0.000206	3.71E-05
Maximum	0.160307	0.095055	0.069049	0.040004	0.039870
Minimum	−0.078205	−0.092189	−0.039137	−0.079436	−0.069948
Std. dev.	0.018646	0.013078	0.012631	0.013085	0.010729
Skewness	3.192659	0.263696	0.920829	−1.154059	−1.147256
Kurtosis	32.39143	25.84039	8.182601	10.15761	11.22779
Jarque-Bera	8103.961	4675.906	270.9991	506.6721	653.6114
Probability	0.000000	0.000000	0.000000	0.000000	0.000000
Sum	−0.489672	−0.226154	0.256656	−0.084740	−0.077153
Sum sq. dev.	0.074401	0.036600	0.034139	0.036640	0.024632
Observations	215	215	215	215	215

Table 7.6: OLS Regression Results of Eq. (7.26), July 18, 1994 to August 28, 1998 (Period 1), 1075 observations $R_t = c_1D_{1t} + c_2D_{2t} + c_3D_{3t} + c_4D_{4t} + c_5D_{5t} + u_t$.

Variable	Coefficient	Std. Error	*t*-Statistic	Prob.
D_1	0.002278	0.000947	−2.404414	0.0164
D_2	0.001052	0.000947	−1.110473	0.2670
D_3	0.001194	0.000947	1.260246	0.2079
D_4	0.000394	0.000947	−0.416095	0.6774
D_5	0.000359	0.000947	−0.378842	0.7049
R-squared	0.006554	Mean dependent var		−0.000578
Adjusted *R*-squared	0.002840	S.D. dependent var		0.013909
S.E. of regression	0.013889	Akaike info criterion		−5.710774
Sum squared resid	0.206413	Schwarz criterion		−5.687611
Log likelihood	3074.541	Durbin-Watson stat		1.678574

estimated by $\hat{c}_1 = -0.002278$. From Tables 7.5 and 7.6, it is seen that the means of the returns on Monday, Tuesday, etc. are indeed the coefficient estimates of the dummies $D_{1t}, D_{2t}, \ldots$ etc. However, if there are other non-dummy quantitative explanatory variables on R_t, then $\hat{c}_j$ is in general not the mean return on the jth day of the week, but just its marginal contribution.

The negative or lower Monday return effect is sometimes addressed as the weekend effect due to the explanation that most companies typically put out bad news if any during the weekends so that Monday prices on average end relatively lower than on other days of the week. This weekend effect sometimes appears only some months of the year. In the U.S., the Monday effect does not typically appear in January. It has also been empirically found that Friday returns on average are the highest in U.S., in some studies before 2002.

7.6.2 Test of Equality of Means

We test the null hypothesis that the means of all weekday returns are equal. This takes the form of testing if the coefficients to the five dummies are all equal, viz. $H_0 : c_1 = c_2 = c_3 = c_4 = c_5$. The results are shown in Table 7.7.

Table 7.7: Wald and *F*-Test of Equal Mean Returns on All Weekdays.

Equation: PERIOD1_REGRESSION			
Null Hypothesis:	$C(1) = C(5)$		
	$C(2) = C(5)$		
	$C(3) = C(5)$		
	$C(4) = C(5)$		
F-statistic	1.764813	Probability	0.133652
Chi-square	7.059252	Probability	0.132790

The Wald chi-square statistic is asymptotic, assuming $\hat{\sigma}_u^2 \to \sigma_u^2$ in

$$\frac{(R\hat{B} - r)^T [\mathrm{R}(X^T X)^{-1} R^T]^{-1} (R\hat{B} - r)}{\hat{\sigma}_u^2} \sim \chi_q^2$$

where there are q number of restrictions. The F-statistic, however, is exact. In general, the asymptotic Wald statistic in more useful in nonlinear constraint and testing. In Table 7.7, the Wald chi-square statistic (d. f. 4) shows that we can reject H_0 only in a critical region with p-value of 13.28 %. The F-test statistic shows that we can reject H_0 only in a critical region with p-value of 13.36 %. Thus, statistical evidence that Monday return is different from the rest is not as strong.

For period 2, we run OLS on $R_t = c_1 N_{1t} + c_2 N_{2t} + c_3 N_{3t} + c_4 N_{4t} + c_5 N_{5t} + u_t$. N_{it} is equivalent to D_{it}. It is the same dummy. In Table 7.8, however, it is seen that though the coefficient of Monday dummy N_{1t} is the only negative coefficient, it is nevertheless not significant with a p-value of 0.41. The test if the coefficients to the five dummies are all equal, viz. $H_0 : c_1 = c_2 = c_3 = c_4 = c_5$, does not reject the null hypothesis at 10 % significance level. The results are similar to those in Table 7.7 and are not shown here.

Has the Monday day-of-the-week effect disappeared after August 1998? It seems so. The day-of-the week effect in U.S. may have disappeared in the late 1990s partly because arbitrageurs would enter to cream away the profit by buying low at close of Monday and selling the same stock high on Friday, earning on average above-normal returns. The arbitrageurs' activities have the effect of raising Monday's closing prices and lowering Friday's closing prices. This would wipe out the observed differences.

Table 7.8: OLS Regression Results of Eq. (7.26), September 7, 1998 to October 18, 2002 (Period 2), 1075 observations $R_t = c_1N_{1t} + c_2N_{2t} + c_3N_{3t} + c_4N_{4t} + c_5N_{5t} + u_t$.

Variable	Coefficient	Std. error	*t*-Statistic	Prob.
N_1	0.000877	0.001055	−0.831321	0.4060
N_2	0.000799	0.001055	0.756916	0.4493
N_3	0.000193	0.001055	0.183048	0.8548
N_4	0.001417	0.001055	1.342474	0.1797
N_5	0.001840	0.001055	1.743269	0.0816
R-squared	0.003815	Mean dependent var		0.000674
Adjusted *R*-squared	0.000091	S.D. dependent var		0.015475
S.E. of regression	0.015474	Akaike info criterion		-5.494645
Sum squared resid	0.256212	Schwarz criterion		-5.471482
Log likelihood	2958.372	Durbin-Watson stat		1.768158

Recently, some studies[35] documented high Monday VIX (volatility index) prices relative to Friday prices, and high fall prices relative to summer prices. This would allow abnormal trading profit by buying VIX futures at CBOE on Friday and selling on Monday, and buying the same in summer and selling as autumn approaches. The day-of-the-week and seasonal effects are not explained by risk premia, but perhaps rather by behavioral patterns exhibiting pessimism or fear of uncertainty, hence greater perceived volatility or VIX index (sometimes called the "Fear Gauge") on Monday for the whole working week ahead, and in autumn when the chilly winds start to blow in North America.

7.6.3 Analysis of Variance

Earlier we saw that $E(R_t|\text{Monday}) = c_1$. Hence also $E(R_t|\text{Tuesday}) = c_2$, and so on. Thus, the population means of Monday returns, Tuesday returns, …, and Friday returns are c_1, c_2, c_3, c_4, and c_5, respectively. We can also test for the equality of the means of each weekday, i. e. c_1, c_2, c_3, c_4, and c_5, using analysis of variance (ANOVA).

The sum of squares treatments (SST) measuring the variability between the sample means of the different days/groups is:

$$\text{SST} = \sum_{i=1}^{5} n_i(\bar{R}_i - \bar{R})^2$$

where n_1 is the number of Mondays in the sample space, n_2 is the number of Tuesdays, n_3 is the number of Wednesdays, and so on. $\bar{R}_1$ is the sample mean of Monday returns,

35 See for example, H. Levy (2010), Volatility Risk Premium, Market Sentiment and Market Anomalies, Melbourne Conference in Finance, March.

$\bar{R}_2$ is the sample mean of Tuesday returns, and so on. $\bar{R}$ is the sample average return of all days.

The sum of squares for errors (SSE) measures the variability within the groups.

$$\text{SSE} = \sum_{j=1}^{n_1}(R_{1j} - \bar{R}_1)^2 + \sum_{j=1}^{n_2}(R_{2j} - \bar{R}_2)^2 + \sum_{j=1}^{n_3}(R_{3j} - \bar{R}_3)^2 + \sum_{j=1}^{n_4}(R_{4j} - \bar{R}_4)^2 + \sum_{j=1}^{n_5}(R_{5j} - \bar{R}_5)^2$$

where R_{1j} is a Monday return for a week j, R_{2j} is a Tuesday return for a week j, and so on.

The population means of Monday returns, Tuesday returns, Wednesday returns, and so on, are $c_1, c_2, \ldots,$ and c_5. Intuitively $H_0 : c_1 = c_2 = c_3 = c_4 = c_5$ is true if the variability between groups (SST) is small relative to variability within groups (SSE). H_0 is false if the variability between groups is large relative to variability within groups.

Analysis of between-group variance and within-group variance leads to test-statistic

$$\frac{\frac{\text{SST}}{(g-1)}}{\frac{\text{SSE}}{(N-g)}} \sim F_{g-1,\,N-g} \tag{7.27}$$

where g is number of groups (here $g = 5$), and total number of days $N = n_1 + n_2 + n_3 + n_4 + n_5 = 1075$.

From the row of unbiased estimates of standard deviations of Monday returns, etc. in Table 7.5, we obtain

$$\begin{aligned}\text{SSE} &= 214^*[0.018646^2 + 0.013078^2 + 0.012631^2 \\ &\quad + 0.013085^2 + 0.010729^2] \\ &= 0.20642. \\ \text{SST} &= 0.001362343\end{aligned}$$

Therefore, via Eq. (7.27), $F_{4,1070} = 1.765$. This is identical with the F-test statistic reported in Table 7.7.

Further Reading

Baker, H. Kent, G. Filbeck, and J. R. Nofsinger (2019), *Behavioral Finance*, Oxford University Press.
Campbell, John Y., Andrew W. Lo, and A. Craig MacKinlay (1997), *The Econometrics of Financial Markets*, Princeton University Press.
Cochrane, John H. (2009), *Asset Pricing: Revised Edition*, Princeton University Press.
Duffie, Darrell (2001), *Dynamic Asset Pricing Theory*, Third edition, Princeton University Press.
Ferson, Wayne (2019), *Empirical Asset Pricing: Models and Methods*, MIT Press.
Thaler, Richard H., editor (2005), *Advances in Behavioral Finance*, Vol. II, Princeton University Press.

8 Euler Condition for Asset Pricing

The main areas of finance have had strong linkages to economics, including microeconomics, where the foundations of optimal consumer and investor choices are laid. Many of the economics giants in the late 1800s and well into the last century labored on mathematical results prescribing optimal consumption and investment choices building on fundamental axioms of rationality and non-satiability in human wants. One key construction is that of a utility function of consumption. A more positive utility number to a bundle of consumption goods than another bundle is simply another expression for preference by the individual of the former bundle compared to the latter. A celebrated study by mathematicians von Neumann and Morgenstern[1] produces the useful result that when probability estimates are introduced into consumption outcomes or utilities, then an individual will prefer a risky gamble to another provided the expected utility of the former is larger. Therefore, we can perform optimization on a set of gambles or choices based on expected outcomes of utility functions of consumption goods.

In this chapter, we consider the necessary Euler condition for utility optimization that leads to asset price modelling. As the theoretical restrictions on the model are nonlinear, we apply a nonlinear method, the generalized method of moments, for the estimation and testing of such models. Many interesting results and constructions in finance theory are exposited in excellent books such as Huang and Litzenberger (1988) and Ingersoll (1987). Similarly excellent books in macroeconomics but using utility-based frameworks are Blanchard and Fischer (1989) and Stokey and Lucas (1989). These classics are shown in the Further Reading list at the end of the chapter. But before that, we recall some basic convergence results and also motivate the idea of method of moments in statistics.

Suppose an infinite sequence of random variables $\{X_n, n \geq 1\}$ converges in some manner to being "close" to X. Convergence almost surely, a. s. or almost everywhere a. e., or w. p. 1 refers to

$$P\Big(\lim_{n\to\infty} X_n = X\Big) = 1$$

Convergence in Probability or in "P" refers to

$$\lim_{n\to\infty} P(|X_n - X| \geq \epsilon) = 0 \quad \text{for any } \epsilon > 0$$

A consistent estimator is a RV that converges in probability to the population parameter. Convergence in Distribution refers to $X_n \xrightarrow{d} X$ where c. d. f. of X_n converges to c. d. f. of X, i. e.,

1 J. von Neumann and O. Morgenstern (1953), *Theory of Games and Economic Behavior*, Princeton University Press.

https://doi.org/10.1515/9783110673951-008

$$\lim_{n\to\infty} F_{X_n}(y) = F_X(y) \quad \text{for all } y \text{ where } F_X(y) \text{ is continuous}$$

The continuous mapping theorem[2] states that if $X_n \xrightarrow{p} X$, then $g(X_n) \xrightarrow{p} g(X)$ if $g(\cdot)$ is a continuous bounded function in X except for discontinuity on a set of measure zero. Similarly, if $X_n \xrightarrow{d} X$, then $g(X_n) \xrightarrow{d} g(X)$ if $g(\cdot)$ is such a continuous bounded function in X. This result is useful for the convergence of sample moments to population moments.

8.1 Method of Moments

Usually i. i. d. RV's or else (strong) stationary and ergodic (more distant RV's in a stochastic process tends toward independence) bounded RVs are sufficient to enable the weak Law of Large Numbers (LLN) or convergence in probability of the sample mean.[3] With sufficient bounds on the moments of the RV's, strong LLN or convergence a. e. can also be obtained for the sample mean. We assume at least the weak LLN.

Suppose X_t is (strongly) stationary ergodic, and $g(X_t, \theta)$ is a continuous bounded function in X_t and θ. Assume $E[g(X_t, \theta)] = 0$ where θ is unique. A Taylor series expansion of $g(X_t, \theta)$ about an estimate $\hat{\theta}$ gives

$$g(X_t, \theta) = g(X_t, \hat{\theta}) + (\theta - \hat{\theta})g'(X_t, \hat{\theta}) + \frac{(\theta - \hat{\theta})^2}{2!} g''(X_t, \hat{\theta}) + \cdots$$

Taking sample average,

$$\begin{aligned}\frac{1}{T}\sum_{t=1}^{T} g(X_t, \theta) = \frac{1}{T}\sum_{t=1}^{T} g(X_t, \hat{\theta}) + (\theta - \hat{\theta})\frac{1}{T}\sum_{t=1}^{T} g'(X_t, \hat{\theta}) \\ + \frac{(\theta - \hat{\theta})^2}{2!}\frac{1}{T}\sum_{t=1}^{T} g''(X_t, \hat{\theta}) + \cdots\end{aligned}$$

Suppose we let both LHS and RHS equal to zero, and define the solution of $\hat{\theta}$ on the RHS to be associated with the sample size T. By the LLN, the LHS converges in probability to the mean zero, so we have no problem with putting the LHS to zero for an asymptotically large sample size T. For the RHS to be zero, we require that for $T \uparrow \infty$, $\hat{\theta} \xrightarrow{p} \theta$. Since θ is unique for the mean of $g(\cdot)$ to be zero, there is no other value to which $\hat{\theta}$ converges that will produce a zero RHS. The other possibility is that $\hat{\theta}$ does not converge as T increases toward ∞. But this cannot be true if the LHS converges to

2 See Jun Shao (2003), *Mathematical Statistics*, Springer.

3 See Kenneth J. Singleton (2006), *Empirical Dynamic Asset Pricing*, Princeton University Press.

zero. Note that in effect $\frac{1}{T}\sum_{t=1}^{T} g(X_t, \hat{\theta}) \xrightarrow{p} 0$ on the RHS. Hence we can solve for the estimate $\hat{\theta}$ by putting $\frac{1}{T}\sum_{t=1}^{T} g(X_t, \hat{\theta}) = 0$. This estimator is a method of moments estimator and has the property that it is consistent as $\hat{\theta} \xrightarrow{p} \theta$. This result is consistent with the continuous mapping theorem since for continuous bounded $g(\cdot)$, $\hat{\theta} \xrightarrow{p} \theta$ if and only if $g(X_t, \hat{\theta}) \xrightarrow{p} g(X_t, \theta)$. The term "method of moments" has also been used in another related but different context of identifying distributions with unique moments.

In the linear regression, $Y_{N\times1} = X_{N\times k}B_{k\times1} + U_{N\times1}$ with $E(U) = 0$. Given the classical assumptions of U being independent of X or a more relaxed condition of $E(U|X) = 0$, we obtain $\hat{B} = (X^TX)^{-1}X^TY$ under OLS. This OLS estimator is unbiased. With the other classical assumption of $\text{var}(U|X) = \sigma_u^2 I$, the OLS estimator conditional on X is consistent as $\text{var}(\hat{B}|X) = \sigma_u^2(X^TX)^{-1}$ is decreasing toward zero as diagonal elements of X^TX increases toward ∞ for stationary ergodic X.

Now consider the same regression $Y_{N\times1} = X_{N\times k}B_{k\times1} + U_{N\times1}$ with $E(U) = 0$, and a similar assumption of independence of U from X. The independence assumption or the weaker $E(U|X) = 0$ implies $E(X_{tj}u_t) = 0$ for each $j = 1, 2, \ldots, k$ and for each $t = 1, 2, \ldots, N$.

Hence $E(X_{tj}(y_t - \sum_{j=1}^{k} b_j X_{tj})) = 0$. This last condition is an "orthogonality condition" that indicates zero correlations between the disturbances and explanatory variables. The k associated sample moments of the orthogonality conditions are

$$\frac{1}{N}\sum_{t=1}^{N}\left(X_{tj}\left(y_t - \sum_{j=1}^{k} b_j X_{tj}\right)\right)$$

for $j = 1, 2, \ldots, k$.

Assuming further that y_t and X_{tj} (for every j) are stationary ergodic (over time), then for each $j = 1, 2, \ldots, k$

$$\frac{1}{N}\sum_{t=1}^{N}\left(X_{tj}\left(y_t - \sum_{j=1}^{k} b_j X_{tj}\right)\right) \xrightarrow{p} E\left(X_{tj}\left(y_t - \sum_{j=1}^{k} b_j X_{tj}\right)\right) = 0$$

Notation-wise, since y_t, X_{tj} are stationary, we could have also used y, X_j within the expectation operator.

The set of k sample moment conditions can also be written in matrix form as:

$$\frac{1}{N}(X^TY - X^TXB) \xrightarrow{p} 0$$

By putting $\frac{1}{N}(X^TY - X^TXB) = 0$, we solve for the method of moments estimator $\hat{B}$.

$$\hat{B} = \left(\frac{1}{N}X^TX\right)^{-1}\left(\frac{1}{N}X^TY\right)$$

This happens to be also the OLS estimator, and as we shall see, also the maximum likelihood estimator when U is multivariate normal.

Another example of the method of moments estimator is as follows. Suppose the demand for goods at time t is y_t. Suppose the demand quantity is given by

$$y_t = d_0 + d_1 P_t + \varepsilon_t$$

where P_t is price of the goods, and ε_t is a disturbance term with zero mean and a constant variance. Typically, $d_0 > 0$ and $d_1 < 0$.

The supply quantity is given by

$$y_t = s_0 + s_1 P_t + \eta_t$$

where η_t is a disturbance term with zero mean and a constant variance. Here $\text{cov}(\eta_t, \varepsilon_t)$ needs not be zero. Typically, $s_0 > 0$ and $s_1 > 0$.

The demand and supply equations can be represented as follows in Figure 8.1. At each time t, the equilibrium price and quantity (simultaneously determined) are reached at the intersection point of the demand and supply at t. At the next time $t + 1$, new occurrences of random disturbances ε_t and η_t would produce a different intersection point and hence a different equilibrium price and quantity. The equilibrium price and quantity at each t are observed price and quantity in the market and is represented by a black dot in the graph. Over time, observed pairs of price and quantity are represented by the scatter of black dots. It is seen that the black dots scatter does not indicate possibility for identifying the demand or supply equations.

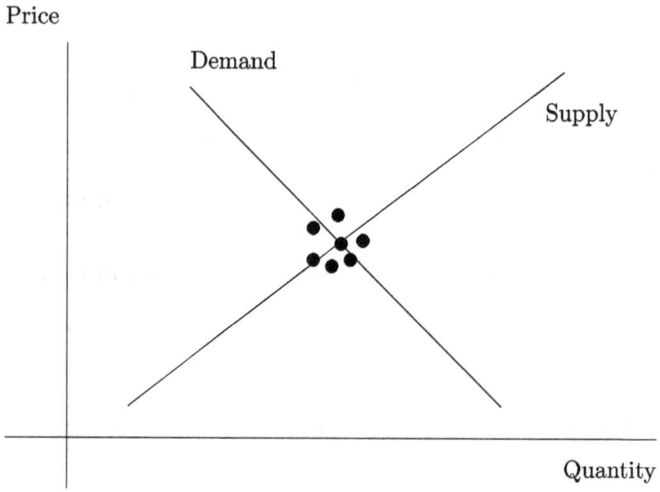

Figure 8.1: Equilibrium Price and Quantity with Stochastic Demand and Supply.

If we solve for the equilibrium price from the demand and supply equations, we obtain

$$P_t = \frac{(s_0 - d_0)}{(d_1 - s_1)} + \frac{(\eta_t - \varepsilon_t)}{(d_1 - s_1)}$$

It is seen that $\text{cov}(P_t, \eta_t) = (d_1 - s_1)^{-1}(\text{var}(\eta_t) - \text{cov}(\eta_t, \varepsilon_t))$. This is in general not equal to zero. Hence it does not make sense to use OLS to perform regression on the supply equation as the explanatory variable price is correlated with the disturbance term η_t. The estimation results would not produce unbiased or consistent estimates. The non-zero correlation implies that price is an endogenous variable (as it also impacts on the disturbances). The undesirable effects if indeed OLS is performed is called the endogeneity bias. It is more specifically a simultaneous equations bias here as it arises out of a simultaneous system of demand and supply.

However, suppose the demand for goods at time t is now given by

$$y_t = d_0 + d_1 P_t + d_2 Z_t + \varepsilon_t$$

where P_t is price of the goods, Z_t is an exogenous variable to both demand and supply, and ε_t is a disturbance term with zero mean and a constant variance. Typically, $d_0 > 0$ and $d_1 < 0$. The supply equation remains the same. Importantly, $\text{cov}(Z_t, \varepsilon_t) = 0$ and $\text{cov}(Z_t, \eta_t) = 0$. The new demand and supply equations can be represented as follows in Figure 8.2.

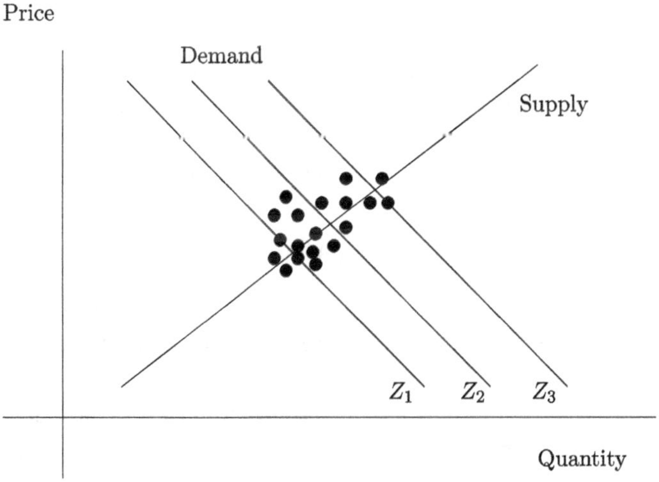

Figure 8.2: Equilibrium Price and Quantity with Stochastic Demand and Supply but Only Demand Driven by Exogenous Variable *X*.

The different levels of Z_t at different t (in addition to different realizations of random ε_t) produce different demand curves (schedules) as shown corresponding to Z_1, Z_2, Z_3.

Over time, observed pairs of price and quantity are represented by the scatter of black dots. Due to additional effect of random Z_t, it is seen that the black dots now scatter along the supply curves (shifted only by random η_t). There is now a possibility for identifying the supply equation, i. e., estimating the supply equation.

The estimation of the supply curve $y_t = s_0 + s_1 P_t + \eta_t$ using the method of moments can proceed as follows. The exogeneity of Z_t provides for $E(Z_t(y_t - s_0 - s_1 P_t)) = 0$ as well as $E(y_t - s_0 - s_1 P_t) = 0$. These two moment conditions help to identify s_0 and s_1 for estimation.

The two associated sample moments of the orthogonality conditions are

$$\frac{1}{N}\sum_{t=1}^{N} Z_t(y_t - s_0 - s_1 P_t)$$

and

$$\frac{1}{N}\sum_{t=1}^{N}(y_t - s_0 - s_1 P_t)$$

Assuming further that Z_t and η_t are stationary ergodic (over time), then these sample moments converge to zeros at least in probability. The set of two sample moment conditions can also be written in matrix form as:

$$\frac{1}{N}(Z^T Y - Z^T XB) \xrightarrow{p} 0$$

where $Z_{N\times 2}$ consists of a first column of ones and a second column of $\{Z_t\}$, $X_{N\times 2}$ consists of a first column of ones and a second column of $\{P_t\}$, and $Y_{N\times 1}$ consists of a column of $\{Y_t\}$. $B = (s_0, s_1)^T$.

By putting $\frac{1}{N}(Z^T Y - Z^T XB) = 0$, we solve for the method of moments estimator $\hat{B}$.

$$\hat{B} = \left(\frac{1}{N}Z^T X\right)^{-1}\left(\frac{1}{N}Z^T Y\right)$$

This is identical with the instrumental variables (IV) estimator discussed in Chapter 6. It is consistent.

Another approach in the use of instrument is the two-stage least-squares (2SLS) method. Suppose the price in the supply curve P_t is explained by an exogenous variable Z_t that has zero correlations with ε_t and η_t. Instead of using Z_t directly as above in the IV regression, we perform a linear regression of P_t on Z_t in the first stage to obtain fitted $\hat{P}_t$.

In the new set of demand and supply equations, $P_t = c_0 + c_1 Z_t + \xi_t$ where $c_0 = (s_1 - d_1)^{-1}(d_0 - s_0)$, $c_1 = (s_1 - d_1)^{-1} d_2$, and $\xi_t = (s_1 - d_1)^{-1}(\varepsilon_t - \eta_t)$. The estimated $\hat{P}_t = \hat{c}_0 + \hat{c}_1 Z_t$. Therefore $\mathrm{cov}(\hat{P}_t, \eta_t) = \hat{c}_1\,\mathrm{cov}(Z_t, \eta_t) = 0$ for any supply residual noise.

But $\text{cov}(P_t, \hat{P}_t) = \text{cov}(c_1 Z_t + \xi_t, \hat{c}_1 Z_t) \neq 0$. Hence $\hat{P}_t$ is a reasonable instrument in place of P_t for the second-stage regression in the supply equation: $y_t = s_o' + s_1' \hat{P}_t + \eta_t'$.[4]

So far, using the method of moments we estimate k number of parameters with k number of sample moment conditions, so the system is exactly identified. Suppose we can find additional moment conditions that fit with the theory, i. e., these moment conditions should also be true if the theory is correct. Then the system is over-identified. The method of moments can then be generalized to handle this situation. At the same time, an interesting test statistic can be developed.

8.2 Consumption-Based Asset Pricing

We saw the intertemporal CAPM that is based on optimizing lifetime consumption. Particularly, the continuous time modeling using Wiener processes as risk innovations makes only the instantaneous means and variances matter in the pricing. This allows aggregating across individuals and imposing a market portfolio (just as in single period CAPM with either quadratic utility or joint normal distribution making only means and variances matter) that allows linear relationship in the expected individual stock returns. Suppose we use another approach in intertemporal asset pricing with discrete time and without specifying the form of the returns distributions except that they have finite moments. Then it becomes hard to aggregate across individual portfolios and introduce a market portfolio return directly into the pricing of individual stock returns. But it is still about the individual investor's lifetime consumption optimization. We refresh this generic pricing approach that can subsume the other approaches when more stringent utility or distributional assumptions are added.

This approach has the advantage of not having to specify (hence no mis-specification) the cdf of the returns distributions, and not having to specify the utility function $U(\cdot)$, except it needs to be bounded, $U'(C) > 0$ and $U''(C) < 0$. The approach allows a nonlinear generalized method of moments (GMM) econometric method to simultaneously (both estimates and test statistic are in one outcome) do estimation and testing of the pricing model. Disadvantages are that we require to assume a single representative agent and asymptotic instead of finite sample statistical results.

The representative individual decision-maker (agent) maximizes his/her expected lifetime utility:

$$\max_{\{C_t, w_t\}} E_0 \left[\sum_{t=0}^{\infty} \rho^t U(C_t) \right]$$

subject to

4 For a more detailed analysis, see Kian Guan Lim (2021), Endogeneity of commodity price in freight cost models, *Journal of Commodity Markets*.

$$W_{t+1} = (W_t - C_t) \sum_{i=1}^{N} w_i R_i$$

and

$$\sum_{i=1}^{N} w_i = 1, \quad \forall t$$

where we assume stationary return distribution of all stock returns R_i and W_t is wealth at time t, with initial condition as W_0. $U(\cdot)$ is von Neumann-Morgenstern utility function, on consumption C_t, and we can think of a unit of consumption good as a numéraire or a real dollar. ρ $(0 < \rho \leq 1)$ is the time discount factor on utility. It means that a more distant consumption unit will be preferred less than a more recent consumption unit. $w_t = (w_1, w_2, \ldots, w_N)$ is the vector of allocation weights of stocks in the portfolio, where N is the number of stocks. Moreover, returns are independent of consumption decisions, and $\lim_{t\to\infty} U(C_t) < \infty$.

Assuming there is an optimal solution to this dynamic optimization problem, we can find a functional equation representation as follows. At each t, there exists a value function $V_t(W_t)$ (we can think of this as an indirect utility function) such that the individual maximizes:

$$V_t(W_t) = \max_{C_t, w_t} U(C_t) + \rho E_t V_{t+1}(W_{t+1}) \tag{8.1}$$

$$\text{s.t.} \quad W_{t+1} = (W_t - C_t) \sum_{i=1}^{N} w_i R_i \quad \text{and} \quad \sum_{i=1}^{N} w_i = 1 \tag{8.2}$$

The above Eq. (8.1) is a recursive equation for each t, and is the Bellman equation. The value function at time t is equal to the utility of optimal consumption at time t plus the expected value of the discounted optimal value function at time $t+1$. Assume derivatives of $U(\cdot)$ and $V(\cdot)$ exist, the individual's optimization is reduced to a single-period problem. The first order conditions (FOC) are as follows.

$$\frac{\partial}{\partial C_t} : U'(C_t) - \rho E_t\left[V'_{t+1}(W_{t+1}) \sum_i w_i R_i\right] = 0$$

$$\Rightarrow U'(C_t) = \rho E_t\left[V'_{t+1}(W_{t+1}) \sum_i w_i R_i\right] \tag{8.3}$$

$$\frac{\partial}{\partial w_i} : \rho E_t[V'_{t+1}(W_{t+1})(W_t - C_t)R_i] - \lambda = 0$$

$$\Rightarrow \rho E_t[V'_{t+1}(W_{t+1})R_i] = \frac{\lambda}{W_t - C_t} \tag{8.4}$$

where λ is the Lagrange multiplier over the portfolio weight constraint in Eq. (8.2)

If we sum the last equation over all weights w_i in Eq. (8.4):

$$\sum_i w_i(\rho E_t[V'_{t+1}(W_{t+1})R_i]) = \rho E_t\left[V'_{t+1}(W_{t+1})\sum_i w_i R_i\right] = \frac{\lambda}{W_t - C_t}$$

From Eq. (8.3), LHS is $U'(C_t)$. So, $\frac{\lambda}{W_t - C_t} = U'(C_t)$. Using Eq. (8.4), we obtain

$$U'(C_t) = \rho E_t[V'_{t+1}(W_{t+1})R_i] \tag{8.5}$$

Consider the Bellman Eq. (8.1). On its LHS, function $V_t(W_t)$ is actually an optimized form of $V_t(W^*_{t+1}(C_t), W_t)$ in which W^*_{t+1} is maximized given W_t via control on C_t and portfolio weights w_i. We can make use of the Envelope theorem. We can therefore take the derivative w. r. t. W_t on the LHS and also a partial derivative on the RHS of Eq. (8.1) to obtain

$$V'_t(W_t) = \rho E_t\left[V'_{t+1}(W_{t+1})\frac{\partial W_{t+1}}{\partial W_t}\right] \tag{8.6}$$

where the RHS is evaluated at optimal C_t and w_t. Employing budget constraint in Eq. (8.2):

$$V'_t(W_t) = \rho E_t\left[V'_{t+1}(W_{t+1})\sum_i w_i R_i\right] \tag{8.7}$$

Equations (8.3) and (8.7) imply $U'(C_t) = V'_t(W_t)$, noting the derivatives are w. r. t. C_t on the LHS and W_t on the RHS. Thus also, $U'(C_{t+1}) = V'_{t+1}(W_{t+1})$. This means the marginal utility of consuming one real dollar less at time t or marginal cost is equated to the marginal benefit or expected marginal utility from investing one real dollar and consuming later.

Substitute $U'(C_{t+1})$ for $V'_{t+1}(W_{t+1})$ in Eq. (8.5) to obtain

$$U'(C_t) = \rho E_t[U'(C_{t+1})R_i] \tag{8.8}$$

Putting $R_i = \frac{P^i_{t+1}}{P^i_t}$ where P^i_t is stock i's price at time t, then

$$P^i_t U'(C_t) = \rho E_t[U'(C_{t+1})P^i_{t+1}]$$

The last equation is called the stochastic Euler equation, and is a necessary but not sufficient condition for any solution to a rational asset pricing equilibrium. This necessary condition is a heavily tested condition in much of empirical asset pricing literature.

We may write the stochastic Euler Eq. (8.8) as

$$E_t[M_{t+1}R_{t+1}] = 1 \tag{8.9}$$

where $M_{t+1} = \rho \frac{U'(C_{t+1})}{U'(C_t)}$ is sometimes called the price kernel or stochastic discount factor (as it discounts the future stock price to the current price), and letting R_{t+1} denote the return to any traded security at time $t + 1$.

The (stochastic) Euler Eq. (8.8) then implies

$$E(R_{t+1})E(M_{t+1}) + \text{cov}(M_{t+1}, R_{t+1}) = 1$$

As the risk-free asset with return R_f also satisfies Eq. (8.9), then

$$R_f E(M_{t+1}) = 1, \quad \text{or} \quad E(M_{t+1}) = 1/R_f$$

Hence

$$E(R_{t+1}) - R_f = -\text{cov}(M_{t+1}, R_{t+1})/E(M_{t+1}) \tag{8.10}$$

or

$$E(R_{t+1}) = R_f + \frac{\text{cov}(-M_{t+1}, R_{t+1})}{\text{var}(M_{t+1})} \times \frac{\text{var}(M_{t+1})}{E(M_{t+1})} \tag{8.11}$$

If we define $\beta_C = \frac{\text{cov}(-M_{t+1}, R_{t+1})}{\text{var}(M_{t+1})}$, and $\lambda_M = \frac{\text{var}(M_{t+1})}{E(M_{t+1})}$ in Eq. (8.11), then λ_M behaves as a market premium (> 0) or the price of common risk to all assets, and β_C is a consumption beta specific to the asset with return R_{t+1}.

The intuition of the consumption beta, β_C is as follows. Suppose the asset's $\beta_C > 0$, and thus its return R_{t+1} correlates positively with $-M_{t+1}$. In turn, this implies a positive correlation between R_{t+1} and C_{t+1} since $U''(C_{t+1}) < 0$. Holding the asset in a portfolio thus adds to the consumption volatility. Since consumption life-cycle theory suggests consumption smoothing (less consumption volatility) as desirable for a risk-averse individual over his/her lifetime, adding to consumption volatility would require risk compensation in the form of higher expected returns for the asset. This is indeed the case as $\lambda_M > 0$.

Equation (8.10) can be re-written as

$$E(R_{t+1}) - R_f = -\rho_{MR}\sigma_M\sigma_R/E(M_{t+1})$$

where ρ_{MR} is the correlation coefficient between M_{t+1} and R_{t+1}, and σ_M, σ_R denote the respective standard deviations. Then

$$\frac{E(R_{t+1} - R_f)}{\sigma_R} = -\rho_{MR}\frac{\sigma_M}{E(M_{t+1})} \leq \frac{\sigma_M}{E(M_{t+1})} = R_f\sigma_M \tag{8.12}$$

In Eq. (8.12), the LHS is the Sharpe ratio or performance of any stock (including the market index) showing its equity premium (or excess return over risk-free rate) divided by its return volatility. The RHS is called the Hansen–Jagannathan bound, which provides a theoretical upper bound to the Sharpe ratio or to the equity premium. (Recall that M here refers to the price kernel or stochastic discount factor, and should not be confused with the market return that also typically uses this notation.) One interesting research agenda in finance is to account for why post World War II U. S. equity premiums have been observed to be too high and have exceeded empirical measures of volatility of the stochastic discount factor times risk-free return (factor).

There had been many years in post World War II period when the annual market Sharpe ratio is well above one but that the volatility of SDF is about 0.8 and risk-free return is about 1.03. This means that there were many post World War II periods when the Hansen–Jagannathan rational bound did not hold. This implies too high a volatility in the per capita consumption on the RHS in order to keep the bound, or else an unexplained high equity premium puzzle on the LHS. The latter implies an extremely high investor risk aversion. This high equity premium puzzle is still an ongoing area of research.

8.3 Generalized Method of Moments (GMM)

The GMM econometric method[5] to perform estimation of parameters and to test the plausibility of a model is based on expectations or moment conditions derived from the theoretical model itself. Assume a stationary stochastic process $\{X_t\}_{t=1,2,...}$ where X_t is vector of random variables at time t. Hence, $\{X_t\}$ is a stochastic vector process. Suppose we have a finite sample from this stochastic vector process as $\{x_1, x_2, \ldots, x_T\}$ of sample size T, where each x_t is a vector of realized values at t that are observable. The subscript t need not be time, and could be in more general context such as sampling across sections at a point in time.

The model is derived based on a set of K number of moment conditions:

$$\begin{aligned} E[f_1(X_t, \theta)] &= 0 \\ E[f_2(X_t, \theta)] &= 0 \\ &\vdots \\ E[f_K(X_t, \theta)] &= 0 \end{aligned} \tag{8.13}$$

where $f_j(.)$ is in general a continuous function with discontinuities, if any, on a set of measure zero, and θ is an m dimension unique vector of unknown parameters with $m < K$. The powerful use of this method arises in cases when $f_j(.)$ is nonlinear in X_t and θ, so that linear regression methods cannot be applied.

5 The GMM is developed by Hansen, L. P. (1982), Large sample properties of generalized method of moments estimators, *Econometrica*, 50, 1029–1054.

The essential idea in deriving an estimate of θ lies in finding a vector $\hat{\theta}$ such that the corresponding sample (empirical) moments are close to zero in some fashion, for finite T.

$$\begin{aligned} \frac{1}{T}\sum_{t=1}^{T} f_1(x_t,\hat{\theta}) &\approx 0 \\ \frac{1}{T}\sum_{t=1}^{T} f_2(x_t,\hat{\theta}) &\approx 0 \\ &\vdots \\ \frac{1}{T}\sum_{t=1}^{T} f_K(x_t,\hat{\theta}) &\approx 0 \end{aligned} \tag{8.14}$$

The Law of Large Numbers would tell us that as $T \uparrow \infty$, these sample moments would converge to

$$E[f_j(X_t,\hat{\theta})]$$

for all $j = 1, 2, \ldots, K$. Hence, if these conditions are approximately zero, then intuitively the vector estimator $\hat{\theta}$ would also be close to θ in some fashion, given that θ is unique. We would also assume some regularity conditions on the moments $E[f_j(.)]$ such that $E[f_j(\hat{\theta})]$ would behave smoothly and not jump about infinitely often (i. o.) as value $\hat{\theta}$ gets closer and closer to θ. This would ensure $\hat{\theta} \xrightarrow{p} \theta$.

Let all the observable values of sample size T be $Y_T \equiv \{x_1, x_2, \ldots, x_T\}$. Let

$$g(Y_T,\hat{\theta}) \equiv \begin{pmatrix} \frac{1}{T}\sum_{t=1}^{T} f_1(x_t,\hat{\theta}) \\ \frac{1}{T}\sum_{t=1}^{T} f_2(x_t,\hat{\theta}) \\ \vdots \\ \frac{1}{T}\sum_{t=1}^{T} f_K(x_t,\hat{\theta}) \end{pmatrix}$$

be a $K \times 1$ vector of sampling moments. Suppose W_T is a $K \times K$ symmetric positive definite weighting matrix which may be a function of data Y_T. The GMM estimator is found by minimising the scalar function:

$$\min_{\hat{\theta}} \Gamma(\hat{\theta}) \equiv g(Y_T,\hat{\theta})^T W_T(Y_T,\theta) g(Y_T,\hat{\theta}) \tag{8.15}$$

Note that if $W_T(.,.)$ is any arbitrary symmetric positive definite matrix, then estimators $\hat{\theta}$ will still be consistent though not efficient. However, given some regularity smoothness conditions about the function $f_i(.,.)$, an optimal weighting matrix function $W_T(.,.)$ can be found so that the estimators $\hat{\theta}$ will be asymptotically efficient, or have the lowest asymptotic covariance in the class of estimators $\hat{\theta}$ satisfying Eq. (8.15) for arbitrary $W_T(.,.)$.

Let vector function $F_{K\times 1}(X_t,\theta) = (f_1(X_t,\theta), f_2(X_t,\theta), \ldots, f_K(X_t,\theta))^T$. Then,

$$g(Y_T,\theta) = \frac{1}{T}\sum_{t=1}^{T} F(x_t,\theta)$$

Let $\Sigma_0 = \sum_{j=-N}^{N} E[F(X_t,\theta)F(X_{t-j},\theta)^T]$ be a $K \times K$ covariance matrix that is the sum of contemporaneous covariance matrix $E[F(X_t,\theta)F(X_t,\theta)^T]$ and $2N$ number of serial covariance matrices $E[F(X_t,\theta)F(X_{t-j},\theta)^T]$.

It is assumed that beyond a fixed N leads and lags, the covariance matrix $E[F(X_t,\theta)F(X_{t-j},\theta)^T] = 0$ for $|j| \geq N+1$. Assume Σ_0 exists and has full rank K.

Note that the covariance matrix of random vector $g(Y_T,\theta) = T^{-1}\Sigma_0$ for an asymptotically large T. By the Central Limit Theorem, as $T \uparrow \infty$, $Tg(Y_T,\theta)^T\Sigma_0^{-1}g(Y_T,\theta) \to \chi_k^2$.

The minimization of Eq. (8.15) gives first-order condition:

$$2\frac{\partial g(Y_T,\hat{\theta})^T}{\partial\hat{\theta}} W_T(Y_T,\theta)g(Y_T,\hat{\theta}) = 0_{m\times 1}$$

conditional on a given weighting matrix $W_T(Y_T,\theta)$. In principle, the above m equations in the vector equation can be solved, i. e.,

$$\frac{\partial g(Y_T,\hat{\theta})^T}{\partial\hat{\theta}} W_T(Y_T,\theta)g(Y_T,\hat{\theta}) = 0_{m\times 1} \tag{8.16}$$

to obtain the m estimates in $m \times 1$ vector $\hat{\theta}$. In this first step, $W_T(Y_T,\theta)$ can be initially selected as $I_{K\times K}$ The solution $\hat{\theta}_1$ is consistent but not efficient. The consistent estimates $\hat{\theta}_1$ in this first step are then employed to find the optimal weighting matrix $W_T^*(Y_T,\hat{\theta}_1)$.

Let $g'(Y_T,\hat{\theta}_1) = \frac{1}{T}\sum_{t=1}^{T}\frac{\partial F(x_t,\hat{\theta}_1)}{\partial\theta}$. Let a consistent estimator of Σ_0 be, for T much larger than N:

$$\begin{aligned}\hat{\Sigma}_0(\hat{\theta}_1) &= \frac{1}{T}\sum_{t=1}^{T} F(X_t,\hat{\theta}_1)F(X_t,\hat{\theta}_1)^T \\ &+ \sum_{j=1}^{N}\left(\frac{1}{T}\sum_{t=j+1}^{T} F(X_t,\hat{\theta}_1)F(X_{t-j},\hat{\theta}_1)^T\right) \\ &+ \sum_{j=1}^{N}\left(\frac{1}{T}\sum_{t=1}^{T-j} F(X_t,\hat{\theta}_1)F(X_{t+j},\hat{\theta}_1)^T\right)^T\end{aligned} \tag{8.17}$$

Then employ $W_T^* = \hat{\Sigma}_0(\hat{\theta}_1)^{-1}$ as the optimal weighting matrix in Eq. (8.15) and minimize the function again in the second step to obtain the efficient and consistent GMM estimator $\hat{\theta}^*$.

The minimized function in Eq. (8.15) is now

$$\Gamma_T(\hat{\theta}^*) \equiv g(Y_T,\hat{\theta}^*)^T\hat{\Sigma}_0(\hat{\theta}_1)^{-1}g(Y_T,\hat{\theta}^*)$$

where the first-order condition below is satisfied:

$$\frac{\partial g(Y_T,\hat{\theta}^*)^T}{\partial \hat{\theta}}\hat{\Sigma}_0(\hat{\theta}_1)^{-1}g(Y_T,\hat{\theta}^*) = 0_{m\times 1} \tag{8.18}$$

As $T \uparrow \infty$, $\hat{\theta}_1, \hat{\theta}^* \rightarrow \theta$, $\hat{\Sigma}_0(\hat{\theta}_1) \rightarrow \Sigma_0$, and

$$T\Gamma_T(\hat{\theta}^*) \equiv Tg(Y_T,\hat{\theta}^*)^T\hat{\Sigma}_0(\hat{\theta}_1)^{-1}g(Y_T,\hat{\theta}^*) \rightarrow \chi^2_{K-m} \tag{8.19}$$

Sometimes the LHS is called the J-statistic, $J_T \equiv T\Gamma_T$. Notice that this test statistic is asymptotically chi-square of $K - m$ degrees of freedom and not K degrees of freedom when the population parameter θ is in the arguments instead. This is because m degrees of freedom were taken up in m linear dependencies created in Eq. (8.19) in the solution for $\hat{\theta}^*$. Equation (8.19) also indicates that a test is only possible when $K > m$, i. e., the number of moment conditions or restrictions is greater than the number of parameters to be estimated.

We can always create additional moment conditions by using instruments. One common instrument is lagged variables contained in the information set at t. If the moment conditions such as those in Eq. (8.13) are generated by conditional moments such as Eq. (8.9), then it is easy to enter the information variables observed at t into the expectation operator in Eq. (8.9), and then take iterated expectation on the null set to arrive at the unconditional moments such as in Eq. (8.13).

For example, a theoretical model may prescribe $E_{t-1}[f_1(X_t,\theta)] = 0$ as a conditional expectation. By the iterated expectation theorem, this leads to moment restrictions in Eq. (8.13). Since X_{t-1} is observed at $t-1$, we can add it as an instrument to obtain $E_{t-1}[f_1(X_t,\theta)X_{t-1}] = 0$, hence another moment restriction $E[f_1(X_t,\theta)X_{t-1}] = 0$. We may say vector $f_1(X_t,\theta)$ is orthogonal to X_{t-1} for any realization of X_{t-1}. Thus, such moment restrictions are sometimes also called orthogonality conditions. The excess number of moment conditions over the number of parameters is called the number of overidentifying restrictions, and is the number of degrees of freedom of the asymptotic χ^2 test.

Now, $g(\hat{\theta}^*) = g(\theta) + \frac{\partial g(\tilde{\theta})}{\partial \theta^T}(\hat{\theta}^* - \theta)$ by a linear Taylor series expansion (mean-value theorem) about the true population parameter θ, where $\tilde{\theta}$ is some linear combination of θ and $\hat{\theta}^*$. $\tilde{\theta}$ is also consistent.

Pre-multiplying by the $m \times K$ matrix, $\frac{\partial g(Y_T,\hat{\theta}^*)^T}{\partial \hat{\theta}}\hat{\Sigma}_0^{-1}$, we obtain

$$\frac{\partial g(Y_T,\hat{\theta}^*)^T}{\partial \hat{\theta}}\hat{\Sigma}_0^{-1}[g(\hat{\theta}^*) - g(\theta)] = \frac{\partial g(Y_T,\hat{\theta}^*)^T}{\partial \hat{\theta}}\hat{\Sigma}_0^{-1}\frac{\partial g(\tilde{\theta})}{\partial \theta^T}(\hat{\theta}^* - \theta)$$

Then

$$\left[\frac{\partial g(Y_T,\hat{\theta}^*)^T}{\partial \hat{\theta}}\hat{\Sigma}_0^{-1}\frac{\partial g(\tilde{\theta})}{\partial \theta^T}\right]^{-1}\frac{\partial g(Y_T,\hat{\theta}^*)^T}{\partial \hat{\theta}}\hat{\Sigma}_0^{-1}[g(\hat{\theta}^*) - g(\theta)] = (\hat{\theta}^* - \theta)$$

Thus,

$$\sqrt{T}(\hat{\theta}^* - \theta) = \left[\frac{\partial g(Y_T, \hat{\theta}^*)^T}{\partial \hat{\theta}} \hat{\Sigma}_0^{-1} \frac{\partial g(\tilde{\theta})}{\partial \theta^T}\right]^{-1} \frac{\partial g(Y_T, \hat{\theta}^*)^T}{\partial \hat{\theta}} \hat{\Sigma}_0^{-1} \sqrt{T}[g(\hat{\theta}^*) - g(\theta)]$$
$$= \left[\frac{\partial g(Y_T, \hat{\theta}^*)^T}{\partial \hat{\theta}} \hat{\Sigma}_0^{-1} \frac{\partial g(\tilde{\theta})}{\partial \theta^T}\right]^{-1} \frac{\partial g(Y_T, \hat{\theta}^*)^T}{\partial \hat{\theta}} \hat{\Sigma}_0^{-1} \sqrt{T}[-g(\theta)]$$

where we employ Eq. (8.18), $\frac{\partial g(Y_T,\hat{\theta}^*)^T}{\partial \hat{\theta}} \hat{\Sigma}_0(\hat{\theta}_1)^{-1} g(Y_T, \hat{\theta}^*) = 0_{m\times 1}$, as $\hat{\Sigma}_0(\hat{\theta}_1) \to \Sigma_0$. Hence we see that the variance of the estimator $\hat{\theta}^*$ is smallest, hence higher efficiency, without additional noise created by the estimator itself.

Since $\sqrt{T}[-g(\theta)] \sim N(0, \Sigma_0)$, then

$$\operatorname{cov} \sqrt{T}(\hat{\theta}^* - \theta)$$
$$= \operatorname{cov}\left\{\left[\frac{\partial g(Y_T, \hat{\theta}^*)^T}{\partial \hat{\theta}} \hat{\Sigma}_0^{-1} \frac{\partial g(\tilde{\theta})}{\partial \theta^T}\right]^{-1} \frac{\partial g(Y_T, \hat{\theta}^*)^T}{\partial \hat{\theta}} \hat{\Sigma}_0^{-1} \sqrt{T}[-g(\theta)]\right\}$$
$$= V \frac{\partial g(Y_T, \hat{\theta}^*)^T}{\partial \hat{\theta}} \hat{\Sigma}_0^{-1} \Sigma_0 \hat{\Sigma}_0^{-1} \frac{\partial g(Y_T, \hat{\theta}^*)}{\partial \hat{\theta}^T} V^T$$
$$= V$$

where $V = [\frac{\partial g(Y_T,\hat{\theta}^*)^T}{\partial \hat{\theta}} \hat{\Sigma}_0^{-1} \frac{\partial g(\hat{\theta}^*)}{\partial \theta^T}]^{-1}$ is an $m \times m$ matrix. We replace $\tilde{\theta}$ with $\hat{\theta}^*$ as they are asymptotically equivalent.

Hence asymptotically,

$$\sqrt{T}(\hat{\theta}^* - \theta) \xrightarrow{d} N(0, V) \tag{8.20}$$

where $V = [\frac{\partial g(Y_T,\hat{\theta}^*)^T}{\partial \hat{\theta}} \hat{\Sigma}_0^{-1} \frac{\partial g(\hat{\theta}^*)}{\partial \theta^T}]^{-1}$.

Equation (8.19) is the test statistic measuring the sampling moment deviations from the means imposed by the theoretical restrictions in Eq. (8.13). If the test statistic is too large and exceeds the critical boundaries of the chi-square random variable, then the moment conditions of Eq. (8.13) and thus the theoretical restrictions would be rejected. Equation (8.20) provides the asymptotic standard errors of the GMM estimator $\hat{\theta}^*$ that can be utilized to infer if the estimates are statistically significant, e. g., from a null of $\theta = 0$, given a certain significance level.

In estimating Σ_0 in Eq. (8.17), the estimator $\hat{\Sigma}_0(\hat{\theta}_1)$ is consistent. However, in finite sample, this computed matrix may not be positive semi-definite. This may result in Eq. (8.19) being negative. Newey-West HACC (heteroskedastic and autocorrelation consistent covariance) matrix estimator[6] provides for a positive semi-definite covariance estimator of Σ_0 that can be used. This takes the form

6 See W. K. Newey and K. D. West (1987), A simple, positive semi-definite, heteroskedasticity and autocorrelation consistent covariance matrix, *Econometrica*, 55(3), 703–708.

$$\hat{\Sigma}_0(\hat{\theta}_1) = \frac{1}{T}\sum_{t=1}^{T} F(X_t, \hat{\theta}_1)F(X_t, \hat{\theta}_1)^T + \sum_{j=1}^{N}\left(1 - \frac{j}{N+1}\right)(\hat{\Omega}_j + \hat{\Omega}_j^T)$$

where

$$\hat{\Omega}_j = \left(\frac{1}{T}\sum_{t=j+1}^{T} F(X_t, \hat{\theta}_1)F(X_{t-j}, \hat{\theta}_1)^T\right)$$

8.4 Estimating Preference Parameters in Euler Equation

Hansen and Singleton tested the Euler condition in Eq. (8.8), viz.

$$E_t\left[\rho(R_{t+1})\frac{U'(C_{t+1})}{U'(C_t)}\right] = 1$$

where $R_{t+1} = P_{t+1}/P_t$ is the return over $[t, t+1]$.

The utility function is assumed to be a power function $U(C_t) = C_t^{\gamma}/\gamma$ for $\gamma < 1$. The risk aversion coefficient is $1 - \gamma > 0$. This utility function is also called the Constant Relative Risk Aversion Utility function as its relative risk aversion parameter $-C_t \times U''(C_t)/U'(C_t) = 1 - \gamma$, is a constant. Suppose the S&P 500 index return is used as a proxy for the market value-weighted return. Let this be R_{t+1}. Then the Euler equation is:

$$E_t[\rho R_{t+1} Q_{t+1}^{\gamma-1}] = 1 \qquad (8.21)$$

where $Q_{t+1} \equiv C_{t+1}/C_t$ is the per capita consumption ratio, as $U'(C_t) \equiv \gamma C_t^{\gamma-1}$. Since there are two parameters, ρ and γ, to be estimated, we require at least three moment restrictions. This will yield one overidentifying restriction. We could employ the lagged values of R_t's or Q_t's as instruments. Here, we form three moment restrictions:

(a) $E[\rho R_{t+1} Q_{t+1}^{\delta} - 1] = 0$,

(b) $E[\rho R_{t+1} R_t Q_{t+1}^{\delta} - R_t] = 0$,

(c) $E[\rho R_{t+1} R_{t-1} Q_{t+1}^{\delta} - R_{t-1}] = 0$

where we let $\delta = \gamma - 1 < 0$ when risk aversion is positive.

Using the GMM method discussed in the previous section, the GMM estimation and test statistics are shown as follows. The quarterly consumption data from 2000 to 2009 used in the analysis are obtained from the public website of the Bureau of Economic Analysis of the U. S. Department of Commerce. In particular the real durable consumption series is divided by population to obtain the per capita durable consumption. Q_t measures the quarterly per capita consumption growth.

From Table 8.1, it is seen that the time discount factor estimate $\hat{\rho}$ is 0.998. The relative risk aversion coefficient estimate is $1 - \gamma = -\delta = 1.3615$. Both are significantly different from zero at p-values of less than 2%. The J-statistic that is distributed as χ^2 with one degree of freedom is 4.12 with a p-value of 0.0425. Therefore, the moment

Table 8.1: GMM Test of the Euler Equation under Constant Relative Risk Aversion. 37 quarterly observations are used. 2000–2009. Standard errors and covariance are estimated using Newey-West HACC. Convergence is obtained after 13 iterations. Instruments are one-period are two-period lagged market returns.

	Coefficient	Std. Error	*t*-Statistic	Prob.
$\hat{\rho}$	0.9980	0.0236	42.30	0.0000
$\hat{\delta}$	−1.3615	0.5149	−2.64	0.0122
Mean dependent var	0.000000	S. D. dependent var		0.000000
S. E. of regression	0.091516	Sum squared resid		0.293129
Durbin-Watson stat	1.897556	*J*-statistic		4.115583
Instrument rank	3	Prob(*J*-statistic)		0.042490

restrictions (a), (b), and (c) implied by the model and rational expectations are not rejected at the 1% significance level, though it would be rejected at the 5% level. The result is broadly similar to those reported in Hansen and Singleton (1982).[7] In this GMM estimation, the covariance matrix of the sampling moments is estimated using the Newey-West HACC matrix estimator with six lags.

Another test of Eq. (8.21) is based on Brown and Gibbons (1985).[8] The Brown and Gibbons study employed an assumption[9] that aggregate consumption each period is a constant fraction of aggregate wealth, i. e., $C_t = kW_t$ where W_t is aggregate wealth of all individuals in the market.

Then, $C_t = kW_t = k[(W_{t-1} - kW_{t-1})(1 + r_{mt})] = (1 - k)C_{t-1}(1 + r_{mt})$ where r_{mt} is the market portfolio return rate over $[t - 1, t]$. Therefore, $C_t/C_{t-1} = (1 - k)(1 + r_{mt})$. We can now express Eq. (8.21) as:

$$E_{t-1}[\rho(1 + r_t)(1 - k)^{\gamma-1}(1 + r_{mt})^{\gamma-1}] = 1 \tag{8.22}$$

where r_t is the return rate of any stock or portfolio (investable asset) over $[t - 1, t]$ that includes the market portfolio and the risk-free asset with return rate r_{ft}.

Using the market portfolio and risk-free asset in Eq. (8.22), we derive

$$E_{t-1}[(1 + r_{mt})^{\gamma}] = \rho^{-1}(1 - k)^{1-\gamma} = E_{t-1}[(1 + r_{mt})^{\gamma-1}(1 + r_{ft})]$$

Since a one period treasury bill with maturity at t has a market price at $t - 1$, the risk-free rate r_{ft} over $[t-1, t]$ is known at $t-1$, i. e., r_{ft}, unlike other risky asset returns r_t, is in the information set at $t-1$, then dividing the equations by $(1+r_{ft})^{\gamma}$ gives the following.

7 L. P. Hansen and K. Singleton (1982), Generalized instrumental variables estimation of nonlinear rational expectations models, *Econometrica*, 50(5), 1269–1286.

8 D. P. Brown and M. R. Gibbons (1985), A simple econometric approach for utility-based asset pricing models, *The Journal of Finance*, Vol. 40(2), 359–381.

9 Theoretical justification for this can be found in Hakansson N. (1970), Optimal investment and consumption under risk for a class of utility functions, *Econometrica* 38, 587–607.

$$E_{t-1}[(X_t - 1)X_t^{\gamma-1}] = 0 \tag{8.23}$$

where $X_t = (1 + r_{mt})/(1 + r_{ft})$, assuming X_t is stationary ergodic.

Equation (8.23) yields the orthogonality or moment condition $E[(X_t - 1)X_t^{\gamma-1}] = 0$ which is testable. Directly using the moment condition and the GMM has the advantage of avoiding distributional mis-specification. It also avoids the need to account for short-term autocorrelation problems if least squares regressions are used (although we require some form of ergodicity to ensure that sample moments converge).

The sample moment corresponding to Eq. (8.23) is

$$\frac{1}{T}\sum_{t=1}^{T}(X_t - 1)X_t^{\gamma-1} = 0$$

for asymptotically large sample size T, and relative risk aversion parameter $1 - \gamma > 0$.

More recent development in the consumption asset pricing has also involved frequency domain econometrics whereby consumption growth can be decomposed into cyclical components with different levels of persistence.[10]

8.5 Other GMM Applications

There is a copious amount of GMM applications. We look at one here whereby a seemingly simple linear regression specification of the Kraus-Litzenberger (1976) three-moment asset pricing model.[11]

Using Taylor series expansion, a representative agent's VM utility function can be expanded as:

$$U(W) = U(\overline{W}) + (W - \overline{W})U'(\overline{W}) + \frac{1}{2!}(W - \overline{W})^2 U''(\overline{W}) + \frac{1}{3!}(W - \overline{W})^3 U'''(\overline{W}) + o(W - \overline{W})$$

where $\overline{W} = E(W)$. Taking expectations on both sides:

$$E[U(W)] = U(\overline{W}) + \frac{1}{2!}\sigma_W^2 U''(\overline{W}) + \frac{1}{3!}m_W^3 U'''(\overline{W}) + o(\overline{W}) \tag{8.24}$$

where $\sigma_W^2 = E[(W - \overline{W})^2]$ and $m_W^3 = E[(W - \overline{W})^3]$ are the variance and the third central moment of end-of-period wealth.

10 See F. Ortu, A. Tamoni, and C. Tebaldi (2013), Long-run risk and the persistence of consumption shocks, *Review of Financial Studies*, 26(11), 2876–2915, and R. Bansal and A. Yaron (2004), Risks for the long run: A potential resolution of asset pricing puzzles, *The Journal of Finance* 59(4), 1481–1509.

11 See A. Kraus and R. H. Litzenberger (1976), Skewness preference and the valuation of risk assets, *The Journal of Finance*, 31, 1085–1100.

These moments can be derived more explicitly as follows. Summation algebras are used as these are explicitly clearer in the case of higher moments. Let original or starting wealth be W_0 and suppose optimal decision is made whereby dollar allocations of this wealth to the one-period investments are W_i in risky asset i (for $i = 1, 2, \ldots, N$) with risky return R_i (1 + return rate) and W_f in the risk-free asset with risk-free return R_f. Thus dollar investment in risky asset i is $W_i = w_i(W_0 - W_f)$ where w_i is fraction invested in the risky asset i, with $\sum_{i=1}^N w_i = 1$. $W_0 = \sum_{i=1}^N W_i + W_f$.

Therefore,

$$\overline{W} = \sum_{i=1}^{N} W_i\overline{R_i} + W_f R_f = (W_0 - W_f)\sum_{i=1}^{N} w_i\overline{R_i} + W_f R_f \tag{8.25}$$

$$\sigma_W = (W_0 - W_f)\left(\sum_{i=1}^{N}\sum_{j=1}^{N} w_i w_j \sigma_{ij}\right)^{1/2} \tag{8.26}$$

$$m_W = (W_0 - W_f)\left(\sum_{i=1}^{N}\sum_{j=1}^{N}\sum_{k=1}^{N} w_i w_j w_k m_{ijk}\right)^{1/3} \tag{8.27}$$

where $\overline{R_i} = E(R_i)$, $\sigma_{ij} = \text{cov}(R_i, R_j)$, and $m_{ijk} = E[(R_i - \overline{R_i})(R_j - \overline{R_j})(R_k - \overline{R_k})]$.

Equations (8.25), (8.26), (8.27) can be re-formulated as the following.

$$\overline{W} = \sum_{i=1}^{N} q_i\overline{R_i} + W_f R_f \tag{8.28}$$

$$\sigma_W = (W_0 - W_f)\sum_{i=1}^{N} w_i\left(\sum_{j=1}^{N} w_j\sigma_{ij}\right)/\sigma_M$$

$$= \sum_{i=1}^{N} q_i\sigma_{iM}/\sigma_M - \sum_{i=1}^{N} q_i\beta_i\sigma_M \tag{8.29}$$

$$m_W = (W_0 - W_f)\left(\sum_{i=1}^{N} w_i \sum_{j=1}^{N}\sum_{k=1}^{N} w_j w_k m_{ijk}\right)/m_M^2$$

$$= \sum_{i=1}^{N} q_i m_{iMM}/m_W^2 = \sum_{i=1}^{N} q_i\gamma_i m_W \tag{8.30}$$

where $q_i = (W_0 - W_f)w_i$, $\sigma_M = (\sum_{i=1}^N \sum_{j=1}^N w_i w_j \sigma_{ij})^{\frac{1}{2}}$, $\sigma_{iM} = \text{cov}(R_i, R_M) = \text{cov}(R_i, \sum_{j=1}^N w_j R_j)$, $\beta_i = \sigma_{iM}/\sigma_M^2$, $m_{iMM} = \sum_{j=1}^N \sum_{k=1}^N w_j w_k m_{ijk}$, $m_M = (\sum_{i=1}^N \sum_{j=1}^N \sum_{k=1}^N w_i w_j w_k m_{ijk})^{\frac{1}{3}}$, and $\gamma_i = m_{iMM}/m_W^3$.

Using the idea of a representative agent (hence market demand and supply are simple constant multiples of the representative agent's demand and supply or allocations), we can think of the market portfolio return as $R_M = \sum_{j=1}^N w_j R_j$ (aggregate portfolio of all the risky assets), and $m_{iMM} = E((R_i - \overline{R_i})(R_M - \overline{R_M})^2)$. The latter divided by the third central moment of market portfolio return, m_M^3, is called co-skewness measure, γ_i, between return R_i and the market return. If this term is positively large when the market return skewness (third central moment divided by cube of standard deviation) is positive, it means that at times when the market return R_M has large moves, the stock return tends to be positive. This stock therefore is a good hedge against a volatile market and is considered a safer stock. Hence it would fetch a lower risk-adjusted return. On the other hand, when market return tends to be volatile and the stock return is negative, then this negative co-skewness needs to be compensated by a higher expected return.

From Eq. (8.24), it is seen that VM expected utility is a function Φ of $\overline{W}$, σ_W, and m_W, ignoring the smaller terms in $o(\overline{W})$. The partial derivatives of Φ with respect to $\overline{W}$, σ_W, and m_W are respectively $\Phi_{\overline{W}} > 0$, $\Phi_{\sigma_W} < 0$, and $\Phi_{m_W} > 0$. The signs are postulated based on the agent's preference for more wealth, less risk, and more positive skewness, everything else being equal.

Then the representative agent would maximize (single-period) expected utility as follows.

$$\max_{q_i, W_f, \lambda} \Phi(\overline{W}, \sigma_W, m_W) + \lambda\left(W_0 - \sum_{i=1}^{N} q_i - W_f \right)$$

where W_0 is starting dollar amount of wealth and λ is the Lagrange multiplier.

Taking FOCs with respect to q_i for every $i = 1, 2, \ldots, N$:

$$\Phi_{\overline{W}} \frac{\partial \overline{W}}{\partial q_i} + \Phi_{\sigma_W} \frac{\partial \sigma_W}{\partial q_i} + \Phi_{m_W} \frac{\partial m_W}{\partial q_i} - \lambda = 0$$

and the FOC w. r. t. W_f is

$$\Phi_{\overline{W}} \frac{\partial \overline{W}}{\partial W_f} - \lambda = 0$$

The wealth constraint (partial derivative w. r. t. λ) is:

$$\sum_{i=1}^{N} q_i + W_f = W_0$$

Using Eqs. (8.28), (8.29), (8.30), we obtain $\frac{\partial \overline{W}}{\partial q_i} = \overline{R}_i$, $\frac{\partial \sigma_W}{\partial q_i} = \beta_i \sigma_M$, $\frac{\partial m_W}{\partial q_i} = \gamma_i m_M$, and $\frac{\partial \overline{W}}{\partial W_f} = R_f$.

Solving the above three sets of first order equations for all i (noting that the second order conditions indicate maximum is obtained),

$$\overline{R}_i - R_f = -\frac{\Phi_{\sigma_W}}{\Phi_{\overline{W}}} \beta_i \sigma_M - \frac{\Phi_{m_W}}{\Phi_{\overline{W}}} \gamma_i m_M \tag{8.31}$$

Now, $\frac{\Phi_{\sigma_W}}{\Phi_{\overline{W}}} < 0$ since the numerator is negative and the denominator is positive. Also, $\frac{d\overline{W}}{d\sigma_W}|_{\Phi,m_W} > 0$, i. e., when we keep Φ, m_W constant. Hence $-\frac{\Phi_{\sigma_W}}{\Phi_{\overline{W}}} = \frac{d\overline{W}}{d\sigma_W}|_{\Phi,m_W}$. We shall write the latter in short-form: $\frac{\partial\overline{W}}{\partial\sigma_W} > 0$, which is the agent's marginal rate of substitution between expected end-period wealth and the standard deviation. Also, $\frac{\Phi_{m_W}}{\Phi_{\overline{W}}} > 0$ since both the numerator and the denominator are positive. $\frac{d\overline{W}}{dm_W}|_{\Phi,\sigma_M} < 0$, i. e., when we keep Φ, σ_M constant. Hence $-\frac{\Phi_{m_W}}{\Phi_{\overline{W}}} = \frac{d\overline{W}}{dm_W}|_{\Phi,\sigma_M}$. We shall write the latter in short-form: $\frac{\partial\overline{W}}{\partial m_W} < 0$, which is the agent's marginal rate of substitution between expected end-period wealth and the cube-root of the third central moment of end-period wealth.

Therefore, Eq. (8.31) can be re-expressed as

$$\overline{R}_i - R_f = \frac{\partial\overline{W}}{\partial\sigma_W}\beta_i\sigma_M + \frac{\partial\overline{W}}{\partial m_W}\gamma_i m_M \tag{8.32}$$

Equation (8.32) should also hold for the market portfolio where $\beta_M = 1$ and $\gamma_M = 1$, hence $\overline{R}_M - R_f = \frac{\partial\overline{W}}{\partial\sigma_M}\sigma_M + \frac{\partial\overline{W}}{\partial m_M}m_W$.

The two marginal rates of substitution $\frac{\partial\overline{W}}{\partial\sigma_W}$ and $\frac{\partial\overline{W}}{\partial m_W}$ can be reduced to one parameter $\phi = -\frac{\partial\overline{W}}{\partial\sigma_W}/\frac{\partial\overline{W}}{\partial m_W} > 0$. Note that ϕ is different from $-dm_W/d\sigma_M$.

Dividing Eq. (8.32) on both sides by $\frac{\partial\overline{W}}{\partial m_W}$, we obtain the following.

$$\left(\frac{\partial\overline{W}}{\partial m_W}\right)^{-1}(\overline{R}_i - R_f) = -\phi\beta_i\sigma_M + \gamma_i m_M$$

$$\left(\frac{\partial\overline{W}}{\partial m_W}\right)^{-1}(\overline{R}_M - R_f) = -\phi\sigma_M + m_M$$

Now, dividing the first equation by the second, we obtain:

$$(\overline{R}_i - R_f) = \left(\frac{-\phi\sigma_M}{-\phi\sigma_M + m_M}\beta_i + \frac{m_M}{-\phi\sigma_M + m_M}\gamma_i\right)(\overline{R}_M - R_f)$$

Hence,

$$\begin{aligned} E(R_i - R_f) = \beta_i&\left(\frac{\phi\sigma_M}{\phi\sigma_M - m_M}E(R_M - R_f)\right) \\ - \gamma_i&\left(\frac{m_M}{\phi\sigma_M - m_M}E(R_M - R_f)\right) \end{aligned} \tag{8.33}$$

can be rigorously tested for its full implications using the GMM.[12]

12 Kian Guan Lim (1989), A new test of the three-moment capital asset pricing model, *Journal of Financial and Quantitative Analysis*, 24 (2), 205–216, is one of the earliest to employ a full test of the moment implications of such skewness models.

An interpretation of Eq. (8.33) is that since $\frac{\phi\sigma_M}{\phi\sigma_M - m_M} > 0$ if m_W is not too positively large, higher stock β_i leads to higher risk-adjusted expected return (assuming $E(R_M - R_f) > 0$). When $m_W = 0$ as in a multivariate normal stock return distribution, then we obtain the Sharpe-Lintner CAPM. For the second term on the RHS, if market return has positive skewness, i. e. $m_W > 0$ but is not too large so that $\frac{m_M}{\phi\sigma_M - m_M} E(R_M - R_f) > 0$, then higher positive co-skewness γ_i in a stock return would reduce the expected return since it is considered a safer stock.[13]

Let r_i's and r_M be the ith asset's excess return and the market excess return rates. μ_M, σ_M^2, and m_M^3 are the mean, variance, and the third central moment of the excess market return. Note that these moments are also those of market return since the risk-free return is treated as a constant for the single period.

β_i is the usual stock i's market beta, σ_{iM}/σ_M^2. This provides a moment condition given by $\text{cov}(r_i, r_M) - \beta_i \,\text{var}(r_M) = 0$. γ_i is stock i return's co-skewness with the market return, $E[(R_i - E(R_i))(R_M - E(R_M))^2]/m_M^3$ which is equivalent to $E[(r_i - E(r_i))(r_M - E(r_M))^2]/m_M^3$. This provides another moment condition given by $E[r_i(r_M - \mu_M)^2] - E(r_i)\sigma_M^2 - \gamma_i m_M^3 = 0$.

The full set of moment specifications in testing the three-moment CAPM, without specifying distributional assumptions (except existence and boundedness of the moments), is as follows.

$$
\begin{aligned}
E\left(r_i - \left[\frac{\phi\sigma_M}{\phi\sigma_M - m_M}\beta_i - \frac{m_M}{\phi\sigma_M - m_M}\gamma_i\right] r_M\right) &= 0, \quad \forall i = 1, 2, \ldots, N \\
E(r_i r_M - \mu_M r_i - \beta_i [r_M^2 - \mu_M r_M]) &= 0, \quad \forall i = 1, 2, \ldots, N \\
E(r_i r_M^2 - 2\mu_M r_i r_M + [\mu_M^2 - \sigma_M^2] r_i - \gamma_i [r_M - \mu_M]^3) &= 0, \quad \forall i = 1, 2, \ldots, N
\end{aligned}
$$

and

$$
\begin{aligned}
E(r_M - \mu_M) &= 0, \\
E([r_M - \mu_M]^2 - \sigma_M^2) &= 0, \\
E([r_M - \mu_M]^3 - m_M^3) &= 0
\end{aligned}
$$

There are thus $3N + 3$ orthogonality conditions with $2N + 4$ parameters ($\beta_1, \beta_2, \ldots, \beta_N, \gamma_1, \gamma_2, \ldots, \gamma_N, \mu_M, \sigma_M, m_M, \phi$) to be estimated. There are $N - 1$ overidentifying restrictions providing a χ_{N-1}^2 test of the model.

Since 1982, the GMM technique has been one of the most widely applied methods for empirical estimation and testing especially of nonlinear rational expectations models in many fields of economics and finance. This attests to its usefulness in many

13 Campbell R. Harvey and A. Siddique (2000), Conditional skewness in asset pricing tests, *The Journal of Finance*, 55(3), 1263–1296, also showed that systematic conditional coskewness in stocks is priced with a negative risk premium in cross-sectional regressions.

situations when low-order (short-term) serial correlations or lack of distributional information hampers empirical investigation. However, its drawback is its reliance on asymptotic theory. Many Monte Carlo and econometric studies had arisen to investigate how inference under the GMM test can be improved in small sample settings.

Further Reading

Blanchard, O. J., and S. Fischer (1989), *Lectures on Macroeconomics*, MIT Press.
Cochrane, J. H. (2001), *Asset Pricing*, Princeton University Press.
Davidson, R., and J. G. MacKinnon (1993), *Estimation and Inference in Econometrics*, Oxford University Press.
Fumio Hayashi (2000), *Econometrics*, Princeton University Press.
Hamilton, J. D. (1994), *Time Series Analysis*, Princeton University Press.
Huang, C.-F., and R. H. Litzenberger (1988), *Foundations for Financial Economics*, North-Holland Elsevier Science Publishing.
Ingersoll, J. E. (1987), *Theory of Financial Decision Making*, Rowman & Littlefield Publishers.
Stokey, N. L., and R. E. Lucas Jr. (1989), *Recursive Methods in Economic Dynamics*, Harvard University Press.

9 Maximum Likelihood Methods

In this chapter, we discuss another major method of estimation and testing in the presence of explicit distributional assumption – that of the maximum likelihood method. Then we consider a very important application, that of generalized autoregressive conditional heteroskedasticity processes.

9.1 Introduction

Consider a Poisson (discrete) distribution with probability mass function

$$f(x_t;\lambda) = \frac{e^{-\lambda}\lambda^{x_t}}{x_t!}$$

where $x_t \geq 0$ is the number of events occurring each time period $[t, t+1)$. The RVs x_t's are independent across time periods. The average number of events each time period is characterized by unknown parameter λ. $\lambda = E(x_t) = \text{var}(x_t)$.

Suppose over T periods, observed x_t's are $\mathbf{x} = \{x_1, x_2, \ldots, x_T\}$. The likelihood function of the (observed) sample (or joint probability mass function) is

$$f(\mathbf{x};\lambda) = \prod_{t=1}^{T} f(x_t;\lambda) = \frac{e^{-T\lambda}\lambda^{\sum_{t=1}^{T} x_t}}{\prod_{t=1}^{T} x_t!}$$

The question is: what is the value of λ that would make this sample most likely? The value of λ that maximizes this joint probability is called the Maximum Likelihood Estimator.

It is like estimating dummy parameter (1 if more balls are blue, 0 otherwise) when out of 20 draws from an urn, 15 are blue. Selecting parameter value = 1 is intuitive as it is consistent with what has been observed.

The log likelihood function of the sample is

$$\ln L(\lambda) = \ln \prod_{t=1}^{T} f(x_t;\lambda) = -T\lambda + \left(\sum_{t=1}^{T} x_t\right)\ln\lambda - \sum_{t=1}^{T}\ln(x_t!)$$

First order condition $\frac{d\ln L}{d\lambda}$: $-T + \frac{1}{\lambda}(\sum_{t=1}^{T} x_t) = 0$. Hence $\hat{\lambda}_{ML} = \frac{\sum_{t=1}^{T} x_t}{T}$. $\frac{d\ln L}{d\lambda} = 0$ is called the likelihood equation. Second order condition $\frac{d^2\ln L}{d\lambda^2} = -\frac{\sum_{t=1}^{T} x_t}{\lambda^2} < 0$ (supposing at least one of the x_t's > 0). The SOC ensures the log likelihood function is maximized.

As another example, consider the MLE of independent sampling of size T from a normal distribution of $x_t \sim N(\mu, \sigma^2)$. The joint probability density function of observing the i. i. d. x_t's or the likelihood function is

https://doi.org/10.1515/9783110673951-009

$$\prod_{t=1}^{T} \frac{1}{\sqrt{2\pi\sigma^2}} e^{-\frac{1}{2}(\frac{x_t-\mu}{\sigma})^2}$$

The log likelihood function is

$$\ln L(\mu, \sigma^2) = -\frac{T}{2}\ln(2\pi) - \frac{T}{2}\ln\sigma^2 - \frac{1}{2}\sum_{t=1}^{T}\left(\frac{x_t-\mu}{\sigma}\right)^2$$

The FOCs are:

$$\frac{\partial \ln L}{\partial \mu} = \frac{1}{\sigma^2}\sum_{t=1}^{T}(x_t - \mu) = 0$$

and

$$\frac{\partial \ln L}{\partial \sigma^2} = -\frac{T}{2\sigma^2} + \frac{1}{2\sigma^4}\sum_{t=1}^{T}(x_t - \mu)^2 = 0$$

The SOCs satisfy the case for maximum.

Solving, the maximum likelihood estimators are:

$$\hat{\mu}_{\text{ML}} = \frac{1}{T}\sum_{t=1}^{T} x_t \equiv \bar{x}$$

and

$$\hat{\sigma}^2_{\text{ML}} = \frac{1}{T}\sum_{t=1}^{T}(x_t - \bar{x})^2$$

The ML estimator $\hat{\mu}_{\text{ML}}$ is unbiased. It is also consistent. But the $\hat{\sigma}^2_{\text{ML}}$ estimator is biased in small sample as it uses the sample size T instead of $T-1$ as the divisor. The difference from the unbiased variance estimator is however very small when T is large. It is asymptotically unbiased, i. e. the bias converges to zero when $T \uparrow \infty$. In general, ML estimators are consistent, but they may be biased in small sample.

Now consider the estimation of a simple linear regression using the maximum likelihood (ML) method. Estimate a and b in $Y_t = a + bX_t + e_t$ where $e_t \sim N(0, \sigma_e^2)$. Suppose X_t is given and sampling size is T. The joint probability density function of observing the i. i. d. e_t's is

$$\prod_{t=1}^{T} \frac{1}{\sqrt{2\pi\sigma_e^2}} e^{-\frac{1}{2}(\frac{Y_t-a-bX_t}{\sigma_e})^2}$$

The log likelihood function is

$$\ln L(a, b, \sigma_e^2) = -\frac{T}{2}\ln(2\pi) - \frac{T}{2}\ln\sigma_e^2 - \frac{1}{2}\sum_{t=1}^{T}\left(\frac{Y_t - a - bX_t}{\sigma_e}\right)^2$$

The FOCs of maximizing the log likelihood function are:

$$\frac{\partial \ln L}{\partial a} = \frac{1}{\sigma_e^2}\sum_{t=1}^{T}(Y_t - a - bX_t) = 0$$

$$\frac{\partial \ln L}{\partial b} = \frac{1}{\sigma_e^2}\sum_{t=1}^{T}X_t(Y_t - a - bX_t) = 0$$

and

$$\frac{\partial \ln L}{\partial \sigma_e^2} = -\frac{T}{2\sigma_e^2} + \frac{1}{2\sigma_e^4}\sum_{t=1}^{T}(Y_t - a - bX_t)^2 = 0$$

Solving:

$$\hat{b}_{\text{ML}} = \frac{\sum X_tY_t - T\bar{X}\bar{Y}}{\sum X_t^2 - T\bar{X}^2}$$

$$\hat{a}_{\text{ML}} = \bar{Y} - \hat{b}_{\text{ML}}\bar{X}$$

$$\hat{\sigma}_{e,\text{ML}}^2 = \frac{1}{T}\sum_{t=1}^{T}(Y_t - \hat{a}_{\text{ML}} - \hat{b}_{\text{ML}}X_t)^2$$

where $\bar{X}$ and $\bar{Y}$ are, respectively, the sample means of X_t and Y_t. It is seen that under normality, the ML estimators $\hat{a}_{\text{ML}}$, $\hat{b}_{\text{ML}}$ are also the OLS estimators for a and b. As for the residual variance, the ML estimator $\hat{\sigma}_{e,\text{ML}}^2$ is consistent but biased in small sample as it uses the sample size T instead of $T - 1$ as the divisor. The difference from the unbiased residual variance estimator is however very small when T is large. It is asymptotically unbiased.

9.2 Maximum Likelihood Estimators

Suppose RV Z_t is i. i. d., and takes sample values $\{z_1, z_2, \ldots, z_T\}$. Let the probability density function of RV Z_t in general be $f(z_t; \Lambda)$ with parameters $\Lambda_{n\times1}$. Function $f(\cdot)$ is assumed to be continuous and smooth. $f(Z_t)$ are also i. i. d. The independence comes from the fact that if Z_{t-1} does not contain information about Z_t, i. e. $P(Z_t|Z_{t-1}) = P(Z_t)$, then $f(Z_{t-1})$ would not contain information about $f(Z_t)$. Note that the weaker zero correlation of Z_t, Z_{t-1} doe not imply zero correlation in $f(Z_t), f(Z_{t-1})$. For example, Z_t^2 could be correlated with Z_{t-1}^2.

Then, for any t

$$\int_{-\infty}^{\infty} f(z_t; \Lambda)\, dz_t = 1$$

that is, area under the probability density curve sums to one. Differentiating the above with respect to parameter Λ,

$$\int_{-\infty}^{\infty} \frac{\partial f}{\partial \Lambda}\, dz_t = 0_{n\times 1} \tag{9.1}$$

If Λ is a vector, i. e. more than one parameter, then the derivative is also a vector. Since score function $\frac{\partial \ln f}{\partial \Lambda} = \frac{1}{f}\frac{\partial f}{\partial \Lambda}$, then $\frac{\partial f}{\partial \Lambda} = f\frac{\partial \ln f}{\partial \Lambda}$. Thus,

$$\int_{-\infty}^{\infty} \frac{\partial \ln f}{\partial \Lambda} f(z_t;\Lambda)\, dz_t = 0_{n\times 1} \tag{9.2}$$

Hence $E(\frac{\partial \ln f(Z_t,\Lambda)}{\partial \Lambda}) = 0_{n\times 1}\ \forall t$, where Z_t in the argument is a (single) RV.

The joint pdf of $\{z_1, z_2, \ldots, z_T\}$ (or Z) is likelihood function

$$L(Z;\Lambda) = \prod_{t=1}^{T} f(z_t;\Lambda)$$

and

$$\int\cdots\int L(Z;\Lambda)\, dz_1 dz_2 \ldots dz_T = \int f(z_1;\Lambda) dz_1 \int\cdots\int f(z_T;\Lambda) dz_T = 1$$

Although likelihood is written as function of Z given Λ, its purpose is really more of being a function of Λ given the observations Z, so that one can find a maximum while searching over the parameter space of Λ.

Moreover, $\ln L(Z;\Lambda) = \sum_{t=1}^{T} \ln f(z_t;\Lambda)$, so $\frac{\partial \ln L(Z;\Lambda)}{\partial \Lambda} = \sum_{t=1}^{T} \frac{\partial \ln f(z_t;\Lambda)}{\partial \Lambda}$. Thus

$$E\left(\frac{\partial \ln L(Z_1, Z_2, \ldots, Z_T;\Lambda)}{\partial \Lambda}\right) = \sum_{t=1}^{T} E\left(\frac{\partial \ln f(Z_t;\Lambda)}{\partial \Lambda}\right) = 0_{n\times 1} \tag{9.3}$$

The expectation operations above are done in short-form. To be precise, the first expectation is integration over multivariate RV Z with independent marginal RV Z_t's. The second expectation is integration over individual Z_t's. It can be readily shown that the LHS is

$$\begin{aligned} E\sum_{t=1}^{T}\left(\frac{\partial \ln f(Z_t;\Lambda)}{\partial \Lambda}\right) &= \int\cdots\int\left(\frac{\partial \ln f(z_1;\Lambda)}{\partial \Lambda}\right) f_1 f_2 \ldots f_T\, dz_1 \ldots dz_T \\ &\quad + \cdots + \int\cdots\int\left(\frac{\partial \ln f(z_T;\Lambda)}{\partial \Lambda}\right) f_1 f_2 \ldots f_T\, dz_1 \ldots dz_T \\ &= E\left(\frac{\partial \ln f(Z_1;\Lambda)}{\partial \Lambda}\right)\int\cdots\int f_2 \ldots f_T\, dz_2 \ldots dz_T \end{aligned}$$

$$+\cdots+E\Big(\frac{\partial \ln f(Z_T;\Lambda)}{\partial \Lambda}\Big)\int\cdots\int f_1 f_2\ldots f_{T-1}\,dz_1\ldots dz_{T-1}$$
$$=\sum_{t=1}^{T}E\Big(\frac{\partial \ln f(Z_t;\Lambda)}{\partial \Lambda}\Big)$$

Taking the second derivative in Eq. (9.1),

$$\int_{-\infty}^{\infty}\frac{\partial^2 f}{\partial\Lambda\partial\Lambda^T}\,dz_t = 0_{n\times n}$$

Now for any single RV Z_t,

$$\begin{aligned}\frac{\partial}{\partial\Lambda}\Big(\frac{\partial \ln f(Z_t;\Lambda)}{\partial\Lambda^T}\Big) &= \frac{\partial}{\partial\Lambda}\Big(\frac{1}{f}\frac{\partial f(Z_t;\Lambda)}{\partial\Lambda^T}\Big)\\ &= \frac{1}{f}\frac{\partial^2 f}{\partial\Lambda\partial\Lambda^T}-\frac{1}{f^2}\frac{\partial f}{\partial\Lambda}\frac{\partial f}{\partial\Lambda^T}\\ &= \frac{1}{f}\frac{\partial^2 f}{\partial\Lambda\partial\Lambda^T}-\frac{\partial\ln f}{\partial\Lambda}\frac{\partial\ln f}{\partial\Lambda^T}\end{aligned}$$

So,

$$\begin{aligned}E\Big[\frac{\partial^2\ln f(Z_t;\Lambda)}{\partial\Lambda\partial\Lambda^T}\Big] &= \int\frac{1}{f}\frac{\partial^2 f}{\partial\Lambda\partial\Lambda^T}f dz_t-\int\frac{\partial\ln f}{\partial\Lambda}\frac{\partial\ln f}{\partial\Lambda^T}f dz_t\\ &= -E\Big[\frac{\partial\ln f}{\partial\Lambda}\frac{\partial\ln f}{\partial\Lambda^T}\Big]\end{aligned}\tag{9.4}$$

Similarly, $\frac{\partial^2\ln L}{\partial\Lambda\partial\Lambda^T}=\sum_{t=1}^{T}\frac{\partial^2\ln f}{\partial\Lambda\partial\Lambda^T}$. Thus,

$$\begin{aligned}E\Big[\frac{\partial^2\ln L}{\partial\Lambda\partial\Lambda^T}\Big] &= E\Big[\sum_{t=1}^{T}\frac{\partial^2\ln f}{\partial\Lambda\partial\Lambda^T}\Big]\\ &= \sum_{t=1}^{T}E\Big[\frac{\partial^2\ln f}{\partial\Lambda\partial\Lambda^T}\Big]\\ &= -\sum_{t=1}^{T}E\Big[\frac{\partial\ln f}{\partial\Lambda}\frac{\partial\ln f}{\partial\Lambda^T}\Big]\\ &= -E\Big[\frac{\partial\ln L}{\partial\Lambda}\frac{\partial\ln L}{\partial\Lambda^T}\Big]\end{aligned}\tag{9.5}$$

Note the expectations operators on the LHS and the last line RHS are integrals over multivariate Z whereas the other expectations are integrals over independent marginal Z_t's. In the last term, $E[\frac{\partial\ln L}{\partial\Lambda}\frac{\partial\ln L}{\partial\Lambda^T}] = E[\sum_{i=1}^{T}\frac{\partial\ln f(Z_i)}{\partial\Lambda}\sum_{j=1}^{T}\frac{\partial\ln f(Z_j)}{\partial\Lambda^T}] = \sum_{i=1}^{T}\sum_{j=1}^{T}E[\frac{\partial\ln f(Z_i)}{\partial\Lambda}\frac{\partial\ln f(Z_j)}{\partial\Lambda^T}] = \sum_{i=1}^{T}E[\frac{\partial\ln f(Z_i)}{\partial\Lambda}\frac{\partial\ln f(Z_i)}{\partial\Lambda^T}]$ since for $i\neq j$,

$$E\left[\frac{\partial \ln f(Z_i)}{\partial \Lambda}\frac{\partial \ln f(Z_j)}{\partial \Lambda^T}\right] = E\left[\frac{\partial \ln f(Z_i)}{\partial \Lambda}\right]E\left[\frac{\partial \ln f(Z_j)}{\partial \Lambda^T}\right] = 0$$

making use of the independence of Z_i from Z_j and Eq. (9.2).

The term on the RHS in Eq. (9.5), $E[\frac{\partial \ln L}{\partial \Lambda}\frac{\partial \ln L}{\partial \Lambda^T}]$, is called Fisher's information matrix of order (sample size) T. This term is also the covariance matrix of random vector $\frac{\partial \ln L}{\partial \Lambda}$. Let $\text{cov}(\frac{\partial \ln L}{\partial \Lambda}) = I_T(\Lambda)$. Hence $I_T(\Lambda)$ is symmetrical. Note also that $E[\frac{\partial^2 \ln L}{\partial \Lambda \partial \Lambda^T}] = -I_T(\Lambda)$. Let $\text{cov}(\frac{\partial \ln f}{\partial \Lambda}) = -E[\frac{\partial^2 \ln f}{\partial \Lambda \partial \Lambda^T}] = I_1(\Lambda)$ or information matrix of order 1 as it is based on only sample size of 1, i. e. $f(Z_t)$.

Since Z_t's are i. i. d., as seen from Eq. (9.5),

$$E\left[\frac{\partial \ln L}{\partial \Lambda}\frac{\partial \ln L}{\partial \Lambda^T}\right] = \sum_{t=1}^{T} E\left[\frac{\partial \ln f}{\partial \Lambda}\frac{\partial \ln f}{\partial \Lambda^T}\right]$$

hence $I_T(\Lambda) = TI_1(\Lambda)$. Similarly,

$$E\left[\frac{\partial^2 \ln L}{\partial \Lambda \partial \Lambda^T}\right] = \sum_{t=1}^{T} E\left[\frac{\partial^2 \ln f}{\partial \Lambda \partial \Lambda^T}\right]$$

hence $-I_T(\Lambda) = -TI_1(\Lambda)$.

The higher the sampling variances of elements of $\frac{\partial \ln f}{\partial \Lambda}$, i. e., the "higher" $I_1(\Lambda)$, the more information the sample data give concerning the parameter(s). We illustrate with an example. Consider sampling from a normal distribution $Z \sim N(\mu, \sigma^2)$. $\ln f(Z) = -\frac{1}{2}\ln(2\pi\sigma^2) - \frac{1}{2\sigma^2}(Z-\mu)^2$. $\frac{\partial \ln f}{\partial \mu} = \frac{1}{\sigma^2}(Z-\mu)$. $\text{var}(\frac{\partial \ln f}{\partial \mu}) = \frac{1}{\sigma^2}$. Hence when σ^2 is very small, the $(1,1)$ element of $I_1(\Lambda)$ or $\text{var}(\frac{\partial \ln f}{\partial \mu})$ is very high, indicating a sample point z_i provides more information about μ than the same sample point providing information on a normal distribution with much higher σ^2.

Recall that the MLE estimator $\hat{\Lambda}_{ML}$ is that which maximizes $\ln L(Z;\Lambda)$ or which sets FOC $\frac{\partial \ln L(Z;\Lambda)}{\partial \Lambda}$ or $\sum_{t=1}^{T}\frac{\partial \ln f(z_t;\Lambda)}{\partial \Lambda}$ to zero. The latter implies setting $\frac{1}{T}\sum_{t=1}^{T}\frac{\partial \ln f(z_t,\mathbf{\Lambda})}{\partial \mathbf{\Lambda}}|_{\mathbf{\Lambda}=\hat{\Lambda}_{ML}} = 0$ for all T. Recall the GMM. By the LLN, the sample moment converges to the population moment:

$$\frac{1}{T}\sum_{t=1}^{T}\frac{\partial \ln f(z_i,\mathbf{\Lambda})}{\partial \mathbf{\Lambda}}\bigg|_{\mathbf{\Lambda}=\hat{\Lambda}_{ML}} \xrightarrow{p} E\left[\frac{\partial \ln f(Z_t,\hat{\Lambda}_{ML})}{\partial \hat{\Lambda}_{ML}}\right]$$

where $\hat{\Lambda}_{ML}$ is fixed given T. By setting the LHS to zero, the RHS also equals to zero. But as we assume in the last Chapter on GMM, together with the smooth regularity conditions, the moment condition has also a unique Λ. Since $E[\frac{\partial \ln f(Z_t,\mathbf{\Lambda})}{\partial \mathbf{\Lambda}}] = 0$, then $\hat{\Lambda}_{ML} \xrightarrow{p} \mathbf{\Lambda}$, i. e. ML estimator is consistent.

Next we show the key result about asymptotic normality of MLE. By the mean value theorem (a similar version uses Taylor series expansion):

$$\frac{\partial \ln L}{\partial \Lambda}(\hat{\Lambda}_{ML}) = \frac{\partial \ln L}{\partial \Lambda}(\Lambda) + \frac{\partial^2 \ln L}{\partial \Lambda \partial \Lambda^T}(\Lambda^*)(\hat{\Lambda}_{ML} - \Lambda)$$

where each element of Λ^* lies between corresponding elements of $\hat{\Lambda}_{ML}$ and Λ. But the LHS equals to a zero vector. Hence

$$\sqrt{T}(\hat{\Lambda}_{ML} - \Lambda) = -\left[\frac{1}{T}\frac{\partial^2 \ln L}{\partial \Lambda \partial \Lambda^T}(\Lambda^*)\right]^{-1} \sqrt{T}T^{-1}\left(\frac{\partial \ln L}{\partial \Lambda}(\Lambda)\right) \tag{9.6}$$

However, in Eq. (9.6),

$$\sqrt{T}T^{-1}\left(\frac{\partial \ln L}{\partial \Lambda}(\Lambda)\right) = \sqrt{T}\left[\frac{1}{T}\sum_{t=1}^{T}\frac{\partial \ln f}{\partial \Lambda}(\Lambda)\right]$$

Note that $E(\frac{\partial \ln f}{\partial \Lambda}(\Lambda)) = 0, \forall i$. The multivariate CLT states that for i. i. d. vectors $u_i = \frac{\partial \ln f(Z_i)}{\partial \Lambda}(\Lambda)$ and $\bar{U} = \frac{1}{T}\sum_{i=1}^{T} u_i$, $\sqrt{T}(\bar{U} - E(U))$ converges to $N(0, \text{cov}(U))$. Then

$$\sqrt{T}\left[\frac{1}{T}\sum_{t=1}^{T}\frac{\partial \ln f}{\partial \Lambda}(\Lambda)\right] \xrightarrow{d} N\left(0, \text{cov}\left[\frac{\partial \ln f}{\partial \Lambda}(\Lambda)\right]\right) \equiv N(0, I_1(\Lambda))$$

The term $[\frac{1}{T}\frac{\partial^2 \ln L}{\partial \Lambda \partial \Lambda^T}(\Lambda^*)] = \frac{1}{T}\sum_{t=1}^{T}\frac{\partial^2 \ln f}{\partial \Lambda \partial \Lambda^T}(\Lambda^*)$ in Eq. (9.6) converges via the weak LLN or in probability to $E[\frac{\partial^2 \ln f}{\partial \Lambda \partial \Lambda^T}(\Lambda^*)]$. As $\hat{\Lambda}_{ML} \xrightarrow{p} \mathbf{\Lambda}$, so $\Lambda^* \xrightarrow{p} \mathbf{\Lambda}$, then $[\frac{1}{T}\frac{\partial^2 \ln L}{\partial \Lambda \partial \Lambda^T}(\Lambda^*)]$ converges in probability to $E[\frac{\partial^2 \ln f}{\partial \Lambda \partial \Lambda^T}(\Lambda)] = -I_1(\Lambda)$.

Using Slutsky's theorem,

$$\sqrt{T}(\hat{\Lambda}_{ML} - \Lambda) \xrightarrow{d} [I_1(\Lambda)]^{-1} Y_{n\times 1}$$

where $Y \sim N(0, I_1(\Lambda))$ and n is the dimension of the vector parameter Λ. The asymptotic covariance (matrix) of $\sqrt{T}(\hat{\Lambda}_{ML} - \Lambda)$ is

$$[I_1(\Lambda)]^{-1}\text{cov}(Y)[I_1^T(\Lambda)]^{-1} = [I_1(\Lambda)]^{-1}$$

Therefore,

$$\sqrt{T}(\hat{\Lambda}_{ML} - \Lambda) \xrightarrow{d} N(0, I_1(\Lambda)^{-1}) \tag{9.7}$$

Hence the maximum likelihood estimator $\hat{\Lambda}_{ML}$ is asymptotically normal.

Thus asymptotic $\text{cov}(\hat{\Lambda}_{ML}) = [TI_1(\Lambda)]^{-1} = [I_T(\Lambda)]^{-1}$. From Eq. (9.7), it is also seen that the ML estimator is asymptotically unbiased since any bias $E(\hat{\Lambda}_{ML} - \Lambda)$ converges asymptotically to zero by virtue of the asymptotic normality. Note that in general, consistency is not identical with asymptotic unbiasedness.

9.3 Cramer–Rao Lower Bound and Asymptotic Efficiency

Suppose $h(Z)$ is any unbiased $n \times 1$ vector estimator of Λ. Then, by unbiasedness,

$$E[h(Z)] = \int\int\cdots\int h(Z)L(Z;\Lambda)dz_1dz_2\ldots dz_T = \Lambda$$

In differentiating the left-hand side, recall that $\frac{\partial L}{\partial \Lambda} = L\frac{\partial \ln L}{\partial \Lambda}$. Differentiating the right-hand side Λ with respect to Λ yields identity matrix I. Therefore, the above becomes

$$\int\cdots\int h(Z)\frac{\partial \ln L(Z;\Lambda)}{\partial \Lambda^T}L(Z;\Lambda)\,dZ = E\left[h(Z)\frac{\partial \ln L(Z;\Lambda)}{\partial \Lambda^T}\right] = I$$

Thus, I is the covariance matrix between $h(Z)$ and $\frac{\partial \ln L(Z;\Lambda)}{\partial \Lambda}$ since the latter is a zero-mean vector. Then, we can specify the covariance matrix

$$\operatorname{cov}\begin{bmatrix} h(Z) \\ \frac{\partial \ln L}{\partial \Lambda} \end{bmatrix} = \begin{bmatrix} \operatorname{cov}[h(Z)] & I \\ I & I_T(\Lambda) \end{bmatrix}$$

Now Λ is $n \times 1$ vector. $h(Z)$ is also $n \times 1$. $\frac{\partial \ln L}{\partial \Lambda}$ is $n \times 1$. So, the RHS is a $2n \times 2n$ covariance matrix that contains four elements of $n \times n$ matrices. A covariance matrix is always positive semidefinite (or positive definite if we rule out zero variance), so we can choose any arbitrary non-zero vector $(p^T, -p^T I_T^{-1}(\Lambda))$, where p^T is $1 \times n$ and $-p^T I_T^{-1}(\mathbf{\Lambda})$ is also $1 \times n$, such that

$$\begin{aligned} &(p^T, -p^T I_T^{-1})\begin{bmatrix} \operatorname{cov}[h(Z)] & I \\ I & I_T(\Lambda) \end{bmatrix}\begin{pmatrix} p \\ -I_T^{-1}p \end{pmatrix} \\ &= p^T\left[\operatorname{cov}[h(Z)] - I_T^{-1}\right]p \geq 0 \end{aligned}$$

The last line above shows the Cramer–Rao inequality. Thus, the covariance matrix of any unbiased estimator, $\operatorname{cov}[h(Z)]$ is "larger than or equal to" the inverse of the information matrix I_T. This means that we can write, for any arbitrary $n \times 1$ vector p, $p^T \operatorname{cov}[h(Z)]p \geq p^T I_T^{-1} p$, a 1×1 number. Clearly, if we choose $p^T = (1, 0, 0, \ldots, 0)$, then $p^T \operatorname{cov}[h(Z)]p$ is equal to the variance of the unbiased estimator of the first parameter in vector $\mathbf{\Lambda}$, and this is bounded below by the first row-first column element of I_T^{-1}, say r_{11}.

Suppose

$$I_T^{-1} = \begin{bmatrix} r_{11} & \cdots & & \\ \vdots & r_{22} & & \\ & & \ddots & \\ & & & r_{nn} \end{bmatrix}$$

Then, any unbiased estimators have variances bounded below by the Cramer–Rao lower bounds $(r_{11}, r_{22}, \ldots, r_{nn})$ respectively. An estimator that attains the lower bound is said to be a minimum variance unbiased or efficient estimator.

We have seen that the ML estimator is consistent and asymptotically normal. It is also asymptotically unbiased although in general, it may be biased in small or finite sample. As ML estimators are asymptotically unbiased, then asymptotically, given the above result for unbiased estimators (any sample size T), ML estimator variances are also bounded below by I_T^{-1}. But in Eq. (9.7) we see that $\text{cov}(\hat{\Lambda}_{\text{ML}}) = [I_T(\Lambda)]^{-1}$. Therefore we can conclude that ML estimators are asymptotically efficient, attaining the Cramer–Rao lower bound. This makes ML a favorite estimation method especially when the sample size is large.

9.4 Likelihood Ratio Test

There is an important class of test statistics of models related to Maximum Likelihood estimation. Suppose we are finding ML estimator $\hat{\Lambda}_{\text{ML}}$ given data Z that are assumed to have known density function f.

Expand using Taylor series around the ML estimator, where higher order terms in the Taylor series are finite.

$$\begin{aligned}
\ln L(z;\Lambda) &= \ln L(z;\hat{\Lambda}_{\text{ML}}) + (\Lambda - \hat{\Lambda}_{\text{ML}})\left(\frac{\partial \ln L(\hat{\Lambda}_{\text{ML}})}{\partial \Lambda}\right) \\
&\quad + \frac{1}{2}(\Lambda - \hat{\Lambda}_{\text{ML}})^T\left(\frac{\partial^2 \ln L(\hat{\Lambda}_{\text{ML}})}{\partial \Lambda \partial \Lambda^T}\right)(\Lambda - \hat{\Lambda}_{\text{ML}}) + o(T) \\
&= \ln L(z;\hat{\Lambda}_{\text{ML}}) + \frac{1}{2}(\hat{\Lambda}_{\text{ML}} - \Lambda)^T\left(\frac{\partial^2 \ln L(\hat{\Lambda}_{\text{ML}})}{\partial \Lambda \partial \Lambda^T}\right)(\hat{\Lambda}_{\text{ML}} - \Lambda) \\
&\quad + o(T)
\end{aligned}$$

The last term $o(T)$ means that as $\hat{\Lambda}_{\text{ML}} \xrightarrow{p} \Lambda$, $o(T)$ becomes negligible with respect to $\ln L(z;\Lambda)$ for $T \uparrow \infty$. We also use short-cut notations $\frac{\partial \ln L(\hat{\Lambda}_{\text{ML}})}{\partial \Lambda}$ and $\frac{\partial^2 \ln L(\hat{\Lambda}_{\text{ML}})}{\partial \Lambda \partial \Lambda^T}$ to mean entering values $\hat{\Lambda}_{\text{ML}}$ into the analytical functions $\frac{\partial \ln L(\Lambda)}{\partial \Lambda}$ and $\frac{\partial^2 \ln L(\Lambda)}{\partial \Lambda \partial \Lambda^T}$, respectively, in place of Λ.

So, asymptotically,

$$\begin{aligned}
&-2[\ln L(z;\Lambda) - \ln L(z;\hat{\Lambda}_{\text{ML}})] \\
&= (\hat{\Lambda}_{\text{ML}} - \Lambda)^T\left[-\frac{\partial^2 \ln L(\hat{\Lambda}_{\text{ML}})}{\partial \Lambda \partial \Lambda^T}\right](\hat{\Lambda}_{\text{ML}} - \Lambda) \\
&= \sqrt{T}(\hat{\Lambda}_{\text{ML}} - \Lambda)^T\left[-\frac{1}{T}\frac{\partial^2 \ln L(\hat{\Lambda}_{\text{ML}})}{\partial \Lambda \partial \Lambda^T}\right]\sqrt{T}(\hat{\Lambda}_{\text{ML}} - \Lambda)
\end{aligned}$$

Now, from Eq. (9.7), $\sqrt{T}(\hat{\Lambda}_{ML} - \Lambda) \xrightarrow{d} N(0, I_1(\Lambda)^{-1})$. As seen earlier, $[-\frac{1}{T}\frac{\partial^2 \ln L(\hat{\Lambda}_{ML})}{\partial\Lambda\partial\Lambda^T}] \xrightarrow{p} I_1(\Lambda)$. From the results in Chapter 6, Section 6.2, we see that the LHS which is a likelihood ratio

$$-2\ln\left[\frac{L(z;\Lambda)}{L(z;\hat{\Lambda}_{ML})}\right] \xrightarrow{d} \chi_n^2$$

i. e., it converges to a chi-square RV with n degrees of freedom, n being the dimension of Λ.

Suppose we want to test $H_0 : \Lambda = \Theta$, i. e., testing if true Λ is a set of values given by Θ, then if the null hypothesis is true, asymptotically

$$-2\ln\left[\frac{L(z;\Theta)}{L(z;\hat{\Lambda}_{ML})}\right] = T(\hat{\Lambda}_{ML} - \Theta)^T I_1(\Theta)(\hat{\Lambda}_{ML} - \Theta)$$

is a test statistic distributed as χ_n^2. In the above, $I_1(\Theta)$ is estimated by

$$-\frac{1}{T}\sum_{t=1}^{T}\frac{\partial^2 \ln f(\Theta)}{\partial\Lambda\partial\Lambda^T}$$

The null is rejected if the test statistic occurs in the right tail of the χ_n^2 distribution at a p-value smaller than the significance level of the test.

9.5 ARCH-GARCH

The landscape of financial econometrics was forever changed and augmented greatly when Robert Engle introduced the Autoregressive Conditional Heteroskedasticity (ARCH) model in 1982. It was an ingeniously embedded tool in specifying the dynamics of volatility coupled with the underlying asset price process. This greatly extended the space of stochastic processes including those in the Box Jenkins approach. ARCH was very successfully extended to Generalized Autoregressive Conditional Heteroskedasticity (GARCH) model by Bollerslev, and to-date there continues to be a huge number of variations of processes building on the embedded tooling idea. We consider such process modelling to be particularly relevant in estimating risks in market prices and in risk management in today's market of high and persistent volatilities. The estimation of GARCH processes using maximum likelihood method is an important application.

For ARMA(1, 1) which includes AR(1) and MA(1) processes,

$$y_t = \theta + \lambda y_{t-1} + u_t + a u_{t-1}$$

the conditional variance $\text{var}(y_t|y_{t-1}) = (1 + a^2)\sigma_u^2$ is constant. Suppose we condition on all lagged information available at t, Φ_{t-1}, then $\text{var}(y_t|y_{t-1}, u_{t-1}) = \sigma_u^2$ is also constant.

Note, however, that conditional mean $E(y_t|y_{t-1}) = \theta + \lambda y_{t-1}$ changes. Similarly, we can show that for

$$y_t = \theta + \lambda x_t + u_t \tag{9.8}$$

where $E(u_t) = 0$, $\text{cov}(u_t, u_{t-k}) = 0$, $k \neq 0$, and x_t, u_t are stochastically stationary and independent, then $\text{var}(y_t|x_t) = \text{var}(u_t) = \sigma_u^2$ is constant. So far we have not modelled anything about the variance of u_t. This is the motivation behind building a conditionally changing variance.

Suppose we model a process on the variance of u_t (not u_t itself – note this distinction) such that:

$$\text{var}(u_t) = \alpha_0 + \alpha_1 u_{t-1}^2 \tag{9.9}$$

This is an autoregressive conditional heteroskedasticity or ARCH(1) model[1] in disturbance u_t. Then, in Eqs. (9.8) and (9.9), we show that $\text{var}(y_t|x_t) = \text{var}(u_t) = \alpha_0 + \alpha_1 u_{t-1}^2 \neq \sigma_u^2$. The conditional variance of y_t indeed changes with past levels of u_{t-1}, although the latter cannot be directly observed.

We can also write Eq. (9.9) in terms of a u_t process as follows:

$$u_t = e_t \sqrt{\alpha_0 + \alpha_1 u_{t-1}^2} \tag{9.10}$$

where $e_t \sim N(0, 1)$. To be precise, Eq. (9.10) implies Eq. (9.9), but the converse is not necessarily true.

Equation (9.10) can also be written as:

$$u_t = e_t \sigma_t \tag{9.11}$$

where $\sigma_t = \sqrt{\alpha_0 + \alpha_1 u_{t-1}^2} = \sqrt{\text{var}(u_t)}$.

It is interesting to know what is the nature of the distribution of the disturbance u_t. From Eq. (9.10), it should be evident that u_t is unconditionally not a normal distribution. However, conditional on u_{t-1}, u_t is normally distributed. Using Monte Carlo simulation with a sample size of 10000, and starting value $u_0 = 0$, a histogram of the distribution of u_t is produced as shown in Figure 9.1.

Clearly, unlike unit normal e_t, unconditional u_t's empirical distribution as shown in Figure 9.1 has a larger kurtosis (>3) than a normal random variable. The Jarque-Bera test statistic rejects the null of normal distribution for u_t.

---

1 The seminal article in this area is R. Engle (1982), Autoregressive conditional heteroskedasticity with estimates of the variance of United Kingdom inflations, *Econometrica*, 50, 987–1008. Its significant generalization is in T. Bollerslev (1986), Generalized autoregressive conditional heteroskedasticity, *Journal of Econometrics*, 31, 307–327.

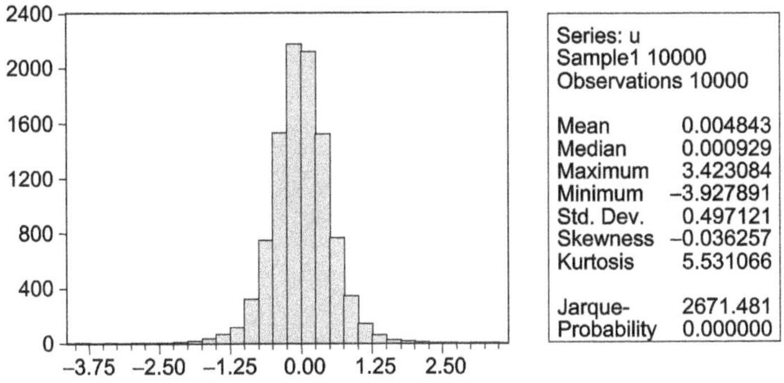

Figure 9.1: Monte Carlo Simulation of Errors $u_t = e_t\sqrt{\alpha_0 + \alpha_1 u_{t-1}^2}$.

When $\text{var}(u_t) = \alpha_0 + \alpha_1 u_{t-1}^2 + \alpha_2 u_{t-2}^2 + \cdots + \alpha_{q-1} u_{t-q+1}^2 + \alpha_q u_{t-q}^2$, we call the conditional variance of u_t above an ARCH (q) process.

Besides Eq. (9.9), another model of changing conditional variance is

$$\text{var}(u_t) = \alpha_0 + \alpha_1 u_{t-1}^2 + \gamma_1 \,\text{var}(u_{t-1}) \tag{9.12}$$

This is generalized autoregressive conditional heteroskedasticity or the GARCH(1, 1) model in u_t. It includes a lagged volatility term.

When $\text{var}(u_t) = \alpha_0 + \alpha_1 u_{t-1}^2 + \alpha_2 u_{t-2}^2 + \cdots + \alpha_q u_{t-q}^2 + \gamma_1 \,\text{var}(u_{t-1}) + \gamma_2 \,\text{var}(u_{t-2}) + \cdots + \gamma_p \,\text{var}(u_{t-p})$, we call the conditional variance of u_t a GARCH(q, p) process with weighted averages of q lagged u_{t-j}^2's and weighted averages of p lagged $\text{var}(u_{t-j})$'s. Due to the large number of parameters that usually has to be estimated in a GARCH process, parsimony typically dictates modelling with low order GARCH(q, p) such as GARCH(1, 1) process.

Suppose a y_t process contains a disturbance random error that behaves according to GARCH in Eq. (9.12). Then

$$\text{var}(y_t|x_t, \Phi_{t-1}) = \text{var}(u_t|x_t, u_{t-1}, \sigma_{t-1}^2) = \alpha_0 + \alpha_1 u_{t-1}^2 + \gamma_1 \,\text{var}(u_{t-1})$$

is no longer constant, but instead, changes with t or more precisely, the information available at t, Φ_{t-1}, even as u_{t-1} and also $\text{var}(u_{t-1})$ change over time. Process such as y_t or u_t itself is said to exhibit conditional heteroskedasticity or dynamic volatility. However, conditional on the lagged observations, it is possible to model the conditional u_t's and also y_t's as normally distributed, though their unconditional distributions are in general not normal.

As an example, if $\text{var}(u_{t-1}) = 0.2$, $\alpha_0 = 0.01$, $\alpha_1 = 0.3$, $\gamma_1 = 0.5$, $u_{t-1} = 0.3$ then $\text{var}(u_t) = 0.01 + 0.3^*0.3^2 + 0.5^*0.2 = 0.137$. We see that the conditional variance of u_t changes over time with new lagged values of residuals and new lagged values of conditional variances.

The GARCH(1, 1) process in Eq. (9.12) can be expressed as

$$\sigma_t^2 = \alpha_0 + \alpha_1 u_{t-1}^2 + \gamma_1 \sigma_{t-1}^2$$

where $\sigma_t^2 = \text{var}(u_t)$. Using lag or backward shift operator L,

$$(1 - \gamma_1 L)\sigma_t^2 = \alpha_0 + \alpha_1 u_{t-1}^2$$

so,

$$\sigma_t^2 = \frac{1}{(1 - \gamma_1 L)}(\alpha_0 + \alpha_1 u_{t-1}^2)$$

which is an ARCH(∞) model. Hence any GARCH(q, p) model can also have an ARCH(∞) representation.

In what follows, we illustrate graphically the volatility clustering effect of different GARCH processes. We simulate sample paths of a process $\{y_t\}_{t=1,2,\dots,200}$ where it is weakly stationary without conditional heteroskedasticity.

$$\begin{aligned} & y_t = \theta + \lambda x_t + u_t \\ & x_t \overset{\text{i.i.d.}}{\sim} N(1, 0.4), \quad u_t \overset{\text{i.i.d.}}{\sim} N(0, 2), \quad \theta = \frac{1}{2}, \quad \lambda = \frac{1}{2} \end{aligned} \tag{9.13}$$

Suppose we chart the path of y_t.

$$\begin{aligned} y_0 &= \frac{1}{2} + \frac{1}{2}x_0 + u_0 \\ y_1 &= \frac{1}{2} + \frac{1}{2}x_1 + u_1 \\ &\vdots \\ y_t &= \frac{1}{2} + \frac{1}{2}x_t + u_t \\ &\vdots \end{aligned}$$

and note that $E(y_t) = \theta + \lambda E(x_t) = \frac{1}{2} + \frac{1}{2}(1) = 1$ and $\text{var}(y_t) = \lambda^2\sigma_x^2 + \sigma_u^2 = \frac{1}{4} * 0.4 + 2 = 2.1$.

The plot of the time-path of y_t is shown in Figure 9.2. It is seen that y_t behaves like a random series with a mean at 1 and the two dotted lines are the two standard deviations away from the mean. In this case, they are $1 \pm 2\sqrt{2.1}$ (about 4 and −2, respectively), with 2.28 % probability of exceeding each way from the region between the two dotted lines.

Next, we simulate sample paths of another process $\{y_t\}_{t=1,2,\dots,200}$ that follows Eqs. (9.8) and (9.12) instead.

$$y_t = \theta + \lambda x_t + u_t.$$

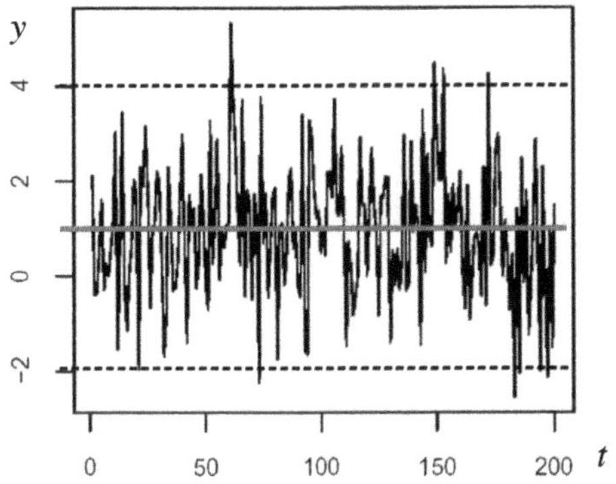

Figure 9.2: Stationary Process $y_t \sim N(1, 2.1)$.

$$x_t \overset{\text{i.i.d.}}{\sim} N(1, 0.4)$$
$$\text{var}(u_t) = \alpha_0 + \alpha_1 u_{t-1}^2 + \gamma_1 \text{var}(u_{t-1})$$

We set initial $\text{var}(u_0) = \sigma_0^2 = 2$. Initial u_0 may be drawn from $N(0, 2)$, but subsequent u_t's are not unconditionally normally distributed. Unlike the constant variance of 2 in the earlier stationary process, this GARCH(1, 1) process will have a changing conditional variance over time.

$$\theta = \frac{1}{2}, \quad \lambda = \frac{1}{2}, \quad \alpha_0 = \frac{1}{2}, \quad \alpha_1 = \frac{1}{4} \quad \text{and} \quad \gamma_1 = \frac{1}{2}.$$
$$y_0 = \frac{1}{2} + \frac{1}{2} x_0 + u_0, \quad u_0 \overset{d}{\sim} N(0, 2)$$

Once u_0^2 and $\text{var}(u_0)$ are obtained, we can use Eq. (9.12) to obtain $\text{var}(u_1)$. Next simulate

$$u_1 = e_1 \sqrt{\alpha_0 + \alpha_1 u_0^2 + \gamma_1 \text{var}(u_0)} \quad \text{for } e_1 \sim N(0, 1)$$

Put $y_1 = \frac{1}{2} + \frac{1}{2} x_1 + u_1$. Next use u_1^2 and $\text{var}(u_1)$ to obtain $\text{var}(u_2)$ via Eq. (9.12). Then simulate $u_2 = e_2 \sqrt{\alpha_0 + \alpha_1 u_1^2 + \gamma_1 \text{var}(u_1)}$ for $e_2 \sim N(0, 1)$, and so on. In general,

$$u_t = e_t \sqrt{\alpha_0 + \alpha_1 u_{t-1}^2 + \gamma_1 \text{var}(u_{t-1})}$$

The plot is shown in Figure 9.3.

Figure 9.3 shows a similar y_t process as in Figure 9.2, with $y_t = 1/2 + 1/2 x_t + u_t$. Its unconditional mean and variance are the same as y_t in Figure 9.2. Unconditional mean and variance of y_t are 1 and 2.1. However, its variance follows the GARCH error process: $\text{var}(u_t) = 0.5 + 0.25 u_{t-1}^2 + 0.5 \text{var}(u_{t-1})$. The figure shows that y_t behaves like a random series with a mean at 1 and the two dotted lines are the two standard deviations away from the mean. In this case, they are $1 \pm 2\sqrt{2.1}$ (about 4 and −2, respectively), with 2.28 % probability of exceeding each way from the region between the two dotted

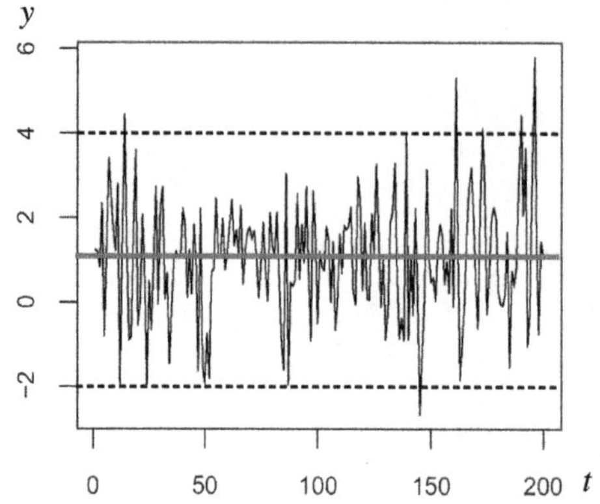

Figure 9.3: GARCH Error Process: Unconditional y_t Has Mean, Variance 1, 2.1. $\text{var}(u_t) = 0.5+0.25u_{t-1}^2+ 0.5\,\text{var}(u_{t-1})$.

lines. There appears to be more volatility. At about the 50th observation, the variance clusters together and y-values persist close to −2.

We provide another simulation using the same $y_t = 1/2 + 1/2x_t + u_t$ with unconditional mean and variance of y_t at the same 1 and 2.1 values, respectively. However, its variance now follows GARCH error process: $\text{var}(u_t) = 0.1 + 0.25u_{t-1}^2 + 0.7\,\text{var}(u_{t-1})$ where clustering or persistence in volatility should be more evident because of the higher $y_1 = 0.7$. This is shown in Figure 9.4.

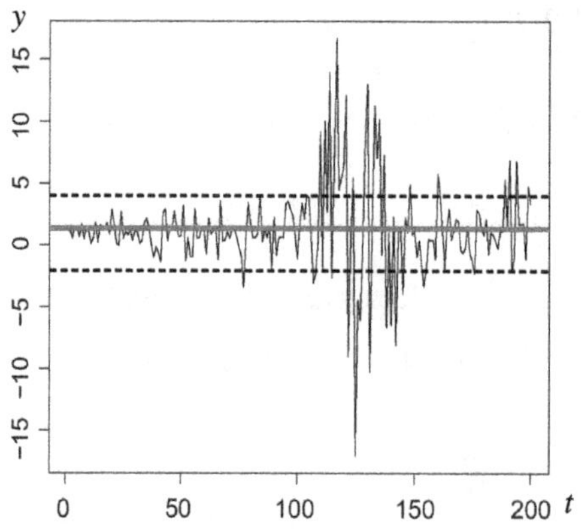

Figure 9.4: GARCH Error Process: Unconditional y_t Has Mean, Variance 1, 2.1. $\text{var}(u_t) = 0.1+0.25u_{t-1}^2+ 0.7\,\text{var}(u_{t-1})$.

Indeed Figure 9.4 shows the persistent and much higher volatility with y_t's exceeding +15 and falling below −15 in the observations from 100 to 150. Thus, we see that GARCH modelling of variance is able to produce the kind of persistence and clustering in volatility sometimes observed in market prices. Similar effects can be observed if in

Figures 9.2, 9.3, 9.4, we fix the 200 values of x_t to be the same. The effects may be even clearer as remove the "noise" of x_t.

In addition to models such as Eqs. (9.8) and (9.12), different impacts of lagged positive and negative u_t's are also modelled by Glosten, Jagannathan, and Runkle (1993),[2] viz.

$$\sigma_t^2 = \alpha_0 + \alpha_1 u_{t-1}^2 I_{u_{t-1} \geq 0} + \alpha_2 u_{t-1}^2 I_{u_{t-1} < 0} + \gamma_1 \sigma_{t-1}^2$$

where $u_t \sim N(0, \sigma_t^2)$, $I_{u_{t-1} \geq 0}$ is an indicator variable taking value 1 if $u_{t-1} \geq 0$, and zero otherwise, and $I_{u_{t-1} < 0}$ is an indicator variable taking value 1 if $u_{t-1} < 0$, and zero otherwise. This is also called a threshold GARCH(1, 1) or TGARCH(1, 1) model. The asymmetric effect is typically shown to be a higher $\alpha_2 > \alpha_1$ for stock return conditional volatilities.

Exponential GARCH(1, 1) or EGARCH(1, 1) is:

$$\ln \sigma_t^2 = \alpha_0 + \alpha_1(|\epsilon_{t-1}| + \theta \epsilon_{t-1}) + \gamma_1 \ln \sigma_{t-1}^2$$

where $u_t = \epsilon_t \sigma_t$, $\epsilon_t \sim N(0, 1)$, and the effect of ϵ_{t-1} on next period σ_t^2 is asymmetric, e. g., if $\alpha_1 > 0, \theta < -1$, then a negative ϵ_{t-1} yields greater increase in σ_t^2 than the decrease in σ_t^2 by a positive ϵ_{t-1}. This models market index price behavior where price level correlates negatively with next period volatility.

Nonlinear GARCH(1, 1) or NGARCH(1, 1) is:

$$\sigma_t^2 = \alpha_0 + \alpha_1 \sigma_{t-1}^2 (\epsilon_{t-1} - \theta)^2 + \gamma_1 \sigma_{t-1}^2$$

where $u_t = \epsilon_t \sigma_t$, $\epsilon_t \sim N(0, 1)$, and the effect of ϵ_{t-1} on next period σ_t^2 is larger the further deviation from a threshold θ. This specification produces leptokurtic (fat-tailed) and skewed distributions in u_t.

Another variation is

$$y_t = \theta + \lambda x_t + \gamma \sigma_t^2 + u_t$$

where $\sigma_t^2 = \text{var}(y_t | x_t, u_{t-1}) = \alpha_0 + \alpha_1 u_{t-1}^2$. Then the y_t process is an ARCH-in-mean or ARCH-M model. This version basically has the variance σ_t^2 driving the mean effect $E(y_t)$.

It is to be noted that GARCH processes are not easily aggregated. For example, if daily returns follow GARCH, then week returns do not follow similar GARCH process. GARCH is a pre-determined (adapted to filtration or information at current time t) changing volatility. Hence it is not a stochastic volatility when the volatility is not adapted to filtration at t.

---

2 L. Glosten, R. Jagannathan, and D. Runkle (1993), Relationship between the expected value and the volatility of the nominal excess return on stocks, *The Journal of Finance* 48, 1779–1801.

9.6 Estimating GARCH

9.6.1 Stationarity Condition

It is interesting to note that while GARCH processes are conditionally non-stationary with changing variances, they are still unconditionally stationary processes. For reasons of data analyses, when we have only one time series or one sample path, it is important to be able to invoke the law of large numbers via stationarity and ergodicity so that sample averages can converge to population moments. We shall show how GARCH processes are also stationary.

If we expand Eq. (9.12):

$$\begin{aligned}
\mathrm{var}(u_t) &= \alpha_0 + \alpha_1 u_{t-1}^2 + \gamma_1 \mathrm{var}(u_{t-1}) \\
&= \alpha_0 + \alpha_1 u_{t-1}^2 + \gamma_1[\alpha_0 + \alpha_1 u_{t-2}^2 + \gamma_1 \mathrm{var}(u_{t-2})] \\
&= \alpha_0(1+\gamma_1) + \alpha_1(u_{t-1}^2 + \gamma_1 u_{t-2}^2) + \gamma_1^2[\alpha_0 + \alpha_1 u_{t-3}^2 + \gamma_1 \mathrm{var}(u_{t-3})] \\
&= \alpha_0(1+\gamma_1+\gamma_1^2+\cdots) + \alpha_1(u_{t-1}^2 + \gamma_1 u_{t-2}^2 + \gamma_1^2 u_{t-3}^2 + \cdots)
\end{aligned} \tag{9.14}$$

We had used the notation $\mathrm{var}(u_t) \equiv \sigma_t^2$ earlier to denote the conditional variance of u_t at t. Let $\sigma_u^2 = E[\mathrm{var}(u_t)]$, being the unconditional variance of u_t. Taking unconditional expectation on both sides, and assuming there exists stationarity so that $\sigma_u^2 = E(u_{t-1}^2) = E(u_{t-2}^2) = E(u_{t-3}^2) = \cdots$, then

$$\begin{aligned}
\sigma_u^2 &= \frac{\alpha_0}{(1-\gamma_1)} + \alpha_1(\sigma_u^2 + \gamma_1\sigma_u^2 + \gamma_1^2\sigma_u^2 + \cdots) \\
&= \frac{\alpha_0}{(1-\gamma_1)} + \frac{\alpha_1\sigma_u^2}{(1-\gamma_1)} \\
&= \frac{(\alpha_0 + \alpha_1\sigma_u^2)}{(1-\gamma_1)}, \quad \text{supposing } |\gamma_1| < 1
\end{aligned}$$

Then, $\sigma_u^2 = \alpha_0/(1-\gamma_1-\alpha_1)$, supposing $\alpha_0 > 0$ and $|\gamma_1 + \alpha_1| < 1$. In the simulation example of Figure 9.3, given the parameters $\alpha_0 = 1/2$, $\alpha_1 = 1/4$, and $\gamma_1 = 1/2$, therefore the unconditional variance of the GARCH disturbance is $\sigma_u^2 = 0.5/(1-0.75) = 2$. In the same way, in the simulation example of Figure 9.4, given the parameters $\alpha_0 = 1/10$, $\alpha_1 = 1/4$, and $\gamma_1 = 7/10$, the unconditional variance of the GARCH disturbance is $\sigma_u^2 = 0.1/(1-0.95) = 2$.

Consider performing a regression of Eq. (9.8)

$$Y_t = \theta + \lambda X_t + u_t$$

where u_t follows GARCH(1, 1) process in Eq. (9.12), i. e.,

$$u_t = e_t \sigma_t \tag{9.15}$$

$$\sigma_t^2 = \alpha_0 + \alpha_1 u_{t-1}^2 + \gamma_1 \sigma_{t-1}^2 \tag{9.16}$$

where e_t is i. i. d. $N(0,1)$ and $\sigma_t^2 = \text{var}(u_t)$. The last definition is acceptable since in Eqs. (9.15), σ_t^2 is pre-determined at t (as it depends on lagged information), and so $\text{var}(u_t)$ on the LHS is equal to $\sigma_t^2\,\text{var}(e_t) = \sigma_t^2$, given $\text{var}(e_t) = 1$.

It is interesting to note that if the classical conditions (A1), (A2), (A3) or (A1′) and (A2′) hold, as seen in Chapter 6, then the OLS estimators of θ and λ are unbiased. This is due to either the independence between X_t and u_t or the conditional moments of u_t's being independent of x_t's.

However, as noted earlier, the dynamic volatility structure of u_t means that even though $E(u_t u_{t-1}) = 0$ (serially uncorrelated), u_t is not serially independent as u_t^2 is correlated with u_{t-1}^2. This non-independence may pose a problem in the convergence of the sampling moment $\frac{1}{T}\sum_{t=1}^{T} u_t^2$ to σ_u^2, the unconditional variance. Thus the BLUE variance result of the OLS estimator is not guaranteed. Even if somehow with more regularity conditions, OLS estimator variance holds, this is also not ideal since it depends on the unconditional variance that can be quite large especially when α_1 and γ_1 are large. However, the maximum likelihood method can be used to obtain consistent and asymptotically efficient estimators.

9.6.2 Maximum Likelihood Estimation

We first consider estimating the GARCH(1, 1) process u in Eqs. (9.15) and (9.16). The procedure can be similarly applied to GARCH(q, p).

We have seen that u_t's are not independent, so we do not want to use the likelihood function of unconditional densities of u_t. However, from Eq. (9.15), conditional RV $u_{t+1}|\sigma_{t+1}$ is independent of RV $u_t|\sigma_t$. This is because conditional RV $u_{t+1}|\sigma_{t+1}$ is constant σ_{t+1}^2 times RV e_{t+1}, i. e. $N(0, \sigma_{t+1}^2)$. Conditional RV $u_t|\sigma_t$ is $N(0, \sigma_t^2)$ and e_{t+1} is independent of e_t.

The joint density or likelihood function of sample values $\{u_1, u_2, \ldots, u_T\}$ (if they are observed or if their estimates $\hat{u}_t$ are observed), is expressed as product of conditional and marginal densities:

$$\begin{aligned}
f(u_1, u_2, \ldots, u_T) &= f(u_T|u_{T-1}, u_{T-2}, \ldots, u_0) f(u_0, u_1, \ldots, u_{T-1}) \\
&= f(u_T|u_{T-1}, u_{T-2}, \ldots, u_0) f(u_{T-1}|u_{T-2}, u_{T-3}, \ldots, u_0) \\
&\quad \times f(u_0, u_1, \ldots, u_{T-2}) \\
&= f(u_T|u_{T-1}, u_{T-2}, \ldots, u_0) f(u_{T-1}|u_{T-2}, u_{T-3}, \ldots, u_0) \\
&\quad \times \cdots \times f(u_1|u_0) \times f(u_0)
\end{aligned}$$

We shall assume the initial values u_0, σ_0 are given. These may be approximated using $u_0 = 0$ (since $E(u_0) = 0$), and $\sigma_0 = \sqrt{\frac{1}{T}\sum_{t=1}^{T} u_t^2}$.

The log likelihood function of the sample data is then

$$\ln f(u_1, u_2, \ldots, u_T) = \left[\sum_{t=1}^{T} \ln f(u_t|u_{t-1}, \ldots, u_0)\right] + \ln f(u_0)$$

Since each $u_t \sim N(0, \sigma_t^2)$,

$$\ln f(u_t|u_{t-1}, \ldots, u_0) = -\frac{1}{2}\ln(2\pi) - \frac{1}{2}\ln\sigma_t^2 - \frac{1}{2}\frac{u_t^2}{\sigma_t^2} \tag{9.17}$$

and each σ_t^2 at t is a pre-determined linear function of $u_0^2, u_1^2, \ldots, u_{t-1}^2$ and σ_0.

If we let parameter vector $\omega = (\alpha_0, \alpha_1, \gamma_1)$, and using say GMM in Chapter 8, Section 8.1, to find consistent estimates $\hat{\theta}$ and $\hat{\lambda}$, then $\hat{u}_t = Y_t - \hat{\theta} - \hat{\lambda}X_t$ can be used as the observed asymptotic equivalent of u_t. We shall keep this in mind when we evaluate the ML estimator ω_{ML}. If $z_t' = (1, u_{t-1}^2, \sigma_{t-1}^2)$, then $\sigma_t^2 = z_t'\omega$.

Differentiating the conditional density in Eq. (9.17) with respect to ω:

$$\frac{\partial \ln f}{\partial \omega} = \frac{1}{2}\sigma_t^{-2}\frac{\partial \sigma_t^2}{\partial \omega}\left(\frac{u_t^2}{\sigma_t^2} - 1\right) \tag{9.18}$$

$$\frac{\partial^2 \ln f}{\partial \omega \partial \omega^T} = \left(\frac{u_t^2}{\sigma_t^2} - 1\right)\frac{\partial}{\partial \omega^T}\left[\frac{1}{2}\sigma_t^{-2}\frac{\partial \sigma_t^2}{\partial \omega}\right] - \frac{1}{2}\sigma_t^{-4}\frac{u_t^2}{\sigma_t^2}\frac{\partial \sigma_t^2}{\partial \omega}\frac{\partial \sigma_t^2}{\partial \omega^T} \tag{9.19}$$

and

$$\frac{\partial \sigma_t^2}{\partial \omega} = z_t + \gamma_1 \frac{\partial \sigma_{t-1}^2}{\partial \omega}$$

The maximum likelihood first order conditions are to set

$$\sum_{t=1}^{T}\frac{\partial \ln f}{\partial \omega} = \sum_{t=1}^{T}\frac{1}{2}\sigma_t^{-2}\frac{\partial \sigma_t^2}{\partial \omega}\left(\frac{u_t^2}{\sigma_t^2} - 1\right) = 0 \tag{9.20}$$

Sometimes $\frac{1}{T}\sum_{t=1}^{T}\frac{\partial \ln f}{\partial \omega}$ or "normalized" likelihood is used. However, the solution for ω_{ML} in Eq. (9.20) above is not straightforward since the equation is not analytical in ω as there is an iteration on $\frac{\partial \sigma_t^2}{\partial \omega}$ and σ_t^2 $(\forall t)$ in Eq. (9.20) is also a linear function of lagged u_{t-i}^2's with coefficients in ω. Therefore an iterative numerical technique is called for.

We first consider the familiar Newton-Raphson method for multivariate solution ω^* yielding $\sum_{t=1}^{T}\frac{\partial \ln f}{\partial \omega}|_{\omega=\omega^*} = 0$ in Eq. (9.20). This ω^* is also the vector whereby $\sum_{t=1}^{T}\ln f|_{\omega=\omega^*}$ is maximum.

Suppose we have a value fixed at ω_k in the kth iteration such that $\sum_{t=1}^{T}\ln f|_{\omega=\omega_k}$ is close to maximum, but we require to improve on this estimate to reach the maximum in the likelihood. We attempt to find this improved estimate in the neighborhood of ω_k.

Using the truncated Taylor series as approximation:

$$\sum_{t=1}^{T} \ln f(\omega) \approx \sum_{t=1}^{T} \ln f(\omega_k) + (\omega - \omega_k)^T g_{\omega_k} + \frac{1}{2}(\omega - \omega_k)^T H_{\omega_k}(\omega - \omega_k)$$

where $g_{\omega_k} = \sum_{t=1}^{T} \frac{\partial \ln f}{\partial \omega}|_{\omega=\omega_k}$ and $H_{\omega_k} = \sum_{t=1}^{T} \frac{\partial^2 \ln f}{\partial\omega\partial\omega^T}|_{\omega=\omega_k}$. Taking first derivative:

$$\sum_{t=1}^{T} \frac{\partial \ln f}{\partial \omega}(\omega) \approx g_{\omega_k} + H_{\omega_k}(\omega - \omega_k)$$

treating ω_k as a constant vector. Suppose maximum is achieved at new ω, i. e., LHS $\sum_{t=1}^{T} \frac{\partial \ln f}{\partial \omega}(\omega) = 0$. Then let the new ω be next iterate ω_{k+1}, so

$$\omega_{k+1} = \omega_k - H_{\omega_k}^{-1} g_{\omega_k}$$

Or,

$$\omega_{k+1} = \omega_k - \left(\frac{1}{T} H_{\omega_k}\right)^{-1} \left(\frac{1}{T} g_{\omega_k}\right)$$

But from Section 9.2 Eq. (9.5), we see that in the case when f is a density function, asymptotically $\frac{1}{T} H_\omega = -\frac{1}{T}\sum_{t=1}^{T} \frac{\partial \ln f}{\partial \omega}\frac{\partial \ln f}{\partial \omega^T}$ evaluated at ω for conditionally independent f. Thus we can approximate $\frac{1}{T} H_{\omega_k} = -\frac{1}{T}\sum_{t=1}^{T} \frac{\partial \ln f}{\partial \omega}\frac{\partial \ln f}{\partial \omega^T}|_{\omega=\omega_k}$. As H_{ω_k} is inherently less stable than $\sum_{t=1}^{T} \frac{\partial \ln f}{\partial \omega}\frac{\partial \ln f}{\partial \omega^T}$, we replace it and use the iterative algorithm

$$\omega_{k+1} = \omega_k + \sum_{t=1}^{T} \frac{\partial \ln f}{\partial \omega}\frac{\partial \ln f}{\partial \omega^T}\bigg|_{\omega=\omega_k} g_{\omega_k}$$

The above is essentially the BHHH algorithm applicable in the maximum likelihood procedure.[3] The iteration stops when the revision in the iterates becomes too small according to criterion set by the econometrician.

The maximum likelihood estimator of θ, λ can also be found. Let $\beta = (\theta, \lambda)^T$. Note that $\frac{\partial u_t}{\partial \beta} = \frac{\partial(Y_t - \theta - \lambda X_t)}{\partial \beta} = (-1, -X_t)^T$. Let $x_t = (1, X_t)^T$.

Differentiating conditional density in Eq. (9.17) with respect to β,

$$\frac{\partial \ln f}{\partial \beta} = \sigma_t^{-2} u_t x_t + \frac{1}{2}\sigma_t^{-2}\frac{\partial \sigma_t^2}{\partial \beta}\left(\frac{u_t^2}{\sigma_t^2} - 1\right) \tag{9.21}$$

$$\begin{aligned}\frac{\partial^2 \ln f}{\partial\beta\partial\beta^T} &= -\sigma_t^{-2} x_t x_t^T - \frac{1}{2}\sigma_t^{-4}\left(\frac{u_t^2}{\sigma_t^2}\right)\frac{\partial \sigma_t^2}{\partial \beta}\frac{\partial \sigma_t^2}{\partial \beta^T} \\ &\quad - 2\sigma_t^{-4} u_t x_t \frac{\partial \sigma_t^2}{\partial \beta^T} + \left(\frac{u_t^2}{\sigma_t^2} - 1\right)\frac{\partial}{\partial \beta^T}\left[\frac{1}{2}\sigma_t^{-2}\frac{\partial \sigma_t^2}{\partial \beta}\right]\end{aligned} \tag{9.22}$$

3 For more details, see E. K. Berndt, B. H. Hall, R. E. Hall and J.A, Hausman (1974), Estimation inference in nonlinear structural models, *Annals of Economic and Social Measurement*, 4, 653–665.

and

$$\frac{\partial \sigma_t^2}{\partial \beta} = -2\alpha_1 u_{t-1} x_{t-1} + \gamma_1 \frac{\partial \sigma_{t-1}^2}{\partial \beta}$$

In Eq. (9.21), conditional on lagged u_t's, $E(\frac{\partial \ln f}{\partial \beta}|u_{t-1}, u_{t-2}, \ldots) = \sigma_t^{-2} E(u_t x_t | u_{t-1}, u_{t-2}, \ldots) = 0$ according to results in Section 9.2, as the conditional expectation of the second term is zero. Then taking unconditional expectation, $E(u_t x_t) = 0$. But in Eq. (9.21), first order condition implies $\frac{1}{T}\sum_{t=1}^{T} \frac{\partial \ln f}{\partial \beta} = 0$. Hence we are solving for $\hat{\beta}_{\mathrm{ML}}$ in $\frac{1}{T}\sum_{t=1}^{T} u_t x_t = 0$ which basically gives the same solutions as in the GMM method.

In Eq. (9.18) when we take the second partial derivative w. r. t. β^T:

$$\frac{\partial^2 \ln f}{\partial \omega \partial \beta^T} = \frac{1}{2}\sigma_t^{-2}\frac{\partial \sigma_t^2}{\partial \omega}[-2\sigma_t^{-2} u_t x_t^T + 2\alpha_1 \sigma_t^{-4} u_t^2 (u_{t-1} x_{t-1}^T + \gamma_1 u_{t-2} x_{t-2}^T$$
$$+ \gamma_1^2 u_{t-3} x_{t-3}^T + \cdots)] + \frac{1}{2}\left(\frac{u_t^2}{\sigma_t^2} - 1\right)\frac{\partial}{\partial \beta}\left(\sigma_t^{-2}\frac{\partial \sigma_t^2}{\partial \omega^T}\right)$$

The conditional expectation

$$E\left(\frac{\partial^2 \ln f}{\partial \omega \partial \beta^T}|u_{t-1}, u_{t-2}, \ldots\right) = \sigma_t^{-4}\frac{\partial \sigma_t^2}{\partial \omega}\alpha_1 (u_{t-1} x_{t-1}^T + \gamma_1 u_{t-2} x_{t-2}^T + \cdots)$$

Taking unconditional expectation on the above, we have $E(\frac{\partial^2 \ln f}{\partial \omega \partial \beta^T}) = E(\frac{\partial^2 \ln f}{\partial \beta \partial \omega^T}) = 0$.

We can then form the expected Hessian matrix

$$E\begin{pmatrix} \frac{\partial^2 \ln f}{\partial \omega \partial \omega^T} & \frac{\partial^2 \ln f}{\partial \omega \partial \beta^T} \\ \frac{\partial^2 \ln f}{\partial \beta \partial \omega^T} & \frac{\partial^2 \ln f}{\partial \beta \partial \beta^T} \end{pmatrix} = \begin{pmatrix} -\frac{1}{2}E[\sigma_t^{-4}\frac{\partial \sigma_t^2}{\partial \omega}\frac{\partial \sigma_t^2}{\partial \omega^T}] & 0 \\ 0 & E[-\sigma_t^{-2} x_t x_t^T - \frac{1}{2}\sigma_t^{-4}\frac{\partial \sigma_t^2}{\partial \beta}\frac{\partial \sigma_t^2}{\partial \beta^T}] \end{pmatrix}$$

that according to Eq. (9.4) is $-I_1(\omega, \beta)$, the Fisher information matrix of order 1. Hence the ML estimators $\hat{\omega}_{\mathrm{ML}}$ via Eq. (9.18) and $\hat{\beta}_{\mathrm{ML}}$ via Eq. (9.21) are consistent and asymptotically normally distributed with covariance matrix $[I_T(\omega, \beta)]^{-1}$ or $[I_T(\Lambda)]^{-1}$ where $\Lambda = (\omega, \beta)^T$.

In the above MLE, conditional normal distribution is assumed on u_t via Eq. (9.15) where e_t is i. i. d. $N(0, 1)$. Suppose this assumption or specification of e_t is incorrect, and the true i. i. d. e_t distribution is non-normal. Although Eqs. (9.1) and (9.2) are tautologically correct for any density f, Eq. (9.4) becomes problematic when the expectation there is taken with respect to the true density whereas the argument contains the incorrect normal density f. Expectation under the true density in Eq. (9.4) is important as later we need to compute the covariance matrix using the sample moments (that converge to population moments under true densities). Thus, if incorrect normal density f is assumed, asymptotically $\frac{1}{T}\sum_{t=1}^{T}\frac{\partial^2 \ln f}{\partial \Lambda \partial \Lambda^T} \neq -\frac{1}{T}\sum_{t=1}^{T}\frac{\partial \ln f}{\partial \Lambda}\frac{\partial \ln f}{\partial \Lambda^T}$.

Using asymptotic theory, however, it can be shown that the ML estimators $\hat{\omega}_{\mathrm{ML}}$ and $\hat{\beta}_{\mathrm{ML}}$ derived under the assumption of conditional normality are generally still consistent and follow asymptotic normal distributions. These estimators are called quasi maximum likelihood (QML) estimators.[4]

$$\sqrt{T}(\hat{\Lambda}_{QML} - \Lambda) \xrightarrow{d} N(0, H^{-1}SH^{-1})$$

where $H = -\frac{1}{T}\sum_{t=1}^{T} E[\frac{\partial^2 \ln f}{\partial\Lambda\partial\Lambda^T}]$ and $S = \frac{1}{T}\sum_{t=1}^{T} E[\frac{\partial \ln f}{\partial\Lambda}\frac{\partial \ln f}{\partial\Lambda^T}]$.

The population moments are replaced by the sample moments

$$\hat{H} = -\frac{1}{T}\sum_{t=1}^{T}\left[\frac{\partial^2 \ln f}{\partial\Lambda\partial\Lambda^T}\right] \quad \text{and} \quad \hat{S} = \frac{1}{T}\sum_{t=1}^{T}\left[\frac{\partial \ln f}{\partial\Lambda}\frac{\partial \ln f}{\partial\Lambda^T}\right]$$

for independent Z_t in the argument of f. It is noted that should the assumed density is actually normal, then $\hat{H} = \hat{S}$, and the asymptotic covariance matrix is $\hat{S}^{-1}$ which is estimate of the information matrix I_1^{-1}.

The QML estimator is however less efficient than the ML estimator if the density is known, i. e. asymptotic variances of the QML estimators are larger than those of the ML estimators if f is known. In the GARCH case, for true f that may be highly leptokurtic (fat tails), the reduction in efficiency can be large. Hence sometimes u_t may be modelled as t-distribution or other distributions with fatter tails. Provided these are the correct densities, the ML estimators based on these would be more efficient.

9.6.3 GMM

Another method that we learn in Chapter 8 is the use of generalized method of moments when the true underlying distribution is not known. Suppose $y_t = \mu + u_t$ (constant mean μ specification), $E(u_t) = 0$, and $E(u_t^2) = \sigma_t^2$, but the distribution of u_t is unknown.

$$\sigma_t^2 = c + \alpha u_{t-1}^2 + \gamma\sigma_{t-1}^2$$

which is a GARCH(1, 1) process.

We can form the following conditional moments using lagged y_{t-i}'s as instruments:

4 See T. Bollerslev, and J. Wooldridge (1992), Quasi maximum likelihood estimation and inference in dynamic models with time varying covariances, *Econometric Reviews* 11, 143–172, and S. Lee, and B. Hansen (1994), Asymptotic theory for the GARCH(1, 1) quasi maximum likelihood estimator, *Econometric Theory*, 10, 29–52.

$$E_{t-1}[u_t] = 0$$
$$E_{t-1}[\sigma_t^2 - u_t^2] = 0$$
$$E_{t-1}[(\sigma_t^2 - u_t^2)y_{t-1}] = 0$$
$$E_{t-1}[(\sigma_t^2 - u_t^2)y_{t-2}] = 0$$
$$E_{t-1}[(\sigma_t^2 - u_t^2)y_{t-3}] = 0$$

By taking iterated expectations over the null information set, we obtain the orthogonality conditions or unconditional moments for estimating the parameters $\{\mu, c, \alpha, \gamma\}$ where there is one overidentifying restriction.

Using the recursive representation of σ_t^2:

$$\sigma_t^2 = c\left(\frac{1-\gamma^t}{1-\gamma}\right) + \alpha\sum_{j=1}^{t}\gamma^{j-1}u_{t-j}^2 + \gamma^t\sigma_0^2$$

where u_0 and σ_0 are assumed as given. Thus the orthogonality conditions can be written in terms of the parameters $\{\mu, c, \alpha, \gamma\}$.

$$E[y_t - \mu] = 0$$
$$E\left(c\left(\frac{1-\gamma^t}{1-\gamma}\right) + \alpha\sum_{j=1}^{t}\gamma^{j-1}u_{t-j}^2 + \gamma^t\sigma_0^2 - (y_t-\mu)^2\right) = 0$$
$$E\left(\left[c\left(\frac{1-\gamma^t}{1-\gamma}\right) + \alpha\sum_{j=1}^{t}\gamma^{j-1}u_{t-j}^2 + \gamma^t\sigma_0^2 - (y_t-\mu)^2\right]y_{t-1}\right) = 0$$
$$E\left(\left[c\left(\frac{1-\gamma^t}{1-\gamma}\right) + \alpha\sum_{j=1}^{t}\gamma^{j-1}u_{t-j}^2 + \gamma^t\sigma_0^2 - (y_t-\mu)^2\right]y_{t-2}\right) = 0$$
$$E\left(\left[c\left(\frac{1-\gamma^t}{1-\gamma}\right) + \alpha\sum_{j=1}^{t}\gamma^{j-1}u_{t-j}^2 + \gamma^t\sigma_0^2 - (y_t-\mu)^2\right]y_{t-3}\right) = 0.$$

Then the GMM method using sample moments and an optimal weighting matrix can be found to find the GMM estimates and a χ_1^2 test of the moments, i. e. test if the GARCH(1, 1) specification of the moment conditions are consistent with the time series data. However, finding the GMM estimators by minimizing the test statistic in this case involves an iterative algorithm that can be unstable. This is especially if γ is large so that large sample convergence is too slow.

9.6.4 Diagnostic for ARCH-GARCH

It is useful to check if a time series $\{y_t\}$ contains conditional heteroskedasticity in its residuals. Note that ARCH (q) is modelled by $E(u_t^2) = \alpha_0 + \alpha_1 u_{t-1}^2 + \alpha_2 u_{t-2}^2 + \cdots + \alpha_{q-1}u_{t-q+1}^2 +$

$\alpha_q u_{t-q}^2$, assuming $E(u_t) = 0$. We may also write this heuristically as a regression of u_t^2 on its lags up to lag q, adding a white noise e_t.

$$u_t^2 = \alpha_0 + \alpha_1 u_{t-1}^2 + \alpha_2 u_{t-2}^2 + \cdots + \alpha_{q-1} u_{t-q+1}^2 + \alpha_q u_{t-q}^2 + e_t$$

GARCH(q, p) for $p \neq 0$ can also have a representation in terms of an infinite number of lags in squares of the residuals. We show this for the case of GARCH(1, 1) in Eq. (9.14):

$$\begin{aligned}
\operatorname{var}(u_t) &= \alpha_0 + \alpha_1 u_{t-1}^2 + \gamma_1 \operatorname{var}(u_{t-1}) \\
&= \alpha_0 + \alpha_1 u_{t-1}^2 + \gamma_1 [\alpha_0 + \alpha_1 u_{t-2}^2 + \gamma_1 \operatorname{var}(u_{t-2})] \\
&= \alpha_0(1 + \gamma_1) + \alpha_1 (u_{t-1}^2 + \gamma_1 u_{t-2}^2) + \gamma_1^2 [\alpha_0 + \alpha_1 u_{t-3}^2 \\
&\quad + \gamma_1 \operatorname{var}(u_{t-3})] \\
&= \alpha_0 (1 + \gamma_1 + \gamma_1^2 + \cdots) + \alpha_1 (u_{t-1}^2 + \gamma_1 u_{t-2}^2 + \gamma_1^2 u_{t-3}^2 + \cdots)
\end{aligned}$$

The last term on the right-hand side shows an infinite number of lags in u_{t-j}^2's. From the section on stationarity, we see that the GARCH process can be expanded in a similar way. Thus, heuristically, a GARCH process may be expressed as follows for an arbitrarily large number of lags N, where we would set u_{t-N-1}^2 equal to some constant. The c_j's are constants:

$$u_t^2 = c_0 + c_1 u_{t-1}^2 + c_2 u_{t-2}^2 + \cdots + c_q u_{t-q}^2 + \cdots + c_N u_{t-N}^2 + e_t$$

It is clear from both the expressions of ARCH and GARCH above that there is autocorrelations (serial correlations) in the square of the residuals. For ARCH(q), autocorrelation in u_t^2 is non-zero up to lag q, and becomes zero after that lag. For GARCH(q, p), $p \neq 0$, autocorrelation in u_t^2 is non-zero for an arbitrarily large number of lags.

Considering Eq. (9.8), suppose we estimate via OLS and then obtain the estimated residuals:

$$\hat{u}_t = y_t - \hat{\theta} - \hat{\lambda} x_t$$

Compute time series $\{\hat{u}_t^2\}$. Then using the Ljung and Box Q-test in Chapter 5, Section 5.10, on the $\hat{u}_t^2$ and its auto-correlogram, to test if correlations $H_0 : \rho(1) = \rho(2) = \rho(3) = \cdots = \rho(q) = 0$. If H_0 is rejected for an auto-correlogram that is significant out to lag q, then ARCH(q) is plausible. If the correlations do not appear to decay or disappear, then a GARCH process is likely. We should also follow up with the Ljung and Box Q-test on

$$\left[\frac{\hat{u}_t}{\sqrt{\widehat{\operatorname{var}}(u_t)}} \right]^2$$

as a confirmation, using the squared normalized noises.

9.7 Applications

We discuss in this section two applications of the maximum likelihood estimation method. The first is to estimate the time discount factor ρ and the risk aversion-related parameter γ. For power utility $U(C_t) = C_t^\gamma/\gamma$, the risk aversion coefficient is $1 - \gamma > 0$. The second is to show how the exchange margin can be set to control for risk using the GARCH process.

9.7.1 Euler Equation Revisited

In Chapter 8, the stochastic Euler equation for asset pricing under power utility as in Eq. (8.21) is:

$$E_t\left[\left(\frac{C_{t+1}}{C_t}\right)^{\gamma-1} R_{t+1}\right] = \frac{1}{\rho}$$

where ρ is the time discount factor, $1-\gamma$ is the constant relative risk aversion coefficient, C_t is per capita consumption at time t, and R_{t+1} is the return of an asset, e. g. a stock or the market portfolio, over period $(t, t+1]$. ML method would be used to estimate the parameters ρ and γ and also test the restriction of the Euler equation.

In using the maximum likelihood method, the idea is to formulate a time series of a RV with a density function that is parameterized by some density parameters as well as the parameters of interest, i. e. γ and ρ.

For more convenient exposition, let $G_{t+1} = C_{t+1}/C_t$, $g_{t+1} = \ln G_{t+1}$, and $r_{t+1} = \ln R_{t+1}$. Then the Euler equation can be expressed as:

$$E_t[\exp((\gamma - 1)g_{t+1} + r_{t+1})] = \exp(-\ln\rho)$$

Assume g_{t+1} and r_{t+1} to be normally distributed conditional on information at t that are restricted to lagged values of g_t and r_t only. Then,

$$\exp\left[E_t((\gamma - 1)g_{t+1} + r_{t+1}) + \frac{1}{2}\operatorname{var}_t((\gamma - 1)g_{t+1} + r_{t+1})\right] = \exp(-\ln\rho)$$

Or,

$$E_t((\gamma - 1)g_{t+1} + r_{t+1}) + \frac{1}{2}\operatorname{var}_t((\gamma - 1)g_{t+1} + r_{t+1}) = -\ln\rho$$

If we further assume $\operatorname{var}_t((\gamma - 1)g_{t+1} + r_{t+1}) = \sigma^2$, i. e. a constant $\forall t$, then

$$E_t((\gamma - 1)g_{t+1} + r_{t+1}) + \ln\rho + \frac{1}{2}\sigma^2 = 0$$

Or,

$$E_t(r_{t+1}) = -(\gamma - 1)E_t(g_{t+1}) - \ln\rho - \frac{1}{2}\sigma^2$$

We can use the above information about the linkage between the conditional expectations of return and consumption growth,[5] but to simplify we use the unconditional expectations to perform the MLE, i. e.,

$$y_t = (\gamma - 1)g_{t+1} + r_{t+1} + \ln\rho + \frac{1}{2}\sigma^2$$

is normally distributed with mean zero and variance σ^2, i. e. $N(0, \sigma^2)$.

Then the density function of y_t is

$$f(y_t) = (2\pi)^{-1/2}(\sigma^2)^{-1/2}e^{-[(\gamma-1)g_{t+1}+r_{t+1}+\ln\rho+\frac{1}{2}\sigma^2]/2\sigma^2}$$

The likelihood function of sample $\{y_1, y_2, \ldots, y_T\}$ is

$$L(\gamma, \rho, \sigma^2) = \prod_{t=1}^{T} f(y_t; \gamma, \rho, \sigma^2)$$

The log likelihood function is:

$$\ln L(\gamma, \rho, \sigma^2) = -\frac{T}{2}\ln(2\pi) - \frac{T}{2}\ln\sigma^2 - \frac{1}{2}\sum_{t=1}^{T}\frac{[(\gamma - 1)g_{t+1} + r_{t+1} + \ln\rho + \frac{1}{2}\sigma^2]^2}{\sigma^2} \tag{9.23}$$

We can then solve for the maximum or first order conditions in Eq. (9.23) to derive the ML estimators $\hat{\Lambda}_{\text{ML}} \equiv (\hat{\gamma}_{\text{ML}}, \hat{\rho}_{\text{ML}}, \hat{\sigma}_{\text{ML}})^T$. We obtain the asymptotically efficient covariance matrix of the estimators as $(\frac{1}{T}\sum_{t=1}^{T}\frac{\partial \ln L}{\partial \Lambda}\frac{\partial \ln L}{\partial \Lambda^T})^{-1} = I_1(\Theta)^{-1}$. We can then apply the asymptotic likelihood ratio test discussed in Section 9.4, $T(\hat{\Lambda}_{\text{ML}} - \Theta)^T I_1(\Theta)(\hat{\Lambda}_{\text{ML}} - \Theta) \sim \chi_3^2$ where the null hypothesis is $H_0 : \Lambda = \Theta$.

9.7.2 Volatility Clustering and Exchange Margin Setting

Trades at Futures and Options Exchanges are transacted at a fraction of the contract price due to leverage. A daily margin account for the trade is required to be maintained at the Exchange so that if the derivative price should change to the detriment of the trader, the deposit in his/her margin account could be withdrawn to cover the mark-to-market loss before the Exchange is able to enforce the trader to put more money

5 For a more general framework, see Lars Peter Hansen and Kenneth J. Singleton (1983), Stochastic consumption, risk aversion, and the temporal behavior of asset returns, *Journal of Political Economy*, 91(2), 249–265.

into the margin account. Hence Exchanges would on a daily basis, or sometimes on a more frequent basis if the market is in turmoil, announce to traders the required margins for each type of derivative contract on a per contract basis. The margins are required for both long and short positions as losses could be incurred either way. The Standard Portfolio Analysis of Risk (SPAN) system developed by CME has been used by many exchanges worldwide to perform their daily margin computations. The SPAN system basically lists an array of margin numbers dependent on scenarios of next day price level or volatility changes.

However, the SPAN estimates may not explicitly take into account the intraday derivative price change patterns nor take into account observable situation variables specific to the local bourse such as trading volumes or frequencies of trades. Since there is plenty of evidence of volatility clustering and contagion effects when market prices moved violently over a prolonged period of several days, modelling volatility as a dynamic process such as in GARCH (including ARCH) is useful for the purpose of estimating risk and developing margins for risk control at the Exchange. Econometric methods such as MLE can then be used to estimate the parameters driving the GARCH process. These estimates can then be used to forecast the volatility for the next day in order to fix the margins.[6]

The optimal setting of margins is closely related to the concept of Value-at-Risk (VaR).[7] Given a historical time series of daily futures price $\{F_t\}$ and its changes $\{\Delta F_t\}$, the probability density function of the daily futures "return" or rate of change may be assumed to be normal, so $\Delta F_{t+1}/F_t \sim N(0, \sigma_{t+1}^2)$, and is depicted as follows in Figure 9.5.

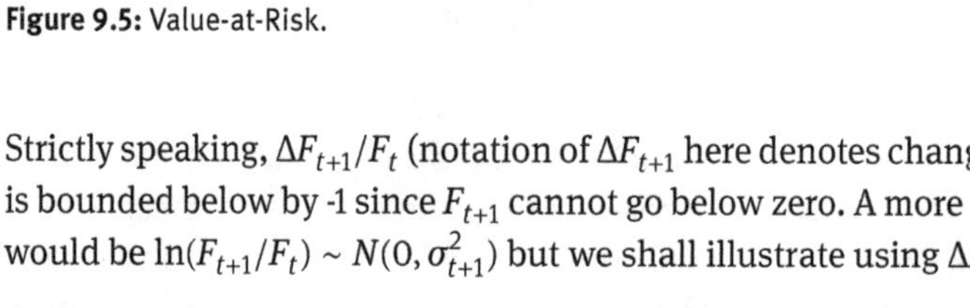

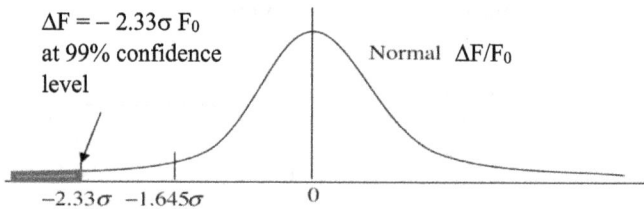

Figure 9.5: Value-at-Risk.

Strictly speaking, $\Delta F_{t+1}/F_t$ (notation of ΔF_{t+1} here denotes change starting at F_t to F_{t+1}) is bounded below by -1 since F_{t+1} cannot go below zero. A more stringent specification would be $\ln(F_{t+1}/F_t) \sim N(0, \sigma_{t+1}^2)$ but we shall illustrate using $\Delta F_{t+1}/F_t$.

6 Perhaps one of the earliest applications of GARCH technology to Exchange risk margin setting could be found in Kian Guan Lim (1996), Weekly volatility study of SIMEX Nikkei 225 futures contracts using GARCH methodology, Technical Report, Singapore: SIMEX, December, 15 pp.

7 See J. Philippe, (2007), *Value at Risk*, Third edition, McGraw-Hill.

In Figure 9.5, the futures price at end of the previous trading day close is F_0. The uncertain or random next day price is F_1. The change is $\Delta F_1 = F_1 - F_0$ which we more conveniently denote as ΔF.

For a normal distribution $\Delta F/F_0$, there is 1 % probability or chance that $\Delta F/F_0 < -2.33\sigma_1$ where σ_1 denoted by σ is anticipated volatility of next day futures "return". See shaded area in Figure 9.5. At 99 % confidence level (or 99 % probability), loss $\Delta F = F_1 - F_0$ would be at most $-2.33\sigma F_0$. This is the daily Value-at-Risk or VaR that is the maximum loss given the 99 % confidence level. The specified confidence level is important, as higher confidence levels would imply possibly larger losses.[8]

Suppose for the following day, $\Delta F/F_0 \sim N(0, \sigma^2)$, and volatility is forecast as $\hat{\sigma}$ in order to estimate the VaR of a long N225 futures contract position. Daily VaR at 99 % confidence level is such that $\text{Prob}(F_1 - F_0 < -2.33\hat{\sigma}F_0) = 1\%$ or $\text{Prob}(F_1 - F_0 \geq -2.33\hat{\sigma}F_0) = 99\%$. The VaR is $2.33\hat{\sigma}F_0$, assuming F_t index is denominated in \$. Note VaR defines loss as a positive term.

Each day t before the next trading day $t + 1$, an Exchange has to decide the level of maintenance margin per contract, $\$x_t$, so that within the next day, chances of the Exchange taking risk of a loss before top-up by the trader, i. e. when event $\{F_{t+1} - F_t < -x_t\}$ or loss exceeding maintenance margin happens, is 1 % or less. Then, x_t is set by the Exchange to be large enough, i. e. set $x_t \geq 2.33\hat{\sigma}_{t+1}F_t$.

Thus at t, forecasting or estimating σ_{t+1} is an important task for setting Exchange maintenance margin for the following day $t+1$. We can model the conditional variance of daily rates of the futures price change $\Delta F_{t+1}/F_t$ as a GARCH(1, 1) process. Assume $E[\Delta F_{t+1}/F_t] = 0$ over a day.

Let $\Delta F_{t+1}/F_t = u_{t+1}$, $u_{t+1} = e_{t+1}\sigma_{t+1}$, and

$$\sigma_{t+1}^2 = \alpha_0 + \alpha_1 u_t^2 + \gamma_1 \sigma_t^2$$

where $e_{t+1} \sim N(0, 1)$. We estimate the parameters $\{\alpha_0, \alpha_1, \gamma_1\}$ using the MLE method for GARCH(1, 1) in Section 9.6.2, and then use them to forecast the following day's volatility $\text{var}(u_{t+1})$ or σ_{t+1}^2 given observed u_t, u_{t-1}, u_{t-2}, and so on.

Further Reading

Campbell, J. Y., Lo, A. W. and A. C. MacKinlay (1997), *The Econometrics of Financial Markets*, Princeton University Press.

Tsay, R. S. (2010), *Analysis of Financial Time Series*, Third edition, John Wiley & Sons.

8 For related bank risk control, it is usual to estimate daily 95 %, 97.5 %, or 99 % confidence level value-at-risk, sometimes doing this several times in a day or at least at the close of the trading day. Sometimes a 10-day 95 % confidence level VaR is also used.

10 Unit Roots and Cointegration

In this chapter, we introduce the important topic of non-stationary process and highlight a major area of econometric research in the last three decades or more on non-stationary process and cointegration. This research has been important in shedding light on some spurious regression results if the underlying process dynamics is not properly understood or investigated. As an application example, we consider purchasing power parity that is one of the tools of determining long-run exchange rate levels.

10.1 Non-Stationary Process

We already have some ideas about stationary stochastic processes in Chapter 5. A random variable that is at least weakly stationary will have constant unconditional mean and unconditional variance as it moves through time. This means that any deviation from some mean level is a just a random draw and has no permanent consequence. If a rate of return goes up this period, at some point in the near enough future, it will come down. This is unlike prices where the price level can continue to increase or decrease without sign of reverting back to old levels. It is in this context that we consider non-stationary processes, especially in relation to security price levels, index levels, commodity prices, and so on.

Consider the process $Y_t = \theta + \lambda Y_{t-1} + \varepsilon_t, \theta \neq 0$, where ε_t is a covariance-stationary process, i. e. $E(\varepsilon_t) = 0$ and $\text{var}(\varepsilon_t) = \sigma_\varepsilon^2$, a constant. $\text{cov}(\varepsilon_t, \varepsilon_{t-k})$ is not necessarily zero for any $k \neq 0$, but is a function of k only. However, as in Chapter 8, for sample moments to converge to population moments, we require ergodicity of ε_t in addition to stationarity. Stronger conditions would be zero autocorrelated identically distributed ε_t (weak-form white noise). Even stronger condition would be that ε_t is i. i. d. Further, $\text{cov}(Y_{t-1}, \varepsilon_t) = 0$. Y_t is covariance stationary provided $|\lambda| < 1$. However, if $\lambda = 1$, then in this case,

$$Y_t = \theta + Y_{t-1} + \varepsilon_t \tag{10.1}$$

Or $(1 - B)Y_t = \theta + \varepsilon_t$, so $(1 - B) = 0$ yields a unit root solution. Thus, Y_t is said to contain a unit root and $\{Y_t\}$ is called a unit root or $I(1)$ process. It is also called a difference stationary process since ΔY_t is stationary with a general stationary noise that needs not be i.i.d but which should have ergodicity. Some literature defines unit root process such that ε_t is i. i. d. (We term this latter case as strong-form white noise.) Independence in ε_t no doubt buys much convenience as the convergence of the sample mean of i. i. d. zero mean RVs to zero is quicker and does not need qualifying conditions on stationarity and ergodicity in time series. In the special case if ε_t is i. i. d. and also if $\theta = 0$, then Y_t is also called a random walk process.

https://doi.org/10.1515/9783110673951-010

For the general stationary-ergodic ε_t, by repeated substitution in Eq. (10.1):

$$\begin{aligned} Y_t &= \theta + (\theta + Y_{t-2} + \varepsilon_{t-1}) + \varepsilon_t \\ &= 2\theta + (\theta + Y_{t-3} + \varepsilon_{t-2}) + \varepsilon_t + \varepsilon_{t-1} \\ &\vdots \\ &= t\theta + Y_0 + \varepsilon_t + \varepsilon_{t-1} + \varepsilon_{t-2} + \cdots + \varepsilon_2 + \varepsilon_1 \end{aligned}$$

Thus, we see that a unit root process in Y_t leads to Y_t having a time trend $t\theta$ as well as a stochastic trend $\sum_{j=0}^{t-1} \varepsilon_{t-j}$. Note that for the unit root process in Y_t, its starting value Y_0 is still a random variable, although Y_0's variance may be very small. Clearly, if

$$\begin{aligned} & E(Y_0) = \mu_0, \\ \text{and} \quad & \operatorname{var}(Y_0) = \sigma_0^2, \\ \text{then} \quad & E(Y_t) = \mu_0 + t\theta \neq \mu_0 \end{aligned}$$

provided $\theta \neq 0$.

Hence, the mean of Y_t increases (decreases) with time according to drift $\theta > (<) 0$. Also,

$$\operatorname{var}(Y_t) = \sigma_0^2 + \operatorname{var}\left[\sum_{j=0}^{t-1} \varepsilon_{t-j}\right] \neq \sigma_0^2$$

The variance of Y_t changes due to the presence of a stochastic trend in the unit root process. For stationary-ergodic ε_t (also, the less general case of ε_t being white noise), $\operatorname{var}(Y_t)$ is increasing in t. Therefore, $\{Y_t\}$ is not covariance-stationary, or we shall simply call it non-stationary.

Suppose RV Y_t is trend stationary, i. e. stationary about a deterministic time trend. By definition, a trend stationary process , unlike a unit root process, does not have a stochastic trend, and thus does not display changing variance over time, although its mean $t\theta$ does change over time. The unit root process, however, possesses both a time trend as in the trend stationary process, and also an additional stochastic trend. The following is a trend stationary process fluctuating randomly about the deterministic trend $\delta + t\theta$.

$$Y_t = t\theta + \delta + \eta_t \tag{10.2}$$

where t is time, θ and δ are constants, and η_t is a stationary-ergodic RV with zero mean. $\operatorname{var}(Y_t) = \operatorname{var}(\eta_t) = \sigma_\eta^2$.

Then

$$Y_{t-1} = (t-1)\theta + \delta + \eta_{t-1}$$

and so

$$\Delta Y_t = Y_t - Y_{t-1} = \theta + \Delta\eta_t$$

where we apply the notation ΔY_t to denote change of Y_t from Y_{t-1}. This notation is different from the notion of infinitesimal change dY_{t-1} at $t - 1$.

Thus

$$Y_t = Y_{t-1} + \theta + \Delta\eta_t \tag{10.3}$$

where $\text{var}(\Delta\eta_t) = \text{var}(\eta_t - \eta_{t-1})$. The latter is $2\sigma_\eta^2$ if we had assumed η_t is i. i. d.

Equation (10.3) may look like the unit root process in Eq. (10.1). However, it is really not so[1] because the stationary noise term $\Delta\eta_t$ carries a special structure (thus, we do not call this a difference stationary process). If we iterate the process through time,

$$\begin{aligned} Y_t &= \theta + (\theta + Y_{t-2} + \Delta\eta_{t-1}) + \Delta\eta_t \\ &= 2\theta + (\theta + Y_{t-3} + \Delta\eta_{t-2}) + \Delta\eta_{t-1} + \Delta\eta_t \\ &\vdots \\ &= t\theta + Y_0 + \Delta\eta_1 + \Delta\eta_2 + \cdots + \Delta\eta_{t-2} + \Delta\eta_{t-1} + \Delta\eta_t \\ &= t\theta + Y_0 + \eta_t - \eta_0 \end{aligned}$$

where $\text{var}(\eta_t - \eta_0) = 2\sigma_\eta^2$ if η_t is i. i. d. Otherwise this quantity would be finite, that is different from the infinitely increasing variance of the stochastic trend in a unit root process.

Here, we may treat the starting value $Y_0 - \eta_0$ as the constant δ. We thus see that for a trend stationary process, the variance of Y_t stays the same even as t increases for i. i. d. η_t. There is no stochastic trend, and the variance of Y_t does not change through time for i. i. d. η_t. The big difference is that the noise at the end of a trend stationary process in Eq. (10.3) $\Delta\eta_t$ does not add up variance as fast as the noise in a unit root process ε_t.

Let us recall. A unit root process as in Eq. (10.1) contains a deterministic time trend plus a stochastic trend. In the special case when $\theta = 0$ in Eq. (10.1), then the unit root process does not have a time trend. The unit root process has increasing variances over time. A process with just deterministic time trend plus a stationary noise, but not a stochastic trend, is called a trend stationary process. Both a trend stationary process and a unit root process can display similar increasing trend (expected values or means) if $\theta > 0$, but the unit root process will display increasing volatility over time

1 One of the earliest and exciting papers to point out this difference is C. Nelson and C. Plosser (1982), Trends and random walks in macroeconomic time series: Some evidence and implications, *Journal of Monetary Economics*, 10, 130–162.

relative to the trend stationary process. This distinction is important to differentiate the two.

More generally, Eq. (10.1) can be represented by ARIMA$(p, 1, q)$ where p and q need not be zero for a unit root process. More general unit root processes or integrated order d processes can be modeled by ARIMA(p, d, q), for $d > 1$.

In Fig. 10.1, we show how the three different processes: a stationary process, a trend stationary process, and a unit root process, would have looked like. Clearly the unit root process can produce large deviations away from the mean.

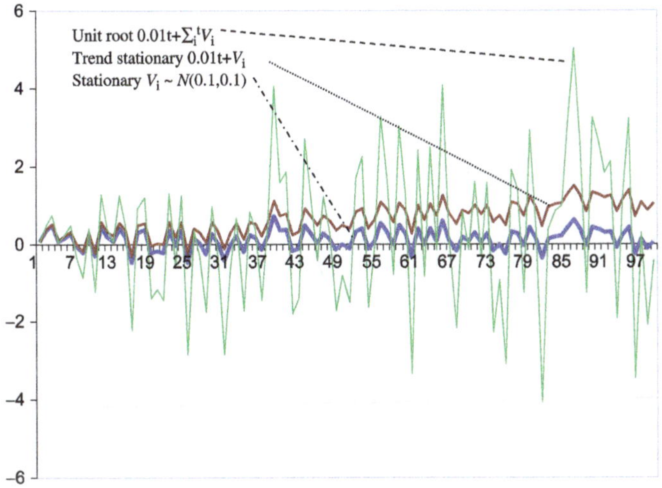

Figure 10.1: Time Series Graphs of Stochastic Processes.

10.2 Spurious Regression

Suppose

$$Y_t = \theta + Y_{t-1} + e_t, \quad e_t \sim \text{stationary-ergodic with mean 0}$$
$$Z_t = \mu + Z_{t-1} + u_t, \quad u_t \sim \text{stationary-ergodic with mean 0}$$

and e_t and u_t are independent of each other. They are also not correlated with Y_{t-1} and Z_{t-1}. $\{Y_t\}$ and $\{Z_t\}$ are unit root processes with drifts θ and μ, respectively. Then,

$$Y_t = t\theta + Y_0 + (e_t + e_{t-1} + \cdots + e_1)$$
$$Z_t = t\mu + Z_0 + (u_t + u_{t-1} + \cdots + u_1)$$

showing their deterministic as well as stochastic trends. Let Y_0 and Z_0 be independent. Then,

$$\text{cov}(Y_t, Z_t) = \text{cov}(Y_0, Z_0) + \text{cov}\left(\sum_{j=1}^{t} e_j, \sum_{k=1}^{t} u_k\right) = 0$$

since $\{e_t\}$ and $\{u_t\}$ are stochastically independent.

Now, Y_t and Z_t are independent. Suppose we set up a linear regression of Y_t on Z_t, with

$$Y_t = a + bZ_t + \eta_t \tag{10.4}$$

η_t is independent of Z_t, and is itself a unit root process, i. e.,

$$\eta_t = \eta_{t-1} + \epsilon_t$$

with stationary-ergodic ϵ_t, $E(\epsilon_t) = 0$, and $\text{var}(\epsilon_t) < \infty$.

Since $\text{cov}(Y_t, Z_t) = 0$, the slope $b = \text{cov}(Y_t, Z_t)/\text{var}(Z_t) = 0$. However, if we expand the regression into its time trend and additive stochastic component, we obtain:

$$t\theta + Y_0 + \sum_{j=0}^{t-1} e_{t-j} = a + b\left(t\mu + Z_0 + \sum_{j=0}^{t-1} u_{t-j}\right) + \left(\eta_0 + \sum_{j=0}^{t-1} \epsilon_{t-j}\right)$$

Divide through by t

$$\theta + \frac{Y_0}{t} + \frac{1}{t}\sum_{j=0}^{t-1} e_{t-j} = \frac{a}{t} + b\mu + \frac{bZ_0}{t} + b\frac{1}{t}\sum_{j=0}^{t-1} u_{t-j} + \frac{\eta_0}{t} + \frac{1}{t}\sum_{j=0}^{t-1} \epsilon_{t-j}$$

Now $\text{var}(Y_0/t)$, $\text{var}(Z_0/t)$, and $\text{var}(\eta_0/t)$ all converge to zero as $t \uparrow \infty$. Thus, as $t \uparrow \infty$, the terms Y_0/t, Z_0/t, and η_0/t should approach zero in mean square sense.

As t increases, the time-averages of the noise terms in e_t, u_t, and ϵ_t also converge to zeros via some version of the law of large numbers due to their stationarity and ergodicity. If these residual errors are (weak-form) white noises, then the weak law of large numbers explained in Chapter 5 implies they would converge to zero in probability. If these residual errors are i. i. d. or strong-form white noises, then the strong law of large numbers explained in Chapter 5 implies they would converge to zero almost surely. We are then left with the following.

$$\theta \approx b\mu, \quad \text{so} \quad b \approx \frac{\theta}{\mu} \neq 0$$

Hence, the regression in Eq. (10.4) between two independent unit root processes produces a slope coefficient b that is non-zero! This is what is termed a spurious[2] (seemingly true yet false) regression result: $b \neq 0$ is obtained when theoretically $b = 0$.

---

2 The spurious regression problem was pointed out in C. W. J. Granger and P. Newbold (1974), Spurious Regressions in Econometrics, *Journal of Econometrics* 2, 111–120.

More specifically, regression method such as OLS, will provide a non-zero estimate of b that is spurious. The point to note is that when we perform OLS regression of a unit root process on another independent unit root process, instead of obtaining the expected zero slope, we are likely to end up with a spurious non-zero slope estimate. In other words, under OLS, the sampling estimate of $\text{cov}(Y_t, Z_t)$ will be spurious and not zero because Y_t and Z_t are unit root processes.

Only when we perform the OLS regression using stationary first differences, i. e.,

$$\Delta Y_t = \theta + e_t \quad \text{on} \quad \Delta Z_t = \mu + u_t$$

or

$$\Delta Y_t = a + b\Delta Z_t + \xi_t$$

where ξ_t is stationary-ergodic, then $b = \text{cov}(e_t, u_t)/\text{var}(u_t) = 0$. Thus, we obtain OLS estimator $\hat{b}$ that converges to $b = 0$.

Spurious regression also occurs to Y_t and Z_t if they are trend stationary instead of being unit root processes. Consider

$$Y_t = t\theta + \delta + \eta_t$$
$$Z_t = t\mu + \gamma + \xi_t$$

where η_t and ξ_t are mean zero stationary-ergodic RVs. We can also assume they are white noises. The noises η_t and ξ_t have zero correlation.

Even though Y_t and Z_t are not correlated,

$$\begin{aligned} Y_t &= \delta + \theta\left[\frac{Z_t - \gamma - \xi_t}{\mu}\right] + \eta_t \\ &= \left(\delta - \frac{\theta\gamma}{\mu}\right) + \frac{\theta}{\mu}Z_t + \left(\eta_t - \frac{\theta}{\mu}\xi_t\right) \end{aligned}$$

So, OLS regression of Y_t on Z_t will give a spurious estimate of $\theta/\mu \neq 0$.

It suggests that the spurious non-zero correlation between Y_t and Z_t (even when they are independent processes) comes from their deterministic trend, not the stochastic trend.

Suppose

$$Z_t = \mu + Z_{t-1} + u_t, \quad u_t \sim \text{i. i. d. with mean 0}$$
$$w_t = \gamma + w_{t-1} + \xi_t, \quad \xi_t \sim \text{i. i. d. with mean 0}$$

are independent unit root processes. Then, in general, a linear combination of the unit root processes Z_t and w_t, Y_t, is also a unit root process as shown below.

$$\begin{aligned} Y_t &= c + dZ_t + w_t \\ &= (c + \gamma) + d\mu + dZ_{t-1} + du_t + w_{t-1} + \xi_t \\ &= (\gamma + d\mu) + Y_{t-1} + (du_t + \xi_t) \end{aligned}$$

is also a unit root process where $c, d \neq 0$. Here, Y_t is correlated with Z_t due to Y_t being a linear combination involving Z_t.

If we perform OLS on $Y_t = c + dZ_t + w_t, d \neq 0$, the effects are as follows. The OLS estimate of d will involve $\text{cov}(Y_t, Z_t) = \text{cov}(c + dZ_t + w_t, Z_t) = d\,\text{var}(Z_t) + \text{cov}(c + w_t, Z_t)$. But the latter is a covariance of two independent unit root processes each with a deterministic trend (and a stochastic trend as well), that produces spurious sampling estimate that is not zero. Thus, the sampling estimate of $\text{cov}(Y_t, Z_t)$ under OLS will also be spurious regardless of the value of d.

At this point, we can almost see when OLS on two related unit root processes such as Y_t and Z_t can or cannot be feasible. It has to do with the covariance of the explanatory variable and the residual variable, $\text{cov}(w_t, Z_t)$. If both the latter are unit root processes, then there is spuriousness.

In summary, suppose unit root processes Y_t and Z_t are truly related as follows: $Y_t = c + dZ_t + w_t$, where disturbance w_t has a unit root and is not correlated with Z_t. Then, it will not be appropriate to perform OLS of Y_t on Z_t since w_t is not stationary. The OLS result will be spurious.

Suppose instead, w_t is a stationary process, and not a unit root process, independent of Z_t. Then, the sample estimate of $\text{cov}(w_t, Z_t) = 0$. This can be seen as follows.

$$\text{cov}(w_t, t\mu + Z_0 + u_t + u_{t-1} + \cdots + u_1) = 0$$

since w_t is independent of Z_0 and all u_t's. In this case, the OLS estimate of d converges correctly to $\text{cov}(Y_t, Z_t)/\,\text{var}(Z_t)$. In the latter, the regression is not spurious only if the disturbance is stationary and not a unit root process. We shall consider this more closely later on the topic of cointegration.

10.3 Unit Root Test

When a time series or stochastic process in time is to be tested for a unit root, the test statistic based on the null hypothesis of unit root can have a more general unit root process as follows. This is on the more general modeling of the residual noise.

Suppose

$$Y_t = Y_{t-1} + \varepsilon_t, \quad \varepsilon_t \sim \text{stationary} \tag{10.5}$$

and ε_t is modeled as AR(k) in ΔY_t

$$\varepsilon_t = \beta_1 \Delta Y_{t-1} + \beta_2 \Delta Y_{t-2} + \cdots + \beta_k \Delta Y_{t-k} + e_t$$

where e_t is i. i. d. The first difference $\Delta Y_t \equiv Y_t - Y_{t-1} = \varepsilon_t$ is stationary. In this case, Y_t is said to be Integrated order 1 or $I(1)$ process with zero drift. The first difference ΔY_t is integrated order 0 or $I(0)$ process and is stationary.

Suppose

$$Y_t = \delta + Y_{t-1} + \varepsilon_t, \quad \varepsilon_t \sim \text{stationary} \tag{10.6}$$

and ε_t is modeled as AR(k) in ΔY_t

$$\varepsilon_t = \beta_1 \Delta Y_{t-1} + \beta_2 \Delta Y_{t-2} + \cdots + \beta_k \Delta Y_{t-k} + e_t$$

where e_t is i. i. d. Then first difference $\Delta Y_t \equiv Y_t - Y_{t-1} = \delta + \varepsilon_t$ is stationary. In this case, Y_t is said to be $I(1)$ process with drift $\delta \neq 0$.

Suppose

$$Y_t = \delta + \theta t + Y_{t-1} + \varepsilon_t, \quad \varepsilon_t \sim \text{stationary} \tag{10.7}$$

and ε_t is modeled as AR(k) in ΔY_t

$$\varepsilon_t = \beta_1 \Delta Y_{t-1} + \beta_2 \Delta Y_{t-2} + \cdots + \beta_k \Delta Y_{t-k} + e_t$$

where e_t is i. i. d. Then first difference $\Delta Y_t = \delta + \theta t + \varepsilon_t$ is trend-stationary. In this case, Y_t is said to be $I(1)$ process with drift $\delta \neq 0$ and trend slope $\theta \neq 0$.

The above Eqs. (10.5), (10.6), (10.7) are all unit root processes. The alternative hypothesized stationary autoregressive processes are, respectively,

$$Y_t = \lambda Y_{t-1} + \varepsilon_t \quad (|\lambda| < 1) \tag{10.8}$$

$$Y_t = \delta + \lambda Y_{t-1} + \varepsilon_t \quad (|\lambda| < 1) \tag{10.9}$$

$$Y_t = \delta + \theta t + \lambda Y_{t-1} + \varepsilon_t \quad (|\lambda| < 1) \tag{10.10}$$

How do we test for unit root processes (10.5), (10.6), or (10.7)? Using the alternative specifications in Eqs. (10.8), (10.9), and (10.10), we can write:

$$\Delta Y_t = \gamma Y_{t-1} + \varepsilon_t \tag{10.11}$$

$$\Delta Y_t = \delta + \gamma Y_{t-1} + \varepsilon_t \tag{10.12}$$

$$\Delta Y_t = \delta + \theta t + \gamma Y_{t-1} + \varepsilon_t \tag{10.13}$$

where $\gamma = \lambda - 1$. For $I(1)$ processes in Eqs. (10.5), (10.6), and (10.7), however, $\gamma \equiv (\lambda - 1) = 0$. Thus, we can test the null hypothesis of a unit root process by testing $H_0 : \gamma = 0$. The alternative hypothesis is that the process is stationary, i. e. $H_A : \gamma < 0$. The theory of unit root testing is more popularly developed for the case of unit root null versus stationary alternative. The case of testing null of stationarity (level stationary or more generally trend stationary) against the alternative of a unit root can be found in KPSS tests.[3]

In practice, before any test is carried out, specifications (10.11), (10.12), or (10.13) are generalized to include lags of ΔY_t so that stationary-ergodic ε_t is pre-whitened to leave a residual error e_t that is mean zero i. i. d. or strong-form white noise. We can use Akaike Information Criterion (AIC) to choose the number of lags k. More rigorously, we also follow up to apply Ljung–Box test to ensure the remaining error is serially uncorrelated. (If the error is asymptotically normal, then this also implies independence or i. i. d. e_t.)

Equations (10.11), (10.12), and (10.13) in general can then be expressed as:

$$\Delta Y_t = \gamma Y_{t-1} + \beta_1 \Delta Y_{t-1} + \beta_2 \Delta Y_{t-2} + \cdots + \beta_k \Delta Y_{t-k} + e_t \tag{10.14}$$

(no constant)

$$\Delta Y_t = \delta + \gamma Y_{t-1} + \sum_{j=1}^{k} \beta_j \Delta Y_{t-j} + e_t \tag{10.15}$$

(there is constant)

$$\Delta Y_t = \delta + \theta t + \gamma Y_{t-1} + \sum_{j=1}^{k} \beta_j \Delta Y_{t-j} + e_t \tag{10.16}$$

(there is constant and time trend) where e_t is i. i. d.

To test if Eq. (10.14), (10.15), or (10.16) contains a unit root, i. e., Y_t is a unit root process, we can run OLS on Eq. (10.14), (10.15), or (10.16) for some k. If $\hat{\gamma}$ is significantly < 0, then we reject H_0 of unit root. If not, then there is evidence of a unit root process. Tests using the specifications with lagged ΔY_t as explanatory variables for pre-whitening are also called Augmented Dickey-Fuller (ADF) tests.

Next, we compute

$$X = \frac{\hat{\gamma}_{\text{OLS}}}{\text{OLS s. e. } (\hat{\gamma}_{\text{OLS}})}$$

This is the usual formula for t-value function, but in this case, it is not distributed as Student's t_{T-n} statistic where T is the sample size and n is the number of parameters, i. e. $n = k+1$ for Eq. (10.14), $n = k+2$ for Eq. (10.15), and $n = k+3$ for Eq. (10.16). It is a nonstandard nondegenerate distribution. The other parameters of constant and slope may occur in the computation of the distribution but are themselves not of interest; they are sometimes termed nuisance parameters .

3 See D. Kwiatkowski, P. C. B. Phillips, P. Schmidt, and Y. Shin (1992), Testing the null hypothesis of stationarity against the alternative of a unit root, *Journal of Econometrics*, 54, 159–178.

Table 10.1: Critical Values for Dickey-Fuller t-Test.

	Sample Size	p-Values (probability of a smaller test value)			
	T	0.01	0.025	0.05	0.10
Case: No constant	25	−2.65	−2.26	−1.95	−1.60
Eq. (10.14)	50	−2.62	−2.25	−1.95	−1.61
	100	−2.60	−2.24	−1.95	−1.61
	250	−2.58	−2.24	−1.95	−1.62
	500	−2.58	−2.23	−1.95	−1.62
	∞	−2.58	−2.23	−1.95	−1.62
Case: Constant	25	−3.75	−3.33	−2.99	−2.64
Eq. (10.15)	50	−3.59	−3.23	−2.93	−2.60
	100	−3.50	−3.17	−2.90	−2.59
	250	−3.45	−3.14	−2.88	−2.58
	500	−3.44	−3.13	−2.87	−2.57
	∞	−3.42	−3.12	−2.86	−2.57
Case: Constant and	25	−4.38	−3.95	−3.60	−3.24
time trend	50	−4.16	−3.80	−3.50	−3.18
Eq. (10.16)	100	−4.05	−3.73	−3.45	−3.15
	250	−3.98	−3.69	−3.42	−3.13
	500	−3.97	−3.67	−3.42	−3.13
	∞	−3.96	−3.67	−3.41	−3.13

Source: W. Fuller, "Introduction to Statistical Time Series," Second edition, New York: Wiley, 1996.

For a correctly specified k in Eq. (10.14), (10.15), or (10.16), the finite probability distribution of the x-statistic (independent of k) is found by simulations. This is reported in studies by Dickey and Fuller.[4] For some sample sizes, e. g., $T = 25, 50, 100, 250, 500$ etc., the critical values of x at probability levels 1 %, 2.5 %, 5 %, 10 % etc., i. e., $P(x \leq$ critical value$)$ = probability levels, are reported in tables.[5] We therefore use the updated Dickey-Fuller (DF) critical values for inference to test the null hypothesis (Table 10.1).

From the Dickey-Fuller table, if sample size $T = 250$, and the computed x– statistic in the case of no constant is less than the critical value of −2.58, then we can reject $H_0 : \gamma = 0$ (or $\lambda = 1$), i. e., there is no unit root at 1 % significance level. From the Dickey-Fuller table, if sample size $T = 250$, and the computed x– statistic in the case of a constant is less than the critical value of −2.88 but greater than −3.14, then we can

4 See D. Dickey (1976), Estimation and Hypothesis Testing in Nonstationary Time Series, PhD Dissertation, Iowa State University and W. Fuller (1976), *Introduction to Statistical Time Series*, New York: Wiley. See also an early but important paper on such statistics, D. Dickey and W. Fuller (1979), Distribution of the estimators for autoregressive time series with a unit root, *Journal of the American Statistical Association*, 74, 427–431.

5 See also updated distribution table in W. Fuller (1996), *Introduction to Statistical Time Series*, Second Edition, New York: Wiley.

reject $H_0 : \gamma = 0$ (or $\lambda = 1$), i. e., there is no unit root at 5 % significance level but cannot reject at 2.5 % significance level. From the Dickey-Fuller table, if sample size $T = 250$, and the computed $x-$ statistic in the case of constant and time trend is between −3.42 and −3.13, then we cannot reject $H_0 : \gamma = 0$ (or $\lambda = 1$), i. e., cannot reject null of unit root at 5 % significance level. It is seen that the more negative is the $x-$ test statistic for $\hat{\gamma}_{\mathrm{OLS}}$, the higher is the probability that the alternative of stationarity is correct.

As another check on whether a process is a unit root process, the autocorrelation function (ACF) of the process is computed. A unit root process will typically show a highly persistent ACF, i. e., one where autocorrelation decays very slowly with increase in the lags.

10.4 Test-Statistic Distribution

Details of the unit root test statistic distribution are beyond the scope of this book, but a sketch of the theory is provided here.[6]

Suppose we ignore the augmentation by lagged ΔY_{t-j}'s and consider that the true data generating process (DGP) of Y_t consistent with a unit root process is as follows.

$$Y_t = e_t + e_{t-1} + e_{t-2} + \cdots + e_2 + e_1 + Y_0 \tag{10.17}$$

where we fix $Y_0 \equiv 0$. Then $E(Y_t) = 0, \forall t$. This DGP implies the regression equation

$$Y_t = Y_{t-1} + e_t$$

which is the no constant case in Eq. (10.5). This can be re-expressed as

$$\Delta Y_t = \gamma Y_{t-1} + e_t \tag{10.18}$$

for the testable hypothesis of a unit root process under the null $H_0 : \gamma = 0$. This is similar to Eq. (10.11) except that the noise e_t is specialized to i. i. d.

OLS regression in Eq. (10.18) with no constant of regression yields

$$\hat{\gamma}_{\mathrm{OLS}} = \frac{\sum_{t=1}^{T} \Delta Y_t Y_{t-1}}{\sum_{t=1}^{T} Y_{t-1}^2}$$

Under the DGP and null hypothesis of unit root process, $H_0 : \gamma = 0$, Eq. (10.17) shows that $\Delta Y_t = e_t$ is an $I(0)$, specifically an i. i. d. process. In the DGP in Eq. (10.17), $Y_{t-1} =$

6 For advanced reading, one can consult P. C. B. Phillips (1987), Time series regression with a unit root, *Econometrica*, 55, 227–301, P. C. B. Phillips (2002), New unit root asymptotics in the presence of deterministic trends, *Journal of Econometrics* 111, 323–353, and P. C. B. Phillips and S. Durlauf (1986), Multiple time series regression with integrated processes, *Review of Economic Studies*, 53, 473–496.

$\sum_{t=1}^{t-1} e_t = Z_{t-1}$, an $I(1)$ process without drift or a stochastic trend. Under H_0, the OLS estimate can be written as

$$\hat{\gamma}_{\text{OLS}} = \frac{\sum_{t=1}^{T} e_t Z_{t-1}}{\sum_{t=1}^{T} Z_{t-1}^2}$$

It can be shown that $T^{-1}\sum_{t=1}^{T} e_t Z_{t-1}$ converges in distribution to $\frac{1}{2}\sigma_e^2(W(1)^2-1)$, and $T^{-2}\sum_{t=1}^{T} Z_{t-1}^2 \xrightarrow{d} \sigma_e^2 \int_0^1 W(r)^2 dr$ where $W(r)$ is Wiener process or Brownian motion such that $W(r) \sim N(0,r)$ for r within the unit interval.

Hence,

$$T\hat{\gamma}_{\text{OLS}} \xrightarrow{d} \frac{\frac{1}{2}(W(1)^2 - 1)}{\int_0^1 W(r)^2 dr}$$

$T\hat{\gamma}_{\text{OLS}}$ converges to the nondegenerate distribution at rate T instead of the standard $\sqrt{T}$ in asymptotic theory. This also means $\hat{\gamma}_{\text{OLS}}$ converges under H_0 at a faster rate T than $\sqrt{T}$ since the variance of $\hat{\gamma}_{\text{OLS}}$ becomes smaller much faster as T increases.

The standard error of $\hat{\gamma}_{\text{OLS}}$ is $\sigma_e / \sqrt{\sum_{t=1}^{T} Y_{t-1}^2}$. Hence, the $x-$ statistic is

$$\frac{\sum_{t=1}^{T} e_t Z_{t-1}}{\sigma_e \sqrt{\sum_{t=1}^{T} Z_{t-1}^2}} \xrightarrow{d} \frac{\frac{1}{2}(W(1)^2 - 1)}{\sqrt{\int_0^1 W(r)^2 dr}}$$

The limiting distribution on the RHS can be numerically evaluated. For finite sample, the distribution of the x-statistic can also be found via Monte Carlo simulation. These form the Dickey-Fuller test statistic distributions.

For OLS regression $\Delta Y_t = \delta + \gamma Y_{t-1} + e_t$ similar to Eq. (10.12) except noise e_t is i. i. d., the limiting distribution of the x-statistic for $\hat{\gamma}_{\text{OLS}}$ is

$$\frac{\frac{1}{2}([W^{\mu}(1)]^2 - [W^{\mu}(0)]^2 - 1)}{\sqrt{\int_0^1 W^{\mu}(r)^2 dr}}$$

where $W^{\mu}(r) = W(r) - \int_0^1 W(r)\,dr$ is a de-meaned Wiener process, i. e. $\int_0^1 W^{\mu}(r)\,dr = 0$. Note that the asymptotic or limiting distribution in the case of a constant $\delta \neq 0$ is different from the case of no constant, but is itself not dependent on the value of δ that is a nuisance parameter here.

For OLS regression $\Delta Y_t = \delta + \theta t + \gamma Y_{t-1} + e_t$ similar to Eq. (10.13) except noise e_t is i. i. d., the limiting distribution of the x-statistic for $\hat{\gamma}_{\text{OLS}}$ is

$$\frac{\frac{1}{2}([W^{\tau}(1)]^2 - [W^{\tau}(0)]^2 - 1)}{\sqrt{\int_0^1 W^{\tau}(r)^2 dr}}$$

where $W^{\tau}(r) = W(r) - \int_0^1 (4-6s)W(s)ds - r\int_0^1 (12s-6)W(s)ds$ is a de-meaned and detrended Wiener process. Note that the asymptotic or limiting distribution in the case of a constants $\delta \neq 0, \theta \neq 0$ is different from the case of no constant and the case of a constant, but is itself not dependent on the value of δ and θ that are nuisance parameters here.

When we consider the cases of Eqs. (10.11), (10.12), and (10.13) with the more general ε_t that is AR(k) that can also be equivalent to an ARMA(p,q) process, the possibility of augmented testing arises. To show this, we make use of the Beveridge-Nelson decomposition[7] that provides a neat way of characterizing an $I(1)$ process.

Basically, the Beveridge-Nelson decomposition informs that a general $I(1)$ process with a stationary ARMA(p,q) noise may be represented equivalently as constant (or initial condition) plus a linear time-trend plus an $I(1)$ process, that is a zero drift stochastic trend, plus a stationary process η_t.

Suppose

$$Y_t = Y_{t-1} + f(t) + u_t \tag{10.19}$$

where u_t is ARMA(p,q), i. e., not a white noise, and $f(t)$ is a deterministic function of t that includes a constant. Let $u_t = \sum_{j=0}^{\infty} \psi_j \xi_{t-j}$ where ξ_t is i. i. d. (strong-form white noise) with mean zero and variance σ_{ξ}^2. Expanding series Y_t in Eq. (10.19), we obtain

$$Y_t = \sum_{t=1}^{t} f(t) + u_t + u_{t-1} + u_{t-2} + \cdots + u_1 + Y_0 \tag{10.20}$$

Assume Y_0 is given. Consider the sum of series

$$u_1 + u_2 + u_{t-2} + \cdots + u_t = \sum_{j=0}^{\infty} \psi_j \xi_{1-j} + \sum_{j=0}^{\infty} \psi_j \xi_{2-j} + \cdots + \sum_{j=0}^{\infty} \psi_j \xi_{t-j}$$

This sum can also be expressed as

$$\sum_{j=0}^{\infty} \psi_j(\xi_1 + \cdots + \xi_t) + \eta_t - \eta_0$$

where $\eta_t = \sum_{j=0}^{\infty} a_j \xi_{t-j}$ and $a_j = -(\psi_{j+1} + \psi_{j+2} + \cdots)$. Now to ensure η_t has finite variance, so that it is well defined in terms of $a_j \xi_k$'s, we require $\sum_{j=0}^{\infty} a_j^2 < \infty$. A sufficient condition is $\sum_{j=0}^{\infty} |a_j| < \infty$ since the latter implies

7 See S. Beveridge and C. R. Nelson (1981), A new approach to the decomposition of economic time series into permanent, and transitory components with particular attention to the measurement of the business cycle, *Journal of Monetary Economics*, 7, 151–174.

$$\left(\sum_{j=0}^{\infty}|a_j|\right)^2 < \infty \Longrightarrow \sum_{j=0}^{\infty}|a_j|^2 < \infty$$

η_t can also be expressed in terms of $\psi_j\xi_k$'s as $\sum_{j=0}^{\infty} -(\psi_{j+1} + \psi_{j+2} + \cdots)\xi_{t-j} = -\psi_1\xi_t - \psi_2(\xi_t + \xi_{t-1}) - \psi_3(\xi_t + \xi_{t-1} + \xi_{t-2}) + \cdots$. For finite variance of η_t, a sufficient condition is $\sum_{j=0}^{\infty} j|\psi_j| < \infty$.

Hence

$$u_1 + u_2 + u_{t-2} + \cdots + u_t = \sum_{j=0}^{\infty}\psi_j(\xi_1 + \cdots + \xi_t) + \eta_t - \eta_0 \tag{10.21}$$

Equation (10.21) can be verified by expanding the LHS and RHS in terms of $\psi_j\xi_k$'s and seeing that the expansions match.

Now let $Z_t = \sum_{j=0}^{\infty}\psi_j(\xi_1 + \cdots + \xi_t)$. We can see that

$$Z_t = Z_{t-1} + \left(\sum_{j=0}^{\infty}\psi_j\right)\xi_t \tag{10.22}$$

hence Z_t is an $I(1)$ process with zero drift and i. i. d. noise term $(\sum_{j=0}^{\infty}\psi_j)\xi_t$. Z_t is a zero drift stochastic trend.

Thus, Eq. (10.20) can be re-expressed as

$$Y_t = \sum_{t=1}^{t} f(t) + Z_t + \eta_t + (Y_0 - \eta_0) \tag{10.23}$$

where Z_t is $I(1)$ process with no drift (a stochastic trend), η_t is a stationary process, and $Y_0 - \eta_0$ may be interpreted as a constant.

A side result from Eq. (10.21) for a large sample size T is the characterization of Z_t.

$$\frac{1}{\sqrt{T}}\sum_{t=1}^{T}u_t = \left(\sum_{j=0}^{\infty}\psi_j\right)\frac{1}{\sqrt{T}}\sum_{t=1}^{T}\xi_t + \frac{1}{\sqrt{T}}(\eta_T - \eta_0)$$

On the RHS, the second term goes to zero since $\text{var}(\eta_T)$ is bounded. ξ_t is i. i. d. so the first term on the RHS converges via the Central Limit Theorem to $N(0, [\sigma_\xi \sum_{j=0}^{\infty}\psi_j]^2)$, i. e., in large sample, ΔZ_t behaves like a normally distributed RV. Let $\Psi = \sum_{j=0}^{\infty}\psi_j$ and $e_t = \Psi\xi_t$. Then (for large sample size T), it is reasonable to assume $Z_t = Z_{t-1} + e_t$ where $e_t \sim$ i. i. d. $N(0, \sigma_\xi^2\Psi^2)$. The asymptotic normal distribution for ΔZ_t would provide support for making simulations of e_t using the normal distribution for large sample.

Equation (10.23) is a general data generating process that implies

$$\Delta Y_t = f(t) + e_t + \Delta\eta_t$$

where we can let $\Delta\eta_t = \beta_1 \Delta Y_{t-1} + \beta_2 \Delta Y_{t-2} + \cdots + \beta_k \Delta Y_{t-k}$, and $f(t) = \delta + \theta t$. This is consistent with the use of Eqs. (10.14), (10.15), and (10.16) for testing the presence of unit root.

10.5 Purchasing Power Parity

Absolute purchasing power parity (PPP) version states that $P_t = e_t P_t^*$, where P_t is UK national price index in £, P_t^* is the U. S. national price index in USD, and e_t is spot exchange rate: number of £ per $.

$$\ln P_t = \ln e_t + \ln P_t^*$$
$$d\ln P_t = d\ln e_t + d\ln P_t^*$$
$$\frac{dP_t}{P_t} = \frac{de_t}{e_t} + \frac{dP_t^*}{P_t^*}$$

The Relative PPP version states that UK inflation rate is equal to the U. S. inflation rate adjusted by the rate of change in the spot rate e_t:

$$\frac{\Delta P_t}{P_t} = \frac{\Delta e_t}{e_t} + \frac{\Delta P_t^*}{P_t^*}$$

Thus, if U. S. inflation rate is 5 %, UK inflation rate is 10 %, both over horizon T years, then $\Delta e_t/e_t = 10\,\%–5\,\% = 5\,\%$, and $ is expected to appreciate by 5 % over £ over T years. e_t is the nominal exchange rate, exchanging e_t number of pounds for one US$. The real exchange rate or real £ per $ is the number of units of real good in the UK that can be obtained in exchange for one unit of the same real good purchased in the U. S. Here, the number of units of real goods purchased in the U. S. per US$ is $1/P_t^*$, supposing US$ per unit of good is P_t^*. The number of units of the same good that can be obtained in the UK by exchanging one US$ is e_t/P_t where we suppose the £ price per unit of good is P_t.

The real exchange rate (real £ per $) is $r_t = e_t P_t^*/P_t$. If the real exchange rate of $ is rising over time, then it means goods prices in the U. S. are becoming more expensive relative to the UK as more units of goods in the UK can be obtained in exchange for one same unit in the U. S. This can happen if nominal e_t increases, or if inflation in the U. S. rises relative to that in the UK. If the PPP holds exactly, then real exchange is 1. Some countries tend to keep their currency's real exchange rate low by own currency depreciation or deflating own goods' prices in order to be competitive in the export markets.

In log form, real exchange rate is

$$\ln r_t = \ln e_t + \ln P_t^* - \ln P_t = 0 \text{ under PPP} \tag{10.24}$$

In reality, in the short run, $\ln r_t$ deviates from zero at any t. We can model $\ln r_t$ either as a stationary process or a unit root process.

Suppose we test $\ln e_t$, $\ln P_t^*$, and $\ln P_t$ separately (see Tables 10.2, 10.3, and 10.4) and they are all unit root processes. Then, it is plausible that $\ln r_t = \ln e_t + \ln P_t^* - \ln P_t$ is also a unit root process. However, it is also possible that $\ln r_t$ may be a stationary process in the following way.

Table 10.2: Augmented DF Unit Root Test of $\ln e_t$. $\Delta \ln e_t = \delta + \theta t + \gamma \ln e_{t-1} + \sum_{j=1} \beta_j \Delta \ln e_{t-j} + \xi_t$. Sample size 42.

ADF Test Statistic	**−1.776037**	**1 % Critical Value**		**−4.16**
Coefficient	**Estimate**	**Std. Error**	***t*-Statistic**	**Prob.**
γ	−0.280485	0.157928	−1.776037	0.0859
β_1	0.392861	0.192132	2.044747	0.0497
β_2	0.121412	0.185310	0.655185	0.5173
β_3	−0.191780	0.184113	−1.041640	0.3059
β_4	−0.081663	0.187675	−0.435129	0.6666
Constant δ	−0.272398	0.178452	−1.526448	0.1374
Time Trend θ	0.004542	0.003192	1.423116	0.1650
R-squared	0.385694	Mean dependent var		1.017981
Adjusted R-squared	0.262833	S. D. dependent var		0.083637
S. E. of regression	0.071809	Akaike info criterion		−2.260947
Sum squared resid.	0.154697	Schwarz criterion		−1.955179

Table 10.3: Augmented DF Unit Root Test of $\ln P_t^*$ (U. S. price). $\Delta \ln P_t^* = \delta + \theta t + \gamma \ln P_{t-1}^* + \sum_{j=1} \beta_j \Delta \ln P_{t-j}^* + \xi_t$. Sample size 42.

ADF Test Statistic	**−1.584216**	**1 % Critical Value**		**−4.16**
Variable	**Coefficient**	**Std. Error**	***t*-Statistic**	**Prob.**
γ	−0.046279	0.029212	−1.584216	0.1236
β_1	1.202727	0.175698	6.845443	0.0000
β_2	−0.747593	0.280181	−2.668249	0.0122
β_3	0.321773	0.275273	1.168924	0.2516
β_4	0.122373	0.181003	0.676080	0.5042
Constant δ	0.140211	0.077081	1.819011	0.0789
Time Trend θ	0.002090	0.001575	1.327341	0.1944
R-squared	0.786908	Mean dependent var		0.047083
Adjusted R-squared	0.744290	S. D. dependent var		0.027333
S. E. of regression	0.013822	Akaike info criterion		−5.556479
Sum squared resid.	0.005731	Schwarz criterion		−5.251711

Table 10.4: Augmented DF Unit Root Test of $\ln P_t$ (U. K. price). $\Delta \ln P_t = \delta + \theta t + \gamma \ln P_{t-1} + \sum_{j=1} \beta_j \Delta \ln P_{t-j} + \xi_t$. Sample size 42.

ADF Test Statistic	**−1.921265**	**1 % Critical Value**		**−4.16**
Variable	**Coefficient**	**Std. Error**	***t*-Statistic**	**Prob.**
γ	−0.062299	0.032426	−1.921265	0.0642
β_1	0.799513	0.168266	4.751490	0.0000
β_2	−0.065058	0.220216	−0.295427	0.7697
β_3	−0.119771	0.218958	1.547006	0.5884
β_4	0.350473	0.177426	0.975319	0.0575
Constant δ	0.122348	0.049615	2.465964	0.0196
Time Trend θ	0.004231	0.002647	1.598458	0.1204
R-squared	0.720435	Mean dependent var		0.067708
Adjusted *R*-squared	0.664522	S. D. dependent var		0.048360
S. E. of regression	0.028011	Akaike info criterion		−4.143815
Sum squared resid	0.023538	Schwarz criterion		−3.839047

Suppose their linear combination

$$\ln r_t = (1 \quad 1 \quad -1)\begin{pmatrix} \ln e_t \\ \ln P_t^* \\ \ln P_t \end{pmatrix}$$

is stationary and not a unit root process. Then the processes $\ln e_t, \ln P_t^*$, and $\ln P_t$ are said to be cointegrated with cointegrating vector (1 1 −1). We shall discuss cointegration in the next section.

If $\ln e_t, \ln P_t^*$, and $\ln P_t$ are cointegrated and $\ln r_t$ is stationary with zero mean, then $\ln r_t$ may deviate from zero, but will over time revert back to its mean at 0. This is the interpretation of PPP (sometimes called the long-run PPP), rather than stating $\ln r_t$ as being equal to 0 at every time t. If long-run PPP does not hold, then $\ln r_t$ may deviate from 0 and not return to it. It can then be described as following a unit root process, viz.

$$\ln r_t = \ln r_{t-1} + \eta_t \tag{10.25}$$

where disturbance η_t is stationary with zero mean.

If Eq. (10.25) is the case, it means that η_t has a permanent effect of causing $\ln r_t$ to move away from 0. This is because if $\eta_1 > 0$, then $\ln r_1 = \ln r_0 + \eta_1$, so new $\ln r_2 = \ln r_1 + \eta_2$ is a stationary deviation from $\ln r_1$ that has permanently absorbed η_1. This can be seen more easily if we consider that Eq. (10.25) is equivalent to process $\ln r_t = \eta_t + \eta_{t-1} + \eta_{t-2} + \cdots$ where the variance of $\ln r_t$ increases with t. We can see that the effect of a past innovation, e. g., η_{t-j} ($j > 0$), stays permanently in the data generating process of $\ln r_t$. This is a feature of a long memory process. Contrast this with a stationary process, e. g.

$\ln r_t = \lambda \ln r_{t-1} + \eta_t, |\lambda| < 1$, where $\ln r_t = \eta_t + \lambda\eta_{t-1} + \lambda^2\eta_{t-2} + \cdots$, and so past innovation η_{t-j} $(j > 0)$ effect is transitory as λ^j reduces toward zero. This is a feature of a short memory process. If in Eq. (10.25) $\ln r_t$ has a drift, then the unit root also incorporates a deterministic trend moving $\ln r_t$ away from zero deterministically as well.

We check the validity of the long-run PPP using Eq. (10.25) by testing the null of unit root of $\ln r_t$. We run OLS on

$$\Delta \ln r_t = \delta + \theta t + \gamma \ln r_{t-1} + \sum_{j=1} \beta_j \Delta \ln r_{t-j} + \xi_t \tag{10.26}$$

where $\Delta\eta_t = \sum_{j=1} \beta_j \Delta \ln r_{t-j} + \xi_t$, ξ_t is i. i. d., and added a constant and a time trend in the regression. The null hypothesis of unit root process of $\ln r_t$ is $H_0 : \gamma = 0$. If unit root is rejected (accepted), then long-run PPP holds (does not hold).

Unit root tests of $\ln e_t$, $\ln P_t^*$, and P_t are shown in Tables 10.2, 10.3, 10.4. Table 10.5 shows unit root test of $\Delta \ln e_t$. Table 10.6 shows unit root test of log real exchange rate $\ln r_t$ via Eq. (10.26).

Table 10.5: Augmented DF Unit Root Test of $\Delta \ln e_t$, the first difference of $\ln e_t$. $\Delta^2 \ln e_t = \gamma\Delta \ln e_{t-1} + \sum_{j=1} \beta_j \Delta^2 \ln e_{t-j} + \xi_t$. Sample size 41.

ADF Test Statistic	**−3.689313**	**1 % Critical Value**		**−2.62**
Variable	**Coefficient**	**Std. Error**	***t*-Statistic**	**Prob.**
γ	−1.304453	0.353576	−3.689313	0.0009
β_1	0.598698	0.287996	2.078844	0.0460
β_2	0.551938	0.238598	2.313254	0.0275
β_3	0.234455	0.218309	1.073961	0.2911
β_4	0.126253	0.180153	0.700812	0.4886
R-squared	0.441254	Mean dependent var		0.001382
Adjusted R-squared	0.369158	S. D. dependent var		0.097641
S. E. of regression	0.077552	Akaike info criterion		−2.147485
Sum squared resid	0.186445	Schwarz criterion		−1.927552

We use U. S. CPI and UK CPI annual data from 1960 to 2001 for the price indexes P_t^* and P_t, respectively. We employ £ per \$ nominal exchange rate for e_t. The log real exchange rate $\ln r_t = \ln e_t + \ln P_t^* - P_t$ is shown in Figure 10.2.

From Table 10.2, the ADF test-statistic with constant and trend of −1.7760 > −4.16 (we use a larger sample size of 50 as approximation to our sample size of 42) at 1 % critical level. It is also greater than −3.18 at 10 % critical level. Hence, we cannot reject that the $\ln e_t$ during 1960–2001 follows a unit root process. All the ADF tests in Tables 10.2, 10.3, and 10.4 show that $\ln e_t$, $\ln P_t^*$, and $\ln P_t$ are unit root processes. Table 10.5 where we do not impose drift or trend since innovations in exchange rate are known to be very efficient shows indeed that $\Delta \ln e_t$ is stationary with mean zero.

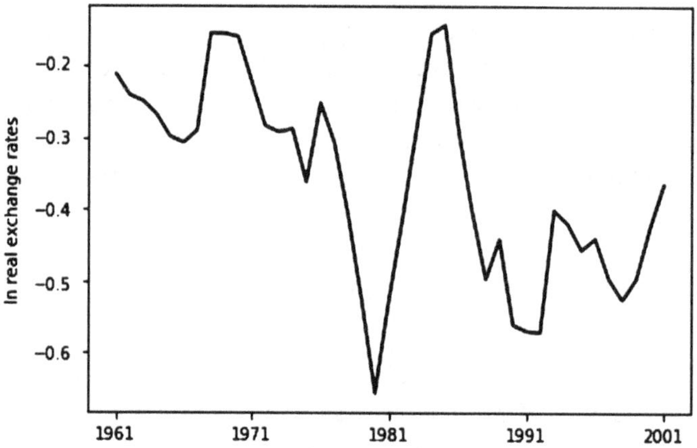

Figure 10.2: Log Real Exchange 1960 to 2001, $\ln r_t = \ln e_t + \ln P_t^* - \ln P_t$.

Table 10.6: Augmented DF Unit Root Test of $\ln r_t$. $\Delta \ln r_t = \delta + \theta t + \gamma \ln r_{t-1} + \sum_{j=1} \beta_j \Delta \ln r_{t-j} + \xi_t$ vide Eq. (10.26). Sample size 42.

ADF Test Statistic	**−3.096016**	**1 % Critical Value**		**−4.16**
Variable	**Coefficient**	**Std. Error**	***t*-Statistic**	**Prob.**
γ	−0.663089	0.214175	−3.096016	0.0042
β_1	0.560278	0.192777	2.906358	0.0068
β_2	0.360211	0.185043	1.946631	0.0610
β_3	0.054125	0.188122	0.287711	0.7755
β_4	0.091169	0.188378	0.483969	0.6319
Constant δ	0.006824	0.027781	0.245636	0.8076
Time Trend θ	0.004848	0.002017	2.403897	0.0226
R-squared	0.422015	Mean dependent var		0.002645
Adjusted R-squared	0.306418	S. D. dependent var		0.084680
S. E. of regression	0.070523	Akaike info criterion		−2.297094
Sum squared resid	0.149205	Schwarzcriterion		−1.992326

The real exchange rate r_t tested via Table 10.6 also indicates it is a unit root process. However, it is borderline at about 10 % significance level and other studies using different sampling periods and perhaps also different currency pairs have produced results indicating the real exchange rate is stationary. Real exchange rate r_t with a unit root process implies that long-run PPP does not hold and that disequilibrium from PPP or deviations r_t from zero do not have tendency to revert back toward zero. It should be noted that the "Prob" p-values in the full regression Tables 10.2 to 10.6 are those of the standard t-test and not the ADF p-values reported in the topline.

Figure 10.2 shows that log real exchange rate in £ per $ appears to be mostly negative, indicating better terms of trade and competitiveness favoring the US from 1960 to 2001.

Sometimes, bank reports show the use of PPP in trying to forecast or make prediction about the future movement of a currency. For example, in the above £ per $ spot rate, actual spot $ value may lie above the theoretical PPP $, and if log real exchange is stationary, a bank report may suggest that $ is undervalued and PPP will bring about a correction soon to see $ trending back to PPP level. However, this could be misleading if the log real exchange rate is a unit root process during the period, and the $ value may indeed continue to move downward or not revert up in the short-term. However, indeed from the 1970s through to the 1990s, the $ did increase in value versus the pound.

10.6 Cointegration

Sometimes two processes may be non-stationary such that they carry unit roots. However, they could have a long-term equilibrium relationship so that over a long time interval, it can be seen that a linear combination of them behaves like a stationary process and they do not drift away from each other aimlessly. We say they are cointegrated with each other. Or it is said they have a long-run common stochastic trend.

To model such a relationship, we proceed as follows. If Y_t, Z_t are unit root processes,

$$Y_t = c + dZ_t + w_t \tag{10.27}$$

where $d \neq 0$, and if w_t is stationary, then Y_t and Z_t are said to be cointegrated with cointegrating vector $(1, -d)$, i. e.

$$(1 - d)\begin{bmatrix} Y_t \\ Z_t \end{bmatrix} = c + w_t$$

is stationary. In this case, OLS of Y_t on Z_t when they are cointegrated indeed produces OLS estimators that are super-consistent, i. e., they converge even faster than normally consistent estimators. In this case, the usual t-statistics inference is valid.

But how do we test for cointegration in Eq. (10.27)? If we know the true parameter values c, d, as in the case of PPP, then it is simply a test of whether $w_t = Y_t - c - dZ_t$ is stationary (not a unit root process). We often do not know the exact linear relationship among unit root variables, i. e., the cointegrating vector, so we cannot rely on a specific cointegrating vector to test if the residual is unit root.

When more unit root processes such as X_t, Y_t, Z_t are involved in a possible system, then there could be more than one independent cointegrating vector. For example, if

$$X_t = a_0 + a_1 Y_t + a_2 Z_t + u_t \tag{10.28}$$

where $a_1 \neq 0$, $a_2 \neq 0$, and u_t is $I(0)$. Further, if also

$$X_t = b_0 + b_1 Y_t + b_2 Z_t + v_t \tag{10.29}$$

where $b_1 \neq 0$, $b_2 \neq 0$, and v_t is $I(0)$. Then Eqs. (10.28) and (10.29) can be solved to obtain

$$(a_1 - b_1)Y_t = (b_0 - a_0) + (b_2 - a_2)Z_t + (v_t - u_t)$$

showing Y_t and Z_t are cointegrated since $v_t - u_t$ is stationary. Similarly. it can be shown that X_t and Y_t, or X_t and Z_t, are cointegrated.

If there were only one cointegrating Eq. (10.28), then $X_t = a_0 + a_1 Y_t + \epsilon_t$ where noise $\epsilon_t = a_2 Z_t + u_t$ contains a unit root process. Hence any pair of X_t and Y_t, or X_t and Z_t, or Y_t and Z_t, is not cointegrated.

Suppose processes X_t, Y_t, Z_t can be either $I(1)$ or $I(0)$. If there were three independent cointegrating vectors, i. e., if we add $X_t = c_0 + c_1 Y_t + c_2 Z_t + w_t$ where w_t is $I(0)$, then on solving the three simultaneous regression equations, we can obtain X_t = constant+stationary noise, and likewise for Y_t and Z_t. Hence all X_t, Y_t, Z_t are $I(0)$.

In summary, for three different unit root processes, only one cointegrating vector implies any linear combination of a pair of the processes will produce an $I(1)$ noise. With two independent cointegrating vectors, they form a basis for the space of cointegrating vectors. When there is more than one cointegrating vector, the OLS method does its usual job of selecting the best linear fit with least squares deviation (presumably from a larger basis when there is more than one independent cointegrating vector). With three different cointegrating vectors, the implication is that the original processes were actually $I(0)$ and not $I(1)$.

More generally, for n different unit root processes, only one cointegrating vector implies any linear combination of $(n-1)$ number of the processes will produce an $I(1)$ noise. With two independent cointegrating vectors, any linear combination of $(n-2)$ number of the processes will produce an $I(1)$ noise, and so on. The basis for the space of cointegrating vectors would be larger when there are more cointegrating vectors. This implies it generally leads to a more optimal OLS fit in the cointegration regressions. When there is statistical evidence that there are n cointegrating vectors, the implication is that the original n processes were actually $I(0)$ and not $I(1)$.

In a more general setup, we could have a vector of either unit root $I(1)$ or stationary $I(0)$ RVs X_t of order $n \times 1$ whereby there are a number of combinations of the elements that could be cointegrated. We can employ the Johansen trace test statistic and/or the Johansen maximum eigenvalue test statistic for the number of cointegrating vectors present in X_t. The Johansen method uses the idea of maximum likelihood ratio test.

Consider the $n \times 1$ dimension Vector Autoregressive Process VAR(p) X_t as follows, where we assume that the elements of the vector process are detrended if any has a time trend.

$$X_t = \mu_0 + \Phi_1 X_{t-1} + \cdots + \Phi_p X_{t-p} + a_t \tag{10.30}$$

where a_t is i. i. d. vector with normal distributions and zero means. Elements of X_t are either $I(1)$ or $I(0)$. Dimension of Φ_i is $n \times n$.

This VAR(p) process X_t in Eq. (10.30) can be re-arranged as:

$$\triangle X_t = \mu_0 + \Pi X_{t-1} + \Phi_1^* \triangle X_{t-1} + \cdots + \Phi_{p-1}^* \triangle X_{t-p+1} + a_t \tag{10.31}$$

where $\Phi_j^* = -\sum_{i=j+1}^{p} \Phi_i$, for $j = 1, 2, \ldots, p-1$ and $\Pi_{n\times n} = \sum_{i=1}^{p} \Phi_i - I_{n\times n}$. Note that if Π and Φ_i^* are estimated, then the original Φ_i's can be recovered as follows. $\Phi_1 = I + \Pi + \Phi_1^*$, and $\Phi_i = \Phi_i^* - \Phi_{i-1}^*$ for $i = 2, 3, \ldots, p$, defining $\Phi_p^* \equiv 0_{n\times n}$.

Equation (10.31) is sometimes called an error correction model (ECM) as it contains the vector term ΠX_{t-1} on the RHS that is stationary. $\sum_{k=1}^{p-1} \Phi_k^* \triangle X_{t-k}$ (autoregressive distributed lags) captures short-run impact on LHS $\triangle X_t$ while Π captures the adjustment toward long-run equilibrium. The latter error correction term can be further characterized as follows. ΠX_{t-1} represents n linear combinations of the elements in vector X_{t-1}. If no $\Pi_{n\times n}$ exists whereby ΠX_{t-1} is stationary, then clearly there is zero number of cointegration vector. This is the case when $\Pi = O$, the zero matrix. In such a situation, the rank of Π is zero. It is important to test if the rank of Π is indeed zero since such a situation means that it is not appropriate to perform OLS linear regression as the results would be spurious.

If the rank of Π is m where $0 < m < n$, then we can always write $\Pi_{n\times n} = \alpha\beta^T$ where both α and β are of dimension $n \times m$. We can define β^T as the m number of linearly independent cointegrating vectors on X_{t-1}. α is adjustment factor. Hence we write Eq. (10.31) as

$$\triangle X_t = \mu_0 + \alpha\beta^T X_{t-1} + \Phi_1^* \triangle X_{t-1} + \cdots + \Phi_{p-1}^* \triangle X_{t-p+1} + a_t \tag{10.32}$$

where $\Phi_j^* = -\sum_{i=j+1}^{p} \Phi_i$, for $j = 1, 2, \ldots, p-1$ and $\Pi_{n\times n} - \sum_{i=1}^{p} \Phi_i - I_{n\times n}$. Hence the rank of Π in this setup would be the number of independent cointegration vectors.

When Π is of full rank, i. e. exhibiting n independent cointegrating vectors, then the implication is that all elements of X_{t-1} (similarly of X_t) are stationary. It is important to test if the rank of Π, m, is at least one so that it is appropriate to perform OLS linear regression. To test for the rank of Π, we proceed as follows.

Consider the maximum likelihood estimation of Eq. (10.32) where residual vector a_t is multivariate normal with covariance matrix Ω. Then the log likelihood function of sample (size T) observations on X_t $(t = 1, 2, \ldots, T)$ is:

$$\begin{aligned} &\ln L(\Omega, \Phi_1^*, \Phi_2^*, \ldots, \Phi_{p-1}^*, \mu_0, \Pi) \\ &= -\frac{Tp}{2}\ln(2\pi) - \frac{T}{2}\ln|\Omega| - \frac{1}{2}\sum_{t=1}^{T} a_t^T \Omega^{-1} a_t \end{aligned} \tag{10.33}$$

The function $\ln L$ can be maximized with respect to $\Phi_1^*, \Phi_2^*, \ldots, \Phi_{p-1}^*, \mu_0$ and these first order conditions are solved, conditional on Ω and Π. The log likelihood function conditional on maximized $\Phi_1^*, \Phi_2^*, \ldots, \Phi_{p-1}^*, \mu_0$ as functions of Ω and Π, $\ln L_C(\Omega, \Pi)$ is then obtained. The latter is called a concentrated likelihood function.

Suppose we perform two auxiliary regressions as follows.

$$\triangle X_t = \mu_c + C_1^* \triangle X_{t-1} + \cdots + C_{p-1}^* \triangle X_{t-p+1} + u_t \tag{10.34}$$

and

$$X_{t-1} = \mu_d + D_1^* \triangle X_{t-1} + \cdots + D_{p-1}^* \triangle X_{t-p+1} + v_t \tag{10.35}$$

From Eqs. (10.34) and (10.35), we can obtain

$$u_t = \Pi v_t + a_t \tag{10.36}$$

where $\mu_c - \Pi\mu_d = \mu_0$, and $C_i^* - \Pi D_i^* = \Phi_i^*$ $(i = 1, \ldots, p-1)$.

We find the OLS estimates in regressions of Eqs. (10.34) and (10.35), and obtain fitted residuals $\hat{u}_t$ and $\hat{v}_t$. $\hat{u}_t$ and $\hat{v}_t$ have sample means as zeros, and are sample-wise othogonal to $(\triangle X_{t-1}, \triangle X_{t-2}, \ldots, \triangle X_{t-p+1})$. Based on the OLS estimates $\hat{\mu}_c, \hat{\mu}_d, \hat{C}_i^*, \hat{D}_i^*$ for $i = 1, 2, \ldots, p-1$, we construct $\hat{\mu}_0 = \hat{\mu}_c - \Pi\hat{\mu}_d$ and $\hat{\Phi}_i^* = \hat{C}_i^* - \Pi\hat{D}_i^*$ for $i = 1, 2, \ldots, p-1$, and employ these estimates in the concentrated log likelihood function

$$\ln L_C(\Omega, \Pi | \hat{\mu}_0, \hat{\Phi}_1^*, \hat{\Phi}_2^*, \ldots, \hat{\Phi}_{p-1}^*)$$

Equation (10.33) can be re-expressed in an asymptotically equivalent form as:

$$\begin{aligned} &\ln L_C(\Omega, \Pi | \hat{\mu}_0, \hat{\Phi}_1^*, \hat{\Phi}_2^*, \ldots, \hat{\Phi}_{p-1}^*) \\ &= -\frac{Tp}{2}\ln(2\pi) - \frac{T}{2}\ln|\Omega| - \frac{1}{2}\sum_{t=1}^{T}(\hat{u}_t - \Pi\hat{v}_t)^T \Omega^{-1}(\hat{u}_t - \Pi\hat{v}_t) \end{aligned} \tag{10.37}$$

From Eq. (10.37), for a given Π, the maximum likelihood estimator of Ω is

$$\hat{\Omega} = \frac{1}{T}\sum_{t=1}^{T}(\hat{u}_t - \Pi\hat{v}_t)(\hat{u}_t - \Pi\hat{v}_t)^T$$

Substituting $\hat{\Omega}$ into Eq. (10.37), asymptotically

$$\ln L_C(\Pi) = -\frac{Tp}{2}\ln(2\pi) - \frac{T}{2}\ln|\hat{\Omega}| - \frac{Tp}{2} \tag{10.38}$$

We can compute the following sample covariance matrices:

$$\hat{R}_{uu} = \frac{1}{T-p}\sum_{t=p+1}^{T}\hat{u}_t\hat{u}_t^T$$

$$\hat{R}_{uv} = \frac{1}{T-p}\sum_{t=p+1}^{T}\hat{u}_t\hat{v}_t^T$$

$$\hat{R}_{vu} = \frac{1}{T-p} \sum_{t=p+1}^{T} \hat{v}_t \hat{u}_t^T$$

and

$$\hat{R}_{vv} = \frac{1}{T-p} \sum_{t=p+1}^{T} \hat{v}_t \hat{v}_t^T$$

The divisor can be T since we are dealing with asymptotics.

Asymptotically, Eq. (10.38), ignoring the constant terms, can be re-expressed as:

$$\ln L_C(\Pi) = -\frac{T}{2} \ln |\hat{\Omega}| = -\frac{T}{2} \ln |\hat{R}_{uu} - \Pi \hat{R}_{vu} - \hat{R}_{uv} \Pi^T + \Pi \hat{R}_{vv} \Pi^T|$$

When Π is restricted to be $\alpha\beta^T$, the first order condition by taking derivative with respect to matrix α of

$$\ln L_C(\Pi) = -\frac{T}{2} \ln |\hat{R}_{uu} - \alpha\beta^T \hat{R}_{vu} - \hat{R}_{uv} \beta\alpha^T + \alpha\beta^T \hat{R}_{vv} \beta\alpha^T|$$

is

$$\hat{\alpha} = \hat{R}_{uv} \beta (\beta^T \hat{R}_{vv} \beta)^{-1}$$

since the derivative of $|f|$ w. r. t. f is a non-zero constant. Substituting $\hat{\alpha}$ into $\ln L_C(\Pi)$, we obtain further concentrated likelihood function

$$\begin{aligned} \ln L_C(\beta) &= -\frac{T}{2} \ln |\hat{R}_{uu} - \hat{R}_{uv} \beta (\beta^T \hat{R}_{vv} \beta)^{-1} \beta^T \hat{R}_{vu}| \\ &= -\frac{T}{2} \ln |\hat{R}_{uu}| |\beta^T (\hat{R}_{vv} - \hat{R}_{vu} \hat{R}_{uu}^{-1} \hat{R}_{uv}) \beta| / |\beta^T \hat{R}_{vv} \beta| \end{aligned}$$

The log likelihood function can thus be maximized by minimizing

$$|\beta^T (\hat{R}_{vv} - \hat{R}_{vu} \hat{R}_{uu}^{-1} \hat{R}_{uv}) \beta| |\beta^T \hat{R}_{vv} \beta|^{-1} \tag{10.39}$$

We now show how to relate canonical correlations between u_t and v_t embodied in Π in Eq. (10.36) to eigenvalues of relevant matrices, and then show the problem of minimization in Eq. (10.39) to be a similar problem of finding maximum eigenvalues.

From Eq. (10.36), we find the canonical correlations between normal vectors u_t and v_t. If elements of random vectors u_t and v_t have non-zero correlations, canonical correlation between the vectors is the maximum correlation between any linear combinations of elements of u_t and any linear combinations of elements of v_t.

Let $\text{cov}(u_t)_{n\times n} = R_{uu}\ \forall t$, $\text{cov}(v_t)_{n\times n} = R_{vv}\ \forall t$, $\text{cov}(u_t, v_t)_{n\times n} = R_{uv}\ \forall t$, and $\text{cov}(v_t, u_t)_{n\times n} = R_{vu}\ \forall t$. Consider a linear combination of u_t, viz. $A_1^T u_t$ (1×1) and a linear combination of v_t, viz. $B_1^T v_t$ (1×1) and their correlation

$$\text{corr}(A_1^T u_t, B_1^T v_t) = \frac{A_1^T R_{uv} B_1}{\sqrt{A_1^T R_{uu} A_1}\sqrt{B_1^T R_{vv} B_1}} \tag{10.40}$$

Without loss of generality, consider only A_1, B_1 or linear combinations where their variances are ones, i. e., $A_1^T R_{uu} A_1 = B_1^T R_{vv} B_1 = 1$. Find $A_{1n\times 1}$ and $B_{1n\times 1}$ that maximizes the correlation in Eq. (10.40).

Differentiating w. r. t. A_1 and then also B_1 to obtain the first order conditions:

$$R_{uv} B_1 - A_1^T R_{uv} B_1 (R_{uu} A_1) = 0 \tag{10.41}$$

and

$$R_{uv} A_1 - A_1^T R_{uv} B_1 (R_{vv} B_1) = 0 \tag{10.42}$$

Let $A_1^T R_{uv} B_1 = \sqrt{\lambda_1}$ and solve for Eqs. (10.41) and (10.42) to obtain:

$$R_{uu}^{-1} R_{uv} [R_{vv}^{-1} R_{vu}] A_1 = \lambda_1 A_1 \tag{10.43}$$

and

$$R_{vv}^{-1} R_{vu} [R_{uu}^{-1} R_{uv}] B_1 = \lambda_1 B_1 \tag{10.44}$$

But the maximized canonical correlation

$$\text{corr}(A_1^T u_t, B_1^T v_t) = A_1^T R_{uv} B_1 = \sqrt{\lambda_1} \tag{10.45}$$

Hence square of the canonical correlation (> 0) in Eq. (10.45) is equal to the eigenvalue of either matrix $R_{uu}^{-1} R_{uv} [R_{vv}^{-1} R_{vu}]$ in Eq. (10.43) or of $R_{vv}^{-1} R_{vu} [R_{uu}^{-1} R_{uv}]$ in Eq. (10.44).

We proceed to find the second largest canonical correlation $\sqrt{\lambda_2}$ involving $A_2^T u_t$ and $B_2^T v_t$ in the same way, except we add the constraint that $\text{corr}(A_1^T u_t, A_2^T u_t) = 0$ and $\text{corr}(B_1^T v_t, B_2^T v_t) = 0$. We can obtain

$$R_{uu}^{-1} R_{uv} [R_{vv}^{-1} R_{vu}] A_2 = \lambda_2 A_2 \tag{10.46}$$

and

$$R_{vv}^{-1} R_{vu} [R_{uu}^{-1} R_{uv}] B_2 = \lambda_2 B_2 \tag{10.47}$$

The second maximum canonical correlation

$$\text{corr}(A_2^T u_t, B_2^T v_t) = A_2^T R_{uv} B_2 = \sqrt{\lambda_2} \tag{10.48}$$

Hence square of the second canonical correlation (> 0) in Eq. (10.48) is equal to the second largest eigenvalue of either matrix $R_{uu}^{-1} R_{uv} [R_{vv}^{-1} R_{vu}]$ in Eq. (10.46) or of $R_{vv}^{-1} R_{vu} [R_{uu}^{-1} R_{uv}]$ in Eq. (10.47).

We can directly find the estimated eigenvalues using the sample covariance matrix of $\hat{R}_{vv}^{-1}\hat{R}_{vu}[\hat{R}_{uu}^{-1}\hat{R}_{uv}]$ in Eqs. (10.44), (10.47), and so on. Let $\hat{b}_i$ and $\hat{\lambda}_i$ be the eigenvector and associated eigenvalue. Let the eigenvalues be ranked from largest for $\hat{\lambda}_1$. Therefore,

$$\hat{R}_{vv}^{-1}\hat{R}_{vu}\hat{R}_{uu}^{-1}\hat{R}_{uv}\hat{b}_i = \hat{\lambda}_i\hat{b}_i$$

or

$$\hat{R}_{vu}\hat{R}_{uu}^{-1}\hat{R}_{uv}\hat{b}_i = \hat{\lambda}_i\hat{R}_{vv}\hat{b}_i$$

for $i = 1, 2, \ldots, m$, $m \le n$. Hence,

$$\hat{R}_{vu}\hat{R}_{uu}^{-1}\hat{R}_{uv}\hat{\beta} = \hat{R}_{vv}\hat{\beta}\hat{\Lambda}$$

for $\hat{\beta} = (\hat{b}_1, \hat{b}_2, \ldots, \hat{b}_m)$ and $\hat{\Lambda}$ is diagonal matrix with diagonal elements $\hat{\lambda}_i$.

Now,

$$\hat{\beta}^T\hat{R}_{vu}\hat{R}_{uu}^{-1}\hat{R}_{uv}\hat{\beta} = \hat{\beta}^T\hat{R}_{vv}\hat{\beta}\hat{\Lambda}$$

We can always normalize the eigenvectors in $\hat{\beta}_{n\times m}$ so that $\hat{\beta}^T\hat{R}_{vv}\hat{\beta} = I_{m\times m}$. Then, $\hat{\beta}^T\hat{R}_{vu}\hat{R}_{uu}^{-1}\hat{R}_{uv}\hat{\beta} = \hat{\Lambda}_{m\times m}$. Therefore, Eq. (10.39) can now be re-expressed as

$$|\hat{\beta}^T\hat{R}_{vv}\hat{\beta} - \hat{\beta}^T\hat{R}_{vu}\hat{R}_{uu}^{-1}\hat{R}_{uv}\hat{\beta}||\hat{\beta}^T\hat{R}_{vv}\hat{\beta}|^{-1} = |I - \hat{\Lambda}||I|^{-1} \tag{10.49}$$

The RHS is

$$\begin{vmatrix} 1-\hat{\lambda}_1 & 0 & 0 & \cdots & 0 \\ 0 & 1-\hat{\lambda}_2 & 0 & \cdots & 0 \\ \vdots & \vdots & \vdots & \ddots & \vdots \\ 0 & 0 & 0 & \cdots & 1-\hat{\lambda}_m \end{vmatrix}$$

Hence the problem of maximizing log likelihood

$$\ln L_C(\hat{\lambda}_1, \hat{\lambda}_2, \ldots, \hat{\lambda}_m) = K - \frac{T}{2}\ln|I - \hat{\Lambda}|$$

where K is a constant, is now maximizing the eigenvalues $\hat{\lambda}_1, \ldots, \hat{\lambda}_m$. However, from Eq. (10.36), $u_t = \Pi v_t + a_t$, so

$$E[u_t v_t^T] = E[(\Pi v_t + a_t)v_t^T] = \Pi E[v_t v_t^T] + E[a_t v_t^T] = \Pi R_{vv}$$

Hence $R_{uv} = \Pi R_{vv}$. As Rank $(\Pi) = m \le n$, therefore Rank (R_{uv}) is Rank $R_{vu} = m$, given Rank $(R_{vv}) = n$ is full. Thus the Rank of $R_{vv}^{-1}R_{vu}[R_{uu}^{-1}R_{uv}]$ is also $m \le n$. Therefore there will be only at most $m \le n$ number of non-zero eigenvalues in $R_{vv}^{-1}R_{vu}[R_{uu}^{-1}R_{uv}]$.

Therefore in large sample, the sample covariance matrix $\hat{R}_{vv}^{-1}\hat{R}_{vu}[\hat{R}_{uu}^{-1}\hat{R}_{uv}]$ should also be estimated to have rank m.

Let the estimated non-zero eigenvalues (or the squared canonical correlations) be $\hat{\lambda}_1, \hat{\lambda}_2, \ldots, \hat{\lambda}_m$. Any sample $(m+1)$th or smaller eigenvalues are likely to be zero or close to zero. This implies that $\ln(1-\hat{\lambda}_{m+1})$, $\ln(1-\hat{\lambda}_{m+2}) \ldots \ln(1-\hat{\lambda}_n)$ are zeros or close to zeros.

In Johansen's maximum eigenvalue test, the null is H_0: Rank $(\Pi) = m$ versus H_A: Rank $(\Pi) = m+1$. Under H_0, the $(m+1)$th eigenvalue, λ_{m+1} is zero. Hence $\ln(1-\lambda_{m+1}) = 0$. Employing the likelihood ratio test on H_0: Rank $(\Pi) = m$ is similar to testing the restriction of $\lambda_{m+1} = 0$ in the log likelihood versus the unrestricted log likelihood. The restricted log likelihood is $\ln L_C^r(\hat{\lambda}_1, \hat{\lambda}_2, \ldots, \hat{\lambda}_m) = K - \frac{T}{2}\ln|I_{m\times m} - \hat{\Lambda}_{m\times m}|$ versus the unrestricted log likelihood $\ln L_C(\hat{\lambda}_1, \hat{\lambda}_2, \ldots, \hat{\lambda}_m, \hat{\lambda}_{m+1}) = K - \frac{T}{2}\ln|I_{m+1\times m+1} - \hat{\Lambda}_{m+1\times m+1}|$ where K is a constant.

The usual likelihood ratio test involving the restricted and the unrestricted log likelihood functions is $-2\ln(L_C^r/L_C)$. This likelihood ratio test is

$$T(\ln|I_{m\times m} - \hat{\Lambda}_{m\times m}| - \ln|I_{m+1\times m+1} - \hat{\Lambda}_{m+1\times m+1}|)$$

which is $-T\ln(1-\hat{\lambda}_{m+1})$. This is ≥ 0 since we employ positive eigenvalues < 1.

Under H_0, this test statistic should be small and close to zero. However, it has a non-standard distribution (not chi-square) since unit roots occur in some of the underlying variables. Reject H_0 if the test statistic is too large.

In Johansen's trace cointegration test, the null is H_0: Rank $(\Pi) = m$ versus H_A: Rank $(\Pi) > m$. In the alternative hypothesis, the rank is at least $m+1$. Under H_0, the sum of all $(m+1)$th, $\ldots$, nth eigenvalues equals to zero. Hence $\sum_{i=m+1}^{n}\ln(1-\lambda_i) = 0$. Similarly, a likelihood ratio test statistic would be $-T\sum_{i=m+1}^{n}\ln(1-\hat{\lambda}_i)$. This is ≥ 0 since we employ positive eigenvalues < 1. Under H_0, this test statistic should be small and close to zero. However, it has a non-standard distribution (not chi-square) since unit roots occur in some of the underlying variables. Reject H_0 if the test statistic is too large. The critical values of these cointegration test statistics are provided via simulations and are available in professional statistical packages.

We illustrate the use of the Johansen method with an application to test the Fisher hypothesis.[8] The Fisher hypothesis posits that in the long run, nominal interest rate and inflation rate move together, so real interest rate (nominal interest rate less inflation rate) are cointegrated.

In the study by Hjalmassson and Pär Österholm (2007), they used monthly data on US short nominal interest rate i_t and CPI inflation rate π_t from January 1974 to October 2006. They found that the null hypothesis of a unit root cannot be rejected for inflation rate. However, they find that the nominal interest rate is "near to unit root". (The

8 Refer to Erik Hjalmassson and Pär Österholm (2007), Testing for cointegration using the Johansen methodology when variables are near-integrated, IMF Working Paper WP/07/141.

power of ADF unit root test is not strong when processes are close to unit root, i. e., the test tends to accept unit root when it may not be.) They then set out to estimate the cointegrating rank of the vector (π_t, i_t). Based on Akaike Information Criterion, they used $p - 1 = 10$ distributed lags.

As there are only two stochastic processes, the number of cointegration, r, is 0, 1, or 2 between the two variables π_t and i_t. Suppose $r = 0$, then $\Pi = 0$ and there is no cointegration. Suppose $r = 2$, then this is the case where all elements of X_t, i. e. both π_t and i_t here, are $I(0)$.

Suppose $r = 1$, then $i_t - b\pi_t$ is stationary (ignoring constant and trend) for some $b \neq 0$, i. e., there exists a cointegrating vector $\beta^T = (1, b)$. This is then consistent with the Fisher hypothesis.

Using Johansen trace and max eigenvalue tests, the study found one cointegrating vector, i. e. $r = 1$, cannot be rejected, where $\Pi = \alpha\beta^T$ and cointegrating vector β^T has dimension $r \times n$ or 1×2 in this case. Usually both the Johansen trace test and the maximum eigenvalue test proceed from a null of $r = 0$ upward to a null of $r = 1$, and so on, until the null is not rejected. The two test results should be consistent and are complementary (Table 10.7).

Table 10.7: Johansen Cointegration Tests.

Null Hypothesis	J trace-statistic	J max eigenvalue statistic
$r = 0$	22.045	16.402
	(0.028)	(0.042)
$r = 1$	5.642	5.642
	(0.220)	(0.220)

Note: The p-values are in the brackets. Source: Erik Hjalmassson and Pär Österholm (2007).

Their Johansen tests showed that the null of $H_0 : r = 0$ is rejected for trace test (i. e., alternative is $r > 0$) and rejected for maximum eigenvalue test (i. e., alternative is $r = 1$). Next, their Johansen tests showed that the null of $H_0 : r = 1$ is not rejected for trace test (i. e.. alternative $r > 1$ is not acceptable) and not rejected for maximum eigenvalue test (i. e., alternative is $r = 2$ is not acceptable). Hence the test conclusion is that $r = 1$. However, their study indicated that when nominal interest rate is nearly $I(1)$ but could be $I(0)$, the cointegrating test may have low power.

Further Reading

Blanchard, O. J., and S. Fischer (1989), *Lectures on Macroeconomics*, MIT Press.
Davidson, R., and J. G. MacKinnon (1993), *Estimation and Inference in Econometrics*, Oxford University Press.
Fumio Hayashi (2000), *Econometrics*, Princeton University Press.
Hamilton, J. D. (1994), *Time Series Analysis*, Princeton University Press.

11 Bond Prices and Interest Rate Models

Modern interest rate theory uses much of the no-arbitrage condition as a workhorse. At the same time, the availability of many new market instruments on interest rates also lends fuel to new models and empirical validation of these models for purposes of forecasting interest rates, managing bond portfolios, and yield risk management. We shall first study interest rate models on risk-free bonds. Then we consider default risks on bonds, and discuss corporate bond yields that include a credit risk spread. We also see how different interest rate models can be tested.

11.1 Interest Rates

By convention, interest rates on a loan or debt are quoted on a per annum basis. Simple interest for a loan over a period t years based on interest rate r is computed as $\$(1+r)^t$ per dollar of loan. If t is less than one, e. g., 3 months, then simple interest is $\$(1+r/4)$. Compound interest is computed based on given rate r, loan period t, as well as the frequency of compounding that must be stated. For example, if the frequency is monthly compounding, then over $m > 1$ months, compounded interest payable is $\$(1+r/12)^m$. Continuously compounded interest based on r p. a., earns total payoff (principal plus interest) of $\$\,e^{rt}$ at the end of t years with an initial investment of $1. The interest component is thus $e^{rt}-1$ at the end of the period. The amount e^{rt} is obtained as a limit, $\lim_{n\to\infty}(1+\frac{r}{n})^{nt}$. There are many ways of getting the exponent; one is to put $y_n = (1+\frac{r}{n})^{nt}$, take the natural logarithms of both sides, and apply L'Hôpital's rule to obtain $\lim_{n\to\infty}\ln y_n = rt$. Then, $y_n \to e^{rt}$.

A bond is a fixed income contract between a borrower (seller) such as a firm or a bank, and a lender (buyer) such as a bank or a buy-side institution, e. g., a pension fund, an investment firm, or a hedge fund. There are many kinds of bonds with different maturities (tenor after which the contract expires) and different payment processes. A common type of Treasury or corporate bond is where buyers pay the principal amount at the initiation, and receive periodic interest payments (or coupon interests) while holding the bond. At maturity of the bond, e. g., end of five years, the borrower or seller pays back the principal to the lender or buyer. There are also bonds that do not provide interest payments during tenor. These are called zero-coupon or discount bonds, and are sold at a discount to the principal value. This discount serves as up-front interest payment in comparison to the standard coupon bond.

A t-period spot interest rate is an interest rate charged on a loan or an interest rate received on a deposit or earned on a bond for holding period from the current time 0 until some future time t without any intermediate cashflow payments. For example, a discount bond bought today at price $B(0,t)$ for redemption at par $1 at maturity time t in the future (time-to-maturity t in terms of number of years) has an effective return

https://doi.org/10.1515/9783110673951-011

rate (non-annualized) of $1/B(0,t) - 1$. The discrete-time spot rate or spot yield p. a. for the discount bond or zero-coupon (ZC) bond is

$$y(0,t) = \left(\frac{1}{B(0,t)}\right)^{1/t} - 1$$

For notational convenience, we denote the spot rate as $y(t)$ when the start point at $t = 0$ is understood.

In most of the advanced analyses of interest rates, due to the heavy use of modeling in continuous-time, it is often convenient to employ continuous-time compounding. Hence, the continuously compounded spot rate (or the p. a. rate to be continuously compounded) is

$$y(t) = \frac{1}{t}\ln\left(\frac{1}{B(0,t)}\right) \tag{11.1}$$

The corresponding effective spot yield factor or return is

$$Y(0,t) = \exp(y(0,t) \times t)$$

The yield-to-maturity (YTM) is an interest rate measure on a bond (whether coupon bond or zero-coupon bond) that is essentially the internal rate of return or discount rate equating the present value of all contractual bond payments to the current bond price. For example, a 2-year coupon bond with half-yearly coupon interest 5 % p. a., par value \$100, and current price \$102, has a current yield-to-maturity of 3.95 %:

$$102 = 2.5/(1 + .0395/2) + 2.5/(1 + .0395/2)^2 + 2.5/(1 + .0395/2)^3 + 2.5/(1 + .0395/2)^4$$

The YTM measure is a function of the time-to-maturity as well as other factors such as credit risk of the bond issuer or borrower, liquidity, tax status, currency, and frequency of coupon interest payments. For a zero-coupon bond with no intermediate interest payments, the yield-to-maturity is identical to the spot rate of the bond.

At any time t, assume the market is trading a continuous spectrum or series of discount bonds with different maturities T at prices $B(t,T)$, respectively. We can then compute from their prices the corresponding spot rates via (11.1). The $(T - t)$ period spot rate $y(t,T)$ for a particular T provides information on the investment return over $[t,T]$. If we plot the graph of $y(t,T)$ against time-to-maturity for the bond or horizon $T - t$, the graph is called a spot rate (spot yield) curve. It is also the yield (yield-to-maturity) curve of the discount bonds. A yield curve is also called the term structure of the yields. For a yield curve to make sense, i. e., useful for comparing bond yields across different maturities, the bonds must have similar factors e. g., similar credit rating, liquidity condition, tax status, currency, and frequency of interest payments, excepting the maturity.

When bonds with intermediate (or coupon) interest payments are first issued, they are typically sold at par value or face value of the bond. The par value is also the redemption value or principal repayment by the borrower at maturity. On day t, if there are many bonds issued at par, each with different maturities n and correspondingly different coupon interest rates y_n, then these coupon rates are also the corresponding yield-to-maturity of the different maturities n. Since bonds at issue (on-the-run bonds) are more liquid, their yield curve (y_n versus n) is an accurate characterization of the maturity effect on the bond yields. This yield curve on par bonds is also called the par yield curve. However, yield curves can also be computed based on bonds of different maturities that have been trading, at prices either below par or above par.

For bonds with coupons, their yield curve is in general different from their spot rate curves. We show how one can obtain the spot rates from the traded prices of bonds on a yield curve. The method is called bootstrapping spot rates. Suppose a 1/2 year to maturity 3 % coupon bond is trading at 99.8 % (of par value). Suppose a 1 year to maturity 2.5 % coupon bond is trading at 99 % (of par value). Suppose a 1.5 year to maturity 2.8 % coupon bond is trading at 98.5 % (of par value). Suppose a 2 year to maturity 3.2 % coupon bond is trading at 98.6 % (of par value).

Using the 1/2 year bond, the 1/2-year spot rate $y_{1/2}$ is obtained as follows: $(1.015/0.998)^2 - 1 = 0.03436$. Let the 1-year spot rate be y_1. Then $0.99 = 0.0125/(1.03436)^{1/2} + 1.0125/(1 + y_1)$. Hence, $y_1 = 0.03558$. Let the 1.5 year spot rate be $y_{1.5}$. Then $0.985 = 0.014/(1.03436)^{1/2} + 0.014/(1.03558) + 1.014/(1 + y_{1.5})^{1.5}$. Hence, $y_{1.5} = 0.03881$. Let the 2-year spot rate be y_2. Then $0.986 = 0.016/(1.03436)^{1/2} + 0.016/(1.03558) + 0.016/(1.03881)^{1.5} + 1.016/(1 + y_2)^2$. Hence, $y_2 = 0.03980$. Thus we can see an upward sloping spot rate curve with spot rates for 6-month, 12-month, 18-month, and 24-month maturities as 3.436 %, 3.558 %, 3.881 %, and 3.980 %.

U. S. Treasury coupon notes and bonds can be stripped into zero-coupon bonds for trading. Bootstrapping enables spot rates to be available for many maturities, being derived from traded bond prices, including from ZC bond prices as well as from discount Treasury bills for maturities shorter than a year. In turn the spot rates enable no-arbitrage prices of other bonds with contractual cashflows to be determined.

We next consider a discrete model of spot rate dynamics over time and show that no-arbitrage bond prices can be derived given the spot rate process. We also show the corresponding dynamics of the spot rate curve.

11.2 No-Arbitrage Dynamics of Spot Rate Curve

For discrete time, $t = 0, \Delta, 2\Delta, \ldots$, etc., suppose spot rate $r(t) \equiv r_t$ at any time t is a spot rate over horizon or period Δ, and is determined at the start of the period. We switch notation of spot rate from $y(t)$ to $r(t)$ here to avoid confusion with the yield-to-maturity since we are dealing more generally with spot rates that need not be yield-to-maturity as the underlying bonds need not be discount bonds.

Assume the spot rates follow a binomial process where in the next period, the Δ-period spot rate realizes one of two values either in an up-state (spot rate increases) or a down-state (spot rate decreases). When the time period or interval Δ shrinks to zero, the spot rate is instantaneous and is called a short rate.

For now, we shall start the modeling using the evolution of this (discrete) spot rate r_t^j where subscript t refers to the time when the spot rate is realized and which applies over the interval $[t, t+\Delta)$, and superscript j refers to the state, u or d. Since the states follow the binomial tree, at $t = \Delta$, there are two states u and d, and at $t = 2\Delta$, there are four states, uu, ud, du, and dd.

Associated with the evolution of the spot rates is the evolution of the risk-free ZC (or discount) bond prices. Assume there are three different maturity bonds at the start, $t = 0$. See the term structure lattice tree in Figure 11.1.

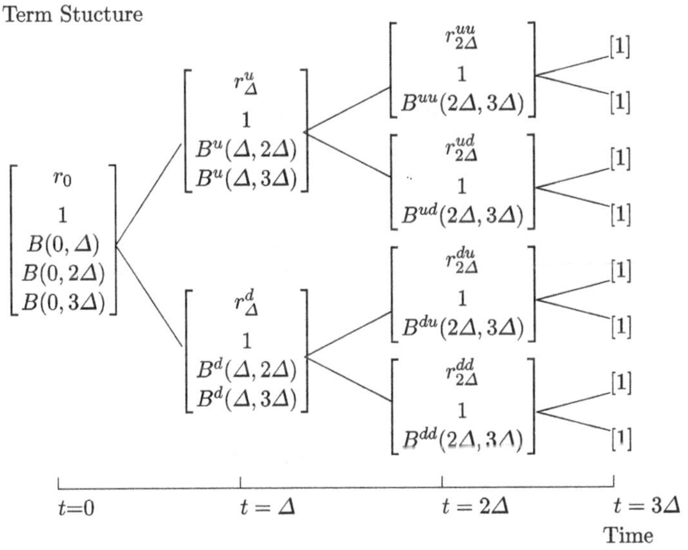

Figure 11.1: Interest Rate Lattice Tree.

At $t = 0$, the ZC bond with Δ period to maturity is priced at $B(0,\Delta) = \frac{1}{1+r_0}$. At $t = \Delta$, state u, the ZC bond with Δ period to maturity is priced at $B^u(\Delta, 2\Delta) = \frac{1}{1+r_\Delta^u}$. At $t = \Delta$, state d, the ZC bond with Δ period to maturity is priced at $B^d(\Delta, 2\Delta) = \frac{1}{1+r_\Delta^d}$. At $t = 2\Delta$, state j (uu, ud, du, or dd), the ZC bond with Δ period to maturity is priced at $B^j(2\Delta, 3\Delta) = \frac{1}{1+r_{2\Delta}^j}$.

Now, consider bonds with two periods until maturity. Here, we have to work backwards just as in binomial option pricing. Suppose at $t = \Delta$, there is a bond with two periods until maturity.

At $t = \Delta$, state u

$$B^u(\Delta, 3\Delta) = \frac{pB^{uu}(2\Delta, 3\Delta) + (1-p)B^{ud}(2\Delta, 3\Delta)}{1 + r_\Delta^u} \tag{11.2}$$

At $t = \Delta$, state d

$$B^d(\Delta, 3\Delta) = \frac{pB^{du}(2\Delta, 3\Delta) + (1-p)B^{dd}(2\Delta, 3\Delta)}{1 + r_\Delta^d} \tag{11.3}$$

Thus, bond prices are priced in a no-arbitrage martingale method, where p is the u-state risk-neutral probability, and $1-p$ is the d-state risk-neutral probability. In more complicated stochastic process of the spot rates, the probabilities may change over time. In simpler spot rate processes, the probabilities remain as constants.

Hence, we see that given the spot rate process – how they take values over time in each possible state – a vector of ZC bond prices of different maturities is also determined via a no-arbitrage equilibrium (whether markets are complete or not). This follows from the First Fundamental Theorem of asset pricing whereby we assume no-arbitrage and hence the existence of an equivalent martingale or risk-neutral probability measure with state probabilities p and $1 - p$.[1]

As seen in Eq. (11.1) and the binomial tree, each time-t state-j vector of ZC bond prices gives rise to a set of spot rates of different maturities at time t and state j. For time in the future, each of these is a contingent spot rate curve. Thus, given the Δ-period spot rate process r_t^j, we see how a no-arbitrage condition can imply a rich stochastic evolution of spot rate curves.

In actual physical situation or reality, the market can only observe a particular realized state j at each time t. Thus, at each time t in a realized (vector) time series, there is only a realized (ex-post) term structure or spot rate curve, although ex-ante there are contingent spot rate curves, each likely to happen with some risk-neutral probabilities according to the evolution of the binomial tree.

Given a particular spot rate model or process described by parameterization of probability p, rate increase factor and rate decrease factor, the no-arbitrage spot rate curve that is theoretically derived at $t = 0$ should ideally be consistent with the observed current market spot rate curve. To do this, we calibrate or estimate the parame-

1 See J. M. Harrison and D. M. Kreps (1979) Martingales and arbitrage in multi-period securities markets, *Journal of Economic Theory* 20, 381–384; J. M. Harrison, and S. R. Pliska (1981), Martingales and stochastic integrals in the theory of continuous trading, *Stochastic Processes and their Applications*, 11, 215–260; J. M. Harrison and S. R. Pliska (1983), A stochastic calculus model of continuous trading: Complete markets, *Stochastic Processes and their Applications*, 11, 313–316; S. Ross (1978) A simple approach to the valuation of risky streams, *Journal of Business*, 51(3), 453–475; J. Jacod, and A. N. Shiryaev (1998) Local martingales and the fundamental asset pricing theorems in the discrete-time case, *Finance and Stochastics*, 2, 259–273.

ters of the spot rate process so that the theoretical curve and the empirically observed curve coincide as closely as possible.

It is instructive to review the pricing of the 2-period ZC bond at time $t = \Delta$ for Eqs. (11.2) and (11.3), respectively, in states u and d. They can be simplified as

$$B^u(\Delta, 3\Delta) = p\left[\frac{1}{(1 + r_\Delta^u)(1 + r_{2\Delta}^{uu})}\right] + (1 - p)\left[\frac{1}{(1 + r_\Delta^u)(1 + r_{2\Delta}^{ud})}\right]$$

and

$$B^d(\Delta, 3\Delta) = p\left[\frac{1}{(1 + r_\Delta^d)(1 + r_{2\Delta}^{du})}\right] + (1 - p)\left[\frac{1}{(1 + r_\Delta^d)(1 + r_{2\Delta}^{dd})}\right]$$

Then, at current time $t = 0$, a 3-period ZC bond has price

$$\begin{aligned} B(0, 3\Delta) &= \frac{pB^u(\Delta, 3\Delta) + (1 - p)B^d(\Delta, 3\Delta)}{1 + r_0} \\ &= p^2\left[\frac{1}{(1 + r_0)(1 + r_\Delta^u)(1 + r_{2\Delta}^{uu})}\right] \\ &\quad + p(1 - p)\left[\frac{1}{(1 + r_0)(1 + r_\Delta^u)(1 + r_{2\Delta}^{ud})}\right] \\ &\quad + (1 - p)p\left[\frac{1}{(1 + r_0)(1 + r_\Delta^d)(1 + r_{2\Delta}^{du})}\right] \\ &\quad + (1 - p)^2\left[\frac{1}{(1 + r_0)(1 + r_\Delta^d)(1 + r_{2\Delta}^{dd})}\right] \end{aligned}$$

In general, let $\tilde{Y}_{0,T} = (1 + r_0)(1 + \tilde{r}_\triangle)(1 + \tilde{r}_{2\triangle}) \times \cdots \times (1 + \tilde{r}_{N\triangle})$, where $N\triangle - T$. Then,

$$\ln \tilde{Y}_{0,T} = \sum_{i=0}^{N} \ln(1 + \tilde{r}_{i\triangle})$$

Let $\tilde{r}_{i\triangle}^C = \ln(1 + \tilde{r}_{i\triangle})$. The LHS is the continuously compounded spot rate, and is the short rate r_u when $\triangle \downarrow 0$. Then,

$$\ln \tilde{Y}_{0,T} = \sum_{i=0}^{N} \tilde{r}_{i\triangle}^C \to \int_0^T \tilde{r}_u du$$

as $\triangle \downarrow 0$ and $N = \frac{T}{\triangle} \uparrow \infty$, and where we drop the superscript C for notational convenience. Hence, in continuous-time,

$$\tilde{Y}_{0,T} = \exp\left(\int_0^T r_u du\right)$$

Then, it is seen that a T year ZC bond price with redemption par value 1 is

$$B(0,T) = E^Q\left[\frac{1}{\tilde{Y}_{0,T}}\right] = E^Q(e^{-\int_0^T r_u du})$$

where Q denotes probability under the equivalent martingale or risk-neutral measure.

More generally,

$$B(t,T) = E_t^Q(e^{-\int_t^T r_u du}) \tag{11.4}$$

We can see that under no-arbitrage condition, ZC bond prices are indeed related to future par bond values discounted by expectation of future random spot rates under the risk-neutral or Q-measure. The risk-neutral rates in the lattice tree can also be used to compute no-arbitrage or arbitrage-free prices of derivatives on the underlying spot rates or underlying bond prices. Therefore, using a correct spot rate model (or short rate model when we refer to instantaneous r_t) is key to finding if current bond prices and interest rate and bond derivatives are correctly priced. Ability to pin-point equilibrium no-arbitrage prices and comparing with actual market prices that may have deviated in the short-run could facilitate profitable trading by buying market-underpriced securities and selling market-overpriced ones. Knowing the equilibrium prices and their parameters could also facilitate construction of accurate hedging positions for related portfolios. We shall develop the idea of spot rate models and estimating spot rate model parameters later.

For now, it is important to recognize that actual physical processes such as movements of realized spot rate curves over time can also provide statistical analyses for risk control. The current spot rate curve (and yield curve of the ZC bonds) can take nearly any shape as it evolves over time. We have seen how the term structure of spot rates determines a bond's price via the present value of sum of discounted bond's contractual cashflows at the related spot rates. Shaping risk is the sensitivity of a bond's price to the changing shape of the term structure of spot rates. More generally, shaping risk refers to risk when the yield curve changes.

To implement a process to manage the yield curve (YC) shape risk in a portfolio, one approach is to find a statistical model (YC Factor model) that reduces most of the possible yield curve movements to a probabilistic combination of a few standardized yield curve movements. A yield curve factor model is defined as a model or a description of yield curve movements that can be considered realistic when compared with historical data. One example is the three-factor model of Litterman and Scheinkman (1991),[2] who found that yield curve movements are historically well described by a

2 R. Litterman and J. Scheinkman (1991), Common factors affecting bond returns, *The Journal of Fixed Income*, 1, 54–61.

combination of three independent movements, which they interpreted as level, steepness, and curvature.

The method to determine the number of factors and their economic interpretation begins with a measurement of the change of key rates on the yield curve. A key rate is the yield on spaced-out specified maturities on a YC. For example, we could find the historical time series of the vector of 1/4, 1/2, 1, 2, 3, 5, 7, 10, 20, and 30 years maturity key rates or yields. The daily change in these key rates or yields provides for computation of the sample 10×10 variance-covariance matrix of the yield changes.

The next step is to try to discover a number of independent factors (fewer than the number of 10 variables in this case) that can explain the observed variance/covariance matrix. The approach that focuses on identifying the factors that best explain historical variances is known as principal components analysis (PCA).

11.3 Principal Component Analysis

Suppose random vector $X_{N\times 1}$ consists of elements Δr_j, each of which is a change in yield of a certain term on a yield curve. For example, Δr_1 could be monthly change in 1/4-year maturity yield, Δr_2 could be monthly change in 1/2-year maturity yield, and so on. Suppose $\mathrm{var}(\Delta r_j) > 0$ and $\mathrm{cov}(\Delta r_j, \Delta r_k) \neq 0$ for $j, k \in 1, 2, \ldots, N$. Let $E(X) = \mu_{N\times 1}$. Let covariance matrix of X be $\Sigma_{N\times N}$ where the jkth element is $\mathrm{cov}(\Delta r_j, \Delta r_k) = \sigma_{jk}$. Let λ_j be the ordered eigenvalues of $\Sigma_{N\times N}$ from largest λ_1 to smallest λ_N, and γ_j $(N \times 1)$ be the corresponding eigenvectors such that $\Sigma\gamma_j = \lambda_j\gamma_j$ for $j = 1, 2, \ldots, N$.

We constrain solutions of eigenvalues and eigenvectors to normalized orthogonal ones so that $\gamma_j^T\gamma_j = 1$. and $\gamma_j^T\gamma_k = 0$ for $j \neq k$. At this point, note that since we do not know the exact Σ and μ, the computed eigenvalues λ_j and eigenvectors γ_j are those of sample estimate $\hat{\Sigma}$ based on X and $\hat{\mu}$, and not of Σ and μ. Denote the computed eigenvalues and eigenvectors as $\hat{\lambda}_j$'s and $\hat{\gamma}_j$'s.

Let $\Lambda_{N\times N} = \mathrm{diag}(\lambda_1, \lambda_2, \lambda_3, \ldots, \lambda_N)$, or columns of $N \times 1$ vectors. Let $\Gamma_{N\times N} = (\gamma_1, \gamma_2, \ldots, \gamma_N)$. $\Gamma^T\Gamma = I_{N\times N}$, $\Gamma^T = \Gamma^{-1}$, so $\Gamma\Gamma^T = I$. We want to be able to find possibly recognizable factors that can explain the covariance matrix, i. e. variances and covariances of X in a maximal way, as much as possible. Suppose we form linear combinations of X, i. e., $Y_j = \gamma_j^T(X - \mu)$. This is the jth (scalar) principal component (PC) of X and there are N of them. Now $Y_{N\times 1} = \Gamma^T(X - \mu)$. The estimated PCs are found as $\hat{Y}_{N\times 1} = \hat{\Gamma}^T(X - \hat{\mu})$.

Properties of $Y_{N\times 1}$ include the following. (a) $E(Y_{N\times 1}) = 0_{N\times 1}$; (b) $\mathrm{var}(Y_{N\times 1}) = E[YY^T] = E[\Gamma^T(X - \mu)(X - \mu)^T\Gamma] = \Gamma^T\Sigma\Gamma = \Lambda_{N\times N}$. Hence the N principal components have zero means and are uncorrelated. The variance of the jth PC is the eigenvalue $\lambda_j > 0$.

From (b), since $\lambda_1 > \lambda_2 > \cdots > \lambda_N$, we can choose $Y_1 = \gamma_1^T(X - \mu)$ with the largest variance λ_1. We can choose $Y_2 = \gamma_2^T(X - \mu)$ with the second largest variance λ_2, and so on.

Now $Y_{N\times1} = \Gamma^T(X-\mu)$, so $\Gamma Y = \Gamma\Gamma^T(X-\mu) = (X-\mu)$. Then $X_{N\times1} = \mu+\Gamma_{N\times N}Y_{N\times1}$. From the latter, taking covariance: $\Sigma_{N\times N} = E[\Gamma Y(\Gamma Y)^T] = \Gamma E[YY^T]\Gamma^T = \Gamma\Lambda_{N\times N}\Gamma^T$. But trace $(\Sigma_{N\times N}) = \sum_{j=1}^N \sigma_j^2$. Also, $\text{tr}(\Sigma_{N\times N}) = \text{tr}(\Gamma\Lambda_{N\times N}\Gamma^T) = \text{tr}(\Lambda_{N\times N}\Gamma^T\Gamma) = \text{tr}(\Lambda_{N\times N}) = \sum_{j=1}^N \lambda_j$.

Choosing first PC as $Y_1 = \gamma_1^T(X-\mu)$ implies $\text{var}(Y_1) = \lambda_1$ has the largest variance with a percentage of total variance $\theta_1 = \lambda_1/\sum_{j=1}^N \sigma_j^2$. Thus the jth PC explains $\theta_j = \lambda_j/\sum_{j=1}^N \sigma_j^2$ percentage of the total variance of X or $\sum_{j=1}^N \sigma_j^2$.

Now, let the jth eigenvector be $\gamma_j = (\gamma_{j,1}, \gamma_{j,2}, \dots, \gamma_{j,N})^T$, for each j. Since $X_{N\times1} = \mu + \Gamma_{N\times N}Y_{N\times1}$, we can write:

$$\begin{pmatrix} \Delta r_1 \\ \Delta r_2 \\ \vdots \\ \Delta r_N \end{pmatrix} = \begin{pmatrix} \mu_1 \\ \mu_2 \\ \vdots \\ \mu_N \end{pmatrix} + \begin{pmatrix} \gamma_{1,1} & \gamma_{2,1} & \cdots & \gamma_{N,1} \\ \gamma_{1,2} & \gamma_{2,2} & \cdots & \gamma_{N,2} \\ \vdots & \vdots & \ddots & \vdots \\ \gamma_{1,N} & \gamma_{2,N} & \cdots & \gamma_{N,N} \end{pmatrix} \begin{pmatrix} Y_1 \\ Y_2 \\ \vdots \\ Y_N \end{pmatrix}$$

The above equation is exact based on the actual means μ_j's and actual eigenvectors of Σ. Since we could only estimate μ_j's and the eigenvectors, the relationship is more usefully expressed as the following.

$$\begin{pmatrix} \Delta r_1 \\ \Delta r_2 \\ \vdots \\ \Delta r_N \end{pmatrix} = \begin{pmatrix} \hat{\mu}_1 \\ \hat{\mu}_2 \\ \vdots \\ \hat{\mu}_N \end{pmatrix} + \begin{pmatrix} \hat{\gamma}_{1,1} & \hat{\gamma}_{2,1} & \cdots & \hat{\gamma}_{N,1} \\ \hat{\gamma}_{1,2} & \hat{\gamma}_{2,2} & \cdots & \hat{\gamma}_{N,2} \\ \vdots & \vdots & \ddots & \vdots \\ \hat{\gamma}_{1,N} & \hat{\gamma}_{2,N} & \cdots & \hat{\gamma}_{N,N} \end{pmatrix} \begin{pmatrix} \hat{Y}_1 \\ \hat{Y}_2 \\ \vdots \\ \hat{Y}_N \end{pmatrix}$$

as seen earlier viz. $\hat{Y}_{N\times1} = \hat{\Gamma}^T(X-\hat{\mu})$.

An alternative estimation of impact on Δr_j's can be developed as follows. It is neither of the above two representations, but makes use of the estimated PCs $\hat{Y}_j$'s as regressors in linear regressions.

We express $\Delta r_j = \mu_j + \gamma_{1,j}\hat{Y}_1 + e_{1j}$ where $e_{1j} \approx \gamma_{2,j}Y_2 + \gamma_{3,j}Y_3 + \cdots + \gamma_{N,j}Y_N$ is residual error associated with regression on only the first estimated PC $\hat{Y}_1$ and with the jth element of X. In the linear regression, we could use monthly sample data Δr_j observations over T months. We use the T observations of X to compute $\hat{\mu}$, $\hat{\Sigma}$, and $\hat{\Gamma}$, hence obtain T observations of $\hat{Y}_1$ as explanatory variable. $\hat{Y}_1$ is the first factor in the regression to explain changes in Δr_j. Thus for $j = 1, 2, \dots, N$, N regressions are performed, each using $\hat{Y}_1$ as explanatory variable.

Similarly, $\Delta r_j = \mu_j + \gamma_{2,j}\hat{Y}_2 + e_{2j}$ where $e_{2j} \approx \gamma_{1,j}Y_1 + \gamma_{3,j}Y_3 + \cdots + \gamma_{N,j}Y_N$ is residual error associated with a regression on only the second estimated PC $\hat{Y}_2$ or second factor, and so on.

Note that $\text{var}(\Delta r_j) = \sum_{k=1}^N \gamma_{k,j}^2 \text{var}(Y_k)$, for each j. Employing sample counterparts for the above equation for j, we obtain the approximate relationship:

$$T\widehat{\text{var}}(\Delta r_j) \approx \sum_{k=1}^{N} \hat{\gamma}_{k,j}^2 T\widehat{\text{var}}(\hat{Y}_k)$$

where T is the sample size in the simple regression. Recall the total sum of squares (TSS) and explained sum of squares (ESS) in Chapter 2 for simple regressions. The LHS is TSS, so the RHS is approximately the TSS.

In the simple regression of $\Delta r_j = \mu_j + \gamma_{1,j}\hat{Y}_1 + e_{1j}$, $\hat{\gamma}_{1,j}^2 T\widehat{\text{var}}(\hat{Y}_1)$ is the ESS. Hence, the coefficient of determination of the simple regression, $R^2 = \text{ESS}/\text{TSS} \approx \hat{\gamma}_{1,j}^2\widehat{\text{var}}(\hat{Y}_1)/\sum_{k=1}^{N}\hat{\gamma}_{k,j}^2\widehat{\text{var}}(\hat{Y}_k)$. Suppose $\hat{\gamma}_{k,j}^2$'s ($\forall k$) are approximately equal, then R^2 of the regression on the first estimated PC $\hat{Y}_1$ is approximately equal to θ_1. Similarly, R^2 of the regression on the second estimated PC $\hat{Y}_2$ is approximately equal to θ_2, and so on.

In practice principal component analysis is a method for dimension reduction in data analysis, so we choose, e. g. only 3 factors, $j = 1, 2, 3$ such that $\theta_1 + \theta_2 + \theta_3$ is close to 1, i. e., the 3 factors explain most of the variations in X. So we can perform a linear regression with dependent variable Δr_j on the first three factors at the same time. If we normalize each estimated PC as $Z_j = \hat{Y}_j/\sqrt{\hat{\lambda}_j}$, so Z_j has unit variance, then we can perform the regression:

$$\Delta r_j = \mu_j + \gamma_{1,j}^* Z_1 + \gamma_{2,j}^* Z_2 + \gamma_{3,j}^* Z_3 + \xi_j$$

where $\gamma_{1,j}^* = \gamma_{1,j}\sqrt{\lambda_1}$, $\gamma_{2,j}^* = \gamma_{2,j}\sqrt{\lambda_2}$, $\gamma_{3,j}^* = \gamma_{3,j}\sqrt{\lambda_3}$, and residual error ξ_j is assumed to be i. i. d. Z_j's are the standardized factors in the YC factor model.

The regression for each j yields estimated coefficients $\hat{\gamma}_{i,j}^*$'s shown as columns in the following table, where i denotes the factor order. $\hat{\mu}_j$ would likely be ≈ 0 and is not important in the analysis.

Table 11.1 shows that for a one standard deviation positive change in the first factor (normalized to have unit standard deviation), the yield for a 0.25-year bond would decline by 0.21 %, that of a 0.5-year bond by 0.22 %, and so on across maturities, so that a 30-year bond yield would decline by 0.31 %. Because the responses (change in yield) are in the same direction and by similar magnitudes across maturities, a reasonable interpretation of the first factor is that it describes (approximately) parallel shifts up and down the entire length of the yield curve. Thus a parallel shift down (increase in factor 1) would lead to downward shifts in all yields across maturities.

Table 11.1: Factors Affecting the Shape of the Yield Curve.

τ	0.25	0.5	1	2	3	5	7	10	20	30
Factor 1	−0.21	−0.22	−0.25	−0.30	−0.33	−0.38	−0.39	−0.38	−0.34	−0.31
Factor 2	0.51	0.45	0.35	0.22	0.15	−0.03	−0.15	−0.27	−0.36	−0.35
Factor 3	0.45	0.26	0.09	−0.34	−0.41	−0.35	−0.18	0.08	0.31	0.42

Note: τ is time-to-maturity in years.

Examining the second factor, we notice that a unitary positive standard deviation change appears to raise rates at shorter maturities (e. g., +0.51 % for 0.25-year bonds) but lowers rates at longer maturities (e. g., −0.36 % and −0.35 % for 20- and 30-year bonds, respectively). We can reasonably interpret this factor as one that causes changes in the steepness or slope of the yield curve. This is also called YC tilting. We note that the $\hat{\theta}_2$ associated with this factor is 17 %, and is much smaller than the $\hat{\theta}_1$ of 77 % associated with the first factor. The relative θ sizes indicate their relative importance as a factor.

The third factor contributes a much smaller $\hat{\theta}_3$ of 3 %, and we associate this factor with changes in the curvature or "twist" in the curve because a unitary positive standard deviation change in this factor leads to positive yield changes at both short and long maturities but produces declines at intermediate maturities. It yields more (convex) curvature.

If a bond portfolio manager anticipates decrease in factor 1 or increase in yield level, since there is an inverse relationship between bond price and yield, he/she would hedge possible loss in long bond portfolio positions by either selling away some bonds to reduce risk exposure and/or sell bond futures or buy puts on bonds. If a bond portfolio manager anticipates decrease (increase) in factor 2 or increase (decrease) in YC slope, he/she would hedge possible loss in long bond portfolio positions by adjusting the long positions toward a bullet structure. If a bond portfolio manager anticipates decrease (increase) in factor 3 or decrease (increase) in convexity of YC, he/she would hedge possible loss in long bond portfolio positions by adjusting the long positions toward a barbell (bullet) structure. Bond portfolio managers may also take speculative positions based on these views.

11.4 Continuous-Time Short Rate Models

In Figure 11.1, we saw how the spot rate process could drive the yield curve and bond prices. The instantaneous equivalent is called the short rate. Short rates need not be the pivot to drive bond prices; it could be instantaneous forward rates as starting points, or even some discrete period interest rates such as LIBOR or the secured overnight funding rate (SOFR). We shall now examine a few continuous-time short rate models.

In the early 1980s, banks and financial institutions were hunting for good models to price bonds with embedded options such as callable bonds, puttable bonds, and convertible bonds. Good models should be a result of equilibrium condition (no-arbitrage condition is an equilibrium market condition that is preference-free) and should also at the start agree or fit with the initially observed market yield curve or term structure,[3] The earliest models start with the modeling of short rate stochastic

3 See T. S. Y. Ho and S. B. Lee (1986), Term structure movements and pricing interest rate contingent claims, *The Journal of Finance*, 41, 1011–1029.

processes, and solving for bond prices under no-arbitrage equilibrium. Calibrating to existing yield curve as another equilibrium condition led to improvements in the models.

We consider the simplest models – single or one-factor interest rate model, whereby the interest rate process is driven by a single innovation dW^P (W^P is Wiener process) under physical measure or empirical measure P.

A continuous time stochastic process that possesses a strong Markov property and that has continuous sample paths (continuous observations in time) with no discontinuity or discrete jumps is called a diffusion process.[4] The application of continuous time mathematics to finance has been largely pioneered by Merton.[5] Many practical discrete Markov processes used in financial modelling can be approximated by diffusion process when the time interval between each observation point becomes very small. Likewise for many diffusion processes, when the interval is very small, we may sometimes choose to use a discrete process to approximate it.

Diffusion processes can be expressed as a stochastic differential equation (SDE) such as the lognormal diffusion process (or sometimes called Geometric Brownian Motion), $dS_t = \mu S_t\,dt + \sigma S_t\,dW_t^P$ where S_t is the underlying asset price at time t, W_t is a Wiener process with $W_0 \equiv 0$, and $(W_t - W_0)$ distributed as $N(0,t)$. μ is the instantaneous or infinitesimal mean or drift of the process, and σ is the instantaneous volatility. This diffusion is often called the lognormal diffusion and is suitable for modeling stock price S_t or commodity price or even currencies, but not suitable for modeling bond prices since bond prices pull to par at maturity. Just as solution of a partial differential equation is a multivariate deterministic function, the solution of a stochastic differential equation is a random variable that is characterized by a probability distribution.

The short rate is the spot interest rate when the term goes to zero. Let the short rate be r. This is the instantaneous spot rate. An example of a diffusion process of the short rate is:

$$dr_t = (\alpha - \beta r_t)\,dt + \sigma r_t^{\lambda}\,dW_t^P \tag{11.5}$$

where, α, β, and λ are constants. In the literature on interest rate modelling, many different models were applied to study interest rate dynamics and the associated bond prices. Many of the models are subsumed under the class represented by Eq. (11.5), and take different forms for different restricted values of the parameters α, β, and λ. When $\alpha = \beta = 0$ and $\lambda = 1$, there is the Dothan model.[6] When just $\lambda = 1$, there is the Brennan-

4 Refer to a classic book such as S. Karlin and H. M. Taylor (1981), *A Second Course in Stochastic Process*, Academic Press.

5 See R. C. Merton (1990), *Continuous-Time Finance*, Basil Blackwell.

6 U. Dothan (1978), On the term structure of interest rates, *Journal of Financial Economics*, 6, 59–69.

Schwartz model.[7] When just $\lambda = 0$, there is the Vasicek model.[8] And when $\lambda = 1/2$, there is the Cox-Ingersoll-Ross (CIR) model.[9]

The Vasicek model $dr_t = (\alpha - \beta r_t)\,dt + \sigma\,dW_t$, for $\alpha > 0$ and $\beta > 0$, is essentially a version of the well-established Ornstein-Uhlenbeck process that is known to be a mean-reverting process with an analytical solution. It can also be rewritten, as

$$dr_t = \kappa(\theta - r_t)\,dt + \sigma\,dW_t^P \tag{11.6}$$

where the equivalence is readily seen when we put $\alpha = \kappa\theta$, $\beta = \kappa$. The mean reversion occurs because when r_t deviates from θ, then there is a drift with positive "speed" κ, that brings future r_{t+dt} back toward θ. The solution to the SDE Eq. (11.6) is:

$$r_t = e^{-\kappa t} r_0 + \theta(1 - e^{-\kappa t}) + \sigma e^{-\kappa t} \int_0^t e^{\kappa u}\,dW_u^P \tag{11.7}$$

where r_0 is the short rate at initial time $t = 0$. The mean or expectation of r_t is

$$E(r_t) = \theta - e^{-\kappa t}(\theta - r_0) \tag{11.8}$$

and the variance is

$$\operatorname{var}(r_t) = \frac{\sigma^2}{e^{2\kappa t}} \int_0^t e^{2\kappa u}\,du = \frac{\sigma^2}{2\kappa}(1 - e^{-2\kappa t}) \tag{11.9}$$

Moreover, in the Vasicek model, r_t is seen to be normally distributed from Eq. (11.7) as it is an integral or summation of normal dW_u. This last feature of the Vasicek model is not desirable as it implies that there is non-zero probability that r_t can attain some negative values. Since r_t is a nominal interest rate, it is not proper for r_t to be negative, or there will be infinite arbitrage by borrowing at a negative cost of funds.

From the mean and variance equations in Eqs. (11.8) and (11.9), it is seen that over time, as t increases, the short rate r_t converges to a stationary random variable about the long-run mean of $\theta > 0$ regardless of the starting point r_0.

Short-rate models in the class of Eq. (11.5) are one-factor models because there is only one-state variable or source of uncertainty affecting the stochastic changes in r_t, i. e. the source from only dW_t. Short-rate models are very important in affecting bond pricing under no-arbitrage rational expectations framework. This is because if

7 M. J. Brennan and E. S. Schwarz (1977), Savings bonds, retractable bonds, and callable bonds, *Journal of Financial Economics*, 3, 133–155.

8 O. Vasicek (1977), An equilibrium characterization of the term structure, *Journal of Financial Economics*, 5, 177–188.

9 J. C. Cox, J. E. Ingersoll, and S. A. Ross (1985), A theory of the term structure of interest rates, *Econometrica*, 53, 385–407.

we assume a full spectrum of discount bonds $B(0, t)$ for maturity t in the future where $0 < t < T$, then each of these can be priced by the following expectation that we saw in Eq. (11.4).

$$B(0,t) = E_0^Q\left(\exp\left[-\int_0^t r_u(\alpha,\beta,\sigma,\lambda)\,du\right]\right) \tag{11.10}$$

where subscript Q to the conditional expectation at $t = 0$ denotes employment of the "risk-neutral" set of probability distribution Q. In the derivatives literature, this is akin to the no-arbitrage condition. In the process of the derivation, the probability measure P is transformed to the Q via the Girsanov Theorem.[10]

If we look at the solution of a short-rate model such as Eq. (11.7), then the RHS of Eq. (11.10) intuitively is solvable and would lead to an expression involving the parameters in the short rate. In turn this is the LHS that is the t-period to maturity discount bond price $B(0, t)$. For many short-rate models, discount bond prices at time t, $B(t, T)$ can be solved as $B(t, T) = \exp[\phi(t, T)-\gamma(t, T)r_t]$ for functions $\phi(t, T)$ and $\gamma(t, T)$ that are dependent on the short-rate model parameters. Thus, theoretical zero coupon bond prices and their derivatives, such as coupon bonds and bond derivatives, are related to the short-rate models and are affected by the parameter values in the short-rate models. In a similar fashion, with more complicated short rate models such as two-factor models,[11] the bond prices can be solved, whether analytically or via numerical methods, in terms of the parameters of the short rate process.

Thus equilibrium no-arbitrage interest rate models can be constructed to find current bond prices, either using a short rate model explicitly specified as in Eq. (11.5) via a SDE or using a discrete lattice model as seen in Figure 11.1. In the lattice model, it is usually possible to find enough degrees of freedom to allow calibration of the lattice parameters to fit the theoretical current bond prices to those observed currently in the market, i. e., fitting the current term structure or current YC. However, using an analytically specified SDE as in Eq. (11.5) where the number of parameters are limited, it is not possible to calibrate the parameters to fit all current bond prices or to fit the current YC exactly. One advantage, however, with using SDE specification under P-measure is that we can use historical time series data to directly estimate the parameters and test the short rate model without invoking the no-arbitrage equilibrium conditions. Of course, even if the statistical specification of the short rate model is found to be acceptable in this case, there is still no guarantee that the model can price bonds and bond derivatives correctly under no-arbitrage conditions.

10 One may refer to M. Musiela and M. Rutkowski (1998), *Martingale Methods in Financial Modelling*, Springer, and R. Rebonato (1996), *Interest Rate Option Models*, 2nd ed., John Wiley & Sons, for more advanced readings.

11 See D. Brigo and F. Mercurio (2001), Two-Factor Short-Rate Models. In: *Interest Rate Models Theory and Practice*, Springer Finance, Berlin, Heidelberg.

If a short-rate model such as Eq. (11.6) is solved in Eq. (11.7), then the analytical probability distribution of r_t is obtained, and this can be used to estimate the parameters via the maximum likelihood method. However, in many cases of short-rate models, including multi-factor models, complete solution of analytical probability distribution of r_t is not possible, and thus the maximum likelihood method cannot be applied. Some distribution-free method, e. g. GMM, may be used. Another approach is to use discrete approximations of the continuous-time short-rate model.

When the time interval Δ between two observations on the short rate is small, Eq. (11.5) may be approximated by an empirical discrete process, i. e. a process that can be tested using empirical data, as follows.

$$r_{t+\Delta} - r_t = (\alpha - \beta r_t)\Delta + e_{t+\Delta} \tag{11.11}$$

where $e_{t+\Delta}$ is an i. i. d. normally distributed random variable with mean $E(e_{t+\Delta}) = 0$, and $\mathrm{var}(e_{t+\Delta}) = \sigma^2 r_t^{2\lambda}\Delta$. Equation (11.11) may be expressed alternatively as $r_{t+\Delta} - r_t = \kappa(\theta - r_t)\Delta + e_{t+\Delta}$. This approximation was used in Chan, et al. and others.[12] We shall next explore the plausibility of several short rate models using regression analyses presented by Eq. (11.11).

11.5 Estimation of Discretized Models

Daily one-month Treasury Bill rates in the Secondary Market from August 2001 to March 2010 are obtained from the Federal Reserve Bank of New York public Web site. The one-month spot rates are treated as proxies for the short rate r_t. The graph of the time series of this rate is shown in Figure 11.2. Treasury bill trades are quoted in terms of discount yield (DY) where the equivalent bill price is $P = \mathrm{FV}(1 - \frac{\tau}{360}\mathrm{DY})$. FV is the face value of the bill, and τ is the day count to maturity. To put the yield computation from bills on the same footing as yields from Treasuy notes and bonds, this DY is converted to a bond equivalent yield (BEY). $\mathrm{BEY} = (\mathrm{FV}/P - 1)\frac{365}{\tau}$. Hence, BEY and DY are related as $\mathrm{BEY} = \frac{365\mathrm{DY}}{360 - \tau\,\mathrm{DY}}$.

It is seen that the p. a. rates increase spectacularly from 2003 to 2007 when the U. S. stock and property markets were booming. The rates collapsed in 2008 and 2009 together with the global financial crisis as governments cut central bank interest rates.

We shall use linear regression method to provide preliminary investigation of the plausibility of the Dothan, Vasicek, Brennan-Schwarz, and the CIR short-rate models.

Dothan's approximate discrete model is

$$r_{t+\Delta} - r_t = \sigma r_t \eta_{t+\Delta} \tag{11.12}$$

12 See K. C. Chan, A. Karolyi, F. A. Longstaff, and A. Saunders (1992), An empirical comparison of alternative models of the short-term interest rate, *The Journal of Finance*, 47(3), 1209–1227.

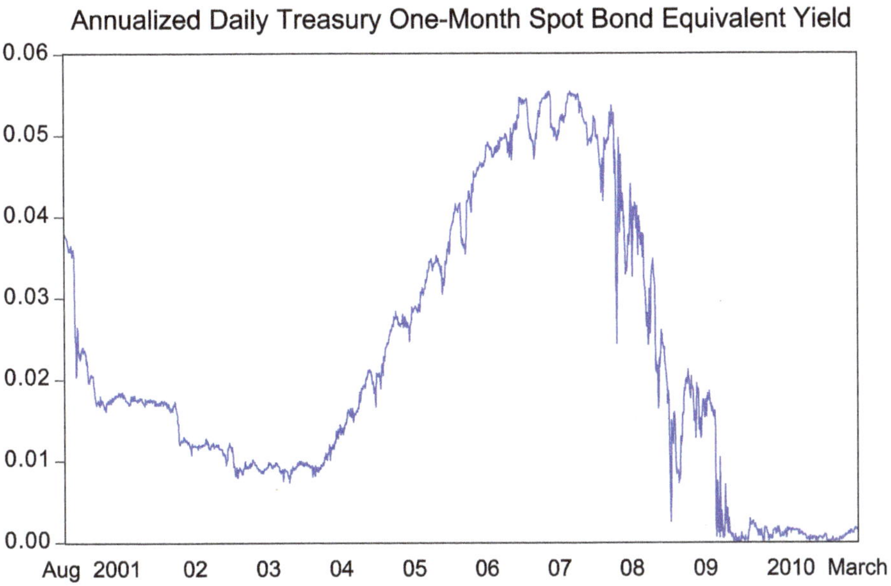

Figure 11.2: Daily One-Month Treasury Bill Rates in the Secondary Market.

where $\eta_{t+\Delta} \sim N(0, \Delta)$. The implication is that $(r_{t+\Delta} - r_t)/r_t \sim N(0, \sigma^2\Delta)$. It should be pointed out here that except for the Vasicek model that is mentioned earlier, all the other three models including Dothan's do not imply normal distribution for the short rates under continuous time. Hence, the discretized version of normal errors is merely an approximation.

Figure 11.3 and the embedded table show that $(r_{t+\Delta} - r_t)/r_t$ is not normally distributed. Thus, Eq. (11.12) may not be a good description of the proxy short rates.

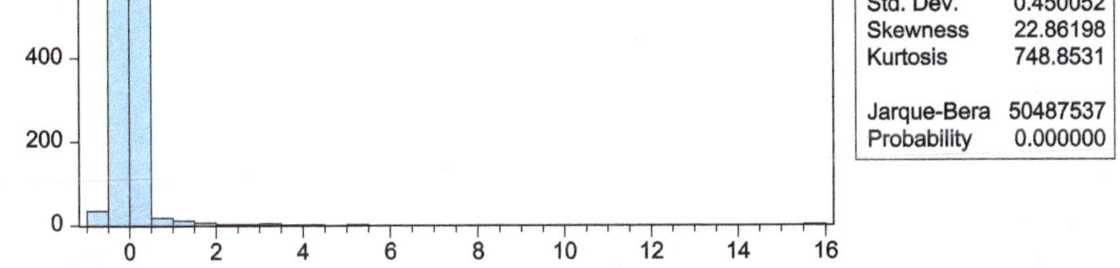

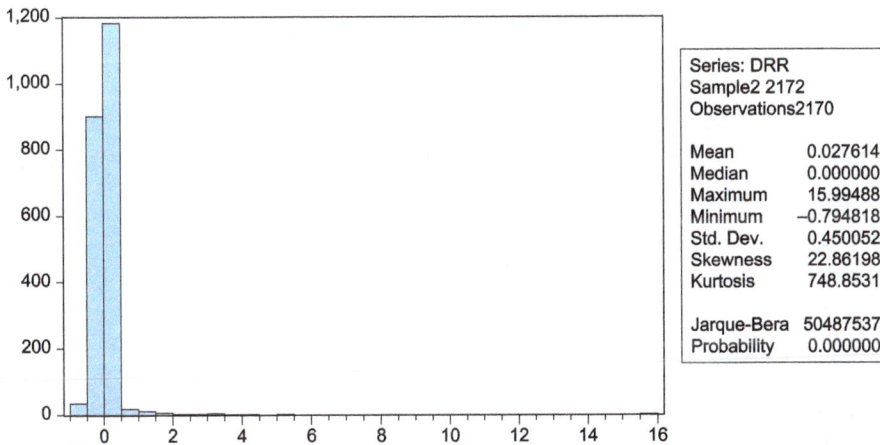

Figure 11.3: Test of Normality of $(r_{t+\Delta} - r_t)/r_t \sim N(0, \sigma^2\Delta)$.

Next, we explore regression using the Vasicek discrete model:

$$r_{t+\Delta} - r_t = (\alpha\Delta) - (\beta\Delta)r_t + e_{t+\Delta} \tag{11.13}$$

where $e_{t+\Delta}$ is i. i. d. normally distributed $N(0, \sigma^2\Delta)$. Let $a = \alpha\Delta$, and $b = -\beta\Delta$. Then, we perform regression

$$\Delta r_t = a + br_t + e_{t+\Delta}$$

The results are shown in Table 11.2. White's heteroskedasticity consistent adjustment[13] is made in estimating the standard errors of estimators. Though the estimates are not significantly different from zero, they neverthelessly have the correct signs. We use $\Delta = 1/365$. $\hat{\kappa} = \hat{\beta} = -365 \times \hat{b} = 0.549$. $\hat{\theta} = 365 \times \hat{a}/\hat{\kappa} = 0.0108$. If the model is correct, it suggests a long-run daily mean of 1.08 % on an annualized basis, and a mean reversion adjustment speed of 0.549. However, the residuals are not normal as seen in Figure 11.4, and this contradicts one implication of the Vasicek model. There is also strong correlation in the residuals.

Table 11.2: OLS Regression $\Delta r_t = a + br_t + e_{t+\Delta}, e_{t+\Delta} \sim$ i. i. d $N(0, \sigma^2\Delta)$. Sample size 2171.

Coefficient	Estimate	Std. Error	*t*-Statistic	Prob.
a	1.63E-05	2.81E-05	−0.579256	0.5625
b	−0.001504	0.001179	−1.275752	0.2022
R-squared	0.000695	Mean dependent var		−1.67E-05
Adjusted *R*-squared	0.000234	S. D. dependent var		0.000977
S. E. of regression	0.000977	Akaike info criterion		−11.02359
Sum squared resid	0.002070	Schwarz criterion		−11.01836
Log likelihood	11968.11	Hannan-Quinn criter.		−11.02168
F-statistic	1.508434	Durbin-Watson stat.		1.653049
Prob(*F*-statistic)	0.219512			

The discrete approximations of Brennan-Schwarz short-rate model is:

$$r_{t+\Delta} - r_t = (\alpha\Delta) - (\beta\Delta)r_t + r_t e_{t+\Delta}$$

where $e_{t+\Delta}$ is i. i. d. normally distributed $N(0, \sigma^2\Delta)$.

Let $y_{t+\Delta} = (r_{t+\Delta} - r_t)/r_t$, then the model implies

$$y_{t+\Delta} = -(\beta\Delta) + (\alpha\Delta)(1/r_t) + e_{t+\Delta}$$

13 See Halbert White (1980), A heteroskedasticity-consistent covariance matrix estimator and a direct test for heteroskedasticity, *Econometrica*, 48(4), 817–838.

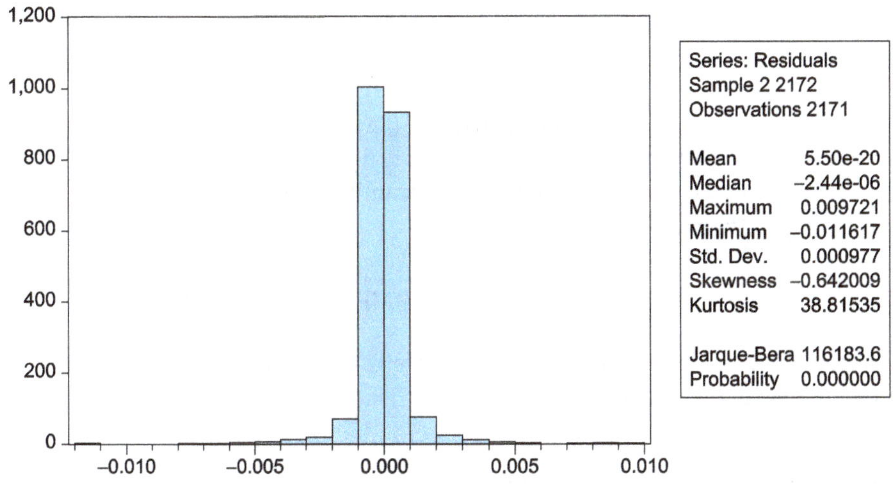

Figure 11.4: Test of Normality of $e_{t+\Delta} \sim N(0, \sigma^2\Delta)$.

Let $a = -\beta\Delta$ and $b = \alpha\Delta$. Then, we perform regression

$$y_{t+\Delta} = a + b(1/r_t) + e_{t+\Delta}$$

The results are shown in Table 11.3. White's heteroskedasticity consistent adjustment is made in estimating the standard errors of estimators.

Table 11.3: OLS Regression $y_{t+\Delta} = a + b(1/r_t) + e_{t+\Delta}, e_{t+\Delta} \sim$ i. i. d. $N(0, \sigma^2\Delta)$. Sample size 2170.

Coefficient	Estimate	Std. Error	*t*-Statistic	Prob.
a	0.000216	0.008442	0.025591	0.9796
b	6.73E-05	1.60E-05	4.209572	0.0000
R-squared	0.032504	Mean dependent var		0.027614
Adjusted *R*-squared	0.032058	S. D. dependent var		0.450052
S. E. of regression	0.442780	Akaike info criterion		1.209432
Sum squared resid	425.0444	Schwarz criterion		1.214669
Log likelihood	−1310.233	Hannan-Quinn criter.		1.211347
F-statistic	72.83674	Durbin-Watson stat		2.181601
Prob(*F*-statistic)	0.000000			

In the regression, the sign of the coefficient of the intercept is not negative, and thus mean reversion adjustment speed is incorrectly estimated as negative.

The discrete approximations of CIR short-rate model is:

$$r_{t+\Delta} - r_t = (\alpha\Delta) - (\beta\Delta)r_t + r_t^{1/2}e_{t+\Delta}$$

where $e_{t+\Delta}$ is i. i. d. normally distributed $N(0, \sigma^2\Delta)$. Let $y_{t+\Delta} = (r_{t+\Delta} - r_t)/r_t^{1/2}$, then the model implies

$$y_{t+\Delta} = c + (\alpha\Delta)(1/r_t^{1/2}) - (\beta\Delta)r_t^{1/2} + e_{t+\Delta}$$

We add a constant c which should be insignificantly different from zero. Let $b_1 = \alpha\Delta$ and $b_2 = -\beta\Delta$. Then, we perform regression

$$y_{t+\Delta} = c + b_1(1/r_t^{1/2}) + b_2(r_t^{1/2}) + e_{t+\Delta}$$

The results are shown in Table 11.4. White's heteroskedasticity consistent adjustment is made in estimating the standard errors of estimators.

Table 11.4: OLS Regression $y_{t+\Delta} = c + b_1(1/r_t^{1/2}) + b_2(r_t^{1/2}) + e_{t+\Delta}$, $e_{t+\Delta} \sim$ i. i. d. $N(0, \sigma^2\Delta)$. Sample size 2170.

Coefficient	Estimate	Std. Error	t-Statistic	Prob.
c	−0.000630	0.001408	−0.447633	0.6545
b_1	7.82E-05	2.64E-05	2.960648	0.0031
b_2	−0.000523	0.007337	−0.071293	0.9432
R-squared	0.009705	Mean dependent var		0.000317
Adjusted R-squared	0.008791	S. D. dependent var		0.012484
S. E. of regression	0.012429	Akaike info criterion		−5.936154
Sum squared resid	0.334769	Schwarz criterion		−5.928298
Log likelihood	6443.727	Hannan-Quinn criter.		−5.933281
F-statistic	10.61857	Durbin-Watson stat		2.018086
Prob(F-statistic)	0.000026			

In the regression reported in Table 11.4, the estimated coefficients are of the correct signs and one of them is highly significant.

$$\hat{\kappa} = \hat{\beta} = -365 \times \hat{b}_2 = 0.191, \quad \text{and} \quad \hat{\theta} = 365 \times \hat{b}_1/\hat{\kappa} = 0.150$$

However, the estimate of long-run mean $\hat{\theta}$ appears too high for a Treasury short rate during this sampling period.

The above preliminary results based on a simple discretized approximation of the various continuous time short rate models do not appear to provide strong support of the models. Similar results are found in a study by Nowman (1997).[14]

14 See K. B. Nowman (1997), Gaussian estimation of single-factor continuous time models of the term structure of interest rates, *The Journal of Finance*, 52(4), 1695–1706.

11.5.1 Black-Derman-Toy Model

To continue with the idea of a lattice tree in Figure 11.1, we show below a popular spot rate model used in industry that carries some of the useful features of the Vasicek model and also allows for calibration to the current term structure. The continuous-time representation of the Black-Derman-Toy (BDT) interest rate model is:

$$d\ln r_t = (\theta(t) - a(t)\ln r_t)dt + \sigma(t)dW_t^Q$$

There are some differences with the original Vasicek model shown in Eq. (11.6). Firstly, the LHS is the change in log of r_t, so that the short rate r_t will not be negative. Secondly, instead of constant long-run mean level and speed of reversion, these are now functions of time, so at different times, they can take different values. Thirdly, the variance is also a function of time. Finally, we use the risk-neutral probability measure Q here for the innovation since we are directly dealing with no-arbitrage prices. There is no need to specify the empirical measure as we do not need to use the historical time series data for estimating the short rate process parameters. The BDT model retains useful features such as mean reversion of the interest rate, and parsimony in the variance process.

For solution, the discrete version of BDT model is

$$\Delta\ln r_{t+\Delta} = (\theta(t) - a(t)\ln r_t)\Delta + \sigma(t)\Delta W_t^Q \tag{11.14}$$

where ΔW_t^Q is normally distributed as $N(0,\Delta)$. The mean and variance at t conditional on $\ln r_t$ are $E_t^Q(\Delta\ln r_{t+1}) = (\theta(t) - a(t)\ln r_t)\Delta$, and $\text{var}_t^Q(\Delta\ln r_{t+1}) = \sigma(t)^2\Delta$.

Starting at $t = 0$ in a binomial process, the log spot rate at $t = \Delta$ is either

$$\ln r_\Delta^u = \ln r_0 + (\theta(0) - a(0)\ln r_0)\Delta + \sigma(0)\sqrt{\Delta} \tag{11.15}$$

with risk-neutral probability $\frac{1}{2}$ or,

$$\ln r_\Delta^d = \ln r_0 + (\theta(0) - a(0)\ln r_0)\Delta - \sigma(0)\sqrt{\Delta} \tag{11.16}$$

with risk-neutral probability $\frac{1}{2}$. Then it is seen from Eqs. (11.15) and (11.16) that $E(\ln r_\Delta - \ln r_0) = (\theta(0) - a(0)\ln r_0)\Delta$, and $\text{var}(\ln r_\Delta) = \sigma(0)^2\Delta$. This is identical with the mean and variance results in Eq. (11.14). Moreover, it can be seen that the binomial process approximates the Wiener process as $\Delta \downarrow 0$. Therefore, another interpretation of the lattice structure in Figure 11.1 is that besides a discrete process in its own right, the discrete lattice process also converges to a continuous-time model as $\Delta \downarrow 0$.

The non-recombining lattice tree in Figure 11.1 is more general and allows for more parameters, but is computationally very heavy as the number of nodes grows exponentially at 2^N when there are N periods. To facilitate computations for a large N (as a way of approaching the continuous-time solution), the lattice tree is made to recombine whenever possible, i. e. numerically feasible (so that the risk-neutral probabilities and the nodal values are all within the feasible spaces), and allows convergence (or finite approximation) to the desired continuous-time process.

We can consider a recombining binomial lattice tree for BDT model as follows. In the next time step from Eq. (11.15),

$$\ln r_{2\Delta}^{ud} = \ln r_{\Delta}^{u} + (\theta(\Delta) - a(\Delta)\ln r_{\Delta}^{u})\Delta - \sigma(\Delta)\sqrt{\Delta}$$

In the next time step from Eq. (11.16),

$$\ln r_{2\Delta}^{du} = \ln r_{\Delta}^{d} + (\theta(\Delta) - a(\Delta)\ln r_{\Delta}^{d})\Delta + \sigma(\Delta)\sqrt{\Delta}$$

For recombining lattice tree, we put $\ln r_{2\Delta}^{ud} = \ln r_{2\Delta}^{du}$, so we obtain $(\ln r_{\Delta}^{u} - \ln r_{\Delta}^{d})(1 - a(\Delta)\Delta) = 2\sigma(\Delta)\sqrt{\Delta}$. Then, $a(\Delta)\Delta = 1 - \sigma(\Delta)/\sigma(0)$. In the BDT model, the volatility process $\{\sigma(0), \sigma(\Delta), \sigma(2\Delta), \ldots\}$ is subjectively specified by the interest rate hedger or else speculator. This in turn fixes the parameters $\{a(\Delta), a(2\Delta), \ldots\}$.

Moreover, if we take the value of an upper node less that of a lower node, we obtain $\ln r_{2\Delta}^{uu} - \ln r_{2\Delta}^{ud} = 2\sigma(\Delta)\sqrt{\Delta}$. Similarly, $\ln r_{2\Delta}^{du} - \ln r_{2\Delta}^{dd} = 2\sigma(\Delta)\sqrt{\Delta}$. This stylized feature of the BDT lattice makes it very easier to specify all the short rate values on each node at a time t when the lowest node is established. For example, if at $t = k\Delta$ $(k > 0)$, the lowest nodal value of short rate is $r_{k\Delta}^{ddd\ldots dd} = X_{k\Delta}$, then the short rates at nodes higher up at $t = k\Delta$ are $X_{k\Delta}\exp(2\sigma[(k-1)\Delta]\sqrt{\Delta})$, $X_{k\Delta}\exp(4\sigma[(k-1)\Delta]\sqrt{\Delta})$, $X_{k\Delta}\exp(6\sigma[(k-1)\Delta]\sqrt{\Delta})$, and so on until $X_{k\Delta}\exp(2k\sigma[(k-1)\Delta]\sqrt{\Delta})$ at the top node.

Given the current term structure or equivalent the current zero coupon bond prices at $t = 0$ of $\{B(0,\Delta), B(0,2\Delta), B(0,3\Delta), \ldots, B(0,N\Delta)\}$,

$$\begin{aligned}
B(0,\Delta) &= \frac{1}{(1+r_0)}\\
B(0,2\Delta) &= \frac{1}{2}\left[\frac{1}{(1+r_0)(1+X_\Delta\exp(2\sigma[0]\sqrt{\Delta}))}\right] + \frac{1}{2}\left[\frac{1}{(1+r_0)(1+X_\Delta)}\right]\\
B(0,3\Delta) &= \frac{1}{4}\left[\frac{1}{(1+r_0)(1+X_\Delta\exp(2\sigma[0]\sqrt{\Delta}))(1+X_{2\Delta}\exp(4\sigma[\Delta]\sqrt{\Delta}))}\right]\\
&\quad + \frac{1}{4}\left[\frac{1}{(1+r_0)(1+X_\Delta\exp(2\sigma[0]\sqrt{\Delta}))(1+X_{2\Delta}\exp(2\sigma[\Delta]\sqrt{\Delta}))}\right]\\
&\quad + \frac{1}{4}\left[\frac{1}{(1+r_0)(1+X_\Delta)(1+X_{2\Delta}\exp(2\sigma[\Delta]\sqrt{\Delta}))}\right]\\
&\quad + \frac{1}{4}\left[\frac{1}{(1+r_0)(1+X_\Delta)(1+X_{2\Delta})}\right]
\end{aligned}$$

and so on.

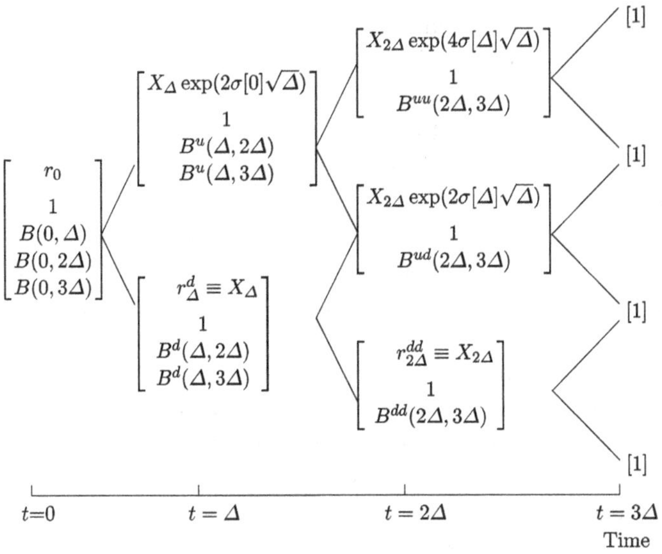

Figure 11.5: Black-Derman-Toy Interest Rate Lattice Tree.

The recombining BDT spot rate tree can be shown in Figure 11.5. We illustrate with only $N = 3$ time steps.

Hence, we can bootstrap to solve for X_Δ given $B(0, 2\Delta)$ (r_0 is known and $\sigma(0)$ is an input). If we assume $\theta(0) = 0$, then from X_Δ we can solve for $a(0)$ using Eq. (11.16). Next we can solve for $X_{2\Delta}$ given $B(0, 3\Delta)$. From $X_{2\Delta}$ we can solve for $\theta(\Delta)$. Therefore, by calibrating the BDT model with inputs of the volatility curve, all the model parameters $\theta(t)$ and $a(t)$ for $t = \Delta, 2\Delta, \ldots$ can be found in Eq. (11.14). Just as the statistical spot rate models have the disadvantage of being not calibrated to the current term structure (partly due to the finite number of parameters in a statistical specification) or bond prices, the calibrated approach in the lattice tree also has the disadvantage that it is clumsy when it comes to forecasting as it has possibly an infinite number of parameters, e. g., $\{\theta(t), a(t)\}$, $\forall t > 0$. These implied parameters may also change over time. There is positive use to understanding how interest rates evolve but normative use such as in forecasting requires more theoretical and empirical studies.

11.6 Credit Spreads

So far we have discussed risk-free Treasury bonds and their interest rates including spot rates and yield-to-maturity. Now we discuss yield-to-maturity of a corporate bond that is higher than that of a Treasury bond with the same maturity since investors would demand compensation of higher yield for bearing default risk in corporate bonds. The excess of a corporate bond yield over the Treasury bond yield of the same maturity is called a credit spread of that maturity. Thus, credit spread also has a term structure.

In Duffee (1998) and Dufresne, et al. (2001),[15] increase in three-month U. S. Treasury bill rate and increase in the slope of the Treasury yield curve both separately would lead to decrease in the credit spread of corporate bonds, especially bonds with longer maturity and lower ratings.

One way of understanding this is that when times are good – boom during a business cycle peak – and demand for loanable funds are high, the short-maturity Treasury interest rates (and other loanable funds rates as well) go up. Likewise, expected next period short-term rate is high. The latter implies that today's long-term rate that accounts for the high expected next period's interest rate would also be high. Higher long-term rates mean that the slope of the yield curve also goes up. In these situation, the market's assessments of the credit risks of corporate bonds are lower, and thus the credit spread (or credit premium, difference between credit risky bond interest and the Treasury interest of the same maturity) would narrow.

On the other hand, when the Treasury yield curve slope starts to decrease and turn negative, then there is expectation of future short rate decreases, a signal of market's negative assessment of future economic prospects.[16] This would cause credit risk premium or credit spread to rise.

To empirically verify this economic intuition, we perform a regression analysis as follows. Monthly spot interest rates of the U. S. Treasury bills and bonds and also Ba-rating bonds from February 1992 to March 1998 were obtained from Lehman Brothers Fixed Income Database. We first construct monthly Ba-rated credit spreads for nine-year term by finding the difference of Ba-rated nine-year spot rate less the Treasury nine-year spot rate. We then construct the Treasury yield curve slope (or its proxy "slope" since the yield curve is not exactly a straight line) by taking the Treasury 10-year spot rate less the Treasury one-month spot rate.

Finally, we also employ the Treasury one-month spot rate (T1M) as the proxy for short rate (very short-term Treasury spot rate). A regression of the credit spread π_t on the one-month Treasury spot and the Treasury slope (TERMSLOPE) using the set of 74 monthly observations is performed.

$$\pi_t = c + b_1 \mathrm{T1M}_t + b_2 \mathrm{TERMSLOPE}_t + \xi_t$$

where ξ_t is residual i. i. d. noise.

15 See G. R. Duffee (1998), The relation between treasury yields and corporate bond yield spreads, *The Journal of Finance*, LIII(6), 2225–2241. See also P. Collin-Dufresne, R. S. Goldstein, and J. S. Martin (2001), The determinants of credit spread changes, *The Journal of Finance*, LVI(6), 2177–2207.

16 A. Ang, M. Piazzesi, and M. Wei (2006), What does the yield curve tell us about GDP growth? *Journal of Econometrics*, 131, 359–403, commented that every recession in the U. S. after the mid-1960s was predicted by a negative yield curve slope within six quarters.

The results are shown in Table 11.5. It is indeed seen that the coefficient estimates on the one-month Treasury spot rate and on the Treasury slope are both negative as indicated. Regression using the three-month Treasury spot rate as proxy for the short-rate yields almost similar results. However, the coefficients for this sampling period are not significantly negative based on the t-tests.

Table 11.5: OLS Regression of Credit Spread π_t on Treasury Short Rate and Slope, 2/1992 to 3/1998 (Sample size 74).

Coefficient	Estimate	Std.Error	t-Statistic	Prob.
a	0.071755	0.022873	3.137055	0.0025
b_1	−0.387103	0.337696	−1.146305	0.2555
b_2	−1.120837	0.907097	−1.235631	0.2207
R-squared	0.024888	Mean dependent var		0.043620
Adjusted R-squared	−0.002580	S. D. dependent var		0.017919
S. E. of regression	0.017943	Akaike info criterion		−5.163593
Sum squared resid	0.022857	Schwarz criterion		−5.070185
Log likelihood	194.0529	Hannan-Quinn criter.		−5.126331
F-statistic	0.906070	Durbin-Watson stat		2.093021
Prob(F-statistic)	0.408730			

The credit spread and the Treasury slope are indeed important factors in the economy. Other factors are of course included in the residual term ξ_t. In a related study, Fama and French (1993)[17] found that in cross-sectional regressions, there is positive effect of term structure slope and also positive effect of default risk premium (credit spread) on risky bond returns.

Further Reading

Garbade, Kenneth D. (1999), *Fixed Income Analytics*, The MIT Press.
Sundaresan, S. (1997), *Fixed Income Markets and Their Derivatives*, South-Western Publishing.
Fabozzi, Frank J. (2007), *Fixed Income Analysis*, John Wiley & Sons.

17 Eugene F. Fama and Kenneth R. French (1993), Common risk factors in the returns on stocks and bonds, *Journal of Financial Economics* 33, 3–56.

12 Option Pricing and Implied Moments

Just as bond prices are derivatives of short rate processes, option prices are derivatives of underlying price processes. The Chicago Board of Trade had started trading options in 1973. The Black–Scholes formula, when endorsed by the academic community, became a popular tool for traders, partly due to its analytical simplicity, and helped in the expansion of the options market.

12.1 Itô's Calculus

We first state the important stochastic calculus result. Note that W_s deenotes the Wiener process at time s.

Theorem 12.1 (Itô–Doeblin Formula). *For* $dX_s = \mu(s, X_s)ds + \sigma(s, X_s)dW_s$,

$$f(t, X_t) = f(0, X_0) + \int_0^t f_t(s, X_s)ds + \int_0^t f_X(s, X_s)dX_s + \frac{1}{2}\int_0^t f_{XX}(s, X_s)\sigma(s, X_s)^2 ds$$

Its differential form is

$$df(t, X_t) = f_t(t, X_t)dt + f_X(t, X_t)dX_t + \frac{1}{2}f_{XX}(t, X_t)(dX_t)^2$$

The latter is often called Itô's lemma. We show below how the Itô's lemma can be used to solve a stochastic differential equation.

Suppose X_t has stochastic differential equation:

$$dX_t = \mu X_t dt + \sigma X_t dW_t \tag{12.1}$$

where μ and σ are instantaneous mean and volatility of dX_t/X_t that are constants. Then, putting $f(X_t) = \ln X_t$, we have, applying Itô's lemma:

$$\begin{aligned} d\ln X_t &= \frac{1}{X_t}dX_t + \frac{1}{2}\left(-\frac{1}{X_t^2}\right)(dX_t)^2 \\ &= (\mu dt + \sigma dW_t) - \frac{1}{2}\sigma^2 dt \\ &= \left(\mu - \frac{1}{2}\sigma^2\right)dt + \sigma dW_t \end{aligned} \tag{12.2}$$

using the Wiener process property that $(dW_t)^2 = dt$ and also $(dt)^2 = (dt)(dW_t) = 0$.

If we take the definite integral on Eq. (12.2) over support $[0, T]$ and define $W_0 = 0$,

https://doi.org/10.1515/9783110673951-012

$$\int_0^T d\ln X_t = \int_0^T \left(\mu - \frac{1}{2}\sigma^2\right)dt + \sigma \int_0^T dW_t$$

Then

$$\ln X_T - \ln X_0 = \left(\mu - \frac{1}{2}\sigma^2\right)T + \sigma W_T$$

and

$$X_T = X_0 \exp\left(\left[\mu - \frac{1}{2}\sigma^2\right]T + \sigma W_T\right) \tag{12.3}$$

This is a strong solution[1] to the Geometric Brownian Motion stochastic differential equation in Eq. (12.1); the solution is a stochastic process $X_t(\omega)$ which in this case is a diffusion process since it is a strong Markov process with continuous sample path. It has a normal probability distribution at any time point t, and is also called a lognormal diffusion process.

12.2 Martingale Method For Black-Scholes Formula

The GBM has a physical or empirical drift term μdt which makes it difficult to price an option directly since it is generally difficult to determine a risk-discounted rate for option returns corresponding to an arbitrary $\mu \neq 0$. The method to price options based on the underlying stock price process such as the GBM in Eq. (12.1) leads to the path-breaking Black-Scholes model. We introduce the Girsanov theorem and use it to transform the GBM under physical or empirical probability measure P to an equivalent martingale or risk-neutral probability measure Q such that the GBM becomes one with a risk-neutral drift.

Theorem 12.2 (Girsanov Theorem). *Define the process $dW_t^Q = dW_t^P + \gamma dt$, where the RHS is an SDE under the P-measure. Assume γ satisfies the Novikov condition*

$$E\left(\exp\left[\frac{1}{2}\int_0^t |\gamma|^2 ds\right]\right) < \infty$$

The LHS W_t^Q is a Wiener process under a different probability measure Q where measure Q is related to P by the Radon-Nikodým derivative $\frac{dQ}{dP} = \exp[-\frac{1}{2}\int_0^t \gamma_s^2 ds - \int_0^t \gamma_s dW_s]$.

1 A weak solution does not enable a mapping of Brownian Motion path $W_t(\omega)$ to solution $X_t(\omega)$ though it may offer a distribution indexed by time. A strong solution would require conditions that initial X_0 has a finite second moment if it is a RV, that X_t has a continuous sample path, and the drift and diffusion coefficients satisfy the Lipschitz condition, i. e., do not change too fast, $|\mu(t,y) - \mu(t,x)| + |\sigma(t,y) - \sigma(t,x)| \leq K|y-x|$, K finite, for some small displacements in X_t from x to y.

The Novikov condition is necessary in order for stochastic integral to be finite. The Girsanov theorem can be used to change the drift of a diffusion process under P-measure and to turn it into a martingale under a different Q-probability measure. Thus, a process $dW_t + \gamma dt$ may have a non-zero drift γdt under the P-measure. But by applying the Q-measure with density $dQ/dP = Z(\omega)$ where Q and P are equivalent probability measures and $E_P(Z) = 1$, we can turn the process into a martingale diffusion process W_t^Q now with zero drift under Q-measure.

Consider a money account process $M_T = M_0 \exp(rT)$ where r is the continuously compounded risk-free rate. M_0 is an initial constant, and M_T is the money in a risk-free deposit or money account that accumulates at the rate of r continuously. Then, employing Eq. (12.3), the discounted price process is

$$\frac{X_t}{M_t} = \frac{X_0}{M_0} \exp\left(\left[\mu - r - \frac{1}{2}\sigma^2\right]T + \sigma W_T^P\right)$$

or,

$$d\left(\frac{X_t}{M_t}\right) = \frac{X_t}{M_t}[(\mu - r)dt + \sigma dW_t^P]$$

Hence, under the P-measure where X_t follows the GBM, the discounted price process has a drift $\mu - r$ which is not zero. To apply Girsanov's theorem and change the drift to zero, we use $\gamma = \frac{\mu - r}{\sigma}$ in the Radon-Nikodým derivative $\frac{dQ}{dP}$ to switch to a different Wiener process $W_t^Q = W_t^P + \frac{\mu - r}{\sigma}t$. Now,

$$\begin{aligned} d\left(\frac{X_t}{M_t}\right) &= \frac{X_t}{M_t}[(\mu - r)dt + \sigma dW_t^P] \\ &= \frac{X_t}{M_t}\left[(\mu - r)dt + \sigma\left(dW_t^Q - \frac{\mu - r}{\sigma}dt\right)\right] \\ &= \frac{X_t}{M_t}[(\mu - r)dt + \sigma dW_t^Q - (\mu - r)dt] \\ &= \frac{X_t}{M_t}\sigma\, dW_t^Q \end{aligned} \tag{12.4}$$

In Eq. (12.4), X_t/M_t is now a martingale under the equivalent Q-measure. Under Q, this probability distribution implies a risk-neutral SDE of X_t as follows

$$dX_t = rX_t dt + \sigma X_t dW_t^Q$$

There is an important connection between no-arbitrage equilibrium asset pricing and existence of an equivalent martingale measure Q. As seen in Chapter 11, the first fundamental asset pricing theorem by Dybvig and Ross (1987)[2] essentially states that no-

2 P. H. Dybvig and Stephen A. Ross (1987), Arbitrage, in J. Eatwell, M. Milgate, P. Newman, eds., *The New Palgrave Dictionary of Economics*, London Macmillan.

arbitrage price obtains if and only if there exists an equivalent martingale measure. Thus, one can employ expectations on the Q-martingale measure to find the current no-arbitrage equilibrium price of any security and derivative without having to construct an equilibrium theory of risk premium. Under this Q-measure, all derivative prices $C(X_t)$ can be solved by taking expectation $E_0(C_t)$ w. r. t. the risk-neutral distribution X_t under Q- measure and discounting by the risk-free return e^{rt}. It is as if investors in the market are all risk-neutral.

The risk-neutral probability distribution of underlying asset price X_t under Q, $N((r-\frac{1}{2}\sigma^2)t, \sigma^2 t)$ is used to price any European derivative $C(X_t, t)$. For a European call, price C_0, on a stock with price S_0, let $X_0 = S_0$. Time to maturity is τ.

$$\begin{aligned} C_0 &= e^{-r\tau}E[\max(S_\tau - K, 0)] \\ &= e^{-r\tau}(E[S_\tau | S_\tau \geq K]P[S_\tau \geq K] - KP[S_\tau \geq K]) \end{aligned}$$

First, $S_\tau \equiv S_0 \exp((r - 1/2\sigma^2)\tau + \sigma\sqrt{\tau}z)$ where $z \sim N(0,1)$. This distribution is under the Q–measure. Then,

$$\begin{aligned} &E(S_\tau | S_\tau \geq K) \\ &= E\left(S_0 \exp((r-1/2\sigma^2)\tau + \sigma\sqrt{\tau}Z) | Z \geq \frac{\ln(K/S_0) - (r - 1/2\sigma^2)\tau}{\sigma\sqrt{\tau}}\right) \\ &= \left(\int_{\frac{\ln(K/S_0)-(r-1/2\sigma^2)\tau}{\sigma\sqrt{\tau}}}^{\infty} S_0 \exp((r-1/2\sigma^2)\tau + \sigma\sqrt{\tau}z)\phi(z)dz\right)/P(S_\tau \geq K) \\ &= S_0 \exp(r\tau)\left[\int_{\frac{\ln(K/S_0)-(r-1/2\sigma^2)\tau}{\sigma\sqrt{\tau}}}^{\infty} \exp\left(-\frac{1}{2}\sigma^2\tau + \sigma\sqrt{\tau}z - \frac{1}{2}z^2\right)\frac{1}{\sqrt{2\pi}}dz\right]/P(S_\tau \geq K) \\ &= S_0 \exp(r\tau)\left[\int_{\frac{\ln(K/S_0)-(r-1/2\sigma^2)\tau}{\sigma\sqrt{\tau}}}^{\infty} \exp\left(-\frac{1}{2}(\sigma\sqrt{\tau} - z)^2\right)\frac{1}{\sqrt{2\pi}}dz\right]/P(S_\tau \geq K) \end{aligned}$$

Doing a change of variable $y = \sigma\sqrt{\tau} - z$, we have

$$E(S_\tau | S_\tau \geq K) = S_0 \exp(r\tau)\left[\int_{-\infty}^{\frac{\ln(S_0/K)+(r+1/2\sigma^2)\tau}{\sigma\sqrt{\tau}}} \exp\left(-\frac{1}{2}y^2\right)\frac{1}{\sqrt{2\pi}}dy\right]/P(S_\tau \geq K)$$

Then

$$E[S_\tau | S_\tau \geq K]P[S_\tau \geq K] = S_0 e^{r\tau}N(d_1)$$

where

$$d_1 = \frac{\ln(S_0/K) + (r + 1/2\sigma^2)\tau}{\sigma\sqrt{\tau}}$$

Next,

$$P(S_\tau \geq K) = P(\ln S_\tau - \ln S_0 \geq \ln K - \ln S_0) = P\left(\ln \frac{S_\tau}{S_0} \geq \ln \frac{K}{S_0}\right)$$

Since $\ln \frac{S_\tau}{S_0} \sim N((r - 1/2\sigma^2)\tau, \sigma^2\tau)$, then

$$\begin{aligned} P\left(\ln \frac{S_\tau}{S_0} \geq \ln \frac{K}{S_0}\right) &= P\left(\frac{\ln(S_\tau/S_0) - (r - 1/2\sigma^2)\tau}{\sigma\sqrt{\tau}} \right. \\ &\geq \left. \frac{\ln(K/S_0) - (r - 1/2\sigma^2)\tau}{\sigma\sqrt{\tau}}\right) \\ &= \int_{\frac{\ln(K/S_0)-(r-1/2\sigma^2)\tau}{\sigma\sqrt{\tau}}}^{\infty} \phi(z)dz \\ &= \int_{-\infty}^{\frac{\ln(S_0/K)+(r-1/2\sigma^2)\tau}{\sigma\sqrt{\tau}}} \phi(z)dz \\ &= N(d_2) \end{aligned}$$

where

$$d_2 = \frac{\ln(S_0/K) + (r - 1/2\sigma^2)\tau}{\sigma\sqrt{\tau}}$$

Therefore,

$$C_0 = e^{-r\tau}(S_0 e^{r\tau} N(d_1) - KN(d_2))$$

or

$$C_0 = S_0 N(d_1) - Ke^{-r\tau} N(d_2)$$

This is the Black-Scholes European call price on an underlying stock without dividends.

12.3 Greeks

Greeks refer to the Greek alphabets used to denote the various partial derivatives of analytical option prices to underlying parameter shifts including changes in the underlying variable. Greeks are (variable) hedging ratios.

Consider the European Black–Scholes call price C_t at time t with exercise or strike price K, maturity at time $T > t$, and underlying asset price following GBM $dS = S(\mu dt + \sigma dW)$. The continuously compounded risk-free rate over $[t, T]$ is r:

$$C(S,t) = SN(d_1) - Ke^{-r\tau}N(d_2) \tag{12.5}$$

where $N(\cdot)$ is the cdf of a standard normal RV and $\phi(\cdot)$ is its pdf,

$$\tau = T - t$$
$$d_1 = \frac{\ln(\frac{S}{K}) + (r + \frac{1}{2}\sigma^2)\tau}{\sigma\sqrt{\tau}}$$
$$d_2 = d_1 - \sigma\sqrt{\tau}$$

Using put-call parity, the European put price is

$$P(S,t) = Ke^{-r\tau}N(-d_2) - SN(-d_1) \tag{12.6}$$

We have employed the Black–Scholes option formula so far, and this is in the context of European stock options. There are other types of European-style options involving commodities, currencies, and futures, which are also based on the Black–Scholes formulation.

Consider a forward contract with current price F for future delivery of commodities, including stock, at time-to-maturity τ. By the cost-of-carry no-arbitrage model, $F = Se^{r\tau}$, or $S = Fe^{-r\tau}$. Substituting this into Eq. (12.5), we have the price of a call option on a forward contract (if we ignore the mark-to-market stochastic interest gains or losses of an otherwise similar futures contract, then this is also the price of a futures call option):

$$C(F,t) = e^{-r\tau}(FN(d_1) - KN(d_2)) \tag{12.7}$$

where

$$d_1 = \frac{\ln(\frac{F}{K}) + \frac{1}{2}\sigma^2\tau}{\sigma\sqrt{\tau}}$$
$$d_2 = d_1 - \sigma\sqrt{\tau}$$

We provide a slightly more general version of the Black–Scholes formula of calls and puts on underlying GBM asset price Z with cost of carry η. Then,

$$C(Z,t) = e^{(\eta - r)\tau}ZN(d_1) - e^{-r\tau}KN(d_2) \tag{12.8}$$

where

$$d_1 = \frac{\ln(\frac{Z}{K}) + (\eta + \frac{1}{2}\sigma^2)\tau}{\sigma\sqrt{\tau}}$$
$$d_2 = d_1 - \sigma\sqrt{\tau}$$

The put formula is

$$P(Z,t) = e^{-r\tau}KN(-d_2) - e^{(\eta-r)\tau}ZN(-d_1) \tag{12.9}$$

Using Eqs. (12.8) and (12.9), if it is a stock option without dividend, $\eta = r$ and $Z = S$. If it is a stock option with continuous dividend yield δ, then $\eta = r - \delta$ and $Z = S$. If it is a futures option, $\eta = 0$ and $Z = F$ since there is no carry cost (as the price for futures is not paid upfront but is settled only at maturity). If it is a currency option priced in US$ for possible gain in currency Y where the domestic US interest rate is r and the foreign currency Y interest rate is r_Y, then $\eta = r - r_Y$ (this amounts to a replication position of borrowing US$ and lending in currency Y, thus receiving payout in Y interest while paying $ interest) and Z is the spot exchange rate in $ per Y.

In the following, we develop the Greeks for the general version of Black–Scholes in (12.8) and (12.9).

From (12.8) and (12.9),

$$\frac{\partial d_1}{\partial Z} = \frac{\partial d_2}{\partial Z} = \frac{1}{Z\sigma\sqrt{\tau}}$$
$$\phi(d_2) = \frac{1}{\sqrt{2\pi}}\exp\left(-\frac{1}{2}(d_1^2 - 2d_1\sigma\sqrt{\tau} + \sigma^2\tau)\right)$$
$$= \phi(d_1)\exp\left(d_1\sigma\sqrt{\tau} - \frac{1}{2}\sigma^2\tau\right)$$
$$= \phi(d_1)\frac{Z}{K}e^{\eta\tau} \tag{12.10}$$

Delta; δ

$$\frac{\partial C}{\partial Z} = e^{(\eta-r)\tau}N(d_1) + e^{(\eta-r)\tau}Z\frac{\phi(d_1)}{Z\sigma\sqrt{\tau}} - Ke^{-r\tau}\frac{\phi(d_2)}{Z\sigma\sqrt{\tau}}$$
$$= e^{(\eta-r)\tau}N(d_1) + e^{(\eta-r)\tau}\frac{\phi(d_1)}{\sigma\sqrt{\tau}} - e^{(\eta-r)\tau}\frac{\phi(d_1)}{\sigma\sqrt{\tau}} \quad \text{using Eq. (12.10)}$$
$$= e^{(\eta-r)\tau}N(d_1) > 0$$
$$\frac{\partial P}{\partial Z} = -e^{(\eta-r)\tau}N(-d_1) < 0$$

Rho; ρ

$$\frac{\partial C}{\partial r} = e^{(\eta-r)\tau}Z\phi(d_1)\frac{\partial d_1}{\partial r} - Ke^{-r\tau}\phi(d_2)\frac{\partial d_2}{\partial r} - KN(d_2)[-\tau e^{-r\tau}]$$
$$= e^{(\eta-r)\tau}Z\phi(d_1)\left[\frac{\partial d_1}{\partial r} - \frac{\partial d_2}{\partial r}\right] + \tau Ke^{-r\tau}N(d_2)$$

$$= \tau K e^{-r\tau} N(d_2) > 0$$
$$\frac{\partial P}{\partial r} = -\tau K e^{-r\tau} N(-d_2) < 0$$

Vega; ν

$$\frac{\partial C}{\partial \sigma} = e^{(\eta-r)\tau} Z\phi(d_1)\frac{\partial d_1}{\partial \sigma} - Ke^{-r\tau}\phi(d_2)\frac{\partial d_2}{\partial \sigma}$$
$$= e^{(\eta-r)\tau} Z\phi(d_1)\left[\frac{\partial d_1}{\partial \sigma}\right] - Ke^{-r\tau}\phi(d_2)\left[\frac{\partial d_1}{\partial \sigma} - \sqrt{\tau}\right]$$
$$= e^{(\eta-r)\tau} Z\phi(d_1)\sqrt{\tau} > 0$$

Note that vegas for the BS European call and put are identical.

Gamma; Γ or γ

$$\frac{\partial^2 C}{\partial Z^2} = \frac{\partial e^{(\eta-r)\tau} N(d_1)}{\partial Z}$$
$$= e^{(\eta-r)\tau}\phi(d_1)\frac{\partial d_1}{\partial Z}$$
$$= e^{(\eta-r)\tau}\frac{\phi(d_1)}{Z\sigma\sqrt{\tau}} > 0$$

Note that gammas for the BS European call and put are identical. Gamma is the largest for calls and puts at the money and close to expiry. Next, the time decay, or theta, is shown as follows.

Theta; θ

$$\frac{\partial C}{\partial t} = -\frac{\partial C}{\partial \tau}$$
$$= -\Bigg((\eta - r)e^{(\eta-r)\tau} ZN(d_1) + e^{(\eta-r)\tau} Z\phi(d_1)\frac{\partial d_1}{\partial \tau}$$
$$- KN(d_2)[-re^{-r\tau}] - e^{-r\tau} K\phi(d_2)\frac{\partial d_2}{\partial \tau}\Bigg)$$
$$= -(\eta - r)e^{(\eta-r)\tau} ZN(d_1) - re^{-r\tau} KN(d_2) - e^{(\eta-r)\tau} Z\phi(d_1)\frac{\sigma}{2\sqrt{\tau}}$$
$$\frac{\partial P}{\partial t} = -\frac{\partial P}{\partial \tau}$$
$$= (\eta - r)e^{(\eta-r)\tau} ZN(-d_1) + re^{-r\tau} KN(-d_2) - e^{(\eta-r)\tau} Z\phi(d_1)\frac{\sigma}{2\sqrt{\tau}}$$

Intuitively, most options have negative θ or time decay, reflecting the fact that their value decreases as the expiry date nears. Time decay is especially fast for at-the-money options. However, unlike other major Greeks, there are exceptions when time decay or θ can become positive. For example, some in-the-money European puts that cannot be exercised until maturity behave like holding ZC bonds, where the value increases as expiry date gets closer. In-the-money European calls on currencies yielding very high interest rates may also have positive thetas. Thus although the sign of θ is mostly negative, it may be positive in some situations.

12.3.1 Delta Hedging

Delta hedging refers to hedging an open option position by taking an opposite position in the underlying with a quantity equal to delta, thus creating a delta-neutral portfolio. Hedging a short (long) position in the underlying can be done by taking a long (short) position in the option by a quantity equal to 1/delta.

Suppose the portfolio is a long (short) position in a stock call option. Delta hedging this long (short) option position consists of short-selling (buying) δ number of stocks. Thus, over a small time interval, the change in value of the delta-neutral portfolio of value $\Pi = C - \delta S$ is close to zero:

$$|\triangle C - \delta \triangle S| = \left|\triangle C - \frac{\partial C}{\partial S} \triangle S\right| \approx 0$$

Dynamic delta hedging refers to a trading strategy that continuously maintains a delta-neutral portfolio through the life of the option portfolio. In this case, the delta of the option portfolio is changing continuously and requires the number of stocks to be continuously adjusted. By continuously maintaining a delta-neutral hedge, the idea is to keep the portfolio value $\Pi = C - \delta S$ approximately constant until the option reaches maturity. The motivation for doing this may be that at time t after the option has begun, the owner has gained value in the option equal to $C_t - C_0 > 0$. To lock in this value, without having to liquidate the options for whatever reasons (including reason of options market being illiquid or having the options as a collateral pledge, and so on), the owner uses delta hedging to try to lock-in $C_t - C_0$ until maturity of option at T.

Consider the call option price $C(S, t)$ at time t. Taking the total derivative and using Itô's lemma gives

$$dC_t = C_t dt + C_S dS_t + \frac{1}{2} C_{SS} (dS_t)^2$$

Hence, the hedged portfolio infinitesimal value change (given fixed δ over dt) is

$$\begin{aligned} d\Pi_t &= dC_t - \delta dS_t \\ &= C_t dt + C_S dS_t + \frac{1}{2} C_{SS} (dS_t)^2 - \delta dS_t \\ &= C_t dt + \frac{1}{2} C_{SS} (dS_t)^2 \end{aligned} \tag{12.11}$$

There are two aspects of Eq. (12.11). Over small discrete trading interval $\triangle$, $\triangle\Pi_t \approx \theta \triangle + \frac{1}{2}\Gamma(\triangle S_t)^2$. Taking expectations on both sides

$$E(\triangle\Pi_t) \approx \theta \triangle + \frac{1}{2}\Gamma E(\triangle S_t)^2 \\ = \theta \triangle + \frac{1}{2}\Gamma\sigma^2 S_t^2 \triangle \qquad (12.12)$$

so a delta-hedged portfolio (e. g., long option short stocks) will still experience some drift. This is shown in Figure 12.1.

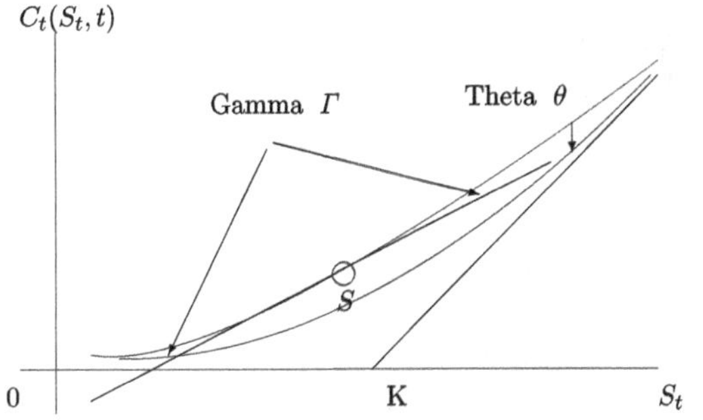

Figure 12.1: Illustration of Delta Hedging.

Figure 12.1 shows the slope of the tangent to the price point S on the upper curve as δ or C_S. At S, if the stock price either increases or decreases, there will be a gap between the new price C_t' and the tangent line representing $C_t + C_S\triangle S_t$. The gap is $\triangle C_t - \delta\triangle S_t$, which is driven by Γ or C_{SS} of the call as seen in Eq. (12.11). The gap is sometimes called the delta-hedging error. Note that whichever way the price S_t may deviate, Γ is positive and is profitable to the trader who is long call and short stock. As time passes, the price curve shifts to the lower one with time decay that is negative as the call is not deep in-the-money. The difference between the two price curves represents time decay or $\theta < 0$, ceteris paribus.

Positive Γ is similar in concept to the convexity in the price-yield relationship of a bond curve. Theoretically, given a stock price $S_t \sim$ GBM, then

$$\begin{aligned} d\Pi_t &= dC_t - \delta dS_t \\ &= C_t dt + \frac{1}{2}C_{SS}(dS_t)^2 \\ &= \theta dt + \frac{1}{2}\Gamma\sigma^2 S_t^2 dt \\ &= -\left[S_t\phi(d_1)\left[\frac{\sigma}{2\sqrt{\tau}}\right] + rKe^{-r\tau}N(d_2)\right]dt + \left[\frac{1}{2}\frac{\phi(d_1)}{S_t\sigma\sqrt{\tau}}\sigma^2 S_t^2\right]dt \\ &= -rKe^{-r\tau}N(d_2)dt \end{aligned} \qquad (12.13)$$

Hence, a long option delta-neutral portfolio has positive gamma, negative theta, and net negative drift as seen in (12.13). On the contrary, sell-side bankers who are short options and hold a delta-neutral portfolio face negative gamma, positive theta, and a net positive drift.

It is seen that Γ is small when the stock is deep in-the-money or deep out-of-the-money, i. e., $\phi(d_1)$ is very small. Thus, a banker holding a delta-neutral portfolio and short in options would prefer if the options did not end close to being at-the-money near maturity, so that the negative gamma would be small in magnitude. On the other hand, an investor holding a delta-neutral portfolio and long in options would prefer if the options end close to being at-the-money near maturity, so that the positive gamma would be large in magnitude and bring about a positive portfolio return.

As shown in Eq. (12.13), delta-hedging on a continuous-time basis still leaves a negative drift $-rKe^{-r\tau}N(d_2)dt$. Where does this come from? If we examine the Black–Scholes European call option pricing formula

$$C(S,t) = SN(d_1) - Ke^{-r\tau}N(d_2)$$

we find that there are two components making up or replicating a call: long position of $N(d_1)$ or C_S or δ number of underlying shares, and short position or borrowing of dollar amount of risk-free bond $Ke^{-r\tau}N(d_2)$.

Delta hedging constitutes only the first component above. That is why there is still a remaining drift term in Eq. (12.13). If we want to replicate a call option exactly in a continuous-time dynamic way, we should buy δ or $N(d_1)$ number of underlying shares and short $Ke^{-r\tau}N(d_2)$ amount of risk-free bonds. If we wish to hedge a long call option, we should short δ or $N(d_1)$ number of underlying shares and buy (lend) $Ke^{-r\tau}N(d_2)$ dollar amount of risk-free bonds. In the latter, the infinitesimal change in the value of the portfolio (now comprising an additional amount of risk-free bond) is

$$d\Pi_t^* = dC_t - \delta dS_t + r[Ke^{-r\tau}N(d_2)]dt = 0$$

Now, we obtain a dynamically perfect hedge, provided that at every instance t, we rebalance our portfolio with a new $\delta = N(d_1)$ and a new amount of risk-free bond equal to $Ke^{-r\tau}N(d_2)$. It is seen in the replicating portfolio $[N(d_1)S_t, -Ke^{-r\tau}N(d_2)]$ for a call option $C(S_t,t)$ that as maturity approaches, if the call is out-of-the-money (OTM) or S_t is below K, then the replicating portfolio behaves more like a bond since $N(d_1)$ is close to zero, and in fact the bond portion is also close to zero. If the call is in-the-money (ITM) when maturity approaches, i. e., $S_t > K$, then $N(d_1)$ approaches 1 while $N(d_2)$ also approaches 1, so that the call value tends towards $S_T - K$.

12.4 Numerical Method in Option Pricing and Hedging

The Black-Scholes option price is analytically tractable. However, most stock options are American style, i. e. the option can be exercised at any time point prior to maturity, unlike the European style options. American options generally do not have closed form analytical solutions though there exist many methods of semi-analytical solutions involving some numerical computations. We show below a popular and common type of numerical method called the lattice tree method. This method is computationally effective and mostly efficient when the option is not path-dependent and the underlying asset's stochastic process is not overly complicated. we show the case of the lognormal diffusion stochastic stock price process.[3]

Figure 12.2 shows the binomial (lattice) tree of stock price evolution in time having two states in each period or interval. The stocks do not issue dividends. In the up-state U, stock return is a factor u, and in the down-state D, stock return is a factor d.

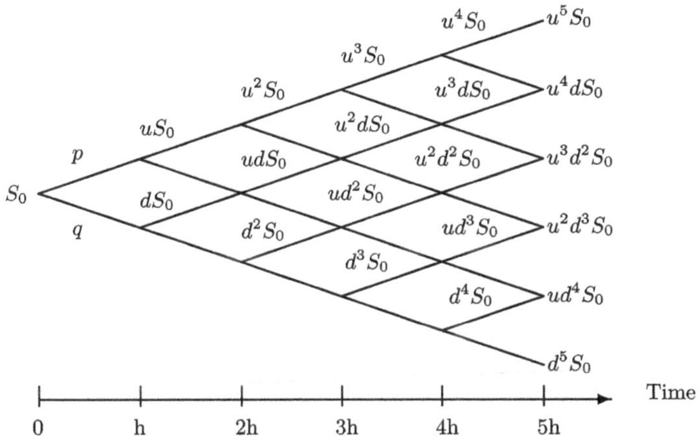

Figure 12.2: Stock Price Evolution (with no dividend).

The time interval at each decision point is h number of years, where h is a small fraction. At $t = 0$, an investor buys $\triangle_0$ shares of stock, costing \$ $\triangle_0 S_0$, and borrows \$ B_0 at risk-free rate (sells \$ B_0 of risk-free bonds) that requires interest payment at the continuously compounded rate r % p. a.

At $t = 0$, total portfolio cost is \$ $\triangle_0 S_0 - B_0$. At $t = h$, the portfolio value can take one of two possible outcomes. In the up-state U, the portfolio value becomes

$$U: \quad \triangle_0 u S_0 - B_0 e^{rh}$$

In the down-state D, the portfolio value becomes

$$D: \quad \triangle_0\, d S_0 - B_0 e^{rh}$$

3 See J. C. Cox, S. A. Ross, and M. Rubinstein (1979), Option pricing: A simplified approach, *Journal of Financial Economics*, 7 (3), 229–263.

If the portfolio is chosen to replicate an option outcome at $t = h$ of option prices C_u at U and C_d at D, then we equate

$$U: \quad \Delta_0 u S_0 - B_0 e^{rh} = C_u \tag{12.14}$$

$$D: \quad \Delta_0\, d S_0 - B_0 e^{rh} = C_d \tag{12.15}$$

Given u, d, r, S_0, C_u, C_d, we solve Eqs. (12.4) and (12.5) to obtain

$$\Delta_0 = \frac{C_u - C_d}{S_0(u-d)} \tag{12.16}$$

$$B_0 = \frac{uC_d - dC_u}{e^{rh}(u-d)} \tag{12.17}$$

The solutions in (12.16) and (12.17) allow the portfolio to replicate the option outcomes at $t = h$. To prevent arbitrage, therefore the total portfolio cost must equal the price of the option at $t = 0$, i. e.,

$$C_0 = \Delta_0 S_0 - B_0 = e^{-rh}\left(\frac{e^{rh} - d}{u-d} C_u + \frac{u - e^{rh}}{u-d} C_d\right) \tag{12.18}$$

Note that the option with prices C_0, C_u, C_d are any option that derives values as a function of the underlying asset or stock price. They can be a call or a put in the current framework. Their exact type is determined by their boundary value or definition of value at maturity, e. g. $C_T = \max(S_T - K, 0)$ for call, and $\max(K - S_T, 0)$ for put. To prevent arbitrage, we must also have

$$u > e^{rh} > d$$

Equation (12.18) shows that we can put pseudo-probability measure

$$p = \frac{e^{rh} - d}{u - d} \in (0, 1)$$

and

$$1 - p = \frac{u - e^{rh}}{u - d} \in (0, 1).$$

Let us call these risk-neutral or Q-probability measures. Then

$$C_0 = e^{-rh} E_0^Q(C_h)$$

where $C_h = C_u$ with probability p, and $C_h = C_d$ with probability $1 - p$. Or

$$\frac{C_0}{e^{r \times 0}} = E_0^Q\left(\frac{C_h}{e^{rh}}\right)$$

which indicates that C_h/e^{rh} is a martingale. According to the fundamental theorem of asset pricing, under this complete market (two states and two securities) where there is no arbitrage, a unique martingale measure exists – in this case, $P_Q(U) = p$ and $P_Q(D) = 1-p$. These probabilities for the U and D states are unique because of market completeness.

From Eq. (12.16), $\triangle_0 = \frac{C_u-C_d}{S_0(u-d)}$ is the lattice tree discrete "delta". This delta on the lattice tree provides a delta-neutral hedge to the option and the underlying shares. From the earlier Eqs. (12.14) and (12.15):

$$\triangle_0 uS_0 - C_u = B_0 e^{rh}$$

and

$$\triangle_0 dS_0 - C_d = B_0 e^{rh}$$

We can see that a short (long) position of call with current value C_0 delta-hedged by long (short) $\triangle_0 = \frac{C_u-C_d}{S_0(u-d)}$ number of shares would lead to constant plus (minus) $B_0 e^{rh}$ in both the up-state and the down-state. Thus the hedge is completely effective and micmics a risk-free bond.

If at $t = h$, it is state U as in Eq. (12.14), after the portfolio assumes the new value under the new price uS_0, an individual holding this portfolio can then rebalance it in such a way that it is a self-financing portfolio, in the sense that there is no cash withdrawal and no fresh capital input. Under state U at $t = h$, the portfolio would be rebalanced to a new portfolio $(\triangle_1^U, -B_1^U)$ such that

$$\triangle_1^U (uS_0) - B_1^U = C_u \tag{12.19}$$

On the other hand, if it is state D as in Eq. (12.15), this portfolio would be rebalanced in a self-financing way to a new portfolio $(\triangle_1^D, -B_1^D)$ such that

$$\triangle_1^D (dS_0) - B_1^D = C_d$$

Moreover, if it is state U, the portfolio $(\triangle_1^U, -B_1^U)$ is selected in such a way that

$$\triangle_1^U u^2 S_0 - B_1^U e^{rh} = C_{uu} \tag{12.20}$$

and

$$\triangle_1^U udS_0 - B_1^U e^{rh} = C_{ud} \tag{12.21}$$

On the other hand, if it is state D, the portfolio $(\triangle_1^D, -B_1^D)$ is selected in such a way that

$$\triangle_1^D duS_0 - B_1^U e^{rh} = C_{du}$$

and

$$\triangle_1^D d^2 S_0 - B_1^U e^{rh} = C_{dd}$$

Solving Eqs. (12.20) and (12.21) for $\triangle_1^U$ and B_1^U, and putting the solutions into Eq. (12.19) gives:

$$C_u = e^{-rh}(pC_{uu} + (1-p)C_{ud})$$

showing how the option prices are attained each state in the next period under self-financing rebalancing. Hence, with no arbitrage there exists Q-measure s. t.

$$C_u = e^{-rh} E_h^Q (C_{2h}|U) \tag{12.22}$$

where $C_{2h} = C_{uu}$ or C_{ud}, and

$$P_Q(UU) = \frac{e^{rh} - d}{u - d} \in (0,1)$$

$$P_Q(UD) = 1 - P_Q(UU) = \frac{u - e^{rh}}{u - d} \in (0,1)$$

Similarly we can show that

$$C_d = e^{-rh}(pC_{ud} + (1-p)C_{dd})$$

and so with no arbitrage, there exists Q-measure s. t.

$$C_d = e^{-rh} E_h^Q (C_{2h}|D) \tag{12.23}$$

where $C_{2h} = C_{ud}$ or C_{dd}, and

$$P_Q(UD) = \frac{e^{rh} - d}{u - d} \in (0,1)$$

$$P_Q(DD) = 1 - P_Q(UU) = \frac{u - e^{rh}}{u - d} \in (0,1)$$

Hence $E^Q(E^Q(\frac{C_{2h}}{e^{2rh}}|\mathcal{F}_h)|\mathcal{F}_0) = E^Q(\frac{C_h}{e^{rh}}|\mathcal{F}_0) = C_0$.

We can always find the present price of an option that matures nh intervals from now by taking suitable expectations based on the Q-EMM. With no-arbitrage, we can find a unique self-financing strategy that can replicate the attainable contingent derivative payoffs in this case in every of the complete states. For a European call for example, the self-financing strategy should end at maturity T with value $C_T = \max(S_T - K, 0)$ where K is the strike price and C_T, S_T are, respectively, the call and stock values according to the state at T. If we choose the factor $u = \exp(\sigma\sqrt{h})$,

$d = u^{-1}$, and $p = (e^{rh} - d)/(u - d)$, then $e^{-r\tau}E^Q(C_\tau|\mathcal{F}_0)$ would converge, as $h \downarrow 0$, to the Black-Scholes option price in Eq. (12.8) for an option with time-to-maturity τ.

The binomial lattice tree in Figure 12.2 can be used to find the arbitrage-free price of a European-style option as well as that of an American-style option. Unlike European-style options, American-style options are different in that the holder or buyer need not wait until maturity, but can exercise the option at any time up until maturity. We show an example of such a pricing in Figure 12.3 as follows.

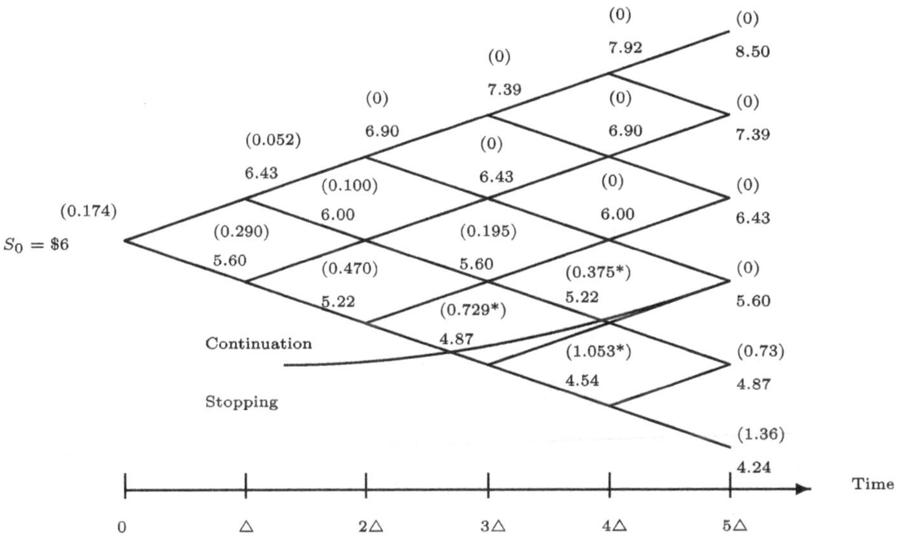

Figure 12.3: American Option Pricing on Binomial Tree. Note: * in the graph denotes the node whereby the American put will be exercised.

Consider an American put option on a stock. The initial stock price is $S_0 = \$6$. The risk-neutral probabilities of stock return factors u and d in the next period are p and $q = 1-p$, respectively. We use the Cox, Ross, Rubinstein (1979) binomial tree calibration employing $u = e^{\sigma\sqrt{\triangle}}$, $d = u^{-1}$, and $p = \frac{e^{r\triangle}-d}{u-d}$. This calibration provides a symmetrical tree in the log returns of the underlying asset price. The size of factor u corresponds positively with the volatility of the underlying asset return.

Assume no dividend payouts, and the time-to-maturity is divided into five periods of equal interval $\triangle$ year. The evolution of the underlying stock price and the associated (European put price) at that state are shown on the lattice tree in Figure 12.3. The strike or exercise price of the American put is \$5.60. In the example, let $\triangle = 1/52$, $\sigma = 0.5$, $r = 2\%$ p. a., so $u = 1.072$, $d = 0.933$, and $p = 0.486$.

The distinction between an American put and a European put is that the American put can be exercised at any time or in this example, at any intervals $j\triangle, j = 0, 1, 2, 3, 4, 5$. The exercise gain is $K - S > 0$ depending on the underlying price S at the particular state or node at time $j\triangle$. In this numerical method, the optimal exercise occurs when the condition $(K - S) > P$ is satisfied, where P is the European put value, i. e., when exercise gain is more than its European value. Then it is not worth to keep the put "alive" by selling it; rather it is more profitable to exercise it. In this case, it happens at node $(4\triangle, UDDD)$ when the exercise gain is $5.60 - 5.22 = 0.38$ which is higher than selling the put at 0.375, and at node $(4\triangle, DDDD)$ when the exercise gain is $5.60-4.54 = 1.06$ which is higher than selling the put at 1.053.

It also happens at node $(3\triangle, DDD)$ when the exercise gain is $5.60 - 4.87 = 0.73 > 0.729$. These occurrences are marked with $(*)$ on the prices that are computed as the discounted expected values under risk-neutral probabilities (p, q). The backward computation of the American put prices then replaces the European prices with the higher exercise prices at the nodes with $(*)$.

It is seen that for this case, the optimal exercise would occur at the earliest instance when exercise gain exceeds the risk-neutral discounted expected price, i. e., at $t = 3\triangle$ if state DDD would be reached, and it would also occur at $t = 4\triangle$ if state UDDD is reached without going through DDD. At time $t = 0$, this American put is priced at \$0.174. An equivalent European put would be priced at \$0.172 at time $t = 0$. Thus, the early exercise premium of the American put here for the period $[0, 5\triangle]$ is \$0.002.

The free boundary in the American put valuation problem is shown on the Figure 12.3 by a curve. The curve ends at the strike price 5.60 at expiry T. The estimated boundary curve separates the stopping or exercise region below (in the put case) and the continuation region above.

While an American put is worth at least as much as, and possibly more than a European put with the same terms – same underlying stock without dividend, same strike price, and same maturity, an American call is, however, worth the same as a European call with the same terms – same underlying stock without dividend, same strike price, and same maturity. This seems counter-intuitive. But examining the rational bound to a European call price at time t, C_t, $C_t > S_t - Ke^{-r\tau}$ since the put-call parity is $C_t = P_t + S_t - Ke^{-r\tau}$. So $C_t > S_t - Ke^{-r\tau} > S_t - K$ (assuming $r > 0$). The last inequality shows that a European call on a stock without dividend would always be worth more "alive" (if sold) than if exercised to obtain $S_t - K$ at any time t before maturity.

However, when a stock issues dividends, its American call would be worth at least and possibly more than its European counterpart. Assume that the stock issues continuously compounded dividend yield q proportional to the stock value. Suppose the ex-dividend stock prices follow the same up-state factor u and down-state factor d. The dividends are continuously distributed as cash so that the effective cost of buying a stock at $t = 0$ is not S_0 in Eq. (12.18) but S_0e^{-qh}. Over discrete interval h, the latter characterization of stock price less the value of dividend gain is an approximation to the continuous time version.

In replicating the option prices in state U with C_u and in state D with C_d based on the ex-dividend prices, the cost of the replicating portfolio is now

$$C_0 = \Delta_0 S_0 e^{-qh} - B_0 = e^{-rh}\left(\frac{e^{(r-q)h} - d}{u-d} C_u + \frac{u - e^{(r-q)h}}{u-d} C_d \right)$$

where the no-arbitrage risk-neutral probability measures for states U and D are now

$$p^* = \frac{e^{(r-q)h} - d}{u-d} \quad \text{and} \quad 1-p^* = \frac{u - e^{(r-q)h}}{u-d}$$

respectively.

This binomial lattice tree can be used in pricing options on stock index, futures, and foreign exchange. In stock index option pricing, replicating the option involves long positions on stocks in the index portfolio and thus the cash dividends of those stocks may be assumed to be continuously received, which reduce the current cost of the long positions. The index itself, upon which the option is defined, is however, measured ex-dividend. Hence the current option price C_0 can be obtained using the risk-neutral probabilities $p^*, 1-p^*$ on the U and D states. For futures options, the computation of option price on the binomial lattice tree can be performed using r as the dividend yield. In doing so, the net cost of carry is zero, since futures do not require outfront payments (ignore the margin requirements). For currency options priced in U. S. dollars, the computation of option price on the binomial lattice tree can be performed using the base (non U. S.) currency's risk-free interest rate r_Y as the dividend yield, so the net cost of carry is $r - r_Y$. When $h \downarrow 0$, the binomial model option prices should converge to those given in Eq. (12.8).

There is however a common situation, particularly for individual stock options, whereby the underlying stock issues dividends only at discrete points in time and by which it may not be a good approximation to assume there is continuous distribution of the cash dividends. This is the case that when an American call is exercised, it is usually exercised just prior to the ex-dividend date when its value would be larger than that of the European call. The binomial lattice tree can be used to price both European and American calls and puts in such a situation. In this tree, an up-state factor is u and down-state factor is d at all nodes whether there is a dividend issue or not in that interval, and these are assumed to represent the volatility structure of the underlying return. However, at a particular interval n, when pre-determined dividend is issued, it is assumed that the stock price drops at ex-dividend by a constant factor $(1-c)$ at whatever stock price at that node. The latter ensures that the lattice tree is recombining. If there had been j up-states and $n-j$ down-states by that interval, the stock price would be $S_0 u^j d^{n-j}$ just before ex-dividend and $S_0 u^j d^{n-j}(1-c)$ at ex-dividend. The European option price is computed by using risk-neutral probabilities p and $1-p$, and discounting backward from maturity until time $t = 0$. For the American call price, the value of the option at each node at $t < T$ is set as the maximum of either the European call value at that node or the exercise value based on the stock price just before ex-dividend on that node.

12.5 Implied Volatility

In the Black-Scholes (BS) model in Eq. (12.5), the variables C, S, K, r, τ are observed, except σ. But using Eq. (12.5), we can imply out the value of σ for any option at any given time. This value is called Black-Scholes implied volatility (IV). Theoretically, the GBM that gives rise to the Black-Scholes model has a constant σ. Hence, if BS model is correct, then for any option chain (series of traded options with different strike prices at the same time point) the IV when plotted against the strike prices should be a flat line. This is, however, not the case. Since the Black Monday stock market crash of 1987, it has been increasingly observed that the plot of option IV (of the same underlying stock) against strike prices often displays a volatility smile.

This means that there is a higher excess demand for ITM or OTM options, thus higher prices, relative to options that are ATM. When ITM calls and OTM puts (when strikes are low relative to underlying asset price) display relatively higher IVs than OTM calls and ITM puts (when strikes are high relative to underlying asset price), the graph would be indicative of a volatility smirk (rather than a smile) or negative volatility skew. It is also recognized that typically OTM puts are priced much higher (termed put premium puzzle). This could be due to very strong hedging demand in times when the market is anxious about potential market drop. The smirk is observed more often in index options. When IV is plotted in a 3D graph against strike and against time-to-maturity, it is called a volatility surface. It is often observed that for the same underlying asset, its longer maturity options typically would yield lower IV relative to its shorter maturity options. Hence the volatility surface is not flat. More complicated models have arisen to improve on the BS model since the IV has shown the BS model to be deficient. There have been subsequent developments in constant elasticity of variance model, local volatility models, stochastic volatility models, jump-diffusion models, and so on.[4]

Though the IV of the BS model may not be the true volatility of the underlying GBM process, there is some information neverthelss in implied volatility from option models. Bates (1991)[5] derived a model for pricing American options on jump-diffusion processes with systematic jump risk and empirically computed the implied volatility during sample period October 1986 to August 1987. The implied volatility from S&P 500 futures options in Bates' model included both the diffusion and the jump volatility. The spikes in Bates' IV in the 7 months prior to the October 19, 1987 stock market crash appeared to foretell the crash. In comparison, the BS IV during the same 7 months period before the crash appeared to be much smaller due to sharply rising

4 See John Hull and Sankarshan Basu (2011), *Options, Futures, and Other Derivatives*, Tenth edition, Pearson India; Espen Gaarder Haug (2007), *The Complete Guide to Option Pricing Formulas*, Second edition, McGraw-Hill.

5 David S. Bates (1991), The crash of '87: Was it expected? The evidence from options markets, *The Journal of Finance*, XLVI(3), 1009–1044.

S&P 500 levels then and the resulting negative volatility skew. The October 19 crash saw the market price level fell a whopping 23 % over two trading days. The conclusion was that the market via the S&P 500 futures options evidenced a strong perception of downside risk during the year preceding the October crash when OTM puts were unusually expensive. There were also negative jumps in Bates' model estimates.

12.6 Model-Free Volatility

Investors pay considerable attention to the forecast of future stock index price and stock index volatility. If the forecast for the future volatility was high, an investors might demand a higher return as compensation for bearing the higher systematic risk in future. Thus the volatility forecast over a specified future period is important to many market players, and a large literature had developed in the estimation of ex-ante volatility. Day and Lewis (1992) and Christensen and Prabhala (1998),[6] for examples, employ the Black-Scholes model to generate the implied volatilities of stock index returns as market forecasts of future volatility. However, it has been shown that the Black-Scholes option IV has inherent flaws due to the assumption that this volatility is constant across time. This flaw is due to the overly restrictive model, and the same kind of flaw could occur in any model as part of the model bias unless the model is truly correct.

While the Black-Scholes implied volatility continues to be a subject of interest, research has moved on to the study of model-free volatility.[7] This is the expected volatility under risk-neutral equivalent martingale probability measure obtained from option prices without using any option pricing model. Britten-Jones and Neuberger (2000)[8] show that the model-free volatility can be expressed as the weighted sum of a continuum of call option prices. In their approach, the underlying price process is not restricted to the log-normal diffusion, thus making the model-free volatility much more appealing than the Black-Scholes implied volatility. Jiang and Tian (2005)[9] and others had introduced a method of estimating the risk-neutral volatility without having to specify the underlying stochastic price process or the return probability distribution exactly.

---

6 See T. E. Day and C. M. Lewis (1992), Stock market volatility and the information content of stock index options. *Journal of Econometrics*, 52, 267–287; and B. J. Christensen and N. R. Prabhala (1998), The relation between implied and realized volatility, *Journal of Financial Economics*, 50, 125–150.

7 See T. G. Andersen and O. Bondarenko (2007), Construction and interpretation of model-free implied volatility. In I. Nelken (Ed.) *Volatility as an Asset Class*, Risk Publications, 141–184.

8 M. Britten-Jones and A. Neuberger (2000), Option prices, implied processes, and stochastic volatility, *The Journal of Finance*, 55, 839–866.

9 George J. Jiang and Y. S. Tian (2005), The model-free implied volatility and its information content, *The Review of Financial Studies*, 18(4), 1305–1342.

Due to its ease of implementation and more importantly its theoretical underpinning, model-free volatility has become an industry standard for constructing volatility indexes, known on the streets as the barometers of fear. In 2003, the Chicago Board of Trade (CBOE) switched from the Black-Scholes implied volatility approach to the model-free methodology to calculate the VIX volatility index. Following the wide acceptance of the revamped VIX for the S&P 500 index, CBOE introduced other model-free volatility indexes for the Dow Jones Industrial Average index (VXD), NASDAQ 100 index (VXN), and Russell 2000 index (RVX). The European markets have also established volatility indexes based on the same model-free approach. The VDAX-NEW volatility index for Deutsche Börse's DAX index, VSMI for Swiss Exchange's SMI index, and VSTOXX for the Dow Jones Euro STOXX 50 index are some of the key European examples. Futures and options written on the volatility indexes had been launched and the trading volumes of these derivative products have also risen considerably.

However, the VXN index, the VIX index, and most of the Exchanges' volatility indexes are constructed only for the most active near term and next near term index options, and thus are indexes of only a 30 day horizon. Moreover, though the index formula is clearly explained in most official sites of the Exchanges, there is typically some ambiguity as to which actively traded options are actually selected by the Exchange for constructing the index, or which options are left out in the formula. Lim and Ting (2013)[10] show an improved method to calculate the model-free volatility for up to a distinctly longer horizon of 450 days. The longer horizon would enable the pricing of index-based derivatives with long maturities. The study includes exploration of the term structure of model-free volatility.

12.6.1 Term Structure of Model-Free Volatility

In this section we show how the term structure of model-free volatility of the S&P 100 index can be derived from the prices of traded S&P 100 European-style options. Using multiple time series of this term structure as it evolves over time, we study some of its properties.

Specifically we find that changes in model-free volatilities are asymmetrically more positively impacted by a decrease in the index price level than negatively impacted by an increase in the index price level, that the negative relationship between daily model-volatility change and daily index level change is stronger in the near term than the far term, and that the slope of the term structure is positively associated with the level of index. There is also a tendency toward a negative slope of the volatility term structure during a bear market and a positive slope during a bull market. These

---

10 See Kian Guan Lim and Christopher Ting (2013), The term structure of S&P 100 model-free volatilities, *Quantitative Finance*, 13, 1041–1058.

significant results have important implications for pricing index derivatives as well as hedging index portfolios.

Let $P(X, S_0, T)$ and $C(X, S_0, T)$ be, respectively, the price of European put and call options with the same time to maturity T and strike price X on the underlying index with current value or price S_0. (Note that the notation of strike or exercise price here is X instead of K to assist in recognizing different derivations in different parts of this chapter). We assume that the underlying index value S_t evolves continuously as an Itô process with drift $r - q$ and volatility σ_t. The instantaneous volatility σ_t can be a function of state and time, i. e. $\sigma(S_t, t)$. The stochastic differential equation for S_t is as follows:

$$\frac{dS_t}{S_t} = (r - q)\,dt + \sigma_t\,dW_t \tag{12.24}$$

where dW_t is a Wiener process, r is the continuously compounded risk-free rate, and q is the continuously compounded stock index dividend yield. We assume for simplicity that r and q are constants.

The stochastic process is under risk-neutral probability as the drift is specified to be risk-free cost of carry $r - q$. Otherwise the drift should be some other constant that is the actual empirical mean of the process.

By Itô's lemma, the function $\ln S_t$ evolves according to

$$d(\ln S_t) = \left(r - q - \frac{1}{2}\sigma_t^2\right)dt + \sigma_t\,dW_t$$

It follows that

$$\frac{dS_t}{S_t} - d(\ln S_t) = \frac{1}{2}\sigma_t^2 dt \tag{12.25}$$

Next, we consider the integrated variance $V(0, T)$ defined as

$$V(0, T) \equiv \int_0^T \sigma_t^2\,dt$$

The variance $V(0, T)$ is the sum of instantaneous variances σ_t^2 realized over time 0 to time T. By Eq. (12.25), we obtain

$$V(0, T) = 2\left(\int_0^T \frac{1}{S_t}dS_t - \log\frac{S_T}{S_0}\right) \tag{12.26}$$

Taking the expectation with respect to the risk-neutral probability measure Q on both sides:

$$E_0^Q[V(0,T)] = 2E_0^Q\left[\int_0^T dS_t/S_t - \ln(S_T/S_0)\right]$$

The first term on the right-hand side is $E_0^Q[\int_0^T dS_t/S_t] = (r-q)T$. If we let σ_{MF}^2 be the annualized model-free variance, then

$$\sigma_{\text{MF}}^2 T \equiv E_0^Q[V(0,T)] = 2(r-q)T - 2E_0^Q\left[\log\frac{S_T}{S_0}\right] \tag{12.27}$$

We consider the forward price of the index with maturity at T, F_0, known at time $t = 0$, and we express $\ln(S_T/F_0)$ as

$$\begin{aligned}
\ln\frac{S_T}{F_0} &= \ln S_T - \ln F_0 - S_T\left(\frac{1}{F_0} - \frac{1}{S_T}\right) + \frac{S_T}{F_0} - 1 \\
&= \int_{F_0}^{S_T} \frac{1}{X}\,dX - S_T\int_{F_0}^{S_T} \frac{1}{X^2}\,dX + \frac{S_T}{F_0} - 1 \\
&= -\int_{F_0}^{S_T} \frac{S_T - X}{X^2}\,dX + \frac{S_T}{F_0} - 1
\end{aligned} \tag{12.28}$$

For any $z > -1$, $\ln(1+z)$ is a strictly concave function and $\ln(1+z) < z$. The left side of Eq. (12.28) is $\ln(1+z)$ with $z \equiv S_T/F_0 - 1$. It follows that the integral $\int_{F_0}^{S_T}(S_T - X)/X^2\,dX$ equals $-(\ln(1+z) - z)$ and hence is strictly positive. We can then rewrite the integral as

$$\begin{aligned}
\int_{F_0}^{S_T} \frac{S_T - X}{X^2}\,dX &= 1_{S_T > F_0}\int_{F_0}^{S_T} \frac{S_T - X}{X^2}\,dX - 1_{S_T < F_0}\int_{S_T}^{F_0} \frac{S_T - X}{X^2}\,dX \\
&= 1_{S_T > F_0}\int_{F_0}^{S_T} \frac{S_T - X}{X^2}\,dX + 1_{S_T < F_0}\int_{S_T}^{F_0} \frac{X - S_T}{X^2}\,dX \\
&= \int_{F_0}^{\infty} \frac{(S_T - X)^+}{X^2}\,dX + \int_0^{F_0} \frac{(X - S_T)^+}{X^2}\,dX
\end{aligned}$$

In the last step, we have used the fact that the asset price S_T, which is unknown at time $t = 0$, is in the range $(0, \infty)$.

Therefore, from Eq. (12.28),

$$E_0^Q\left[\ln\frac{S_T}{F_0}\right] = -e^{rT}\int_{F_0}^{\infty} \frac{C(S_0, X, T)}{X^2}\,dX - e^{rT}\int_0^{F_0} \frac{P(S_0, X, T)}{X^2}\,dX$$

since $E_0^Q[S_T] = F_0$. Now,

$$\ln \frac{S_T}{S_0} = \ln \frac{S_T}{F_0} + \ln \frac{F_0}{S_0}$$

Thus,

$$E_0^Q\left[\ln \frac{S_T}{S_0}\right] = -e^{rT} \int_{F_0}^{\infty} \frac{C(S_0, X, T)}{X^2}\, dX$$
$$- e^{rT} \int_0^{F_0} \frac{P(S_0, X, T)}{X^2}\, dX + (r - q)T$$

since $F_0 = S_0 \exp((r-q)T)$. Substituting this equation into Eq. (12.27), we obtain the following.

$$\sigma_{MF}^2 T \equiv E_0^Q[V(0,T)]$$
$$= 2e^{rT}\left(\int_0^{F_0} \frac{P(X, S_0, T)}{X^2} dX + \int_{F_0}^{\infty} \frac{C(X, S_0, T)}{X^2} dX\right) \qquad (12.29)$$

This formula is model-free because it uses option prices directly without having to use any option pricing formula.

The European option put-call parity states that

$$C(X, S_0, T) - P(X, S_0, T) = S_0 e^{-qT} - e^{-rT} X = e^{-rT}(F_0 - X)$$

Suppose there is a continuum of options and because put (call) price is a monotonically increasing (decreasing) function of X, there exists a unique strike price $X_\star$ such that $C(X_\star, S_0, T) = P(X_\star, S_0, T)$. From the put-call parity,

$$X_\star = S_0 \exp((r-q)T)$$

which is the forward price of the index at $t = 0$, F_0. Thus F_0 can be found as the strike price where the call and put curves intersect. F_0 may not be readily observable otherwise.

The model-free or risk-neutral variance for maturity T in Eq. (12.29) is estimated using numerical method. Firstly, spline-smoothing or other smoothing method is performed to fit a cubic curve on the discrete number of option prices where the European options all have a maturity of T. A small number close to 0 is used as the lower bound of the call option prices, and similarly a large number several times F_0 is used as the upper bound of the put prices. The intersection point F_0 is also determined.

Secondly, numerical integration is carried out to find the area under the OTM puts and OTM call price curves divided by square of strike prices. The model-free variance is shown as the shaded area in Figure 12.4. Model-free volatility is then computed as the square root of the model-free variance.

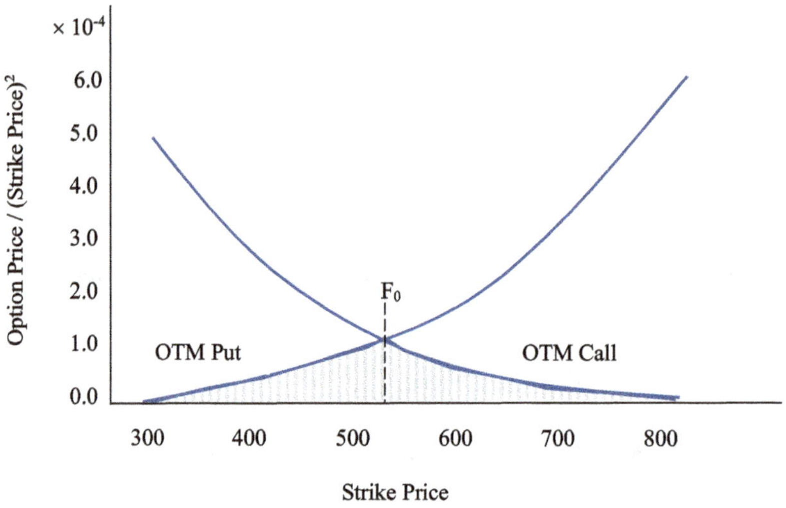

Figure 12.4: Computing Model-Free Variance of on S&P 100 Index.

The figure consists of put prices $P(X, S_0, T)$ and call prices $C(X, S_0, T)$ on December 10, 2003. Their ticker symbol is XEO. The underlying index is OEX or the S&P 100 index created by CBOE. On this date, the closing value of this index was 525.33. A number of put and call XEO contracts (cash-settled) based on OEX (S&P 100 Index) are traded or have dealer quoted prices. For a subset of these derivative contracts with maturity T on June 9, 2004, about half a year later, the mid-points of bid and ask quotes for the puts and calls are shown in the figure using circle symbols. The corresponding X-axis number refers to the strike price X at which the put or call would trade. All option prices on the curves do not violate the no-arbitrage conditions.

We obtain end-of-day S&P 100 Index option quotes, volume traded, and open interest from Optionmetrics along with the zero-coupon riskfree interest rate curve. Our sample period starts from July 23, 2001 when the European-style XEO began trading. After excluding November 3, 2004 as the data for that day are diagnosed to be incorrect, we have a total of 2,621 trading days by end of December 2011 for our sample.

For any given trading day, we calculate σ_{MF} for each available maturity date of the options. Suppose σ_1 is calculated from the near term options and σ_2 from farther term options. The days to maturity for these two terms are τ_1 and τ_2, respectively. Suppose $\tau_1 \leq z \leq \tau_2$. Then the annualized z–day model-free variance is estimated using interpolation as follows.

$$\sigma_{MF}^2 \frac{z}{365} = \frac{\tau_2 - z}{\tau_2 - \tau_1} \sigma_1^2 \tau_1 + \frac{z - \tau_1}{\tau_2 - \tau_1} \sigma_2^2 \tau_2 \tag{12.30}$$

Using adjacent maturity variances for interpolation, the model-free volatility σ_{MF} is estimated for 8 constant-maturity volatilities of $z = 30, 60, 90, 120, 150, 180, 360$, and 450 days. We provide in Table 12.1 summary statistics of model-free volatility estimates of the 8 different constant maturities.

Table 12.1: Model-Free Volatilities of 8 Different Constant Maturities.

Maturity in Days	30	60	90	120	150	180	360	450
Mean	21.51	21.78	21.95	21.85	21.73	21.62	21.55	21.57
Std. Dev.	9.37	8.63	8.04	7.35	6.73	6.39	5.71	5.64
Minimum	8.64	9.41	10.23	10.69	10.88	11.11	12.26	12.53
5th Percentile	10.94	11.56	12.23	12.58	12.78	12.91	13.44	13.55
10th Percentile	11.92	12.38	12.97	13.24	13.39	13.51	14.10	14.30
25th Percentile	14.77	15.37	15.96	15.97	16.08	16.16	16.46	16.58
Median	19.70	20.38	20.76	20.92	21.03	21.12	21.32	21.41
75th Percentile	25.25	25.68	25.76	25.71	25.96	25.91	25.62	25.44
90th Percentile	34.42	33.20	32.00	31.43	30.73	29.79	28.95	28.70
95th Percentile	39.29	38.65	37.15	35.72	34.23	32.45	31.00	31.38
Maximum	75.38	67.97	60.89	56.72	45.48	45.35	40.32	41.02

This table presents summary statistics of the model-free volatility estimates σ_e, in percentages on an annualized basis, calculated directly from option prices. Eight constant maturities are obtained from linear interpolation over sample period July 23, 2001 to December 30, 2011. The means and standard deviations (Std. Dev.) along with percentiles for the model-free volatility of the different constant maturities are reported. The table shows that the percentage annualized model-free volatility estimate σ_e has an overall mean during the sample period in the range of 21.51 to 21.95 for the eight different constant maturities. However, the standard deviation or variability of σ_e decreases with a longer constant maturity.

12.6.2 Information in Model-Free Volatility

The S&P100 model-free volatility captures information embedded in the series of puts and calls traded or price-quoted on any trading day. As the European-style puts and calls have a maturity T, the volatility information is forward-looking and provides a forecast of the aggregated daily volatility from the trading day until future T. However, the model-free volatility estimates are based on a risk-neutral equivalent martingale probability measure different from the empirical or physical probability measure. Therefore the estimates would differ from the physical or empirical measure of future volatility by a quantity typically known as the volatility risk premium. However, the risk-neutral volatility should contain information about future realized volatility up to time T.

As we have eight different maturity periods, the realized volatilities have to be computed separately. At time or day t, the ex-post realized volatility for a horizon of τ, e. g. 30 days, is computed as

$$\frac{1}{\tau}\sum_{i=t+1}^{t+\tau}(\ln S_i/S_{i-1})^2$$

Daily mean drift is close to zero and noisy, so the mean adjustment is often not added in the literature.

Define ex-post realized volatility at t up to horizon τ as $RV(t,\tau)$. Let the model-free volatility estimate at t of up to horizon τ be denoted as $\sigma_{MF}(t,\tau)$. We perform a simple OLS regression:

$$RV(t,\tau) = a + b\sigma_{MF}(t,\tau) + \epsilon_t$$

where a, b are the constants of intercept and slope respectively, and ϵ_t is a stationary zero mean noise uncorrelated with the explanatory variable. To avoid the problem of serial correlation in the regression, we use non-overlapping data. Serial correlation can lead to inefficient forecast in small sample. For $\tau = 30$, we obtained the time series of the dependent variable as $RV(t,30)$, $RV(t+30,30)$, $RV(t+60,30)$, and so on. Corresponding explanatory variable values as a time series are $\sigma_{MF}(t,30)$, $\sigma_{MF}(t+30,30)$, $\sigma_{MF}(t+60,30)$, and so on. For $\tau = 60$, we obtained time series for the dependent variable as $RV(t,60)$, $RV(t+60,60)$, $RV(t+120,60)$, and so on. Corresponding explanatory variable values as a time series are $\sigma_{MF}(t,60)$, $\sigma_{MF}(t+60,60)$, $\sigma_{MF}(t+120,60)$, and so on. Regression is performed for $\tau = 30$, 60, 90, 120, 150, and 180. Non-overlapping data implies fewer than 20 observations for the cases of $\tau = 360$, and 450, so these cases are not reported.

For comparison, we also compute an empirical measure forecast using the GARCH method. As estimating accurate GARCH parameters requires a long time series, we provide one year of past daily returns data for each set of new GARCH parameter estimates. The GARCH parameter estimates are then utilized to construct the GARCH forward-looking forecast of volatility. We follow the methodolgy in Ederington and Guan (2005).[11]

The GARCH future volatility estimate at t for horizon τ is denoted as $GV(t,\tau)$. We estimate $GV(t,30)$, $GV(t,60)$, $GV(t,90)$, $GV(t,120)$, $GV(t,150)$, and $GV(t,180)$ for each $t = 1, 180, 360$, and so on, i. e. on a half-yearly window rolling forward in time. For

11 See Louis Ederington and Wei Guan (2005), Forecasting Volatility, *Journal of Futures Markets*, 25, 465–90.

finding the first set of GARCH parameters, we utilize an extra set of one year daily index data over the period July 3, 2000 to July 20, 2001. Again, we did not use overlapping data, and pair each GV forecast $GV(t,\tau)$ at a time-point t with an ex-post realized volatility $RV(t,\tau)$ and a model-free forecast $\sigma_{MF}(t,\tau)$.

Table 12.2 presents results of the regressions of ex-post realized volatility on the model-free volatility for eight constant maturities over the sample period July 23, 2001 to December 30, 2011. Out-of-sample mean forecast errors and RMFE (root mean forecast errors) are also reported in comparison with the GARCH forecasting method. From Table 12.2, it is evident that all the slope estimates are significantly positive at the 1 % level for $\tau = 30, 60, 90, 120$, and significant at the 5 % and 10 % levels for cases $\tau = 150$ and $\tau = 180$ respectively. In all cases, tests based on the null of slope being one are not rejected at the 5 % level. Except for the case $\tau = 30$, the p-values are all large, above 0.3. Thus there is sufficient statistical evidence that the model-free volatility contains information and predictability about future realized volatility of the index returns.

Table 12.2: Regression of Ex-Post Realized Volatility on Model-Free Volatility.

Regression	**30-day**	**60-day**	**90-day**	**120-day**	**150-day**	**180-day**
constant	−0.058***	−0.005	−0.023	0.007	0.022	0.042
(t-value)	(−3.066)	(−0.181)	(−0.585)	(0.092)	(0.265)	(0.525)
slope	1.142***	0.879***	0.978***	0.858***	0.757**	0.682*
(t-value)	(13.587)	(7.034)	(5.486)	(2.509)	(2.030)	(1.89)
R^2	0.602	0.452	0.436	0.249	0.186	0.166
average RV	18.26	18.52	18.73	19.51	18.35	18.72
mean (RV-MFV)	−0.31	−0.62	−0.32	0.16	−0.44	−0.01
mean (RV-GV)	−0.34	−0.10	0.63	0.65	0.22	0.66
RMFE (RV-MFV)	7.68	8.57	8.24	10.46	10.14	9.73
RMFE (RV-GV)	5.08	5.38	6.33	6.60	5.86	5.85

Note: ***, **, and * denote significance levels of 1 %, 5 %, and 10 % respectively based on two-tailed tests of the null of zero.

RV, MFV, and GV denote realized volatility, model-free volatility, and GARCH volatility forecast in annualized percentage terms. Across time series indexed by t for the respective matched pairs of RV-MFV and RV-GV, we report the means $T^{-1}\sum_t^T[RV(t,\tau) - \sigma_{MF}(t,\tau)]$ and $T^{-1}\sum_t^T[RV(t,\tau) - GV(t,\tau)]$, as well as the square roots of the means of the squares of the out-of-sample forecast errors or root-mean-forecast-square-error (RMFE). The results in the last five rows of Table 12.2 show that the GARCH volatility forcasts have lower RMFE than that of MFV when compared with realized volatility. Strictly speaking, the model-free volatility estimates are based on a risk-neutral equivalent martingale probability measure different from the empirical or physical probability measure of the GARCH estimates and the realized volatility estimates. Therefore the comparison with GARCH is on a different footing as the volatility risk premium enters into the model-free volatility estimates before it can be compared with a physical measure statistics. In this sense, it is not surprising that RMFE(RV-GV) is smaller than RMFE(RV-MFV) due to the presence of the volatility risk premium.

Next, we study the relationship between the estimated term structure of model-free volatility and the underlying stock index dynamics, thus providing a better understanding of the fear gauge. Figure 12.5 shows the time series of S&P 100 index in Panel A, and the time series of constant-maturity volatilities for $T = 30, 60, 90, 120, 150, 180$, and 360, in the other 7 panels of B to H. To save space, we do not show the case of $T = 450$. It is noticeable that when the S&P 100 index is on a down trend, the model-free volatility is on the up trend, and vice-versa. For example, there is a sharp market decline in August 2001 and this is accompanied by a sharp rise in the model-free volatility from about 20 % to more than 40 % in Panel B for 30-day constant maturity. This sudden increase in volatility is smaller for other maturities, yet still quite substantial with the volatility reaching 25 % and above.

We also observe that in July 2008, the S&P 100 index drops to 320 points while at the same time volatilities for various maturities rise to 40 and over 70 points. By the end of 2011, the index rises to 600 points while model-free volatilities across all maturities fall to about 20 points. These observations suggest that a bullish (bearish) market is accompanied by decreasing (increasing) model-free volatility.

Panels B to H of the figure show that the pattern of time series of model-free volatility for different constant maturities are qualitatively the same. Their average daily values are also close to each other in a tight range though the range of values shortens as maturity increases. The key observation is that there appears to be an inverse relationship between the level of the S&P100 stock index and the level of its model-free volatility.

To analyze properties of the model-free term structure with respect to exogenous explanatory variables, an obvious candidate is the level of the index itself and the change of the index levels. In Table 12.3, we report the correlation between the day-to-day change in the model-free volatility $\Delta\sigma_{t,\tau}$ (rewriting $\sigma_{MF}(t,\tau)$ as $\sigma_{t,\tau}$) and the day-to-day change in the S&P100 index level ΔL_t. Note that we drop the subscript MF to model-free volatility at time t to simplify notation. Table 12.3 also reports sample estimates of the first-order serial correlation of $\Delta\sigma_{t,\tau}$.

Table 12.3 shows that $\Delta\sigma_{t,\tau}$ is negatively correlated with ΔL_t for all 8 constant maturities, τ. This evidence of "fear gauge" is well documented for VIX and the S&P500 index, and appears also to hold for the S&P100 index. The contemporaneous correlation coefficients are significant at the 1 % level. The negative correlations for the various constant maturities are in the range −0.708 to −0.532, and does not become weaker at longer term maturity, though the variability of the model-free volatility appears to decrease in maturity with increasing smoothness with maturity.

There is also evidence of a significant negative correlation with lagged model-free volatilities, though the negative correlations in the range −0.222 to −0.046 across ma-

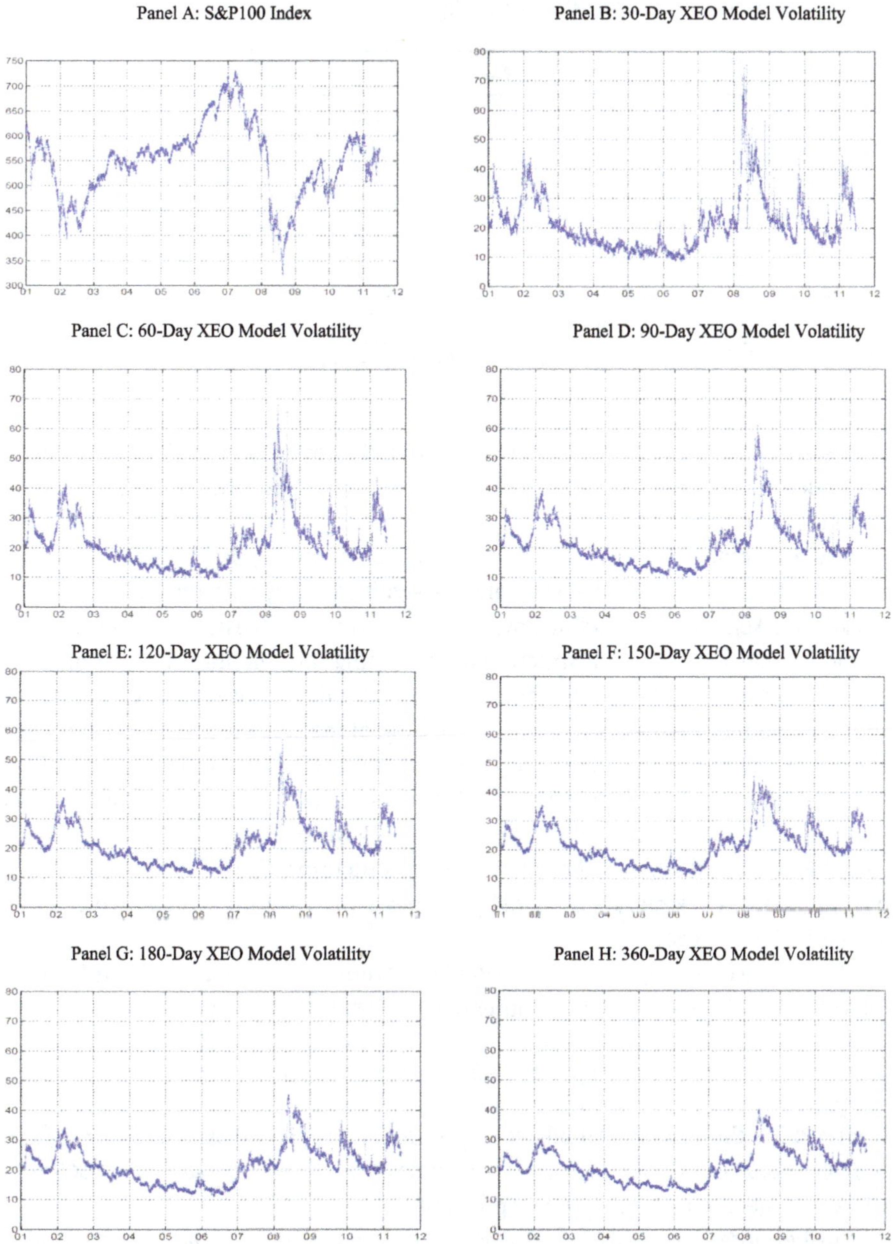

Figure 12.5: The Figure consists of 8 panels. Each panel shows a plot of the time series. The annualized model-free volatilities are in percentages. The horizontal axis shows the calender years in 2-digit convention. The sample period is from July 23, 2001 through December 30, 2011.

Table 12.3: Autocorrelations of Model-Free Volatility.

Constant maturity	Correlation with ΔL_t	First-lag auto-correlation
30-day	-0.655^{***}	-0.202^{***}
60-day	-0.600^{***}	-0.222^{***}
90-day	-0.708^{***}	-0.176^{***}
120-day	-0.679^{***}	-0.117^{**}
150-day	-0.629^{***}	-0.123^{***}
180-day	-0.532^{***}	-0.144^{***}
360-day	-0.596^{***}	-0.048^{*}
450-day	-0.650^{***}	-0.046^{*}

Note: *, **, and *** indicate 1 % , 5 %, and 10 % levels of significance, respectively.

turities are weaker in magnitudes compared with the correlations with ΔL_t. The negative autocorrelations in $\Delta\sigma_{t,T}$ also reduces in magnitude when the maturities increase above 180-day.

The preliminary evidence in Table 12.3 indicates that the daily change in model-free volatility, $\Delta\sigma_{t,T}$, co-varies negatively in a significant way with the daily change in index level, ΔL_t. For each trading day, we could form an OLS estimate of the slope of the model-free volatility term structure by regressing the volatility on the term. This is a crude estimate as the number of observations per day in the regression is small at eight data points. We then run an OLS regression of the slope estimates on the index levels across all the trading days. The OLS estimate of this slope of slopes is a positive 0.00010 with a standard error of 0.00014. Thus there is some preliminary evidence that the volatility term structure slope varies positively with index level. When the stock market is bullish, it appears the volatility term structure slope becomes slightly positive. When the stock market is bearish, it appears the volatility term structure slope becomes slightly negative.

We run the following panel regression to determine a linear relationship of model-free volatility with index level and other relevant explanatory variables:

$$\sigma_{t,T} = \delta_0 + \delta_1 t + \delta_2 T + \delta_3 L_t + \delta_4 \sigma_{t-1,T} + \delta_5 \sigma_{t-2,T} + u_t \tag{12.31}$$

where T takes the various annualized values 30/365,60/365, 90/365, 120/365, 150/365, 180/365, 360/365, and 450/365, t is number of days into the sample divided by 365, and u_t is a zero mean noise that is independent of L_t.

Furthermore, we specify $\delta_2 = \theta_0 + \theta_1 L_t + v_t$ where θ_0 and θ_1 are constants, and v_t is a zero mean noise that is independent of L_t for all t and T. The other coefficients of δ_0, δ_1, δ_3, δ_4, and δ_5 are constants.

Substituting the dynamics of δ_2 into Eq. (12.31), we obtain:

$$\sigma_{t,T} = a_0 + a_1 t + a_2 T + a_3[TL_t] + a_4 L_t + a_5 \sigma_{t-1,T} + a_6 \sigma_{t-2,T} + \epsilon_{t,T} \tag{12.32}$$

where $a_0 = \delta_0$, $a_1 = \delta_1$, $a_2 = \theta_0$, $a_3 = \theta_1$, $a_4 = \delta_3$, $a_5 = \delta_4$, $a_6 = \delta_5$, and $\epsilon_{t,\tau} = u_t + \tau v_t$ has zero mean, is stochastically independent of L_t and assumed to be contemporaneously uncorrelated with $\sigma_{t-1,\tau}$ and $\sigma_{t-2,\tau}$.

The panel data has trading days $t = 1, 2, \ldots, T$ ($T = 2622$) during sample period July 23, 2001 to December 30, 2011.For each trading day t, there are cross-sectional data associated with each of the constant maturity, $\tau = 30/365, 60/365, \ldots, 450/365$. The time-series cross-sectional or panel regression of Eq. (12.32) has dependent variable values stacked as

$$Y_{8T'\times 1} = \begin{pmatrix} \sigma_{3,1} \\ \sigma_{3,2} \\ \vdots \\ \sigma_{3,8} \\ \sigma_{4,1} \\ \sigma_{4,2} \\ \vdots \\ \sigma_{4,8} \\ \sigma_{5,1} \\ \vdots \\ \vdots \\ \sigma_{T,8} \end{pmatrix}, \quad X_{8T'\times 7} = \begin{pmatrix} 1 & \frac{3}{365} & \frac{30}{365} & \frac{30}{365}L_3 & L_3 & \sigma_{2,1} & \sigma_{1,1} \\ 1 & \frac{3}{365} & \frac{60}{365} & \frac{60}{365}L_3 & L_3 & \sigma_{2,2} & \sigma_{1,2} \\ \vdots & \vdots & \vdots & \vdots & \vdots & \vdots & \vdots \\ 1 & \frac{3}{365} & \frac{450}{365} & \frac{450}{365}L_3 & L_3 & \sigma_{2,8} & \sigma_{1,8} \\ 1 & \frac{4}{365} & \frac{30}{365} & \frac{30}{365}L_4 & L_4 & \sigma_{3,1} & \sigma_{2,1} \\ 1 & \frac{4}{365} & \frac{60}{365} & \frac{60}{365}L_4 & L_4 & \sigma_{3,2} & \sigma_{2,2} \\ \vdots & \vdots & \vdots & \vdots & \vdots & \vdots & \vdots \\ 1 & \frac{4}{365} & \frac{450}{365} & \frac{450}{365}L_4 & L_4 & \sigma_{3,8} & \sigma_{2,8} \\ 1 & \frac{5}{365} & \frac{30}{365} & \frac{30}{365}L_5 & L_5 & \sigma_{4,1} & \sigma_{3,1} \\ \vdots & \vdots & \vdots & \vdots & \vdots & \vdots & \vdots \\ \vdots & \vdots & \vdots & \vdots & \vdots & \vdots & \vdots \\ 1 & \frac{T}{365} & \frac{450}{365} & \frac{450}{365}L_T & L_T & \sigma_{T-1,8} & \sigma_{T-2,8} \end{pmatrix}$$

with parameter vector $B_{7\times 1} = (a_0, a_1, a_2, a_3, a_4, a_5, a_6)'$, and where $T' = T - 2$. The subscript τ is represented by a group number, e. g., 1 associated with 30/365, 2 associated with 60/365, 3 associated with 90/365, and so on.

In the regression, $Y = XB + E$ where $E_{8T'\times 1} = (\epsilon_{3,1}, \epsilon_{3,2}, \ldots, \epsilon_{3,8}, \epsilon_{4,1}, \epsilon_{4,2}, \ldots, \epsilon_{4,8}, \epsilon_{5,1}, \ldots, \epsilon_{T,8})$, and E has covariance matrix $I_{T'\times T'} \otimes \Sigma_{8\times 8}$. Σ is the covariance matrix of $\epsilon_{t,\tau}$ for each t, and has its ijth element as $\text{cov}(u_t + \tau_i v_t, u_t + \tau_j v_t)$. Note that we assume $\epsilon_{t,\tau}$ has cross-sectional heteroskedasticity, but that $\epsilon_{t+k,\tau}$ and $\epsilon_{t,\tau}$ are not correlated for any $k \neq 0$ and any τ.

The best linear unbiased estimate $\hat{B}' = (\hat{a}_0, \hat{a}_1, \hat{a}_2, \hat{a}_3, \hat{a}_4, \hat{a}_5, \hat{a}_6)$ is found via generalized least squares (GLS) as

$$\hat{B} = (X'[I \otimes \Sigma]^{-1}X)^{-1}X'[I \otimes \Sigma]^{-1}Y$$

The estimates are conditional on estimated $\hat{\Sigma}$ based on the initial estimated residuals. The estimates $\hat{B}$ are reported in Panel A of Table 12.4. The table also reports the Durbin-Watson (DW) statistics, indicating negative residual error correlation at 5 % significance level. To ensure the regressions are not spurious due to any presence of unit roots, we also test the fitted residuals for unit roots using the Augmented Dickey-Fuller (ADF) test statistic. In all cases, the presence of unit root is rejected at less than 1 % significance level, indicating stationarity in the regression or else a cointegrating relationship that enables OLS to be an appropriate tool.

We perform a second GLS regression to confirm results by taking the first difference of Eq. (12.32):

$$\Delta\sigma_{t,\tau} = b_0 + b_1[\tau\Delta L_t] + b_2\Delta L_t + b_3\Delta\sigma_{t-1,\tau} + b_4\Delta\sigma_{t-2,\tau} + \xi_{t,\tau} \tag{12.33}$$

where $b_0 = \delta_1$, $b_1 = \theta_1$, $b_2 = \delta_3$, $b_3 = \delta_4$, $b_4 = \delta_5$, and $\xi_{t,\tau} = \Delta\epsilon_{t,\tau}$. The results are shown in Panel B of Table 12.4. Finally, we consider if asymmetric changes in L_t may impact changes in the model-free volatility differently. To model this, we separated ΔL_t into its positive and negative parts:

$$\begin{aligned}\Delta\sigma_{t,\tau} = c_0 + c_1[\tau\Delta L_t] + c_2\Delta L_t^+ + c_3\Delta L_t^- \\ + c_4\Delta\sigma_{t-1,\tau} + c_5\Delta\sigma_{t-2,\tau} + \eta_{t,\tau}\end{aligned} \tag{12.34}$$

where $\Delta L_t^+ = \max(\Delta L_t, 0)$ and $\Delta L_t^- = \min(\Delta L_t, 0)$. The results are reported in Panel C of Table 12.4.

Table 12.4: Panel Regression Results Explaining Changes in Model-Free Volatilities.

Panel A	a_0	a_1	a_2	a_3	a_4	a_5	a_6
Estimate	0.9505***	0.0010***	−0.1385	0.0003	−0.0013***	0.8846***	0.1001***
(t-value)	(6.309)	(7.696)	(−1.271)	(1.268)	(−4.812)	(128.75)	(14.593)
Adjusted R^2	0.99						
DW-Statistic	2.39						
ADF-Statistic	−90.85						
Panel B	b_0	b_1	b_2	b_3	b_4		
Estimate	0.0014	0.0398***	−0.0957***	−0.0947***	−0.0005		
(t-value)	(0.351)	(22.479)	(−44.792)	(−16.105)	(0.931)		
Adjusted R^2	0.291						
DW-Statistic	2.28						
ADF-Statistic	−90.59						
Panel C	c_0	c_1	c_2	c_3	c_4	c_5	
Estimate	−0.0361***	0.0400***	−0.0874***	−0.1033***	−0.0995***	−0.0055	
(t-value)	(−6.709)	(22.644)	(−38.038)	(−45.819)	(−16.896)	(−0.939)	
Adjusted R^2	0.294						
DW-Statistic	2.27						
ADF-Statistic	−90.88						

Note: *, **, and *** indicate test significance levels at 1 %, 5 %, and 10 %, respectively.
Unit root tests of the fitted regression residuals based on Augmented Dickey-Fuller statistics are also reported. Null of unit root is strongly rejected with p-values smaller than 0.01 for all panel regressions.

The results in Table 12.4 show strong evidence of negative contemporaneous relations between changes in daily index price returns and changes in the model-free volatility across all maturities. Specifically, estimates $\hat{b}_2$ in Panel B and estimates $\hat{c}_2$ and $\hat{c}_3$ in Panel C are all significantly negative at significance levels of less than 1 %. The results are consistent with a significantly negative $\hat{a}_4$ in Panel A. This result for S&P100 is consistent with results using implied volatilities on the S&P500 as in Whaley (2000)[12] and Ostdiek and Whaley (1995).[13]

In Panel C, we see that $\hat{c}_2 = -0.0874$ while $\hat{c}_3 = -0.1033$. Their average is about the same as estimate $\hat{b}_2$ in Panel B. The results indicate that a 1 % decrease in index price level is associated with a larger positive increase in the fear gauge or model-free volatility of 0.1033 % than a 1 % increase in index price level leading to a lesser decrease of 0.0874 % in model-free volatility. This asymmetric impact is tested under the null of $H_0 : c_2 = c_3$. Using the covariance matrix of estimates obtained in Panel C GLS regression, the t-statistic, d. f. 2619, for the difference in the coefficient is $\frac{0.0159}{0.00158} = 10.070$. Thus $\hat{c}_2$ is significantly different from $\hat{c}_3$.

When we combine the estimated coefficients, $\hat{c}_1[\tau\Delta L_t] + \hat{c}_2\Delta L_t^+$ in Panel C produces negative impacts on model-free volatility of −0.0841, −0.0808, −0.0775, −0.0743, −0.0710, −0.0677, −0.0480, and −0.0381 for the various maturities of $\tau = 30/365, \ldots, 450/365$. Similarly, when we combine the estimated coefficients, $\hat{c}_1[\tau\Delta L_t] + \hat{c}_3\Delta L_t^-$ in Panel C produces negative impacts on model-free volatility of −0.1001, −0.0967, −0.0934, −0.0902, −0.0869, −0.0836, −0.0639, and −0.0540 for the various maturities of τ. Thus, it is seen that the negative partial correlations between changes in index price level, whether positive or negative changes, and changes in model-free volatilities, becomes weaker as the horizon increases. Again, this could be due to the smoothing effect of changes in longer maturity model-free volatilities.

Finally, we see that the expected slope of the term structure conditional on information at time t is $E_t(\delta_2) = \hat{\theta}_0 + \hat{\theta}_1 L_t = -0.1385 + 0.0003L_t$ (from Panel A) at time t. Thus, for index level higher than $0.1385/0.0003 \approx 462$, the conditional expected term structure of model-free volatility slope is positive, while for index level below ≈ 462, the conditional expected term structure of model-free volatility slope is negative. This would suggest that upward sloping term structure occurs during a bullish market, which is characterized by low volatility and more days with positive daily returns. On the contrary, downward sloping term structure of model-free volatility tends to be associated with a bearish market. The implications are similar to those of the interest yield curve.

The above stacked regression in Eq. (12.32) can also be re-arranged as:

12 See R. E. Whaley (2000), The investor fear gauge, *Journal of Portfolio Management*, 26, 12–27, 2000.

13 Fleming J. Ostdiek and R. E. Whaley (1995), Predicting stock market volatility: A new measure, *Journal of Financial Markets*, 15, 265–302.

$$\begin{pmatrix} Y_1 \\ Y_2 \\ \vdots \\ Y_8 \end{pmatrix} = \begin{pmatrix} X_1 & 0 & \dots & 0 \\ 0 & X_2 & \dots & 0 \\ \vdots & \vdots & \ddots & \vdots \\ 0 & 0 & \dots & X_8 \end{pmatrix} \begin{pmatrix} B_1 \\ B_2 \\ \vdots \\ B_8 \end{pmatrix} + \begin{pmatrix} e_1 \\ e_2 \\ \vdots \\ e_8 \end{pmatrix} \tag{12.35}$$

where $Y_i = (\sigma_{3,i}, \sigma_{4,i}, \sigma_{5,i}, \dots, \sigma_{T,i})'$, $e_i = (\epsilon_{3,i}, \epsilon_{4,i}, \epsilon_{5,i}, \dots, \epsilon_{T,i})'$,

$$X_i = \begin{pmatrix} 1 & \frac{3}{365} & \frac{\tau_i}{365} & \frac{\tau_i}{365}L_3 & L_3 & \sigma_{2,i} & \sigma_{1,i} \\ 1 & \frac{4}{365} & \frac{\tau_i}{365} & \frac{\tau_i}{365}L_4 & L_4 & \sigma_{3,i} & \sigma_{2,i} \\ 1 & \frac{5}{365} & \frac{\tau_i}{365} & \frac{\tau_i}{365}L_5 & L_5 & \sigma_{4,i} & \sigma_{3,i} \\ \vdots & \vdots & \ddots & \vdots & \vdots & \vdots & \vdots \\ 1 & \frac{T}{365} & \frac{\tau_i}{365} & \frac{\tau_i}{365}L_T & L_T & \sigma_{T-1,i} & \sigma_{T-2,i} \end{pmatrix}$$

and $B_i(7 \times 1) = (a_{0i}, a_{1i}, a_{2i}, a_{3i}, a_{4i}, a_{5i}, a_{6i})'$, for $i = 1, 2, 3, \dots, 8$. Assume $\text{cov}(e_i) = \sigma_i^2 I_{T' \times T'}$. If we perform eight separate OLS time series regressions $Y_i = X_i B_i + e_i$ for each $i = 1, 2, 3, \dots, 8$, the OLS estimates $\hat{B}_i$ for each i are consistent, conditional on estimated $\hat{\sigma}_i^2$ using the initial fitted residuals.

By stacking up the individual OLS equations into Eq. (12.35), letting $B_1 = B_2 = B_3 = \dots = B_8 = B_{7\times1}$, the $X^*_{8T'\times7}$ matrix becomes $X^* = (X_1^T, X_2^T, \dots, X_8^T)^T$. The stacked residual vector $U = (e_1, e_2, \dots, e_8)^T$ now has a covariance matrix $\text{cov}(U)_{8T'\times8T'} = \Sigma_{8\times8} \otimes I_{T'\times T'}$. Applying GLS, the estimates for $\hat{B} = (X^{*\prime}[\hat{\Sigma}\otimes I]^{-1}X^*)^{-1}X^{*\prime}[\hat{\Sigma}\otimes I]^{-1}Y$ conditional on estimate $\hat{\Sigma}$ based on initial fitted residuals. The covariance $\Sigma \neq I_{8\times8}$ provides information additional to those used in the separate individual OLS regressions, and leads to GLS that is consistent and more efficient than the individual OLS estimates. The use of information Σ in the stacked regression of Eq. (12.35) is sometimes called the Seemingly Unrelated Regression (SUR).[14]

The time series plot of the S&P100 index price levels together with the estimated volatility term structure slope $\hat{\theta}_0 + \hat{\theta}_1 L_t$ are shown in Figure 12.6.

The figure plots the time series of S&P 100 index and the time series of the Estimated Slope of the Model-Free Volatility Term Structure obtained from the Panel Regression results. The horizontal axis shows the calender years in 2-digit convention. The figure shows that the estimated volatility term structure slope tends to move in tandem with the index price level.

During the period July 2001 to March 2003, in the aftermath of 9/11, the Enron scandal, and the Second Gulf War in the spring of 2003, S&P100 index stayed on the low side of 500 and below 500 for the most part while the daily volatility term structure estimated slopes were mostly negative. During the boom period or easy credit period from mid-2003 to July 2008, the S&P100 rose steadily past 600 while the volatility

14 See A. Zellner (1962), An efficient method of estimating seemingly unrelated regressions, and tests for aggregation bias, *Journal of the American Statistical Association*, 57, 348–368.

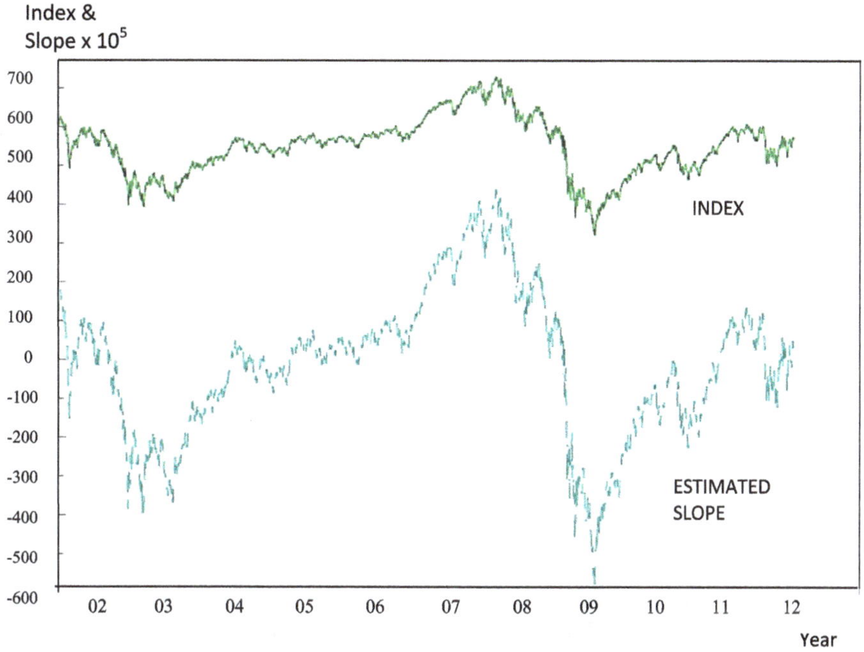

Figure 12.6: S&P 100 Index and Estimated Slope of the Model-Free Volatility Term Structure.

term structure slope became highly positive. Thus there is clear evidence that upward sloping volatility term structure occurred during boom times. The collapse of the U. S. housing mortgage market and subsequent global financial crisis from August 2008 to September 2010 ushered a bear market seeing the index plunged below 500 and the volatility term structure slope slipping into negative territory throughout. From September 2010 to 2012, there had been some stabilization and a half-hearted recovery in the market before the onslaught of the European debt crisis, and the index had climbed back above 500 while the volatility slope rose into the positive territory.

12.7 The Bakshi-Kapadia-Madan (BKM) Model

Besides model-free volatility, the second, third, and fourth distribution-free moments of the underlying stock or else index return could be implied simultaneously from an option chain, i. e., at any time, there exists traded option prices on the underlying with different strike prices. The method is slightly different from that in the previous section.[15]

15 See G. Bakshi, N. Kapadia, and D. Madan (2003), Stock return characteristics, skew laws and the differential pricing of individual equity options, *Review of Financial Studies* 16, 101–143.

The fundamental theorem of calculus implies that for any fixed F:

$$f(S) - f(F) = \int_F^S \frac{df}{du} du = \int_F^S f'(u)du$$

Hence,

$$\begin{aligned} f(S) &= f(F) + 1_{S>F} \int_F^S f'(u)du - 1_{S<F} \int_S^F f'(u)du \\ &= f(F) + 1_{S>F} \int_F^S \left[f'(F) + \int_F^u f''(v)dv \right] du \\ &\quad - 1_{S<F} \int_S^F \left[f'(F) - \int_u^F f''(v)dv \right] du \end{aligned}$$

Note that $f'(F)$ is independent of u. (The assumption of smooth derivatives of the f-function may impose some limitations on the model-free processes such as excluding those with discontinuities.) Then,

$$\begin{aligned} f(S) &= f(F) + f'(F)(S-F) + 1_{S>F} \int_F^S \int_v^S f''(v)\, dudv \\ &\quad + 1_{S<F} \int_S^F \int_S^v f''(v)\, dudv \end{aligned}$$

Performing the integration over u yields:

$$\begin{aligned} f(S) &= f(F) + f'(F)(S-F) + 1_{S>F} \int_F^S f''(v)(S-v)\, dv \\ &\quad + 1_{S<F} \int_S^F f''(v)(v-S)\, dv \\ &= f(F) + f'(F)(S-F) + \int_F^\infty f''(v)(S-v)^+\, dv \\ &\quad + \int_0^F f''(v)(v-S)^+\, dv \end{aligned}$$

Now let $f(S) = [\ln(F_T/F_t)]^m$, for $m = 1,2,3,4$, where current index futures price F_t is given, and F_T is random index futures price at maturity time T. F_T replaces S. Let F_t replace F. The f function becomes contingent claims payoffs based on F_T given F_t.

Then $f(F) = f(F_t) = [\ln(F_t/F_t)]^m = 0$. Also $f'(F) = df/dS|_{S=F} = m[\ln(F_T/F_t)]^{m-1}(1/F_T)|_{F(T)=F(t)} = 0$.

Let $v = K$ (exercise price). Then

$$\begin{aligned} f''(K) &= d^2f/dS^2|_{S=K} \\ &= m(m-1)[\ln(F_T/F_t)]^{m-2}(1/F_T)^2 - m[\ln(F_T/F_t)]^{m-1}(1/F_T)^2|_{S=K} \\ &= (1/K)^2[m(m-1)[\ln(K/F_t)]^{m-2} - m[\ln(K/F_t)]^{m-1}] \end{aligned}$$

So, for $m = 2$, $f''(K) = (1/K)^2 2[1 - \ln(K/F_t)]$. For $m = 3$, $f''(K) = (1/K)^2[6\ln(K/F_t) - 3[\ln(K/F_t)]^2]$. For $m = 4$, $f''(K) = (1/K)^2[12[\ln(K/F_t)]^2 - 4[\ln(K/F_t)]^3]$.

Suppose we let $R_T = \ln(F_T/F_t)$. Then for $m = 2$,

$$\begin{aligned} R_T^2 &\equiv [\ln(F_T/F_t)]^2 \\ &= \int_{F_t}^{\infty} \frac{2(1 - \ln(K/F_t))}{K^2}(F_T - K)^+ dK \\ &\quad + \int_0^{F_t} \frac{2(1 + \ln(F_t/K))}{K^2}(K - F_T)^+ dK \end{aligned}$$

For $m = 3$,

$$\begin{aligned} R_T^3 &\equiv [\ln(F_T/F_t)]^3 \\ &= \int_{F_t}^{\infty} \frac{6\ln(K/F_t) - 3(\ln(K/F_t))^2}{K^2}(F_T - K)^+ dK \\ &\quad - \int_0^{F_t} \frac{6\ln(F_t/K) + 3(\ln(F_t/K))^2}{K^2}(K - F_T)^+ dK \end{aligned}$$

For $m = 4$,

$$\begin{aligned} R_T^4 &\equiv [\ln(F_T/F_t)]^4 \\ &= \int_{F_t}^{\infty} \frac{12(\ln(K/F_t))^2 - 4(\ln(K/F_t))^3}{K^2}(F_T - K)^+ dK \\ &\quad + \int_0^{F_t} \frac{12(\ln(F_t/K))^2 + 4(\ln(F_t/K))^3}{K^2}(K - F_T)^+ dK \end{aligned}$$

Now let $\tau = T - t$, and let $V_t(T) = E_t^Q(e^{-r\tau}R_T^2)$, $W_t(T) = E_t^Q(e^{-r\tau}R_T^3)$, and $X_t(T) = E_t^Q(e^{-r\tau}R_T^4)$. Also, $E_t^Q(e^{-r\tau}(F_T - K)^+) = C_t(\tau, K)$, and $E_t^Q(e^{-r\tau}(K - F_T)^+) = P_t(\tau, K)$.

Then we obtain

$$V_t(\tau) = \int_{F_t}^{\infty} \frac{2(1 - \ln(K/F_t))}{K^2} C_t(\tau, K) dK$$

$$+ \int_{0}^{F_t} \frac{2(1 + \ln(F_t/K))}{K^2} P_t(\tau, K) dK$$

$$W_t(\tau) = \int_{F_t}^{\infty} \frac{6\ln(K/F_t) - 3(\ln(K/F_t))^2}{K^2} C_t(\tau, K) dK$$

$$- \int_{0}^{F_t} \frac{6\ln(F_t/K) + 3(\ln(F_t/K))^2}{K^2} P_t(\tau, K) dK$$

$$X_t(\tau) = \int_{F_t}^{\infty} \frac{12(\ln(K/F_t))^2 - 4(\ln(K/F_t))^3}{K^2} C_t(\tau, K)\, dK$$

$$+ \int_{0}^{F_t} \frac{12(\ln(F_t/K))^2 + 4(\ln(F_t/K))^3}{K^2} P_t(\tau, K)\, dK$$

So $$\mu_t(\tau) \equiv E_t^Q(R_T) \approx e^{r\tau}\left(-\frac{1}{2}V_t(\tau) - \frac{1}{6}W_t(\tau) - \frac{1}{24}X_t(\tau)\right). \quad (12.36)$$

$$\mathrm{var}_t^Q(\tau) = e^{r\tau}V_t(\tau) - \mu_t(\tau)^2 \quad (12.37)$$

$$\mathrm{Skew}_t^Q(\tau) = \frac{e^{r\tau}W_t(\tau) - 3\mu_t(\tau)e^{r\tau}V_t(\tau) + 2\mu_t(\tau)^3}{[e^{r\tau}V_t(\tau) - \mu_t(\tau)^2]^{3/2}} \quad (12.38)$$

$$\mathrm{Kurt}_t^Q(\tau) = \frac{e^{r\tau}X_t(\tau) - 4\mu_t(\tau)e^{r\tau}W_t(\tau) + 6\mu_t(\tau)^2e^{r\tau}V_t(\tau) - 3\mu_t(\tau)^4}{[e^{r\tau}V_t(\tau) - \mu_t(\tau)^2]^2} \quad (12.39)$$

12.8 Intraday Moments and Trading

To show how we can utilize the implied moments for intra-day trading, we perform back-testing using intra-day E-mini S&P 500 European-style options time-stamped (to the second) traded price data on weekly index futures series (EW1, EW2, EW4) from August 2009 to December 2012. Transactions data are also obtained on the E-mini futures prices. These options typically trade actively 2 weeks before their expiry. Consider only the E-mini futures options data on trades between 0830 and 1500 h due to less liquidity outside the regular trading hours. Riskfree rates are based on 4-weeks Treasury bill rates reported in the Fed Res Report H. 15. We use as many strike prices within each 10-minute trading interval. We use at least 2 OTM and 2 OTM puts for constructing the moments in each 10-minute interval. As the theory requires an infinite number of options, it is necessary to use numerical method to find the smoothed OTM call and OTM put price curves against exercise price K. We use piece-wise hermite interpolation which is more stable compared to cubic splines. The smoothed curves are used for finding the numerically integrated values for $V_t(\tau)$, $W_t(\tau)$, and $X_t(\tau)$. These are then used to compute the risk-neutral mean $E_t^Q(R_T)$, risk-neutral volatility $\sqrt{\text{var}_t^Q(\tau)}$, risk-neutral skewness $\text{Skew}_t^Q(\tau)$, and risk-neutral kurtosis $\text{Kurt}_t^Q(\tau)$ from Eqs. (12.36) to (12.39).

Table 12.5 shows averages of moments across all 10-minute intervals on all dates, sorted by their different time-to-maturity (in days n). Annualized mean risk-neutral (RN) volatility is quite stable across n. RN skewness is negative. RN kurtosis exceeds 3 and decreases with maturity.[16]

We have each trading day, a 10-minute interval time series of estimated RNV, RNS, and RNK. We test to ensure each of the series is $I(0)$ by using the Augmented Dickey-Fuller tests. Unit root is rejected for all cases at $< 1\%$ significance level, i. e., their non-standard "t-value" is highly negative.

We fit the intraday time-series moments data using eight competing models: a benchmark Random Walk Model (RW), an Autoregressive (AR) lag-one Model, an Autoregressive Moving Average Model (ARMA(1, 1)), an Autoregressive (AR(1)) Model with GARCH (generalized autoregressive conditional heteroskedastic) error – AR(G), Vector Autoregressive (VAR) lag-one Model where all three lagged risk-neutral moments (RNMs) enter as regressors, Vector Autoregressive (VAR) lag-one Model with GARCH errors for each of the three vector elements – VAR(G), Vector Error Correction Model (VECM), and the Local Autogressive (LAR) lag-one Model. Experimenting with higher lag-orders generally does not yield any clearer results or improvement in analyses. As the lag-order is understood, we do not clutter the notation and leave out the lag-one notation. In what follows, each interval $[t, t+1)$ is 10-minute within a trading day.

For the RW Model, for each RNM:

$$\text{RNM}_{t+1}(\tau) = \text{RNM}_t(\tau) + \epsilon_{t+1}$$

where ϵ_{t+1} is an i. i. d. noise.

For the AR Model, for each RNM:

$$\text{RNM}_{t+1}(\tau) = b_0 + b_1\text{RNM}_t(\tau) + \epsilon_{t+1}$$

where b_0 and $b_1 < 1$ are constants and ϵ_{t+1} is i. i. d.

16 See Kian Guan Lim, Ying Chen, and Nelson Yap (2019), Intraday information from S&P 500 Index futures options, *Journal of Financial Markets*, 42, 29–55.

Table 12.5: Descriptive Statistics of S&P 500 Risk-Neutral Moments.

Time-to-Maturity n	1 Day	2 Days	3 Days	4 Days	5 Days	6 Days	7 Days	8 Days	9 Days	10 Days
Risk-Neutral Volatility $\sqrt{\mathrm{var}_t^Q(\tau)}$ (%)										
No. of Obs.	2628	2769	2594	2277	1920	1987	1784	1471	1205	1224
Mean	21.05	19.85	18.97	19.07	20.49	20.31	20.35	20.89	20.43	21.41
Risk-Neutral Skewness $\mathrm{Skew}_t^Q(\tau)$										
No. of Obs.	2628	2769	2594	2277	1920	1987	1784	1471	1205	1224
Mean	−1.01	−1.03	−1.07	−1.17	−1.26	−1.12	−1.08	−1.05	−1.03	−1.02
Risk-Neutral Kurtosis $\mathrm{Kurt}_t^Q(\tau)$										
No. of Obs	2628	2769	2594	2277	1920	1987	1784	1471	1205	1224
Mean	6.28	5.72	5.76	6.28	6.53	5.16	4.68	4.49	4.37	4.14

For the ARMA Model, for each RNM:

$$\mathrm{RNM}_{t+1}(\tau) = b_0 + b_1 \mathrm{RNM}_t(\tau) + \epsilon_{t+1}$$

where b_0 and $b_1 < 1$ are constants and ϵ_{t+1} is MA(1), with $\epsilon_{t+1} = \alpha\epsilon_t + \varepsilon_{t+1}$, $\alpha < 1$, and ε_t i. i. d.

For the AR(G) Model, for each RNM:

$$\mathrm{RNM}_{t+1}(\tau) = b_0 + b_1 \mathrm{RNM}_t(\tau) + \epsilon_{t+1}$$

where b_0 and $b_1 < 1$ are constants and $\mathrm{var}(\epsilon_{t+1}) = \alpha_0 + \alpha_1 \mathrm{var}(\epsilon_t) + \alpha_2 \epsilon_{t+1}^2$ with constants $\alpha_0 > 0$, and $\alpha_1 + \alpha_2 < 1$.

For the VAR Model:

$$\begin{pmatrix} \mathrm{RNV}_{t+1}(\tau) \\ \mathrm{RNS}_{t+1}(\tau) \\ \mathrm{RNK}_{t+1}(\tau) \end{pmatrix} = B_0 + B_1 \begin{pmatrix} \mathrm{RNV}_t(\tau) \\ \mathrm{RNS}_t(\tau) \\ \mathrm{RNK}_t(\tau) \end{pmatrix} + e_{t+1}$$

where B_0 is a 3×1 vector of constants, B_1 is a 3×3 matrix of constants, and e_{t+1} is a 3×1 vector of i. i. d. disturbance terms.

For the VAR(G) Model: the above VAR Model is used except that each element of the vector error e_{t+1} is modelled as GARCH(1, 1).

For the VECM Model:

$$\begin{pmatrix} \triangle\mathrm{RNV}_{t+1}(\tau) \\ \triangle\mathrm{RNS}_{t+1}(\tau) \\ \triangle\mathrm{RNK}_{t+1}(\tau) \end{pmatrix} = \Gamma_0 + \Gamma_1 \begin{pmatrix} \mathrm{RNV}_t(\tau) \\ \mathrm{RNS}_t(\tau) \\ \mathrm{RNK}_t(\tau) \end{pmatrix} + \Gamma_2 \begin{pmatrix} \triangle\mathrm{RNV}_t(\tau) \\ \triangle\mathrm{RNS}_t(\tau) \\ \triangle\mathrm{RNK}_t(\tau) \end{pmatrix} + e_{t+1}$$

where Γ_0 is a 3×1 vector of constants, Γ_1 and Γ_2 are 3×3 constant matrices, and e_{t+1} is a 3×1 vector of i. i. d. disturbance terms.

For the LAR Model:

$$\text{RNM}_{t+1}(\tau) = b_{0,I_d} + b_{1,I_d}\text{RNM}_t(\tau) + \epsilon_{t+1}$$

where I_d denotes a subset of the sample points on day d. In the current context, this subset consists of sample data from the latest time point before forecasting, i. e. 12:00 pm, to a lagged time point not earlier than 8:40 am. The statistical procedure in which this subset I_d is selected is explained in the next subsection. LAR basically selects an optimal local window to perform the regression fitting where structural breaks do not occur. While it has the advantage of providing a better fit and possibly better forecast in time series that are not smooth and that may have breaks, the disadvantage is that if the time series is not smooth, the shorter sampling window may yield forecasts and estimates with larger standard errors. The maximum likelihood regression method, equivalent to least squares in cases of normal random errors, is utilized, except that in the LAR case, the selection of window adds to the regression procedures.

12.8.1 Forecasting Performance

After the regression models are estimated, the estimated coefficients are used to provide a fitted model for the purpose of predicting the next period or future RNMs. Parameters are estimated in the window on the same day from 8:40 am to 12:00 pm, after which the fitted model is used for forecasting during 12:10 pm to 2:50 pm. Unlike daily or weekly methods, we do not use rolling windows over the 10-minute intervals within a trading day. This helps in focusing on days with highly liquid transactions at start of day trading to fix the parameters for forecast and trading for the rest of the day. As mentioned before, some days whereby there are insufficient risk-neutral moments for estimation during 8:40 am to 12:00 pm are excluded from the sample.

Forecasts are made for RNMs pertaining to different horizons τ of one up to ten days. The various models are as follows.

For the RW Model:

$$E_t(\text{RNM}_{t+1}(\tau)) = \text{RNM}_t(\tau)$$

where the subscript to the expectation operator denotes a condition on the information at t.

For the AR Model, for each RNM:

$$E_t(\text{RNM}_{t+1}(\tau)) = \hat{b}_0 + \hat{b}_1\text{RNM}_t(\tau)$$

where $\hat{b}_0$ and $\hat{b}_1$ are estimated parameters.

For the ARMA Model, for each RNM:

$$E_t(\mathrm{RNM}_{t+1}(\tau)) = \hat{b}_0 + \hat{b}_1 \mathrm{RNM}_t(\tau) + \hat{\alpha}\hat{\epsilon}_t$$

where $\hat{\epsilon}_t = \mathrm{RNM}_t(\tau) - \hat{b}_0 - \hat{b}_1 \mathrm{RNM}_{t-1}(\tau)$.

For the AR(G) Model, for each RNM:

$$E_t(\mathrm{RNM}_{t+1}(\tau)) = \hat{b}_0^G + \hat{b}_1^G \mathrm{RNM}_t(\tau)$$

where $\hat{b}_0^G$ and $\hat{b}_1^G$ are estimated parameters based on maximum likelihood procedures recognizing the GARCH variance in the residuals.

For the VAR Model, for all three RNMs at once:

$$E_t \begin{pmatrix} \mathrm{RNV}_{t+1}(\tau) \\ \mathrm{RNS}_{t+1}(\tau) \\ \mathrm{RNK}_{t+1}(\tau) \end{pmatrix} = \hat{B}_0 + \hat{B}_1 \begin{pmatrix} \mathrm{RNV}_t(\tau) \\ \mathrm{RNS}_t(\tau) \\ \mathrm{RNK}_t(\tau) \end{pmatrix}$$

where $\hat{B}_0$ and $\hat{B}_1$ are the estimated parameters.

For the VAR(G) Model, for all three RNMs at once:

$$E_t \begin{pmatrix} \mathrm{RNV}_{t+1}(\tau) \\ \mathrm{RNS}_{t+1}(\tau) \\ \mathrm{RNK}_{t+1}(\tau) \end{pmatrix} = \hat{B}_0^G + \hat{B}_1^G \begin{pmatrix} \mathrm{RNV}_t(\tau) \\ \mathrm{RNS}_t(\tau) \\ \mathrm{RNK}_t(\tau) \end{pmatrix}$$

where $\hat{B}_0^G$ and $\hat{B}_1^G$ are the estimated parameters based on GARCH(1, 1) errors e_{t+1}.

For the VECM Model, for all three RNMs at once:

$$E_t \begin{pmatrix} \mathrm{RNV}_{t+1}(\tau) \\ \mathrm{RNS}_{t+1}(\tau) \\ \mathrm{RNK}_{t+1}(\tau) \end{pmatrix} = \hat{\Gamma}_0 + (\hat{\Gamma}_1 + I) \begin{pmatrix} \mathrm{RNV}_t(\tau) \\ \mathrm{RNS}_t(\tau) \\ \mathrm{RNK}_t(\tau) \end{pmatrix} + \hat{\Gamma}_2 \begin{pmatrix} \Delta\mathrm{RNV}_t(\tau) \\ \Delta\mathrm{RNS}_t(\tau) \\ \Delta\mathrm{RNK}_t(\tau) \end{pmatrix}$$

where $\hat{\Gamma}_0$, $\hat{\Gamma}_1$, and $\hat{\Gamma}_2$ are the estimated parameters.

For the LAR Model:

$$E_t(\mathrm{RNM}_{t+1}(\tau)) = \hat{b}_{0,I_n} + \hat{b}_{1,I_n} \mathrm{RNM}_t(\tau)$$

where $\hat{b}_{0,I_n}$ and $\hat{b}_{1,I_n}$ are the estimated parameters in I_n.

12.8.2 Error Metrics

To measure the forecasting performances of these models, we employ three error metrics or loss functions.

The root mean square error (RMSE) is defined as:

$$\text{RMSE} = \sqrt{\frac{1}{T-1}\sum_{t=1}^{T-1}\left(\text{RNM}_{t+1}(\tau) - E_t(\text{RNM}_{t+1}(\tau))\right)^2}$$

where T is the number of periods of forecasts, each period being a 10-minute interval.

The mean absolute deviation (MAD) is defined as:

$$\text{MAD} = \frac{1}{T-1}\sum_{t=1}^{T-1}\left|\text{RNM}_{t+1}(\tau) - E_t(\text{RNM}_{t+1}(\tau))\right|$$

The mean correct prediction (MCP) percentage is defined as:

$$\text{MCP} = \frac{1}{T-1}\sum_{t=1}^{T-1} J_{t+1} \times 100$$

where indicator $J_{t+1} = 1$ if $(\text{RNM}_{t+1}(\tau) - \text{RNM}_t(\tau))(E_t(\text{RNM}_{t+1}(\tau)) - \text{RNM}_t(\tau)) > 0$, and $J_{t+1} = 0$ otherwise.

Table 12.6 reports the out-of-sample statistical performances of all the models. The autoregressive models are lag-one models. Results are reported for each of the RNMs of volatility, skewness, and kurtosis. For each RNM category, the regression results of all maturities are pooled. There is a total of 8,534 observations for each RNM regression. Every trade day from August 24, 2009 to December 31, 2012, the RNMs computed in each 10-minute intervals from 8:40 am to 12:00 pm are used to estimate the parameters of each model. The estimated or fitted model is then used to forecast the RNMs for each 10-minute interval from 12:10 pm to 2:50 pm. The error metrics or loss functions of RMSE, MAD, and MCP are shown in the table. The MCP is the percentage of times that the forecast of directional change in the RNM is correct.

Table 12.6: Out-of-Sample Error Metrics for Forecasting Models.

	Risk-Neutral Volatility			Risk-Neutral Skewness			Risk-Neutral Kurtosis		
	RMSE	MAD	MCP %	RMSE	MAD	MCP %	RMSE	MAD	MCP %
RW	0.662	0.174	50.00	0.647	0.463	50.00	4.001	2.490	50.00
AR	0.580	0.175	58.15	0.511	0.374	70.75	3.252	2.174	68.98
ARMA	0.598	0.175	59.66	0.581	0.424	69.44	3.619	2.373	68.10
AR(G)	0.498	0.162	61.18	0.521	0.378	70.27	3.230	2.131	69.63
VAR	0.654	0.210	58.35	0.541	0.387	69.87	3.465	2.255	68.40
VAR(G)	0.569	0.182	63.04	0.625	0.433	67.83	3.387	2.209	68.27
VECM	3.619	0.396	60.36	1.358	0.544	63.20	7.995	3.092	61.99
LAR	0.526	0.159	68.67	0.535	0.374	71.01	3.391	2.110	70.23

The results in Table 12.6 provide clear indications of the following. Firstly, the VECM performs the worst; this shows that more complicated models with more than one lag could yield less accurate forecasts. Similarly, the VAR Model does not perform well as there may be multi-correlation of the RNMs in a finite sample setting. Secondly, across all RNMs, the AR(G) Model, the LAR Model, and the AR Model perform better than the rest in terms of lower RMSE, lower MAD, and higher MCP. For the more volatile RNV processes, the LAR appears to perform slightly better in MAD and MCP. These latter models are all autoregressive in nature. Remarkably, all methods perform better than the RW in terms of MCP higher than 50 %. In summary, there is statistical evidence of a lot of intraday information that can be utilized to successfully make rather accurate predictions of next period RNMs over short intervals of 10-minutes.

12.8.3 Option Trading Strategies

Using the forecasts generated by the seven competing models of AR lag-one, ARMA(1, 1), AR(1) with GARCH error, VAR lag-one, VAR(1) with GARCH errors, VECM, and LAR, we attempt to construct a trading strategy to benefit from the accurate forecast of the various future moment changes. RW is excluded as it has served its purpose for benchmark comparison in the forecast assessments. We now add the benchmark case of perfect knowledge forecast (PK) whereby prediction of moment increase or decrease is 100 % correct.

We construct three different trading strategies corresponding to the forecasts of the three RNMs. The trading strategies are designed to capture option price changes consistent with the forecast changes in the RNMs.

Table 12.7 reports the average $ trading profit per trade according to the different forecasting methods on risk-neutral volatility and according to threshold signals. Trading cost per option contract is $0.225, and this has been deducted to arrive at the net trading profit. The trading strategy involves creating a volatility portfolio each 10-minute interval as follows: long an OTM call and short delta amount of underlying asset, together with long an OTM put and short a delta amount of underlying index futures. The respective deltas are based on the strike prices of the call and the put, and are computed using the Black-Scholes model. Since option price depends on both underlying and volatility, the use of delta is to hedge option price change due to underlying and not volatility.

At the end of the interval the positions are liquidated at market prices. Prediction is done on moments with the same maturity. If the predicted next interval risk-neutral volatility is higher (lower) than the current risk-neutral volatility by at least the threshold percentage, the above portfolio of long (short) call and long (short) put is executed. The execution now and liquidation next interval constitute one trade. There can be more than one trade per interval if different maturity moment forecasts exceed the

Table 12.7: Profitability of Trading Strategy using Risk-Neutral Volatility Prediction.

Threshold	Signal 0.0 %		Signal 5.0 %		Signal 7.5 %		Signal 10.0 %	
	Profit	#Trades	Profit	#Trades	Profit	#Trades	Profit	#Trades
PK	1.91**	7137	2.56**	2152	3.39**	1264	4.31**	773
	(7.86)		(4.51)		(3.98)		(4.50)	
AR	−1.01	7137	−0.32	1403	0.46	921	0.87	664
	(−4.14)		(−0.52)		(0.56)		(0.90)	
ARMA	−0.96	7137	−1.40	1175	−0.54	719	−0.56	457
	(−3.92)		(−2.08)		(−0.55)		(−0.46)	
AR(G)	−1.06	6455	−0.90	1243	−0.21	806	0.24	570
	(−4.14)		(−1.34)		(−0.23)		(0.24)	
VAR	−0.71	7137	−0.61	3121	−0.05	1962	0.59	1296
	(−2.88)		(−1.66)		(−0.09)		(0.91)	
VAR(G)	−0.69	6455	−0.69	2817	−0.07	1754	0.61	1144
	(−2.68)		(−1.80)		(−0.14)		(0.90)	
VECM	−0.87	7137	−0.80	2175	−0.64	1265	−1.30	954
	(−3.57)		(−1.26)		(−0.74)		(−1.31)	
LAR	−0.20	7137	0.09	2050	1.33	1235	0.84	884
	(−0.80)		(0.15)		(1.55)		(0.98)	

Note: **, * denote significance at the one-tailed 1 %, and 2.5 % significance levels, respectively. #Trades refers to number of trades.

threshold, or there may be no trade in a particular interval if a non-zero threshold signal is used. The portfolio has zero cost as the net balance of the cost in the call, put, and underlying asset is financed by borrowing at risk-free rate. The overall cost of the portfolio can be expressed as:

$$\pi_t^{\text{Vola}} = C_{t,\text{OTM}} - \Delta_{C_{t,\text{OTM}}} F_t + P_{t,\text{OTM}} - \Delta_{P_{t,\text{OTM}}} F_t - B_t$$

B_t is chosen such that $\pi_t^{\text{Vola}} = 0$. Outlay for F_t the index futures is assumed to be zero for the initial futures position. The numbers within the parentheses are the t-statistics based on bootstrapped variances calculated for the average profit. The bootstrap is carried out over 2,000 iterations. Overall, the table results show that risk-neutral volatility forecasts cannot lead to a profitable options trading strategy.

Table 12.8 reports the average $ trading profit per trade according to the different forecasting methods on risk-neutral skewness and according to threshold signals. Trading cost per option contract is $0.225, and this has been deducted to arrive at the net trading profit. The trading strategy involves creating a skewness portfolio each 10-minute interval as follows: long an OTM call and short a number of OTM puts equal to the ratio of the call vega to put vega. Also short a number of underlying assets equal to the call delta less the same vega ratio times put delta. The respective vegas and deltas are based on the strike prices and other features of the call and the put and are computed using the Black-Scholes model. The portfolio is hedged against option price change due to underlying and due to volatility.

Table 12.8: Profitability of Trading Strategy using Risk-Neutral Skewness Prediction.

Threshold	Signal 0.0 %		Signal 10.0 %		Signal 20.0 %		Signal 50.0 %	
	Profit	#Trades	Profit	#Trades	Profit	#Trades	Profit	#Trades
PK	2.81**	7137	2.97**	5657	3.00**	4291	2.68**	2406
	(9.33)		(8.98)		(7.96)		(5.56)	
AR	1.42**	7137	1.74**	5178	1.88**	3290	1.16	1507
	(4.76)		(5.01)		(4.30)		(1.81)	
ARMA	1.39**	7137	2.01**	4101	1.84**	2645	0.52	1384
	(4.65)		(5.04)		(3.73)		(0.76)	
AR(G)	1.48**	6455	1.80**	4661	1.97**	2928	1.03	1317
	(4.66)		(4.85)		(4.21)		(1.46)	
VAR	1.59**	7137	1.94**	5246	1.75**	3336	1.02	1562
	(5.28)		(5.58)		(4.18)		(1.67)	
VAR(G)	1.62**	6455	1.91**	4710	1.78**	2961	0.91	1372
	(5.19)		(5.23)		(3.96)		(1.39)	
VECM	0.45	7137	0.91**	5115	0.53	3439	0.02	1685
	(1.50)		(2.55)		(1.21)		(0.03)	
LAR	1.40**	7137	1.62**	5458	1.83**	3647	1.06	1622
	(4.65)		(4.67)		(4.43)		(1.67)	

Note: **, * denote significance at the one-tailed 1 %, and 2.5 % significance levels, respectively. #Trades refers number of trades.

At the end of the interval the positions are liquidated at actual market prices. Prediction is done on moments with the same maturity. If the predicted next interval risk-neutral skewness is higher (lower) than the current risk-neutral skewness by at least the threshold percentage, the above portfolio of long (short) call and short (long) puts is executed. The execution and liquidation next interval constitute one trade. There can be more than one trade per interval if different maturity moment forecasts exceed the threshold, or there may be no trade in a particular interval if a non-zero threshold signal is used. The portfolio has zero cost. The overall cost of the portfolio can be expressed as:

$$\pi_t^{\text{Skew}} = C_{t,\text{OTM}} - \left(\frac{\upsilon_{C_{t,\text{OTM}}}}{\upsilon_{P_{t,\text{OTM}}}}\right) P_{t,\text{OTM}} - \left(\Delta_{C_{t,\text{OTM}}} - \left(\frac{\upsilon_{C_{t,\text{OTM}}}}{\upsilon_{P_{t,\text{OTM}}}}\right) \Delta_{P_{t,\text{OTM}}}\right) F_t - B_t$$

B_t is chosen such that $\pi_t^{\text{Skew}} = 0$. Outlay for F_t the index futures is assumed to be zero for the initial futures position. The numbers within the parentheses are the t-statistics based on bootstrapped variances calculated for the average profit. The bootstrap is carried out over 2,000 iterations.

Except for VECM, all other forecasting models, with thresholds < 50 %, yield significantly positive profits per trade at 1 % significance level. Persistence of RN skewness over the 10-minute intervals could be a reason for the predictable profits.

Table 12.9 reports the average $ trading profit per trade according to the different forecasting methods on risk-neutral kurtosis and according to threshold signals. Trading cost per option contract is $0.225, and this has been deducted to arrive at the net trading profit. The trading strategy involves creating a kurtosis portfolio each 10-minute interval as follows: long X at-the-money (ATM) calls and X ATM puts and simultaneously short one out-of-the-money (OTM) call and one OTM put, where $X = (C_{t,\text{OTM}} + P_{t,\text{OTM}})/(C_{t,\text{ATM}} + P_{t,\text{ATM}})$. The ATM (OTM) options are chosen as far as possible to have similar strikes. Aït-Sahalia et al. (2001)'s study shows for a predicted increase in kurtosis, RN probability would increase in prices closer to ATM strike and decrease in prices at far OTM. Hence we expect increase in kurtosis to lead to increase in ATM options relative to their counterparts.[17] The overall cost of the portfolio is:

$$X(C_{t,\text{ATM}} + P_{t,\text{ATM}}) - (C_{t,\text{OTM}} + P_{t,\text{OTM}}) = 0$$

Table 12.9: Profitability of Trading Strategy using Risk-Neutral Kurtosis Prediction.

Threshold	Signal 0.0 %		Signal 10.0 %		Signal 20.0 %		Signal 50.0 %	
	Profit	#Trades	Profit	#Trades	Profit	#Trades	Profit	#Trades
PK	2.92**	682	2.70*	377	3.53	228	4.35	87
	(2.98)		(2.01)		(1.86)		(1.15)	
AR	0.71	682	2.82	319	5.78*	137	4.00	33
	(0.71)		(1.72)		(2.09)		(0.63)	
ARMA	0.55	682	2.85	241	1.99	128	5.33	41
	(0.55)		(1.44)		(0.68)		(0.82)	
AR(G)	0.60	623	2.57	286	5.72	121	4.64	29
	(0.56)		(1.43)		(1.85)		(0.63)	
VAR	1.37	682	2.16	328	4.42	142	4.18	38
	(1.39)		(1.33)		(1.52)		(0.74)	
VAR(G)	1.36	623	2.22	301	3.93	129	4.52	36
	(1.28)		(1.27)		(1.25)		(0.76)	
VECM	0.79	682	3.82**	374	3.75	192	1.10	60
	(0.79)		(2.69)		(1.75)		(0.32)	
LAR	−0.89	682	1.64	374	3.65	188	2.25	45
	(−0.88)		(1.17)		(1.65)		(0.38)	

Note: **, * denote significance at the one-tailed 1 %, and 2.5 % significance levels, respectively. #Trades refers to number of trades.

At the end of the interval the positions are liquidated at actual market prices. Prediction is done on moments with the same maturity. If the predicted next interval risk-neutral kurtosis is higher (lower) than the current risk-neutral kurtosis by at least the

17 See Y. Aït-Sahalia, Y. Wang, and F. Yared (2001), Do option markets correctly price the probabilities of movement of the underlying asset? *Journal of Econometrics*, 102, 67–110.

threshold percentage, the above portfolio of long (short) ATM calls and puts, and short (long) OTM call and put is executed. The execution and liquidation next interval constitute one trade. There can be more than one trade per interval if different maturity moment forecasts exceed the threshold, or there may be no trade in a particular interval if a non-zero threshold signal is used. The portfolio has zero cost. The numbers within the parentheses are t-statistics based on bootstrapped variances calculated for the average profit. The bootstrap is carried out over 2,000 iterations.

From Table 12.9, it is shown that there are only two cases of significant profits. However, there is no evidence of consistent profits.

The empirical results indicate that forecasting risk-neutral volatility and kurtosis may not lead to any profitable options trading strategies. However, real-time statistical forecast of risk-neutral skewness may be profitable in options trading.

Further Reading

Adam S. Iqbal (2018), *Volatility, Practical options Theory*, Wiley.

John Hull and Sankarshan Basu (2011), *Options, Futures, and Other Derivatives*, Tenth edition, Pearson India.

Kerry Back (2005), *A Course in Derivative Securities: Introduction to Theory and Computation*, Springer Finance.

Peter James (2002), *Option Theory*, Wiley.

List of Figures

https://doi.org/10.1515/9783110673951-013

List of Tables

https://doi.org/10.1515/9783110673951-014

About the Author

Kian Guan Lim

Kian Guan Lim is Overseas Union Bank Chair Professor in the quantitative finance area at Singapore Management University. He holds a PhD in financial economics from Stanford University. Lim has consulted for major banks in risk validation and has taught in various business executive development courses. He has published in *Journal of Financial Markets, Finance and Stochastics, Journal of Financial and Quantitative Analysis, Journal of Financial Economics, Review of Economics and Statistics*, and many other refereed journals in quantitative finance, derivatives, computational statistics, risk analytics, investment analyses, commodities, machine learning, accounting, real estate, maritime economics, transportation, operations research, and so on. He has been active in university administration including being vice-provost. Lim is the recipient of the Singapore Public Administration Medal (Silver) in 2012 and the SMU Distinguished Educator Award in 2021.

https://doi.org/10.1515/9783110673951-015

Index

https://doi.org/10.1515/9783110673951-016